ALSO BY ROGER G. KENNEDY

Architecture, Men, Women and Money
American Churches
Men on the Moving Frontier
Minnesota Houses

ORDERS FROM FRANCE

ORDERS FROM FRANCE

THE AMERICANS AND THE FRENCH IN A
REVOLUTIONARY WORLD, 1780–1820

ROGER G. KENNEDY

upp

UNIVERSITY OF PENNSYLVANIA PRESS
1990

First edition published in the United States 1989 by Alfred A. Knopf, Inc., New York, and simultaneously in Canada by Random House of Canada Limited, Toronto. Distributed by Random House, Inc., New York.

Paperback edition first published 1990 by the University of Pennsylvania Press, by arrangement with Alfred A. Knopf, Inc.

Grateful acknowledgment is made to the University of North Carolina Press for permission to reprint an excerpt from *Goethe, the Lyrist,* translated by Edwin H. Zeydel. Copyright © 1955 by the University of North Carolina. Reprinted by permission.

All credits for illustrations and all acknowledgments of permission to use illustrations will be found on p. 527.

LIBRARY OF CONGRESS CATALOGING-IN-PUBLICATION DATA

Kennedy, Roger G.
    Orders from France: the Americans and the French in a revolutionary world, 1780-1820/Roger G. Kennedy.
        p.   cm.
    Reprint. Originally published: New York: Knopf, 1989.
    ISBN 0-8122-1328-9
    1. United States—Civilization—1783–1865.   2. United States—Civilization—French influences.   3. Architecture, French—United States.   I. Title.
[E164.K46   1990]
973—dc20   90-33174
                                                           CIP

Manufactured in the United States of America

For McGeorge Bundy

CONTENTS

ACKNOWLEDGMENTS

Like that well-known Franco-American Blanche Du Bois, I have been the beneficiary of the kindness of strangers in getting this book written. I have also gotten along with the help of my friends, including those members of my family who went into involuntary service as a trial audience for the first or second version of some of these tales, over dinner and while trapped for long distances in automobiles—Frances Kennedy, Robert and Ruth Bowers.

I now offer thanks all around, in the order in which I find correspondence in my files.

Thanks to:

Catharine Bashir for help with the North Carolina Barings, and to Nicholas Baring, of Baring Brothers, for help with the London ones.

Gene Waddell for help on Mr. Jefferson's biloggial plans for Monticello I, for reading several versions of chapters, and making the suggestions noted in the endnotes.

Susan Pearl of Riverdale for help on "Baron" van Steir; Marjorie G. McNinch, Betty Bright B. Low, Elizabeth Gray Kogen, and the staff of the Hagley Museum and Library.

Constance C. Cooper of the Historical Society of Delaware, and the staff at Eleutherian Mills for much research and discovery of material related to Pierre Bauduy and the Du Ponts.

Mrs. Dorothy Garesché Holland of St. Louis and other Bauduy family decendants, and William W. Laird and other Du Pont descendants, John C. Rumm of the Joseph Henry Papers, Mary-Jo Kline of the Aaron Burr Papers, W. W. Abbot of the Papers of George Washington, and Charles (Monte) Harris of the Thornton Papers.

Jeff Cohen and John Van Horne of the Latrobe Papers for help on John

Craig, Nicholas Biddle, and ten or twenty other matters from the beginning to the end of this book. John H. Walker of the National Gallery for leads to George Hadfield and Maria Cosway.

Nicholas B. Wainwright and Beatrice Garvan for other Biddle and Latrobe-related assistance. Robert Gamble, Samuel Wilson, Jr., Harriet Bos, Mary-Louise Christovich, and Arthur Scully, Jr., for help with Alabama and Louisiana matters, together with S. Frederick Starr, whose encyclopedic knowledge of European architecture from the Urals to the Sabine has been immensely helpful.

Michael Zuckerman, informed reader, critic, and friend. Brooke Hindle, Robert Vogel, John H. White, Gary Kulik, Tom Crouch, Reidar Norby, Robert Post, Arthur Molella, Lonn Taylor, Edward Ezell, Rodris Roth, Susan Myers, Anne Golovin, Douglas Evelyn, Barbara Clark Smith, and Terry Sharrer, who come to mind as having helped with specific passages of the text (I recall at the moment poison ivy, Danish translation, giant cane, clipper ships, and Philadelphia cabinetmakers, especially) and stand as representatives of a score or more other patient and obliging colleagues at the National Museum of American History.

To the best of editors, Corona Machemer, who has endured four or five versions of this book, and improved each of them. To Naomi Glass, who has organized my office and much of the rest of my life, and to Joyce Ramey, who knows more about this manuscript in the physical sense than any living person, and without whom it might have stayed with its third or even seventh iteration.

Jim Roan of the Smithsonian Libraries and the staff of the Flower Memorial Library of Watertown, New York. Molly Roberts, Dana Leventhal, and Michael Orscheln, who searched out the answers to many an enigma.

Robert Alexander of the University of Iowa, Alexander De Conde of the University of California, Leonard Eaton of the University of Michigan, Alan Gowans of the University of British Columbia, Marcus Cunliffe of George Washington University, Milton Cantor and Miriam Levin of the University of Massachusetts, William Stinchcombe of Syracuse University, and Michael Tomlan of Cornell University, Theodore Caplow, Richard Guy Wilson, and Mack Thompson of the University of Virginia, John J. McClusker of the University of Maryland, Sidney Mintz of Johns Hopkins, Richard Candee of Boston University, Egon Verheyen of George Mason University, Joseph Borome of City College, Eugene Ferguson of the University of Delaware, John S. Pancake of the University of Alabama and Rockbridge Baths, Virginia, James S. Ackerman of Harvard, Thomas J. Schaeper of St. Bonaventure University, Paul V. Turner, of Stanford, who knows all about Joseph-Jacques Ramée, and many other useful things. Milton Lomask, who knows Aaron Burr; and John A. Jackson, Jr., who knows all about the Great Silver Scheme; and Calder Loth, whose grasp upon the architectural history of the Commonwealth of Virginia is as complete as such things should be.

The Reverend Euclid Marrier of Antwerp, New York, and J. Winthrop Aldrich, host, guide, and mid-Hudson guide; Marcus Grant, now in New Zealand, who has unraveled the Masonic mysteries of the Leray estate; Ford Petross of the Library of Congress and Pamela Scott of the Papers of Robert Mills; David Moltke-Hansen of the South Carolina Historical Society; the Archivist of St. Lawrence University, Bruce Naramore of the Clermont State Historic Site, Ruth Piwonka of everything on the Hudson, Edith Pilcher of Castorland and Schenectady; the staffs of the Remsen-Steuben Historical Society of Remsen, New York, the Union College Library, the Remington Museum in Ogdensburg, and the St. Lawrence County Historical Society.

Paul Cohen, Mary Carey, and Wendy Shadwell of the New-York Historical Society, and James Corsaro of the New York State Library; Betsy H. Bradley of the Statue of Liberty, and June A. V. Lindqvist and the staff of the Public Libraries of the islands of St. Croix and St. Thomas for Virgin Island matters; Pamela D. Arceneaux of the Historic New Orleans Collection, and Vartan Gregorian and friends at the New York Public Library of the City of New York.

Anne Perotin, Laure Quoniam, Michel Gallet, and Jean-Marie Perouse de Montclos in Paris, Eileen J. O'Brien of Watervliet, New York (for Thurman matters), Douglas Bucher of Albany for the Hooker brothers, Joseph Newell of New Orleans (for Nolte), Desmond Fitz-Gerald the Knight of Glin, for the Irish elements of Sam Smith's architecture, Clay Lancaster in deepest Kentucky, and another Kentuckian, T George Harris, editor, host, and Kentuckian in New York; Charlie Dunham, Suzanne Wylie, and David Guldenzopf of the domain once owned by Leray de Chaumont; Hakon Lund in Copenhagen, for information and guidance as to the Danish work of Joseph-Jacques Ramée.

Latrobe's sketch of the view of Richmond from Broad Rock Island,
showing the Virginia capitol

I

A WAY OF LOOKING

AT THINGS

There is a little island in the James River of Virginia where boatmen can rest amid the rapids on a smooth rock one hundred feet across. Local fishermen have known it over three centuries as Broad Rock Island, though at the end of the eighteenth century its proprietor called it Bushrod Washington's Island; and the city of Richmond, now responsible for the welfare of its population of chipmunks and muskrats, asserts that it should be known as Belle Isle.

In April 1797, a man six-feet-two-inches tall, thin, with wire-rimmed spectacles, came to the island with a sheaf of paper and a set of watercolor paints. If a boy had been fishing from the broad rock, he might have found the sight of any painter unusual; but this visitor was as rare as a Jacobin duke or a friendly weasel: here was an architect come to admire the work of other architects.

Benjamin Henry Latrobe made a wonderful watercolor sketch that day of the Virginia state capitol, designed by Thomas Jefferson and Charles-Louis Clérisseau. With a little artistic license, he depicted it as a Parthenon set in a shanty town, gathering into a picturesque cluster around it the little houses of the mill hands who had produced flour for William Byrd III, an improvident Tory squire who had failed to make much of the water power available where the James pitched sharply downward. (Byrd, who chose the wrong side in the

War of Independence, was the last of his line to live in the mansion at Westover, not far downriver.)

Though Latrobe had a genius for water-powered machinery and might have done better with the site, he too was a failure at that moment, an engineer and architect trying to start again after a bankruptcy. Of uncertain nationality, with a French name, an English passport, and a largely German education, he had been disappointed in his expectations of an estate in Pennsylvania left by his American mother. His prospects did not seem bright.

The capitol building Latrobe sketched was even more exotic than he was. Designed by a Frenchman trained in Italy and an Albemarle County squire then living in Paris, it was a loose version of the Maison Carrée, a Roman temple in southern France. This was the second temple-form building in the Western Hemisphere. The other was Prince William's Chapel in Sheldon, South Carolina (1753), a site so far out of the way that the Virginia capitol (1758–89) was the true precursor of the neoclassical age in America, of which Latrobe was to become the foremost practitioner.

A true multinational who became a passionate American patriot, Benjamin Henry Latrobe was born in Yorkshire, the son of a Pennsylvania German woman and a Moravian clergyman descended from French Huguenot refugees.* After studying in Moravian schools in Germany from the ages of twelve to twenty, he traveled in Italy and France, then returned to England to become an apprentice, first to the engineer John Smeaton and subsequently to the rising architect Samuel Pepys Cockerell. In the early 1790s, he struck out on his own, designing two distinguished country houses,† but the revolution in France and the world war it provoked destroyed the independent practices of many architects, and Latrobe lacked the necessary political connections to obtain commissions of state like the Bank of England.‡ He went bankrupt. His wife died, and his children were taken from him to be raised by her relatives. In the fall of 1795, he boarded the American ship *Eliza* at Gravesend to start again. He thought he was bound for Philadelphia, but bad weather or a better chance for captain's profits sent the *Eliza* to Norfolk, Virginia, instead.

As engineer or architect, Latrobe could create small masterpieces on any provocation, even on a bet. Not long after landing in Norfolk, and a few

---

*Latrobe's mother, Anna Margaretta Antes—the Pennsylvania German—was the granddaughter of a Roman Catholic abbot and abbess, who became Protestants, married, came to America, acquired large land holdings, and supported the missionary activities of the Moravians.

†The better of them, Hammerwood Park in Sussex, is (as of 1988) undergoing loving rehabilitation by a young physicist named David Pinnegar.

‡The bank was a Tory job, obtained by John Soane through his earnest solicitation of the Pitt family. Cockerell's commission for the Admiralty Building came from the same sources; as his first names suggest, he came of the family of the diarist and Admiralty politician.

months before he went on his sketching expedition to Broad Rock Island, he
made his first American design. It was the outcome of

> a trifling Wager laid against me by Captn. Pennock that I could not
> design a house . . . which should have only 41 feet front; which should
> contain on the Ground floor, 3 rooms, a principal Staircase, and back-
> stairs . . . the front door of which should be in the Center. I won the
> Wager . . .

> About two months afterwards, I dined at the Eagle tavern in Rich-
> mond[, where a neighbor to the house in Norfolk was seated nearby and]
> related, that some time ago, a Frenchman was at Norfolk, who had given
> Captn. Pennock the most preposterous design . . . From his description,
> interlarded with many oaths and imprecations against the Frenchman, I
> learnt that my own design was meant . . .

A man signing himself "B. Henry Latrobe Boneval" and speaking in the
accent of a childhood spent more upon the continent of Europe, including
France, than in England, caused some confusion among the merchants of
Norfolk. These seafarers had seen many men of many nations in many places,

Benjamin Henry Latrobe by Carl Von Breda

but never before an engineer, poet, playwright, diarist, watercolorist, and artist of architecture and invective.

After picking up a few odd jobs in Virginia, Latrobe received the commission for the Bank of Pennsylvania in Philadelphia and his career was launched. His works included many private houses, churches, and large public works such as waterworks in Philadelphia and in New Orleans. He is perhaps best known for his cathedral in Baltimore and the interiors in the national Capitol that remain from his long years struggling with that building. He was a friend of Thomas Jefferson's and, through Jefferson, had a strong influence on the design of the University of Virginia. For another friend, Henry Clay, he provided the plans to make Lexington, Kentucky, a classical village. For Aaron Burr, as we shall see, he might have designed the neoclassical capital of an empire, or at least of a satrapy.

Latrobe was also a formidable traveler, and thanks to the wondrously illustrated volumes of his American journals, published in recent years, we can travel with him, to see the United States in its neoclassical age through his eyes. He is a good companion, wise and full of anger at the right things, despising the right enemies, loyal to the right causes and to the right friends. Aside from an anachronistic disdain for commerce, he can be trusted—and will be trusted throughout this work—to give us a clear impression of the terrain he traversed.

1

FRENCH NEOCLASSICISM
AND OTHER MATTERS

"Neoclassical" is a term that engenders much bickering among scholars; it does not have neatly mitered edges, but it is useful nonetheless. In architecture it describes buildings that make use of the post and the lintel and/or the arch in the ways the Greeks and the Romans used them. When a post is brought forward, it becomes a column; when it remains a part of a wall, but is discernably advanced from it, it is a pilaster. When a lintel is laid across the top of two posts and elaborated with certain devices favored by the Greeks, it becomes an entablature. When a gable roof is added to cover the box behind, *voilà!*—the Parthenon or the Virginia capitol.

The Greeks (and neoclassical architects severely Grecian in their taste) seem to have been more interested in the appearance of a building than in one's experience inside it; that is, they were conscious of its effect as an object set

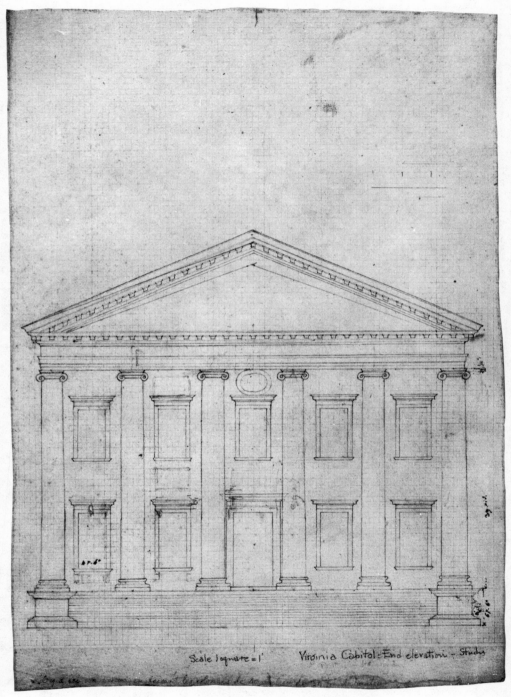

Front elevation of the Virginia capitol by Thomas Jefferson

View of Broadway and City Hall, looking north from Ann Street;
watercolor by Baron Axel Leonhard Klinckowstrom

in a landscape, and gave less attention to its effect (in a psychological sense) on a person walking through its interior space.* In contrast, the Romans had a flair for interior space; they contrived grand impressions through the use of the arch, the vault, and the dome. The neoclassical period was willing to consolidate the accomplishments of the Greeks and the Romans, often placing a recollected Pantheon—a building dominated by a dome—within the shoe-box-with-columns form of the Parthenon. This is what Latrobe himself did in creating, in 1798, his Bank of Pennsylvania, a more original work than the Virginia capitol.

The Virginia capitol and the Bank of Pennsylvania both asserted the color scheme and surface treatment for neoclassical buildings in America. A brilliant cream replaced the tawny or russet of brick. Walls were covered by seamless stucco or by precisely laid, carefully trimmed blocks of light-colored stone. When stone and a client rich enough to afford it were not available, wood painted white would do, or brick painted yellow, buff, ochre, or white.

*Since I wrote this sentence, a friend has instructed me about Pausanias's account of the post-Parthenonic achievements in interior space on the part of Iktinos. But the same friend assures me that what I have said is as true as any general principle not aspiring to include all exceptions.

The transformation of one city may illustrate what neoclassicism brought to the United States. Prerevolutionary New York had been dark, steep, angular, and harsh. Stepped gables faced the street; brick and stone structures showed their seams and joinings. Though there were a few "Georgian" red-brick cubes set uncomfortably here and there, much of the town looked as if it had been built by an elderly, impatient Dutch bricklayer who kept changing his mind.

One by one, in the 1790s, new buildings appeared amid the disarray, cool, bright, serene, and symmetrical. Columns and pilasters confirmed a geometric grid ordaining a classical balance. Surfaces were smoothed, shapes were clarified. Brick was still used for ambitious buildings, perhaps of clay from the same kilns as before, but now stuccoed over and pierced by larger windows and doors. There was more glass to reflect the sky, more stucco shining white in the sunlight. This was an architecture full of pride, enlightened, proclaiming the coming of a new age.

The Anglo-Dutch red-brick-and-white-trim of the past was associated in the minds of many, including Thomas Jefferson, with British colonialism. Jefferson dismissed the buildings of William and Mary College and the hospital at Williamsburg as "rude, mis-shapen piles, which, but that they have roofs, would be taken for brick-kilns." Another important figure in this story, Pierre Pharoux—not so celebrated as Jefferson but better trained as an architect— reached the same judgment. Indeed, he put it into much the same words, though on artistic grounds alone: Independence Hall in Philadelphia, he wrote, was "a pile of bricks, as is also the library, over the door of which they have put a fine statue of Franklin, like a saint in a niche . . ."*

Orders

In 1796, the Virginia capitol, in its uncouth setting, would have attracted any architect's eye; but the classically trained, like Latrobe, might well have grimaced at the notion of the Orders amid such disorder. Latrobe liked puns, but not obvious ones. He also liked system and comprehensiveness, and might therefore have delighted in the thirty-odd meanings of the word "order" provided by the *Oxford English Dictionary*. They range from "Holy Orders" to "lower orders" by way of mercantile orders, Orders in Council, orders of magnitude, of chivalry, and of files.

---

*In his own city plans Pharoux showed a penchant for grand Parisian avenues meeting at acute angles, like those his countryman Major Pierre-Charles L'Enfant recommended for Washington City. He thought Philadelphia depressingly "uniform" in its unbroken rectilinear grid: "The city is built in lines, the streets are all at right angles." (Pharoux, in the *Castorland Journal*, p. 125—see chapter 5.)

Among this catalogue are four uses of the word that together provide a grid for some discussion of how the capitol came to be in Richmond, how Latrobe arrived upon Broad Rock Island, and quite a lot besides.

Two of those uses are before us already: first, the opposite of "disorder," and second, that which has leaped to the minds of English-speaking architects since Inigo Jones. "The Orders" are the specific styles of classical architecture characterized by the type of column each employs; by a somewhat sloppy extension common in nineteenth-century America, "the Orders" came to mean columns in general.

The other two definitions most important to us can be distinguished from each other by their familiar companion verbs. We have "May I take your order?" and "May I have your orders?": thus are the orders of merchants and waiters distinguished from those of presidents and generals. Though we will attend to both—two political proclamations, the Declaration of Independence of 1775 and the Monroe Doctrine in 1818, set the limits to the period we discuss—that does not mean there will be much space given here to battles and elections and revolutions. The merchants and architects who are our chief actors were not much awed by orders issued by politicians and military men; and alliances among families and family firms rather than among dynasties and governments moved most of the events in this story.

In fact, familial and commercial alliances shaped the actions of states more often than the other way around in the neoclassical age. When they could not arrange such accommodations, merchants found ways through, over, and under the economic policies of kings, parliaments, and presidents. Famous fortunes were created out of disorderly practices like smuggling and privateering, even piracy, a profession with its own classical precedents (the grave Athenians, creators of the stateliest sort of architecture, were prone to piracy on a grand scale). And after a millennium and a half not distinguished for tranquil money-getting, the eighteenth-century royal governor of New York Lord Bellomont and the colony's rising merchant-prince Robert Livingston brought things up to date by engaging in a partnership with Captain Kidd.*

---

*This episode is well summarized in the *Dictionary of American Biography* entries under William Kidd (vol. 10, p. 367) and Robert Livingston (vol. 11, p. 317). The British *Dictionary of National Biography* entry for Kidd (vol. 11, pp. 93–95) is a compendium of errors, compounded by the smug assertion therein that the great Macaulay's account is "more than usually inaccurate." The dictionary is more than usually vague about the differences between New York and Massachusetts, Livingstons and Livingstones. But we need not worry so much about pirates as about engineers, where the dictionary is even worse—see chapter 5.

Captain Kidd permits an early exposition of this work's policy on notes. In the main text are those of possible interest to general readers; in the back matter, references and those notes useful only to scholars and others of relentless curiosity. I do not "note" things of such common knowledge that a court might take them within "judicial notice," but I strive to do so when assertions are cranky or when I hope someone else will pursue the idea.

Thus, a partnership of a politician, a merchant, and a pirate set the tone for an epoch in which mercantile opportunity made it unusually difficult to draw distinctions between what was public policy and what was private interest.

The Color of Irises

Commerce and architecture are the two most important strands braided into this narrative. There is a third, the color of which is blue, the tint of the iris, the fleur-de-lis.*

The architecture that survives from the formative years of the American Republic shows the imprint of French taste, easily recognized if one sets one's eye for the color of the fleur-de-lis in architecture, in the way one sets one's eye for blue or red or yellow in a field of wildflowers. Let us return to the New York City of 1810 and look about its new City Hall. Over on Mott Street, there is the first Saint Patrick's Cathedral, a work of the same French architect. These two celebrated buildings gave a sudden, cool grace to a town that had been growing along its haphazard Dutch pattern and now began to extend itself northward along the grid established by that Frenchman.

In the 1790s comprehensive exercises in town planning were carried out for the first time in the state of New York by another Frenchman, Pierre Pharoux, whose comments on Philadelphia we have noted; the towns were Tivoli, Athens, and probably Rome (the latter two did not acquire their neoclassical names until a little later).

Pharoux was also the author of New York's first estate plan on a grand scale, that for Baron von Steuben, near Remsen, and its second, if my conjectures are correct (see p. 68ff.), for James Leray, near Watertown. Another French architect, Joseph-Jacques Ramée, had more ambitious opportunities twenty years later, designs for James Duane of Duanesburg, for the Ogdens of Ogdensburg, and for the campus of Union College, near Schenectady. Union was to be formed about a rotunda in linked wings like those shown from the 1770s onward in many French competition designs for the Ecole des Beaux-Arts; its design preceded by five years a similar concept, that of Mr. Jefferson's University of Virginia at Charlottesville.

The main body of *Orders from France* is confined to the period after the Franco-American alliance achieved a victorious outcome in war and established an independent United States in 1783. One expects to find an iris-colored tincture in American architecture of that time—at least until the French and

---

*I suppose my choice of the fleur-de-lis rather than the Tricolore may offend some revolutionary spirits. At the other extremity of the political spectrum, black is available, the color of the three toads on the flag of Clovis, founder of the Merovingian dynasty of France.

the Americans fell out with each other and had their own brief, informal war in the late 1790s. But it should be noted that that color was present considerably earlier and remained discernible considerably later. Thus, for example, in the 1760s, gardens designed by Claude-Joseph Sauthier surrounded the palace of the governor of North Carolina and several other plantations in that colony; there were a half-dozen French-designed towns in North Carolina and as many, even earlier, in Georgia. And a chain of French-engineered fortresses girdled the exposed shoreline of the United States, from Maine, around the Florida Keys, and on westward to Mobile and Louisiana (see Appendix I).

The French, in fact, made a specialty of garrison towns and fortress building; designs developed along their own Rhineland frontier reappeared in the eighteenth century from the Upper Volga to the lower Mississippi. In the United States, New Orleans, Detroit, and Saint Louis took their initial configurations while they were under French rule; and around 1800 most of the coastal cities of the newly independent nation depended on the architectural skill of Frenchmen to protect them against attack from the sea. From an architectural point of view, the Star-Spangled Banner first waved over a French fort, and the torpedoes damned by Admiral David Farragut emerged from apertures designed by Napoleon's former aide General Simon Bernard.* Colonel Anne-Louis de Toussard, whom we will meet as a painter and hunting companion, was the commander of the defenses of Philadelphia and author of a primer for American artillerists.† Boston's Fort Independence and Baltimore's celebrated Fort McHenry were the work of Jean Fontin. Fort Monroe in Virginia, like the famous defenses of Mobile Bay, were by Bernard, assisted by a man who once was a draftsman for Latrobe and who bore the name of the great painter Poussin. (William Tell Poussin belongs to a later age; his service as an emissary from France to the United States was as disastrous as his service as a draftsman for Latrobe—for which see p. 398.)

Major Charles L'Enfant was the most famous of the French military engineers to branch out into American city planning and architecture. Yet we can

---

*Bernard instituted general use of an instruction manual devised by Charles Lallemand, whom we will meet in another role. Bernard served the United States for sixteen years before returning to France in the 1830s, where he became minister of war (twice), aide to King Louis Philippe, and a peer of France. He was already a Napoleonic baron.

†Toussard's friend Joel Barlow provided to his brother-in-law and head of the Army ordnance department, George Bomford, the sobriquet for the first American fifty-pound guns, the "Columbiads." Named for Barlow's epic poem (see pp. 391, 417), they replaced French forty-two-pounders as America's standard heavy weapons.

Bomford is a principal player in the drama of the final days of Benjamin Henry Latrobe's architectural career in Washington. As we will see, his partner in an effort to help Latrobe was George Graham, who, as acting secretary of war, placed Bernard in charge of America's coastal defenses.

It happens that Bomford was also the nominal designer of the house Oak Hill, in Loudon County, Virginia, where James Monroe wrote the state papers that were combined to form his famous Doctrine (see p. 420ff.).

measure the strange propensity of our national memory to select against giving due credit to French influence—a phenomenon that might be called "gallavoidance"—by the fact that L'Enfant has not yet gained the attention of a modern biographer (or an accurate one of any period); nor has so much as a county been named in his honor. Yet he was trusted to plan not only the capital city of the United States but also the major buildings of that city and the nation's first "company town," Paterson, New Jersey.

A Matter of Style

French fortresses.

America's first professionally designed gardens: French as well.

Cities modeled on Versailles, such as Williamsburg, Virginia, and Washington, D.C., and cities modeled on French fantasies: Castorland, Scioto, Gallipolis, Azylum, Aigleville, Speranza, Tivoli, Demopolis, Arcola. From bellicose Le Champ d'Asile in Texas to whimsical Fontaine Laval in Maine, French urban planners girdled trees in arboreal wilderness and scratched lines across desert earth.

What was French about all this work? French in what ways? And what is French about French neoclassicism? Distinguishing the influence in America of French neoclassical style from that of British neoclassical style is not easy, despite endless, earnest pedagogical essays making the effort. Indeed, there was so much cultural cross-pollination between Britain and France that there is scarcely a single aspect of architectural style to be found in the one country without a like in the other.

Soon after Howard Mumford Jones published his *America and French Culture, 1750–1848,* a book admirably broad in literary scope but, like most of its day, eschewing the artifactual, Carl Becker admonished Jones and other historians not to discourse too much about French "influence" in America. "Contacts of Americans with things French is one thing; . . . estimating the influence of French culture on American culture is another."

That has been good advice for nearly sixty years. Estimates of influence are not very useful when simple observation confirms that as Frenchmen moved about America, they made architecture that is seldom distinguishable from that produced by British designers working in the same regions. Still, despite Becker's admonition, other writers have tried to provide field guides to distinguish French from British influences in America, Talbot Hamlin among them. Such overreaching was an error on the way to other errors, as this passage illustrates:

> Specifically French architectural details had . . . limited influence in America. Certain planning ideals, such as curve-ended or elliptical rooms

and ingenious relationship of many varied room shapes and sizes, were generally accepted. Occasional conceptions monumental in type can be traced to the same source. That is almost all ... Gradually during the 1790s the French influences waned.

It is not true that French influences waned during this period. Even earlier, while they were subjects of the king of England, Americans were not necessarily governed by English fashions in art. They traded with the king's enemies, the French, engaged French designers, and luxuriated in French fashion. Later, after they became politically independent, casting themselves loose from the British empire, they were even more likely to look to France for architectural ideas. In fact, those influences were so strong that there is plenty of work for us to do in following Frenchmen going about their influential work, without spending much energy parsing out which of those shapes and sizes of buildings (or gardens or cities or fortresses) created by them should be thought to be "specifically" French.*

We follow Becker, not Jones or Hamlin. In the neoclassical period there was so much commercial traffic passing back and forth from one nation to another that neither aesthetic nor economic autarchy could survive. The early history of the United States was not that of a frail infant growing to maturity distinct from Europe. Its first surge of economic growth, in the 1790s, was made possible by the exigencies—indeed, the distress—of Europe and of Europe's colonies, including those of France. As war swept every ocean except those of the polar regions, and every continent except Australia and Antarctica, commerce thrived at a pace, scale, reach, and freedom from restraint unprecedented in human affairs.

While all this was occurring, the language of architecture, like the language of commerce, became more and more multilingual. Even among the noncommercial classes in France there had been a generation-long fit of anglomania. The courtiers of Louis XVI adopted British accents and laid out English gardens, while across the channel aristocrats of a Whig coloration were very French in dress, in architecture, and sometimes in accent. So intermingled was taste that the greatest cookbook writer of the age, Brillat-Savarin (in his *Physiologie du goût*), cautioned that no wise person waxes metaphorical or solemn in the use of the word "taste" itself.†

*From 1750 onward, there were plenty of curve ends and elliptical rooms and ingenious geometry for Americans to observe in the work of Robert Adam, Sir Robert Taylor, and James Gibbs in Britain. As to "monumentality," one can call the building of large buildings a French idea if one likes; but what is one to do with huge piles of British masonry stretching across the horizon of Yorkshire, like Castle Howard or Wentworth Woodhouse, or along the Thames embankment? Are we to make Somerset House into a French building because Sir William Chambers, its architect, studied in France? It is wearisome and unproductive to fret at a great man like Hamlin, but he was wrong on all counts.

†Brillat-Savarin was in America in the 1790s, forced to squander his gastronomic talent teaching

So we may observe the work of Frenchmen in America and note certain French qualities in that work, when obvious enough, without attempting to make distinctions where only gradations and impressions are to be found. It is sufficient for our purposes to note the degree to which commerce, architectural fashion, and affairs of state induced behavior. Sometimes all three acted in concert; sometimes they vied with one another to determine the outcome of the biographies we follow in the pages to come.

2

ARCHITECTURE AND MONEY

Architecture is by its nature obtrusive in size and expensive in scale. Architects, because of the public and collective nature of their art, often work at commercial intersections, amid crowds of agitated people; real architects—as distinguished from the contrivers of projects—do their work where the hurly-burly is headiest. Much of the story of the early economy of the United States can be interpreted as if it were the story of the creation of a class of clients.

Architecture in any country, and at any time, is the joint product of a designer with a skill in engineering and a client with a skill in money-making or money-keeping. Becoming a client manifests a strong desire to assert oneself publicly, a desire seldom conscious but nonetheless very powerful. A client and a designer create a sort of joint persona. They express what they both want the public to think of them. Mercantile people are accustomed to thinking about marketing—the art of impressions. Merchants are therefore more conscious of such matters than, for example, subsistence farmers or feudal princes in remote regions.

In my *Architecture, Men, Women and Money,* examples of this thesis were seen in familiar buildings, or buildings that ought to be familiar, created in the New World between 1600 and 1860. *Orders from France* is a book about a shorter span of time, roughly from 1780 to 1820. (We give, at the outset, some earlier examples just to provide orientation.) Some of the themes of the preceding work reappear, illustrated in greater detail. Chief among them is the observa-

---

school and playing in a pit orchestra among the other Frenchmen who largely composed the stock of musicians for the theater. But he did instruct a Boston cook, whose only previous training had been as chef for the archbishop of Bordeaux, in the correct method of cooking eggs with cheese, and he left us an accurate history of the tactics used by his compatriot Captain Collet to accumulate his first fortune, selling sorbet on the streets of New York.

He also tried to warn Mme de Staël, critic, novelist, patron and mistress of art and artists, against extending too widely her holdings in the Adirondack back country (see p. 40).

tion that a transfer of taste often accompanies a transfer of money repeated often enough to permit an expectation.*

In the late eighteenth century there was immense though irregular traffic in goods, persons, ideas, and fashions between France, the United States, and the West Indies, especially with that portion of the island of Hispaniola the French called Saint-Domingue, now called Haiti. By "irregular" I mean to suggest that this traffic was often illegal as well as discontinuous. Many of the people who carried it on built houses in the French fashion in the United States. The richest of them had traded with the French islands and had gathered there architectural ideas that, mingled together with French classicism, gave shape to houses and gardens from the Saint Lawrence to Blowing Rock, North Carolina. Sometimes the Caribbean influences are not easy to spot: there might, for example, be no verandas or piazzas; but more often than not there were.

The first example offered here of the intrusion of French patterns of building into the English colonies is one of those structures that owes its existence to the West Indies though it owes its shape to Normandy by way of Scotland. It demonstrates that these traffic patterns defying the laws of nations in the interests of profit did not first produce revenue and architecture in America in 1783. They had done so from the very beginning.

Mount Pleasant

A grand Philadelphia house of 1765, Mount Pleasant might be expected to be a typical product of the most confident days of the first British empire. In the early 1760s, that portion of the North American continent ruled by the British, which had been at war with France off and on for a half century and more, was at war no longer: William Pitt the elder had organized a series of victories across the globe and had driven France from North America. At this apogee of British pride, Mount Pleasant was erected on the highest point of a hill above the Schuylkill River. Knowing where and when it was built, we should not wonder that it was given pride of place in a centerfold in volume 1 of *Great Georgian Houses of America,* reprinted in 1970 by Dover.

When we ask the natural question "Who paid for it?" we are led immediately away from the Georgian—indeed, away from the English. Mount Pleasant was built by a Scots trader, Captain John Macpherson. Macpherson was not a famous man, though he was briefly rich. He seems to have been one of those Scotsmen who formed their artistic affinities by living in Holland or elsewhere

*Some may find this emphasis distasteful. Well, money matters. It mattered to all the characters in our story, and we are trying to understand them as well as ourselves.

in northern Europe where French taste held sway before making their way to America—like other Scots traders we will come to know in these pages, the Livingstons of Jamaica and New York (see p. 31), the Hopes of Boston, London, and Amsterdam (see p. 244), and the Parishes of Hamburg, Antwerp, Philadelphia, and Parishville (see p. 242). It was not necessary, however, that he learn to be French in France or anywhere beyond his homeland.

Art historians have tended to describe Mount Pleasant as Anglo-Palladian in style. What we know about Captain Macpherson suggests instead that it is neither English nor Palladian but Franco-Caledonian. The Caledonian part of this term is simple enough: the Romans called Scotland by this name—Sir Walter Scott immortalized it as "Caledonia, stern and wild." The other portion may require a little explanation.

In the sixteenth century, Andrea Palladio designed villas as headquarters for Venetian plantations on the mainland of Italy. Two centuries later, English gentlemen laid their own versions of these villas heavily on the English countryside, magnifying his name and his dimensions, seeking to emulate the defining qualities of his works: their symmetry, their horizontality, and their way of spreading themselves in loggias and linked dependencies to enfold the terrain.

Mount Pleasant comes of a different tradition in Italian villa design: pleasure palaces in the country for bankers, courtiers, clergymen, and owners of distant

Mount Pleasant, as drawn for the Architects' Emergency Committee's
Great Georgian Houses of America

Entrance Facade of The
Mount Pleasant Mansion at Philadelphia Pennsylvania
Erected in 1761 by Captain John Macpherson

estates. This was the tradition introduced to the aristocracy of France by Sebastiano Serlio, contemporary and competitor of Palladio. French aristocrats did not (or were not permitted to) deny themselves the beguilements of the court for very much of the year; Paris and Versailles were far more dominant in their lives than was London for the landed gentry of England, and when they came to vouchsafe occasional visitations upon their agricultural estates, they kept to tall, tight châteaux under high, un-Palladian roofs. These fortress-houses departed from stone so far as to use bricks, but they seldom were stuccoed in the Palladian fashion. Nor were they expansive; they held their elbows in, so to speak—their courtyards were cramped in a garrisonlike fashion.

Mount Pleasant was not built by a Frenchman, yet it looks much like a reduced version of a château in Normandy. This is a clue to the character of its builder, a lowland Scot who hated everything British.

The "Auld Alliance"

The eighteenth century was a time of strange alliances. One of the strangest was the friendship between desolate and barbaric Scotland—much of it perpetually beyond agriculture and even beyond grazing, foggy when not under snow, bleak, swept by Arctic winds and Nordic raids, inhabited largely by grouse, deer, seabirds, and bandits, ruled by uncouth lairds—and smiling, fertile France, the center of Western civilization.

A succession of Scottish kings had been taking French ladies as their queens since the twelfth century; sovereigns in Edinburgh and Paris had striven together to limit the sway of competitors based in London. Courtly ladies and gentlemen had exchanged gifts and offered to Scotsmen of lower degree examples of how to make use of the accoutrements of French fashion. Half a millennium of emulation made subtle but discernible changes in the rough Caledonian landscape.

The alliance had its sentimental and aesthetic side, but at its heart was a common antipathy to England. By 1700, that antipathy was no longer running regularly into border warfare; it was expressing itself, as such feelings often do, in mercantile competition.

Scotland was an independent commercial rival to England, sending its own settlements to New Jersey and South Carolina. In 1698, the Scots even planted their own colony in South America, on the coast of Panama, called New Edinburgh. Their ambitions were frustrated, however, by the commercial interests of the City of London and by the Dutch courtiers surrounding the newly installed King William III of England—who was also chief of state of Holland, prince of Orange (the principality of his ancestors in the south of France), and, it was contended in London, Scotland's king as well. William prevented the Scots from obtaining funds from the merchants of Hamburg and ships from the merchants of Holland; the colonists of New Edinburgh set out so weakened that they were unable to resist the inevitable counterattack from Spain and perished. Scottish anger, often felt after Scottish humiliation, was focused on the English; when Queen Anne succeeded William, her ministers could buy union with Scotland only by offering the lowland magnates very large inducements.

Maritime Scotland was eager for freedom to compete with England, and the Highlanders were avid for alliance with France. Louis XIV recognized a succession of Stuart princes as kings of Scotland and in 1708 sent an armada to escort the "Old Pretender" back to his throne. The wind, as usual, favored the English; but in 1715 the earl of Mar rose again with his Highlanders, opening the east coast of Scotland to the French. Louis XIV died at that moment, however, and the regent of France, false to the alliance, dallied with the English; Mar went into exile, and the English banned the use of the name of the Jacobite MacGregors in Scotland, an inconvenience redressed only in 1774.

In 1717, some of the leaders of "the '15" returned aboard Spanish ships. This tiny revolt was quickly dispersed, but in 1745 a genuine rebellion arose in Scotland, financed by the French. Prince Charles Stuart gathered the Highland chiefs behind him and led a Scottish army deep into England. His retreat was full of heroics, and his life would have come to a more graceful end had he died with his men at Culloden. Instead, he lived on and on, through a dissolute and discredited old age, until his death in 1788. But the memories of Bonnie Prince Charlie lived on as well: his kilts and smiles, his youth and grace, the charm he had learned in France.

In the eighteenth century, the lowland lairds ignored the ruckus in the Highlands when they could and came to prosperous terms with Britain. But they abandoned only the politics and religion of France, not its instruction in architecture. Before his death in 1710, one of them, Sir William Bruce, made the same kind of attentive tour of France as his English counterparts made of Palladio's Italy. After Bruce led the way, other Scottish architects, like William Adam, patriarch of a celebrated clan, made their own visits to French châteaux, such as Balleroy, in Normandy, and Blérancourt, and made free use of French forms when they came home to the lowlands. The outbuildings of Bruce's Kinross, obvious exemplars for those at Mount Pleasant, are equally obvious in their indebtedness to Blérancourt. They were built in a style we are therefore free to call Franco-Caledonian, common to Mount Pleasant, to Henry Livingston's Teviotdale, on the Hudson (see p. 67), and to Bruce's Kinross, Raith, Mertoun, and Auchidenny—designs that were the models, reduced in scale, for many houses built by ambitious merchants and planters in America when they were able.

The Château de Balleroy, in Normandy

In John Macpherson's youth, the "auld alliance" with France was very much alive. The evidence for this statement lies upon the façade of Mount Pleasant. Other evidence is to be found only "by inquiring within," as the expression used to go among the mercantile classes.

The Economic History of Mount Pleasant

Though architecturally Mount Pleasant is Franco-Caledonian, what little we know of its economic history suggests that it is Creole-Caledonian.

No one has yet been successful in finding ledgers or even dispatches by which Macpherson reported his mercantile adventures. It is conventional to call him a privateer, since privateering was the chief means of gaining wealth among Scotsmen based in Philadelphia during the last years of the wars of the 1750s against France.

A privateer was a shipowner authorized to prey upon the commerce of a nation with which his own was at war. This authorization and a somewhat limited range of victims distinguished him from a pirate. Many seafarers of

Scottish origin chose to base themselves in the Chesapeake, especially in the port of Norfolk, and in Philadelphia; many were even willing, most of the time, to limit their activities to attacking the subjects of the king of France. The Caribbean was their theater of war; predation was their business.

These fierce seafarers often combined privateering with "the Mount and Cape trade." "The Mount" was Monte Cristi, a Spanish port on the island of Hispaniola; "the Cape" was Cap François, directly across a pleasant, sheltered bay and ruled, rather diffidently, by the French. French regulations denied to Americans flying the British flag access to the purchase orders of planters of the Cape who desired to feed their slaves on Pennsylvania grain. British regulations denied such merchants the right to carry sugar, rum, or molasses produced by those slaves to American ports, where a great thirst and an appetite for sweets awaited.

Merchants like John Macpherson found a way: they picked up a Spanish passport, a Spanish flag, and a few Spanish crewmen in the Mount; sailed serenely across the bay to the Cape; became Spanish for a day's unloading of grain and reloading of sugar products; sailed back to the Mount; returned their rented passport, flag, crewmen, and nationality; and made for home under their own colors.

If one repeated this process often enough, one might become rich enough to build Mount Pleasant.

We shall return to the Cape, a lucrative and terrible place, several times in this tale. Mount Pleasant had its own tragedies. It, too, was a place accursed. Macpherson overspent himself, and lost his mansion to his creditors. In 1779 it was purchased by Benedict Arnold to give to Peggy Shippen, his Tory bride. Already on his way toward becoming the most famous traitor in the chronicles of America, the general was a man desperate for fame and for fortune— desperate enough for any devices.

Arnold's business practices were squalid even for those ugly times; his first business experience was among the notoriously corrupt West Indiamen of New Haven, Connecticut, and he spent most of the 1760s shuttling back and forth to the sugar islands, following the example of larger figures like Macpherson, with smaller results. He tried smuggling and land speculation, including an effort to lay his hands on forty thousand acres near Lake Champlain, once a French seigneury.* While still a hero of the revolutionary cause, he was trading with the enemy; when caught in one especially noxious transaction, he was reprimanded, and his hurt pride gave him yet another incentive to switch sides for money.

Benedict Arnold never inhabited Mount Pleasant. If his treason had been successful, he might have presided there like a British satrap in India or Ireland or even Scotland, places where "native" revolts recently had been suppressed.

*His sometime partner William Constable had more success in such matters (see p. 40).

But he failed. After the war, he built himself another mansion overlooking the waterfront, at Saint John, New Brunswick, and returned to the West Indies trade. Unlucky again, he became a British secret agent against the French in the Caribbean, then a smuggler pretending to be an American. Finally, he put all his earnings into a fling for a merchant's killing and lost. He died in 1801, bankrupt, like Macpherson.

He reappears only once in this narrative, in an incident of the early 1790s, in association with Charles Maurice de Talleyrand-Périgord, who was much more fortunate than Arnold in his American real-estate transactions (see p. 102n.).

The story of Mount Pleasant has been offered here to establish the pattern of this book, which is intended to be read not as architectural history but as the history of the relationship of architecture to mercantile activity. Architecture lasts longer than many other works of humankind and is therefore available longer to give some tactile firmness to general statements about economics and to ground commercial biography in specific places.

Architecture, as distinguished from sculpture, has an inside that can be explored, an inside that can also be *shared* over long periods of time. One generation may return to architecture that was important to its predecessors. Having shared space with them, it may understand them better, especially if they left messages about how they felt about that space. Comparing our feelings about an object or a space with the feelings of others is a means to achieving an imaginative intimacy with them. This must be important to many of us, or we would not exert ourselves, as we do, to visit such places as Monticello or Tintern Abbey.

And so there is somewhat more architectural history here, and more biography of architects, than is conventional in social or economic history, and somewhat more economic and social history than is found in conventional art histories. The biographies of architects stitch together their clients, who are often representative of a significant body of people possessing ready money at a particular time and are for that reason especially interesting to social historians. This point of view is American and thus somewhat commercial. Americans have been known as a people interested in money, perhaps because they are aware of the flexibility money imparts, and may be distinguished from those whose status relationships are more fixed, whose desire for flexibility is less pronounced, and whose habit of movement, in status and in space, is less active.

Within these broad objectives, our theme is the commerce in ideas, aesthetic concepts, technology, farm and livestock products, consumer goods, talent, and political ideals between France and the United States in the years between 1783 and 1820.

II

THE
MULTINATIONALS

Given a choice in the matter, any large historical observations herein are grounded upon specific artifacts—a habit carried over from years in banking, wherein one learns to go beyond the balance sheet of a used-car dealer to "kick the tires." The grounding offered here is architecture.

A work of architecture requires a setting if it is to be understood at all; a building makes no sense in isolation, like a boxed mushroom purchased at a market. Architecture appears in life like a mushroom in the forest floor, amid a compost of experience.

Chaumont, an ancient château on the Loire in "the Garden of France," owned by a family of West Indies merchants, was like that; so were other houses of the Lerays: their villa at Passy, between Versailles and Paris, and their stone headquarters among the granite knuckles, bogs, and rivulets of the northwestern Adirondacks. So, too, were the neoclassical mansions built along the Hudson by their contemporaries and occasional partners in commerce and patronage the Livingstons.

The château of Chaumont has never been an ingratiating place. It stands, snarling at the landscape, huge and squat, to be approached through a fortified entry across a double drawbridge. For centuries, however, the question for a succession of noble ladies was not how to enter but how to leave this dank and

The Château de Chaumont

gloomy place. They all wished to be elsewhere: Diane de Poitiers, mistress of
Henry II; Catherine de' Medici, sorceress and queen; and considerably later,
Mme de Staël.

In the middle of the eighteenth century, Chaumont was acquired by a new
châtelain, who had quite another view of the place; he was delighted to be there.
Jacques Leray, a slave-trading merchant of Nantes, became a landed gentleman
with the acquisition of the château, which was to him the summit of an ascent
from noisome docks and the bickering of traders. Chaumont was his new
headquarters, and he surrounded it with many fertile acres.

By 1808, however, the largest holdings of the Leray family were not to be
found along the silver loops of the Loire, among vineyards and grain fields.
They were scattered, in lots of fifty thousand or more acres, between the Saint
Lawrence River and a squalid village that since has grown to be the city of
Syracuse, New York. A new seigneury had been acquired, centering on a
mansion that could be found only be traversing a blank stretch on the map

known as the Tug Hill upland. Today that eerie, treeless moorland of sandstone and marsh is still a blank. It lies to the left, westward, as one follows the Lerays' southern access road, now Route 120. Lost in the brush, over to the right somewhere, is Castorland, the largest of the American land speculations of the Lerays. Beyond Tug Hill, on the shore of Lake Ontario, are the remains of Basle, the seaport of Castorland, with twenty thousand unoccupied building sites.

Following the Tug Hill route, one can either pass through Talcottville, made notable in our time as the home of the critic and historian Edmund Wilson, or take a short detour to Constable Hall and Constableville, relics of William Constable, one of those who enticed the Lerays into diversifying their holdings into this unprepossessing terrain. Finally, one comes to Leraysville and the Leray mansion. It is a most unexpected sight, gleaming white amid freshly mowed lawns and giant trees. It is especially unexpected in its present context, for it is visited only upon gaining security clearance from the lean young men at the entrances to a Special Forces training unit.

The Leray mansion is now the residence of the commanding general of the Tenth Mountain Division at Camp Drum, a busy place: armored vehicles cruise

The Leray mansion

about, setting up dust clouds. Barracks, helipads, and PXs line the old route from the southeast, by which we entered. This was the route of plantation workers reporting to labor for James Leray, grandson of Jacques, the lord of Chaumont. Distinguished visitors were encouraged to approach instead from the northwest, past a model village and artificial lake, traversing a "romantic" or "English" garden as their carriages wound uphill to the formal parterres in front of the central, stuccoed mass of the house.

Remnants of carriage roads and bridges that once spanned water courses suggest that there was another "English" or "Chinese" garden on the southeast side, with specimen elms and pines. Across that side of the house there was probably a piazza or veranda in the West Indian mode, raised one story off the ground, like that still seen on the rear side of Constable Hall. (Greek-revival columns replaced the piazza in the 1820s, and lawns have replaced the parterres.)

In Leray's day, after entering a door at the center of the main block, one passed through a wide stair hall into two octagonal drawing rooms at the rear, leading onto the piazza. The octagons could be opened together (and still are) for large gatherings; the spirit of Paris in the 1780s, before the French Revolution, survived in Leraysville well into the 1820s: émigré musicians, painters, and memoirists found some reward there for the long, dusty, bleak journey across the Tug Hill wasteland to James Leray's outpost.

The tall windows admitting light into the linked octagonal parlors, and the floor plan of which those parlors are the most conspicuous elements, are of interest not only for their aesthetic value but because they can teach us something about political and economic history. They are also clues to the designer of the Leray mansion and of a group of houses on the other side of the Adirondacks, along the Hudson.

Following those clues was made easier by some of the technological devices in use at Camp Drum for other purposes. The photographs and rough floor plans of the Leray house could be juxtaposed with photographs and floor plans of the Hill, a Livingston house bulldozed only recently from its site in the Hudson Valley, and a Van Rensselaer house still extant nearby. One can easily discern the similarity of the porticoed façades of the three, though all received their porticoes well after their initial construction.

Computer graphics, used to strip away the porticoes and all other accretions known to be remodelings, revealed nearly identical, three-bay façades. The floor plans, superimposed and brought to the same scale, showed hallways, stairways, and linked drawing rooms in roughly the same positions, and even a strange, triangular vestibule connecting the sets of twin parlors to the piazza. There were differences, of course, which we will come to examine in greater detail. But the likenesses would require further inquiry even if a neoclassical mansion and a vast landscape plan in the midst of the Adirondack back country were not enough to get us started.

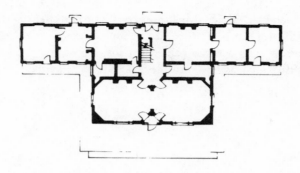

Floor plan and conjectural elevation of the Leray mansion as built, c. 1808
(computer-generated by James Stokoe; a piazza may be added at will)

This section contains a report on what was learned in satisfying our curiosity about how the commanding general of Camp Drum happens to be lucky enough to live in a sophisticated neoclassical villa and about what the Livingstons, the Van Rensselaers, and the Lerays might have had in common beyond façades and floor plans.

Place names are a considerable aid in unraveling this tale, marking, as they do, the extent of James Leray's real-estate investment. When he moved into his mansion, he controlled more than four hundred thousand acres, a large portion of the northwest corner of New York. Though he habitually approached his estates as we have, from the south via Syracuse and Constableville, on several occasions he came from the east by way of the hamlet of Gouverneur, to call upon his partner, Gouverneur Morris. He would then enter the Leray lands after crossing borders marked by the townlets of Belfort and Antwerp and proceed, as we can, by way of Lake Bonaparte, named for Joseph Bonaparte, former king of Naples and of Spain, and repurchaser from Leray; Alexandria Bay, named for a daughter of James Leray; and Cape Vincent, named for his son. There is

Chaumont Bay, and the villages of Chaumont, Theresa (for another daughter), Plessis (for a friend), Deferiet (for his mistress), Brownville (for his overseer), and Burrs Mills (presumably for Aaron Burr, into whose family Vincent married). There is even a town named for his dog.

This is helpful, but it is far from the whole story. For that we need a little larger map.

3

THE EMPIRE OF

COMMERCE

The first recorded French appearance off the shores of North America occurred in 1534, when Jacques Cartier began to expose the fish and beaver of the Saint Lawrence Valley to the commercial appetites of Europe. Eighty-five years before Henry Hudson, French explorers probed the mouth of the Hudson; and French visitors were planting gardens in Maine in the sixteenth century. Thereafter, imperial France occupied itself with exploiting the trade of the Saint Lawrence and the Mississippi, while the British struggled to establish their entrepôts along the Atlantic Coast. Then, in 1613, a British expeditionary force from Virginia wiped out a French beachhead at Port Royal, and the struggle between the two great imperial powers for control of the North American continent began. During the reign of King Louis XIV, the governor general of his North American dominions, the comte de Frontenac, mounted a campaign to exclude all European competitors from America north of the Spanish dominions. He surveyed the lakes and rivers glinting in silver sequence from Montreal to New York City and saw in them a fissure in the British empire.

France had governed the northern third of that route for a hundred years: the Champlain Valley was organized along French postfeudal lines, protected by fortresses designed by the world's best military engineers. From their border province, French invaders thrust southward nearly every year, slicing down the valleys to sever New England from Britain's "bread colonies" to the south. Sainte-Hélène burnt Schenectady in 1690; Rouville ravaged Deerfield in 1704; Rigaud bypassed Albany to attack western Massachusetts again in 1746, as Léry appeared deep in the Mohawk Valley. Lorimer followed the Mohawk route in the next year, and nearly effected a junction with Montcalm, who took Fort William Henry, near the headwaters of the Hudson.

It would be a mistake, however, to assume that imperial contests totally distracted the minds of Americans from opportunities for trade. During the

"French and Indian Wars" (as we still tend to call the battles fought in North America during the worldwide conflicts between Britain and France in the eighteenth century), British colonials in America were not averse to dealing with the French, or with the "Indians" in alliance with France. Indeed, it was difficult to avoid an occasional swap of furs or fish, powder or ball, cloth or tobacco. The interior of the continent had been reached by Frenchmen well ahead of the British; traders from Montreal were busy in Wisconsin while the British were gingerly threading their way through the Berkshires of western Massachusetts. And the French possessions in the West Indies were like sweet tropical fruit, attracting a swarm of seafaring Yankee merchants.

Larger occasions were opened by the treaties of 1763, when the French gave up their North American possessions to Britain. Though the Champlain Valley seigneuries were wiped out, French culture was not extirpated among the populace; a huge region beginning not far to the north of Albany remains "French Canada." Nor did the pervasiveness of French culture diminish in the central Hudson, especially among the squirearchy. French Huguenots of the seventeenth century were joined by Creoles* in the eighteenth, each intermarrying in turn with Dutch and Scottish families having their own reasons for not being especially fond of the English (the Livingstons, for example; see below).

Indeed, in the eighteenth century, any cultivated person, from Archangel to Panama, looked to Paris as the most civilized of cities. France set the aesthetic tone, though the czar of all the Russians or the king of Spain or the king of England or the president of the new United States might at the time be at war, de facto or de jure, with the king of France or the French Republic; and this was as true in Mr. Jefferson's Albemarle County, Virginia, as in Dutchess County, New York. It became especially so after relations with France warmed from the deferential neutrality that followed the truce of 1763 to outright alliance in 1778, when France went to war beside the American rebels against British rule. To mark the occasion, Benjamin Franklin, in Paris, took into his arms the aged Voltaire, in the presence of a multitude fully aware that it was an affectionate gesture of cultures as well as of persons.

This political and collective enfolding was the proclamation of a diplomatic success: Franklin's assignment had been to broaden into an international conflict an American civil war, being fought with reciprocal savagery between those loyal to the British king and Parliament and those who sought independence, and this had been accomplished.† During the eight-year contest eventuating in

---

*The term "Creole" is used here to mean someone of French culture born in the West Indies.

†Franklin was in America for only four years in the whole span of time from 1758 to 1785. He had lived so long abroad that it must have been difficult for him to recapture his Philadelphia patois when he was ready to come home and play his role as an elderly Poor Richard, or, as the French backers of John Paul Jones translated the title of Franklin's almanac, *"Le Bonne Homme Richard."*

the independence of the United States, warfare again spread from North America across the globe. But though the aid of the Dutch and the Spaniards and even the complicity of the empress of Russia were not insignificant, these others did not make their presence felt as did the French upon the main course of events on the North American continent. The French were America's most important allies. There were three times as many Frenchmen as Americans present at the decisive battles around Yorktown. In 1783, Britain finally acquiesced in the independence of the United States by a treaty signed in the capital of France.

The most energetic and attractive of the French aristocracy had been at the elbows of American diplomats in conference and at the side of American soldiers in battle. Thousands of the healthiest young citizens of France were on American soil, engaged in a common cause with the battle-weary Continentals and those of the militia who remained very long in arms. Even after the "allied" troops went home—and all of them did not choose to go—French taste continued to be transmitted to America by French visitors, curious at first and then necessitous, as postrevolutionary America became a haven from revolution in France.

During the French and American alliance of the first part of this period, men like Thomas Jefferson, already deeply imbued with French philosophical ideas, were passionately francophile, and even devotees of the British constitution admired French culture. John Adams, for example, was an avid reader of Crèvecoeur and Chateaubriand (see p. 89).

Americans, then, had what Mr. Jefferson described as a canine appetite for books on French theory and French design; in the 1790s they displayed a canine appetite for French "flight capital" as well. As a result, the region between the Adirondacks, Lake Ontario, and the Saint Lawrence became economically a French and Flemish province. David Parish, Flemish by dint of his headquarters at Antwerp, added his 150,000 acres to the larger holdings of the comte de Survilliers, better known as Joseph Bonaparte, and of Leray de Chaumont. Nearby were the piquant little estates of the prince de Grouchy, the princes Murat, Mme de Staël, and the marquise de La Tour Du Pin.

Other capital from France was reinvested in New York timberlands, ironworks, shipyards, and farms, and in French communities in Texas, Alabama, Ohio, Missouri, Maine, Pennsylvania, Kentucky, and Indiana. The sponsors of these ventures were Bourbon loyalists, regicides who voted for the death of Louis XVI, Orleanists, Bonapartists, liberals, republicans, and those out of patience with all French factionalism.

Uncritical Francophilia had only a few years to bloom. The peace that ensued from the Treaty of Paris of 1783 was an uneasy one, frequently interrupted by skirmishes. American seafarers had long since become bold in challenging both of the world's leading commercial powers; the fleet of France as well as that of England sought to exclude all others from the rich markets and sources of raw materials in the West Indies. Then, in 1789, the kingdom of France entered into its own long agony. Over twenty-six years of bloodshed, the helical course of true revolutions was to take the French through a republican phase, an oligarchic phase, a military dictatorship, an empire, and back to a Bourbon monarchy, though a monarchy irreversibly altered from that of 1789. Relations between the United States and France declined into a "quasi-war" from 1797 to 1799, from which they never truly recovered, though the British once again had to fight them both from 1812 to 1815—a conflict that was disgraced by the burning of the capital cities of the United States and Upper Canada, and which settled very little.

The Livingstons and the Lerays

A merchant as such can be attached particularly to no country.
His mere place of residence is, as merchant, perfectly accidental.
—ROBERT MORRIS

As easily as fish through broken weirs, commerce and architectural style moved together about the North Atlantic, indifferent to the porous constraints of the imperial powers. "Mercantilism" as a system of political economy devoted to the restraint of trade did not appeal to mercantile interests, and commerce had its own laws (if not "laws," then "forces"); the Dutch West India Company, which controlled cities and vast reaches of inland territories, summoned to its purposes the shrewd and ambitious of all nations and established in New Netherland the quintessential multinational corporate outpost.

"The scrapings of nationalities," Peter Stuyvesant called the people of New Netherland. Until 1674 they were ruled by the Dutch, but they spoke fourteen European tongues, not to mention native dialects useful for commerce. Albany served the fur trade; New Amsterdam, the West Indies trade. Yankees migrating westward as early as 1690 across the old Dutch possessions along the Hudson heard in the streets of Albany and New York Croatian, Swedish, Norwegian, several German dialects, French, Gaelic, English, and even, on occasion, Dutch.

These "Dutch" towns were as squalid as the entrepôts of the multinational mercantile system in India, Java, or China. Albany's garbage was dumped out its windows, and "the problem of its removal," in the absence of sewers, was resigned to "a little army of wandering pigs." The shoreline was a jumble of sheds, shanties, and saloons. On the rising ground above the flood line were the merchants' houses. Carts of pelts and hogsheads were pushed uphill on un-greased axles, through the shrieking pigs and the garbage. Multilingual sum-monses would call for pulleys to elevate the trade goods beyond pilferage and offal, and up they would go—the evidence of commerce disappearing into attic warehouses with ornamented gables much beloved by antiquarians.

In New York City, once New Amsterdam, a nostalgic interest in the old "Gothic" buildings grew in inverse proportion to the number of surviving examples. Commerce was represented throughout the mid-Atlantic trading region by cramped little brick structures with steep roofs often displaying ornamental stepped or scalloped gable ends. Bridgetown, on Barbados, looked like this, as did Charles Town, South Carolina: very quaint, and very closely associated with the slave trade of the seventeenth and early eighteenth centuries. The streets of New Amsterdam and of Newport, Rhode Island, were main-tained by a tax on that trade.

New Amsterdam's founding was not an expression of any imperial Dutch ambition; it was the outpost not of a nation but of a slave-trading corporation. This was characteristically Dutch; the Netherlands had passed from a culture of late-medieval city-states to the world of the multinational corporation without much of a pause to consider self-contained nationalism. The inhabitants of diminutive and water-logged Holland could not aspire to autarchy. They had neither the dry space for agriculture nor the resources for heavy industry. So the Dutch, wherever they were, broke the rules laid down by the great imperial powers to constrain commerce.

The burghers of New York kept on breaking them during the relatively brief period when they were ruled by the British, between the 1670s and the American Revolution. The trade of the world put in to the landings they built as they deployed their profits into land in patroonships up the Hudson. The mere conversion of patroonships into manors did not change these merchants' behavior: they did not become English merely because they were conquered by the duke of York. The first generations of "patroons" did not live on the land, nor were they "squires" in the purely agricultural way of the English; they owned land largely for speculation.

The center of their trading world was the Caribbean. The Hudson River was a highway of the West Indies country and an extended anchorage of West Indies traders becoming squires. It carried furs and lumber to exchange for slaves, wheat to exchange for sugar (and feed the plantations), brown tannin to exchange for indigo and scarlet-powdered cochineal. Tidal as far as Albany, the river was the largest and longest of the streams by which the Atlantic penetrated the continent. By the end of the eighteenth century its shores were lined with verandaed cottages—the Dyckman House at 204th Street and Broad-way in Manhattan, for example—that some people call "Dutch colonial," though they were not at all like the strict, gabled, brick merchants' houses of

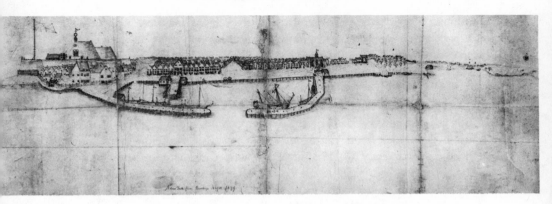

"The Labadist General View" (New York from Brooklyn Heights),
1678–1680, by Jasper Danckaerts

Bridgetown or old New Amsterdam, whose relatives are still to be seen in remote Columbia County and Dutchess County villages.*

The nature of the trade that paid for these structures is still suggested in the slave quarters of the ancestors of Franklin Roosevelt, preserved at Hyde Park. Under Dutch rule, New Netherland had a higher proportion of black slaves than Virginia. Nearly a century later, New York's Dutchess and Orange counties had more Negroes per capita than North Carolina.

Though fur trading and land speculation were also important to the Livingstons, members of a clan of great interest to us as major patrons of architecture, this Francophile family of Scotch and Dutch descent was always alert to the "sell" as well as to the "buy" side of the slave-and-sugar trade. After they acquired their own sugar plantations, like Aleppo on Jamaica, these holdings thrived and provided some of the building funds for a dozen houses on the Hudson in the 1790s. (An entire branch of the family, those descended from Philip Philip [*sic*—1741–87], made their lives and built their houses on Jamaica. All but one of his ten children were born there.) The sugar warehouses of the Livingstons were built both in New York and on Jamaica; the largest of these was given the attention of their Huguenot partners, the Bayards and the Gouverneurs. (In the 1790s, when Robert Morris, an old West Indiaman, commissioned Gouverneur Morris to represent their joint interests in Paris, it was largely to pry open further existing apertures to the French West Indies.)

The name Livingston should not lead us to think that those who bore it

---

*These are not specifically Dutch, either. They are to be found in compacted urban places from "Catfish Row" in Charleston, South Carolina, to Dutch cities like Haarlem and English ones like Ipswich—wherever the Atlantic trading community was formed into close quarters.

would take as their models the English squirearchy. They were a clan founded
by a patriarch (the Reverend John Livingston) so vehemently opposed to
English rule of Scotland that in 1665 he went into exile in Holland. His
descendants married Dutch women for a century and enriched his loyalty to
the "auld alliance" of Scotland and France against England with prejudices
acquired during the three bloody wars between Holland and England of the
seventeenth century. By the 1790s, Livingston ships and Livingston sons could
be found in Calcutta and Cartagena, off Vera Cruz and Singapore, and the
Livingstons were ready to enter into transactions with the greatest merchant
families in the world, such as the Lerays of Nantes and Chaumont.

These two clans grew powerful first through adept participation in the
slave-and-sugar economy of the West Indies and, second, from backing the
winning side in the American war for independence. The Lerays were vastly
richer and more famous than the Livingstons until, through a succession of
strange events, they became investors in the kind of New York real estate the
Livingstons understood and they did not. Other merchant clans were drawn
in—the Parishes of Hamburg, the Hopes of Amsterdam, and the Barings of
Exeter and London—and all deposited upon the landscape architecture that still
stands, reminding us of their participation in the enormous commercial contests
of the neoclassical period.

We will take up each in accordance with the timing of their major investments in American affairs. Their commercial and artistic influence thereupon
waned at about the same pace, leaving behind a palace near Haarlem, a château
near the Loire, a string of villas along the Hudson, and another set near the
intersection of the Saint Lawrence and Lake Ontario.

Multinationality on the Hudson

As we have seen, the Hudson and Mohawk valleys were parts of the Atlantic
trading system centering upon the West Indies, and profoundly permeated by
French culture. Wheat and furs passed down to saltwater on small, shallow draft
vessels and were then transferred to ocean-going craft to take them to Jamaica
(legally) or to the French islands (not so legally much of the time). Sugar came
back; the Livingstons and other great merchants found distilling as profitable
as transshipment and smuggling.

The trading patterns of the Atlantic deposited upon the shores of the Hudson
many Frenchmen and many people of indistinct nationality—like the Livingston clan—whose taste was French. In the 1620s, the first clergyman in New
Netherland, the Reverend Jonas Michaelius, offered his first sermon; it was
given in French because so many of his parishioners spoke that language. Later,
in the 1680s and 1690s, this congregation of Walloon—French-speaking—

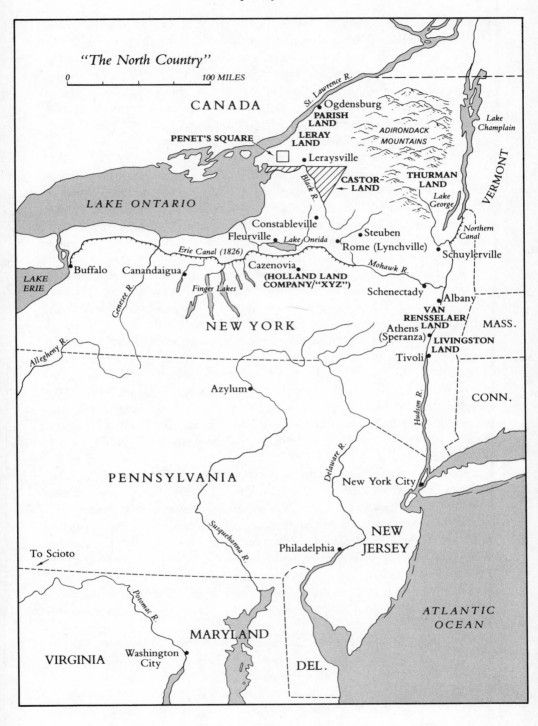

"The North Country"

0 _____ 100 MILES

CANADA

St. Lawrence R.

• Ogdensburg

PARISH
LAND

LERAY
LAND

PENET'S SQUARE

• Leraysville

ADIRONDACK
MOUNTAINS

Lake
Champlain

CASTOR-
LAND ←

THURMAN
LAND

Black R.

LAKE ONTARIO

Lake
George

VERMONT

Northern
Canal

• Constableville

Fleurville   Lake Oneida

• Steuben

Rome (Lynchville)

Schuylerville

Erie Canal (1826)

Mohawk R.

LAKE
ERIE

• Buffalo   Canandaigua •

Cazenovia

(HOLLAND LAND
COMPANY/"XYZ")

Schenectady

• Albany

MASS.

Genesee R.

Finger Lakes

NEW YORK

VAN
RENSSELAER
LAND

Athens
(Speranza)

LIVINGSTON
LAND

CONN.

Allegheny R.

• Tivoli

Hudson R.

• Azylum

PENNSYLVANIA

Delaware R.

New York City

Susquehanna R.

NEW
JERSEY

To Scioto

• Philadelphia

Potomac R.

ATLANTIC
OCEAN

MARYLAND

VIRGINIA   Washington
City

DEL.

Protestants was reinforced by French Huguenots. Villages like New Paltz and Hurley still retain Walloon-country qualities, and dynastic names like De Lancey, Gouverneur, and Bayard carry into the daily experience of the tele-phone-delivery clerks of several Madison Avenue branches of Gristedes' super-markets the consequences of the revocation of the Edict of Nantes.

After 1790, French Creole refugees from the revolutions on Saint-Domingue began settling in Red Hook, Hyde Park, Poughkeepsie, and Rhinebeck, and some were quickly integrated into the Francophile society of the area: a son of the marquis de Cardillac, lately of Le Cap, married Catherine Livingston. Among the arrivals to Red Hook was Pierre de La Bigarre, who married Margaret Beekman, whose sister married Peter William Livingston. The eldest son of Henry Walter Livingston married Catherine de Grasse de Pau, grand-daughter of the Admiral de Grasse, whose sails were such a gratifying sight off Yorktown in 1781. In New Orleans, later, Edward Livingston married Louise Moreau de Lassy, a Creole and widow of a Creole.

This conjugality was achieved so easily that it might seem in retrospect unseemly. But imperial contests did not distract the Hudson River Franco-philes, even contests fought very close to them: the funeral fires of the French and Indian Wars were scarcely cool. And even during the height of those contests, puffs of powder smoke only occasionally obscured a clear mercantile view of things. Their willingness to put trade ahead of other matters dismayed some of their allies. Chief Hendrick of the Mohawks told the Albany Congress of 1754 that men like Philip Livingston were little employed in fighting the French or hostile Indians but instead were busy seizing the land of friendly Indians, leaving only "the very spot we live in and hardly that." Others observed Governor De Lancey doing a brisk business with the French in powder, lead, and guns.

Beaver pelts from Montreal brought high profits, and so did outfitting the British armies sent against the French. Lord Bellomont, the royal governor, complained that Robert Livingston's chief interest in war with France was in profiteering from provisioning, saying that he had "pinched an estate out of poor soldiers' bellies." Perhaps he was unfair; but it is certain that the French were simultaneously trading partners and imperial opponents. Peter Livingston was not alone in entering into a series of transactions with the French and their allies the Spanish, though he did so ineptly and brought about his bankruptcy and the breaking of the Livingston entail (his right to inherit all the manor as elder son).

When the wars with France came to an end in 1763, affinities for French culture could be more candidly expressed. The Livingstons, the Van Rensse-laers, and the Van Nesses set up a French school for their younger children in New Rochelle also attended by Gouverneur Morris. Thereafter, the offspring of these Francophile squires were as eager to see Paris as was Thomas Jefferson.

Fifteen years later, in 1778, when France became a wartime ally, merchants among the leaders of the independence movement were drawn into even closer political and commercial ties to France. This should not lead us, however, to think that they were any more exclusive in their trading patterns during this period than they had been during the French and Indian Wars. Robert Morris, the author of the epigraph for this chapter, was the chief financier of that struggle, steadfast, and full of resource. In his ultimate adversity, in a debtor's prison twenty years later, this service gained him poignant testimony of the esteem of George Washington, who dined in jail only once in his life, when he had a long, reminiscent visit with Morris in his cell in Philadelphia. Yet, as a merchant, "as such," Morris smuggled and speculated and, it was said, felt free to trade with the enemy during the Revolutionary War.

The Livingstons became the leaders of the "French party" in New York. Patronage disputes with the pro-British Federalists reinforced their ancient Francophilia; and in the 1790s the Livingstons left the Federalists to close ranks with those other Francophiles, Aaron Burr and Thomas Jefferson.

French statesmen exerted themselves mightily to bring about that immensely important defection, one of the causes of the Jeffersonian triumph of 1800. Before the United States had a secretary of state, the Continental Congress had a chief of the Department of Foreign Affairs. The French minister, the chevalier de La Luzerne, boasted that his influence had secured that post for Robert R. Livingston. Certainly Chancellor Livingston* was compatible with the French, a fact of considerable importance in his skillful direction of the negotiations leading to the Treaty of Paris and the end of the Revolutionary War.

Livingston refused George Washington's offer to become minister to France in 1794 but accepted the post from Thomas Jefferson in 1801. Henry Walter Livingston had already served in Paris as secretary to the American minister, Gouverneur Morris (himself of Huguenot lineage), in the early 1790s, and the family proprietorship of the ministry to France was sustained when the Chancellor was succeeded by his brother-in-law, John Armstrong, husband of Alida Livingston. When Edward Livingston assumed the post in the 1830s, he was already a foreign associate of the Institute of France.

Traffic between the central Hudson and Paris included many shipments of furniture, glass, and books—and architectural plans. Janet Livingston Montgomery asked her brother Robert, during his ministry to France, to send her a "hansom" plan for a house, the Château de Montgomery. Other shipments were recorded in letter books, vouchers, and place names such as La Bergerie (built by another Livingston sister after leaving an earlier residence, De Veaux Park), John R. Livingston's Masséna, and Pierre de La Bigarre's Château de Tivoli. Indeed, the most enduring achievements of these squires who assumed their full role as the oligarchs of a new and very prosperous trading nation in

---

*"Chancellor" is the title carried by the chief judge of the court of chancery. (See Gilbert and Sullivan.)

the 1790s were an array of French-designed country mansions, gardens—as we shall see—and villages.

4

THE MEN OF THE WEST

The Caribbean economic empire extended as far as Africa and the great slaving ports of Nantes in France, Liverpool and Bristol in England, Newport and another Bristol in Rhode Island, and New York City.

Sugar was not the only product of the West Indies, but it was the most important. Sugar and slaves provided capital to be reinvested. Though the slaving ports themselves did not burgeon with diversified industry, capital and confidence gained there emboldened a set of entrepreneurs who could bully their way into other opportunities, especially in textiles. This was the progression in Rhode Island, in Lancashire, and in France.

There was scarcely one of the original thirteen United States not dependent to a large degree upon the West Indies. Sugar-producing slaves in the West Indies consumed vast quantities of fish from New England, grain from the "bread colonies" (Pennsylvania and its neighbors), and rice from South Carolina. As we have seen, Hudson River squires were often West Indiamen as well; even the remote Mohawk Valley of New York was shipping wheat to the Caribbean.

No city on the eastern seaboard of the United States could have grown as it did without the West Indies trade. Faneuil Hall in Boston, the Redwood Library in Newport, the Apthorp and Livingston houses of New York, mansions in Fairmont Park in Philadelphia, and the lovely, galleried houses of Charleston's Battery were built of the same materials as the quay at Nantes and the warehouses of Bristol—a compound of sugar and the sweat of slaves.

There might have been some lingering redolence of the sweat of Black workers even in the perfumed corridors of Passy and in the central courtyard of the Château de Chaumont, for Jacques Leray was the son of René, mayor of Nantes, who presided over a chamber of commerce taking this view of the triangular trade with Africa and the West Indies: "What commerce can be compared to that which obtains men in exchange for commodities?"

"From the port of Nantes," we are told, "their ships sailed the seven seas, and the owners rapidly accumulated a fortune. They did extensive business, especially with the West Indies." Exchanging ever-increasing numbers of Black people for ever-increasing amounts of sugar and sugar products constituted the primary transactions contributing to a noble suffix-of-place for the name of the

Leray family: after they acquired the château, their orders went out signed "Leray de Chaumont," then, somewhat later, "Le Ray de Chaumont."*

We know what the Lerays' "extensive business" entailed, and we know something of the conditions aboard a slave ship, and so we can moderate our rejoicing that its benefits included the ability to purchase "the most beautiful of the French châteaux, the famous . . . Chaumont sur Loire."

In 1770, in order to press closer to Paris, where economic policy was being made, the Lerays supplemented their inventory of residences with an estate near Versailles, at Passy. The property had a manor house and a guest cottage, which soon was tenanted, free of rent, by Benjamin Franklin.

René Leray had not been discernibly aesthetic in his interests; but at Chaumont, Jacques developed an atelier for ceramic and glass artists. Among the most successful of their products were thousands of copies of Giovanni Battista Nini's medallion of Franklin.

The Contest for the Seas

Though the Lerays played at being landowners on the Loire and patrons of the arts, maritime commerce with the Caribbean was never far from their minds.

In the 1780s, they led lesser merchants into an alliance with the young aristocrats crowding into commands in a rebuilt French fleet. Old titles and new money were invested alongside the resources of the state in the imperial contest with Britain. Immense sums were lavished upon the navy. New international alliances were fledged, including a burgeoning understanding with the rebellious colonials of British America.

M. Leray, the generous landlord, might forgo the rent of M. Franklin and, later, of Admiral John Paul Jones, but he did not forgo their assistance in recouping the balance of power with perfidious Albion. The supplying of John Paul Jones with ships and provisions from Leray's own purse was part of this long campaign. Jones got free rent, free ships, and French crews trained in the Atlantic traffic. His charge was to gain for France the vast and increasing commerce of the Caribbean and to secure the routes leading from the coasts of Europe to the ports of Saint-Domingue.

The flagship of Jones, one of Leray's tenants, was given its name, *Le Bonhomme Richard,* by another, Franklin. When Jones got through with the British, *Poor Richard,* they hoped, would not be poor much longer.

The French fleet itself, of course, was the main interest of the merchants of the west of France who were represented in Paris by Jacques Leray. The duc

*Thomas Schaeper informs me (in a letter of February 24, 1986) that Jacques-Donation Leray always wrote his name as I have spelled it. His son James began to spell it somewhat more grandly, as Le Ray. James's son Vincent spelled it always, apparently, Le Ray.

de Choiseul invited him to become a minister of state to King Louis XVI to advise on "matters related to commerce." The king was himself the only Bourbon to have an interest in the fleet, an interest solicited by Leray and by M. Ozanne, the king's tutor, who was a naval architect.

Choiseul and his cousin Choiseul-Praslin, who held the Ministry of Marine as a family fiefdom, escalated the rebuilding of the French fleet after its humiliations in the wars ending in the truce of 1763. Christopher Lloyd, in the *Cambridge Modern History,* summarized their need for men like Leray: not satisfied with the support they received directly from the crown, they "turned . . . especially to the merchant classes of the south and west, as a result of which no less than fifteen ships of line were built by subscription . . . [and] Choiseul and his successors developed the chief naval ports of France and the West Indies."*

The French maritime contest with Britain consumed 160 million livres—the fleet bankrupted the national treasury even more than subsidies to the rebellious colonists—but the result was victory. George Washington observed after Yorktown: "Whatever efforts are made by land armies, the navy must have the casting vote in the present contest."

Only one part of that contest was fought in the Chesapeake. The French struggle for commercial supremacy with Britain spanned the globe, from Canton to Australia, from Patagonia to Baffinland. To give a sense of the importance of Saint-Domingue in that contest, we can note that, also in 1789, Britain's entire colonial trade was five million pounds, while that of France with Saint-Domingue alone was eleven million.

William Pitt, trained in the city of London to be the most competent practitioner in economic statesmanship of all British prime ministers, saw Saint-Domingue as a commercial and military objective and the source of precious sugar to pay for attacks on other commercial and military objectives. Sixty thousand British casualties† were spent in an effort to capture Saint-Domingue from, or deny it to, the French commercial empire.

On the French side, the subvention of raiders like John Paul Jones, the outfitting of privateers and ships of line, and the importation of dissident British craftsmen were all aspects of economic warfare. Jacques Leray's ceramic factory at Chaumont made use of such dissidents, and so did his cotton-spinning plant, the first in France, according to at least one source, to compete with the

---

*Various Lerays actually lived or owned properties in the West Indies, including the mistress of Gouverneur Morris, Mme Foucault, sister of James Leray. One "J. le Ray," but almost certainly not our James or our Jacques (according to Thomas Schaeper, who has dogged their footsteps and written me to this effect on March 14, 1986), was a witness to a wedding of a child of one set of relatives of Pierre Bauduy (see chapter 17) at Saint Marc in 1772 and made a timely sale of his plantation, slaves, and animals to another set, the Provenchères, in 1792. We will soon have occasion to unravel the connections among these other clans of West Indies traders.

†At least. Some estimates are considerably higher.

Jacques-Donation Leray (artist unknown)   *James Leray (artist unknown)*

British.* Like his British counterparts, Leray grew rich, not only through trade, the object of war, but through the outfitting of war itself. Several famous British country houses were built with money made supplying British uniforms; for a huge fee Leray performed the same service to the French.†

Investing in America—the Third Phase

The private war fought by the Leray family against Great Britain to protect trade routes to the Caribbean led them to further investment in America. First had been slaves and plantations. Then they outfitted John Paul Jones, sponsored Franklin, and sent arms, ammunition, and other supplies through their agents to other enemies of Britain—the Danes, the Spaniards, and, from time to time, the pirates. A deeper commitment began when they accepted payment in congressional scrip.

After the peace of 1783, the new American government was unwilling to recompense the Lerays for the inflationary depreciation in that scrip, requiring, in effect, that they make an investment in the stability of the Continental Congress. It was a bad investment.

Many other holders of depreciated currency took equivalent losses, but Jacques Leray was tenacious. In 1785, he sent his son James to America to press his claims. After four years, and the personal intervention of Franklin with

*I cannot be certain of this assertion; it is drawn from Thomas Wood Clarke's beguiling but excessively enthusiastic picture of Leray in his *Emigrés in the Wilderness,* pp. 8–22, and comes without citation.

†Supplying the French also enriched American merchants; see p. 102n.

President Washington, all James could collect was nine thousand dollars. But he did obtain a wife, who was by American standards an heiress, and some very useful documents. He returned to France in 1790 accompanied by the former Grace Coxe of Sydney, New Jersey, and certificates assuring the French revolutionaries that, as a (new) American citizen, his French estates were exempt from expropriation.

Also in Paris, however, lying in wait for Leray and his brother-in-law Paul Chassanis—two rich and idealistic young men ripe for plucking—was William Constable. Since Leray had passed some very pleasant time among the Coxes and the Stocktons, country squires of Princeton and Bordentown, perhaps he might prefer America to revolutionary France. Perhaps he might bring some of his friends. Constable was as eloquent about the beauties of the Saint Lawrence Valley as Joel Barlow about the Ohio (see p. 91). Leray and Chassanis were persuaded, and assembled a syndicate to make their largest investment in America. They bought shares in the Company of New York, the purchaser from Constable of thousands of acres around the imaginary city of Castorland. Each member received a suitable medal. On one face, in assurance of the fecundity of this vale of ease, was the head of the goddess Ceres. On the other was a maple tree, oozing sap, and, of course, a recumbent beaver (in Latin, *castor*), suitable for skinning.

Castorland was never much of a success, and its few settlers straggled away after Napoleon permitted most royalist émigrés to return to France in 1802. Leray, however, pushed more chips on the table, making further investments in American real estate and buying the property of the company at auction. (The Company of New York finally expired, owing its creditors, especially James Leray, over a half million francs.)

As Leray's American commitments grew, his wife left France for the United States, in 1799. He followed in 1802 and settled in Burlington, New Jersey, where he could keep an eye on a tract of eighty thousand acres in Pennsylvania, west of Azylum, part of which he sold to Mme de Staël, his tenant at Chaumont. Later, she and her father, the Swiss-born financier Jacques Necker, followed Leray's lead again and invested in northern New York, to the considerable satisfaction of the eager seller, Gouverneur Morris.

The Opulent Years

The stone mansion built *in absentia* for James Leray de Chaumont upon his New York lands (near Watertown) was the wonder of the neighborhood. Jean-Jacques Milbert, a French scientist who was acquainted with opulence in France itself, said that it rivaled the "best-known châteaux and estates of France for its luxury and furnishings" and that it included "a large drawing-room, billiard and music rooms [probably the twin octagons], a library and two independent

Vincent Le Ray (artist unknown)

sections reserved for guests and friends." And in Leraysville one can still hear legends about James Leray and his companion, Mme Janika de Fériet; his butler, his footman, and a dozen more servants; his coach, with six outriders in livery; and his superbly handsome son, Vincent.

Leray's house was the center point of holdings that once covered the better part of four counties; one of them, Saint Lawrence County, is the size of the state of Rhode Island.

Here, under the direction of Vincent Le Ray, towns were laid out, iron was mined and smelted, and sheep were raised. Relationships with international bankers extended to David Parish, with results soon to be noted, and into the ranks of two new financial operators based in Philadelphia, Stephen Girard and Nicholas Biddle. Vincent Le Ray was a frequent visitor at Biddle's country seat, Andalusia, joining him there in charades played in French and English.

Things went well enough at first, despite the irritating restrictions put upon trade on the Saint Lawrence by Mr. Jefferson's nonintervention policies. Jefferson, seeking to diminish the number of humiliations suffered by Americans, whose naval forces he had much reduced, thought it best to keep them away from the British fleet; congenitally pro-French and anti-British, from 1807 onward he attempted to penalize the British by forbidding Americans to trade with them. It was an unsuccessful strategy, largely beneficial to smugglers. Nonetheless, an export business developed on the Saint Lawrence for potash, produced by boiling down lye into "black salts." Boiling required enormous quantities of wood, denuding the landscape. At Leraysville, however, the great white pines were permitted to remain in a two-hundred-acre park traversed by "intersecting footpaths which traverse streams, ascend hillocks and plunge into little valleys affording every species of scenery for . . . interest and delight. Every part of the estate . . . bears the impress of Europe." (These gardens may, in fact, have borne the impress of either of two highly trained designers, Pierre Pharoux or Joseph Ramée, or of both.)

Somewhat later, another romantic park was laid out to surround the residence of James Leray's friend Janika de Fériet, a redoubtable woman who has left us an old and rather indistinct picture of her house, another of herself, and a carefully composed autobiography. According to her account, the de Fériet family came from Lorraine and had been ennobled by the duke thereof in 1521. Her father was a minor official in the Ministry of Finance, and her brother, Baron Ferdinand, became a successful broker in New Orleans. All her life she wore a locket bearing a miniature of Mme de Staël, and she claimed to have been a friend both to de Staël and to Lady Hester Stanhope, the English explorer.

Janika de Fériet was an accomplished pianist and, judged by her portrait, a most attractive woman. She arrived in America in 1816 upon the *Bellone,* chartered by Leray, as a companion to his daughter, Countess Teresa de Gonvello. She was soon Leray's own companion, living at first in a small house on the estate, then building her own porticoed establishment nearby, which she called, demurely, the Hermitage. The house "was built of gray stone" and the main floor "consisted of four immense rooms, each with its own fireplace." There was a conservatory "containing orange and lemon trees." In that climate, fueling a conservatory must have required the clearing of almost as large a stretch of the "pine plains" as did the reduction of charcoal to "black salts." Within the "pleasure-ground," however, there were groves of virgin pines, gardens, and in a remarkable survival of West Indian patterns, "outhouses were used for a kitchen and for the servants, none of whom lived in the mansion."

Janika de Fériet lived there for fifteen years. Early in her tenure as proprietress, she assumed the title "madame" and "rode for miles over the countryside, dropping in [on the] . . . houses of her friends . . . [especially the] aristocrats in the neighborhood," who dropped in on her as well. She was said to be "intimate with the American landed gentry as well as the French." But she was very discriminating.

The New and the Not-Quite-So-New

Perhaps, among saints, the latest to achieve sainthood enthusiastically welcome the next. Or perhaps there are provisional saints, who gain tenure because of the enthusiasm they show for the following cohort. They are in heaven. Down here, fresh-fledged respectables are apt to feel that they have filled the quota. When they can, they close the door after them.

Thus it was that Janika de Fériet was cool to the yet more newly rich, and the Lerays de Chaumont showed little desire to hobnob with indelicate people

Mme Janika de Fériet; probably a self-portrait

Mme de Fériet's painting of "The Hermitage," c. 1820

who reminded them of their own mercantile origins. Besides, who would have thought that another West Indies slave trader would arrive in the remotest corner of New York to play *grand seigneur?*

Yet in the early 1830s a stone mansion even larger than that of Mme de Fériet began to rise between Chaumont and Deferiet. It was at Lafargeville, upon an enclave ten miles square called Penet's Square. Fifty years earlier, Pierre Penet of Nantes had escorted Benjamin Franklin from that city to Paris and had gained a commission to engage in the ammunition business with the American revolutionaries. It appears that (unlike the senior Leray) he insisted upon payment in cash. He was able, after 1783, to buy some land in New York and to wheedle more—the whole square, in fact—from the Oneida Indians. Thereafter, with a North American base secure, he followed the lanes of commerce southward to the West Indies, where he did more trading, in slaves and land.

On Saint-Domingue, Penet met a tough young man named Jean-Frédéric de La Farge. They got along well together, until Penet died mysteriously, by drowning. Then La Farge went on to do even better on his own; soon he had acquired land in both Louisiana and New York, including his major holding, Penet's Square. Nearly fifty years of age, he also acquired a sixteen-year-old wife, of a social standing somewhat more elevated than his own—the daughter of the by then impoverished, but artistically gifted, Saint-Dominguan planter M. Binsse de Saint-Victor.

We must pass over La Farge's transactions with Joseph Bonaparte for the moment. We bring him and his wife into this part of our story only to reflect upon how rapidly Creole merchants became invidiously genteel. We are told by a local historian that the young wife of La Farge was never happy in Lafargeville, for her husband "was considered merely a businessman" and "was never quite accepted as a social equal by the Le Rays, the Bonapartes, Mme de Fériet, and the other aristocrats of the neighborhood."

Had Mme La Farge known them well enough, she might have understood their irritability. The mid-1820s were bitter years for the Le Rays and for Mme de Fériet. The potash business had expired; the iron business was flagging; and the Erie Canal was for them a disaster. Their scrubby terrain did not attract settlers, who could instead go westward along the canal toward the rich lands of the Western Reserve of Ohio.

In the Genesee Valley, the Wadsworths and the Churches were welcoming the emigrants. In his neoclassical villa in Canandaigua, Thomas Jefferson's secret agent and spoilsman Gideon Granger presided over a vast domain, acquired with the leverage of the postmaster generalship, and delighted in reselling it at escalating prices (see p. 288). But James Leray, who had weathered the economic distress of 1819, emerged too weak financially to survive the second crisis, of 1823–25. The Château de Chaumont and the estate at Passy had already been sold. Leray promised his New York creditors that he would "do everything in my power to procure the money." He sold "contracts at an immense loss," trying to get earlier payment from those who were buying portions of his land in installments. His sons "were now around me in the wilderness trying to improve my situation . . . my plans for rest and enjoyment [in France were] . . . abandoned . . . I must remain in the woods." He promised to sell the whole property "at public auction" if he was unable to fulfill his obligations in full by 1832.

In order to pay, he had to be paid; and those who owed him money were as numerous as those to whom he was in debt. From the willingness of his debtor and creditor neighbors to give him a testimonial dinner in that year, it appears that he did not press for payment too hard, though he was being goaded by the heirs of his old friend David Parish and also those of Gouverneur Morris, his companion on the voyage from Hamburg to New York in 1802.

In September 1834, Leray was back in America for the last time, winding up his affairs. A notice of foreclosure on most of his American properties was posted in October 1835. The old man was "compelled . . . to meet many . . . neighbors in the court house of Watertown to ask the forbearance of my creditors." He died in 1840.

Mme de Fériet made fitful efforts to develop her estate, founding the town of Deferiet. She complained that Vincent Le Ray was not so considerate of her as was his father. In 1841, she finally returned to France; she died two years later, at Versailles. Her house burned to the ground in 1871. Vincent Le Ray outlived his father by many years, and the Le Ray holdings in northern New York outlived them both. There was a Le Ray land office until 1910, when, apparently, the French members of the family sold their last bits and pieces of the Adirondacks.

5

GREAT INVENTIONS

Architecture is, as was suggested earlier, a collective art. Architects may choose to draw alone, but people who only draw are not architects but draftsmen. To be an architect, one must create buildings, a process requiring the participation of others. The art itself only exists in community. Moreover, architecture is not only public in its origins but public in its consequences; it sets itself before a public, though it may be at the end of a lane or upon an island. Therefore, more than in any other art except skywriting, an understanding of architecture requires an understanding of its circumstances.

In the 1790s, some architects left France because there was little for them to do except to make temporary exhibitions, parade grounds, *fêtes,* and political spectacles. Joseph Ramée found new opportunities in Germany, Denmark, and the United States; he was preceded to America by Pierre Pharoux and Simon Desjardins and others who will figure in these pages.

These émigrés were supported in their efforts to find their professional footing by the international community of merchants: people like Leray de Chaumont, of Paris, Saint-Domingue, and Watertown, New York; and the Livingstons, of Jamaica and New York. West Indian sugar paid for land in New York and Pennsylvania, and upon that land cities might be built.

In the state of New York in the 1790s, the planning of new cities offered new careers to French architects. The French have been good at this sort of thing; it apparently appeals to their tidiness, their desire for order. In 1690, Jean-Baptiste Colbert, the controller general of finance under the Sun King, Louis XIV, ordained that there would be an elite corps of planners, called *experts-jurés,* whom the king would pay to make surveys and appraisals, inspect buildings, and design improvements. To qualify as *experts-jurés,* architects had to be thoroughly trained. To sustain their qualification, they had to demonstrate that they were relatively pure of the corruption attending the real-estate booms that enthralled and cluttered Paris from the time of Colbert to the eve of the revolution.

Simon Desjardins was first listed as an architect *expert-juré* in Paris in 1782. Pierre Pharoux received that distinction in the revolutionary year of 1789. Their duties included making inspections and meticulous reports of their daily activity to bureaucrats in the royal service. Their habit of journal keeping was most useful, not only to shareholders who had invested a great deal of money in a distant, American real-estate speculation but, two centuries later, to historians looking for leads in some forgotten architecture.

Memoirs and a Journal

The War of American Independence was over. The Livingstons and other families in their network of clans—the Van Nesses, the Van Rensselaers, and the Schuylers—had picked the winning side. Commerce and population were on the upswing. Squires who owned land up and down the Hudson were finding ready buyers among that increasing population. Rich already from West Indian commerce, they built largely, confident that they would grow richer still from the growth in value of land.

The Livingstons alone produced a dozen houses on a monumental scale in the decade of the 1790s. Three—The Hill, Arryl House (also known as the Chancellor's House), and Masséna—have gained legendary associations with

French or Italian architects. Though the legends are demonstrably false in their details, and later historians may scoff at their errors, these tales are all we have—and besides, they lead us in the right direction.

A Dutchess County chronicler, General John Ross Delafield, reported in 1941 that there was "a tradition" that The Hill was "planned by an . . . architect whom Henry Walter Livingston had met when he was abroad." Delafield wrote "Italian" where I have inserted ellipses. Since Livingston was attached to the American ministry in Paris and spent very little other time abroad, "French" seems a likelier signpost.

In the 1870s, Mrs. Martha Lamb informed the readers of *The Homes of America* that John R. Livingston's Masséna was from a design "by Brunel . . . an exact copy of the chateau of Beaumarchais, in France." Masséna and the residence of Beaumarchais have nothing whatever in common; but there is something floating about here in local memory—something about the kind of intercontinental trade in which Pierre Augustin Caron de Beaumarchais, the Livingstons, and Leray de Chaumont were engaged, and something, too, about an architect from France, who was associated, two generations later, with the name Brunel, or "Bunel"—both Marc Brunel and his son Isambard Kingdom Brunel having become famous in the interim. Beaumarchais too was famous by then, thanks largely to Mozart and Rossini.*

The same set of Livingston-Beaumarchais-Brunel associations forms a nimbus around Arryl House of Robert R. Livingston. In the 1940s, Harold Eberlein and Cortlandt Hubbard wrote that the Chancellor, admiring "French domestic architecture of the Neo-Classic type . . . is said to have had Bunel [*sic*] design Arryl House on lines suggested by the Chateau of Beaumarchais."

It would be pleasant to report that the many biographies of the great engineer Sir Marc Isambard Brunel would help us sort these things out. Brunel *was* in America from 1792 to 1799, and Chancellor Livingston's well-catalogued correspondence *does* include several letters to Brunel. But beyond that we can rely on little that Brunel, his biographers, or the encyclopedists who have followed them, have to tell us. The pages to follow present a reconstruction of the events of that period in his life, in which only those of his biographers' assertions that are unrebutted by contrary evidence are accepted, a precaution made necessary by the discovery of documents casting doubts upon the entire traditional tale.

Brunel Remembered

For most men, a knighthood, the patronage of dukes, and the acclamation of his peers would have been enough. In 1840, Sir Marc Brunel was celebrated

---

*Courtier and watchmaker to Louis XV, Beaumarchais went on to participate in the financing

Sir Marc Isambard Brunel in 1813,
by J. Northcote

for tunnels and dockyards, steam tugs, printing presses, machines to produce cannons and the rigging for Her Majesty's Navy, and floating landing piers. His ingenious shield was protecting the workers burrowing under the Thames to complete the tunnel commissioned by the duke of Wellington. He was famous as well for his experiments: nine-hundred-foot timber bridges to cross Russian rivers, hurricane-proof bridges for islands in the Indian Ocean, swing bridges for Liverpool, and his celebrated low-temperature containers for the liquefaction of gases.

Accomplishments of this scale and variety might have satisfied him. But never since the Renaissance has there lived a man more avid for glory. His disciple and first biographer, Richard Beamish, admitted that Brunel had "acute sensibility to . . . a too anxious desire for . . . sensitiveness to . . . and a love of approbation." Recently discovered evidence permits us fairly to surmise that this love of approbation led to the composition of the filigree of imaginative detail Beamish and others have passed along to us about the six years Brunel spent in America. We might leave it in place, ornamental and impressive for its inventiveness, but for the fact that it forms a screen between us and the reputations of several other people.

It is impossible in retrospect to sort out how many of Brunel's autobiographical creations were his own and how many can be attributed to Beamish, but

---

of the American Revolution and in smuggling on a grand scale, as well as to write the plays upon which were based Rossini's *The Barber of Seville* and Mozart's *The Marriage of Figaro*.

it is difficult not to charge Brunel with the prime responsibility. Members of his own family—in particular, his great-granddaughter Celia Brunel Noble—repeated versions of these stories in print and said they were relying upon family reminiscences. So strong was the old man's personality that they, like Beamish, did so despite the fact that they were "unable to obtain any notes or correspondence relative to the eventful coup d'essai" of his engineering life in America, though they had "often heard Brunel speak of his sojourn in America."

The Castorland Journal

Readers of family memoirs expect puffing. On the other hand, reference works like the *Dictionary of National Biography* and the encyclopedias *Britannica* and *Americana* imply that their consumers are protected. Yet these authorities have embalmed Brunel's inventions for the past hundred years, and have permitted their reappearance in biographies published as recently as 1974.

Contrary views are not enthusiastically received, as Robert Alexander, an American architectural historian, found some years ago when he uncovered some of Brunel's fabrications: he could find no publisher. Recently, however, a free-lance writer in Schenectady, Edith Pilcher, published a history of the Company of New York, in which she called attention to the *Castorland Journal*, a longhand manuscript report to the company from its American representatives, which confirms many of Alexander's opinions. Other local historians have collaborated in providing portions of the documentation that appears below. Chief among them has been Ruth Piwonka, resident expert on the upper valley of the Hudson.

The *Journal* is a cornucopia of information about architectural and engineering work done along the Mohawk and the Hudson. Its two primary authors, Desjardins and Pharoux, provided a companion volume, just a year or two older, to the most important document in the architectural history of America, the journals of Benjamin Henry Latrobe (who arrived in 1796). It is true that a little piecing together is required; Pharoux and Desjardins were reporting to investors, as architects and engineers administering those investors' legal and business affairs. They wrote in great detail about the tasks performed for their employers but gave only the most tantalizing references to the work done by Pharoux on his own time, for others. He and Desjardins did find occasion, however, to make frequent references to an apprentice they picked up along the way—Marc Isambard Brunel.

Marc Isambard Brunel in 1798,
as engraved by Saint-Mémin

Heroes Ashore

In early July 1793, Brunel, a deserter from the French West Indies squadron, made use of a false passport to escape the Terror and get aboard the American ship *Liberty*, bound for New York. Also aboard—and the ship's most eminent passengers—were Pierre Pharoux and his fellow commissioner of the Company of New York, Simon Desjardins.* Pharoux and Desjardins were on their way to survey the company's property along the Black River between Lake Ontario and the western slope of the Adirondacks—the two hundred thousand acres known as Castorland.

Soon after they arrived, the two commissioners proceeded up the Hudson, while Brunel stayed in New York City, looking for work. Then the French West Indies squadron, carrying old shipmates who might recognize him, appeared in the harbor; in some haste Brunel followed his new friends upriver.

He found them in Albany. Desjardins and Pharoux were both professionals;† Brunel was without any training to qualify him to assist them in planning an entire province. But Pharoux, recalling that the young man had proven himself "a good sailor and a man of resolution" during a storm on their Atlantic crossing, took him on as an apprentice surveyor; and in the fall of 1793 the three

---

*We will board this craft again: its other passengers included the lawyer Bancel de Confoulens and his brawling family, on their way to Scioto and Maine (see p. 92n.).

†While both Pharoux and Desjardins were equally qualified in architecture and engineering, the journal, in a section obviously written by Desjardins, identifies Pharoux as "a celebrated architect and engineer" with experience as a surveyor. Desjardins was apparently well known to his addressees and felt little need to explain himself (see Pilcher, p. 31). Diligent efforts have been made to discover any private work Pharoux may have performed in Paris, aside from his duties to the crown, but all I have found is his address: 15, rue de Cléry.

men set out westward toward the company's domain. They found, as they no doubt expected, beaver ponds; they also found rocks, swamps, brambles, and the harsh beauties of the Adirondack "backs"—and squads of French surveyors already at work on several other tracts in the region. A Swiss-French-Dutch syndicate (including most of the participants in the celebrated "XYZ Affair"—see p. 117) employing John Hooker as its architect was developing the region around the town named Cazenovia for Théofil (or Théophil) Cazenove, a Swiss-Dutch-French-American developer.* Pierre Penet was promoting his ten-mile-square project near the outlet of Lake Ontario, Pharoux reported, by providing immigrants with a "map of the city of 'Fleurville,' with all its fortifications . . . in which he would give graciously a building lot to those who would buy his lands." The only difficulty was that Fleurville did not exist, and the site, in fact, belonged to another speculator, "Mr. Scriba . . . who had bought it of the State of New York."

Northeast of Fleurville was the vast reach of bog and heath to be occupied by Castorland, with its chimerical capital, Castorville, the city of beavers, and its imaginary entrepôt, Basle. Each city would cover two thousand acres divided by avenues into fourteen thousand dwelling sites. Two thousand lots were reserved for churches, theaters, and other public buildings. Six thousand acres were set aside to accommodate a class of peasants and artisans, and twenty thousand acres to be sold to provide money to build canals and highways.

In no time Pharoux and Desjardins were at work blazing the trajectories of avenues and splashing through swamps that might someday become reflecting pools, as Pharoux made the sketches for his portfolio of American works. A few—only a tantalizing workaday few—of these sketches are to be found in the *Castorland Journal:* "a shelter of bark," a design for a mill, with "a sketch of the Falls." Perhaps they worked together on an essay in maritime engineering: "a pine tree four feet in diameter to be cut, for a canoe twenty seven feet long, for which he [Pharoux] made the model."

Their route from Albany took the commissioners past the farm of Mme de La Tour Du Pin (see pp. 105–6), where they were welcomed, and the even more isolated outpost of Baron Friedrich Wilhelm von Steuben, once aide-de-camp to Frederick the Great, then major general in the Continental Army, now another land speculator. Steuben had been rewarded by Congress with sixteen thousand acres south of Castorland; he held court in a log house at Starr Hill (now the town of Steuben), south of the confluence of the Moose and Black rivers.

Moonlighting, Pharoux made a detailed plan for Steuben's rough terrain, centering upon "a little pond in the English style to receive all the waters"

---

*It was either Théofil Cazenove or his cousin Pierre, mayor of Georgetown, who later commissioned a house in Washington from Latrobe.

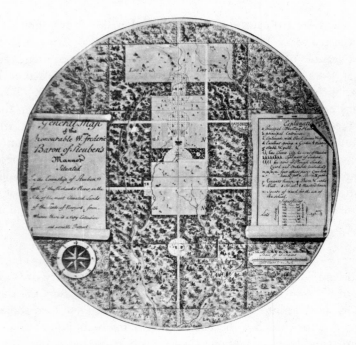

Pierre Pharoux's estate plan for Baron von Steuben

drained from the upper meadow. There would be a French formal garden next to the house, where one could take the air after dinner before strolling graveled walks around the pond and meadow.

Then Pharoux found his own cabin site. He "visited the two great rocks" still to be seen at the confluence of the Black and Independence rivers "and took the alignment and location of a house that I intend to build on the plateau above [amid] fine meadows without trees . . . From its summit there is afforded a beautiful view of the Black River . . . Saw the graves of two Indians on the top of the plateau, exactly on the place most convenient for the house . . . fished and caught trout."

Pharoux never had to decide whether or not to disturb those Indian graves. He drowned in the Black River, which had seemed so beautiful to him, on September 21, 1795.

He had only eighteen months, but within that span he created a series of plans for gardens, houses, and villages for the Francophile squires of the Hudson and Mohawk valleys. His productivity was prodigious; he was able as well to leave the only notes on the condition of early American engineering worthy of comparison with those of Latrobe, and enough gritty detail to enable us to salvage some grains of useful fact from the ooze of legend about Brunel.

Canals and Inventions

Of all the "eventful coups d'essai" of Brunel's American career, his biographers single out as especially striking his role in proposing the routes—"the projection of . . . [New York's] canals . . . [and the] improvement of [its] rivers. His ingenuity soon suggested the means of freeing the beds from masses of rock and imbedded trees . . . and . . . evading falls and cataracts . . . He may therefore be considered as the pioneer of those great inland communications, which have tended so largely to promote the commercial prosperity of the States."

The Brunel family version, arising from evenings "in later years, [when] he enjoyed talking of those journeys in the American backwoods," was that the "scheme for making canals to link up the Hudson with the great lakes [*sic*], and the St. Lawrence, as proposed by Desjardins, Pharoux and Brunel, became one of the most important projects of the day."

In fact, the Northern and the Western Inland Lock Navigation Companies had been chartered by the New York Legislature in March 1792, and construction had been under way for more than a year on both New York's western and northern canals when the Frenchmen arrived in Albany in the fall of 1793. There is no evidence that Brunel made suggestions for the modification of the routes contemplated by the legislature; but as Pharoux and Desjardins journeyed westward toward Castorland with Brunel in tow, Pharoux observed the lamentable state of work already done on the bypass of a stretch of rapids on the Mohawk route, called Little Falls.* His comments reached the ears of Philip Schuyler, squire, Revolutionary general, father-in-law of Alexander Hamilton, canal promoter, and a formidable political power, "who did not like to be contradicted in his opinions, and drew a thousand pounds a year as head of the

---

*While Pharoux was not mean-spirited, there was nothing tepid about his professional opinions. In 1793 or early 1794, on his way to Philadelphia, he inspected the new bridge at New Brunswick: "They . . . attempted to place piles without pile drivers . . . Their masonry was only a mass of loose irregular stones." When he reached the capital, he found it "dreary . . . and uniform." As we have had occasion to note earlier, he thought Independence Hall no better than "a pile of bricks." (*Castorland Journal*, pp. 125–27.)

Pharoux and M. de La Forest, the French consul general in Philadelphia, went out to survey another canal project under construction, the Delaware and Schuylkill. Brunel was then in Philadelphia as well, and it seems likely that his education continued as Pharoux pronounced the "ditch part . . . well made and leveled, but in every place where there should be any architectural work the canal is interrupted . . . [The] single bridge is a brick arch . . . not high enough to allow barques to pass with their masts . . . A light wooden bridge might have been thrown across for a tenth part of the cost." (*Castorland Journal*, p. 216.) Several Brunel biographers refer to a visit to the bookshop of Moreau de Saint-Méry in Philadelphia at this time, and so does Pharoux. (*Castorland Journal*, pp. 125–27.)

*Possibly John Thurman, as engraved by
Saint-Mémin; though the portrait appears
in mid-19th-century records as "Dr. Hill,"
descendants of John Thurman believe
it to be a portrait of Thurman*

enterprise." Schuyler could scarcely be expected to agree that "those thousand pounds might better be spent in paying a European engineer."

Brunel was being trained in engineering, if not in tact. He was also being introduced to some people who did not object to candor and who would help him make something of his American exile.

Chief among these was Squire John Thurman. We have only a few scraps of paper to tell us anything about this wonderful man, who tried to create an industrial complex amid the granite outcrops, bogs, boulders, and blue mountains of the Adirondacks, where the Hudson is a roistering, unpredictable young river. Around the time he met Pharoux,* he wrote his friend John Whitehurst, a clock manufacturer in Derbyshire, that a decade or more earlier he had "quit Trade and taken to settle New Lands where the sound of the Axe was not known or any Human Being visited . . . It is now a large settlement."

A New York merchant of conservative sentiments, Thurman had occupied the Revolutionary War years with an architectural grand tour of Europe: though he had been an early petitioner for a correction in the behavior of the British government, he had stood aside from the conflict. This might have categorized him as a Tory, but he was sufficiently well considered by his peers, like Schuyler and the Livingstons, to be speedily reincorporated into the

*Thurman chanced to meet the French travelers on their voyage down the Hudson from Albany at the end of 1793, after they had completed their first western tour and just before Pharoux made his winter expedition to Philadelphia.

committee system of New York merchants after his return. Brunel, as reported by Beamish, agreed with the impression of Thurman conveyed by Pharoux and Desjardins; he was "charming . . . with a gayety quite rare for a man somewhat advanced in years." (He was sixty-one in 1793.) His gaiety was understandable: he had chanced upon a kindred spirit. "Learning that M. Pharoux was an architect, he turned his conversation to that subject. This worthy man [Thurman] had travelled in Europe with good result, for he had observed much, and knew how to appreciate the great men of the day."

Among those great men, in New York, was Schuyler, and among Thurman's means of "appreciation" was sufficient knowledge of engineering to assess what Schuyler did not know. The two had been asked by the state legislature to join another up-country squire, Simeon de Witt, in appraising land condemned for canal purposes. Early in his study of the matter, Thurman had reported some doubts about Schuyler's methods, and Pharoux agreed. He told Thurman what he thought of Schuyler's "hydraulic endeavors," especially the "incompetence" of the retaining walls.

Thurman asked Pharoux to make a detour to his own lands, north of Albany, in the spring. Thurman now owned property that had been a French seigneury until 1763; he was delighted to have a French engineer to help him with its improvements and to "inspect the labors on the Northern Canal," which, passing two townships owned by Thurman, was to link Lake Champlain to the Hudson. "There was only wanting a good engineer to make it a success," Thurman told Pharoux.

When Pharoux acceded to Thurman's request in May of 1794, he took along a companion: "M. Pharoux embarked with M. Brunel . . . in Mr. Thurman's bateau." Brunel remembered this as "the turning-point in his life." He spoke of "un homme sage" and a sponsor, with whom "a fortuitous connection . . . determined his destiny . . . the . . . profession of a civil engineer." This was, however, not his description of Pharoux, who *did* provide his training as well as his introduction to Thurman, but of *Thurman*. Perhaps that was because Pharoux had been forgotten by the world, whereas Thurman was, according to Beamish, "still remembered with reverence in New York."

The *Castorland Journal* gives us somewhat more detail than usual about this incident, not because it was a turning point in the life of Brunel but because the shareholders deserved an explanation for an unusually extended bit of moonlighting by Pharoux. Desjardins felt it appropriate to explain that "service for our friend [Thurman] and for the state [was] . . . essential for the interests of this great enterprise." By the middle of June 1794, Desjardins had been waiting a month at baron von Steuben's headquarters. He was much relieved when the baron's secretary told him on the fourteenth that "Pharoux was on his way." On Sunday the fifteenth, "Pharoux and the two other surveyors arrived" with oxen to begin laying out a road to Castorland. The moonlighting, however public-spirited, was over. The real work had to begin again.

That was not how Brunel remembered matters. He was, as always, center stage; Castorland was now the sideshow. The hero could not be presented as merely tagging along on Pharoux's inspection of work already under way—no indeed: Thurman "engaged them [Pharoux and Brunel] to survey a line for a canal . . . M. Pharoux was confided the conduct of the operations; but as difficulties accumulated, the superiority of Brunel's genius became so apparent, that . . . M. Pharoux did not hesitate to resign the command into the hands of his gifted companion."

Along Wood's Creek, in 1793, Brunel and Pharoux watched "the contractors, busy in removing from the creek some fallen trees . . . no mechanical appliances were used . . . They appeared not even to know the use of a ladder, much less of a crane, or of the simplest labor-saving power." Here was an opportunity for French engineering. In October, Pharoux provided another consultation to Thurman, "on the return of his lands, and the completion of the clearing out of Wood Creek." Beamish extols Brunel's "ingenuity in . . . freeing the beds from masses of . . . embedded trees."*

The *Journal* tells us that "M. Pharoux concluded to pass the [rest of] the winter [of 1793–94, after his Philadelphia sojourn] in New York, as a place more proper [than Albany] for making known his talents." Brunel, with no training as an architect, had no such choice to make. He spent the winter with Desjardins in Albany and then "also decided to go to New York, to arrange his commercial affairs."

These "commercial affairs" must not have been too demanding, for in the spring Brunel was ready to take a place beside Pharoux "in Thurman's bateau." It does not appear that he returned to New York City very soon or spent much time there. Its city directories do not list him, though his biographers assert that he not only was in the city but indeed was its chief engineer. It is more likely that he spent much of the next five years applying the lessons he learned from Pharoux to the mills and mines and roads being built within the eight hundred square miles of the town of Thurman. The bachelor proprietor of that community recruited many young artisans (county records tell us of Joseph Holder, the machinist; Daniel McGinnis, the master of spinning machines; James Smalley, the calico printer; Jeremiah Harrington, the maker of millstones; John Jones, the weaver; and Enos Gover, the cooper).

It is possible that Brunel or Pharoux, or both of them, worked on Thurman's

---

*Embedded in this tale may be the origin of a model under construction in England as part of the celebration of Brunel's genius. It is based upon a set of specifications, found in Brunel's papers, of a device for clearing out tangles of timbers, brush, and stones of the sort that clog Wood's Creek. In the *Castorland Journal* there is not a word about such a machine, but perhaps this work was in fact Brunel's first major invention. (The drawings are undated.)

headquarters, a house he called Elm Hill, near Johnsburgh Corners. It was a frontier citadel so important that "for many years the territory west of the Hudson River and north of Athol was known among the friends in England, Ireland and America as Elm Hill." From there Thurman directed the construction of roads, sawmills, grist mills, potash-rendering plants, and stores. His distillery and malt house provided a market for the rye grown by his tenants. His woolen mill gave employment to newcomers to this remote area west of Lake George. In 1797 Thurman converted it into a cotton factory and added a calico-printing plant; it may have been the first in America.

Everything stopped after he was gored to death by a bull in 1809. The region has not yet recovered from that event, though his neighbors and tenants gave his name to hamlets named Johnsville, Thurman, Thurman Center, and Thurman Station.

According to Beamish, "the connection formed with Mr. Thurman opened to Brunel other and more brilliant opportunities for the exhibition of his constructive talents. Success attended all his efforts; and thus . . . he had achieved a name."

A name: that is what he wanted.

Brunel and Pharoux

Though the *Castorland Journal* speaks only of "commercial affairs" attempted briefly by Brunel in New York City, his biographers have much confused the history of American architecture with the assertion that he "shortly became a busy architect," and with dazzling success. One of them, Paul Clements, offered as proof four drawings found in a British private collection. These drawings may be by Brunel; one carries the notation, made in some hand at some time, "Brunel . . . New York." But if they are his, they are prentice work, probably carried out as exercises under the instruction of Pharoux.

The first, Clements tells us, is for a bank for Wall Street. Possibly; but it could also be a courthouse for some speculative village, a possibility we will pursue.

Clements says of a second drawing that it is "almost certainly his design for the United States Capitol building," though it is instead quite clearly a fanciful imperial column set in the midst of a reminiscence of the place de la Concorde. Clements's third drawing, a concatenation of arcaded drums, pediments, heroic statuary, and urns, described as a combination of "splendor with light and charming detail," he asserts to be "Brunel's Capitol Scheme itself." Such an attribution would corroborate the following account, stitched together from the elements of Brunel's tale as passed along through Beamish, Lady Celia

Brunel's "design for the United States Capitol building"

"Brunel's Capitol Scheme itself"

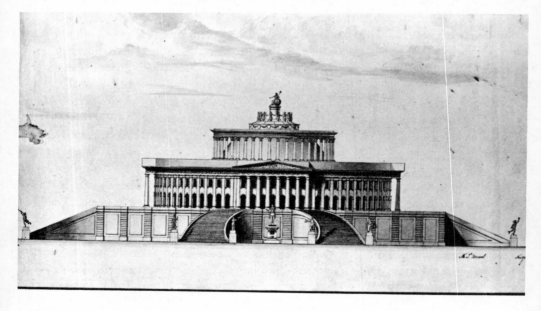

Noble, Lionel Rolt (another Brunel biographer), and Clements and accepted by the editors of the *Encyclopaedia Britannica:*

"Brunel and his friend M. Pharoux, an architect, it must be remembered, by profession, responded to an invitation to send in plans for a new structure [to house] . . . the great council-chamber of the nation at Washington."* His next exploit was to submit a winning design, "so superior in arrangement, elegance and grandeur of design . . . that the judges were relieved from all difficulty of selection . . . [Though] principles of economy . . . robbed the nation of a noble structure worthy of its greatness . . . the judges pronounced it outstanding, and the intelligentsia of New York and Washington buzzed with delight."

Perhaps the kindly Pharoux did pronounce it outstanding and even buzz with delight. But the Capitol competition had already been completed, and awards were made, in 1792—too early for Brunel or Pharoux. Even Dr. William Thornton's postcompetition submission arrived early in 1793, before Pharoux and Brunel reached America—and the current Architect of the Capitol assures me that there is no record of any entry from abroad by a twenty-four-year-old sailor named Brunel.

Unless a huge chunk of the record of the Capitol competition is missing— and the subject is, if anything, overresearched—there was no invitation to, no submission by, and no buzzing about Brunel or Pharoux. Of course, at a later stage in his life Brunel may have felt free to compose his own version of a proper Capitol, if not for the United States, then for some republic or other. He had idle hours on his hands as early as 1794; any young architect might wish to show his mentor what he might have submitted if he had been on the scene of a famous architectural competition just a year earlier. But we can wish that Brunel had been more generous in what he said thereafter about his teacher.

6

THE FURTHER CAREER
OF PIERRE PHAROUX

The biographers of Marc Isambard Brunel have confused this already complex scene with the story, often repeated, that "when New York demanded a play-house, his plans were chosen and he built the Park Theater." Beamish adds the rancorous twist that this was another triumph over Pharoux. In fact, the

---

*Rolt and Lady Noble refer to a competition for "a new Congress Building at Washington."

Park Theater competition of 1794–95 was won by two other Frenchmen, the Mangin brothers (see p. 112). It is doubtful that either Pharoux or Brunel had anything to do with the Park. Instead, the *Journal* says Pharoux first sought "to make his talents known" by entering the competition for the City Hotel with "two different plans . . . and three for the public baths[,] there being at this time none of any note in the city." Both assertions square with newspaper accounts of the time.

Though a tavern and a public bath are hardly monumental compositions, they would have been conspicuous in the absence of others. While he was at work on the baths, Pharoux says, he "also prepared plans at the request of Mr. Livingston, for his house on the battery [*sic*], and two others for Mr. Harison's house on Chatham Place." Which "Mr. Livingston"? Edward Livingston did tell the Common Council of plans for a house on Pearl Street, on the Bowery, in 1794. Though he went off to Congress, he returned to become mayor of New York in 1800, with a "residence at No. 1 Broadway, the windows overlooking the Battery." His brother Robert R. Livingston lived at no. 5. Another brother, John R. Livingston, and their lawyer, Richard Harison, completed new residences in the neighborhood at dates permitting the inference that they could have been designed by Pharoux. (John R. Livingston wrote Robert in November: "My castle as you call it is almost complete but the arrangements of so

City Hotel, New York

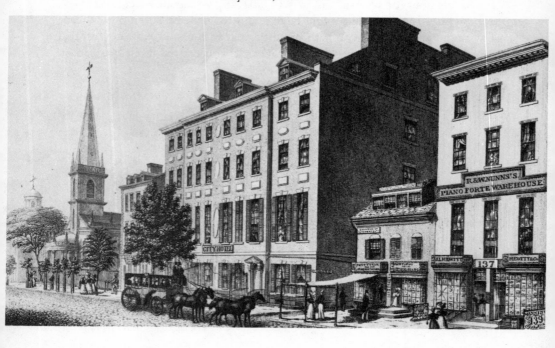

Arcade Bath as it appeared in 1828

large a house will take some time yet." He was describing the process of design for a huge country house—if not a "castle," then almost a château. The architect, perhaps because of interruptions and absences, did indeed take more than a year. The house was to be called Masséna, and we will come to it, in its extravagantly picturesque setting, in a moment.)

In 1795, Harison moved into 227 Broadway. If this was the house built to Pharoux's designs, it is a pity that we cannot judge much of his skill from the indistinct old pictures of its exterior, depicting it as like its neighboring structures (occupied by Aaron Burr and John Jacob Astor). But in the same year, John R. Livingston moved into a considerably more interesting new residence at 65–67 Broadway. His establishment was actually two houses, side by side. Dr. David Hosack was living in the south half while engaged in creating a botanical garden and orangerie on the present site of Rockefeller Center (for the use of this garden by Alexander Hamilton, see p. 121).* Like other Livingston houses built thereafter, 65–67 Broadway is itself somewhat like an orangerie, with considerably more glass than any twentieth-century owner would be likely to present to a busy and unruly city street.

It may seem strange that, legends aside, these houses have not been attributed to an architect or an engineer. An explanation may be that the gentry who built

---

*65–67 Broadway is a block off the Battery itself, but is in the Battery district, just below Trinity Church. Hosack, a professor at Columbia, gave his nursery to the college. Columbia held on to the property, giving the Rockefellers only a ground lease for Rockefeller Center, not a fee title.

John R. Livingston's house on Broadway, in about 1810; from "Broadway,
Grace and Trinity Churches, N.Y.C." by William Strickland

towns, houses, and public buildings along the Hudson and the Mohawk wished
to be thought of as people of taste, quite capable of making their own designs.
By the time the legends about the Livingston houses on the Hudson were
hatched, in the middle of the nineteenth century, amateurism had faded, and
association with European "celebrity architects" was becoming an aspect of
American striving for place. (American celebrities like Stanford White and
Frank Lloyd Wright were waiting in the wings.) Marc Brunel and his son,
Isambard Kingdom Brunel, were already famous in the 1850s. A forgotten
Frenchman named Pharoux would have provided no kudos by association.

Country Houses

In 1795, after he completed his city venture, John R. Livingston commenced
construction of a country villa, seven bays wide and five deep, with an octagonal tower impaled upon the back, bearing a cupola. He called the place after
André Masséna, a soapmaker, West Indies trader, smuggler, fruit dealer, and
military genius who became a marshal and duke of France. Marshal Masséna
was very celebrated at the time. A city in the far north of New York bears
his name, and the elegant Joseph A. Smith of South Carolina, the first American
to visit Greece to study architecture, was honored to take time off from his
grand tour of Italy to study fencing under him.

Masséna, after remodeling in the 1850s

In that account of the house in the 1870s which has already caught our attention, Martha Lamb was led to the odd assertion that it was a facsimile, managed by Brunel, of the Hôtel de Beaumarchais (she, and others, spoke of a "chateau" of which there was none).* Another account, contemporary with Mrs. Lamb's, says that Masséna "covered a great deal of ground." It certainly did, especially after it was enlarged and given an Italianate shell by new owners in the 1850s. The interior had already been altered, probably within its first decade, to make the house more useful in the winter to the growing Livingston family. It had centered around a great "tribune," an octagonal space rising from ground level, past two floors to a dome and cupola. Mrs. Lamb wrote that "Livingston sacrificed the dome in order to multiply upper bedrooms," apparently slicing across the octagon at the second-floor level.

The other legendary Brunel-Livingston association with which we began this section leads to an estate nearby, owned by John Livingston's brother Robert.

*Beaumarchais, to whom earlier reference was made in connection with Leray de Chaumont, married an elderly aristocrat, purchased a title of nobility, and became a secret agent of the king of France and avid speculator in currency and commodities long before he turned to drama and to supplying the American insurgents during the Revolutionary War. It is a pity he did not in fact influence American architecture as much as he, and his forty vessels bearing military supplies, influenced American politics. With this second reference, we must pass him and his story by and think only of Masséna, the rabbit-skinner-grown-to-be-marshal.

Chancellor Robert R. Livingston
by John Vanderlyn

The Chancellor's House was built in 1792–93. His descendants sometimes called
that residence Arryl, to memorialize his initials, R.R.L., but "Aitch" might be
more appropriate: artists of the next three generations loved to sketch its high
central mass and four lower pavilions, spreading east and west and forming two
very French paved courtyards.

On the south side of the house was a greenhouse, possibly suggested or
planned by Dr. Hosack (see p. 121), who came to own a country house in the
neighborhood. "The conservatory ran the whole depth of the house on the
south side and here on great occasions the dinner and supper tables were set,
the tables being so constructed that large plants rose from their centres." In the
sheltered space between the two pavilions on the other side, the Chancellor
would set out "orange, lemon and myrtle trees in tubs, after the contemporary
French manner." The house within "he embellished with many things he
brought from France—books, paintings, furniture, silver, Gobelin tapestries."

It may be that when Chancellor Livingston's widowed sister, Janet Montgomery, asked that he send her a plan from France (see p. 35), she was following
his own happy precedent of nearly a decade earlier; the possibility of a mail-
order design for the Chancellor's House might explain a strange passage in the
Castorland Journal.

In August 1796 (Pharoux had died the preceding September) Desjardins
reported receiving from Paris a "power of attorney . . . from the father of my
friend Pharoux." On the strength of that document he "went to the Consulate"

Arryl House

and obtained permission to remove some items from Pharoux's estate. He "then
sent to the Chancellor the portfolios with which I was charged, and they gave
me a discharge from the inventory."

It is possible that the Chancellor had ordered a plan from Paris in 1792 or
early in 1793, that only preliminary sketches had arrived, and that he had to
settle for supervision only of the final stages of his house by the sender—Pierre
Pharoux. Perhaps the detailed drawings were to accompany Pharoux to America but were lost in the revolutionary hubbub before his departure (he did leave
a portfolio in Nantes; see below). Perhaps they finally arrived in 1795. The
Chancellor wanted some items from the papers of Pharoux; he went to considerable pains to obtain them. This may simply have been because he had paid
for them, though, like his friend and partner James Leray de Chaumont,
Livingston may have been fond of Pierre Pharoux and had a sentimental interest

The Hill

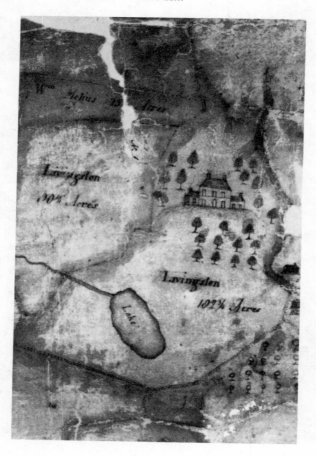

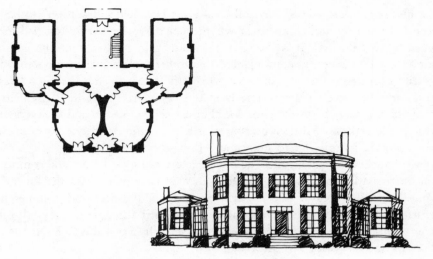

*Floor plan and conjectural elevation of The Hill as built
(computer-generated by James Stokoe)*

in a set of plans by him, even if they had arrived too late to be useful.

We will come back to that missing portfolio, and to James Leray, in a moment. First we should explore a third Livingston mansion, The Hill.

The *Castorland Journal* makes its first reference to work by Pharoux for the Livingstons in 1794. Henry Walter Livingston had just returned from Paris, full of ideas about geometrical neoclassicism; his father, Walter (cousin of the brothers Robert R., Edward, and John R.), began writing to friends about adding a pair of "octogens" to his house at Teviotdale, a Franco-Caledonian structure not unlike Mount Pleasant (see chapter 2). But the owner of Teviotdale died, his neoclassical "octogens" unbuilt, in 1797, and it was left to Henry Walter, upon inheriting his share of the estate, to begin construction of a full-scale neoclassical villa, known as The Hill.

Nothing had been built along the Hudson to equal its confident elegance—it was a lyrical exercise in ovals, to counterbalance the severe rectilinearity of the Chancellor's house. Photographs taken just before it was burnt and bulldozed in the 1970s do not do it justice. By then it had acquired a huge, ungainly portico and its wings had doubled in height. It was a blithe, breezy, cheerful villa when first built, as we can see in an illustrated map of the estate. Large windows surveyed the river and the Catskills from two linked oval parlors. Curved glass corridors swept back to semioctagonal wings largely composed of glass on the view side.*

---

*It has sometimes been said that Purcell and Elmslie's masterpiece of 1911, the Harold Bradley

This is the house said by General John Ross Delafield's "tradition" to have been "planned by an . . . architect whom Henry Walter Livingston had met when he was abroad." It was a convenience that, in 1793 or 1794, he would not have had to adopt his cousin Janet Montgomery's device of asking someone to send plans from France. For those two years Henry Walter had easy access to an architect from France—one he could easily have met in Paris. Pierre Pharoux had traveled in the same social circles as Livingston and Gouverneur Morris and came to America bearing dispatches to the American government from Morris, its minister to France and Livingston's employer.

Morris was the friend, colleague in land and wool speculation, and companion on transatlantic voyages of James Leray de Chaumont (and the lover of Mme Foucault, Leray's sister). Leray was also a political and commercial associate of many of the Livingstons—at least until 1807, when they fell out over a misdirected shipment of merino sheep.* It was Leray who engaged Pharoux for the work in Castorland.

Henry Walter Livingston, Morris's secretary, and Pierre Pharoux, the dispatch bearer for Morris, were both gentlemen-professionals. They met all the leading figures of President Washington's cabinet in Philadelphia, then the capital of the United States. Leray joined Morris in vouching for Pharoux in letters to Thomas Jefferson, Alexander Hamilton, and the President himself. They must have thought well of him; heavy investments in America were not to be put at risk by recommending to America's new leaders anyone who would not do them proud. Furthermore, Leray asked that his brother-in-law, the New Jersey magnate and economist Tench Coxe, escort Pharoux about the capital.

Henry Walter Livingston's The Hill, of 1796–99, was, it seems to me, the prototype of a design simplified to produce two other American houses, both of which are still here, though in somewhat altered form. Both have Pharoux connections.

We have already visited the first, the headquarters of James Leray, beyond the Adirondacks and far beyond the reach of the kind of skilled craftsmen available along the Hudson. Not for him would there be glass-lined corridors and oval rooms; yet otherwise the two houses were remarkably similar. Leray's house was also remodeled in the 1820s, and also gained a portico, some Greek-revival interior trim, and probably a fresh coat of stucco to hide the effects of a fire. But when we imagine away those changes, we find another villa, its

---

"bungalow" at Woods Hole, Massachusetts, looks like a sea bird poised for flight. It does—and so too did Henry Walter Livingston's house, a hundred years earlier, when glassiness and lightness and the tautness of the musculature stretching backward were far more daring.

*In his biography of Robert R. Livingston, George Dangerfield reported that Leray, "with more prudence than was quite seemly," kept four of Livingston's five sheep on his own property "to enrich his own flock" (p. 430).

octagons echoing the ovals of The Hill, its wings straightened, its interior dispositions simplified.

The resemblances between the two may be explained by a notation in the *Castorland Journal* that on July 6, 1793, just before he embarked for America, "not finding his portfolio . . . [Pharoux] entrusted the care of his goods not yet arrived to Mssrs. Baudry and Boulogne, and gave them the keys to his trunks." Baudry was Dr. Jean Baptiste Baudry, agent of James Leray de Chaumont.

That portfolio could have contained drawings for a house for Leray (and further drawings for Chancellor Livingston as well). They remained in Baudry's hands as he awaited instructions to build. We know that Leray did not proceed, as he had intended, to establish himself in America. He kept delaying his departure, finding himself surprisingly comfortable in France: his estranged wife had left him free to develop his relationship with Janika de Fériet; and, as we have noted earlier, the revolutionary authorities had assented to his contention that during his earlier stay in the United States he had become an American citizen and thus immune from confiscation. (He was a very rich and sometimes a very generous man.) So he did not emigrate in 1795; he waited, and Dr. Baudry waited, presumably keeping a set of plans in his portfolio.*

A generation later, Vincent Le Ray, son of James, wrote to an American historian, Franklin Hough, that it was not until 1805 or 1806 that his father finally decided to build a house in America. Baudry, with a set of plans in hand, preceded him to prepare things for his arrival. According to Vincent Le Ray, it was Baudry who selected the site and supervised construction of the house that was to serve as the headquarters of 150,000 acres of Leray lands.†

---

*Dr. Baudry, physician and agent for Leray de Chaumont, is not to be confused with all the Bauduys (including the architect Pierre Bauduy) who enter our story in Part Four—though the latter, as we shall see, had their own connections to the Lerays.

Furthermore, Dr. Baudry was not only the holder of a crucial portfolio for Pierre Pharoux, he was also friend and counselor to a third architect, Joseph-Jacques Ramée, a principal character of Part Six. This is a fact adding piquancy to the resemblance between two neoclassical barns. One is on the grounds of Henry Walter Livingston's The Hill, which may be the work of Pharoux in the 1790s. It is unique in America except for the other on the grounds designed by Ramée for Livingston's first cousins, the Duanes of Duanesburg, dating from about 1815. (Mrs. James Duane was Maria Livingston, sister of Walter and aunt of Henry Walter.)

These buildings may be coincidentally in the same style, unrelated otherwise. Or they may be connected through Baudry. Or, on another hand, they may represent links in a chain among Leray, his architect, Pharoux, and David Parish, who purchased more than 150,000 acres of northern New York from Leray, and was the sponsor of the American work of Ramée. We will have something more to say about all this.

†We do not have to attribute to Pharoux all the linked octagonal or oval drawing rooms built in the United States between the War of Independence and the War of 1812. Those in Alexander Hamilton's The Grange, built in 1802, for example, were likely the result of General Schuyler's and Hamilton's observation of The Hill as they passed it on their travels between Schuyler lands and Hamilton's rented quarters in New York City. But so far as I can tell, aside from The Grange, there were none without a Pharoux connection.

Bread-and-Butter Drawings

As carpenters began work on the Leray villa near the Saint Lawrence, another country house, its near duplicate in elevation and linked-octagonal plan, was being completed east of the Hudson. It was the manor house of Jacob Rutsen Van Rensselaer at Claverack. Perhaps it too was just a simplified emulation of The Hill. But the possibility exists that it was Pharoux himself who suggested that simplification to Van Rensselaer, in the form of one of the architectural "bread-and-butter letters" he was accustomed to leave with his hosts.

The *Journal* contains casual references to "a sketch of a plan for M. [Andrew B.] de Haussy and another for an enlargement of M. Desjardin's house . . . a plan for M. [Pierre] de La Bigarre . . . Stayed with M. [Honoré] Chauraud. Made a plan of his farm and buildings." On January 26, 1795, Pharoux left Albany in the morning. He dined "at Mr. Van Rensselaer's, on the other side of the river, and arrived in Claverack . . . at nine in the evening."

The logistics of travel at the time suggest that his host for dinner was John Jeremias Van Rensselaer, a first cousin of Jacob Rutsen. John Jeremias held court at the family stronghold, Fort Crailo, in what is now the town of Rensselaer. Jacob Rutsen had not yet inherited his share of his father's estate at Claverack, but could have been one of those to whom Pharoux left plans for houses they might build someday. In 1803 he inherited his father's inland estate, including a knoll beside the mill pond. He replaced an old house on that knoll with a central cube nearly identical to Leray's, across the Adirondacks, but never got around to adding wings or formal gardens to complete the scheme.*

Speranza

Pharoux had not completed his commissions for the Livingstons. During the winter of 1794–95, he made a series of entries in the *Journal* about plans for "the city of Speranza . . . which the Livingstons have employed him to make."

---

*There were other connections among the Leray Mansion, The Hill, and the Van Rensselaer house.

Cornelia, sister of Henry Walter Livingston of The Hill, married James Leray de Chaumont. She was born in 1780, and first married (April 29, 1802) John Juhel. From that marriage sprang a daughter, also named Cornelia, who married James's son, Vincent.

Further, Richard Morris Esselsteyn (1775–1825) of Claverack, a surveyor and engineer, went to the vicinity of the Leray Mansion in 1801 to work for Leray's agents, Mssrs. Smith and Delamater. I believe the plans for the Leray Mansion were in hand as early as 1794, but, in any case, it was commenced in 1806 and completed in 1808. Esselsteyn returned to Claverack in 1806, where he had grown up upon the adjacent property to the site of the Robert and Jacob Rutsen Van Rensselaer house, which was commenced at about that time.

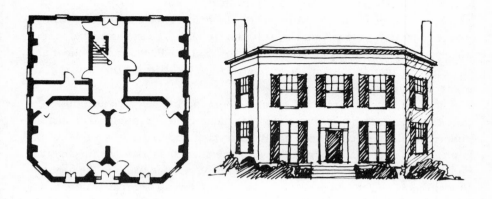

*Floor plan and conjectural elevation of the house of Jacob Rutsen
Van Rensselaer as built (computer-generated by James Stokoe)*

John R. Livingston of Masséna had formed a family syndicate to develop a port city on the west bank of the Hudson, now incorporated into the town of Athens (pronounced "Ay-thens"). It is easy to forget now that the Hudson is salt as far as Albany; it was entirely possible to develop a deep-water port at Speranza for whalers and West Indies traders to exchange wheat for sugar. (John Thurman thought he could reach world markets from manufacturing establishments a hundred miles farther upstream.)

In early January, Pharoux "worked on the plan . . . on the map . . . a plan of the church . . . [and laid] out the streets and lots." Two of the streets were named for Mary and Eliza, the wives of Edward and John R. Livingston. On February 7, he was still "busy on the plans for Speranza and the various public edifices to be constructed there." On April 14, 1795, he "finished the plan of Speranza, and sent it to M. de St. Mémin, who will get it engraved."

Charles B. J. Fevret de Saint-Mémin is as well known in the world of portraiture as Brunel is among engineers. After serving with the guards of King Louis XVI, he fled to America in 1794. He was encouraged to become a portraitist by John R. Livingston and made several profile portraits and a few landscapes before he returned to France in 1814. Many of them are now to be found in the Corcoran Gallery and the National Portrait Gallery in Washington, D.C. Among them are four architectural engravings; they depict a "church" and other "public edifices." The whole collection is attributed to the engraver, though Saint-Mémin was not an architect. In the Corcoran's files the buildings are assigned to Asylum, or Azylum, the Susquehanna project (see p. 93) with which he had weaker connections than those that bound him to the Hudson and the Livingstons.

The Saint-Mémin collection at the Corcoran does not include an engraved map of Speranza, but one is to be found in the New York State Library at Cooperstown. It is called "the Pharmix map," because, apparently, an 1884 history of Greene County reported that a "large map, made by one P. Pharmix, was engraved, and a few copies are still to be found." The signature was in such a tight configuration that it could easily be read as "P. Pharmix," but it was the same as that found on the garden design for Baron von Steuben: "P. Pharoux."

The most powerful of the Corcoran engravings depicts a courthouse of a peculiar cruciform design, revolving around a central rotunda, with piazzas connecting the splayed projections. It fits precisely upon the "footprint" of the courthouse on the map Pharoux drew for Speranza, and Saint-Mémin engraved and signed. More important, it fits the terrain. When one walks in the footsteps of Pharoux, along the ridge above Athens, four views appear that he might have intended as balm for litigants' eyes, from his four piazzas: the Hudson and the Berkshires, the Catskills, the fields, and the forest.

The second Corcoran engraving shows a church, with a cupola on top, and a portico with six attenuated columns (see p. 76). And on the Speranza map of 1794–95 were two churches, two six-columned buildings facing each other across "Church Square"—like those Asher Benjamin, Elias Carter, and Ithiel Town made a Yankee village "standard" after 1800.

The Corcoran's sketch of a market reposes easily on the site shown for it

The "Pharmix" map of Speranza

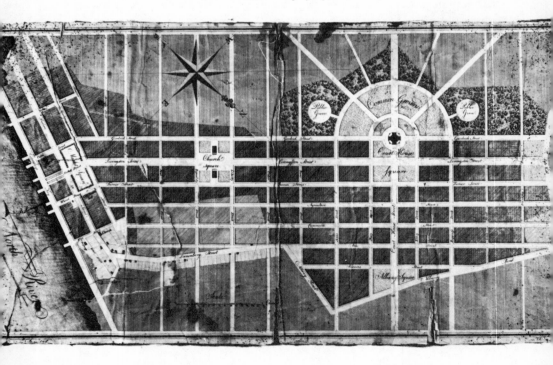

Courthouse Square, Speranza

Court House by Pierre Pharoux(?), engraved by Saint-Mémin

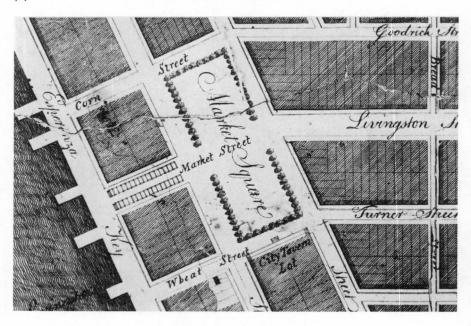

Market Square, Speranza

Market by Pharoux(?), engraved by Saint-Mémin

Tavern by Pharoux(?), engraved by Saint-Mémin

in Pharoux's map. Architectural historians might see it as related to the designs of the French neoclassicists Etienne-Louis Boullée and Claude-Nicolas Ledoux, but at Speranza it would have been seen as the frontispiece to stalls full of root crops, apples and peaches, honey and jam, wool, wheat, corn, and rye, brought down from hillside farms and laid out just above the quayside, where seafarers and merchants could chose among them as they walked up Market Street to Market Square, parallel to Wheat Street and Corn Street.

The last "Saint-Mémin" building at the Corcoran is a heavy, utilitarian tavern. It too has its place at Speranza, across from the market, on the "City Tavern Lot," facing Market Square. It resembles the City Hotel in New York, and it may have had another iteration, not in Speranza or Athens but in Rome. In the *Castorland Journal,* Pharoux tells us that on May 8, 1795, Dominick Lynch, the founder of Rome, New York, "made me some proposals for the city which he wishes to lay out at Ft. Stanwix." Lynch had purchased the site from the Livingstons, and the Castorland Company had undertaken "to buy a lot . . . to raise another store . . . which should serve as an entrepot of the Company." Since Pharoux was already designing the company's stores else-where, it is not surprising that there is a plan for Lynch's city, in the archives of Rome, dated no later than 1796, very much like the plans of Pharoux for Speranza and for another French speculation, Tivoli.

Church Square, Speranza

Church by Pharoux(?), engraved by Saint-Mémin

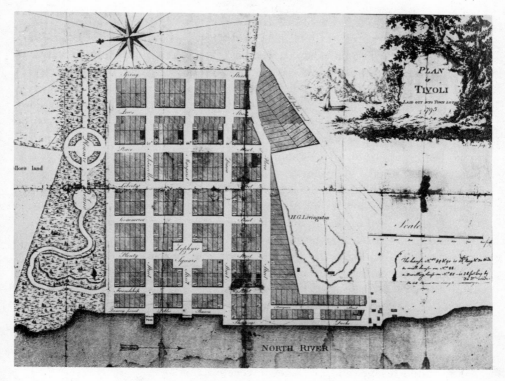

Plan of Tivoli by Pharoux(?), engraved by Saint-Mémin

Tivoli and the Black River

Pharoux's *Journal* entry for March 22, 1795, says he had "made a plan for M. de La Bigarre," a West Indian adventurer who settled into the Hudson Valley enclave of Saint-Dominguan Creole refugees. Pierre de La Bigarre, as we observed earlier, married an heiress whose sister married Peter William Livingston, began buying up land among the Livingston holdings, and laid out his own speculative community just south of the Chancellor's house. His Château de Tivoli was surrounded by a high brick wall with a classical "postern gate." Stories grew up that it was a true château, with walls and moats like a French fortress. One account of it says: "The House (one end of which was octagonal in shape) was probably erected between 1798 and 1802." Perhaps it then looked like Masséna.

The gardens of Tivoli were much admired in the 1840s by the landscape designer and publicist Andrew Jackson Downing. Taken together with the city plan of Tivoli, they might have provided a synthesis of the "English gardens" Pharoux laid out for Steuben and the plan of Speranza.

Tivoli seems to have been the last of the series: Castorville, Basle, Fort Stanwix, and Speranza. None of them could have been criticized for being "all in straight lines," like Philadelphia; yet even they were not fully representative of what Pierre Pharoux might have done had he designed his own ideal city. But for the charms of Niagara Falls, we might know the whereabouts of such a plan. In August 1796 Desjardins recorded in the *Journal* that he "saw M. de St. Mémin, on the project of engraving a map of Castorland . . ." They fell to talking with "M. de Valdenuit, [who was living in Saint-Mémin's house and who had been] one of my neighbors of Champaigne . . . is devoted to the arts, and wishes to make a journey to Niagara." Desjardins's account rushes on to talk about Niagara; that is the last we hear about a grand design upon which Pharoux was working during the summer of 1795.

He had returned to Castorland. On September 21, his "zeal" to complete his surveying, and perhaps to return to architecture, led him to try to cross the rain-swollen Black River on a raft. The raft was "drawn into the falls by the violence of the current . . . Money, instruments, provisions, all were lost"—and with them poor Pharoux.

One of the first settlers of Castorland wrote his obituary: "An event . . . has much hindered the prosperity of this colony. The death of a young man of much talent . . . sent from Paris, to render a wild and hitherto unknown country fit [for] . . . a new born society, to divide the lands, open roads, begin the first labors, build bridges and mills, and invent machines . . ."

Soon after James Leray arrived in northern New York in 1803, he asked to be shown the little island at the mouth of the river where the body of Pierre Pharoux had been found. Among the rocks of the island he placed a marble tablet bearing these words: "To the Memory of Peter Pharoux . . . This Island is Consecrated." Many clients have done less for their architects. But it seems likely that the house at Leraysville that Dr. Baudry began building two years later was Leray's true memorial to Pharoux.

Postmortem: Brunel and Aaron Burr

Marc Isambard Brunel was not in the habit of drawing from his own experience for cautionary tales; rueful self-mockery was not his tone. Nor could he bring himself to admit that the eminence of his celebrated middle age was at some remove from his years of obscurity in America. When he came to give an account of the means by which he escaped into celebrity, he did not emphasize his dependence upon the largesse of the Thurmans or that of Chancellor Livingston; nor, especially, did he choose to discuss his most eminent patron, Aaron Burr.

In their celebrated duel in 1804, Burr had killed Alexander Hamilton and had thereby made Hamilton in death the hero he aspired to become in life. Attitudes among the gentry toward dueling had changed; it was no longer honorable to shoot an opponent, and Burr was popularly considered a murderer—and a seditious murderer at that, for he had gone on to engage in a larger sort of duel with the Sage of Monticello, Thomas Jefferson, for control of the Mississippi Valley.

There is, as we have seen, copious evidence of Brunel's dependence upon Livingston and the Thurmans and, as we will see in a moment, even more graphic demonstration of his acquaintance with Burr. Yet Brunel informed his biographers that it was Alexander Hamilton who selected him for friendship. According to Brunel, he was in the habit of dining with his "particular friend," who, recognizing his mechanical genius, sent him to London to aid the British fleet in its struggle against Napoleon by means of one of his wondrous inventions—a mass-produced "block" for rigging.

There is no reference to Brunel in Hamilton's papers, but in the European journal of Aaron Burr there are many entries written in 1811 and 1812 from England, during his exile, about the interest in mechanical contrivances he shared with Brunel. They discussed mechanized shoemaking equipment and chemical experiments, and there is preserved a letter from Brunel to a Mr. Randolph introducing Burr for further discussions. However, the strongest testimony that the two had become acquainted in New York during the late 1790s is a fine drawing signed by Brunel; it is to be found among the Hurst Collection of Brunel documents from which Paul Clements drew those discussed earlier, but for some reason he did not think it worthy of reproducing. Dated 1796, it is clearly a proposal to set an elaborate baroque front upon the residence, Marble Hill, for which Burr had entered a lease commencing early in the next year.

This is an extraordinary document, showing the progress of Brunel's skill in draftsmanship together with the regress of his architectural taste. The "Capitol" drawing, made while Pharoux was around to counsel him, was, if ungainly, in the latest style of the "visionary architects." The proposal for Burr, though beautifully rendered, is for a building fifty years out of date, like that proposed by Major Pierre-Charles L'Enfant for Robert Morris (see p. 99).

The Burr-Brunel connection is not only of interest to architectural historians; it is a link through Baron von Steuben to that consummate scoundrel James Wilkinson, and to the military adventures in the West that led to the contest between Burr and Jefferson that is the subject of Part Seven.

In the first two weeks of December 1793, a new tone creeps into the *Castorland Journal;* Pharoux and Desjardins speak with surprising asperity of their interview with Thomas Jefferson, in which they report that he grimaced when they replied to his inquiry as to their expectations for Castorland by saying that "many of the best families would come before long, to seek in this

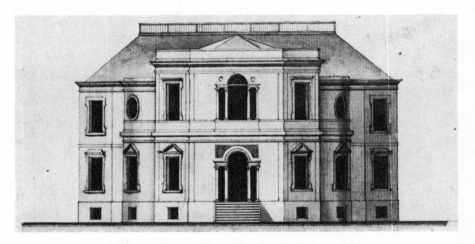

*Brunel's design "for Colonel Burr of New York," of a "projected
improvement for his country house," Marble Hill*

*Marble Hill in 1790, when it was the country house of John Adams
(also known as Richmond Hill Mansion)*

country the tranquility of true liberty." This was a time when Jefferson was readying for his departure from the cabinet, having been defeated by Hamilton in a series of tests of strength, convinced that the "monarchical" Federalists were triumphant and that his public life was at an end.*

That "grimace" was no doubt a commentary on his own view of the prospects for his brand of American liberty. But such was their state of mind that they read it to be yet another expression of American "hatred for foreigners." The *Journal* continues:

> Europeans are distrusted here. The merchant fears that the newly arrived stranger will share with him the profits of trade; the farmer that he will enhance the price of land; the land broker, that he will expose his speculations; the man of reputation, that he will detect his weak points, and the ambitious man, that among these emigrants there may be those who will eclipse him by their talents . . . They monopolize all, concentrate all, everything for self, nothing for others, such is the governing principle of this nation.

From whom would they have so quickly derived the instances to support such sweeping conclusions? Whose disappointments with ungrateful Americans, whose smarting about talents eclipsed, land prices raised, and speculations exposed might lead to such a judgment? They were having their own problems in securing remittances from James Leray through his brother-in-law Tench Coxe, but that would hardly have been enough had their interview with Jefferson not been given a gloss, a week later, by an embittered and frustrated Baron von Steuben.

Traditionally, he has been presented as happily retired in his log cabin at Steubenville, though Samuel Flagg Bemis, more than sixty years ago, ferreted out the truth: Steuben was so angry at his treatment by the American government and people that he had proposed to the king of Spain that he would take a group of hardened revolutionary warriors with him to form a buffer state between Mexico and the United States, a "frontier military colony," upon a Spanish land grant. At the time of his death, not long after his long discussions with Pharoux, Desjardins, and Brunel, he was planning a trip to Madrid to consummate this plan, which anticipated both the proposal to Joseph Bonaparte by Joseph Lakanal (see Part Eight) and, with a twist or two, that of James Wilkinson to the Spanish authorities in 1805–06, which may or may not have been known to his then partner, Aaron Burr (see Part Seven).

At this stage Steuben was closer to the Spanish authorities than was Wilkin-

---

*Claude Bowers, in a typical passage in his *Jefferson and Hamilton,* tells us that Jefferson was contemplating "going home. . . . Soon the negroes would be running down the hill road to meet the carriage, to touch his clothes, to kiss his hands" (p. 239).

son, who used Steuben as his intermediary. We are free to wonder whether or not Brunel had occasion to mention the matter to Burr in London in 1811—or had he already done so in New York in 1796?

To the memory of Marc Isambard Brunel many volumes have been dedicated. It is just as well that we do not rely on either those volumes or his own memory of the circumstances under which he escaped his ignominious American years. Chancellor Livingston told William Constable that he sent the young man to England to promote a steamboat scheme, and all accounts agree that he did embark aboard the packet *Halifax* in the summer of 1799, bound for yet another series of triumphs—this time, real ones.

He left behind him certain unfulfilled obligations. There was, for example, at least one American child: years later, according to Lady Celia Noble, American cousins came to call on the famous Brunels in London. Lady Noble's account of the American cousins is remarkably candid in the light of family lore about a long, celibate American vigil, spent thinking only of the lady he left behind in France—Lady Noble's grandmother.

A poignant document in the New York State Library records how Brunel chose to recognize what he owed the Thurmans: in August 1812, John Thurman's nephew Richard wrote Brunel, whom he addressed as "Isambard," reminding him that when Richard was his uncle's agent in Essex County, Brunel—"a stranger, nay a foreigner"—had appeared on the scene. Soon the Thurmans were persuaded that he was "a Gentleman endorsed with learning, Genius, & a great share of Mechanical ingenuity, & by no means wanting in honor & . . . honesty."

Sometime later, probably in 1799, Thurman learned that Brunel was "about to leave me . . . [but he was] arrested at the moment of departure for a debt he could not pay." Though Thurman "had no reason to suspect [that Brunel] would ever return," the great engineer drew "upon my friendship & generosity for relief." His "necessities" were relieved. Then, recalled Thurman, "he takes his leave; without thanks, or even an acknowledgement of the debt."

For years, apparently, they corresponded. Brunel was working his way upward in London; as Thurman recalled, "While it was out of your power . . . I never . . . requested you to pay me; but . . . [then] you informed me that the generosity & liberality of the British government had . . . amply rewarded your services." Probably in 1811, Thurman finally asked Brunel to buy for the "wife I love" a plate, perhaps of silver, thereby repaying the debt. Brunel "did not comply" but instead told his bankers to send twenty pounds sterling, not even the "full amount."

Thurman felt he had a "just claim on [Brunel's] Honor & Gratitude." More important, the two had been friends; it was his "silence and apparent neglect" that hurt. Keeping open the possibility that he was wrong about Brunel, he said he hoped for a reply. There is no sign that it ever came.

III

AMONG

THE GREAT ONES

It was useful for merchants to be "multinational"; their opportunities were not geographically limited, nor was it profitable to limit themselves to patriotic trade. But in the eighteenth century the term did not connote, as it often does today, massive, conspicuous, overweight assemblages of bureaucratized routineurs, whose chief power lies in inertia, and whose chief weakness lies in their inability quickly to adapt. Earlier multinationals made a virtue of rapidity and invisibility as they worked in units small enough to find apertures through archaic national policies.

But transatlantic traffic in eminent persons was not limited to those in the drab of commerce. Other great ones came aboard as well, trailing clouds of glory past, and of glory promised. The Middle Ages were not so distant, as yet, for inconspicuousness to be available to all ranks of society. Princes, dukes, and marquises could not easily render themselves invisible while seeking to avoid harassment or decapitation. Heirs to kingdoms, even if they were most unlikely to reign, were objects of awe. Awe is a pleasant response when one is prospering, but it can quickly turn to derision when one is on one's uppers.

And there was another category of displaced persons whose comings and goings were likely to be of avid interest to the people among whom they were seeking asylum. These were eminent politicians whose careers had been interrupted by exile. Between 1785 and 1820, the French centrifuge sent into exile royalists of both Bourbon and Orléanist varieties, Bonapartists and Moreauites, republicans and anarchists, clericals and anticlericals. Some of these were doubly notable for being aristocrats as well as the leaders of factions.

A few came in relative comfort, like the Bonaparte brothers Jerome and Joseph and the Bonaparte nephews the princes Murat. Some were received as celebrities, like the future king Louis Philippe and his brothers. Others survived in the United States periods of disagreeable obscurity. Among these were Jean Victor Moreau, the only true competitor to Napoleon among the generals of the Republic; Jacques-Pierre Brissot de Warville, who gave his name to one of the great parties of the first, moderate phase of the revolution, the Brissotins; and Charles Maurice de Talleyrand-Périgord, who directed the foreign policy of France under more regimes and to greater personal gain than any other statesman in its history.

Americans were dazzled, bemused, and moved to moralizing: how the mighty had fallen! Charles Nisbet, of Carlisle, Pennsylvania, wrote to an English friend that in Philadelphia "the awful and depressing events of the present age have rendered great changes . . . familiar." He had observed the duc de Rochefoucauld-Liancourt housed with a barber and "obliged to clean his own shoes," and the Vicomte de Noailles living in two rooms "in the house of a Seceding Minister." The vicomte was still rich enough, it seems, to keep "sundry ci-devant French Barons, Counts and Marquises employed in the Labor of Agriculture." He kept himself employed as well. He was remembered as a man whose "form was perfect—a fine face, tall, graceful, the first amateur dancer of the age, and of very pleasant manners. He became a trader and speculator . . . every day at the coffee-house or exchange, busy, holding his bank book in one hand," ready to strike a bargain.

Nisbet said he found a former admiral at work as journeyman to a Baltimore potter, and another marquis an ironsmith in Philadelphia; but not many émigrés had recourse to vocational training. Grousing was a more common response to altered circumstances. Some attempted to eke out their remittances in coffee-houses and pastry shops. Others fell to trading on their ancient names to sell dubious schemes. There were enough titled mountebanks to provide new characters for American folklore—mendicant dukes and dauphins. Mark Twain, as was his habit, took an abundance of frontier clichés and, in *Huckleberry Finn,* turned a sordid reality into a myth of the frontier itself.

Twain's comedy arose from compassion disappointed. Tales of dauphins in captivity, like princes in the Tower, elicit from us fantasies of better outcomes. Anyone with half a heart wants to believe that guiltless young ones do not die of starvation or suffocation. Even Napoleon's rather pallid son, "L'Aiglon," became a figure of myth. Did he escape his comfortable captivity of twenty years in the hands of his mother's parents, the emperor and empress of Austria? Was a substitute found to die for him, in the full glare of the world's rapt attention? Eaglets and dauphins abounded on the American frontier in the 1830s and 1840s; L'Aiglon was reported in several sightings in the Adirondacks.

7

TRANSATLANTIC CROSSINGS

Having completed his last work, an essay attacking the traffic in slaves, Benjamin Franklin died in April 1790. It was not until July 11 that the news reached Paris, where he had constructed the alliance that culminated in the first victorious war of the United States and the last victorious war of the Bourbon monarchy.

"Franklin is dead." The comte de Mirabeau brought the news to the National Assembly, and "a shiver ran through the audience." After gaining control of his own emotions and of his famous sense of timing, Mirabeau uttered these words: "He has returned to the wellsprings of divinity, that genius who set America free and bathed Europe in torrents of light."

As is true of most funeral orations, this one both simplified and exaggerated the truth. Still, Franklin had certainly been helpful in bringing France to the aid of the American armed forces after the first three years of the revolutionary conflict, and it is quite reasonable that a French statesman should see that aid as crucial, since the war required five more years to win. Mirabeau was not speaking as a historian; he was speaking for people on both sides of the Atlantic who had been comrades in the global disorder stirred by Franklin.

That disorder had subsided; peace had reigned for seven years, and in that summer of 1790 Franco-American relations were salubrious. France had entrusted power to a set of statesmen—Mirabeau among them—who, like those in power in the United States, aspired to controlled revolution. Robespierre was only in the audience; it would be three more years before the Terror sent royalists and republicans to the scaffold together.

Franklin's funeral provided the final ceremony of a golden summer of hope and amity. Majestic obsequies took place under the huge dome of the Halle aux Blés, hung in black cloth; the assembly, gathered by the city of Paris, gazed upon a portrait of Franklin mounted on a pedestal. In the front row sat Arthur Dillon, father of Henriette de La Tour Du Pin (see p. 51); the marquis de Lafayette, representing the heroes of the war for American independence; Mirabeau; the duc de La Rochefoucauld, a leader of the liberal aristocracy; the mayor of Paris; and Abbé Sieyès, who lasted as a politician almost as long as Talleyrand.

Few of these celebrators of Franco-American friendship would survive the next seven years to bemoan the outbreak of a "quasi-war" between the two countries in 1797. Like us all, they were thinking of their present as defined by their past; seven years before, in 1783, they had celebrated a common victory over the British, a war brought to an end by a treaty signed in Paris. Seven thousand Frenchmen had served in America, comrades with Washington and Hamilton and the other heroes of the scrupulous revolution led by these gentry to achieve political independence without too much social change.

Seeds of Revolution

We cannot know how any of the French who were exposed to American ideas returned with a determination to apply them at home, but it is safe to say that America's return gift to the Bourbons was an insurrectionary spirit. Its most famous embodiment was Lafayette. From 1786 to 1792 he was a power in France. Handsome, willful, spoiled, noble in aspiration though slow of mind and incurably flighty in action, he was the wrong man to negotiate a peaceful outcome from a tense and complex situation. Lafayette had a defect of some importance: he was unable to distinguish appearance from reality. Yet he had a friend, a genuinely devoted friend, who was already experienced in the management of revolution. That man was the American representative in Paris from 1785 to 1789, Thomas Jefferson.

Jefferson was more than a diplomatic representative of the newly united states; he took a role in French politics. In August 1789, a committee drafting a constitution for France asked him to join them. He wisely demurred, but he was in constant demand for other, less systematic services. One evening he received this note from Lafayette:

> I beg for liberty's sake you will break every engagement to give us dinner . . . We shall be some members of the National Assembly—eight of us whom I want to coalize as being the only means to prevent total dissolution and civil war.

Jefferson took pains to cover his back. He was the representative of a Federalist government, and that government was already apprehensive about the prospect of "total dissolution" of the monarchy. Power was slipping from the hands of Brissot, Lafayette, Mirabeau—the moderates—into those of the Jacobins; and Jefferson was already being charged with a failure to anticipate— or, worse, with a desire deliberately to accelerate—that slippage. His direct superior, John Jay, secretary for foreign affairs (Jefferson himself was later to become the first American to carry the title secretary of state), was one of the first to lose confidence in Jefferson and his friends. Having written them off, Jay was already systematically at work building an alliance with the British.

Jefferson protested to Jay that he too was trying to slow the pace of change in France. Accordingly, he was even ready to report his meetings with his revolutionary friends to the Bourbon minister of foreign affairs, the comte de Montmorin. Jefferson assured Jay that Montmorin, "so far from taking umbrage at the use made of my house . . . earnestly wished I would habitually assist at such conferences . . . moderating the warmer spirits." Before the warmer spirits prevailed, and before the ensuing conflagration, Jefferson's hopes were high: "I will agree to be stoned as a false prophet if all does not end well in this country. Here is but the first chapter in the history of European liberty." Jefferson was writing the reciprocal of Brissot's three-volume love letter to "hundred times happy America."

Brissot

Jacques-Pierre Brissot shared with Mirabeau the leadership of the moderate party in the early years of the revolution. He was, for a time, one of the agile ones who thrived upon disorder.

Son of an innkeeper and a governess for the children of the duc d'Orléans (many characters in this portion of this story were associated with that household), Brissot became a lawyer successful enough to add an aristocratic caboose to his name, "de Warville," in the same way that Robespierre became "de Robespierre," Danton "d'Anton," Dupont "Du Pont de Nemours" (see p. 188), and Jacques Garnier "Garnier de Saintes" (see pp. 344–5).

He then abandoned law for literature and journalism and, to his immense credit, for propagandizing for the abolition of slavery. The power of slave-

Brissot (artist unknown)

owning Creoles was still very great at court, and Brissot paid for views then thought extreme by a sojourn in the Bastille; but in 1788, as leader of the Friends of the Negroes, he could travel to Philadelphia, "whence he returned with his Quaker-like appearance and manner much intensified." He did not find there exactly the simple spirit he expected: he was disappointed in "the growing luxury and refinement of the cities in America, as a sign of decay of republican simplicity." He was not so simple himself. Quaker-like, he could put a journey to several uses—moral fervor is not incompatible with shrewd business judgment. His Philadelphia trip was a scouting expedition for a group of French real-estate speculators, and also for a British syndicate that hoped to corner the American debt to France for a quick resale in Europe.

Brissot's political theories bubbled out of that same deep well of fantasy as his images of wondrous wealth in American real estate. He imagined dreamscapes where free Negroes roamed arm-in-arm with French intellectuals and American yeomen. To the doubts of a more skeptical traveler from France, the marquis de Chastellux, he responded, "You wish, sir, to destroy this enchantment! Cruel man!"

Home again in Paris, he lived surrounded by his prattling children in two cold rooms and was able to write those volumes on "hundred times happy America." He was already chief of a Gallo-American Society as well as the Friends of the Negroes. Now he plotted to reorganize French society around a constitutional monarch; thus one might "free the people and immortalize oneself."

But the people, once feeling the rush of freedom, were not to be constrained by a monarchy, constitutional or otherwise; they wanted blood and called forth Robespierre and the Terror. Louis XVI, Brissot's briefly constitutional monarch, went to the guillotine, and soon thereafter Brissot followed him to the ultimate test of immortality. France mobilized against invasions from the terrified and furious monarchies of Europe and turned to America for assistance. But though it was announced at the Jacobin Club that the Americans were on their way—"Washington is at sea!"—it took one hundred and twenty years for him to arrive, and by then he was General John Pershing.

Military Exchanges

In a fervent gesture of transatlantic fraternity, the French Assembly had made honorary French citizens of Thomas Paine, James Madison, Washington, Alexander Hamilton, and, somewhat later, the poet Joel Barlow (see p. 390). Washington, however, was unavailable for European campaigns; he was fully occupied with the presidency and appalled by regicide and the Terror. Even more disgusted with the French was Hamilton, the only other military figure on that list of honorary citizens; he was engaged in resisting even the mildly revolutionary spirits of the Jeffersonians. But there were a few underemployed heroes of the American Revolution who did offer their services. George Rogers Clark wrote from his post at the falls of the Ohio River that he was willing to conquer Spanish Louisiana and Mexico for France and was commissioned a brigadier general in the French Revolutionary Army.* "Light Horse Harry" Lee pursued a commission as a French general for active service in Europe until he was dissuaded by the excesses of the Terror.

Neither Lee nor Clark saw active duty; but other Americans held high posts in the armies of France, with important results for the frontiers of the United States (see p. 314). With less effect, Colonel William Tate led a handful of undisciplined and drunken men against the coast of Wales. This first American expeditionary force did not impress the Welsh; Tate went to jail.

In 1798, a more formidable expedition set out to assault the Celtic fringe of the British Isles. With only a handful of Americans aboard, a French fleet deposited an expeditionary force on the west coast of Ireland. Led by two soldiers whose major appearance here would be premature (we will find one of them empire-building in Texas and the other seeking absolution at Monticello), the French joined hands with the survivors of a premature Irish rising, routed the British at Castlebar, and conducted an admirable war of hares against hounds as Lord Cornwallis, the loser at Yorktown fifteen years earlier but the inevitable winner in Ireland, closed in. "The year of the French" ended in another bloody slaughter of the Irish; the French in charge were carefully preserved for later heroics.

Chateaubriand and Crèvecoeur

Of more permanent effect than any of these military adventures were the periodic tours of inspection of America made by French intellectuals whose writings were intended to instruct their countrymen what to think of America (and who powerfully shaped what Americans thought of themselves) and the longer sojourns in America by French architects, whose stories unfold throughout this book, giving some density to the vaporizings of those who worked only with words.

The most influential of these visitors—in terms of the impressions of America arising in France and the investment decisions made as a result—were François-René, vicomte de Chateaubriand, poet, playwright, and pamphleteer, and J. Hector Saint Jean de Crèvecoeur, farmer and essayist.†

Chateaubriand visited America before either the American or the French

---

*It was not unreasonable for the French to expect Clark's aid; in 1778–79 he had had the help of French guides in his attack on the British post of Vincennes.

†Crèvecoeur had been born Michel-Guillaume-Jean Saint-Jean, but he revised this for literary

revolution, but he belongs in this part of the story because he instructed many political refugees as to what to expect. He came in search of the Northwest Passage, expecting it in the neighborhood of Schenectady. Though he remained only briefly among the virgin timber and virgin literary possibilities of the region, he was its most competent creator of folk heroes until the advent of Washington Irving and James Fenimore Cooper.

No piping shepherd or hoary-handed husbandman, Chateaubriand wrote his American romances while sitting with a hamper beside his chair in Saint James's Park in London. But thousands of Frenchmen took him seriously as an expert witness to the glories of America. Many Americans did as well: the states of Mississippi and Alabama each created a town, "Atala," named for one of his tales (Alabama gave its an extra *l*); and, as we shall see, Vincent Nolte, the greatest sugar speculator in New Orleans and a patron of architecture, thought his own accomplishments small beside those of Chateaubriand.

Crèvecoeur was made of sterner stuff. He explored America from Niagara to Florida, and married an American, Mehetable Tippet, of Yonkers; Thomas Jefferson was present at the marriage of their daughter, America-Frances. For a decade Crèvecoeur farmed in Orange County, on the north side of the Hudson Highlands, introducing alfalfa and the vetches to America.

An uncompromising conservative, Crèvecoeur took a somber view of the prospects for an American republic after observing a civil war between Connecticut and Pennsylvania settlers on the Susquehanna in the 1770s. During the revolution he was on the Tory side and went back to France; he returned to America in 1783.

Though acknowledging that "there is something truly ridiculous in a farmer quitting his plough or his axe, and then flying to his pen," Crèvecoeur wrote a supple and sinuous English. His *Letters from an American Farmer* have been criticized for playing into the Rousseauian myths about America; but in fact he had few illusions. The line "Trade knows no enemy" is his. His *Farm Life* provides an honest sense of American rural reality.

8

INNOCENTS ABROAD

George Grieve is largely remembered as the translator of the works of Crève-coeur. He was a young American, often an amiable though crankily idealistic

---

purposes though he admitted that neither he nor his august ancestors had ever owned the estate at Crèvecoeur, and he had no connection to Hector save through reading Homer.

guest of Benjamin Franklin and the Lerays de Chaumont at Passy. Later, however, he became obsessed with the faded courtesan Mme Du Barry, and as the French Revolution increased in fervor, so did Grieve. Du Barry, by 1789 a decaying woman encrusted in paint and jewels, was for him the embodiment of the corruption and cruelty of the ancien régime. He took possession of her house and did not relent until he had prevailed upon the Terror to send her, screaming in fear, to the guillotine in 1793.

Even before the Terror gave full play to the demons in many like George Grieve, there were wiser beneficiaries of the old regime than Mme Du Barry. Many anticipated the course of events and took steps to protect themselves. In the late 1780s, and not for the last time, "flight capital" was available in Paris for investment in America. It was boiled off by the heat of revolution. Exports were heavy in jewels, gold, silver, paintings, bric-a-brac, and furniture. There were quick profits to be made by unscrupulous dealers like Richard Cosway (see p. 445). American bankers, like more scrupulous Swiss bankers of the twentieth century, accumulated in their vaults caches of wealth payable to persons some of whom never made it past their political difficulties to demand payment.

Other Americans, like Joel Barlow (see p. 390), made tidy sums finding real estate in the United States in which French liquidity might be reinvested. Some of Barlow's customers followed their money to the backwoods. They did not go unobserved, for such glamorous departures gave rise to "violent discussions and much gossip." The Atlantic ports were full of elegant luggage. Citizens observed "one of the strangest spectacles of this astonishing period" as deep-dyed aristocrats took ship for an experimental republic—"an old society seeking sanctuary in the temple of Liberty."

Many of these glittering and beribboned anticipators of disaster were bound for the resort on the Ohio promised them by the Scioto Company. Aside from Barlow, who was in Paris as its chief salesman, its promotors included the marquis de Lezay-Marnésia; a lesser figure, Duval d'Esprémesnil; and a company of nobles, parliamentarians, and high officers in the armies of Louis XVI.*

---

*There is a long and honorable history in France of sagacious leaders of imperiled minorities looking to America for refuge. That history commenced in the 1560s, when the first Protestant colony in America was established with the encouragement of Admiral Gaspard de Coligny, on the coast of what is now South Carolina, which was then territory disputed among Spain, France, and Britain. When the Spaniards exterminated Coligny's Huguenot colonists in 1562, they left a proclamation that such ferocity was due these intruders not as Frenchmen but as Protestants.

Ten years later, on Saint Bartholomew's Eve, the broken body of the admiral himself lay in his own courtyard in Paris, at the feet of his relentless enemy the duc de Guise. Packs of killers, hired by the relentless Guise, went about the city cutting down Huguenots; those lucky enough to escape went into exile, as Coligny knew they must. Accordingly, Britain and Ireland received a class of devoted Protestant artisans and tradesmen. South Carolina acquired that Huguenot merchant class still guiding its fortunes, and America received the genius of B. Henry Latrobe—after several skips.

Lezay-Marnésia was so persuaded by Crèvecoeur's paeans to the simple life that he actually went to America to seek it; he returned convinced that he had found "a world where earth, principles and men move together in a natural and tranquil liberty, illumined by the fear of God." Duval never inspected his Sciotan holdings; he sent his lawyer to join a hundred courtiers, coach makers, gilders, confectioners, glass blowers, watchmakers, and scene painters who had made the four-thousand-mile journey to Ohio.* They found no city awaiting them, but only eighty log cabins laid out in rows of twenty on the swampy margin of the swollen river below a bluff. Blockhouses had been hastily created at the corners to stand off the Indians. This was Gallipolis, the metropolis of Gauls (pronounced by its twentieth-century natives "Gallo-police").

Though its condition was squalid and its land title defective,† its location was splendid, not far upstream from Louisville, named after the king of France; from Kentucky counties named Bourbon and Fayette; from towns named Paris, Versailles, and Marietta, for Queen Marie Antoinette.‡

In 1793, the emigrants began with a ball—so it was always said of French colonies—and ended by drifting away. Title to their land was successfully disputed by the Ohio Land Company, a rival organization of speculators. The Scioto colony was abandoned, though a few of the settlers moved to twenty-four thousand acres awarded to them by a Congress made conscious of their plight; some bought their asylum all over again, from the Ohio Company.

---

*Duval's lawyer was Bancel de Confoulens, who made the passage of inspection to America in company with Pierre Pharoux and Simon Desjardins, bound for Castorland.

Duval heard of the debacle at Scioto and instructed Bancel to avoid Castorland—perhaps because its location was said to be on the baleful-sounding Black River, perhaps because its sponsors were even more inexperienced than he was. Instead he was sent to Maine, where some other Scioto investors, led by the strong-minded Mme Bacler de Leval, had found some rocky land that had a spring so effulgent that she called her settlement Fontaine Leval.

Fontaine Leval—such a lovely name! Bancel wrote Duval to come and bring with him plaster of paris, olive oil, rum, almanacs, and the latest fashions in clothing. But Duval had another appointment—with the guillotine.

†Barlow probably believed he was providing well for his French friends; there is no proof he understood that he was a salesman for a fraud organized by William Playfair of Edinburgh and William Duer of New York.

Playfair was the nephew of the remarkable architect James Playfair, whose Cairness House anticipates Louis Sullivan's Owatonna Bank in ways we cannot here pause to examine, and cousin of William Playfair, an even more famous architect of villas and classical monuments. William Playfair the promoter, Barlow's partner, was another tinkerer, inventor, and international speculator. He lacked the versatility of Marc Brunel and the stamina of Robert Fulton; and, sad to say, we lack the space for his story.

‡My favorite examples of French place-names in America are two in Arkansas: Low Freight *(l'eau froid)* and the bogus Indian Tchemanahaut *(chemin en haut).*

Azylum

In our discussion, in chapter 6, of the architecture associated with French reinvestment and colonization in New York, in the eighteenth century, we discovered that historians have misattributed the most interesting neoclassical architectural drawings made for those purposes by assigning them to Azylum, a Pennsylvania venture set upon the beautiful bend in the Susquehanna River, now between the towns of Wyalusing and Towanda.

These are Indian names; Azylum was built on dark and bloody ground. Not far away was the region of the "Wyoming Massacre" of 1778, when the Iroquois eradicated a group of American settlements, and of a much larger destruction wrought by the retaliatory expedition under General John Sullivan, which obliterated many villages and sought to starve out the survivors by destroying their apple orchards and 160,000 bushels of corn. Amid the relics of these border battles, the little village of French refugees was established.

The newcomers included Louis-Marie, vicomte de Noailles, Lafayette's brother-in-law. Noailles had fought for American independence and had returned to France full of a passionate reforming idealism. He had been elected to the Estates General, and espoused the abolition of feudal privileges in 1789. At the same time, he and others bought the land for Azylum and commenced construction of a village later reported by the duc de Rochefoucauld-Liancourt to have "attained an uncommon degree of perfection, considering its infant state." He himself purchased eight hundred acres "to give to his children in case they should have no resources."

Azylum was centered upon a Grand Maison of squared logs, three stories high, with French windows and two baronial fireplaces in its Great Hall. Tradition tells us that the Grand Maison was intended to be the house of Marie Antoinette, had she succeeded in her attempt to escape France. Perhaps it was an *architecture parlante,* but speaking false. A more skeptical visitor, the comte de Moré, saw it as a trap. This "immense building," he suggested bitterly, was to appear as if it might "house all the important people they expected . . . The Pope, the sacred college, even dethroned sovereigns, still dizzy from the boat on their arrival, were to occupy apartments there, and buy American land."

Scattered about this primeval palace were inns, fifty-odd houses, a chapel, a theater, a smithy, a distillery, and a bakery. Azylum became a required stop on the backwoods tour by distinguished visitors. But its rural charms faded; when Napoleon reopened France to these émigrés in 1802, most of its inhabitants abandoned Azylum. Though "perfect in its way," it was not to the taste of many Parisians.*

*Noailles actually made money on his venture in Pennsylvania; it might have been better had

Royal Visitors

Among the last visitors to Azylum was a future king of France, Louis Philippe, the eldest son of the regicide duc d'Orléans.* The duke so loathed his royal cousins, and so loved the adulation of the mob, that he hired a multitude of pamphleteers to stir up the populace. The republican tide rose, bearing on its scarlet froth the duke, now become "Philippe Egalité." He voted for the execution of King Louis XVI while elegant courtiers of his persuasion gossiped and consumed ices in the exquisite little opera boxes of the convention hall. But when the drama proceeded to the next act, Philippe Egalité himself stood on the great stage before the guillotine.

Louis Philippe, his son, had joined the Jacobin Club; but Paris became too dangerous, and in 1792 he went off to the frontier to fight in the revolutionary army. The time came for his commander, Dumouriez, to explain to him that he might be the next of the descendants of Louis XIII to fall before the fury of the Terror. Louis Philippe defected to the Austrians with Dumouriez in 1794. He passed the first period of his exile teaching in Switzerland as "M. Chabos," appeared in Hamburg as "M. Ludovic," and emerged to tour Scandinavia, as far as Lapland, as "M. Muller." Then he headed for America.

When he reached Philadelphia in March 1797, he was joined by his brothers, the duc de Montpensier, who made excellent drawings and gouaches of American scenes, and the comte de Beaujolais. These were younger brothers, who had been freed after nearly four years in a Jacobin jail. Louis Philippe was by then of a wider world than France, handsome, sensitive, with a gift for striking language and, when he was young, for wry wit. His American memoirs are piquant but too brief—we wish he had told us more about his stay in Philadelphia. Other chronicles say that during its course he paid court to the daughter of Thomas Willing, the town's leading banker (this was before the ascent of Stephen Girard). Perhaps this story persists because no historian can bear to give up the apothegm attached: the old gentleman is reported to have said that if the situation of Louis Philippe did not improve, he was not good enough for her, and if it did, she was not good enough for him.

From Philadelphia, Louis Philippe, now calling himself "Mr. Orleans,"† set forth on a tour, accompanied by his brothers and his valet: Washington, Nashville, Louisville, Pittsburgh, Niagara Falls, back to Philadelphia, through

---

he remained there. Like many others who had served under Rochambeau in the war for American independence, he agreed to join in the effort to reconquer Saint-Domingue and reimpose slavery upon it. He died of his wounds in Cuba in 1802.

*Among the progeny of King Louis XIII were those of the senior branch, the Bourbons, who became his successors, Louis XIV through XVIII, and the junior branch, the house of Orléans.

†In my life as a financial manager, I have had the pleasure of working beside a prince who found

Louis Philippe by James Sharples

New England to Maine, down the Ohio again, and then down the Mississippi to New Orleans, sleeping, on occasion, three, and sometimes four, men to a bed, as was the custom in the West.

After a stint in New Orleans, the three scions of the house of Orléans enjoyed a tropical idyll in Havana, where a royalty-struck old lady provided them a house, carriages, servants, and romantic introductions. But *la dolce vita* too came to an end, in December 1799, when at Napoleon's insistence they were packed out of Cuba. Off again—to the Bahamas, Nova Scotia, New York, and London. Finally, Louis Philippe (apparently no more bound in sentimental attachment to Miss Willing of Philadelphia than was, later, Jerome Bonaparte to Miss Paterson of Baltimore—see p. 353) married an Italian princess (Jerome married a German one) and retired to raise oranges outside Palermo. It was from this second southern sojourn that he was summoned by the quiet Revolution of 1830 to succeed his cousin Charles X.

Louis Philippe remained a king for eighteen years. Toward the end, he became nearly as fat, vain, and self-indulgent as his Bourbon cousins, but he was still credible when he came to the throne, proclaiming that he had carried the tricolor under fire and that he was devoted to the principles of the

---

it convenient in the United States to identify himself as "Mr. X"—"X" being the name of his country. Therefore I do not find it mannered or disingenuous for Louis Philippe to have chosen a "patrianymic" during his visit here. Many well-dressed Frenchmen shortened their noble names to American lengths.

Revolution. For a while, until he bored a generation spoiled for kings by the memory of an emperor, he was affectionately known as "the Citizen King," wandering the streets and keeping open to his subjects the doors of the Palais Royal.*

L'Enfant

From 1790 to 1830, and beyond, the backwoods of America were full of imposters and mountebanks—and highly competent, well-trained French civil engineers. The first of them to be defeated by American folkways was Major Pierre-Charles L'Enfant, displaced professional person. He trod the muddy paths of the kings and dukes and heirs presumptive, philosophers, merchants, and literary men, and he was no happier than they were for the experience.

L'Enfant, the son of one of the court painters of Louis XV, was trained in engineering before volunteering to join the American forces fighting for independence. Commissioned a lieutenant at the age of twenty-three, he survived the winter at Valley Forge, was wounded at Savannah, captured by the British at Charleston, and released by them in 1782, and joined Steuben in his expedition to the frontier to force the British to evacuate some of their posts in accordance with the Treaty of 1783.

His first architectural works were a series of patriotic stage sets, beginning with a pavilion in Philadelphia to celebrate the birth of the dauphin in 1782. Then there was a domed banquet hall and pavilions to seat six thousand people on the occasion of New York's adherence to the federal Constitution in 1788, and some splendid baroque church fittings ordered by Saint Paul's Church on Broadway, to accompany the funeral monument of the hero of the American assault on Montreal, General Montgomery. Permanency and magnitude were promised by the commission to convert the old City Hall in New York into the first Capitol of the United States. On a gallery of L'Enfant's redesigned building, given the name Federal Hall, the most important structure in the city, George Washington was inaugurated as President on April 30, 1789. The Senate and the House of Representatives met within L'Enfant's grand spaces, and the business of government was carried forward.

The tale of L'Enfant's great adventure, the planning of the federal city of Washington, has been often told: his initial success in persuading Hamilton, Jefferson, and Washington that it should be "proportioned to the greatness . . . of a powerful Empire"; his unwillingness to settle for a conventional

---

*When he was deposed in the Revolution of 1848, he left to us a characteristic exit line: "I shall never abdicate—at least until I have consulted my wife" (quoted in Becker's translation of Louis Philippe's *Diary of My Travels in America,* p. 201).

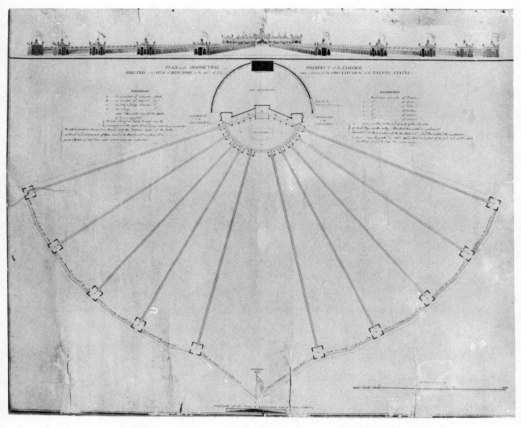

L'Enfant's "Plan and Geometrical Prospect of the Edifice Erected in the City of New York on the 23rd of July, 1788, in Honor of the Constitution of the United States"

rectilinear grid as "a mean continence . . . wanting a sense of the really grand and the truly beautiful"; his aspiration instead to the grandeur of Versailles; and his loss of the support of Washington and Jefferson as he insisted, over their repeated remonstrances, upon having woodcutters hew out all the avenues, inducing construction crews to start buildings and streets. His canal, with its wharves, bridges, and aqueducts, would have been sufficient for a metropolis, though Washington had not yet enough inhabitants for a village. He was ultimately dismissed by a government that admired his enthusiasm but could ill afford it.

When Thomas Jefferson came to offer to L'Enfant models for American public buildings, they were not fit for either an artisan or a yeoman republic. Instead, he drew on his memories of Paris to commend the enormous colum-

Federal Hall (New York City Hall as remodeled by L'Enfant)

niated façade of Ange-Jacques Gabriel's place Louis XV (now the place de la Concorde) and the equally "imperial" east façade of the Louvre. The smallest building he offered as an example to poor L'Enfant was the domed and colonnaded Hôtel de Salm, occupying an entire city block. Then Jefferson gave the major a roll of plans for imperial cities. L'Enfant had asked for maps of ports in many countries, but Jefferson's contributions were almost entirely French. L'Enfant provided as a result the "footprint," the general scheme, of Versailles. The White House was set in the position of the Trianon, the mall in the place of the baroque axis of Louis XIV, and the Capitol took the place of the palace of absolutism. Altogether, his own difficulties with scale were not alleviated by the leader of the Republicans.

From these follies L'Enfant was rescued, briefly, by Alexander Hamilton and the Federalists. He was sent off to design and build a "company town" around the falls of the Passaic River at Paterson, New Jersey. Perhaps the commissioners of Paterson should have been warned by his locution in laying before them a plan that "far exceeds anything of the kind yet seen in this country"—it far exceeded as well what they could afford. Once again it was Hamilton who obtained for him a series of reprieves. At last, his vaunting ideas could no longer be reconciled with the resources of the promoter of Paterson, the Society for the Establishment of Useful Manufactures, and he was dismissed again.

It is very strange how little we actually know of L'Enfant's contribution to our architecture aside from the planning of Washington. Perhaps the best clue to why he did not build a more commodious practice is his failure to accommodate the two best clients he could have found in America, Robert Morris, the financier of the revolution, and Stephen Girard, who would later become the financier of the War of 1812.

During the summer of 1794, L'Enfant's Federal Hall was as fresh and new as his reputation. His fame as a designer of cities was still in the minds of those who did not know the details of the imbroglio in Washington. He was a Personage; and a rising merchant in Philadelphia, Girard, was not sure so great a man would deign to talk with him about the town house he wished to build at 23 North Water Street to assert his new prosperity. Girard, and all Philadelphia, knew L'Enfant was at work on the palace of Morris, another West Indies merchant, who had combined his role in revolutionary finance with very profitable smuggling and privateering operations.

Girard asked Paul Bentelou of Baltimore, apparently more eminent socially, for a note of introduction to the architect. Bentelou's wife forgot to pass along Girard's request, so unimportant was it. Girard had to write a second time. Like so much about L'Enfant, this project for the client who would become the richest man in America is shrouded in mystery. Girard built his house. We have a picture of it (it was later replaced by warehouses): an utterly conventional late-eighteenth-century five-story brick structure with a parapet linking two end chimneys. It appears that L'Enfant's reputation caught up with him. Hearing that Girard might be thinking of employing L'Enfant, Bentelou warned him off.

Fifty years ago, President Nicholas Murray Butler of Columbia University deposited in its Avery Library a set of handwritten lecture notes by Professor William Hindley. Hindley devoted a lifetime of passionate advocacy to the thesis that every large and handsome structure built in New York City between 1785 and 1810 not positively attributed to somebody else was a work of L'Enfant's. Hindley had little to go on, but he posited an association between L'Enfant and the furniture maker Duncan Phyfe, demonstrated, he said, by a L'Enfant sketch of Phyfe's remarkably handsome store and showroom on Fulton Street. Josiah Wedgwood had his John Flaxman to design his best wares, said Hindley; Phyfe had his L'Enfant. There is an undeniable similarity between the attenuated grace of Phyfe's best work and those structures we can definitely associate with L'Enfant.

What makes Mr. Hindley's list interesting is not that it proves that L'Enfant created all those architectural designs Hindley assigned to him. Rather, it is a handy checklist for further research. There was a burst of building in New York. It produced a hundred structures that might have been designed by any one of the three or four French architects who were in the city. Twoscore of these buildings have remained into our own time; they can enliven walks about the city. Hindley's list provides an invitation to scrutinize the last mansion on Battery Park, at 9 State Street; the Rufus King House in Jamaica; the Crosby Mansion in the Bronx; the Prince House in Flushing; the Van Cortlandt House in the Bronx; Gracie Mansion in Manhattan; and the Cortelyou House in Flatlands. All of these were built or remodeled while L'Enfant was available to do the work.

This is not to say that he did them; probably he did not. There is little in his impoverished old age to suggest that he had either the savings or the associations of an architectural practice of any size. If he received many commissions for money, some of it would probably have stuck with him.

9

A FEASTING OF

TIGERS

In the summer of 1795, the city of New York was still rebuilding. The great fire of 1776 had destroyed most of its older buildings; and the revolution, most of its social structure. The upper third of its population had been Tories, who departed with the British at the end of the War of Independence. An occupying army and the presence of a large number of refugees had brought their usual consequences: speculation, the commercialization of sexuality on a large scale, and the corruption of the legal system.

By that time, some civility had been restored. Not only were French architects beginning to give neoclassical elegance to the city's demeanor, but French statesmen-in-exile were available to improve the tone of its conversation. Some of them joined other cosmopolitans gathered for quiet suppers. In a few weeks, with the beginning of the mosquito season, the fear of yellow fever would disperse them to healthier places; now the most conspicuous insects were an unusually brilliant display of fireflies, and the diners-out strolled in groups of twos and threes among these little visitors from the stars, talking and gesturing, laughing and evoking memories and expectations. Among them one evening were Charles Maurice de Talleyrand-Périgord; his companion in America, Bon-Albert Briois de Baumetz; an Anglo-Indian named Thomas Law; the marquis and the marquise de La Tour Du Pin; and Alexander Hamilton, recently retired from the cabinet of President George Washington to repair his fortunes by the practice of law, and aspiring to become a gentleman planter.

Talleyrand

Talleyrand was the forsaken son of a noble couple who had pronounced him unfit for a title because he had fallen as a child of four, and the bones of his broken leg had knit badly, leaving him deformed. His feelings hardened too, into an ambition supple, resilient, and sharp-edged. He became, successively, priest, abbot, and bishop under the ancien régime; prince and grand chamberlain under Napoleon; and president of the Council under the restored Bourbons. He was the ultimate survivor; in his treacherous way, he was also the ultimate patriot. Loyal always to France but to nothing else, he was the bishop who proposed the confiscation of the property of the Church by the revolutionary French in 1789. After his sojourn in America he would be foreign minister and betrayer of the Directory and then of Napoleon; he emerged, smiling his porcelain smile, in the same capacity for the restored Louis XVIII. The model French diplomat, he was ambassador to the Court of Saint James's for governments headed by Danton, Robespierre, and—a generation later—Louis Philippe, who asked him to take the foreign ministry once again, in 1830. "Treason," he once noted, "is merely a matter of dates."*

It was said of Talleyrand that he believed in neither God nor the devil, but few clergymen could match his command of liturgical drama. Between his proposal to "purchase" the estates of the Church with paper money and his excommunication in 1791, he presided at a commemoration of the fall of the Bastille, celebrating the Mass with three thousand priests in tricolor scarves, leading the singing of the "Te Deum" accompanied by an orchestra of twelve hundred before three hundred thousand people.

He was equally impressive in smaller groups. But he was, of course, not universally admired.

Such men do not exert themselves for causes like American independence, though in his youth Talleyrand did confess a tepid admiration for that experiment in republican government. His enthusiasm grew a trifle when the Terror threatened to recall him from his post in London to put him on trial for his life and the British would not keep him. He was willing then to bestow himself upon Philadelphia. While in England, he had been introduced to Alexander Hamilton's sister-in-law Angelica Schuyler Church; like many other women, she was fascinated by him, and she wrote her friends in Philadelphia and New York that he should be received as a sage.†

---

*Patriotism by more conventional standards does not seem to be the only guarantee of long life; long after the deaths of Jefferson, Hamilton, and John Adams—even after the departure of the last surviving signer of the Declaration of Independence, Charles Carroll of Carrollton—Talleyrand and Aaron Burr lived on in relatively comfortable old age.

†She had married John Barker Church, a mysterious Englishman who had come to her under

Talleyrand (artist unknown)

Mrs. Church, it turned out, was not a very good guide to postrevolutionary America, for she had lived long in London and did not understand how persistent was Quaker, Puritan, and Dutch Reformed morality in the land of her birth. Talleyrand's private and public reputation had preceded him, and he confirmed it often, promenading "with a coffee-colored mistress on each arm." Accordingly, he was treated not as a sage but as a libertine. Besides, he was known to be politically treacherous. President Washington declined to receive him. Talleyrand "found himself dwarfed, out of his element, even somewhat ridiculous, in this country he had hoped to dazzle, instruct, and direct."

Not surprisingly, though his American visit lasted long enough for Talleyrand to recoup his fortunes in successful American speculations, he grew spiteful as a rejected savant. Upon his return to power in 1797, he informed the Directory that America had no national character because "her population is composed of fishermen and woodcutters." Fishermen, he said, have no country, and woodcutters "no memories to attach to anything." Americans were there-

---

an assumed name but who became both a good husband and rich. During the Revolutionary War, Mr. Church (his real name) supplied, under a succulent contract, the French forces fighting as allies to the Americans. A decade later, Angelica Church, now living gracefully in Britain, operated a sort of aristocratic "underground railroad" for those French émigrés who met her standards of deportment.

Talleyrand also asked that perjured and despised turncoat Benedict Arnold, who was then living in London, for letters of introduction to America. Arnold was forced to give him a reply: "I am the only American who cannot give you letters to his own country." (See Rosengarten, p. 202.)

fore a nation that, having no farmers, did not observe the "products of ... toil ... through all the stages of growth so endearing to the farmer" or "follow up the destiny" of their products, so that if they left their homes but remembered to bring along their axes, they left "no regrets behind." His displeasure, and his consequent misunderstanding of American character, were to lead him into a rare display of diplomatic ineptitude in the negotiations of 1797–98 known as the XYZ Affair (see p. 117). The undeclared war between France and the United States that ensued might have been avoided had he not insisted on bribes to carry on serious discussions.

Cameo Roles

Bon-Albert Briois de Baumetz, a lawyer and minor noble from Artois, had been a member of the Constituent Assembly, one of the sequence of parliaments assembled in Paris as the revolution became increasingly violent. Disguised as a sutler, he escaped the terror that swept to the guillotine many other members of that body. Later, encouraged by Talleyrand, he went on to Calcutta to sell American real estate to Indian merchants, a venture in which he was not successful, despite his backing by that Dutchman of French-Swiss extraction, Théofil Cazenove, who had already attracted to American real estate the surplus funds of many Dutch investors.

Talleyrand's enthusiasm for India, and for schemes to separate Indians from some of their fabled wealth, was reinforced by tales of "elephants and palanquins" he had heard from another shipboard companion, the only English member of the dining group, Thomas Law. The son of a rising North Country cleric who became bishop of Carlisle and produced a pride of remarkable sons (John and George became bishops; Edward became a great defense lawyer, arguing the case for Warren Hastings in 1787), Law became a land speculator; soon after joining the East India Company and reaching one of its lucrative posts, he charmed into matrimony a rich Brahmin widow. Not long afterward, she left him a rich widower; and, dreaming dreams of vast acres of unencumbered real estate, he set his affairs in order in London and took ship to the New World.

Everyone seems to have liked Law, though he was not financially persuasive to the sequence of French visitors who made his house in Washington City a required stop on their grand tours. After Talleyrand came the philosopher-poet Chateaubriand, the duc de Rochefoucauld-Liancourt, and, in 1797, the future king Louis Philippe, to whom Law explained that Americans did not form villages because "they prefer isolation, and each builds on his own property to increase its value." He could make nothing of those who denied the benefits of speculation to those who, like himself, had bought large tracts

Thomas Law by Gilbert Stuart

of land anticipating hordes of happy villagers, coming onstage early, in operatic fashion.

Law thought operatically and was in fact quite a creditable poet. A businessman he was not; he was that most vulnerable of men, a naive speculator. He lost his first wife's fortune and then that of his second, Eliza Custis, the granddaughter of Martha Washington and adopted child of the President himself. Henriette de La Tour Du Pin said of this "most eccentric of Englishmen, who are all more or less so, that when preoccupied with an idea, the house might have collapsed without his lifting his eyes." But he had an eye for architecture and for architects: he befriended Benjamin Henry Latrobe, William Thornton, and a third architect who will be introduced in Part Four, Pierre Bauduy.

Law's brother-in-law George Washington Parke Custis commissioned George Hadfield, another friend of the charming speculator, to design Arlington House (see *Architecture, Men, Women and Money*); and their brother-in-law Armistead Peter received from Thornton his largest residential design, for Tudor Place. These two are the finest houses remaining in Washington from Law's lifetime. His own residence is there too, on Sixth Street S.W., a block south of the Arena Stage. It is the carrier of ironies: built by an earlier speculator who had gone bankrupt investing in the growth of Washington City, it was occupied by the Laws while their fortunes were declining in the same kind of speculation. It is now a diminutive appendage to a collation of high-rise condominiums of a density capable of making either Law or his speculative predecessor extremely rich.

The Marquise and the Muttonchop

The Marquise de La Tour Du Pin was more Irish than French, though one French historian claimed her to be the "exquisite type of Frenchwoman, simple, intelligent, courageous and good." She was the daughter of Arthur Dillon, commander of the famous regiment of Jacobite refugees who had fought for the Bourbons. Her father-in-law had been minister of war under the first, moderate revolutionary government; her husband had been minister to Holland. The old marquis went to the guillotine in 1794; Henriette and the heir to the marquisate, her husband, were permitted to go into exile in America through the intervention of the mistress of Jean Tallien, whose Terror in Bordeaux was even more brutal than Robespierre's in Paris. (Tallien, it may be noted, married a beautiful comtesse in 1794. He became the official historian of Napoleon's expedition to Egypt and died in his bed in 1820.)

Such eminent visitors could often count upon the hospitality of Alexander Hamilton's relatives by marriage the Van Rensselaers and his father-in-law, General Schuyler, who adopted Mme de La Tour Du Pin as his "sixth daughter." Schuyler, she said, "found them a place to live chez M. Van Buren, 'a school of American ways.'" What a school! There, only twelve years old at

Mme la Marquise de La Tour Du Pin
(artist unknown)

the time, was Martin Van Buren, who was to become eighth President of the United States and quite capable of contending in guile with Talleyrand himself.

Henriette de La Tour Du Pin was no fool. She understood Law and had no illusions about Talleyrand, of whom she saw rather more than she wanted after their return to France in 1796. She knew, as he did not, what American "woodcutters" were like, having spent two years on a hillside farm in the southern fringes of the Adirondacks. It requires a little effort for us to swallow whole the romantic image of her life there, presented by the French historian Bernard Fay, but if it could be true of anyone, it would be true of her: "She lived the life of a farmer-philosopher, milking her cows, making her butter, superintending her slaves and servants, giving bits of ribbon to the Indian women, who adored her, and winning over the braves by the charm of her smile and the splendor of her manners."

Historians have tended to present the marquise's sweet side, but she could be tart too. She was also one of the best memoirists of a period when writing memoirs achieved the highest reaches of literary art. Of Talleyrand she said: "As he had no moral quality himself, by singular contrast he had a horror of that which was evil in others. To listen to him without knowing him, you would have believed that he was a worthy man." While she lived on her farm she was visited by the "philanthropic grand seigneur" the duc de Roche-foucauld-Liancourt, who had chosen to go about caparisoned as a noble savage, "covered with mud and dust . . . he had the appearance of a shipwrecked sailor escaped from the pirates." (Though she herself once received Talleyrand with a meat cleaver in her hand, that was because she was surprised slaughtering a sheep.) She disapproved of Rochefoucauld, "a first gentleman of the Chamber," going about in "this bizarre get-up," and agreed with Mrs. Van Rensselaer, who "sized him up from the first as . . . very ordinary."

She was scornful too of the celebrated Lafayette, who, she said, treated his heroic wife "with the most cruel indifference" and "numerous infidelities." She saw him as "soft even to foolishness," full of "a foolish confidence"; when "that imbecile" came to write his "dull memoirs," he managed to "render the details" of the early years of the American Revolution "so insipid" that she was glad to have heard the same stories romantically told by Hamilton.

"She loved her farm, her country dog and the starry sky." The farm and the dog are gone; the sky is still there, blue-black, with just enough starlight, on some nights, to show a crumbling rectangle of stone, the foundations of a farmhouse probably built of locally sawed siding with a split-shingle roof of timber cut on the Schuyler land and a lean-to kitchen. Her sheepfold would have been close by the house to be a little safer from the wolves.

Her château in France, Le Bouilh, to which she returned after leaving America, remains amid its vineyards, to be seen just before one crosses the river Gironde to enter the city of Bordeaux. It was one of the extravagant intentions

*Project for the Château de Bouilh by Victor Louis
(only the wing on the left was built)*

of the ancien régime, a grandiose hulk still inhabited (in 1988) by descendants of the marquise. It was to have been the culmination of the theatrical classical style of Victor Louis, the architect of the Grand Théâtre in Bordeaux—still, after two hundred years, the most magnificent in France. Louis, who began his work for the La Tour Du Pins in 1786, had planned two huge wings connected by a screen of pillars, with an enormous, open, domed pavilion at the center, like a cut-away version of the Pantheon, and the whole assemblage was to be set upon a Piranesian arcade cut from a limestone cliff. As the date suggests, life impinged upon art, and only one wing of Le Bouilh was completed. But the marquise, her husband, and their son huddled there quite comfortably until that son chose the wrong side in the July Revolution of 1830 and was forced to emigrate to Switzerland.

The house that survives seems oddly familiar to Americans; the ancien régime fuses into the antebellum so that in a dim light it is like a southern mansion built at the end of the 1850s, with its French windows at veranda level, its white columns, and a stone arcade holding the main mass far above the ground.* It is, of course, more ambitious than any of the creations of Henry Howard and Samuel Sloan†—it is of stone, not simulated stone—but like so many of their mansions, it too is a fragment of a huge plan, incomplete even in its details: its column capitals were left uncarved, blocks of stone awaiting the return of the Good Old Days Before the War.

---

*There is only one other mansion in France as southern American as Le Bouilh: the Hôtel de Gallifet, the Parisian palace where Talleyrand lived for ten years. It was built by a West Indies merchant and appears even today like a hot-climate house longing to surround itself with verandas but forced to accommodate itself to an urban site and to settle for one façade of columns and another with columns merely implied.

†See *Architecture, Men, Women and Money.*

The château at Bouilh was fairly typical of the prerevolutionary scale of Victor Louis, who planned a group of city houses for the shore of the Garonne, in Bordeaux itself, in the form of an interminable "palace" of a thousand pilasters, relieved only by a curve at the center thirteen hundred feet across. The Adirondacks, the dog, and even the starry sky itself would stand abashed by such arrogance. In Paris in the 1780s, Louis designed a huge real-estate development, with shops and residences, called the Palais Royal, which was built around the gardens of the palace of the Orléans branch of the royal family in an effort to relieve the debt burdens of the duc d'Orléans, the voluptuary father of Louis Philippe. It was much admired by Thomas Jefferson, who contemplated a speculation of his own for "a whole square in Richmond improved on some such plan."

The marquise de La Tour Du Pin, née Henriette Dillon, seems to have been overwhelmed neither by architectural pomp nor by adversity. It is probable that she was, as she said, reluctant to abandon her hillside farm and take her station at Le Bouilh; many years later, she recalled feeling "no pleasure at returning to France."

10

ALEXANDER HAMILTON

Talleyrand, on the other hand, was delighted to return to a career of statesmanship, patriotism, and larceny on a grand scale. He was a virtuoso in the exploitation of "conflict of interest," and found it incomprehensible that Alexander Hamilton's financial genius had not produced private gain from the public treasury during the years when Hamilton was in charge of that Treasury. During the summer of 1795, after Hamilton had retired from office, Talleyrand observed his friend toiling to make up for time lost in public service. He left us an account of another late supper party in New York, that summer. On his way to his destination he took a roundabout walk and saw a candle still burning in the windows of Hamilton's office. When he entered the supper room, he remarked to his host: "I have just come from viewing a man who had made the fortune of his country, but now is working all night to support his family."

But however impractical Hamilton seemed to Talleyrand, he was the one American, said the savant-bishop, who "divined Europe . . . I consider Napoleon, Pitt and Hamilton as the three greatest men of our age, and if I had to choose among the three, I would unhesitatingly give first place to Hamilton."

The feeling was mutual. Hamilton assayed Talleyrand to be "the greatest of modern statesmen"—an assessment made long before Talleyrand had showed his full repertory of statesmanship, after returning to Europe at the end of 1795.

Talleyrand and Hamilton, like most of us, had little difficulty in appreciating their own virtues and in welcoming the affirming radiance of those same virtues when observed in others. Hamilton's admiration of Talleyrand centered, he said, on the indifference of the bishop to any unpleasant side effects of the policies he thought advisable: he knew "when it was necessary both to suffer wrong to be done, and to do it."

Hamilton also knew how to do right by a friend. Even if we set aside Brunel's claim to Hamilton's patronage, there are records of many other instances in which the former secretary of the treasury, though leader of a pro-British faction in a country enjoying a relatively brief interlude between British wars, honored many friendships with Frenchmen of high and low estate.

Hamilton's attachment to the former bishop of Autun, and the reciprocal affection of Talleyrand for Hamilton, tell us much about the character of both men. It tells us even more about the epoch in which one came to power but once and briefly and the other often and remuneratively.

After George Washington became President in 1789, he had brought Hamilton into his cabinet as secretary of the treasury. In that post Hamilton had labored to create a party favorable to commercial and to British interests, a policy against which Thomas Jefferson contended with increasing fury. Jefferson was forty-six, middle-aged by eighteenth-century standards; Hamilton was barely into his thirties. Hamilton never knew Europe; Jefferson was returning from the happiest years of his life, spent in Paris, a city more comfortable to this professed Arcadian than anywhere in the countryside. Hamilton's entire training in finance had been as a clerk for a merchant in slaves and sugar on the island of Saint Croix; Jefferson had managed a complex of plantations and, with John Adams, had renegotiated the entire national debt—with architectural consequences (see p. 441). But it was Hamilton who, in *The Federalist Papers* and as secretary, dealt with the growing financial difficulties of the new nation.

The United States had enormous land and natural resources, a benign climate, and an energetic population with remarkable mechanical skills and a useful tradition of tinkering. But the states of which it was composed were heavily indebted to those nations (including the French and Dutch) who had made money available to buy the armaments and the time of soldiers and sailors that had gone into establishing their independence. Few bankers were willing to make further funds available to pay the costs of that independence, and the population as a whole showed little disposition to be taxed either to repay debt or to defend itself. After all, taxation for defense, past and present, was chief among the burdens Americans had fought a revolution to avoid.

Hamilton arduously and successfully constructed a new credit system, including an effective taxing process and the first Bank of the United States. (For the further history of that institution, and its successor, see p. 276.) Though he could discern his nation's requirements and was prescient of its financial future, Hamilton was, it seems, blind to the ways his own emotional needs could drive

Alexander Hamilton, painted posthumously in 1806 by John Trumbull

him into blighting his own prospects. In the fall of 1794 he had become, in effect, secretary of war, in the absence, on private speculative business in Maine, of Secretary of War Henry Knox. He then wheedled the old President into raising a disproportionately large expeditionary force to cope with the insurrection in western Pennsylvania often called the Whiskey Rebellion. The friends of Thomas Jefferson and of John Adams were justifiably suspicious of the uses Hamilton might make of such a force, especially after he had the President pass to him the command of the army in the field. But to Hamilton's chagrin, the "rebels" melted away. There was no heroic victory. By the end of the year, Hamilton seemed a little ridiculous. Sensing this, he resigned from the cabinet and began a series of faintly ludicrous efforts to prevent the presidency of Adams and secure it for himself.

Hamilton became a lawyer-planter and political plotter in New York, and Jefferson a planter-lawyer and political plotter in Virginia. Observing them at work, Adams furiously charged this "dark and insidious . . . intriguer" within his own party of undermining his presidential administration while "Jacobins . . . and French hirelings" (e.g., Jefferson) attacked from outside. The friends of Adams and the friends of Jefferson were of one mind on few things in the late 1790s, but they agreed that Hamilton was capable of planning to topple constitutional government with a military coup. Adams thought Hamilton so furious in his ambition as to be willing to plunge his country into "all the Bloodshed and distractions of foreign and civil War at once." Jefferson knew

Hamilton to be too cold to arouse a popular following but feared him nonetheless. "A colossus . . . Without numbers he is a host within himself."

Hamilton's reputation was mixed during his lifetime, but all shadows were bleached out by the manner of his death in the famous duel with Burr; if the goal was reputation, Burr, not Hamilton, lost that duel. Something had been said or implied by Hamilton so heinous as to make its way under Burr's usually elephant-thick skin, something that provoked him into uncharacteristic anger, anger Hamilton made strangely feeble efforts to alleviate. Yet even the customarily skeptical Theodore Roosevelt came to see Burr as diabolic and, in Hamilton, that "touch of the heroic . . . of the purple . . . of the gallant, the dashing, the picturesque." (In photojournalism, one would see this as a montage, in which Hamilton fuses into Roosevelt himself.)

Hamilton had every reason to be a snob and has often been charged with being a monarchist. He certainly aspired to be a country gentleman, and held democracy in no more exalted esteem than did Talleyrand. Yet he and John Adams brought the United States into a working alliance with Toussaint Louverture, the Black revolutionary (see p. 149).*

Talleyrand was able to forgive Hamilton for assisting Toussaint. He was unwilling to forgive Aaron Burr for killing Hamilton.

Hamilton and Patron

Hamilton's political career is as familiar as Jefferson's but his role as a patron of architecture and horticulture is not. As we have seen, from the outset of his tenure in the Treasury he exerted himself to succor the career of Major L'Enfant, his comrade-in-arms at Valley Forge; and he was (at least in part) responsible for a burst of commissions for John McComb, Jr., and McComb's occasional partner Joseph Mangin.

Aaron Burr and Hamilton were participants in many architectural as well as political contests, even after Jefferson's triumph in 1800 crowded both of them out of center stage. Jefferson has had ample appreciation for his contributions to architecture; they have not. Even in Natchez they have not had sufficient thanks for "springing" that city's first neoclassical architect from his murder charge (see p. 118n.). Yet they were both important patrons, though less important than they wished to be. John McComb, Jr., the son of the contractor-builder who had designed and built the President's House, New York's residence for General Washington, was Hamilton's favored architect. Burr's was Latrobe.

While the Federalists dominated the politics of the city of New York,

---

*Toussaint himself spelled his name as here, not in the French fashion, L'Ouverture.

McComb was more likely than Latrobe to be given large public commissions; but even McComb could not count on them unless he was able to recruit the services of one or another of the French designers who were lightening and clarifying the city along neoclassical principles. By that time L'Enfant was disgraced and Pierre Pharoux was dead, but Joseph Mangin was available, so McComb went into partnership with Mangin to respond to the great opportunities bubbling up in the city. Though it was no longer the political capital of both the state of New York and the nation, it was becoming the commercial capital, and it required amenities.

The firm of Mangin and McComb was prepared to provide them. Mangin was a recent immigrant from France, sprung from a tribe of architects: Charles Mangin, probably his uncle, established a practice extending from Russia to Paris; Mangin père et fils offered plans for improvements to the Louvre in 1790; and Mangin père collaborated in schemes for the "beautification of Paris" during the hopeful days before the revolution degenerated into the Terror.

We do not know when Joseph Mangin abandoned hope of a practice in Paris and came to America, but it seems that he did not come unsponsored. George Washington used presidential influence to secure for him the commission to design further fortifications for New York, and soon he was city surveyor. He and Casimer Goerck, a German engineer, made the official city maps and laid out a portion of the growing grid of streets cutting into the meadows north of the old Dutch town (as Mangin and Goerck streets still demonstrate).

In 1796, the minutes of the Common Council noted that "Monsr. Mainshin" had become one of its three surveyors, working on dockage, fortifications, and street layout. (It seems likely that it was in this phase of his career that he was the employer of Adrien Boucher* and also of Marc Isambard Brunel.

"Monsr. Mainshin" did very well at first. He designed the state prison in Greenwich Village and, a little later, the first Saint Patrick's Cathedral, on Mott Street, some portions of which survive, remodeled after a fire into an even odder composite than its initial classical cube with a gothicized broken pediment, anticipating Philip Johnson's Chippendale AT&T Building of 1984. The Mangin brothers built the Park Theater at about the same time.

In the summer of 1794, Joseph Mangin and John McComb, Jr., went into

---

*In the late 1790s, Boucher went from New York to Savannah, where he provided the city with its first neoclassical interior, the grained-vaulted vestibule of the Houstoun-Johnston-Screve house on Reynolds Square, and made the plans for the town's dominant building, the Exchange, and for the City Hall. He taught classes in "the five Orders" of architecture and disobeyed the segregation orders of the town, for which he was jailed, with results so lively as to require a lengthy telling. A book could be written about neoclassical architects and the clients who got them out of jail. Aside from Levi Weeks, the contractor for The Grange, and his client Hamilton, there were Bartholomy Lafon and Edward Livingston (see p. 402) and Adrien Boucher and Thomas Gibbons, whose story I have saved for my book on the Greek revival.

*The first Saint Patrick's Cathedral in New York, as remodeled in 1809–15
(drawn by C. Burton, engraved by Hatch & Smillie)*

business together to complete a joint project, the Equestrian Circus for a Mr. Ricketts on Greenwich Street. Their great opportunity came with the City Hall competition in 1802, from which ensued the finest surviving monument to Franco-American cooperation (the Statue of Liberty has many virtues, but it does not compare with the New York City Hall as a work of architecture). That competition brought them into direct competition with Burr and Latrobe. The former had prevailed upon the latter to enter the contest, though, said Latrobe, "he knew my individual feelings to be in favor of Mr. Jefferson's election in 1800." Others apparently had the same information; for, despite Burr's assurance to Latrobe that he had obtained every vote on the council "save one," the Federalist majority of the New York Common Council preferred McComb.

Knowing (we are free to suppose) that he was overweighted, McComb turned to Mangin, whose fine design sense appears together with McComb's practicality in the winning proposal. Mangin and McComb's masterpiece was instantly recognized as such, and it remains the paradigm for urbane elegance in the city.

The Park Theater, 1797–98

So much has been written of that magnificent but inviting, elegant but strong, monumental but airy building that it requires no further description here. Besides, it is there; it can be experienced directly, and should be, even when the traffic to Brooklyn is heavy on the bridge nearby and the smog lies low upon the FDR Drive. (See also the illustration on p. 6.)

City Hall was the chief contribution to New York of two men whom Latrobe, with typical fervor in defeat, in a letter to his brother Christian called "a New York bricklayer & a St. Domingo Frenchman." There is no way of knowing whether Latrobe had a shred of evidence to connect the Paris-educated Mangin to Santo Domingo (the Spanish usage), but the association has stuck, as closely as Hamilton's to a "Scots Peddler."

Latrobe's letter gives us a clue to a greater mystery than Mangin's origins— Mangin's subsequent career. The context of Latrobe's nastiness was telling his brother the news that though he had been denied the pleasure of building his "best design," for City Hall, he had been importuned by that "very city of New York" to undertake the draining of the "Collect Pond." This was in November 1804. It seems that a previous plan, to build an elaborate series of docks on the site, had been submitted by Mangin and rejected as impractical. (Latrobe, to his credit, did not underline the connection.) This is our last sighting of Mangin. Abruptly, after the City Hall project, he disappeared.

The Descendants of City Hall

The works of Joseph Mangin not only survived him but provided him with innumerable artistic descendants in obscure townships of New York and the trans-Appalachian West. The parentage of some of these cannot be tested; but any traveler, then as now, can confirm that French architectural forms proliferated after his death among people whose most indelible architectural experience could well have been the New York City Hall.

Up-country builders who never saw Versailles could visit New York City and marvel at Mangin and McComb's echo of the style of Louis XV. Among them was Philip Hooker of Albany, who reiterated its pattern of very large windows set in a grid of pilasters in his Albany Academy. Admitting another debt, he proudly told his patron Stephen Van Rensselaer that the city jail he proposed to design for Albany "would be copied from the new jail recently constructed in New York City." He was speaking of Mangin's State Prison.

The Academy set the upstate style.* Its progeny appeared where the Erie Canal deposited yeomen-emulators across the migration routes of Americans from the Hudson to the Mississippi, in Chautauqua County and Lewis County, along the Finger Lakes of Central New York, in the Pennsylvania counties northwest of Pittsburgh, and all the way to Cleveland. In Ohio, it was taken up and given new vitality by carpenter-builders like Willie Smith and Jonathan Goldsmith.

Hooker was not capable of the French glassiness and finesse of ornamental detail of City Hall, but his combination of a pilastered arcade and large French windows, and the superb site of the Academy, fixed it indelibly in the memories of a generation of westering people. They had never seen anything so fine in their own back-country villages, or even in Springfield, Hartford, or—dare I say it?—Boston.†

Philip Hooker's brother, John, found his employers one hundred and fifty

---

*Hooker was a Yankee practitioner with a good eye for business and another good eye for the newest French fashions. In Albany, among his political cronies, he was commissioned to design a new state capitol, banks, churches, houses, and markets. Most of them were built in the eighteenth-century New England manner of Charles Bulfinch and Asher Benjamin; but Hooker was quite capable of acknowledging the instruction of the émigré architects who in his youth were giving New York City the look of a provincial French town.

From 1800 to 1830 this quick, adaptable, and charming architectural politician gave good value to the merchant-squires, led by the Van Rensselaer and Clarke clans. When I wrote about Hooker in *Architecture, Men, Women and Money,* I did not know enough of New York's economic history to understand how likely it was that these up-country oligarchs would be prone to French architectural ideas. They had been so for a century and remained so for nearly a generation after the departure of Mangin and Pierre Pharoux.

†If there are Bulfinch admirers with us, I am prepared to assert that to my eye the hundreds of

Albany Academy, 1817

miles farther west of Albany, among the Franco-Dutch-Swiss proprietors of the Holland Land Company. We have recently learned from the research of William Stinchcombe that its owners probably included a former bishop and ambassador—Talleyrand. Talleyrand might have been amused that he re-enters this story by way of an obscure upstate carpenter-builder trying, with imperfect success, to follow French fashion. Yet so it was in Cazenovia, while in New York City, Talleyrand, in more elegant company, was surveying French architects directly at work upon a more elegant scene.

---

pilastered houses with French windows built across western New York and all the way to Painesville, Ohio, owe more to the Mangin brothers, by way of Philip Hooker, than to Bulfinch.

Others might prefer to follow the paper trail of influence back to the triumphal arches of Rome or to the upper pilasters of its Colosseum. There is a sober joy in tracing the origins of the pilastered houses of Jonathan Goldsmith and Charles or Willie Smith to Roman antiquity as filtered by the Palladian tradition—indeed, there is a sketch by Palladio of the Mausoleum of the Deified Romulus on the via Appia (to be found in Lewis p. 46) that could be a first draft by Goldsmith, almost three centuries later, and fifteen centuries after an unknown Roman designed a tomb for the son of the last pagan emperor of Rome. I hope to be able to amplify this thesis in a chapter on "The Persistence of the Pilaster" in another book. But not here.

Théofil Cazenove, who had lived and worked with Talleyrand in Paris in the 1780s, became the chief promoter of land speculations in Pennsylvania and New York, with Talleyrand as his silent partner. They had other ventures around Cazenovia together with other Swiss investors, Jean Conrad Hottinguer of Zurich, and Nicholas Hubbard and Pierre Bellamy of Geneva.

In Paris, in 1798, these speculators in American lands reassembled for other purposes when Talleyrand had the temerity to solicit bribes from the chief American negotiator, John Marshall, to secure a settlement of American claims against France and a pause in French predations upon American shipping. His intermediaries in the famous "XYZ Affair" were Hubbard, as the now forgotten "W," Hottinguer as "X," Bellamy as "Y," and Lucien Hauteval as "Z." So many fronts and proxies had been used in the land transactions, and such elaborate alphabetic "covers" in Paris, that it is doubtful that anyone knew how much they all had in common: in the American delegation, Marshall and his brother, James, were themselves investors in the same New York real estate as Cazenove and Talleyrand.

While the XYZ Affair was unfolding in Paris, Cazenove was managing not only his own investments in New York but Talleyrand's as well. Their agents at Cazenovia had engaged John Hooker to design a brick hotel in Utica, in 1797, where he showed what he could do with the pilaster-and-French-window

A house with pilasters (detail)
in Ashville, New York

theme learned from his brother, and carried farther in courthouses at Whitesboro in 1807 and Cazenovia in 1810.

Recent evidence from other sources adds to that list mansions for John Lincklaen and Samuel Forman between 1805 and 1813, in Cazenovia. Forman's frame house was razed in 1937, but Lorenzo, Lincklaen's wonderful estate at the head of a lake, set in fine gardens and ancient trees, is still there to remind us of the skill of the Hookers, and if I am right, of the Mangins, by distant derivation.

11

THE GRANGE

During the last years of his life, Hamilton labored—often, as Talleyrand recalled, late at night—to set himself up as a country gentleman, in a proper country house. To the extent that he was able to pause at any time for simple, unambitious enjoyment, it was as he contemplated the valley of the Hudson from the veranda of that house, which he called The Grange.* That name is only part of an enigma wrapped (to borrow a portion of a complex Churchillian metaphor) in a bundle of misconceptions, some of which are so peculiar as to imply deliberate deception.

We shall attempt to penetrate this riddle and, in the process, to suggest a reconsideration of some historical writing centering upon it, in which the snobberies of Hamilton's friends have compounded the calumnies of his foes. Misconceptions about his origins, his character, and his policies have afflicted our understanding of his time, especially of Franco-American relations.

As is our practice, we begin our inquiry by standing in a specific place—in this instance, before a Creole house set in a Creole horticultural garden.

The Grange was—but is no longer—situated superbly, overlooking the Hudson River, on thirty-five carefully landscaped acres, between what are now 140th and 147th streets, not far from the present site of Columbia University. The gardens alone would have justified the interest of posterity; they were extensions of a system of experiment stations in West Indian horticulture, one upon the spine of the island of Tortola, another on the milder slopes of the plantation island of Saint Croix. A third, on an islet off Hispaniola, was provided for research as the result of an intersection of friendship, slave revolt, and Hamiltonian foreign policy, as we shall see.

---

*The contractor was Ezra Weeks, who also served in that capacity for McComb and Mangin's City Hall. The brother of Ezra was the architect-builder Levi Weeks, who was able to go on to build a career in Natchez because he was acquitted of a charge of murder in 1799; his co-counsels were Hamilton, Aaron Burr, and Brockholst Livingston.

The Grange

Shorn of its thirty-five acres, deprived of its barns, outbuildings, and tenant house, unkempt, unvisited, and virtually unknown, Hamilton's country house languishes at 287 Convent Avenue on upper Manhattan Island. After many remodelings and other indignities, it has passed into the hands of the National Park Service, which is now struggling to treat it properly. They have not had much encouragement from the editors of the Hamilton Papers, who thought fit to describe it disparagingly: "In neither size nor architecture was the Grange comparable to the famous plantation mansions occupied by some of Hamilton's contemporaries among southern slaveholders and politicians."

It may not be Monticello, but compared with Friendship Hill, the Pennsylvania "plantation" of Albert Gallatin, or with the country houses of James Monroe, James Madison, or John Marshall—or, indeed, with Mount Vernon—The Grange is a respectable piece of work. Yet historians slighting it have drawn upon the testimony of Allan Hamilton, Hamilton's grandson and biographer, who judged it "never an architectural triumph, although it is a type of the comfortable house of the period." Such a biographer is not to be trusted: we are put on notice that The Grange did not comport with the impression of Hamilton that his family wished to leave in the national memory. It was more in their interest to suggest that Hamilton did not care about it very much; in their view he "remained a city dweller until the day he died, and the Grange was essentially a 'retreat' and a hobby."

Hamilton's own testimony is directly contrary to this view of the matter. If he had been accorded the respect due his direct expression, a place might have been found for this wonderful house in Fort Tryon Park, or in its own park.

There is something in the very name of the place that urges us to assess it for ourselves, to look at it with fresh eyes. That name is ambiguous—it is both Creole and Scottish, both the name of a castle and that of a plantation. Which association was in Hamilton's own mind? Let us begin by thinking of it not as it is, cramped between two apartment houses of an ugliness unusual even in an unusually ugly neighborhood, but as it once was, set among a group of estates so beautiful as to attract as residents such romantic spirits as the painter John James Audubon and the poet Edgar Allan Poe.

Old watercolors show that The Grange in its horticultural setting was very handsome, and certainly not to be dismissed as a "hobby." Its design had been commissioned from the most celebrated architects in the city of the time, and it was intended to be a country seat considerably larger than "retreats" like Jefferson's Poplar Forest. It contained a kitchen, a family dining room, and service rooms on the lower floor,* and, on the main floor, a library, two guest rooms, and two large, octagonal rooms that abutted each other and could be opened to provide a ballroom. The third floor provided another living room, for the family, and three bedrooms.

The house was worth $25,000 at Hamilton's death, and he spent nearly that much money on it. (It is probably safe to multiply this by nearly 400 to get 1980s building costs.) Hamilton did not treat this ambitious undertaking as a hobby; he was very serious about it, stretching the ethics of his profession to borrow from an estate of which he was a trustee to find his equity and taking a mortgage for the balance. (The Hamiltons did have a "hobby farm" in which they lived while The Grange was being completed.)

He wanted to live as a country gentleman. The Grange, he said, was "always . . . a sweet asylum from care and pain."

Sweet Asylum

There is a tender letter from Hamilton to his wife about The Grange, written on one of his endless business trips to raise the fees to pay for its building program. He asks her to see to it that the tulip trees, hemlocks, and white pines are put in the right places. Hamilton loved gardens and trees; he exchanged seeds as well as political gossip with old friends like Charles Cotesworth Pinckney of South Carolina and, as a gentleman farmer, produced market crops of strawberries, cabbages, and asparagus.†

---

*In the manner of French houses or of Jefferson's Farmington, near Louisville, Kentucky, this was a "raised basement."

†Hamilton was indeed a gentleman farmer, as was Nicholas Biddle. Historians of the New Deal

"View of Elgin Garden on Fifth Avenue" (David Hosack's nursery), c. 1812

Three of Hamilton's friends will appear and reappear in these pages, in part, but only in part, because of their interest in medicine and in horticulture. All three were doctors: Edward Stevens, a central figure of Part Four; David Hosack, who supplied the plants for the botanical park intended to be seen from the piazzas of The Grange, from which plants would be exchanged with Hosack's nursery on Fifth Avenue; and William Thornton.

Hosack was professor of botany and *materia medica* at Columbia College (at the same time that Mozart's librettist Lorenzo da Ponte was professor of classics).* In 1798, after the college refused to establish a botanical garden, he talked his friends into buying land for the purpose on the "middle road" between the city and upper Manhattan, to produce plants grown from seeds from the West Indies and obtained from the Jardin des Plantes in Paris (rescued from revolutionary destruction by Joseph Lakanal; see p. 344).

---

era pre-empted that role for Jefferson and Andrew Jackson, to serve as precursors of the Sage of Hyde Park; but the arch-Federalist and the arch-Whig were farmers too, and Biddle was a better one than that occasional agrarian Jackson.

*A grandson of da Ponte became a merchant and patron of architecture in New Orleans.

The Meaning of "The Grange"

What's in the name The Grange?

Hamilton's need for confirmation of his genius, both by power and by wealth, arose, perhaps, from his impoverished and dependent youth. He had achieved the heights by ascending a painful road. "Bastard brat of a Scotch peddler," John Adams may have called him in private; for posterity Adams wrote that he was a "Scottish Creotian Bolingbrook . . . born on a speck more obscure than Corsica."

The man Hamilton spoke of as his father, James Hamilton, was not a peddler—indeed, he was sprung from an eminent Scottish family—but he was an improvident plantation manager. His mother had been married to a man named James Michael Levien, whom she deserted to accompany Hamilton. She bore him two sons and was herself deserted by him. Alexander made his own way.

Alexander Hamilton was not physically impressive—he stood only five feet seven, dwarfish beside Thomas Jefferson and George Washington—but he was attractive to both sexes, and he enjoyed the affections of a sequence of important and highly discriminating older men, including Washington, whose second administration, from 1793 to 1797, he dominated from his post at the Treasury.

Hamilton, the illegitimate child of uncertain fatherhood, solicited, all his life, the approval of a chosen set of surrogate fathers. He was born on the Caribbean fringe of the British social system. His youth was spent among violent, promiscuous, alcoholic planters, from whom he was rescued by Thomas Stevens, a planter of Saint Croix, who raised him as a member of his own family and sent him off to be educated in New York. There he lived as a person of precarious status until he captured as a wife the daughter of one country squire, Philip Schuyler, and adopted as his model another, George Washington.*

Throughout the 1790s Hamilton strove to acquire the means to secure for himself a country estate, the physical symbol of a settled and continuous condition. Since he was a hard-working attorney for commercial clients, his "seat" could not be far from the center of the city; but on Morningside Heights, not long before his death, he was finally able to find a proper frame for his self-image.

It is part of the lore of The Grange that he gave it that name in order to establish a link with the gentry from which sprang his putative father, James Hamilton, a clan whose half-ruined castle in Scotland is called The Grange. But

---

*Washington had earlier taken as his own models the Fairfaxes, who carried the only hereditary baronetcy to be found among the English residents of America.

it is also true that after Alexander Hamilton's mother was deserted by that scion of an ancient clan, she went to live on Saint Croix, found shelter in the home of Thomas Stevens, and died, on February 19, 1768, at the home of her relatives the Lyttons, who lived at a plantation also called The Grange.*

At his own Grange, Hamilton was master, though master of an adopted terrain and living in a house constructed largely of material floated down the Hudson from the lands of the Schuylers.† The Grange reveals its Creole qualities (indistinguishable from what we might also call its French qualities) only slowly, as if under questioning. Some faded paintings show it when Hamilton first built it, a cubical building with a "captain's walk" on its roof, "piazzas along the sides . . . with tall French windows from floor to ceiling, opening from the two octagon rooms onto the piazzas." There they were again, those tall French windows, piazzas, and linked octagons. The Livingstons had set the tone for the Schuylers. There was, through them all, a connection back to the meeting of Pierre Pharoux and Alexander Hamilton, in Philadelphia in 1794.

It is often said that his West Indian origins were an embarrassment to Alexander Hamilton; but he did not act as if they were when it came to the most courageous statecraft of his career, his support of the rebellion of the Blacks there against the French (see Part Four), or when he was at ease at home, where he was free to call himself "a Creole."

---

*The name was not uncommon: it was given the Drummond-Baring house in Hampshire, to be visited shortly, and, in French translation, to the estate of the marquis de Lafayette.

†Hamilton's father-in-law also supplied the paint and oil and a great deal of advice: the house, for example, should be framed of timber covered with clapboards lined on the interior with brick to keep out rats and mice. (For this correspondence between Hamilton and his father-in-law about The Grange, see volume 25 of the Hamilton Papers.)

LOUISIANA

Ohio R.

Mississippi R.

•Philadelphia

TEXAS

Rio Grande

Galveston•

New Orleans

ATLANTIC OCEAN

Barataria Bay

M E X I C O

GULF OF MEXICO

•San Luis Potosí
(Silver mines)

•Mexico City

•Vera Cruz

CUBA

Le Cap

JAMAICA

SAINT DOMINGUE

CARIBBEAN SEA

PACIFIC OCEAN

Saint Domingue and the Silver Routes

0   500 MILES

VENEZUELA

IV

SAINT-DOMINGUE

It is one thing to exercise a little more vigorously than usual that desire, common to all of us, Freudians and non–Freudians alike, to reshuffle ancestry. It is quite another to attempt to rewrite the history of an entire people and an entire epoch. This is what was done during much of the nineteenth century with respect to the history of the people of Haiti (or "Hayti," as Allan Hamilton wrote it). The founding fathers of many amiable American and French families had been dependent, directly or indirectly, consciously or not, upon the traffic in sugar and slaves in the West Indies, and on that unhappy island in particular. It was most disagreeable to deal directly with the subject, even if one had none of the special reasons to eschew it of the Hamilton family or of those who strove to make Thomas Jefferson into a saint.

The history of European invasions of Hispaniola began with Columbus, who gave the island its name and introduced to it the cultivation of sugar. In 1697 it was divided into two portions. The western portion, shaped like a hand severed at the wrist, pointing toward Jamaica, was assigned to France; it was called by the French Saint-Domingue and is now known as Haiti. The eastern portion was Spanish Santo Domingo and is now the Dominican Republic. Together, these were, at the end of the eighteenth century, "the pearl of the Antilles," a jewel for any empire. It was, however, more fragile than a pearl.

It was destroyed, as an engine producing surplus wealth, by the most terrible war in a time of terrible wars.

Until quite recently, histories of the French West Indies in this period offered a picture of a sudden, isolated holocaust arising from the granting of freedom to its slaves by a French revolutionary Assembly infatuated with oratory and idealism. This act of folly, the traditional story ran, set loose a Caribbean Reign of Terror that was compounded by the barbaric outrages of Negro "brigands"; the idyllic life of the white planters on the island was destroyed, and with it the prosperity of all, White and Black.

This much is true: in fifteen years of warfare after 1789, a once lucrative colony, superb in climate and fertility, was reduced to ruin. The human cost was three hundred thousand Blacks, sixty thousand French soldiers and sailors, at least as many British, and nearly the entire White population on the island— about thirty thousand people in 1789.

The cataclysm was not isolated. Simultaneous revolts occurred in British Jamaica and Spanish Cuba; the Haitian revolution was but the largest and fiercest of a continuous series of slave rebellions in the West Indies. The causes and consequences of these disorders are so discomfiting to some historians, however, that it has been their practice to present them as separate from the history of Europe and of the United States. They were, in fact, most painfully conjoined, and their political and sociological effects upon the United States were larger than we have been taught to believe. For example, Creole émigrés reinforced in Baltimore and New Orleans a Mulatto culture distinct from that of the upland rural South. The West Indian pattern of White men producing an entire class of educated offspring of color was stronger in New Orleans than anywhere else on the mainland. Manumission following "miscegenation" (in the view of others in the old South) became common after the influx of refugees from Saint-Domingue.

Louisiana, Maryland, Maine, Missouri, Massachusetts, Ohio, Pennsylvania, New York, and the Carolinas suddenly acquired a new set of citizens and, with them, a Creole culture. The sugar-refining and furniture-manufacturing industries of the United States were transformed by an influx of skilled Creoles, and a conspicuous gunpowder and textile complex began to grow along the Brandywine, in Delaware, financed and to some extent managed (as we will see) by Creoles.

A failure to give sufficient weight to the consequences of the revolution in Saint-Domingue has thrown off-kilter many histories of the neoclassical period. A balance is required. Too much counterweight is now a risk to be preferred to too little, too long delayed. Henry Adams was right a century ago: "The prejudice of race alone [has] blinded the American people to the debt they owed to the desperate courage of five hundred thousand Haytian negroes who would not be enslaved."

Adams was bold enough to tell his countrymen that the defeat of Napoleon's scheme for a restoration of the New World empire of France had been at the hands of the Negroes of Saint-Domingue and that its beneficiaries were the people of the United States.

Yet the effects of Negro resistance to the reimposition of slavery were even wider and earlier than Adams suggests, and they began to work their way through the history of the North Atlantic region even before Thomas Jefferson came to power. In its effort to conquer Saint-Domingue and to restore slavery to the island in the 1790s, the British army squandered its resources and became enfeebled. For five crucial years thereafter it could offer little aid to the monarchic alliance arrayed against the infant French Republic. That republic survived and evolved into the empire of Napoleon, who also contemplated an American empire—a dream that was relinquished only in 1803, when he was frustrated by the collapse of his expedition against Saint-Domingue. Baffled, impoverished of men and equipment, requiring funds to finance excursions closer to home, Napoleon was willing to sell Louisiana for some hard cash plus some forgiveness of a set of annoying claims by Americans aggrieved by earlier French predations.

The Louisiana Purchase decisively turned the energies of many in New England and the central colonies westward. Though others continued to brave the seas made dangerous by protracted warfare between the British and French, despite Jefferson's embargo on much of their traditional Atlantic trade, the combination of his implied invitation to go west and his impediments to commerce upon the waters to the east surely had its effects. One thing is sure: the last bonanza benefits to American traders from the West Indies trade were garnered during Toussaint's rule in Saint-Domingue.

After the fall of Toussaint and the desolation of the island, and after Jefferson's embargo and the Louisiana Purchase, the West Indies attracted less and less American energy, and the West attracted more and more. The destruction of Saint-Domingue as an engine of wealth did not alone turn Americans westward, but a poll taken in 1808 on the docks of Philadelphia, among young men planning their futures, would, I think, have yielded quite a different geographic orientation from one taken ten years earlier. Toussaint Louverture was as important to that shift in orientation as anyone except Napoleon and Thomas Jefferson.

As late as the War of 1812, Americans had good grounds to remember with gratitude the Negroes of Saint-Domingue. Had the British retained the strength, in the 1790s, to strangle the French Republic in its infancy, had a resurgence of French imperialism under the banner of revolution not required the outpouring of the blood and treasure of Britain in warfare upon the continent, only a minor portion of Britain's resources would have sufficed for an effective campaign, in 1812, to intimidate the United States or reduce it to

dependent status. But thanks to the revolt on Saint-Domingue and its consequences, Britain had not that surplus of force, and the rational statesmen of
London and Westminster therefore computed that the cost of reconquest of a
former colony in North America would be more than the cost of economic
domination of the cotton-growing South.

There might have been other reasons for withholding their hand in moments
of anger or avarice, but it was a boon to the United States that such a
computation was possible. The benefit side of the ledger displaying the fruits
of conquest was likely to be smaller, net of costs in blood, treasure, and the
destruction of conquered assets, than the potential yields over time to the mills
of Manchester of a subservient southern plantation system. Twenty-two years
of war against France had exhausted the British. Impotence is a better guarantee of restraint than miscalculation or morality.

12

THE BENEFITS

OF TOIL

American independence was first recognized by the great powers of Europe in
1783, at the Treaty of Paris. Rejoicing in its victories, exalted in its heroism,
justified in its sacrifices, France received the embarrassed British at its capital
and meted out its demands. After five years of conflict, and such vast exertions
as to rupture its social fabric and open the way to revolution, France demanded,
and received, the West Indian island of Tobago and a slaving station in Senegal.

What can be the explanation of this apparent abnegation? Not, surely, that
Tobago had the honor to be the birthplace of Dr. William Thornton. That little
sugar island must have been precious on other grounds. It was. It is easiest for
us to gauge its value if we think of its product not as a white powder used
to sweeten but, instead, as a silvery dust like platinum, a dust of such price as
to justify making war to secure its sources. And the slaving station? It was the
processing point for the work force needed to produce more of that magical
substance.

In 1783, any French minister who could add and subtract might have felt
justified in exchanging millions of acres of North American land for a few
hundred producing sugar. At the beginning of the eighteenth century, imports
from Britain's West Indian and mainland colonies were about equal, but the
former grew much more rapidly than the latter. By the time of the American

Revolution, the West Indies sent home twice the value of goods from all of North America. In 1798, income drawn by British investors from the West Indies was four times as great as that gleaned from the rest of the world.

As early as 1700, the 166 square miles of Barbados were more valuable than the aggregate value of New England, New York, and Pennsylvania. Jamaica replaced Barbados as the primary source of sugar to Britain, exporting five times the value of the products of Pennsylvania and the other "bread colonies." From 1714 to 1773, Britain imported from Montserrat three times what it got from Pennsylvania. Imports from Nevis, the diminutive birthplace of Alexander Hamilton, were twice those from New York; those from Antigua were over three times those from all of New England. On the other side of the export-import balance sheet, British exporters sold to Barbados and Antigua as much as to New York. Pennsylvania was not so good a market as Montserrat and Nevis.*

When Eric Williams was still laboring in scholarly vineyards, before he became the prime minister of Trinidad and Tobago, he assembled for us some further details about the role of the Caribbean in the British economy: Bristol might have returned again to the condition of a fishing village had it not become, in the seventeenth and eighteenth centuries, a great slaving port. "Sumptuous mansions, luxurious living, liveried menials, were the produce of the wealth made from the sufferings . . . of the slaves bought and sold by Bristol merchants." Most of those slaves went to the West Indies; Bristol merchants, returning home, brought with them the products of those slaves' labor. The sugar trade soon "was worth to Bristol twice as much as all her other overseas commerce."

In the spring of 1790, the blue estuary of the Severn seemed as lovely as ever, flecked by white sails seen from a distance. Now, however, they were the sails of fleets of slave ships returning home, sluiced down from their deliveries to the West Indies, bearing slave-produced rum and sugar. On the horizon they provided Wedgwood decoration as they worked their way home against the tide.

Bordeaux and Nantes

Bordeaux, on the broad reaches of the Garonne, was the home port for traffic in the same products as Bristol. On its wharves those trade goods were sold and capital accumulated.

We can imagine Henriette de La Tour Du Pin, before the revolution, sitting

---

*Cuba was still the Patagonia of the Caribbean, largely unvexed by European agriculture, a vast cattle ranch with a few starveling plantations.

at her leisure in her garden at Le Bouilh, looking across the river as flotillas, graceful and sleek, passed across the horizon, ships come to anchor off Bordeaux, "the magnificent quay of the Garonne."

Stendhal found Bordeaux to be "unquestionably the most beautiful city in France. It slopes down toward the Garonne, and from all sides there is a fine view of that lovely river, so crowded with ships that it would be impossible to stretch a rope from one shore to another without passing over one of them." The mercantile oligarchs of Bordeaux built so well that "you are constantly being brought up short by the sight of a magnificent house" built, more often than not, from West Indian profits. By 1833 the city was acclaimed for its "completely epicurean way of life, a far cry from the crafty and ambitious hypocrisy of Paris . . . [without] the slightest affectation."

It was a way of life made possible by wealth compounding at a rate as notorious in France as among the fabled West Indians of London: in the eighteenth century, the French islands were more productive than those the British settled, planted, and exhausted earlier. In 1717, one slave on Saint-Domingue produced four times more than one on Jamaica. In 1737, it was reported that a plantation in the French islands was nine times as profitable as the tired cane fields of British Barbados. French sugar could be sold in the markets of Europe at half the cost of the British product.

Bordeaux was the sugar port of France; Nantes was its slaving port.

It was the Dutch who instructed the French (as they had the British and the Americans—see *Architecture, Men, Women and Money*) about the profits to be made in facilitating such "laborious toil." In 1661, a lone Dutch ship conducted the West Indies trade for Bordeaux. Two decades later, the city had more than fifty vessels serving the plantations. Twenty-five more were based at Nantes. The slave trade accelerated rapidly as the eighteenth century progressed, with Nantes traders in the lead. Eric Williams recently estimated that eight hundred thousand Blacks were carried to Saint-Domingue between 1680 and 1776, an average of between twelve thousand and fifteen thousand annually toward the end of the period. There are profits to be made in replenishing a labor supply: despite the addition of one hundred thousand newly imported slaves to Saint-Domingue, and some natural increase among those already there, Williams tells us, there were nineteen thousand fewer Blacks on the island in 1776 than in 1763.

This ghastly record accounts for only the loss of human life after the cargoes reached the island. Many more Blacks died along the way, and with them some Whites. Mortality among the human cargoes of Nantes reached 34 percent in 1732. Death was not accepted passively, however; there are reports of a battle on board one out of fifteen voyages, on the average. In 1775, the Blacks captured the *Diane,* and on the *Concorde* all but three of the Whites were killed.

In the last years of the ancien régime, Saint-Domingue was unrivaled in wealth. Its production of sugar, already huge, doubled between 1783 and 1789. Bordeaux and Nantes poured in further investments—said to be one hundred million pounds sterling.

All subsequent historians owe much to C.L.R. James's *The Black Jacobins,* from which I have drawn this reminder: "If in no earthly spot was so much misery concentrated as on a slave-ship, then on no portion of the globe did its surface in proportion to its dimensions yield so much wealth as the colony of Saint-Domingue."

Slavery on Saint-Domingue

It is impossible to give oneself over for many days to reading memoirs of Saint-Domingue in the last two decades of French rule without hallucinating. I do not recommend the experiment. The reports left to us jangle one against the other, like colors seen in a fever, too bright for life against a sky too dark for daylight. They are the stuff of nightmare. Discordance dances with discordance, the hideous with the exquisite. The pencil to illustrate these stories would be that of Hieronymus Bosch.

Let me offer this from M. Girod-Chantrans, a Swiss, writing in 1785:

> There were about a hundred men and women of different ages, all occupied in digging ditches in a cane-field, the majority of them naked or covered with rags. The sun shone down with full force on their heads. Sweat rolled from all parts of their bodies. Their limbs, weighed down by the heat, fatigued with the weight of their picks and by the resistance of the clayey soil baked hard enough to break their implements, strained themselves to overcome every obstacle. A mournful silence reigned. Exhaustion was stamped on every face, but the hour of rest had not yet come. The pitiless eye of the Manager patrolled the gang and several foremen armed with long whips moved periodically between them, giving stinging blows to all who, worn out by fatigue, were compelled to take a rest—men or women, young or old.

Here is a report by an anonymous French planter of a scene not far distant, possibly at about the same time:

> In the center of the garden were flowers and fruit trees; also, displaying its choicest treasures, was an immense sapodilla, whose long flexible branches, covered with fruit, touched the grass and made a vast salon of verdure; beneath its foliage the table was set. It appeared to me that I had never beheld a more brilliant scene. Imagine twelve lovely and elegantly dressed women seated at a round table covered with everything luscious—

the most deliciously prepared things and fruits of diverse colors and odors filled graceful baskets.

The table encircled the tree, which was entwined with garlands and resembled a column of flowers. Lanterns were strung among the branches like fruits of fire, and candles were placed upon the table in enormous bouquets of jasmine that seemed to replace the brilliance of the sun, which had just hid behind the mountains. The sky was serene, only a zephyr moved the leaves, and a murmuring brook could be heard nearby.

We were refreshed by the wines of France and the fine liqueurs of Italy and Martinique. Champagne soon had its usual effect, and brought gaiety to the table with bright banter and songs of love: I was in my element. Placed between the beautiful Madame d'E. and the seductive Madame N., surrounded by cakes, fruits, and flagons, I had my lyre brought and sang impromptu couplets, interrupted only by a dozen glasses.

It may have been the beautiful Madame d'E. or the seductive Madame N. who was the unnamed hostess in another story—a woman famous for her charm and easy grace who became accustomed to a ready supply of slaves, replaceable with the next shipload. When one cook displeased her, she had the wench thrown into the fire.

By the late 1780s, forty thousand Negroes were landing on the island every year; fierce new recruits were not easily or quickly broken to servitude. So many spirits to tame, so many hearts to break! Firmness was required. A description of the disciplinary devices the French employed penned by C.R.L. James has been criticized by subsequent writers for abandoning a chilly, "objective" tone. But one may be permitted a slight rise in temperature when recalling scenes like these:

> There was no ingenuity that fear or a depraved imagination could devise which was not employed: . . . irons on the hands and feet, blocks of wood that the slaves had to drag behind them wherever they went, the tin-plate mask designed to prevent the slaves eating the sugar-cane, the iron collar. Whipping was interrupted in order to pass a piece of hot wood on the buttocks of the victim; salt, pepper, citron, cinders, aloes, and hot ashes were poured on the bleeding wounds. Mutilations were common, limbs, ears, and sometimes the private parts, to deprive them of the pleasures which they could indulge in without expense. Their masters poured burning wax on their arms and hands and shoulders, emptied the boiling cane sugar over their heads, burned them alive, roasted them on slow fires . . .

There were Creoles of Saint-Domingue inclined by nature toward generosity, ease, and grace. Pierre de Vaissière, a historian writing early in this century, found evidence of them. But life in such a place at such a time did not endorse such qualities; it made brutes of masters and of slaves. Vaissière concluded that the island was a graveyard for hundreds of thousands of Blacks, and the graveyard as well for the sensibilities of tens of thousands of owners. Some of the great families of France contributed younger sons and scapegraces to rot in the island sun. We are told that before 1789 one could expect to find there "de Vaudreils, a Chateauneuf, or Boucicault . . . passing his life between a bowl of rum and a Negro concubine."

Hatred was as heavy in the air as heat. The great planters despised the "petits blancs," the overseers, clerks, and dockside trash. The Blacks were patronized by the Mulattoes, who were arranged by law into 128 degrees, according to their proportion of White and Black ancestors. Free Blacks victimized the unfree. The Spaniards, on the east side of the island, were traditional enemies of the French on the west side. Men sent from Paris to govern the planters regarded the posts of governor and intendant as a lucrative purgatory, whether they came with a royal prerogative in hand or a charter from a revolutionary assembly. Brissot, the leader of the moderates in the Assembly, rising to espouse the vote for Mulattoes, depicted the Creole as a man in whose heart there was "at the same time . . . hatred against the man of color who claims his rights, against the merchant who claims his debts, against a free government which wishes that justice be done to all."

13

DISASTER

Two representative chroniclers of the traditional view of the history of Saint-Domingue were the otherwise admirable Frances Childs, upon whom we have relied for much of our knowledge of the lives of French émigrés in the United States in the revolutionary period, and the Honorable John W. Fortescue, whose history of the British army appeared in a series of volumes from 1905 to 1910.

From Childs comes the statement that on Saint-Domingue "the social equilibrium was an extremely delicate one, maintained only by the most rigid enforcement of the color line." We have seen what "rigid enforcement" meant in practice. But we may ask: Was there in fact a "social equilibrium" to be suddenly disrupted? Childs tells us there was, and asserts further that "into this situation came the revolutionary philosophy, theories of representative government, and civil rights." Fortescue picks up the story: when the revolutionaries in Paris granted a constitutional government (in theory) to the island, "dissensions" between Blacks and Whites were "naturally kindled" and then "artfully inflamed." He goes on to tell us that "the violent language of Brissot and others of the Negro's Friends encouraged the hot-headed mulattoes to organize an insurrection."

The truth is otherwise: there was no social equilibrium on Saint-Domingue, or anywhere else in the empire of sugar and slaves spanning the Atlantic from the Madeira and Canary archipelagoes and the lonely islet of São Tome on the east, to the experimental plantings of Louisiana and Florida on the north, or Brazil on the south. Slave uprisings began almost with the first shipload of slaves to arrive in the Western Hemisphere and persisted throughout the seventeenth and eighteenth centuries. There was a rising on Saint Kitts in 1639. Scarcely a year passed without an attempt. In 1700, three hundred slaves revolted on Saint-Domingue; in 1733, the slaves of Saint John took the whole island and held it for six months, until they were beaten by the combined forces of the Danes, the British, the French, and the Dutch. Jamaica was in a constant state of insurrection until 1739, when the "maroons," an army of escaped slaves, were recognized as masters of their own mountain enclave. A new rising on Saint-Domingue, led by François Macandal, failed; the Dutch in Surinam reached an accommodation with the "bush Negroes" in 1761, but race warfare began again on this southern flank of the plantation system in the 1770s.

Nor was there any general chorus of reassurance from Europe for the planters. John Locke, that maker of clever colonial constitutions, was willing to tolerate slavery; but he recognized it for what it was, a state of war, with violence ordained by its very nature. Adam Smith was a true friend of the Negro (though he took, perhaps, too general a view of the character of any people). In his *Theory of Moral Sentiments* he spoke of the magnanimity of the Negro in contrast to his "sordid master," and of the Africans as "nations of heroes" and the slave owners as "the refuse of the jails of Europe." His position, though as sentimental as that of Rousseau, was clear. Condorcet agreed: "If one wished to find a man in the isles of America, it would not be among the people of white skin that one would find him."

Voltaire, Diderot, Helvétius, Tom Paine—all the great names of the French Enlightenment weighed in against the planters and the slave system. By the end of the century, no literate person could feel upright as a slave owner; no practical person could feel secure; and no person of sensibility could ignore the heavy judgment of the poets, novelists, and playwrights of the time. Even that high Tory Dr. Samuel Johnson drank a toast to slave insurrection. Economists, following the lead of Adam Smith, joined the flotilla of enlightened opinion, though they muffled their oars, as they conventionally do, with assertions that their fervor was not fervor at all but an unavoidable synthesis of statistics. Eleuthère Irénée Du Pont de Nemours, a physiocrat who will emerge in another role later in this tale, anticipated Smith by seven years, arguing that slaves had no incentive to industrious labor and would always be at war with their masters. Benjamin Franklin agreed.

It was not the inflammatory Brissot who laid the match to the powder; the sugar fields were already aflame. Nor was it a set of strange ideas, suddenly emerging in 1789 and then disrupting a slave-and-sugar "equilibrium." The system had been at war with the slaves themselves from its beginning; as the century came to a close, it came under attack by White people of conscience.

On Saint-Domingue itself, tension was accumulating: abrasion between the seigneurial class and the royal governors became bitter enough to induce some of the Patriots to think of cutting themselves free of the homeland. Their peers had shown the way from Virginia to Georgia; and others would, soon enough, throughout Latin America.

The regime of the seigneurs was threatened by the growing population of freshly imported, "unseasoned" slaves, and it was also at odds with the petits blancs. Saint-Domingue, even without its slaves, might have experienced a revolt of White workers, like that on Barbados earlier.

Mulattoes outnumbered the Whites, owned much property, and were getting richer. As a result, they too were restless; and by 1790 they had the means and the will to mount a revolt of their own.

The Tragedy Unfolds

In the final years of the ancien régime, the vivid example of slaveholding planters in the South of the United States encouraged the Saint-Dominguan seigneurs to form a Colonial Assembly—for Whites only. The fall of the Bastille, in 1789, reminded the planters that they had economic as well as racial considerations to keep in mind. They began, uneasily and incoherently, to compete with the royalist bureaucracy for the favor of the Mulattoes. After all, some of these were their own cousins, and people of wealth, and they all had something to fear from the now inflamed petits blancs, the island's sans-culottes. The royal governor in turn replied in the spring of 1790, encouraging his bureaucrats to strike up their own alliance with the Mulattoes, even "to treat them as friends and whites." The planters responded by lynching those Mulatto leaders who dared take such protestations seriously, and the Mulattoes rose in a brief, aborted insurrection.

Many of the rich Mulattoes were well represented in Paris, where their influence in the Assembly might even gain them the right to vote at home. The Colonial Assembly of White planters, at Saint-Marc, took up the cry of "No taxation without representation"—representation, that is, upon the southern American pattern, by Whites only. Anticipating South Carolinians a generation later, they passed a nullification resolution: no act of the central legislature in

France would be valid in Saint-Domingue unless it gained their concurrent support.

The Assembly in Paris was deadlocked. Some of the Friends of the Negroes were abolitionists. Some among the men of the Gironde (representing the maritime interests) entered an alliance with the well-subsidized agents of the planters—a few favored enfranchising Mulattoes and free Blacks. Vincent Ogé, an eloquent Mulatto, despairing of forward movement in Paris, went to London and was encouraged by abolitionist leaders there—and, one suspects, by imperial interests as well. He landed in Saint-Domingue in October, accompanied by many Mulattoes who had fought in the American War of Independence.* After a bungled effort to detonate a Mulatto rising, he was captured, tortured, and put to death. The brutality meted out to his followers by the Whites is too horrible to recount here, but its recollection provided precedents for later ingenuity in torture on the part of the Blacks and Mulattoes.

After 1790, as Louis XVI became a barely royal, constitutional king, the "Patriots," those advocating independence—for Whites—on Saint-Domingue, grew more vocal. Things were getting out of hand in Paris; one Saint-Dominguan delegate to the National Assembly declared it to be "drunk with liberty." On the island itself, in March 1791, the royal governor was murdered by his own soldiers, removing one more symbol of order and authority, and the planters assumed power in defiance of Paris.

Soon that power was tested by a slave rebellion led by Boukman, a gigantic Black priest of an African religion, whose followers massacred and tortured and were massacred and tortured in turn. Boukman was killed; but before his death the struggle of the Blacks had gained the adherence of a forty-five-year-old man of genius, Toussaint Louverture. So frail in his youth that he was called "Little Stick," he was to become one of the great leaders of the revolutionary period.

In November 1791, three commissioners arrived from Paris to try to bring peace to the island. They failed. By April 1792, a force composed of royalists, Negroes, both free and former slaves, and Mulattoes was besieging the "Patriots" in Port-au-Prince, and Toussaint was raising another army of former slaves and free Blacks in the mountains of the north. In July 1792, a new set of commissioners, representing the more radical coalition then in power in Paris, set forth for Saint-Domingue. Childs describes them as of "extreme Jacobin opinion which only failed to put a mulatto on the Commission."

The strongest of the three was Leger-Félicité Sonthonax, who, Childs writes, was "of the worst possible type . . . to the colonists a symbolic monster set upon their destruction." Fortescue tells us that these monsters "at once allied themselves to the blacks, in order to enrich themselves with the plunder of the

---

*Substantial numbers of both Black and Mulatto Saint-Dominguans were recruited for the American campaigns of the French armed forces in 1778 and 1779.

Toussaint Louverture (artist unknown)

whites." As a matter of fact, Sonthonax was no "extreme Jacobin" but a Brissotin. His temperament was fervent, but he was no bloody terrorist; in fact, the "extreme Jacobins," led by Robespierre, were at the time engaged in a strange dalliance with the planters' representatives in Paris. Yet in the end the party of Robespierre did accommodate itself to the pressures of the Convention, in Paris, for Negro emancipation. As for Sonthonax—we shall see.

Childs continues the story, from the perspective of the planters, as she heard it from their descendants in the United States: Sonthonax "indulged in a ruthless anti-white policy, setting up a miniature revolutionary tribunal, deporting large numbers of unsympathetic whites and inaugurating a veritable reign of terror."

Upon Sonthonax's arrival, he was warned by the president of the planters' assembly that the Patriots had "not brought a half-a-million slaves from the coasts of Africa to make them into French citizens." Sonthonax responded that he was there to see to the observance of the decree of April 4, 1792, which enfranchised the free Blacks and free Mulattoes but did not emancipate the slaves, and to terminate the lingering resistance of the royalists. This, with Mulatto assistance, he did, calling those who opposed him among the petits blancs "aristocrats of the skin." Toussaint, with his army of former slaves, played a waiting game, edging closer to an alliance with Sonthonax.

A civil war had become a confusion of race wars; now it was compounded by an international commercial and ideological war.

A new French governor arrived, who was himself a planter. Though he had a Mulatto wife, he took the side of the counterrevolution: not quite royalist, perhaps, but distinctly hostile to Sonthonax. The sailors of the fleet bringing him to the island were, of course, White. When they landed, they found an island governed by Sonthonax but increasingly dependent upon the army led by Toussaint. In Le Cap, a fracas between the followers of Sonthonax and the governor became a pitched battle between sailors from the fleet and ten thousand Blacks; the governor was driven from the shore. Two-thirds of the city was destroyed by fire; and as the fleet withdrew from the flames, it took with it thousands of White refugees, whose horrid recollections have determined much of the historiography of these events. Some contemporary observers, however, saw the bestiality as reciprocal. A Captain Bickford of Salem, Massachusetts, who was in Le Cap, wrote, "The white troops . . . take no prisoners, but kill everything black or yellow, leave the Negroes dead upon the fields."

Sonthonax had vanquished his foes among the Whites, but he was isolated, surveying the embers of Le Cap amid a throng of black faces. In June, he moved to secure the allegiance of the armed Blacks, proposing a decree of abolition limited to them only. On August 29, 1793, he declared that slavery was abolished in the northern province of the island, and asked his colleagues charged with attempting to hold the rest of the island to extend the abolition to regions under their control.

Meanwhile, the "Patriots" had turned to the British on Jamaica, who had their own rebellious Blacks to worry about and were already nervous enough. London soon heard demands for an expeditionary force to invade Saint-Domingue. After the king of France was executed, on January 21, 1793, Britain and Spain had entered the war against revolutionary France; and in September, a British force from Jamaica landed in Saint-Domingue. In January 1794 the National Assembly in Paris endorsed Sonthonax's strategy, issuing a formal decree of abolition. The revolution celebrated its alliance with the Blacks. Danton, one of the radicals who succeeded Brissot, rose in the Assembly and cried: "Citizens, today the English are riddled! Pitt and his plots are done for!" Sonthonax, however, returned to France in June, having been arrested by an envoy of Robespierre.

That spring, British expeditionary forces captured Martinique, Saint Lucia, and Guadeloupe; but the French sent to recapture these islands Victor Hugues, a Jacobin petit blanc who had been a public prosecutor during the Terror. His character is viewed differently by the winners and the losers in his ensuing campaigns, but no one disputes his success. Fortescue says of him that he "ought to have shared the fate" of Robespierre and his party—the guillotine—but admits that he "possessed . . . audacity and vigour as well as brutality, and as a leader of an excitable race like the negroes was most formidable." Sir Harry Johnston calls him "one of the great personalities of the French Revolution to whom nothing was impossible."

As Toussaint watched from Saint-Domingue, Hugues formed an army of former slaves, recaptured Guadeloupe, and carried the war to the British on Grenada and Saint Vincent. While he was picking off the Windward Islands, the Blacks on Jamaica rose against the British. The course of the war turned decisively. Toussaint, having reflected upon the news from Paris, became a general in the French Republican Army and turned his fury upon the enemies of France.

For the next five years, the British lavished men, money, and supplies on a vain attempt to capture "these pestilent islands, in the expectation that thereby they would destroy the power of France, only to discover, when it was too late, that they had practically destroyed the British army." British troops were no better able than French to withstand heat, fever, malnutrition, and guerrilla warfare. Only a fragment of their forces was able, ultimately, to survive. Fortescue concluded that by 1798, the West Indian campaigns had cost England "little fewer than 100,000 men, about half of them dead, the remainder permanently unfit for service."*

An extra push in Flanders, or in Italy, might have extinguished the French Republic; a concentration of forces against the ragged armies led by Generals Moreau, Hoche, Humbert, and Bonaparte might have ground them to bits, one by one. But, instead, Britain was distracted by the West Indies. It could not mobilize sufficient strength in Europe to put the republican genie back in the bottle. The way was open for Napoleon.

Napoleonic Politics

Sonthonax returned to Saint-Domingue in 1796. Robespierre had fallen and been replaced by the Directory, a corrupt oligarchy; Sonthonax was now a commissioner of the Republic. As he attempted to impose its authority over the Mulattoes in the south of the island, he encountered stiff resistance from their leader, Benoit-Joseph Rigaud. The following year, he fell out with Toussaint as well (Toussaint and Rigaud were themselves increasingly at odds). Ultimate power now resided with the Blacks. Sonthonax could not bring himself to accept an ancillary role. He was a man of genuine republican

---

*Other historians have revised these figures downward, but not enough to diminish substantially the magnitude of the drain upon British military resources.

principles, relatively free of either sentimentality or race hatred, but he needed to be in charge. The same could be said of Toussaint. Their animosity increased. It became clear that it would be healthier for Sonthonax if he departed for France, leaving Toussaint, in effect, the ruler of the island.

Toussaint Louverture knew he would not be left unchallenged. Former plantation owners in Paris, in London, and in the United States were soliciting expeditions against him. He warned the French Directory not to attempt "to re-establish slavery in San Domingo . . . it would be to attempt the impossible." In the next year he demonstrated his point by driving the British completely off the island, both that portion formerly held by France and the Spanish colony to the east.

The Directory sent a new governor to the island, General Marie-Joseph-Gabriel-Théodore, comte d'Hédouville. Though he was expelled by Toussaint, as Sonthonax had been, it was not until he had deliberately spread germs of division between Rigaud and Toussaint. A fresh civil war broke out, in which, as we shall see, the United States took an active part.

Toussaint's army was largely composed of Blacks, but many of his officers were White. He made it a practice to appoint White officials to important posts, while Rigaud and his Mulattoes sought alliances with the remnants of the planter class.

Rigaud was defeated and fled to France, where he was received by Napoleon in 1801 with these words: "General, I blame you for only one thing, not to have been victorious."

Toussaint, assisted by the Federalist government of the United States, had triumphed—for the moment. After Rigaud's defeat, he turned eastward, marching against the Spanish, and added their territories to his dominions. He was, in effect, the independent sovereign of a multiracial state, supreme on the entire island, though still nominally a French general.

His most poignant necessity was food for people trying to survive in the charred remains of cities and amid burned-out cane fields. Food could come only from the United States. As he searched the horizon in that direction, he could see signals aplenty, but they were most confusing. The natural allies of revolution might be thought to be the Jeffersonians, who were about to assume power in 1800. But along the southern coasts of America, especially in Virginia and South Carolina, the signs were of implacable hostility. His natural enemies might have been expected to lie within the aristocratic circle around Alexander Hamilton, no longer in government but powerful nonetheless. Yet the Hamiltonians were Toussaint's consistent friends.

How can this apparent anomaly be explained? Was it only that Jefferson and the southern slave owners feared Blacks more than they loved liberty, and that Hamilton, Adams, and the high Federalists loved commerce more than they feared slave rebellion on other people's plantations?

A popular image of Toussaint, composed at the time
(there are no completely authentic portraits)

Such sardonic simplicities give part of the answer, but only a small part. There was no neat Mason–Dixon Line between slave and free colonies. There were more slaves per capita and over a longer period in portions of the Hudson Valley (like Dutchess County) than in Piedmont Virginia or North Carolina.

Nor were the circumstances of Jefferson's youth or maturity more likely to engender fear of Blacks than those conditioning Hamilton. On Saint Croix, Blacks outnumbered Whites by ten to one, a far higher and more explosive proportion than was true of Jefferson's Piedmont Virginia, where the ratio was probably two or three Whites to every Black. And the two men were equally well acquainted with, or threatened by, the propinquity of Blacks later in life; in his prosperous middle years, Hamilton, like his kinsmen the Schuylers, had as many Black house slaves as Jefferson.

The keys to racial attitudes do not lie in such matters, but in the affinity-repulsion mechanisms deep in the unconscious, where they lurk, appearing only in occasional glimpses. Hamilton did not seem to harbor antipathies toward

Blacks, though he was well acquainted with the prevailing prejudices and practices of his time (he had worked for a slave trader when a boy on Saint Croix). He supported their manumission, and told his beloved friend John Laurens that he believed their "natural faculties are probably as good as ours." Scholars have pointed out that though he was secretary of the Manumission Society, he did not take as forceful a position against slavery during the Constitutional Convention as did his Federalist colleagues Rufus King and Gouverneur Morris. But he did not take a forceful position on anything in Philadelphia. He made one great, but coolly received, speech, and then fell into one of his periods of lassitude and depression, abandoning the antislavery fight to Morris.

Jefferson was another case; as a Virginia politician, he had reason to be careful to avoid admitting agreement with Hamilton's view of Blacks, but it appears that he had no desire to do so even when such an admission might have been relatively safe. In the "Notes on Virginia," written for an audience of abolitionist French philosophes, he admitted instead to "the suspicion" that "the Creator may perhaps have" consigned Blacks to a lower "rank in the scale of being" than Whites. When talking to his southern colleagues, he may have cleared up any suspicion and expressed himself as he did in 1807, in a moment of exasperation, to the British minister to the United States. Blacks, he said, were "as far inferior to the rest of mankind as the mule is to the horse, and as made to carry burthens."

The records of the Constitutional Convention demonstrate the remarkable consistency of the high Federalist stance against slavery, especially on the part of men in Hamilton's immediate circle. Gouverneur Morris was willing to abandon the entire enterprise at one point rather than give implicit moral sanction either to the slave trade or to the continued ownership of slaves. The southerners united to oppose meddling with the ownership of slaves once the trade had done its work, though Virginians expressed disgust with the trade that had brought their work force to them, while Carolinians were heard to defend it. Virginians had more slaves than the declining tobacco and wheat plantation system could support and wished to sell them off without the competition of new slaves from Africa. The Carolinians were expanding their plantation system westward and wished to purchase labor at the cheapest possible price.

A "dirty compromise" was finally worked out. New England received commercial advantages and a government capable of protecting commerce. The South succeeded in delaying until 1808 the possibility of any legislation to terminate one kind of commerce, the slave trade, and baked protection for slavery itself into a dozen provisions. The final Constitution preserved the unity of thirteen disparate colonies and commenced the process of knitting them together into a nation. The moment to strike effectively against slavery, and in the interest of Blacks, was lost; yet it is noteworthy that Morris, King, and other Federalists who later were sympathetic to Toussaint were the last to abandon the fight.

It is with this record in mind that we may understand why Claude Bowers and partisans of Jefferson have been so avid in their disparagement of Morris. Their task was to elevate a sage into a saint; so Morris, a witty and consistent antagonist to his views and a living reproach to his inconsistencies, was intolerable. When Bowers describes Morris as a man of "no morals to speak of . . . resembling Hamilton only in his antipathy to democracy and in his cynical skepticism of republican institutions," we are free to wonder what passion led so meticulous a writer to lose control of his tautologies.

And when Bowers chooses to say that the horror that Morris expressed at the excesses of the Terror, after he succeeded Jefferson as minister to France, can be dismissed as "[aligning] himself ardently with the reactionaries . . . and against the Revolution," we may be induced instead to make closer inquiry into Jefferson's propensity to be more disposed to any French government, even one headed by Robespierre or Napoleon, than to any set up against France—especially, perhaps, one headed by a Black man and a former slave.

14

AMERICAN CONNECTIONS

As far back as 1784, Jefferson became anxious about the effects of commercial rivalries in the Caribbean upon relations between his cherished France and the United States. He wrote James Monroe from Paris that French merchants were becoming "very clamorous against our admission into the West Indies": they were offended especially by American competition against them in the trade of Saint-Domingue. Jefferson, never very sympathetic to those of his countrymen who neither planted nor sowed but traded instead, was not loath to propose limitations on the clandestine trade carried on by Yankees. Anxiety and distaste were joined by panic when to the prospect of discord with France over grubby matters of commerce was added the far more hideous specter of Negro insurrection spreading from the West Indies to the plantations of those North Americans who planted, sowed, and reaped with Negro labor.

There were other voices, even more clamorous, demanding an end to American dalliance with the rebels of Saint-Domingue. By 1793 there were several thousand Creole refugees in the port cities of the United States, many of them rich and persuasive. By 1795, further insurrections on Saint-Domingue had so added to that number that settlements of angry Creoles were widespread, and not only on the seaboard. Their influence extended beyond politics into the field of architecture—an aspect of the matter to which we return shortly.

Jefferson was George Washington's secretary of state from 1790 through 1793. In that post he could reinforce the old general's private desire to "crush the alarming insurrection of the negroes of San Domingo," whom Jefferson called "the cannibals of the terrible Republic." Offsetting these views were those of Adams and Hamilton. All were alike in their aversion to disorder; but despite his occasional rhetoric to the contrary, Jefferson was willing to support all revolutions against colonial oppression except the next one. Hamilton could look beyond an increase in existing disorder toward the future victory of a strong leader like Toussaint. A Hamiltonian kind of order, and ports open to American shipping, commended themselves to the majority of Washington's cabinet.

Jefferson departed for Monticello at the end of 1793 to resume farming, architecture, and schemes of faction. Thereafter, Washington looked more benignly upon a Negro republic consuming large quantities of hides, lumber, livestock, salt fish, rice, furs, grapes, tar, and flour, including flour from Washington's own mills. His friends and partners at Alexandria and Georgetown were busy unloading cargoes of rum, sugar, coffee, and molasses from Saint-Domingue.

Both the French and the British set about to disrupt Yankee intrusions; in the last months of Jefferson's tenure as secretary, three hundred American vessels were seized by the British. Federalist policy, however, called for amity with Britain, not with France. To the Francophile Jefferson's disgust, John Jay was sent by President Washington as special minister to Great Britain. In 1794 Jay concluded a treaty with Britain that removed the British threat to the sea lanes to Saint-Domingue.

Talleyrand and the French Directory responded by arming "87 cruizers . . . at sea" and noted with satisfaction that what remained of French administration of Saint-Domingue "had subsisted, and individuals been enriched, with the product of those prizes . . . They felicitate themselves that American vessels are daily taken." The Americans were not felicitated; the new secretary of state, Timothy Pickering, called the French actions "atrocities and piracies . . . committed on our defenseless commerce." The new President, John Adams, began to defend that commerce at sea and gave support to Toussaint in exchange for his shutting his ports to French privateers. John Quincy Adams, supporting his father, began speaking of a "free and independent" Saint-Domingue, "in close alliance and under the guarantee of the United States."

Jefferson had assured the French that their hold on the island would not be weakened by American action. Hamilton and the Adamses, father and son, were willing to "avoid the explicit recognition of any regular authority . . ." Pickering went further: "We shall never receive from the French Republic indemnification for the injuries she has done us. The commerce of St. Domingue represents the only means of compensation, and this I have no doubt we will obtain."

Statesmen may have used temporizing language; but in truth, during much of the period from 1796 to 1800 the ships of the United States and France behaved as if the two nations were at war. Especially after the U.S.S. *Constellation* went into battle with the French frigate *Insurgente* in February 1799, there were grounds for calling the conflict "Mr. Adams's quasi-war."

Though Adams was willing to return to negotiations with the French despite the XYZ Affair, Hamilton and Pickering were prepared to go to war in the full, declared, and jurisprudential sense. They did not wish to see French revolutionary contagion spreading into the Western Hemisphere and were prepared to gamble that "if left to themselves . . . the Blacks of St. Domingo will be incomparably less dangerous than if they remained the subjects of France; she could form with them military corps . . . as no European or other white force could resist."

Hamilton himself, a "bastard son" of the West Indies, may even have harbored some sympathy for those who rose against the planter class. After all, neither his political aspirations nor the interest of his law practice required that ambitious, frustrated, and desperately overworked man to play John Locke to Toussaint Louverture. Yet he diverted himself from his own debt-ridden urgencies and in 1799 delivered to Toussaint a plan for a constitution for Saint-Domingue. He was by now in open disagreement with President Adams, who had sent negotiators to Paris to seek a settlement with Talleyrand.

Hamilton's draft constitution was a document of considerable importance. It was not only a sign that he was more committed to the survival of Toussaint's government than was Adams; it also showed how his view of government had evolved since he and James Madison collaborated on *The Federalist Papers*. * Now he recommended a President for life, supported by a junto, and universal military service for males. Upon this Hamiltonian model, in February 1801 the Central Assembly of Saint-Domingue, consisting of seven Whites and three Mulattoes, under the eye of Toussaint, drafted the constitution of the Republic.

Edward Stevens

In chapter 11, it was suggested that we cannot be sure about which "Grange" was dominant in Alexander Hamilton's memory when he chose this name for his country estate. This question suggests another: How certain can we be that Hamilton was really Hamilton? During his lifetime, many people, including those who knew him very well, believed that his father was not James Hamil-

---

*It was also, of course, what he thought appropriate in other circumstances.

ton, scion of lairds, but instead Thomas Stevens, merchant of the island of Saint Croix.

Henry Cabot Lodge, writing in 1882, said that "every student of the period [was] familiar with the story, which oral tradition had handed down, that Hamilton was the son of a rich West Indian planter or merchant, generally supposed to have been Mr. Stevens, the father of Hamilton's early friend and school-fellow." James Yard, Stevens's brother-in-law, told their mutual friend Secretary of State Timothy Pickering that "the remark had been made a thousand times—that they must be brothers."

A connection to an unsung Creole merchant (a "peddler" perhaps?) had little to commend itself to Hamilton's heirs. They went to some pains to snip away any connections between Hamilton and either Thomas Stevens or his son, Edward. Here, for example, is the reference to Edward Stevens in Allan Hamilton's biography of his grandfather:

> The early friendship that existed between Hamilton and Edward Stevens led to no greater intimacy in later life. Stevens was one of the few friends who did not particularly distinguish himself, and about whom little is heard. He grew up to be a worthy doctor, but was a negative character, and his sole public service was rendered in a consulship to Hayti. The letters that passed between the two were of the most formal character, and there is no display of extraordinary interest in any of them, despite the promising beginning.

On the contrary, Henry Adams reported the uniform assessment of Edward Stevens by his contemporaries as "a very able man"; and, in fact, Allan Hamilton was fully aware that Stevens distinguished himself as a research scientist in human digestion and as a diplomat. (Stevens's only real peer as a gentleman-doctor-botanist was his friend William Thornton, the gentleman-doctor-botanist-architect. As we shall see, Thornton attempted to redress the damage meted out to Stevens for serving the foreign policies of Hamilton against the purposes of Thomas Jefferson; in turn, Stevens served as executor of Thornton's West Indian estates, including a botanical "experiment station" on Tortola.) Stevens saved Hamilton's life during the yellow fever epidemic of 1794 and that of Mrs. Hamilton as well. Hamilton wrote a letter to the newspapers saying that their recovery "under God, [was due] to the skill and care of my friend Doctor Stevens, a gentleman lately from the island of St. Croix." Nor was there anything "formal" in their correspondence; Stevens was the author of one of the most intimate letters to survive in Hamilton's correspondence (see p. 341n.).* No "negative character" would have been chosen by Secretary of

*Nor did their intimacy languish in later life; they kept in touch until Hamilton's death. Through Stevens, Hamilton entered into correspondence with one of his most fervent overseas admirers, Ernst

State Pickering and by President John Adams, with Hamilton's advice, for a mission to Toussaint Louverture—a mission that might have changed the history of American slavery and, accordingly, of much else.

Stevens upon the Great Stage

Edward Stevens was born on the island of Antigua in 1754. Despite the joint efforts of Hamilton's family and Jefferson's admirers to derogate him, he was a great man: diplomat between nations and races, botanist, merchant, pioneering investigator of the human digestive system, soldier, planter, economist, and financial adviser to Toussaint Louverture. He represents a path not taken, a linkage of the American Revolution to revolutions against colonialism elsewhere, regardless of race.

Stevens's father sent Edward and Hamilton to study at King's College (now Columbia University) in New York; Stevens went on to get his medical degree from the University of Edinburgh in 1777. There his researches into human digestion were so distinguished that he was asked to join the faculty. (This we know from a letter left us by Thornton, a fellow medical student, who came from Tortola, just across a narrow channel from Saint Croix.)

Stevens's career in research and teaching in Scotland was set aside by Hamilton's call to join him in the revolutionary armies of the United States. His military career was as brief as his career in medical research. Though, according to Thornton, he "fought gallantly," he was "recalled by his father to finish his studies."* (This seems to have been in 1781 or 1782.)

After getting his license to practice medicine, Stevens returned to Saint Croix, once again at the call of his father. He found time for extensive research into the flora and fauna of Puerto Rico, but he was chiefly occupied as a practitioner of medicine and manager of the family sugar lands. He was not altogether satisfied, it seems; for he thought of following other ambitious West Indians to Demerara, on the swampy north coast of South America. He was dissuaded by Thornton on the ground that "the unhealthiness of the Country might perhaps deprive [the world] for ever of one of its chief ornaments." In 1793, he chose Philadelphia instead and settled into practice there just in time to save the lives of Hamilton and his wife during an epidemic of yellow fever. The fever was bad enough; an equal peril was the bleeding therapy that had

---

Frederik von Walterstorff, governor-general of the Danish West Indies. Stevens had married Hester Kortright, a sister of Cornelius and Sarah Kortright, who both married von Walterstorffs—Sarah, the governor-general. (I am indebted to Elizabeth Bradley for this information.) Hester Stevens had previously been married to William Amory, a friend of Hamilton's, who died early in the 1790s.

*Another Edward Stevens became a militia general in Virginia and is easily confused with our medical student.

been prescribed for them by Thomas Jefferson's friend and physician, Dr. Benjamin Rush. Stevens contended successfully against both the disease and the remedy. His distinctions at Edinburgh were supplemented by the renown won in controversies with Rush: he was asked to lecture in New York, as a faculty member at Columbia Medical School, in 1794–95 (when he could have dined with Hamilton, Hosack, and—Pierre Pharoux?).

Hamilton and Stevens, doctor and patient, looked alike, as many in Philadelphia commented. To this observation was added the interesting datum that they were just over two years apart in age. (Hamilton gave his birth date as January 11, 1757; Stevens was christened on November 14, 1754, in Saint John's Cathedral in Antigua.) As we have noted, it was generally believed, contrary to the Hamilton family story, that Thomas Stevens was father to them both.

Timothy Pickering became acquainted with Stevens through Hamilton. The secretary of state was searching for a wise diplomat who knew the West Indies and whose prejudices against Negroes were not too rampant. Pickering was determined "to conciliate the good will of the Negro government, & to give protection and assistance to our citizens engaged in . . . commerce." Such a task demanded an agent of "integrity, ability, a cautious disposition & a familiar knowledge of the French language." He sent for Stevens, who was known as "very intelligent, and a worthy man." When Stevens entered his room, "at the first glance, I was struck by the extraordinary similitude of his and General Hamilton's faces; I thought they must be brothers."

Pickering inquired of Yard, Stevens's brother-in-law, who also came from the West Indies, and "it seemed apparent that he thought them near of kin." More than twenty years later, Pickering tried to satisfy his curiosity by drawing out a clear answer from Yard; what could be the harm? Hamilton had been dead a long time. Yard added confusion: Mrs. Hamilton had died in the 1760s, but now, in 1822, Yard reported that "General Hamilton's mother died but two or three years ago."

Pickering thought it odd that Hamilton, "the reputed father of the General, became a planter in Granada," and apparently a man of means, while it was Thomas Stevens who provided for Hamilton's education. Yard would go no further. "In cases of this sort," Pickering concluded, "the possibility of kindred blood gives rise to some surmises, or strong suspicions, of which no proof is attainable." Henry Cabot Lodge, writing Hamilton's biography sixty years deeper into Victorian decorum, put the presumption the other way round: we should defer to Hamilton's preference for an aristocratic though illegitimate paternity, despite the "meagre statement of Hamilton himself, and the careless and unsupported account given" to support that statement by his son, "in the absence of convincing proof to the contrary."

In 1798, John Adams and Pickering gave other signals: when Pickering wrote Adams for instructions for Stevens on February 20, 1799, he archly referred to him as "the brother-in-law of Mr. Hamilton, just appointed to go to St. Domingo." They both were well acquainted with the Schuylers, Hamilton's in-laws, and knew that Stevens was not among them. And in 1801, after Adams and Hamilton had fallen to feuding amid the debris of the Federalist party, Adams listed four instances of appointments he had made for which Hamilton should have been grateful; they were all made to members of Hamilton's family or to Hamilton himself except—and was it an exception?—Stevens's appointment as consul general to Saint-Domingue.*

A Mission to Toussaint

Stevens carried instructions from Pickering and Hamilton to come to terms with the "distinguished negro General Toussaint." He went to work immediately upon arrival to strengthen the bonds uniting the two young powers in the New World, the one ruled by Whites, the other by Blacks.

In 1798, the Federalists in Congress passed a trade embargo against France and its colonies, amended a month later to open an exception for Saint-Domingue. Jefferson derided this provision as "Toussaint's clause" and charged that its proponent, Stevens, "may be considered as our Minister to Toussaint." Toussaint acknowledged the relationship by sending a special emissary, Joseph Bunel, to act in effect as his minister to the United States. Secure in the knowledge that he could draw upon the financial acumen of Alexander Hamilton, Stevens became Toussaint's adviser on tax policy. Soon, reciprocally, he was Toussaint's advocate to the councils of the administration of John Adams, insisting that the ruler of Saint-Domingue was no tyrant but "mild and humane—[bent on] encouraging agriculture and establishing useful Regulations for the internal Government of the Colony." Pickering agreed that the Black consul was "amiable and respectable." An independent Toussaint could be a useful ally.

To secure this result, Stevens and Pickering agreed on the "absolute Necessity of supporting Toussaint by every legal measure." The United States entered an active co-belligerency with the Black republic. American arms and uniforms outfitted its armies; American bankers held its reserves.

Stevens told his superiors that "Toussaint has on his Side most of the Blacks, and all the Whites of the Colony." On the other side, under the command of General Rigaud, were the Mulattoes, described by Stevens as "the best Horse-

---

*Stevens was convoyed to the island by Captain Thomas Tingey, U.S.N., a friend he shared with Benjamin Henry Latrobe. It was to Tingey, who was later commander of the U.S. Navy Yard in Washington, that Latrobe wrote describing in affectionate terms another friend, his client John Craig, father-in-law of Nicholas Biddle. (See p. 254.)

men in the Colony. From Indolence and Pride these People seldom travel on foot, and being accustomed to ride from their Infancy [presumably to distinguish them from the Negro field-hands], they acquire a Facility of managing a horse, which renders them superior to the Negroes."

Stevens warned his government that the French were arming the Mulattoes in order to "invade the Island of Jamaica and the southern states of America . . . [a] diabolical Attempt to extend the destructive Influence of French Principles and to add another Million to those who already crouch under the Iron Sceptre of modern Liberty, and Equality." He acknowledged that this scheme might seem "wild and impracticable," but the French seemed bent on it, sending recruiters to Saint Thomas and Guadeloupe. Toussaint had no appetite for such a "counterpart of the Egyptian Expedition" upon which Napoleon was embarked at the time.

Providing men and ships to the French, Rigaud took up their quarrel with the Americans. "12 of Rigaud's Barges, strongly armed and manned by 500 Negroes and Mulattoes" attacked a little American flotilla. Stevens, aboard the schooner *Experiment,* joined its crew as they repulsed the boarding parties; but the wind dropped, and the large American sailing craft were becalmed and at the mercy of the long-oared barges. The brigs *Daniel* and *Mary* and the schooner *Washington* were captured by Rigaud's men.

Toussaint's navy recaptured the American brigs; but, in riposte, Rigaud's barges defeated a small force of Toussaint's sent to blockade Jacmel, Rigaud's headquarters. At the urgent call of Stevens in March 1800, the frigates *Boston, Connecticut, Constitution,* and *Richmond* appeared in Saint-Dominguan waters. This American fleet obliterated Rigaud's flotilla and took up the blockade. While they were cutting off Rigaud's supplies, Stevens found arms and food for Toussaint on Jamaica and delivered them under convoy of the American fleet. The *General Greene,* the *Experiment,* and the *Augusta* prowled offshore as Toussaint ground down the Mulatto army. When that was not enough, the American fleet turned its guns on Rigaud's fortress and assured Toussaint's victory in the "War of Knives."

The working alliance of the governments of Toussaint Louverture and John Adams brought the United States into hostilities with other French garrisons in the West Indies. The French governor of Guadeloupe declared war on the United States, and French officials in Guiana did the same. Stephen Decatur, skipper of the *Delaware,* a converted merchant ship, captured a French privateer, explaining that "the French have been making war on us for a long time." Thomas Truxton, vying for honor, captured a French frigate and announced that its captain had charged him with having "caused a War with France," and that "if so I am glad of it." French corsairs skulked among the islands, preying upon the American merchantmen trading with Toussaint, who responded to Stevens's urging and closed his ports to armed French vessels.

The Congress of the United States rushed to augment a fleet to "sweep" the West Indies, the primary theater of war, and the coastline of North America as well. By the end of 1799, the navy could announce that it was strong enough "to rid those seas . . . of French commissioned armed vessels as of the pirates which infest them." Six hundred American ships were plying the sea lanes to the West Indies, most of them making for ports controlled by Toussaint.*

The old West Indiamen were back at sea, delightedly renewing their commerce with Saint-Domingue. American vessels swarmed into its ports; thirty-two were reported in Le Cap on a single day in July 1801. Trade between the United States and Saint-Domingue became seven times that between the island and France.

15

THE SLAVE OWNERS

ATTACK

The mercantile interests of New York and New England were vanquished in the election of 1800. The new administration, headed by Thomas Jefferson, took a different view of slave insurrections. Though Edward Stevens, having followed up Hamiltonian constitution-making with counsel in the intricacies of Hamiltonian finance, spoke of bringing Toussaint into a three-way, Hamiltonian understanding with the British, Jefferson, in his initial discussion with

---

*At home, the war was fought with weapons of which we have been made thoroughly aware by later historians, particularly those who admire Thomas Jefferson more than John Adams. Despite Hamilton's opposition, the extreme Federalists passed the Alien and Sedition Acts, permitting expulsion of foreigners (presumably Jacobins) by presidential decree and making illegal vehement criticism of the government. The latter action was clearly contrary to the First Amendment to the Constitution, though not to British practice—similar measures to contend with Jacobin sedition were adopted at the time in Great Britain.

In response, Jefferson and his friends threatened to dismember the Union. The Kentucky and Virginia Resolutions brought the doctrine of nullification (already proclaimed by the slave-holding plantation owners of Saint-Domingue) into serious American political dialogue. It contended that individual states could nullify acts of Congress in accordance with their own theories of constitutionality.

We can always look to Claude Bowers to assert the orthodox Jeffersonian position on such matters, so let him state his case. The resolutions, says Bowers, "were primarily intended as a protest against interference with freedom of speech and the liberty of the press, and only"—proceeding to quote another Jeffersonian apologist, Frank M. Anderson, writing in 1899—" 'incidentally they gave expression to a theory concerning the nature of the federal union.' " That theory was not thought to be "incidental" by the founders of the Confederacy, but let it be. (Bowers speaks on nullification in his *Jefferson and Hamilton*, p. 408.)

the British Minister, made it clear that thenceforward, such things would not be considered. Stevens had shown, he said, "too great bias in favor of England," and Stevens must go. He was replaced by Tobias Lear, George Washington's private secretary.*

It was Lear's assignment to cut the connections between Toussaint and the United States, in response to southern—and northern racist—fears that a contagion of abolitionism might be carried in the holds of trading vessels. As far back as 1793, Jefferson had told James Monroe that he was "convinced that all the West India islands will soon remain in the hands of people of colour & a total expulsion of the whites sooner or later take place. It is high time we should foresee the bloody scenes which our children, certainly, and possibly ourselves (south of the Potomac) have to wade through." His foreign policy in the West Indies was a search for means to avert these horrors.

During the 1790s, while the Jeffersonians were organizing themselves to assume power, one of their devices was the deployment of terror of contagion or combustion from Haiti. In 1799 Jefferson wrote: "We may expect . . . black crews, & supercargoes & missionaries thence in the southern states; and when the leaven begins to work," where might it spread? The "combustion," once introduced, would be uncontrollable, and "we have to fear it."

Fear of slaves—fear of Blacks—pervaded Jeffersonian and Jacksonian politics. The moment the Federalists were out, the new government set about to gain its first object, the destruction of Toussaint's regime.†

Northern Quandaries

The views of the New England merchants were clear enough; so were those of the southern slave owners. But during the last years of the Adams administration, Jeffersonians of the middle colonies were in a quandary. We will have occasion later to observe the behavior of the chief among Jeffersonian financiers of Philadelphia, Stephen Girard, and the party's chieftain in Baltimore, Senator Samuel Smith. Albert Gallatin of western Pennsylvania, their leader in the

*That was not the end of the career of Edward Stevens, but it did terminate his role as a participant in geopolitics. We shall return to him when we have seen the outcome of Mr. Jefferson's "Revolution of 1800" upon the revolution in Saint-Domingue. We must also defer until we return to Stevens some explanation for the peculiar choice Jefferson made for his replacement. There were other contenders—earnest, loyal Jeffersonians among them. Yet these eminent men, two of whom were also important in the biography of Latrobe, lost this patronage plum to a man who was neither a Jeffersonian nor distinguished for his accomplishments.

†It is an arresting fact that this was one of the political differences between Jefferson's faction and that of Aaron Burr. Another fact worth bearing in mind is that the successors to the southern Federalists, the southern Whigs headed by Henry Clay, were less virulent in this regard than were their antagonists, the Jacksonians. All this must be the subject of another book.

House of Representatives, had the uncomfortable task of finding reasons to oppose Federalist legislation opening trade to Toussaint.

In a speech to the House, the most ignoble of his public career, Gallatin did his part for the Jeffersonian strategy of using racial hatred for political ends. Saint-Domingue had a "black population"; if Toussaint succeeded, "the interest . . . will be wholly black." As to Toussaint himself, "the General is black, and his agent here [Bunel] is married to a black woman in this city." Gallatin generously admitted that Toussaint "had behaved well to Americans," and blandly disclaimed any racial animosity—he "only intended to show that it would be with a black population we must treat."

The color scheme was established. Now for the arabesques of the argument: Gallatin expressed "abhorrence against the attempts of other countries to divide the people of a nation from their Government." (Such "abhorrence" bloomed quickly, it seemed. Many Americans present on the floor of the chamber had been grateful for the French intervention at Yorktown that had accomplished the division of themselves from their government in England.) Commerce with Saint-Domingue might be "lucrative," but it was "wrong in itself," for it encouraged the independence of the island. And Jeffersonian foreign policy deemed that independence "extremely injurious to the interests of the United States."

This Swiss-born apostle of Voltaire, swept into public life by the whiskey-distilling Jacobins of western Pennsylvania, once had welcomed the revolution in France as the cause "of mankind against tyranny." But White Jacobins were one thing, Black Jacobins another. American revolutionaries and Parisian sans-culottes may have been intemperate, even violent; but the people of Saint-Domingue had been "initiated to liberty only by rapine, pillage, and massacre" and were by no means likely to prefer "peaceful cultivation . . . to . . . plunder and predations." Their unhappy experience under their former masters excited his compassion, but he was "unwilling . . . to constitute a whole nation of freed slaves . . . and thus to throw so many wild tigers on society."

No man, said Gallatin (in words repeated, with little alteration, in a thousand speeches on that floor for the next sixty years), wished more than he did "to see an abolition of slavery when it could be properly effected." *But*—always "but"—in the meantime, there were the economic interests of the plantations to be protected. Better return the Saint-Dominguans to slavery under France than to open the southern states to "invasion" or to subversion by Black agents who "might visit the States of South Carolina and Georgia, and spread their views among the negro people there, and excite dangerous insurrections among them."

Senator James Jackson of Georgia, normally more independent in his views, held to the party line as late as 1805 and proclaimed himself in debates of that year as willing to go "whole lengths" to "prohibit the trade of San Domingo;

. . . the usurped government of that unfortunate island must be destroyed." For that destruction of a "Negro government," Jefferson's son-in-law, John Wayles Eppes, "would venture to pledge the Treasury of the United States."*

Gallatin built an anti–Saint-Dominguan alliance among border-state and northern Jeffersonians:† young John Breckinridge of Kentucky was for an embargo on trade to the island; Samuel L. Mitchell of New York,‡ torn between his loyalty to Jefferson, his affection for Aaron Burr, and the interests of his merchant constituents, was willing to condemn that trade as "illicit" and "contrary to the law of nations." When Mitchell retired from the Senate in 1804, Logan of Pennsylvania offered legislation to cut it off. Then Aaron Burr, near the end of his tenure as vice-president, earned a final dose of antipathy from Thomas Jefferson: he intervened to defeat that motion, breaking a tie.

Tacit Understandings

The new secretary of state, James Madison, in his first conversation with Napoleon's emissary Louis-André Pichon, adjusted Hamiltonian policy only a little; the American government was "taking things just as they were without pretending to judge them." But Pichon knew the climate had changed more than that. Planters like James Delaire had already been closeted with the President-elect, and they were confident their views would prevail, "however advantageous the independence of these revolters might appear to the mercantile faction."

In September 1800, the Treaty of Mortefontaine§ with France brought Mr. Adams's quasi-war to an end, and Madison issued to Tobias Lear the party line of the new regime: "The United States would withdraw from Saint-Domingue rather than hurt relations with France."

A Napoleonic colony was to be preferred to a Negro republic in the West Indies, especially when France intended the reimposition of slavery and, thus, some alleviation of the fears of the slave owners. Those fears were rising; the governor of South Carolina spoke of the "similar . . . situation of the southern States and St. Domingo . . . in the profusion of slaves . . . exposed to the same

---

*Jackson's bitter foe in Georgia politics, Mayor Thomas Gibbons of Savannah, was the patron of Adrian Boucher and a defender of free Blacks. See my *Greek Revival America*.

†Throughout this period, Mr. Gallatin of Pennsylvania anticipated the position of Mr. Buchanan of Pennsylvania, President of the United States in the years 1857–61, staunch friend of the slaveholders and staunch opponent of abolition—except in some heavenly future, when it could be "properly effected."

‡Mitchell was another of the remarkable group of doctors, like Stevens, who studied at Edinburgh and later went into politics.

§Mortefontaine was the estate of Joseph Bonaparte. Leray de Chaumont was also present at the treaty making.

insurrections . . ." The lieutenant governor of Virginia took seriously a warning that the Saint-Dominguan rebels might "operate against us" a domestic rising. Georgia and South Carolina even suspended the slave trade, to keep out Blacks who might carry the Caribbean contagion.

The Federalists had found arms and food for Toussaint. Now the administration of Thomas Jefferson loaned France three hundred thousand dollars for relief of the Whites on the island.

The charming M. Pichon, and his equally charming wife (so admired by biographers of Jefferson, such as Claude Bowers), moved rapidly to outflank the cautious Madison and secure assurances from the President himself that a Napoleonic campaign against Toussaint would not be troubled by intrusions of American frigates—memories were fresh of the American fleet at the siege of Jacmel, the stronghold of Rigaud's Mulattoes.

On July 20, 1801, Pichon paid a call on the President. Did Jefferson approve of the regime of Citizen Toussaint? Jefferson "did not approve." If France were to send an expedition against it, would the Americans once again interfere? On the contrary, it would be possible "without difficulty" to arrange "a concert with the United States in order to accomplish more quickly the conquest of the colony." Once Napoleon achieved the armistice with England then under negotiation, "nothing would be easier than to furnish your army and fleet with everything; and to reduce Toussaint to starvation."

Pichon could scarcely restrain his joy. But Jefferson was not quite through. He assured the French representative that Britain would see things likewise. She would "doubtless participate in a concert to repress this rebellion" (this from Thomas Jefferson!), moved not only by "her fears for her own colonies, I am sure," but also—supplying a phrase upon which Napoleon was to pounce with eagerness—to prevent Saint-Domingue from "becoming another Algiers in the seas of America."

That was all that Talleyrand and Napoleon needed. Off went instructions to their agents in London. Back came word that Lord Addington, the British foreign secretary, on a pleasant morning at Wimbledon, acknowledged that "the interest of the two governments is absolutely the same, namely, the destruction of Jacobinism [in general] and that of the blacks in particular." Comforted by this assurance, Talleyrand wrote his ministers that the "Spaniards, the English, and the Americans look upon the Black Republic with equal anxiety."

Through all these events, there courses a profound current of racial hatred and fear of slave insurrection. The sentiments of the southern planters were candid and might have been expected. Those of Napoleon were at the outset hidden; but, emboldened by the sudden onrush of respectable opinion in his favor, they emerged in the full fervor of a Corsican married to a Creole. He spoke of Toussaint's government as "Africans . . . utterly uncivilized . . . did not even know what a colony was." He quietly had harried out of the French army the Saint-Dominguan Mulatto Thomas-Alexandre Dumas, one of its ablest commanders.* He announced that he would not leave an epaulet on the shoulders of a single Black man and began driving out of public life those White officials who were willing to work in good faith toward rebuilding Saint-Domingue under Toussaint's rule.†

The United States having been tranquilized, Napoleon proceeded to remove the second obstacle to a reconquest of Saint-Domingue: on October 1, 1801, peace was declared at Amiens between Britain and France. The seas were safe for an invasion force. The final tragedy for the Island in the Sun, for the first multiracial government in the New World, and for sixty thousand Frenchmen, was under way.

Twenty thousand men were aboard the first fleet, under the command of Napoleon's brother-in-law General Victor Leclerc; his wife, Pauline Bonaparte, who saw herself as a Caribbean queen, carried in her ship the full appurtenances of a court: musicians, actors, hairdressers. The pretense was that Leclerc was coming to aid in Toussaint's pacification of the island; but when that old realist saw Samana Bay crowded with Leclerc's fleet, he knew that the thirty thousand rifles he had purchased from America would not be enough, nor would the army he had created.

Toussaint acknowledged the inevitable: "We shall perish. All France is come to overwhelm us." But he determined to fight, rejecting the advice of Tobias Lear to surrender.

Leclerc's instructions from Napoleon were detailed and explicit: Toussaint was to be lured into Le Cap to swear fidelity to France, kidnapped, and shipped off to prison. His White administrators would then be sent to France for punishment for political miscegenation. If Toussaint refused the trap, there was to be "a war to the death" until he was captured and shot. Other Black leaders were to be assured of protection; but after Toussaint was gone, "all the black generals whatever their status [would be] deported."

It was war to the death—so many deaths. Leclerc's emissary was intercepted on his way to Toussaint. He was found to be bearing proclamations of Leclerc's authority, and hostilities began. Le Cap had been damaged in 1793, when the first, celebrated emigration of Whites took place; in 1802, the city felt the true nature of Napoleonic warfare. Only fifty-nine of two thousand houses remained. Toussaint told his generals: "We have no other resource than destruction and fire . . . The soil bathed with our sweat must not furnish our foes with

---

*Dumas, father and grandfather of novelists, had refused to offer the deference Bonaparte required during the Egyptian campaign.

†One of these "conspirators" warned Bonaparte that Toussaint, whom Napoleon persisted in calling a "revolted slave," might be driven into the arms of the British; but the Emperor refused to consider a compromise with "gilded Africans." (For "revolted slave," see James, p. 272; for "gilded Africans," p. 271.)

the smallest sustenance. Tear up the roads. Throw corpses and horses into all the fountains, burn and annihilate everything . . ."

A third of the White settlers still remained—perhaps ten thousand of them. But already nearly one hundred and fifty thousand Blacks had died. As C.L.R. James summarized the situation: "The population, corrupt enough before, had been trained in bloodshed and soaked in violence." Toussaint held out as long as he could keep his forces together; but eventually, sickened by more than a decade of bloodletting, he surrendered to Leclerc. The terms he accepted were, of course, soon violated. He was arrested and deported to a French prison,* where he slowly starved to death. His end came in April 1803.

Command of the Blacks passed to Toussaint's deputies, Jean-Jacques Dessalines and Henri Christophe, who had no illusions and, now, little remorse. In February 1802, Napoleon announced the reinstitution of slavery in Guadeloupe. This was a clear signal to the Blacks on Saint-Domingue. The pace of killing increased. Leclerc had shot his prisoners—five hundred at one time. (A regiment of conscripted Poles had to be sent home after refusing to join in these mass executions.) Now lots of one thousand Blacks were put onboard ship at Le Cap and drowned. But Caribbean fever could not be fought with such devices, and the Blacks would not abandon the fight. Leclerc died before Toussaint; his executioner was not starvation but fever. In his way, he too died in exile.

Of the thirty-four thousand troops who ultimately served under Leclerc, all but two thousand were casualties of war or fever. He announced just before his death that his army was destroyed. One of his officers looked about and said: "This is no longer a war. It is a fight of tigers." But ten thousand more men were on their way from France.

The comte de Rochambeau had stood beside Washington. In 1802, after the death of Leclerc, his son took command in Saint-Domingue. To track down Negroes in the hills, the French brought a thousand dogs from Cuba, where they were given an affectionate send-off by planters who had used them to control Blacks who had revolted there in sympathy with Toussaint. The dogs were landed to the kisses of planters' ladies; the French sponsored gladiatorial spectacles in which the animals tore living Negroes apart. It was reciprocal slaughter. On one occasion, Rochambeau executed five hundred Blacks; as each one went to the scaffold, Dessalines hanged a White person, a few miles away, on a scaffold of his own.†

And so it went on, horror for horror, until, in November 1803, Rochambeau had had enough: the truce between Britain and France, arranged at Amiens in

*The ship that carried him to France was called the *Creole*.
†In a landscape made hideous by their own predations, a score of old heroes of the American Revolution were drawn into an endless and terrible war between races. The vicomte de Noailles, once aide to Lafayette, abandoned his career as the most desirable dancing partner, and occasional banker, in Philadelphia to fight in this ignominious campaign against liberty. General Humbert, the embodiment of a career open to talent (see p. 370), fought to deny such careers to men of dark skins.

1802, came to an end, and he surrendered to the British who were now hovering offshore as the French had hovered off Yorktown. The terms were ignominious: to escape the fury of the Blacks, Rochambeau consigned his few remaining followers to British prisons. Sixty thousand and the island of Saint-Domingue had been lost to France.

Dessalines set himself up as emperor of the ruins. His crown, furnished by Philadelphia merchants, was brought to the coronation, in October 1804, by the *Connecticut*. His coronation robes were tailored in London. The following spring, he ordered the massacre of most of the remaining Whites on the island, excepting only certain experts in what we would now call "technical assistance," and clergymen; perhaps he recalled the role of some clergymen in France, led by Abbé Grégoire, in seeking abolition for the Blacks.

The planter class, exterminated on Saint-Domingue, succeeded in a considerable transfer of persons and assets to Cuba, where they held tenaciously to the customs of the ancien régime: powdered wigs and contredanses, a fondness for naming oneself after one's plantation, and slavery. Though Napoleon's response to the loss of Saint-Domingue was to encourage the manufacture of sugar from beets and, therefore, to diminish the economic value of the plantations these refugees hewed out of the Cuban bush, the refugees from Saint-Domingue remained rich enough to assure that that island remained the last part of the Northern Hemisphere to emancipate its slaves, in 1886.

Cuba became the ultimate refuge of a Creole of amiable disposition and architectural talent, Pierre Bauduy, whose sojourn in the United States produced a series of very fine buildings and a powder-and-wool business that grew into an immense multinational corporation.

There are other mercantile interests to be accounted for before we come to the story of Bauduy, interests whose views toward the Caribbean and Latin America presaged in a melancholy way those policies of the United States that have made its relations with Cuba a somber and sordid chronicle extending to the present day.

Tobias Lear

With this in mind, there is special reason to pick up another thread, Thomas Jefferson's choice of Tobias Lear, Federalist and secretary to George Washington, to be consul to Saint-Domingue. This was believed to be a lucrative position; yet Lear was preferred over other claimants such as William Lee, a steady Jeffersonian, and Dr. Erich Bollmann, an economist and friend of Latrobe's, who had other claims upon Jefferson's attention.*

*I mention these also-rans because they emerge as important characters later on. Lee used all the

It was no minor appointment, nor was it a hasty choice. It was, I believe, the outcome of a masterly Jeffersonian intrigue. Stevens and Pickering had left themselves vulnerable to the kind of attack that could only be mounted by the high-minded and inexperienced Lear.

In April 1799, when Stevens arrived in Saint-Domingue under escort from the United States Navy, he had with him aboard the *Kingston* a large supply of provisions for the inhabitants, who were "in the extremest Distress" because of the French and British blockades. Pickering had instructed him to finance the cost of his mission out of the sale of those provisions, and Toussaint was rightly expected to see this shipment "as earnest of further supplies" if he joined the Americans in opposing French privateering.

While this was a beneficent step for the inhabitants at large, it did not please the profiteers on the island, who were doing very well selling smuggled goods at high prices and had a powerful friend in the previous American consul, Jacob Mayer. Mayer was described (and no doubt treated) by Stevens as "the basest and most treacherous Character I ever met with . . . a disgrace to the American name . . . never sober after dinner." This one of Stevens's opinions was echoed by Tobias Lear.

Mayer circularized the planters on the island with advice not to sell their produce to replenish the *Kingston,* on the grounds that all the ports would soon be open and prices would escalate upward. Mayer then wrote his friends in Philadelphia that Stevens was making speculative profits on the goods aboard the *Kingston* and buying up coffee to his own advantage.

Stevens not only broke the profiteers' monopoly on food supplies but expressed a determination to "put a stop" to the smuggling of arms to the French forces on the island, carried on by "several Mercantile Houses in America," probably Mayer's correspondents in Philadelphia. He wrote Pickering that he knew these merchants had been "disconcerted" by his "stiffness" in ending their "clandestine trade."

This set of Philadelphia merchants (quite distinct from those working with Stephen Girard; see p. 169) made an alliance with the slave-owning southern planters. They encouraged the idea that the Black "combustion" might be contained even before Mr. Jefferson could gain the presidency; George Wash-

---

persuasion he could muster to gain the post awarded to Lear but was given Bordeaux instead. As it happened, his experience there had important consequences: first, for the development of American textile technology, and next, for an invasion of Texas by Napoleonic veterans. He also performed certain confidential tasks so well for Jefferson's Virginian successors in the White House that he was given an important role in the replacement of his friend Latrobe by another friend, Charles Bulfinch, as architect of the Capitol. These matters will be discussed later. Bollmann is just another of those speculator-promoters who bubbles to the surface in chaotic times. He is important largely because he was one of the chief reasons for one of Latrobe's financial collapses, though he was also a bit player in the drama often called "Burr's Conspiracy."

ington himself could accomplish that, if he was willing to undermine the policies of his Federalist successor, John Adams; the key to Washington might be held by Lear. Washington was in retirement at Mount Vernon, back among the slave owners of Virginia. Perhaps he could be reminded of his old fears of Toussaint. But he could not be approached directly: the Washingtons, especially Martha Washington, did not like Jefferson.*

Somehow, entrée was obtained to George Washington. The former President was growing wheat for export and wished to be further engaged in the Saint-Domingue trade. He turned for guidance to the Philadelphia merchants (but not, it seems, to the group headed by Girard).

On June 6, 1799, Washington wrote Clement Biddle that he had some "flour on hand," that he had been reading not only the "Gazettes" but also the "Dispatches . . . received from Mr. Stevens our Consul"—dispatches, one can assume, to the Department of State. "Permit me to ask what effect this event [the reopening of trade with Saint-Domingue] has had, or is likely to have, on the price of that article . . . I will do nothing until I hear from you."

What did Biddle reply? What information did he convey from disconcerted merchants to a fearful slave owner? His letter has been lost. Washington got off a private letter to the secretary of state on August 11, 1799, stating that "friends, as well as enemies of our Government" had spoken "in severe terms" of a new "monopoly," now, they said, enforced by Stevens.

Washington did not reveal his sources, nor did he trouble much to investigate their veracity. But on the same day, to make sure of things, the old man, with Lear at his elbow, wrote the secretary of war, asking "how stands the charge, in verity and truth with respect to the Consul General's [Stevens's] purchase of coffee, and breach of trust; or in other words taking advantage of his official knowledge to monopolize that article at a low price? This thing made a good deal of noise . . . and if true, proves him unworthy, altogether, of public confidence; and denominates him a mercenary [word illegible] one who would do anything for lucre."

It took a while for Stevens to hear of the charges made against him, and by that time Lear was on the way to replace him. Stevens responded to the "false and groundless Calumnies that have been propagated against me both openly and secretly by some persons, who have acted solely by motives of Envy, Jealousy, and Disappointed Ambition." But Washington was dead now, and the damage was done.

Even that was not the end of the matter. Albert Gallatin became secretary of the treasury and, thus, the man to pay Stevens's accumulated expenses.

---

*Martha Washington once said that the second-worst day of her life, next only to that of her husband's death, was when she had to receive President Thomas Jefferson in a state visit to Mount Vernon.

Thomas Jefferson was President and saw himself as chief attorney to the secretary in difficult cases. That presented by the claims of Stevens was so difficult that it was only extinguished by the claimant's death and that of his "friendly agent," Dr. Thornton, nearly thirty years later.

Thornton was slow to enter the lists, perhaps because he was conscious of the political risks of doing so—otherwise we might not enjoy his contributions to the architecture of the University of Virginia. By 1825, Stevens was living in the West Indies, still seeking repayment of his expenses. Finally Thornton, in Washington, found it safe to press, pursuing the elderly Pickering for further evidence and attempting to catch the conscience of old Jeffersonians in the Senate and of Henry Clay, now secretary of state.

Stevens did collect some of what was due him. One can examine the obstacles put in his way by searching the National Archives for an exchange on the matter between Jefferson and Gallatin. It does no more honor to either than Gallatin's "Black speech" to the Congress.

After his dismissal, Stevens seems to have lived again in Philadelphia for a year or so. Around the time of Hamilton's death, in 1804, he returned to their boyhood home on the island of Saint Croix.

He stayed in touch with his old friends: the New-York Historical Society possesses letters of introduction written by Stevens to Dr. Hosack (the classmate of Hamilton's and Stevens's at Columbia who provided plant stock to The Grange, who occupied a house I have suggested was designed by Pierre Pharoux, and who attended Hamilton after his duel with Burr). One of these letters, dated October 6, 1823, introduces Stevens's youngest son, who wished to visit New York after studying medicine in Edinburgh and London. Hosack noted upon it his recollection of Stevens's experiments as a student in Edinburgh leading to discoveries among the intricate workings of the human digestive system. There are other letters, as yet unpublished, among the Thornton papers, expressing Stevens's friendship with William Thornton and with his widow, for whom he served as executor of the architect-physician's estate in the West Indies.

Some recent discoveries in the library on the island of Saint Thomas indicate that Stevens built himself a prosperous practice there, not only in medicine but also as a planter and sugar agent. His plantations included Grove Place, Brook Hill, and Upper Love. Aside from winding up Thornton's West Indian affairs, he was also "executor of Harcourts estate." Some of his letters in the Historical Society of Pennsylvania are written by him as "Attorney" (meaning financial agent) for "Newton's Sugars" to the New York firm of Gouverneur and Kemble, a family connection of Gouverneur Morris.

Dr. Edward Stevens died on Saint Croix in October 1834, at Grove Place. Its ruins are still visible—next to a gravel pit.

Kingdom in the Sun

While Edward Stevens was pulling his life together again in Philadelphia, during the first baffling term of the Jefferson administration, his old friend Hamilton was spiraling into desperate, suicidal courses, as if seeking Aaron Burr's bullet. Hamilton's eldest son led him onward, provoking a political duel; Philip Hamilton died from a gunshot fired on the New Jersey Heights. His second child, Angelica, was driven insane; and his wife became a constant neurasthenic invalid. Hamilton had his rendezvous with Burr on those same heights just after Independence Day in July 1804. Soon thereafter, Stevens left the United States for the last time and returned to live on Saint Croix.

Toussaint Louverture had been found dead by his jailers on April 27, 1803. We have no direct means of knowing what that event meant to either Hamilton or Stevens; Hamilton was too frenzied to give time to reflection on what might have been—in another man's life, in another country. His constitution for Toussaint had been ground under the boots of an invasion sanctioned by the President of the United States. The constitution of his own country, for which "no man in the United States has sacrificed . . . or done more," had been reduced by that same President, he wrote, to a "frail and worthless fabric."

And Stevens? In October 1801, the ineffable M. Pichon reported to his superiors in France that he had just had a conversation with the doctor, from which it was apparent that Stevens was still corresponding with Toussaint; he had expressed a candid admiration for Toussaint's boldness and magnanimity, which left Pichon gasping. The French minister was especially incredulous when Stevens told him of Toussaint's efforts to bring Whites back into the life of the island. "A masterpiece of hypocrisy," said Pichon.

I do not feel that Stevens regarded them so, nor should we. One day in 1987, in the library on Saint Croix, recalling that Stevens had access to the same facility (probably ampler then than now, for in his day the island was more prosperous), I began to consider the possibility that his ruminations might have been led, after some reading in the history of the Middle Ages, in this direction:

The extraordinary in history may not seem so baffling if we do not require it to be unique in all its aspects. Partial analogues can help. The multiracial regime of Toussaint Louverture, for example, stood magnificently isolated in its own time, but its aspirations were not utterly unprecedented. In the holiday season of the year 1130 after Christ, a benign spell seemed to have been cast upon another island, Sicily. People emerged from their huts and their castles, squinted into the sunlight, and began picking up the debris. On Christmas Day, a new king was crowned in Palermo Cathedral, Roger II, a Norman knight, born of an Italian mother, reared by Arab and Greek tutors. He was a man accustomed to warfare but disposed to peace. He made Arabic, Greek, and Latin his official languages. Arabs, Greeks, Normans, Lombards, and the descendants of Phoenicians and Carthaginians all had their places in the most tolerant state known in the Middle Ages. Arabic, Greek, and Latin inscriptions were placed in the mosaic of the Palatine Chapel, to remind the worshipers of the kinship of people of brown skin and fair, of blue eyes and dark. A Greek assumed the Saracenic title of emir of Palermo. Christian churches and monasteries flourished, while Muslims managed the finances of the island and manned the shock troops of the army.

The "kingdom in the sun" lasted scarcely a century; multiracial and tolerant governments do not easily survive the fierce antagonisms of any age.* *Homo homini lupus,* as one aspirant to the consulship to Saint-Domingue said in another context (see p. 417). The imperial ambitions of mainland powers brought the Norman experiment to an end.

Toussaint Louverture had only two or three years of relative peace. What he aspired to accomplish for his "kingdom in the sun" would have been as much a miracle as Roger II's feat.† His achievement was the more admirable for his having to accomplish it without the skillful bureaucracy and army inherited by Roger of Sicily.

In the face of the studied and ferocious opposition of France, Spain, and Britain, Toussaint had begun the reconstruction of Saint-Domingue, appointing experienced White officials to civil administration and suppressing racial violence. He had been willing to execute his own nephew for starting a pogrom against the Whites.

Swords and Pruning Hooks

Perhaps this analogy of Toussaint Louverture to Roger II may seem a little overdrawn. But there were those who did base their careers upon the assumption that Toussaint had brought a multiracial serenity to the island, and even to the island's islands, such as Tortuga, off the north coast. Thanks to Toussaint and to Edward Stevens, this almost uninhabited islet became another of the botanical-experiment stations of Hamilton's circle of physician-botanists: Stevens, William Thornton, and David Hosack.

An ambitious young scientist, Pierre-Jean-François Turpin, had joined the forces sent by the French government to Saint-Domingue in 1794. There he

---

*"Kingdom in the sun" is not Stevens's term (or mine) but a title chosen by Lord Norwich for his book about the Norman kingdom (New York, 1970).

†I might be criticized for this comparison, but let it stand: Toussaint, like all of us, is to be judged for what he steadfastly endeavored to achieve, not what fate allotted to him.

came under the tutelage of a botanist who introduced him to the lurid complexities of its tropical flora at about the time that Stevens was investigating those of Puerto Rico.

Turpin was ordered to return to France with his unit. He wished to escape a military career and had the immense good fortune to come to the attention of General Leclerc, who had a scientific side. Leclerc sent him back to the island with permission to devote himself to science.

Once again upon Saint-Domingue, Turpin had a second stroke of luck: he met Stevens, and possibly Toussaint. Stevens assigned Turpin to take the whole island of Tortuga as a field of study, to develop botanical gardens and experiment stations, presumably with the encouragement of Toussaint.

These activities continued until Leclerc came to the island himself, not in the role of the sponsor of research but as an agent of destruction. Turpin's little venture in horticulture on Tortuga was wrecked, along with so much else.* Probably with Stevens, Turpin went to the United States, where he met the renowned scientist Alexander Freiherr von Humboldt. It was yet another happy association; he returned with Humboldt to France.

Turpin's story is illustrative of a great lost opportunity, one that may have included more brief instances of multiracial science, agriculture, architecture, or economics. It is said by some that a few French architects and engineers remained in Saint-Domingue even after the fall of Toussaint and the reciprocal slaughters of the bloody decade that followed. No one has been able to identify the designers of Sans Souci, the great palace built by Henri Christophe, one of Toussaint's successors (the Haitian scholars at work on its restoration in 1986 told me that they believe Christophe had the benefit of the advice of Frenchmen).

But after a moment of golden dawn, the night returned. History has no tools to suggest how deep was that sudden night: no recital of great events, distant in time and place, can give a sense of such a calamity after so much hope. We can report the comings and goings of generals and governors and armies, but it is much harder to give a sense of the desolation left in their passage. Saint-Domingue was reduced to rubble. It was not Toussaint or his "brigands" but war, constant war—civil, racial, and imperial—war itself that desolated the fairest island in the Caribbean.

---

*I have been unable to determine what remnants may remain of Turpin and Stevens's gardens on Tortuga—perhaps about as many as there can be found on the mountaintop of Tortola, where exotic plants still remind the visitor of the horticultural researches of Dr. Thornton.

V

THE TRANSFER OF ART AND TECHNOLOGY

During the first five decades of its independent life, the United States was short of capital, incapable of financing the discoveries of those few Americans capable of research into chemistry or physics, and industrially primitive. This was a developing country.

In its infancy it was succored by the fortuitous arrival of gifts presented by the adversities of others. From the distress of France and Saint-Domingue it acquired both talent and technique to aid in its ascent toward industrial power. Several examples of the transfer of French technology to the United States will be shown in Part Five; others will appear when we come to the career of William Lee. Its weakness was obvious to both Britain and France; they responded as their imperial interests required. The British attempted to constrain their former colonists within the status of colonial—now neocolonial—suppliers of raw commodities, such as cotton and wheat. The French aided the American industrial system so that it might contend against British mercantile imperialism.

After 1793, however, the United States could no longer rely upon old friends like the marquis de Lafayette to promote trade and the transfer of technology across the Atlantic. Many were forced into exile, put to death or into prison. The Americans lost an active ally as France turned away from Atlantic matters

toward the conquest of Europe. Then, in 1802, Napoleon's dream of a Caribbean kingdom, to be supplied from a restored French empire in Louisiana,
briefly and disastrously distracted him from the European theater of war.

Yet, in the meanwhile, technical skills and capital accompanied to the United
States people dislodged by revolution from their orderly anticipations. As we
have seen, French "flight capital" was already active in America; now it
fertilized the growth of industry along the Hudson, the Brandywine, the
Patapsco, and the Schuylkill.

After Alexander Hamilton passed from the scene in 1804, the fiscal and the
industrial system he had nurtured came to depend upon the financial acumen
of two French-trained immigrants to the United States, Albert Gallatin and
Stephen Girard.

16

STEPHEN GIRARD

The Girards were a family of French origin but increasingly indeterminate
nationality who had grown rich in the West Indies trade. Jean, brother of
Stephen, was one of hundreds of eager young men from France who were
drawn to Le Cap and to Saint Eustatius, a Dutch free port. In the early 1780s,
these harbors received seven hundred and fifty vessels with twenty-four thousand sailors aboard.

Stephen Girard spent a lifetime avoiding attention; he has often been misun-
derstood and misdescribed. For example, he was, contrary to legend, neither an
orphan, a bachelor, nor a miser. He was emotionally and politically complex
and cannot be confined within the picture of a grasping, aesthetically inert
Scrooge often presented in survey courses or their literary equivalents.

He was a son of Bordeaux, which explains something: from that beautiful,
turbulent, and callous place the Girard family's maritime interests spread across
the Atlantic to the West Indies. He first went to sea in 1764, as a cabin boy
on a run to Port-au-Prince. It was to Port-au-Prince, again, that he went on
his first voyage as a licensed "officer of a ship," in 1774. Two years later, he
put into Philadelphia from another trip to Saint-Domingue, and stayed. He did
not lose touch with Bordeaux; the chief reason he did not become involved
in the revolt of the British colonies was that he felt himself still to be "a
Frenchman trading with the West Indies." He prospered in a triangular partnership with his father, in Bordeaux, and his brother, Jean, in Le Cap, on Saint-
Domingue. Girard remained neutral in his sentiments even after he entered a
partnership with an American, Isaac Hazlehurst, whose daughter Lydia was to
become the wife of Benjamin Henry Latrobe.

Stephen Girard by Bass Otis

It is a pity that that partnership had no architectural consequences, for Girard displayed an alert aesthetic sense as he gave employment to Saint-Dominguan refugees such as Jean-Baptiste Laurent and Charles Domballe, whom he set up as cabinetmakers after they remodeled his country house. Indeed, the elegant furniture they provided for both his houses impelled the infusion into Philadelphia of French "Directoire" taste.*

Girard purchased other handsome, though somewhat old-fashioned, furniture from Bordeaux, but he was not extravagant. Instead of commissioning Latrobe to design a new building to serve as his banking house, he picked up the slightly used Bank of the United States, designed in 1793 by Samuel Blodgett, probably with some help from one or another of the Irish draftsmen then working in Philadelphia. Architects do not enjoy losing commissions that way: in 1818, Latrobe bemoaned the fact that Girard "may, I presume, do as he pleases . . . What a change from the captain of a schooner for our father . . ." (This was in a letter to Hazlehurst's son, which accounts for the slight tipping of the scales: "our father" was Girard's partner, not his employer.)

The most famous instance of Girard's strict taste was his insistence upon a plain, bare, but fireproof building for the "college"—a school for orphan boys—he endowed. That insistence, in his will, resulted in a design by Thomas U. Walter as retrograde as anything L'Enfant might have produced or as the house Girard actually built on Water Street. But Nicholas Biddle, a rising

---

*As a result, that style had been popular for twenty years before the arrival of Joseph Bonaparte in 1816, with his purloined paintings and jewels.

banker full of a passionately Hellenophile spirit, used all his wiles on Walter and on Girard's executors to make Girard College into a temple compound. It remains today chief among the temples made customary by Biddle thereafter in those cities where ran his writ as president of the second Bank of the United States. (See *Architecture, Men, Women and Money*.)

Our interest here is not the endowing testator but in the living Girard, a man remarkable but not unique in the consistency of his operating principles. He represented a group of people, some literary and some mercantile, who adjusted serenely to the revolutionary changes of their time. They were capable of forming political alliances and doing business whether the other party was a slave or a king.

Girard and Toussaint

In 1797, Girard had shrewdly cast himself as a friend to Toussaint Louverture, asking a mutual friend named Thibeaux to intercede for him in the interest of

Stephen Girard's "retrograde" house on Water Street in Philadelphia

Girard College, 1833–34

a "very important . . . venture" he had in mind. Thibeaux wrote Toussaint that he had been working among "the good patriotic merchants" of the United States "to come to the aid of our brave defenders by sending them provisions." He described Girard as "a good French citizen, good patriot . . . merchant of Philadelphia, owner of one of the best commercial houses in the city and well able to come to the aid of San Domingo."

Specifically, Toussaint was asked to speed the return of Girard's brig *Sally* to its home port so "that it may continue to go to your relief." Thibeaux followed up by sending letters to General Pageot, commander of the French forces in the north of the island, telling him how rich Girard was and how excellent his credit; "moreover he is naturally disposed to help our brave defenders." Thereafter, Girard continued to do a sparkling business with Saint-Domingue (including, strange to say, large shipments of Windsor chairs).

It would be an error to dismiss Thibeaux's description of Girard's sentiments as pure puffery. Girard was a Jacobin. In 1793, he was told by a Saint-Dominguan correspondent that the enfranchisement of the Mulattoes was "bait" offered to induce the Blacks to return to their labor on the plantations, in "scandalous disregard of our [White] color." But Girard made no secret of his support of the decree of enfranchisement and increased his investments in vessels intended for the Saint-Dominguan trade.

For this, his brother, Jean, reproached him. "Oh, Revolution! How many reasons have I for cursing it." He warned that the revolution would spread to the United States—"nothing is impossible." The response was dry; speaking of possibilities, said Stephen, "for my part, I believe that if all these rascally aristocrats were in Guinea peace would have been restored long ago."

Jean persisted. "The creatures who are now governing," supported by troops "composed of the dregs and offal of France, sent here in order to punish us," were permitting the "impertinence of the class which I abhor." As for the officers of the revolutionary army, they belonged "to the infamous caste of incendiaries and assassins . . . I cry out for vengeance!"

Stephen answered in some irritation: "You ought to remember there has never been a revolution without unpleasant results. Let the mulattoes, the gossips, and politics alone and attend to the task of gathering up of the remains of your fortune." When France declared war on Britain, Jean, who had dallied, now considered "my fifty negroes I have in the mountains as lost. After such a reverse of fortune is it possible I can look favorably on the French Revolution?"

Stephen Girard was not impressed by his brother's preference for invective rather than action, but he was quick to offer succor to his friends who suffered from the revolution, in France or in Saint-Domingue. His correspondent in Marseilles was guillotined, and Girard aided his widow. He provided housing and money to Saint-Dominguan refugees, but refused to complain about the huge losses his own firm suffered when its warehouses were burnt during the pillage of Le Cap. "I am one of those . . . to whom the sacking of the city will be most disastrous, but we must be philosophical and try to recoup ourselves elsewhere."

After the election of Jefferson in 1800, provisions brought on Girard's ships continued to sustain the regime of Toussaint, not as an act of charity, of course, but undeterred by the policies of the administration. Girard was getting a little deaf, it was said—deaf to inhibitions upon trade, deaf to the preferences of his brother and to the outcries of the planter-refugees, and deaf to the racial fears of the President.

Other Entrepreneurs

Girard converted earnings from the West Indies trade into a banking empire and, later, proved that a private bank could be as potent in the defense of national solvency as the Treasury itself (see p. 262). Along the way, he provided financing to entrepreneurs who made use of French machines, French chemical research, French managers, French salesmen, and French capital.

He gave aid to smaller concerns as well: there was the Philadelphia bookshop of the jurist Moreau de Saint-Méry, friend of Talleyrand and civil governor of Paris just long enough to receive the keys to the Bastille. (Moreau received them from the militia, which had taken them from the royal commander of that fortress, and passed them on to Lafayette, who in turn presented them to George Washington.) And there were entrepreneurs on a larger scale: the Du Ponts, a "philosophal" father and two sons, one charming and the other practical, and their partner, Pierre Bauduy.*

When Pierre Bauduy arrived in Wilmington, Delaware, in 1791, it was a town of six hundred or seven hundred houses. It had a library, but its only large building was "the Work House . . . whose extent and white steeple [drew] . . . attention to it." After he departed, three decades later, it had a half-dozen fine neoclassical buildings, all probably of his design, including its town hall, a church, at least three residences, and a bank. Along the way he managed to play an essential role in the inception of America's largest textile and explosives complex. (When we come to Part Eight, we will learn how some of those explosives were used by another French father with two sons, who, like Stephen Girard, came from a maritime family of the southwest of France. Louis Lafitte was a native of Bayonne; he and his sons became pirates. They had this much in common with the Du Ponts: their partner was also an architect. His name was Bartholomy Lafon, a man of talents as diverse as those of Bauduy, Dr. Thornton, or Benjamin Henry Latrobe.)

17

PIERRE BAUDUY

Edward Stevens left us little to remember him by. Pierre Bauduy left us much. This is fortunate, for his memory is as beneficent as Stevens's in helping us give a more affirmative picture of French Creole contributions to American culture. The two of them were probably exceptions. Bauduy brought beauty into the world, reminding us not to generalize too glibly about the proprietors of slave and sugar plantations even on Saint-Domingue (where his career began) or on

---

*In our search for Pierre Pharoux, we were led to the agent of Leray de Chaumont, Dr. Baudry, and to the portfolio left by Pharoux with Baudry in 1793. We had no occasion then to worry about confusing Dr. Baudry with the M. Bauduy who has now joined our pilgrimage. They were involved simultaneously in neoclassical architecture and multinational commerce; they knew many of the same people; they were both amiable products of the not-very-amiable Creole culture. I have had some difficulty in keeping them straight.

Pierre Bauduy; self-portrait in middle-age

Cuba (where it ended). Perhaps the function of such an exception was to be a rebuke to their excesses. He was like Wade Hampton II, who demonstrated that among the upland cotton magnates of the Carolinas a man could live gently, humorously, and intelligently, in a fruitful and satisfying conversation with painters, writers, and architects (see *Architecture, Men, Women and Money*). Bauduy and Hampton were remarkably free of envy and rancor. They lived graceful and humane lives, and elevated, somewhat, the nasty lot among whom they found themselves.

During this period, guerrilla warfare between slaves and masters was endemic throughout the Caribbean. Planter families became accustomed to moving from one burned-out holding to another. Often, one or more members of the family would be missing after each successive move. Genealogies become confusing. The father-in-law of Pierre Bauduy, Jean Bretton des Chapelles, bore the same name as a contemporary who was killed by his slaves on his plantation in Louisiana. Probably they were cousins; families were constantly intermarrying and traveling between the Mississippi Valley and Saint-Domingue.

Governance of Louisiana and Saint-Domingue shifted back and forth between Spain and France; Whites engaged in constant battle with Blacks; the sugar-and-slave system was for its owners a lucrative life of self-imposed terror. The pursuit of wealth required a career of violence; yet planters wrote memoirs full of grievance against the "outrages" of those whom they ripped out of Africa to provide that wealth.

They were also capable of outrages of their own. In *Architecture, Men, Women and Money* I recounted the means by which Wade Hampton I restored order after a slave revolt in Louisiana, including ornamenting a mile of roadside with the heads of his defeated enemies. On Saint-Domingue, other restorers of order, perhaps recalling Napoleon's pledge that he would not leave an epaulet on the shoulders of a Black, captured Maurepas, a free Black of European culture who became one of Toussaint's generals. They forced him to watch as his wife and children were drowned, and then nailed his epaulets to his naked shoulders.

Yet, amid all this, some individuals distinguished themselves by kindness. Some were able to effect a transition in their own lives from a privileged youth within a culture corrupted by slavery into a new industrial world which had its own corruptions but was, at least, free of the incubus of economic exploitation justified by racial hatred and endorsed by law. After a crucial transfer of industrial technology from France to the United States, some of these planters became relatively benign industrial managers such as Pierre Bauduy.

Swanwyck

This entire volume commenced as the result of an expedition to try to find one of the buildings long attributed to Bauduy. I had asked friends among architectural historians whether there were any houses in America properly to be called "villas" in the Regency or Directoire or Gustavian style. By that I meant the sort of lovely stuccoed houses to be seen amid green lawns and duck ponds, graceful and unpretentious, clear in intention and unfussy in detail, in suburbs of small maritime trading towns from Sweden to Portugal. They are rare in America.

I was told that one villa like that had appeared in the report of the Architects' Emergency Committee during the 1930s and that though the photographs of the house were "discouraging," the sketches were more hopeful. It was listed as "Swanwick, A Regency House," and the location was Farnhurst, Delaware. The report, I found, was republished as a Dover reprint in 1970; though it did not attribute the house to any architect, and though the photographs were indeed discouraging, the sketches were wonderful. Farnhurst turned out to be a forgotten by-station between Wilmington and New Castle, and the house was ultimately discovered under its proper spelling, "Swanwyck."

It was well worth the search. Under the stains and the fungus and the chipped paint, behind the sagging porch-posts, there appeared to be exactly what I was looking for, the sort of house a merchant of modest means might build about 1800. More important for my purposes at the time, it might just as well have been built in the 1980s, if a client had the taste and an architect the talent.*

---

*I have yet to find a client or an architect to build something like Swanwyck, though Mary Mix Foley has subsequently called Swanwyck "perhaps the first modern house" (*The American House*, p. 128).

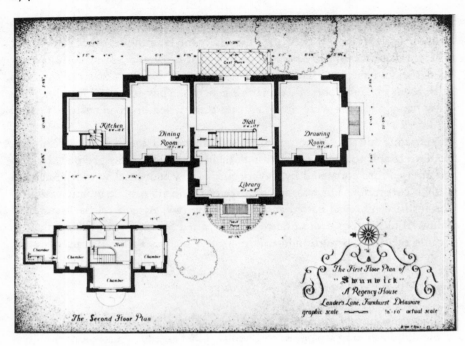

Floor plan and front elevation of Swanwyck Manor, as drawn
c. 1936 by the Architects' Emergency Committee

One can, if one wishes, draw distinctions between a Regency house and a French villa of the Directoire period, but such quibbles are as trivial as the differences in trading practices between merchants based in the French versus the English West Indies. A villa Swanwyck certainly is, even today—a travesty villa, a Blanche Du Bois of a villa, deprived of one of its playful little porticoes, which must have collapsed after the Architects' Committee gave it a dose of emergency photography. The dreary suburb surrounding it was built on landfill where waterbirds once sported.

According to family recollection, Swanwyck was a gift from Pierre Bauduy to his daughter, Cora, and her husband, Jean-Pierre Garesché, after they were married, on May 26, 1813. As a visitor came to call upon the newly married couple, it would first be glimpsed shining white through the foliage, amid its gardens upon the grassy point of land Bauduy had chosen. The evening sun might leave pockets of shadow in the panels recessed into its taut skin of plastered brick, and pick out the band of Grecian ornament stretched under the eaves.

This is a Regency house, not a Greek-revival temple; but there is an anticipation, a hieroglyph of a temple form in its barely discernable pilasters and the implied portico in its little five-arched, semicircular piazza. Under the diminutive saucer-dome of that piazza our imaginary visitor might pause for a last look across the western estuary to the far shore disappearing into the evening haze, then, entering the door to the library, find herself in a sunny room with tall French windows. Today, all that is left of what was once, almost certainly, a brilliantly colored interior are the plain black marble fireplaces. But it is easy to let fantasy recreate the tints of the rugs and hangings and paintings. Perhaps Cora Bauduy persuaded her father to provide landscapes or still lifes like those he tossed off for his friend Colonel Toussard at Fort Mifflin, not far upstream (see p. 186).

After several years of searching the records, I cannot state with certainty that Pierre Bauduy was the designer of his daughter's house. In fact, there are no certainties whatever with regard to his architectural career; the best that can be done is to give what evidence there is as we go along from one building to another that, from time to time, people have attributed to his skill. There appear to be no Bauduy architectural drawings or plans, not even an architectural contract between him and anyone else.

But the attributions are of long standing; and, perhaps more to the point as an explanation for why there are no better records, the reasons for erasing his authorship in some instances are obvious, and the means were at hand. There was ample motivation to deny him his due as one of the chief instruments whereby French and French Creole capital and technology were transferred to the United States. The means will become clear as we proceed.

No Saint-Dominguan left a more important physical legacy to the United

States than Pierre Bauduy. Furthermore, his skill in finance, his marketing ingenuity, and his network of useful friendships were essential to the founding and the successful growth of the Du Pont Company in its first two decades. He was also a respectable portraitist, a writer who could, when it suited him, be touching or funny or mordant, and a master of the art of discovering parallel interests among people who might seem to be incurably disharmonious.

This is his story, beginning with his antecedents on Saint-Domingue.

The Bitter and the Sweet

In 1697, Spain acknowledged in the Treaty of Ryswick that France was in effective occupation of the westerly portions of the island of Hispaniola. It was about that time that one Louis de Bauduy settled there. His origins, like those of the founders of many of the first families of Virginia, are obscure. But through the diligence of a number of family historians, chief among them Dorothy Garesché Holland, we know quite a lot about him and his progeny. By 1742, he owned fifty-three slaves. His quarrelsome son Pierre, born in 1703, acquired more as a result of shrewd business practice and litigation against his brother, Thomas. He also so alienated his wife and daughter, "both women . . . of great determination," that they attempted to escape to France, whereupon he secured *lettres de cachet* requiring the former to return to Saint-Domingue, "a place she detested," and the latter to be clapped into a convent.

Pierre "was . . . furious with the entire family." His wife was equally so, and with sufficiently demonstrable reason to secure a legal separation—no mean achievement in eighteenth-century France. Their son, Jean, proved to be as contentious as either of his parents. Though he lost his first lawsuit against them, he was shrewd enough to break the will by which his father subsequently disinherited him in favor of his sister, who had been released from her convent only to be poisoned by her husband.

By the time of the American Revolution, Jean Bauduy had become rich enough to designate himself Jean-Baptiste de Bauduy de Bellevue, after his largest plantation, which produced six hundred thousand pounds of sugar every year. But riches evidently produced no more tranquility for him than for his father. Jean-Baptiste was said to be a man of "the most . . . violent and imperious will" and sufficiently flagrant in his infidelities to be notorious even in a society where constancy would have been noteworthy. He was a militant reactionary "who made himself . . . obnoxious to the democratic whites by his fierce invectives against their leaders."

The family history characterizes him as "a spendthrift and prodigal" who hired superintendents by whom he was "constantly swindled . . . forever in debt

Swanwyck in 1927; it looks much the same today

and forever in trouble." As the revolution on Saint-Domingue exploded about him, he repaired to Bellevue, beat off one attack by a band of Blacks, and, with his nineteen-year-old younger son, Alexandre, prepared to make the place into a little fortress. "Desperate and weary of a life which he had shamefully misspent," according to his own description (in his will dated October 10, 1791), he drunkenly defied the "brigands," who, he said, would have taken his life "were it not for the firm and intrepid countenance which I and my friends have been able to maintain."

His other son, Pierre, was not numbered among those friends; nor were the parents of Pierre's wife, who had already emigrated to Philadelphia. Pierre was placing as much distance as possible between himself and his irascible and dissolute father. Jean-Baptiste, of course, saw it otherwise: during the first attack on the estate, he wrote in his will, "instead of flying to the aid of his father, he [Pierre] stayed peacefully in . . . town." Warming to the subject (and, one suspects, warmed to it by avaricious neighbors), he went on to charge his son with cowardice: "To avoid danger . . . he has hastened to leave for New England [Wilmington or Philadelphia, actually] leaving me at the mercy of the brigands." Next, Jean-Baptiste repeated the family curse. The weapon of money was used, again, to perform symbolic murder of the son: "Because of these lawful grounds and the cowardly neglect, I denounce the legitimate rights of . . . my eldest son."

In the place of Pierre, Jean-Baptiste substituted two of his companions. "I leave . . . Ferdinand, Baron de Mullenheim, my friend who did not desert me in time of danger, the sum of 40,000 livres . . . [and] to M. Nicolas Hilaire, who . . . has helped repulse my assassins, the sum of 30,000 livres." To a woman "in the colony where she resides at this time under the name of Madame ———" he left 10,000 livres, and the same amount to a White or Mulatto child who bore his name.

As a final gesture, he left an angry bequest. If, as we suspect he hoped, his legitimate children died without issue, all his sweat-and-blood-and-alcohol-stained plantations would go to "his Most Christian Majesty, Louis XVI, my sovereign and master, King of France, begging him in said case to accept my estate for himself and his to enjoy it." A besieged planter on Saint-Domingue, full of spite, was making a gift to an imprisoned king.

Within a few weeks, the "brigands" revisited Bellevue, surrounded the house, and taunted those inside to confront them. Jean-Baptiste was at dinner, perhaps with his friends Mullenheim and Hilaire. He lurched to his feet, gestured to his guests that he would deal with the "assassins," walked to the door, and was met by the volley of a firing squad.

Somehow, Alexandre escaped to Baltimore. He married, lived for a few years in Wilmington and Philadelphia, and then returned to Saint-Domingue "at the head of a troop of creole gentlemen," part of Leclerc's expedition. Among the few in that company to escape yellow fever and the armies of Toussaint and Dessalines, he survived as well the vengeful rage of Rochambeau, which settled, for reasons unknown to us, into a personal vendetta against Alexandre Bauduy. After Saint-Domingue, he joined Napoleon's disastrous occupation of Spain and survived again, to take a safe billet as governor of Corfu. Though he became an aide to Napoleon during the hundred days of Napoleon's rule between his return from Elba in 1815 and his final abdication, he was pardoned by the Bourbons and died in 1826 as Baron Alexandre de Bauduy, general and chevalier of the Legion of Honor.

The life of his brother, Pierre, was more complicated.

Pierre Bauduy, sometimes called "de Bauduy" and often, by his wife and others, "Bellevue," was born in France in 1769, during the period of his mother's attempt to diminish her exposure both to her husband and to Saint-Domingue. Pierre likewise avoided the island as long as he could. Though he entered the army at seventeen, his education was broader than we might expect:

Pierre Bauduy in his youth; probably a self-portrait

the painting on the cover of this book is believed to be that rarest of art forms—an equestrian self-portrait. It depicts Pierre Bauduy as a lieutenant of the Chasseurs of Picardy.

After the fall of the Bastille in 1789, Bauduy resigned his commission, and in 1790 he married Juliette Bretton des Chapelles. His father insisted that they come to Saint-Domingue, where for a year they tried to live "peacefully" in Port-au-Prince. On September 27, 1791, however, two weeks before his father rewrote his will, Pierre Bauduy and his wife set sail for the United States on one of Stephen Girard's ships.

Getting Settled

Family memoirs written later in the nineteenth century propound an illusory background that would, if true, have made the accomplishments of Bauduy less remarkable. He was not "descended from a noble old French family and accustomed to all the luxuries that rank and wealth could give." He was the son of a nouveau-riche planter. Like many people of portable and adequate means, he escaped Saint-Domingue, but he had special reason to emigrate: a cursed family.

Family memoirists assert that "the horrors of the Revolution came upon him as a thunder-clap and stripped him of all he possessed." The revolution, as we have noted, was scarcely a surprise; like many other émigrés of the 1790s, Bauduy came with sufficient capital to set himself up, not in his father's slave-provided opulence, yet comfortably. Once in America, he and most of his peers plied the bourgeois pursuits they had traditionally plied.

Bauduy landed at Philadelphia and went on to Wilmington, a smaller place offering a better opportunity to make an artistic mark, and found a house on Market Street, at the Sixth Street corner. His father-in-law, M. Bretton des Chapelles, and Mme Bauduy's sisters were installed in a "mansion near the Delaware River."

The next acquisition was a workshop that some family recollections say was a coach works purchased from Robert Morris. Bauduy was not impoverished, but he had to work, and there was a market for elegant signs "for shops and inns" and for miniatures. There is a tale recounted in family and local histories that one of his signs (extant until recently) hung outside either a coach shop or a tavern, and depicted Phaëthon driving the chariot of the sun. It was so affecting that when George Washington passed by, his magisterial eye was drawn to it. Upon being told who was its author, he is reputed to have said, "Ah, those French, they are never too proud to work!"

Certainly Pierre was not. That sign may have hung over his own workshop

Juliette Bauduy by Pierre Bauduy

"Phaeton" coach sign by Pierre Bauduy

and buildings on Market and Hanover streets. He listed himself as "Pierre Bauduy, gentleman coachmaker."

Elizabeth Montgomery, a Wilmington historian of the nineteenth century, quoted an unnamed source as recalling that Pierre Bauduy was "an enterprising man of affable manners possessing great taste in fine arts . . . a useful citizen and kind neighbor." "Mrs. B.," said Montgomery, "was a handsome and accomplished lady." One of Bauduy's surviving paintings, his official version of his wife, depicts her startled at her washbasin. Neither he nor she was pompous.

In 1794, Jean Garesché, another emigrant from Saint-Domingue, arrived and settled into Wilmington in grander style, with a retinue of slaves.* The

*Sustained by sugar revenues from the portion of the island then under British control and remitted through the apothegmatic Philadelphia banker Thomas Willing (see p. 94), Garesché was later to support Bauduy during a decline in the fortunes of the powder and textile businesses, a merger of interest confirmed when two of his grandsons married Bauduy's daughters. Garesché's grandsons had other connections to our story beyond Swanwyck and the Bauduy daughters. They

Gareschés were a typical family of Protestant maritime bourgeois, like the de La Trobes, progenitors of Benjamin Henry Latrobe. They too had fled France after the revocation of the Edict of Nantes in 1685 and had found a new living among other exiles in Dublin and in Cork; from there Garesché branches spread out to the Low Countries, according to family tradition. Other members of the family returned to France, practicing their religion with discretion, and prospered in the Saint-Domingue trade. They acquired plantations on the island, but the head of the family, a slave trader and merchant, remained in La Rochelle, where he became mayor in 1791. A brother of the mayor was a deputy to the Estates General, took the "tennis court oath," and served into the early years of the revolution, but wisely withdrew into the provinces in 1792. He reappeared in November 1792 to stand beside Garnier de Saintes as president of the Council of La Rochelle (see pp. 344–5).

Jean Garesché, who came to Wilmington from Saint-Domingue, was the third of these brothers. It seems probable that he gave Bauduy one of his earliest architectural commissions, recorded in a signature, "P. Bauduy," as legal witness to the purchase of two small houses, on two and a half acres on Kent and French streets, combined to form a more commodious establishment. Behind them an elaborate garden was laid out, bordered by poplar trees, extending to the next square. "Fruit trees were interspersed throughout the square, and fanciful walks" led to an octagonal brick building with a gazebo on its top "encircled by a balcony, with seats and stands for flower-pots."

A Church and City Hall

Pierre Bauduy was versatile. The baptismal records of the Roman Catholic congregation at Wilmington show another, similar signature, for "Rev. P. Bauduy," as the officiant at a baptism in 1797. Except in the case of an infant about to die, such duties were then performed by Father Cibot, a friend who had been superior general of a mission in Saint-Domingue, or by Reverend Patrick Kenney.

Kenney, who arrived in the Delaware Valley sometime after 1800, left a diary for the years from 1811 to 1828 reporting Bauduy as a frequent host. This is useful information, for Kenney was by that time the lone and overworked Roman Catholic clergyman in a Protestant community. Bauduy was a donor to his first church building, Saint Peter's, at Sixth and West streets, when the congregation finally assembled the resources to begin construction in 1816.

---

were educated by Abbé Carles, who served a term in the Asylum Colony. One of them, Vital Garesché, became a shareholder in the Vine and Olive Colony at Demopolis, Alabama (see Part Eight).

Wilmington Town Hall

He may also have been its architect. Kenney's diary has lamentable lacunae in this period, but it does report meetings at Bauduy's house. In 1887, a Bauduy family historian recorded that the church "was dedicated under the invocation of Saint Peter, his [Bauduy's] own patron Saint, in compliment to himself." Another, somewhat later, states that it was "built . . . largely through M. Bauduy de Bellevue's efforts; he was the architect."

Saint Peter's became Wilmington's cathedral, and survives, though it was completely remodeled in 1916. Old photographs show a brick structure with a dark, Gothic-survival interior.

Bauduy's fingerprints are a little easier to read on the Wilmington Town Hall opposite the site of his house, at Sixth and Market streets. Here we have not only family recollections and correspondence, including an equivocal letter of 1800, but also an unequivocal attribution in a "History of Wilmington" compiled by the newspaper *Every Evening* in 1894: "The architect, Pierre Bauduy, seems to have attempted an improvement on the architecture of the Philadelphia State House. He succeeded; he raised its floor much higher . . . and thus made it a more imposing edifice. He also impressed his idea of architecture upon the town." The chief means for impressing that idea was by laying across the red brick of the front façade a belt of white stone bearing larger medallions, or blocks. Another of these stone necklaces, which became one of his trademarks, can be seen on the building he (probably) designed for the Delaware National Bank.

Bauduy's ideas were not fully developed in the city hall design of 1798.* While he was prepared to improve on the forms he found in Philadelphia or in a dozen other towns along the coast, he was not ready, as yet, to "impress" anything genuinely expressive of the French taste of his own time. The cosmopolitan—and the painter—in him were still subordinated to the new and dutiful citizen of a young country only uneasily edging toward its own architecture, away from the brick piles characterized by Pierre Pharoux and Thomas Jefferson as remnants of its colonial past.

Eden Park

It is apparent that the effort of Bauduy's father to will his plantations to his titled drinking companions and to the Bourbon monarchy were not upheld by the revolutionary courts of France or by the government of Toussaint. In 1801, Bauduy made his last return trip to Saint-Domingue, selling property to release capital from family plantations there to investments in powder, land, wool; to remodel and enlarge a twenty-nine-room brick house outside Wilmington called Monckton Park;† and to free himself, finally, from his temporary expedients as a coach maker. Symmetrically, he freed his remaining slaves in the United States.

We can tell from a surviving watercolor that the house was a large brick cube sporting a small portico and cupola. Bauduy substituted Eden Park as his name for the pedestrian, British, Monckton Park; straightaway he began to turn

---

*Though willing to give it appropriate shape, Bauduy does not seem to have been too abashed by civic propriety. At Christmastime two years after the city hall was completed, he and some friends applied to the sober-sided city fathers to permit a party in an inner, ceremonial room he had designed. They were refused, but "Pierre Bauduy and his associates procured a . . . key and opened the large room and by violence forced the door and held their entertainment." (Perhaps he merely used a key he had retained from the construction period.) Ladies, it seems, were present, for a fan, said to have been carried at this "unauthorised ball" by his daughter, Juliette, now reposes at the Historical Society of Delaware. Some accounts of the break-in state the date as Christmas 1800, but it must have been the following year, since his wife's meticulous chronology, annexed to the memoirs of Mimi Garesché, states that Pierre was in South America over Christmas 1800, returning the following June. (See Holland, p. 34.)

†The property had been owned by a Foxite Whig named George Haines, who during the years of the American Revolution divided his time between his primary business in Philadelphia and the West Indies. On Haines's return to England in 1791, he sold the property to Robert Morris, who may have been acting as agent for Louis Philippe de Ségur, another of Lafayette's tribe of relatives, who sold it in turn to Pierre Bauduy.

the grounds into a garden and expanded the estate from 180 acres to 330.*
Though he had it ditched and drained, the ground was still so soggy as to defeat
one of his better ideas, the employment of Basque shepherds on stilts to watch
after his sheep (see p. 209).

18

THE BASIS
OF ECONOMICS

*A knowledge of order and of natural and physical laws should
serve as the basis of economics.*
PIERRE S. DU PONT DE NEMOURS

During the "quasi-war" against France, in 1797 and 1798, a frenzy of fear of
Jacobinism swept across the United States. Its most familiar consequences
were the Alien and Sedition Acts, intended to quiet radicalizing and to send
packing those feared to be French agents. These laws were not directed only
at the French, however; they had economic purposes as well: to diminish
competition from Irish refugees from the risings of 1798 as well as from
skilled Frenchmen. Some state legislatures were prepared to go even further
and to deport—or at least to deny employment to—French engineers and
technicians.

Had these exclusionary devices succeeded, the nation would have been denied
necessary new skills, and the advance of the American nation into the industrial
age would have been slowed. Aaron Burr, always the sardonic voice of reason
in such matters, arose during a debate in the New York legislature on a proposal
to exclude from state offices all foreign-born military officers to suggest, by a
solemn listing, that if it was Jacobin riffraff the Federalists feared, they might
better turn their apprehensions in the directions of a monarchist coup: the
government of the United States had entrusted nearly all its fortresses to the
design and command of French royalist officers.

Burr's irony was persuasive to his fellow legislators and has been of equal
interest to architectural historians. It was based upon a current inventory of the

---

*The impulse to ennoble a residence classically also led Joel Barlow, a classical scholar, to call
his country estate Kalorama, rather than, shall we say, Belle View or even Bellevue. I have been unable
to reconstruct Bauduy's garden plan. Here he may well have reciprocated with Irenée Du Pont, the
botanist, whom he had assisted with architecture. I like to think the garden was romantic, like those
of Joseph-Jacques Ramée or Pierre Pharoux, rather than as severe as those of Claude-Joseph Sauthier
(see Appendix I).

Eden Park as remodeled by Pierre Bauduy (artist unknown)

Frenchmen who were capable of assisting the developing United States with talent trained in the finest schools of military engineering in the world. Those present in 1798 stood in the great tradition of L'Enfant and Pharoux and did not even include, since they were not in command of fortresses, Marc Isambard Brunel, the brothers Mangin, and Stephen Hallet.

Among the officers given as examples by Burr were the commander of West Point, Chevalier de Rochefontaine, and the commander of the approaches to Philadelphia, Colonel Anne-Louis de Toussard (sometimes spelled Tousard), late of the staff of General Lafayette. Toussard's headquarters were at Fort Mifflin, just below Philadelphia, which had been erected by L'Enfant upon the ruins of an earlier fort, where in 1777 another character important to us, General Samuel Smith, became a national hero (see p. 273ff.).

A few years later, Burr might have put in argument another reason for valuing Toussard's presence: his role in the development of American military technology. This is the point, however, for us to note his contribution to the advancement of the artistic talents of Pierre Bauduy. Toussard found his commandant's "house damp . . . and so had canvass stretched on frames and set onto the walls. Many of the guests, notably M. Bauduy . . . after dinner, when the wine warmed them generously perhaps . . . would amuse themselves by painting figures, still lifes, or landscapes on these conveniently canvassed walls; and so these walls became a gallery of . . . art."

The site of Fort Mifflin was commonly called Mud Island, suggesting why the walls of its commandant's house were likely to be damp. The building given murals by Bauduy was almost certainly that house. (There is a strong possibility that the building, like the fort, was designed by L'Enfant. It stands today somewhat damaged by a recent fire but still a fine neoclassical design. But where are the murals?)

Historians of law think of Toussard primarily in association with Andrew Jackson's test of the rights of neutrals;* historians of technology know him as an early investigator of interchangeable parts, produced in quantity. He appears here because it was he who (according to a story repeated so often that it has by now become a part of folk wisdom, despite a lack of contemporary documentation) took a friend hunting with such poor powder that the friend, a chemist and botanist named Irenée Du Pont, concluded that there was a fine market for better stuff than that which had spoiled their sport.†

The Du Ponts advance into this tale at this point, led by the patriarch of the clan, as is his due.

High Finance

Solitary composition has no witnesses. A pity. We have to rely upon our imagination to find Thomas Jefferson writing Maria Cosway under the laminated dome at Monticello, in remembrance of a sunny day at the Grain Market (see p. 445). We must supply our own images of Pierre Samuel Du Pont de Nemours as he wrote his *Philosophy of the Universe* in the observatory of Mazarin College in Paris. Searching the stars for laws of order in the heavens, he hid from the Terror as the tumbrils rolled and the crowd outside cried for blood.

One wonders what Du Pont might have done had he turned his adaptable energies toward architecture, what forms of order he might have conceived. As it was, he and his sons were fortunate in discovering Pierre Bauduy as an

---

*In 1814, Toussard was French consul in New Orleans and was arrested by Andrew Jackson during Old Hickory's erratic tenure as military governor of that city, causing one of Jackson's characteristic series of judicial embarrassments. (See Nolte, pp. 221–23.)

†Benjamin Henry Latrobe cited Toussard as late as 1813 as a victim of the continuing prejudice against French military engineers and, in that period, wrote him a peculiar letter from which we can deduce that the colonel was plotting some sort of chicanery involving the bribing of foreign officials—probably Spanish—for trade advantages, presumably like those John Craig had received during the Silver Scheme (see p. 254; for Latrobe's views, see Talbot Hamlin, *Latrobe*, p. 386).

Pierre Samuel Du Pont de Nemours
(artist unknown)

architect who could provide such shapes for their houses. Bauduy had some additional advantages: he could also find the land for these houses; he could locate plant sites and equity capital, secure credit, and provide sales management for them.

Pierre Du Pont was a member of the upper tier of the French bourgeois class. Born in Paris in 1739, he was that noblest of creatures, a popularizer, translating unappetizing economic theories into pamphlets and articles digestible by a large public. In his early thirties, he went off to Poland to assist the high-minded but doomed regime of King Stanislas in schemes for public education. Those plans—like Poland itself—were sliced to pieces by Prussia, Austria, and Russia, and Du Pont went home to France to try for economic reform. Once again the natural order failed to reproduce itself upon earth; Du Pont turned to translating Ariosto, to economic theory, and to meditations on his Polish experience that became very useful to the educational reforms of Joseph Lakanal (see p. 378).

Du Pont was recalled from bucolic retirement to represent the French in negotiations for the independence of the United States. He then became a minister of state for commerce in the last days of the Bourbon regime; and as a constitutional monarchist he represented Nemours, the location of his farm, in the revolutionary assemblies. He adjusted his name to accord with this dignity: earlier, he had severed "Du" from "pont"; now he added "de Nemours." (His corporate descendants re-elided "Dupont"; in referring to the family, we will defer to their usages whenever those usages were consistent.)

His moderate views attracted the ire of Robespierre, however, and he hastily retired, first to the observatory and then to the countryside. He was discovered, captured, and imprisoned; the fall of Robespierre occurred just in time to save him from the guillotine. He clung to his royalist views, though; and in 1799, after his house was sacked by a mob, he concluded that it was best to seek refuge in America; he settled at Point Breeze, on the northern coast of New Jersey.

Though, before departing, he wisely warned the members of the French Directorate of their folly in promoting Napoleon, he was bold enough to return to Napoleonic France in 1802. There he was available to Thomas Jefferson to convey the messages to Napoleon that ultimately led to the Louisiana Purchase.

While his two sons remained in America (and were no longer "de Nemours") to find opportunities for a holding company of French investors formed at this point, the senior Du Pont lived a quiet, literary life in France until the first Bourbon restoration. In 1814, he thought it safe to reappear on the great stage as secretary of the provisional government, then as Councilor to King Louis XVIII. He was a little premature. Napoleon's emergence from Elba in 1815 was the final disappointment. Du Pont de Nemours embarked again for the United States. He died two years later, in a house near Wilmington designed by Pierre Bauduy.

The Sons

The two sons of Pierre Du Pont de Nemours were of complementary temperament and demeanor. One was the expansive, charming Victor, who had been in the French consular service in the 1790s and had reconnoitered the United States for the family. He often served as the family's ambassador to the outside world, but he was not a good man for business. His brother was the suspicious, inhibited, crafty chemist, botanist, and engineer, Eleuthère Irénée (E. I.) Du Pont (called Irénée). In another time Irénée might have followed his training under Lavoisier to become a research chemist; in the ebullient atmosphere of developing America, his genius for business made him an entrepreneur.

The first American venture of the Du Ponts' holding company, a land development scheme, could not bear the combined burdens of selecting a site and appeasing the old physiocrat's ideals; it failed. Victor was then sent to New York to set up a merchant bank. But the banking business never flowered; nor was Victor lucky in a subsequent trading venture.

Relying upon the friendship between his father and President Jefferson, recently elected, and upon Jefferson's desire that France extinguish the regime of Toussaint Louverture, Victor Du Pont returned from a trip to Paris in 1802 with his pockets full of orders from Talleyrand to supply provisions for the forthcoming expedition of Leclerc. He promptly entered into the first, and worst, of a series of Du Pont–Bauduy partnerships, with Alexandre Bauduy, not Pierre. Alexandre, inheritor of his father's bellicose nature, was spoiling to return to the wars on Saint-Domingue and on friendly terms with Leclerc. He

Eleuthère Irénée Du Pont (artist unknown)

was evidently used as an intermediary: "If . . . Leclerc will arrange with me to take $100,000 . . . payable in drafts—which Bauduy thinks he certainly will—I will give Livingston* 50,000 for his share . . . and I will pocket the remaining 25,000. This is the sort of safe investment that poor dear Papa loves."

Papa was soon poorer, however; for the government of Napoleon failed to honor Leclerc's drafts, and Victor Du Pont's fortune began its decline into a cheerful bankruptcy.†

Meanwhile, another Bauduy–Du Pont scheme had been hatched, probably in the summer of 1801. Whether or not we believe the story of the frustrated hunting expedition with Colonel Toussard, the two Du Pont brothers had seen fit, during the preceding year, to return to France to persuade their investors to permit them to accumulate the necessary machinery to begin a powder-making business. They obtained $36,000 and returned to seek the right place to install their manufactory.

Thomas Jefferson extolled the virtues of the Potomac Valley, but Irénée found "the country, the people, the location . . . worthless." On September 19, 1801, he concluded instead that he would return to his new friends Bauduy and Toussard "at Wilmington to see the Brandywine."

---

*Probably Chancellor Robert R. Livingston, minister of the United States to France. Here is the link between a Bauduy–Du Pont–Livingston partnership and the Leray-Livingston partnership.

†In 1805, Victor's creditors were led by Hamilton's brother-in-law John Barker Church. As we will see, the Paris "holding company" followed the New York trading company into the abyss at a crucial moment.

The visit went well. Bauduy wrote Irénée that he was "very eager that you should settle in our neighborhood." The response was cautious. Americans were not only using state legislation and the Alien and Sedition Acts to diminish the competition of French engineers and the agitation of French Jacobins, they were also making it very difficult for foreigners to own real estate. The Du Ponts engaged the services of Alexander Hamilton (at Talleyrand's suggestion?) to seek a special act from the Delaware legislature, like those of modern developing countries, favoring immigrants who brought with them desirable technical secrets. Hamilton was not successful; so Pierre Bauduy as a citizen became even more important to the Du Ponts' plans: he would begin by acquiring the real estate, and then, perhaps, he might help avoid future complications. In response to Irénée's request, he set about "to arrange your naturalization."

Naturalization was a business necessity, not an act of sentiment. These canny émigrés did not manifest a passionate desire to Americanize. Paris, where the partnership agreement was signed, was still "headquarters," and they probably thought of their venture as they might one on Saint-Domingue or Martinique. It was an "off-shore investment."* All the correspondence from which I have been quoting was carried on in French; so was most of the firm's business throughout this generation. And it was expected that the capital invested would return to Europe; when this occurred too slowly to suit them, even Pierre Du Pont's daughter was prepared to sue to force more rapid repatriation (see p. 216).

Irénée, based in New Jersey, would budge only if inducements were offered, though he acknowledged to Bauduy that Wilmington offered "the ease of making shipments and the pleasure of being near you and your family." That pleasure was increased by the knowledge that in 1801 Bauduy had succeeded in extricating considerable sums from Saint-Domingue. It was becoming apparent that the capital secured in France would not be sufficient to launch the powder works, and, besides, "dear Papa" did indeed like his investments to be as "safe" as possible.

The caution of the senior Du Pont was understandable. The device of a limited-liability corporation was not yet available to shelter entrepreneurs. Instead, most business was done through partnerships with each partner personally liable for all losses. This is why so many of the characters in this book went through bankruptcy court. And powder works, with their propensity for explosion, were riskier than some other undertakings. Thus, not only did Pierre Du Pont de Nemours ration his resources, putting only half of what he had in America in the Brandywine adventure (much of the rest went to the unfortunate Victor); he also was on the lookout for a further hedge. The Du

---

*The Bauduys were, it is true, beginning to feel themselves as American as French, but only from force of circumstance. As Pierre put it, quoting a French proverb: "Where a goat is tethered, there he will feed."

Ponts needed "an American capitalist . . . whose credit was essential, not only for the money his shares represent, but for his influence then and now with the banks." They needed Pierre Bauduy.

There were two banks immediately germane to their purposes: that of Bauduy's friend Stephen Girard and the Bank of Delaware, the first financial organization in the state and the first anywhere to enter into a full-scale correspondent relationship with Girard. Bauduy had been one of its founders, in 1795, and was a director. Irénée worried that Bauduy might slip away to Saint-Domingue; Toussaint was inviting some planters of genial reputation to return. Irénée hoped that such a radical notion would not "interfere with your idea of interesting yourself in our business—an idea that will always be agreeable to me."

In January 1802 Irénée wrote again, probing further: what were Bauduy's plans? Pierre replied that he and his family were settled in Wilmington and that he did not like the look of things in "the colonies," by which he meant Saint-Domingue and the other sugar islands; he would continue to "sell my property in them . . . whenever I can."

Left to their own devices, the two sons of the philosopher moved in concert to envelop Bauduy. Irénée signed letters, "I salute you and embrace you with all my heart." On December 12 Pierre replied: "If you settle in this neighborhood I shall be glad of a share in your enterprise . . . Believe in my sincere friendship." Four days later, with "esteem and . . . friendship which I promise you for life," Bauduy sent a prudential note about the purchase of the potential mill site: "I suggest your buying . . . in my name. If our man [the seller] knew your plans . . . he might ask much more. These gentlemen do not always keep their word."

In April 1802, a parcel along the Brandywine River that has become perhaps the most celebrated in American industrial history was purchased in the name of William Hamon, a brother-in-law of Pierre Bauduy and a naturalized American citizen.

Then for some months the skein unraveled. Bauduy was still distracted by the notion that he might spend part of every year in Saint-Domingue, a possibility that finally flickered out only two years later, when Dessalines massacred nearly all the remaining Whites on the island. Victor was busy with his schemes to supply Leclerc; Pierre Du Pont was back in France. That left Irénée to move to Delaware and negotiate with Bauduy.

In August, Victor wrote Irénée: "Above all, decide on something with Pierre. It seems to me . . . his last proposition is perfectly reasonable . . . As a shareholder I . . . tell you that when manufacture begins, the acquaintances and credit of Bauduy could not be too highly paid . . . Pierre's presence in San Domingo would just now be of great service to me . . . but I yield his services to you . . . You have a bad habit of wishing to do too well."

Victor Du Pont (artist unknown)

Irénée complained to his father that Victor had provided him with only $6,000 from family funds; he had been forced to turn to a friend of Bauduy's for credit "in purchasing materials." Bauduy himself had offered $8,000 "and his assistance in the construction of the mills, but I think he asks too large a share in the profits." Irénée was thus inclined to refuse his offer, "though his great energy, his loyalty and his reputation in this neighborhood would have been very helpful." Victor wrote him that Bauduy's support was essential.

It is probable that at this point the tender bud of the whole Du Pont chemical empire might have perished of a chill emanating from the heart of Irénée. Only Victor's warmth, arising from embarrassment for cash, sustained the potentiality of the family's enormous future fortune. Keep Bauduy in, he implored Irénée; and could Irénée ask Pierre for a loan of $2,000 "for three weeks or so?"

Despite his growing aversion to Pierre, Irénée "could" and did—and more besides. He and Victor drew up a partnership agreement in which Bauduy agreed to assume personal liability for all obligations required to provide funds for the powder works. Dated August 25, 1802, it is one of the primary documents in the history of the American economy.

Before their agreement was signed, the Du Ponts extricated another contribution from Bauduy. Instead of the $24,000 they were expected to invest, they put in only $16,470.90. Bauduy took up the slack, committing his $8,000 in equity and guaranteeing an additional $18,000 in long-term debt on top of his readiness to arrange short-term credit with the bank of which he was a director.*

Victor continued to caution Irénée against "wishing to do too well" at Bauduy's expense. Shortly after the first powder was actually manufactured, in May 1804, he reported that "Bauduy is nervous . . . you must remember his devotion and good nature. . . . [T]he work on the farm† annoys him . . . He receives none of the produce . . . done by the men of the manufacture, who might otherwise be employed at labor by which he might profit." Bauduy, said Victor, hesitated to speak of it; "he thinks you are oversensitive and does not want to vex you . . . but try to avoid sending the powder men to work on the farm."

Somewhat later, Irénée asked Victor not to "blame too severely the coldness and sensitiveness of my nature" and complained that Bauduy had been so bold as to suggest to outsiders that he was a partner. Irénée, it appears, had remonstrated. To this, Bauduy exclaimed: "I am responsible for all the money this business should owe and I am not a partner!" Victor, at wit's end, admonished Irénée: "You are wrong . . . in trying to avoid the admission that Bauduy was a partner and not an employee." Treading lightly, he went on: "This was not from injustice on your part nor . . . concealment, but the result of your education and your French prejudice." The embattled older brother, on the brink of financial disaster, came close to losing his temper: "Can two rational men for such a trifle risk the existence of an establishment that should make their reputations and even their fortunes?"

These two did. They were ill suited for a marriage of convenience.

Pierre Bauduy's ebullient nature opened him to the opinions of the world; he was very conscious of how he was seen. He felt that "it is always a good thing to have friends and a big family. Unhappy the man who shuns society." Such a man can be expected to exert himself to keep society from shunning him and to maintain his honor before the world.

Irénée, crabbed and cold, inhabited an emotional environment tight and fearfully constricted. To such a man, any effort by Bauduy to inflate his apparent role in the firm in the opinion of the world would seem an indignity; Bauduy was by his very nature a threat—he was too large, too robust, too hearty.‡ Irénée Du Pont was not alone among men of his class and training in feeling their model of a good businessman scandalized by Bauduy's propen-

---

*Colonel Toussard, it may be noted, was allocated three shares as a promotional fee—and, quite possibly, to use to induce government officials to provide powder contracts. Some years later, Du Pont père told his shareholders that these shares "had been held in reserve . . . to be given to certain persons who had much influence . . . a kind of influence that was unnecessary with the upright Jefferson" (B. G. Dupont, vol 8, pp. 45 ff.).

†Apparently Irénée was using men from the plant to work on his farm.

‡It is possible that these disputes had as much to do with the principals working their way toward

sity to distract himself with the arts. Architecture was useful enough; one needs a house. A garden is the avocation of a gentleman, especially one trained in France. But painting! One of Bauduy's drier cousins, Pierre Provenchère, wrote other members of the family that, instead of selling gunpowder, "the new consciousness of painting in which he finds he has talent occupies him completely."*

Bauduy was a threat in other ways. Once he had been necessary, because of his associations with the banks; but now Irénée complained to his father: "It is in his power at any time to refuse me the use of his signature at the bank of which he is a director—which could ruin me but would be easy for him, as is customary among Americans . . . he is much better known than I am and has all kinds of advantages."

Soon after the news of Victor Du Pont's bankruptcy reached Wilmington, there was a meeting of the board of the bank. One can imagine the feelings of Irénée when after a day or two he received this note from Bauduy: "I saw at our meeting that our directors were uneasy and that the subject was avoided from courtesy." The president of the bank had urged him to write the creditors of the Du Pont–Bauduy partnership in Philadelphia that "we had nothing in common with the New York house . . . they fear we are partners."

This touch of peevishness was directed at Irénée, not at Victor. To the latter, Pierre wrote courteously about his difficulties, urging him to bring his family to stay at Eden Park in "warmth and friendship." Victor replied with thanks— and with more soothing words about Irénée: "Do not be angry with him, you know he is naturally uncommunicative . . . I cannot urge you too strongly, my friend, to do justice to Irénée's goodness of heart; to persuade yourself he has no hatred toward you, and to attribute only to the natural melancholy of his nature all that you can find cold in his manner . . . Remember, too[,] that a house divided must fall."

19

ARCHITECTURAL MATTERS

It would be irksome to follow every ebb and flow of this embattled relationship, as irksome as it must have been for the directors of the Bank of Delaware

---

the forms of corporate or partnership organization as with differences of character. But my own experience among venture capitalists suggests that the former process is often a proxy for, or a formalized ritual expressing, the latter.

*Provenchère approved of artistic interests if they were profitable. Alexandre, the soldier in the family, was blamed only when he guessed wrong; "he buys at the sales pictures which he counts on

to respond to the financial requirements of each fluctuation of the relationship among these volatile Frenchmen. The directors met in a neoclassical room in a neoclassical building, all very serene and tidy. We can get some relief from the unhappy chronicle of a collapsing partnership if we follow them into that space, a progression made easier because we possess an old engraving of the bank and of the directors' room.

After a decade, however, there was a trend in those fluctuations, and some of those board members began to adjust their positions as it became clearer that the Du Ponts would emerge as the winners. Bauduy was their fellow director, and his credit had made possible the entire enterprise; but there was no use in being sentimental. From 1812 onward he was clearly losing the struggle; and after his departure from the scene a decade later, no one contested with the Du Ponts in their dominance of the city and, indeed, the entire trading territory of the bank.

Yet there is an untidiness under these smooth surfaces: some records are missing. Though, as we suggested earlier, there is nothing neat about the records of any phase of the architectural career of Pierre Bauduy, one might have expected that a commission to construct a headquarters for the Bank of Delaware would provide an exception. Bankers tend to be careful about such things; only when there is a reason to destroy documents do they tend to act against the impulses of a retentive psychological type. There must have been such a reason, for once again Bauduy's reputation rests only on folk memory and newspaper clippings.

Soon after the building was completed, in 1816, the design of the Bank of Delaware was attributed to him, but a careful search of the bank's surviving records by Barbara Benson and Constance Cooper of the Historical Society of Delaware

found no mention of Bauduy as architect of the bank building. The minutes are rather strange. They mention buying the lot for the building; approving the rear portion, which was added to the original design; and payments for some small parts of the work. But they do not speak of hiring Bauduy, approving his design, or paying for the major construction costs or Bauduy's fee. It seems as though they talked around the project, rather than directly dealing with it.

That is certainly one explanation. Bauduy was so much a part of the life of the bank, from the date of its incorporation nearly twenty years earlier, that accepting his contributions to design and construction might have occurred

---

returning to him four times what he paid for them." Richard Cosway had a rival (see p. 445; Holland, appendix, for Provenchère, June 2, 1805).

The Bank of Delaware

without comment. One thing seems certain: no other architect would have been engaged in that way.

The front elevation bears some relationship to a side elevation of Latrobe's Bank of Pennsylvania, built sixteen years earlier. Bauduy—it was almost certainly he—was an observant man; but he was no copyist, for his design for Wilmington is a more coherent and compelling work than Latrobe's effort three years later, in New Orleans, to reduce his grand-scale Pennsylvania Bank to a scale like that required for Wilmington. Latrobe's Bank of Louisiana, designed in 1820, just before his death, does have more interesting interior spaces, though the comparison is not entirely fair, because the antiques merchant operating in the New Orleans building has salvaged more of the original appearance of Latrobe's work than has been possible for the Delaware Academy of Medicine, which has occupied the Bank of Delaware building since it was moved* and, apparently, largely gutted.

Perhaps it was Latrobe's example that led him onward, but Bauduy (if it was

---

*From its original location at the northeast corner of Sixth and Market streets to Lovering Avenue and Union Street.

Baudry) had moved well beyond the indecisive colonial style of the Town Hall and Saint Peter's Church. The bank is a sleek cube, with closely laid bricks in Flemish bond, under a hipped roof. The detailing is suave, with the surface broken by sunken panels like those of Swanwyck, and by Baudry's characteristic white stone belt course and panels. The skin of this building is drawn tight over the cube and pressed inward by the curve of the inset doorway, a graceful piece of sculpture, with slim columns set below a Venetian window; the Renaissance tradition was still alive, but not so oppressively as to be followed without wit.

Eleutherian Mills

The Bank of Delaware building, like Swanwyck, is without any clearly French characteristics. Cosmopolitans like Pierre Baudry spoke several languages with fluency and worked in the international architectural style we may choose to call "Regency." The houses that he provided the Du Ponts, however, do suggest a French Creole at work; they have piazzas—galleries of a West Indian origin—combined with a Gallic elegance of massing and a piquancy of interior space that is unusual in American houses not designed by Frenchmen.

There were three buildings along the Brandywine that served as Du Pont residences and were probably designed by Baudry. One is gone; another is owned by the Hagley Museum; and the third remains in the hands of a Du Pont descendant.

The cautionary "probably" is necessary, because it is no easier to uncover Baudry's role in the residential history of the Du Pont family than in their economic history. It has not been in the Du Ponts' interest to credit their departed partner with very much. There are traces of Baudry in the masses of memoirs, diaries, and sponsored research left for us, neatly catalogued and impeccably preserved, by a family of amateur and professional historians committed to giving posterity their side of the story—but only traces. At times one feels as one does after trying to descry some shred of wisdom or virtue in the opponents of John, duke of Marlborough, in the histories of his descendant Winston Churchill.

Let us begin with the most famous of Du Pont residences, the Director's House at Eleutherian Mills (the name of the manufactory and of the house) built for Irénée Du Pont. In his prospectus for the powder works, that prudent man stipulated that it should occupy "the highest point of land . . . placed in such a position that the whole plant may be seen from its windows . . . The construction of this house should be limited to what is absolutely necessary for the director and his family."

This fairly represents Irénée's aesthetics: straight to the point. In such a disrupted life as his, however, there was room for associations with the past

Eleutherian Mills

implying continuity; and so Irénée asked Victor to send along to him, in 1802, some reminiscences of the house their father had called Goodstay during his first American exile in New Jersey, a place of repose amid a community of exiles, some from France itself and some from the West Indies. The house seems to have been constructed by a refugee from Saint-Domingue. The peculiar, attenuated columns on the upper tier of its gallery—Corinthian capitals so "primitive" as to seem sophisticated abstractions of the classical—suggest the conception of a Frenchman who had learned about galleries in Saint-Domingue.*

I do not suggest that Bauduy had a hand in the design of Goodstay—merely that someone like him did. But Irénée asked Bauduy to work on the plans for Eleutherian Mills, after writing Victor to be sure that he made use of "two drawings of the piazza from the back . . . being careful to mark in inches the size of the mouldings."

The Goodstay columns appeared first at Eleutherian Mills and then at Victor's house, Lower Louviers. They are, I think, symbols of the continuing influence—aesthetic, economic, and emotional—of the patriarch, Du Pont père, though he was by then back in France; it was as strong along the Brandywine as the smell of powder.

---

*The attenuated columns of Mount Vernon may have been brought to George Washington's mind by buildings he saw on his voyage to Barbados. See *Architecture, Men, Women and Money*.

Sketch of the rear façade of Goodstay, attributed to Victor Du Pont

On August 22, 1802, Bauduy wrote Victor: "This morning we put the shovel in the earth at Irénée's." Four days later: "Irénée is well and we are putting our shoulders to the wheel. I hope that the construction will move rapidly." By October, Irénée was complaining. He wrote Victor: "Bauduy made me build a bigger house than I would have wanted." It was only forty-six by thirty-one feet, with a lean-to wing thirty-one by seventeen; but Irénée worried about the upkeep of this "enormous and damned house," a two-story stone-and-stucco cube with a steep, high roof with dormers. It has been extensively remodeled, but the memory of the West Indies remains in the two-story gallery, and the taste of Paris appears in an elegant spiral stairway rising to a little dome.

We are told in the guide to the house in its current role as a museum that "the 'original drafting' of the plans for the dwelling was done by Pierre Bauduy, a bilingual St. Dominguan and a shareholder in the powder company, who also supervised the construction." This generous recognition of Bauduy's architectural contributions is relatively recent. Irénée wrote his father in February 1803 about the "really astonishing" progress made since August, including "a large house and barn of stone and a large part of the refinery," but neglected to mention Bauduy's part in it, a tradition sustained until the last few years.*

*The "large house" here may be one of the powder buildings—e.g., the Doying House. It would be appropriate in that case for Irénée not to have mentioned Bauduy.

Upper and Lower Louviers

A house across the Brandywine from Eleutherian Mills, called Upper Louviers, was once the residence of Admiral Samuel Francis Du Pont. It was destroyed in the late 1970s after a multitude of remodelings had made it difficult to determine with certainty either its design or the precise date of its Greek Doric portico. Taken alone, this little, graceful, four-columned item, though festooned with an unusually fetching ironwork balustrade, might not seem to justify much interest. But if its date is 1802, as we are told by the only professional report made upon the house before its demise, that portico is one of the earliest architectural artifacts of the Greek revival in America.*

This anonymous study, commissioned in 1960 by Elise Du Pont Elrick, notes that a house "was already there in much simpler form when Bauduy bought the property in 1802." No evidence is given for this; but the author says that whenever Upper Louviers was built, and by whom, its "proportions, ceiling heights, and paneling" show it "to have been the house of a person of some pretensions and taste. Pierre Bauduy is said to have a house on the property, presumably after he bought it, and as I know of no other such house on it, I believe it must have been this very house. I have heard it was."

It seems likely that Upper Louviers, complete with its stocky portico, was built by Pierre Bauduy. This would have been before 1808, when he began to place greater symbolic distance between himself and the Du Ponts, moving to the other side of Wilmington and beginning the reconstruction of Eden Park.

Lower Louviers, down the Brandywine a few hundred yards, has an even more complicated story; but there is no doubt about the Du Pont family version.

It is an expansive, almost extravagant place, designed about 1810 for Victor Du Pont. The powder works were prosperous, and Victor, his bankruptcy five years past and unabashed by a second failure (at storekeeping in Angelica, New York, in the Genesee Valley), was ready to build. He got a successful composite of a Franco-English bow-fronted villa and a two-story adaptation of the "West Indian" gallery† essayed only by George Washington at an earlier date.

---

*I am grateful to Charles Brownell for the information that some of Latrobe's Greek Doric columns from the Bank of Pennsylvania, just one year older (1799–1801), were saved from its demolition. One of them is in Wilmington, re-erected as the Soldiers and Sailors Monument, with a new capital by A. D. Mullett.

†The reasons for the quotation marks are set forth in *Architecture, Men, Women and Money*. The "living porch," an invention of the Western Hemisphere, began to appear around the Caribbean trading territory as far north as the Hudson Valley and as far south as Trinidad about 1735. No earlier positive sightings have been reported north of Brazil.

Upper Louviers in 1862

With all this in mind, we can enter the somewhat selective memory of Victor's wife, Josephine, recorded many years afterward in *Our Travels in America*. Everybody but Victor is at fault in her chronicle, and no one but a Du Pont accomplishes anything. As Bessie G. Du Pont gently said in a joint biography of Victor and Josephine, *Travels* is "less a narrative of the events of her life than an explanation for her descendants of her husband's changes of occupation and of purpose."

But Josephine's work is important, for she is the sole source of several traditions:

She says that in 1806, Pierre Bauduy had "bought land opposite the powder yard—across the river—intending to build a house for himself." (Actually, Bauduy had owned the land since 1802, about the time he procured the site of the powder yard.) "Soon a charming house was built for us for which Irénée made the plans himself. One day as we stood on the piazza of his house after breakfast and saw the progress that had been made on our future home, I said,—'My dear brother, I feel gratitude growing on each floor.' 'Don't say that,' he answered laughing, 'or I will build it to the skies.' "

Everything is wrong with this account, except the charm of familial felicity.

Irénée did not design houses, especially "enormous and damned" houses, even, we may suppose, for his brother. That Bauduy might have designed her house must have been an unacceptable thought to the loyal old lady; Bauduy had sued the family, making dreadful allegations against them, and had embarrassed Victor's political career. Even before that, also before the house was designed and built, even while the two were friends, Bauduy had added to Victor's burdens during the discomfiting sojourn at Angelica by requiring him constantly to mediate by mail between this importunate West Indian and the saintly Irénée.

Lower Louviers stands today, facing the river, with a grand façade of slim columns terminating in those Goodstay capitals. It is one of America's finest surviving Regency/Directoire country houses, next only, perhaps, to Gore Place. French windows extend its elliptical parlor onto a living porch considerably more ample than the decorative little balconies of British or French convention. It is an American house, and its present owner, William W. Laird, Jr. (a descendant of Irénée Du Pont), has sustained it as the finest of its kind in private hands.

As recently as 1960 a family study, to be found in the library of the Hagley Museum, asserted that "this lovely thing" was "designed by . . . Irénée, for his brother Victor." The same document protests that Bauduy was out of the picture by 1802, citing the reminiscences of Josephine Du Pont and a 1955 study by Thomas B. Hartmann, also to be found there. But Hartmann, we find, said only that "E. I. Du Pont supervised the building" after "the land was purchased from Bauduy" in 1808.

This gives us six crucial years, from 1802 to 1808, with an experienced architect, Bauduy, available on the premises. Hartmann, it must be admitted, was not himself very precise; the house, he said, "was designed by E. I. Du Pont with advice from Thomas Jefferson." That tale apparently was derived from the reminiscences of Evalina Du Pont (1840–1938). Mr. Laird wrote me in the summer of 1984 recalling a conversation he had with "Cousin Lina" in 1926. She said "that E. I. . . . designed, or had designed, what he thought Victor wanted," with a breezy gallery like those Victor had seen while he was French consul in Charleston, South Carolina. "She claimed [that E. I.] consulted an architectural expert whom she thought might have been Thomas Jefferson (or Peter Bauduy)* about the original design . . . There is no letter from Jefferson about Louviers Lower House, but there is considerable correspondence about the powder mills."

Another house having tall columns in the Goodstay pattern was built a year or two after Lower Louviers. This was Marengo, which stood until quite

*The parenthetical comment is Mr. Laird's.

recently on the Newport Pike, near Wilmington. Its builder was William Warner, a West Indies merchant who came to Wilmington at about the same time (1796) as Bauduy, well before the arrival of the Du Ponts; he went bankrupt at the same time as Bauduy, who owned 176 acres at "the Warner Farm," and he and Bauduy were engaged, perhaps together, in speculation in merinos and cotton manufacturing. If Warner had an architect, it was Bauduy.

20

GORKY PARK
AND EDEN PARK

The partnership with Pierre Bauduy, like gunpowder, had to be handled gingerly; it was too profitable to abandon. As the Jefferson administration drew to its end, Irénée was complaining to his father of Bauduy's "injustice, bad faith and hatred . . . greed and ambition." But they proposed, nonetheless, to enter a new joint venture. They needed each other more than they loathed each other.

In 1808, each had important friends in Paris and Washington. The Bauduy dining room was open to any distinguished visitor from France who happened along, within a wide political spectrum. Louis Philippe had dined there in 1797, and the republican general Moreau (described by another guest as "a sportsman, a determined drinker and smoker . . . come to declare war on our woods") in July 1806.

Some of these acquaintances (though neither the future king nor the celebrated general) were mobilized into a private and profitable conspiracy to outwit the settled economic policies of Britain, France, and the United States. Shrewd, powerful, highly placed people gathered forces on both sides of the Atlantic to smuggle animals for breeding purposes, a necessary preliminary to the movement of technology to make cloth of the wool they were to produce.

The novel and the motion picture Gorky Park are unlikely to linger in the memory of the race very much longer—already, apparel makers are asked fewer questions about the pricing of sable coats. But this bloody tale of espionage did remind many of us about the monopoly value of wild Siberian sables. In order to obtain breeding stock of these animals and get them out of the Soviet Union, this story went, the villains were willing to kill, cover up, and kill again.

The best way to understand the venture known as Du Pont, Bauduy & Co. is to think of merino sheep and Eden Park as we have learned to think of sables and Gorky Park. The chief difference between the two situations is that one

Lower Louviers, river-front elevation, in the late 1860s(?)

was fiction and the other history. Patriotism actually did conspire with avarice to justify illegal trade in sheep, whereas fictional avarice had to triumph over patriotism in order to induce high government officials to a trade in sables. Enormous profits could be secured from the successful smuggling of either animals (the plural is the necessary form, for the objective in each instance was to transfer a pair to a new place of reproduction).

At the outset, the traffic in sheep was merely difficult, not illegal. When Irénée Du Pont returned to the United States in 1801, having acquired investors for the manufacture of black powder, he brought with him a merino ram named Don Pedro, whose wool was of an astonishing length and silkiness. Don Pedro spent the next few months at Goodstay; and in the spring, the bill of lading for Irénée's move from there to the Brandywine included "Seven Sheeps." They were, of course, half-breeds, but worth inestimably more than the scruffy animals running along the hillsides of the Livingston estates on the Hudson or under the care of George Washington Parke Custis at Arlington House, on the Potomac.

Don Pedro was then established on the estate of one of Chancellor Livingston's neighbors. The Chancellor, now minister to France, had cause to know there was a decent prospect of a surcease in the Napoleonic wars, a brief passage when sheep might slip through the fleets of France and Britain. In 1802, during a truce between Britain and France (the Peace of Amiens), both Livingston and David Humphreys, formerly minister to Spain, sent merinos to their estates in the United States.

The Du Ponts were not so quick, but they did the best they could. E. I. Du Pont re-acquired Don Pedro from Livingston's neighbor, asking Victor to go up the Hudson "and to bring back the Ram, Don Pedro, of whom we have the greatest need," and after Britain and France resumed their warfare in 1803, he pressed their father to find means to run the British blockade and the French counterblockade to secure "a couple Spanish rams and two or three sheep . . . for my little farm . . . the expense would . . . easily be covered by selling the second ram. Since Mr. Livingston sent Spanish sheep here, their reputation has gone up rapidly."

Irénée told his father that he and Victor could keep five hundred merino sheep on their land along the Brandywine and that Bauduy had room for fifteen hundred more on his larger place at Eden Park.

At the same time, Bauduy was also pursuing merinos in partnership with Dr. William Thornton, the director of the Patent Office. In 1805, he jocularly reported to Irénée that he had been drawn into the dissipations of the Federal City, where he met both Thornton and our old friend Thomas Law, who wrote Irénée, "Pray remember me affectionately to Mr. Baudui and his amiable family." But Bauduy's "dissipations" had a business purpose. In 1809, Bauduy and Thornton were sufficently cozy for the former to impart to the latter a secret method of marking sheep to prevent rustling. Thornton urged Bauduy to join him in a speculation: "My thirty or forty thousand acres of gold mine land excellently adapted to rear sheep in North Carolina . . . the Shepherds might be employed in getting gold while attending the flocks."

These two sugar planters from the West Indies, now turned to technology transfer, sheep raising, and amateur architecture, apparently knew each other well. (There may even have been, through their mutual friend Dr. Thornton, an association between Edward Stevens and Bauduy.) In 1804, while Bauduy was arranging for the naturalization of Pierre Du Pont de Nemours, he also asked Thornton, at the Patent Office, for another favor for the senior Du Pont: a patent on a machine illustrated by a drawing by Bauduy. The artist was a little diffident about his sketch, but Thornton assured him that "I am not of the opinion that you are rusty in your drawing. Your drawing is very well executed."

In the fall of 1812, Thornton wrote Irénée Du Pont to convey his affectionate regard to "our worthy Friend Bauduy and his good family. Tell that jolly son of Momus to come down and cheer us with his company. He owes us a long visit. If he does not come soon, I shall say he is bribed by Napoleon." Thornton had written Bauduy that he was becoming "very sheepish," but it was not easy to smuggle sheep through the British and French blockades and the American embargo. Napoleon's customs agents were alert. Thornton told Bauduy that Jefferson's protégé Edward Coles, "just from France," had been annoyed that French officials "examined his bags lest they should have merinos sewed up" in them. Bauduy pressed into service his brother-in-law in Paris, the marquis de Sassenay. (Sassenay was accustomed to occasional tasks as a secret agent.) The marquis was to find "six ewes and six rams from the Rambouillet strain" and send them by a special presidential route: "They must pass as belonging to Mr. Jefferson."

Bauduy explained that the French government should be glad to make four-legged contributions to the transfer of technology to a developing country. The sheep and the wool they produced were weapons of economic warfare against England. That nation of wool gatherers and manufacturers had been enriched by revenues from the sale of powder and wool to the United States. Bauduy and Du Pont had already virtually eliminated the market for British powder. Now the partners proposed to cut into the traditional British market for textiles. Bauduy wrote Sassenay, "Your government should realise that the biggest blow to England would be to make things easy so this country could do without English goods . . . If we can find good wool, we would discontinue the import of English wool."

Obviously, Bauduy and Irénée Du Pont had been rehearsing their speeches, for the latter wrote his father, "The greatest harm that can be done the English is to destroy their trade . . . it is only by American industries that England can be fought."

Dr. William Thornton by Gilbert Stuart

This was the argument put to Thomas Jefferson, even after he had, with infinite pain, set the government of the United States upon an opposite course. He had imposed the Embargo of 1807, overriding the argument that the transfer of European technology and, by implication, breeding stock, was essential to the development of domestic manufacture. The embargo was a very expensive effort to keep the ports of the United States unpolluted by British or French goods and thus keep the system neutral in the Napoleonic wars.

Then Jefferson heard a siren song all the way from Paris. His old friend Pierre Du Pont de Nemours suggested an exception to the embargo for the President's personal profit:

> ... Because you are returning to administer your estates after governing with wisdom and honor, you will be permitted to buy a small flock. Try to arrange it while you are still in power. Have your Ambassador ask officially to buy and send you sixty sheep and twenty rams ... Your excellency might at the same time send me a formal letter authorising me as a sufficiently well-known member of the Agricultural Society, to supervise the selection and shipping ...
>
> And I would ask in return that in your friendship you would permit my son Irénée ... your manufacturer of powder ... to have a quarter of the sheep and two of the rams, or three, in case of accidents.

Jefferson's complicity was essential for anyone to win the race for breed stock. The Du Ponts were in the lead, but there was a late entry: Dr. Thornton tried his own approach to Jefferson, asking the President to use his influence to help Thornton go to France himself and bring sheep back with him. With Jefferson's support, Thornton told Bauduy, "I will show you the conversion of your Friend Thornton into Argus the 2nd."

The Du Ponts moved to slow down the competition with an offer to Thornton of some of the sheep they might smuggle through. Naively, he replied that he was willing to assist in their venture as well, "though I cannot obtain permission for your Sheep" in a formal sense. Smuggling was easy— "They may be landed in the river's Bank"—and, if not exactly legal, smuggling of sheep was patriotic, "for the Government cannot be displeased with an Act that will benefit the whole nation."

While Thornton was writing sententious letters, the Du Ponts struck their deal. In March 1809 the President issued instructions through the secretary of the treasury, Albert Gallatin, to instruct the collector of the port of New York to allow the *Mentor* to sail for France through the British blockade and bring back the Du Ponts' sheep. Irénée wrote his father, "The embargo will not trouble you."

Jefferson got his sheep, and gave them for stud without charge. The Du Ponts did not feel so constrained. By November 1809, Irénée reported to his father that merinos "are spreading all over the country with astonishing rapidity" and at astonishing prices. Two rams and two ewes were sold for a total price of six thousand dollars. (Government officials like George Graham [see Part Eight] were paid five dollars a day at the time, and the same six thousand dollars could have built over a hundred cottages for shepherds, according to my rough estimates.)

A Baltimore newspaper said "the heretofore barren hills" of the Brandywine "are clothed with rich verdure, and covered with sheep." The *National Intelligencer* said that "in the neighborhood of Wilmington, patriotism and public spirit is unparalleled in raising and procuring Merino sheep."

Bauduy wrote to Paris for books on sheep raising. Jefferson wrote Pierre Du Pont for shepherd dogs. Bauduy obtained his own, using them to tend the six hundred sheep kept at Eden Park. His only known polemical work (a letter to the Philadelphia Society for Promoting Agriculture) extolled the virtues of a shepherd dog named Montagne, of "immense strength, great mildness in his ordinary deportment, though ferocious towards other dogs." That ferocity had ample outlet; in protecting Bauduy's sheep "at least 20 dogs have been killed in my barnyard or on my farm by him." Bauduy illustrated his letter with one of his drawings, showing a benign but wary Montagne, looking, as is often the case with favorite dogs, very like his master.

Bauduy had reason to be pleased: the dogs, it seems, were more effective in tending sheep than the Basques that Bauduy also imported, together with their traditional stilts. They kept bogging down in the swampy soil at Eden Park, which, though ditched and drained, was still too soggy for appurtenances intended for the rocky Pyrenean foothills. (One of the reasons Thornton had offered his North Carolina meadows was to prevent this outcome.) The antics of the stilted shepherds became a joke even to Bauduy's daughter, who wrote a friend to come to join her in "the wonderful woods of Eden Park. Don't be frightened if you see the God Pan, for this will be our sheperd on his stilts, who really looks like him."

There they were: "Argus the 2nd," "the great god Pan," and three amateur neoclassical architects, Jefferson, Thornton, and Bauduy. It is frustrating that in all their correspondence about sheep there is not a word about architecture, unless we accept this wisp from Thornton to Bauduy in 1809: "Mr. Jefferson lives on a mountain where he enjoys nothing naturally but prospect, for he has neither wood nor water ... Adieu my worthy friend ... may your enjoyments not be confined to prospects alone!"

Whole Cloth

Irénée Du Pont was not much given to his father's propensity for theory; on occasion he roused himself to a practical man's derision for physiocratic foolishness about yeoman farming. That might be an amiable way to live in a state of nature, but manufacturing, said Irénée, "is a creation of wealth . . . It is taking wool at $1 and selling it again at $6 or $7 when it has received its metamorphose from our industry."

In 1808, a new Du Pont–Bauduy partnership moved to secure that "establishment" by building a cloth factory on Bauduy's two-hundred-acre tract of land across the Brandywine from the powder works. At the same time, the partners extended the powder-making partnership that would have terminated in 1810. A millrace was dug in the first year, the mill building constructed in the next. French technological skill was mobilized: a new engineer, Raphael Duplanty, designed the plant; and Ferdinand Bauduy, Pierre's son, was sent to the Low Countries and France to acquire fresher information (the sort of state-of-the-art material imported by William Lee a few years later; see p. 365).

Setting up one's offspring in business was conventional among the French bourgeoisie; and Irénée Du Pont was willing to assist the Bauduys, beginning with the education of Ferdinand, in whom he had a special interest (see p. 213). In 1812, while Ferdinand was in Europe, another textile venture, Bauduy, Garesché and Company, was put together to provide for him and for the master of Swanwyck, Bauduy's son-in-law. Its investors were largely members of the Bauduy family, but among them was Irénée Du Pont. Another millrace was dug, another dam and the foundation for a mill were laid up, downstream from Eleutherian Mills. After Ferdinand's death, in 1814, these assets were folded into Victor and Charles I. Du Pont and Company.

A friendship, by necessity, still persisted between Victor Du Pont and Pierre

Du Pont, Bauduy & Co. label (or cartoon?)

Bauduy. As Lower Louviers was under construction, Victor wrote his brother that he was sorry that Irénée acted as though any reconciliation with Bauduy would "amount to nothing . . . I have always thought you exaggerated his faults and make the worst of them . . . but . . . it has become more important than ever to deal wisely with him, and treat him well and to make him more willing to call himself our friend." Victor feared Bauduy might add to his shares in the business those of the French stockholders, who were tiring of "these overseas investments." He then "would have nearly the whole thing. He may think of this if coldness and quarrels furnish him with pretexts—he will never do it if friendship, union, and harmony exist . . . keep the peace if it's possible."

There were, however, clouds on the horizon: the scarcity value of merinos was diminishing. Napoleon's invasion of Spain and Portugal in 1808 led to an insurrection of the Iberian peoples. The British stoked the fire with supplies and landed an expeditionary force. Battles blazed across the countryside; sheep owners were forced to sell their stock into international markets. In 1810 William Jarvis, American consul in Lisbon, picked his way "among the scenes of warfare and blood, ever attentive to the interests of my country . . . I have profited of an opportunity . . . and purchased two thousand of the best blooded sheep in Spain."* Twenty thousand refugee sheep landed in America, and a rhymester wrote:

> I'll risque my fame and fortune, too,
> Quoth I, on what a ram can do.
> Scarce did my hobby 'gin to thrive,
> 'Ere thousand Spanish rams arrive,
> And what I dreamed not of before,
> My ram turned out to be a bore.

Healthy merinos could still provide respectable income, however, when they were raised in conjunction with a manufactory, like that of Du Pont, Bauduy & Co., to which they could assure a steady supply of wool. That was where, as Irénée Du Pont knew, the real profits were generated. Other plants, not so well provided, went under in a brief panic in 1811; Bauduy reported that "many cloth manufacturers will follow" the bankruptcy of one of their competitors in Bordeaux. There were over four thousand sheep grazing the outskirts of Wilmington to supply the Brandywine mill, but more might be needed when the United States finally went to war with Britain. Bauduy moved to diversify his sources; he guaranteed purchases from sheep raisers in the Philadelphia area as well.

Bauduy searched for other opportunities. He speculated in French currency, sharing this interest with David Parish (see p. 222) and Joel Barlow (see p. 392), who acted as an intermediary between Bauduy and his Sassenay relatives in

---

*Two sheep of the first shipment went to ex-President Jefferson, two to President Madison.

France. He organized a private water company to build wooden pipes along the streets of Wilmington to reservoirs, and sold water at retail. (The Spring Water Company sold out to the city in 1810, after eight years in business.)

Powder and Wool

Meanwhile Bauduy was also proving his value in the powder business: he was often absent from the meetings of the directors of the Bank of Delaware because he was "on the road," selling gunpowder in Boston, New London, and Washington. Stephen Girard became a customer, and John Jacob Astor ordered twenty-five thousand pounds a year for his fur traders.

"The government really hopes for our success," Bauduy wrote Irénée. "Mr. Jefferson will help us as much as he can because of his friendship with your father."

That friendship produced a steady stream of government orders; and after Jefferson's retirement, Bauduy saw to it that the Madison administration was not short of powder, either. The path to Madison's good graces was paved with French books: in October 1809 Irénée wrote the President that a shipment of the latter had been received from his father and that "my partner, Mr. Peter Bauduy, will do himself the honor of waiting upon you in Washington to make delivery."

For powder makers, the War of 1812 was a bonanza. In 1813, Irénée Du Pont wrote: "We have just signed a contract with the United States government for 200,000 powder [sic], which will give us a good year." Though he permitted himself meals with his family or visitors, Irénée was always available to direct his men from the gallery at Eleutherian Mills with a speaking trumpet. Below, "day and night, two shifts of workmen packed the military powder in canisters, kegs and barrels, and piled them gingerly into stout wagons, lined with straw."*

The powder business was almost secure by 1816. But the fragile Du Pont–Bauduy textile venture lay exposed to the wrath of Manchester. After the War of 1812 the British moved quickly and massively to recapture the woolen market, dumping cheap goods into the United States and driving American competitors out of business. With no factories to consume their wool, sheep producers along the Brandywine and the Delaware had no alternative to

---

*However gingerly gunpowder may be handled, its natural function is to explode. This it insists upon, bidden or unbidden. In 1816, Napoleon's Marshal Grouchy appeared on his way southward, just in time for one of the occasions when the Du Pont–Bauduy powder works demonstrated these properties. He had been late in arriving at the battle of Waterloo, with consequences to be noted in Part Eight. Many unintended explosions occurred subsequently along the Brandywine. After an especially large one, in 1890, the Du Ponts finally moved out of Eleutherian Mills. They did not return until powder making ceased, in 1921.

slaughter: merino steaks were regular entries on local menus. "Thirty manufac-
turies for either wool or cotton, within twenty miles" of Wilmington, tried
to secure legislative protection. President Madison, however, like President
Jefferson before him, did not approve of tariffs, and most of the thirty manufac-
turies failed. There were only four of them left in the New Castle County
census of 1820; a decade later there were only two. Du Pont, Bauduy & Co.
was not among them.

Even without international foes, the Brandywine textile business probably
would not have survived, for it was a Victor Du Pont project, only grudgingly
supported by Irénée. Victor, the family's financial albatross, insisted that a place
be found in management for a charming Englishman named William Clifford,
who married Amelie, Victor's daughter. Not long thereafter Clifford was found
already to have a wife and child, in England. He was sent packing; but without
either his or Duplanty's skills, the business failed. Down with it went $32,000
originally invested in Bauduy, Garesché and Company by Pierre Bauduy, his
son, nephews, and brother-in-law; $8,000 invested in this abortive attempt at
conjugality by Irénée Du Pont; and some portion of $37,703.15 owed by Victor
and Charles I. Du Pont and Company to E. I. Du Pont and Company.

After Pierre Bauduy withdrew from the textile business, in 1815, the plant
and machinery were turned over to a new partnership, intended, apparently,
to give Victor a base for his political interests (he served in the Delaware
legislature) and to provide employment for his son. Charles I. Du Pont and
Company made kersey for the United States Army until 1856, when the
company was dissolved.

Union and Disunion

During one of the boom years, 1811, Pierre Bauduy proudly told the marquis
de Sassenay about the textile plant: "Our new establishment is doing well." His
son, Ferdinand, was under Sassenay's care in Paris, and Pierre wanted him to
learn all he could about "the dyeing process . . . his fortune depends upon it."
Six months later came another paternal injunction: "Tell Ferd to work . . . The
branch of industry he is studying has such a great future in this country!"*

Ferdinand's fortune was almost made, but in quite a different way. He fell
in love with Irénée Du Pont's daughter, Victorine. Both families disapproved.
His father wrote Sassenay, in Paris, "She is mismatched and her parents can

---

*Ferdinand Bauduy was the product of the best education provided by Father William Dubourg's
Sulpicians in Baltimore. He studied at Saint Mary's College in Baltimore during the period when
Maximilian Godefroy was professor of architecture there, before Dubourg went off to contend, in
New Orleans, with the ecclesiastical broils reported by Latrobe and with the educational theories of
Joseph Lakanal. For more on Godefroy and Lakanal, see pp. 238 and 344ff.

never be my friends. To tell the truth I am trying to be a Christian and wish my enemy well. I have never had such an antipathy toward anyone like the father, and no doubt, he feels the same toward me. Father, mother, daughters, are all false and dishonest and nothing would be worse than to be related to such people."

In 1813, Bauduy was still opposed to any intermarriage with the Du Ponts, "a very odd family." Irénée returned the disfavor. He wanted no part of the Bauduys, "this strange family"; and as for Ferdinand, "it is the factory he wants to marry . . . I am much dissatisfied with both the father and the son." But Victorine was a very strong-minded woman; soon Victor sent another letter to Paris. Victorine, he explained, had "been in love" with Ferdinand "since they were children . . . Irénée now says that he never refused Ferdinand, though he and all his people—who are very proud, very irritable, and very sensitive— took it for refusal and he will do what he can to bring about a reconciliation."

The "strange" and "odd" families were united on November 9, 1813, in a ceremony conducted by Father Patrick Kenney of Saint Peter's Church.

On the twenty-first day of the following January Ferdinand died of pneumonia. Pierre wrote Irénée: "I left your house stricken with horror . . . May sorrow unite us; be my friend, I have lost the best one I ever had . . . Let us throw a veil over the past, my friend . . . I cannot write one word to Victorine—her grief adds to mine. As long as my heart beats she will have her place as my daughter—she whom my son loved so dearly."

End of a Partnership

In the 1940s, William S. Dutton produced a history of the Du Pont Company "as seen by Du Pont men." There were, of course, several kinds of Du Pont men, the Victor variety being more compatible to salesmen like Pierre Bauduy than the Irénée variety. Dutton spoke for the latter. Victor's bankruptcy was an embarrassment, and so was the failure of the woolen mill, described as "Victor's project" after he had "returned from the Genesee." The senior Du Pont's firm in Paris had functioned as a sort of family holding company, but it failed with twelve shares of the powder company's stock as its only assets. Dutton told his readers that Irénée only "lent his credit to help his brother Victor," whereas in fact Irénée, not Victor, was the Du Pont equity holder. Dutton attributed to Victor other disappointments: "In addition to . . . the woolen business" Irénée "aided in setting up a cotton mill and later a tannery . . . One after another they failed."

Who was to blame? An effort to transfer the onus of failure from Victor Du Pont to Pierre Bauduy has colored all economic and architectural histories of the Brandywine based upon the memories of the Du Pont family. The first family memoir was that of Victor's wife, Josephine. Upon it, Bessie Du Pont based her view that "Bauduy was a shrewd business man, skillful in the art of manipulating credit; he was not a loyal friend or partner." To her, Bauduy's only virtues were that he was "fond of his children and very proud of his son. While he was hoping that Victorine Du Pont would some day marry Ferdinand, his methods were amiable and considerate," but that conduct precipitously changed after Ferdinand's death.

Of course, "that conduct" merely returned to normal; Bauduy and Irénée Du Pont had been at odds for years. After the death of Ferdinand Bauduy, there was nothing to hold the partnership together. The bickering began anew. Pierre wrote to Du Pont senior to protest against Irénée's expanding the business by purchasing additional property.* Unforgivably, he wrote to the other European stockholders as well. He began to negotiate a termination of the powder partnership, arguing that "enormous sums" due the shareholders were "being buried on the Brandywine." He was short of cash, having buried so much of his own fortune in sheep farms. He wrote Irénée that he also wished to withdraw from the cloth factory. Irénée totted up their respective prospects from that failing venture and replied that "complaints about the cloth factory do not concern me, for since the time Mr. B. took control of that establishment . . . I have nothing to do with it."

This assault from outside the family struck while Du Pont de Nemours was embarrassed by Victor's failure and his own, and had the further effect of dividing one set of the old gentleman's children from another: Bauduy's complaints were persuasive not only to Mme de Pusy, daughter of the patriarch's second wife, but probably to that wife herself. Bessie Du Pont, writing in 1930, charged Bauduy with "doing all he could to increase Mme de Pusy's unreasonable irritation against her step-brothers." Worse, caught between his sons and his womenfolk, even Du Pont de Nemours "was influenced . . . and wrote letters to his sons that made Irénée profoundly unhappy and Victor very angry."

Irénée wrote back a "temperate, respectful letter . . . urging his father to return to America." Du Pont de Nemours did not come; but another shareholder, Jacques Bidermann, sent his son to Wilmington to see what value there might be in the American shares in the light of Bauduy's claims. Antoine Bidermann "came on to Delaware, where the reserve of his manner did not promise a friendly decision." But he went through the books of the company, sided with the sons; and after the Du Ponts bought out Bauduy, the young inspector "took his place in the powder company, a change that made the greatest possible improvement in the happiness of the Du Pont family." One can imagine that it did.

---

*It is astonishing that Bauduy, a member of the French bourgeois class of the eighteenth century, could so miscalculate the relative weights of family and abstract justice in the mind of Du Pont senior.

By then, Du Pont de Nemours too had come to America, where he made his own study of the record and agreed that "my daughter Pusy . . . has said much that was very untrue and very dangerous." Irénée, he now said, "is a great man with courage and perseverance ten times greater than I would have dared to expect." These conclusions did not endear Pierre to his wife, who remained in Paris exhorting him to come home. "Her letters were all alike, and she wrote very often," said the family chronicler. In America "at last his great ability was appreciated," but she insisted that his "duty was to France—and to her." He did not return, and she did not come to America. The American members of his family felt the estrangement. Nursing their wrath, they were sure "he most positively wanted never to see Mme de Pusy again."

It is probable that they never wanted to hear of Pierre Bauduy, either, or to be reminded of these unhappy family matters. *Surely,* he could not have been essential to the formation of the Du Pont Company—*surely* not the designer of the architecture of their daily lives. And so it has come to be believed, ever since the partnership was formally dissolved, on February 15, 1815.

During the lifetime of this partnership, Pierre Bauduy received, in cash, for his shares and in distributions for sales commissions and dividends, $108,690.31.* He began as a rich man and ended, despite these very large remittances, a relatively poor one. Among his skills, it seems, was not the retention of money.

There can be no doubt that Irénée Du Pont worked a miracle in salvaging his company after it was stripped of cash to pay off Bauduy. His brother and father were insolvent, and Bauduy, once a formidable ally, had become a competitor.

Many former employees of the Du Pont Company went with Bauduy, who, Dutton reported, "copied Irénée's machinery and methods and coaxed away some of his sales agents. He denied the adequacy of the settlement made with him and instituted a lawsuit that was to drag through the courts for eight years before being decided against him."

In truth, Bauduy needed little refreshing to "copy" either methods or machinery; he had been on the site for a decade, a site he had procured. But he was in no position to be a forceful litigant, because, as we shall see, he was no longer in the country. On the other hand, he was probably not a good powder maker, and Irénée certainly was. Bauduy, said Dutton, had stubbornly resisted Irénée's constant efforts to raise quality control and had been slipshod in his safety requirements.

Bauduy the salesman was more of a threat than Bauduy the producer of "Brandywine Powder," at his new plant at Eden Park; he produced magnificent designs for powder bags and labels. Animosity became a road show: in May

---

*Eight years of litigation were involved in this accounting. It can still be disputed. There were intricate offsets and counterclaims, "draws," and advances. But this is as good a number as any.

Label for Eden Park Mills's Eagle Rifle Powder

1817, Irénée went on a marketing expedition to Washington and found "Mr. Bauduy . . . very conspicuous." The secretary of the treasury "is presenting him to everyone." Irénée met him at the home of the French minister, M. de Neuville, and at Analostan (see p. 397), where they were both the guests of General Mason. Sales were going slowly, "and . . . it is to that miserable Bauduy that I owe this . . . annoyance."

Especially annoying was the harsh reminder of what Bauduy had meant to the partnership in its fledgling days. A flood of government orders had emanated from the national capital. Now, when Irénée went to Washington, he found himself "without friends, without acquaintances, scarcely knowing anyone to speak to—but forced to assert myself, absolutely against my nature, in order to counterbalance the audacity and great impudence of that infernal Mr. B. whom I meet everywhere."

Competition from Bauduy in the powder business was bad enough, but competition from the British textile empire was almost too much for Irénée Du Pont. He struggled to salvage his powder company, and the threat from Bauduy receded: his labels were charming, but what went inside did not continue to sell after the charm had spent itself. Ultimately, quality, persistent management, and well-tested plant and equipment prevailed, and Du Pont was able to withstand the depression of 1818, as Bauduy was not. The economy contracted in a deflationary collapse comparable to that of 1931.* Wholesale prices fell, and kept falling, with no buyers. Manufactured goods bringing three dollars in 1815 would barely sell for one dollar in 1820.

*One cannot compare "depressions" in an economy like that of 1818, into which the market only partially penetrated, with that of 1893 or, certainly, 1931. One can compare the rate of decline of prices in the market sector, however, and those rates were comparable.

Irénée Du Pont met these disasters with a steadfastness and doggedness beyond the capacity of the volatile Bauduy. In 1818, an explosion devastated the Du Pont powder works. Irénée found the money to rebuild. He also displayed another kind of sturdiness, which emerged as he carried on the business after Bauduy was no longer allocated the warmer side of the partnership. This was a sturdiness of morality, a sense of decent behavior unusual among his peers; he began paying one hundred dollars a year to the widows of those killed in the explosion, at a time when normal wages ran about three hundred dollars a year. It was also a shrewd recognition that the loyalty of workers was important to the manufacturing process.

Pierre Bauduy was not so fortunate. In the boom years before 1818, he expanded, as was his nature. He kept spending his cash reserves and then borrowed large sums from his relatives to purchase land. There had been the 35-acre mill site on the Brandywine, the 333 acres at Eden Park, 119 acres at Bedford Farm, 176 acres at the Warner Farm, 1,000 acres at Pencador and Saint George. After the crash, his debts were overwhelming. And he had troubles specific to him, within the general economic gloom. His merinos fell prey to hoof rot and died by the hundreds. He was forced to sell land into a depressed market and, finally, in January 1819, his powder works, to Jean Garesché, his son-in-law, the seigneur of Swanwyck.* Leaving Eden Park—the mansion, the sheep folds, and the powder plant—to the care of his spoiled and restless son-in-law, he went off to Cuba to begin again.

The End of the Road

For two years, Pierre Bauduy, his wife, and three of their children lived at Vedado in Cuba. Then he bought a coffee plantation called Santa Elena, near Matanzas, converted it to the cultivation of sugar, and renamed it Recouso. His son-in-law Aristide des Chapelles bought another coffee plantation, which he renamed Eden Park.

Cora Bauduy Garesché, at Swanwyck, reported sorrowfully her father's frenetic efforts to recoup his fortunes. "He attempted various projects but ill-fortune seemed to attend the latter years of his life . . . He had a noble heart, warm affections, and he was generous to a fault . . . he . . . possessed a wildly speculative mind and embarked on many visionary schemes which finally ended disastrously . . . in Cuba . . . he doubtless might have succeeded had he been content to plod patiently for a few years . . . his temperament was too ardent and his imagination too vivid to be a quiet planter."

An obituary in a Wilmington newspaper tells us something of the events

*The Bauduy-Garesché powder business lasted four decades longer, to everyone's surprise.

preceding his death, on August 25, 1833: "Being naturally endowed with a strong and active mind, and great energy," he was easily distracted. "He was commissioned by the Spanish government to visit some of the other islands, with a view to introduce into Cuba, their improvements in the manufacture of sugar and the cultivation of coffee . . . He was made a citizen of the island—a privilege which, on account of the jealous disposition of the Spaniards toward foreigners, is conferred only as a mark of great honor.

"When cholera made its appearance at Matanzas, he was ready in a moment to sacrifice his comfort, and risk his life in relieving the miseries of . . . his slaves," who, said a newspaper report, "found in him a faithful friend . . . His exertions on behalf of others were too great for his bodily powers, and he brought on an attack of the disease in his own person."

He died in quite a different way from his father, Jean-Baptiste.

VI

BRASS
AND SILVER

Abank building, a town hall, a powder mill, and a row of villas along
the Brandywine are not the first things one would expect as mementos
of a slave revolt on Saint-Domingue. Nor does everyone who parks
in the loop of driveway before the commanding general's quarters at Camp
Drum expect to find there a demonstration of the revolutionary displacement
of French real-estate investment. But in the architectural history of the north
country of New York there are even stranger things to be found. In a little
neo-Gothic church in Antwerp, New York, there are vaulted aisles purchased
with Mexican silver brought there by French necessities. The ruins of a grand
villa along the west bank of the Saint Regis River, a town house, now museum,
in Ogdensburg, and a college campus in Schenectady show the hand of a
distinguished French landscape designer and architect whose fees were paid
from specie secured in Vera Cruz.

A little explanation will be offered in the next two chapters; though they
are rather short and choppy, they are meant only to introduce a longer and more
stately narrative. Chapter 21 begins with an account of the entourage of David
Parish, which produced the second phase of north-country neoclassicism, in
1811–12 (James Leray had provided the first in 1806–08). Written by Vincent
Nolte, one of that entourage, it serves to ground, in a few objects personal and

tactile, the broader context within which a sequence of adventurers struggled to secure Mexican silver between 1805 and 1818 and transfer some of the wealth it produced from the shores of Mexico to the north slope of the Adirondacks. That silver, and French desires to obtain it, precipitated the events in Parts Six, Seven and Eight. They would be incomprehensible without our having come to them through Part Four: events on the Mexican borders of the United States followed from events on Saint-Domingue. Had things gone otherwise in sugar and silver markets—speaking broadly enough to include wars and insurrections, treaties and alliances made because of a concern for sugar and silver—the economy of the United States and its politics, and its architecture upon the Potomac, the Saint Lawrence, and the lower Mississippi, would have been quite different.

21

PRELIMINARIES TO BUSINESS: ARCHITECTURE

David Parish was attended by

an excellent French cook;

a French painter of miniatures, a man already far advanced in years, a punster, who, like Shakespeare's Falstaff, was not only witty himself, but furnished ample material for the wit of others;

the French architect Ramée . . . builder of the . . . Bourse in Hamburg . . . Ramée was to put up for him, at Ogdensburg, a suitable residence, a church, and other buildings [there] and . . . in a smaller place, to which Parish had already given the name of Parishville.

The American Antwerp

Joseph Ramée* did not execute that church in Ogdensburg, but he did complete another, which stands today in Antwerp, New York, a town named for the city in which David Parish struck up a working partnership with Talleyrand.

*"Joseph" is how Ramée signed himself in America. He was born Jean-Jacques and was known in Europe as Joseph-Jacques.

Saint Michael's Church, Antwerp, New York

The American Antwerp is not thriving in the 1980s; the brick stores along the one block of Main Street are visited by a few local people to gossip away the time—unemployment is high in Antwerp—or in search of last-minute items forgotten when they made the trip to the supermarkets of Watertown or Gouverneur. There are only ruins left from the woolen and grist mills that once lined the now crumbling millrace. The town need make no apologies for its architecture, however. One of the millwrights trained by Ramée built a very handsome stone house, which remains, not far from the church, with an upstairs parlor in free-classical taste. The bridge over the Indian River and the millrace beside it are finely crafted, with elegant arches and well-trimmed ashlar.

The "French architect" did not always understand the craft traditions of his Yankee associates; but even in his years as Baumeister of the Hamburg Bourse he could have been proud of a church like that which stands in Antwerp, on its green hillside overlooking the millpond. It is confident, tension-free, unemphatic, rising to a straightforward spire without embellishment. The pointed windows are punched in, not scooped out; one does not get any sense of the mass of the brickwork, nor is there any Gothic tension of weight and structure. No grand gestures here—just a building doing its work, sure of its role. The interior has been spared remodelings except for a little scroll-saw work along the balconies; the aisles are classical corridors, somewhat like the entranceway of Latrobe's Decatur House in Washington.

This little church, in an out-of-the-way place, is, I think, the best of the essays in that odd, classicized Gothic favored by the first generation of architects to return to Gothicism after the United States established its independence.*

I came upon Antwerp, New York, and its church as a result of inquiries into the means by which Talleyrand, Parish, and a cabal of international bankers managed to extricate more than seventy million pesos, worth something around a billion 1988 dollars, from Mexico. As usual, the search was for tangible consequences. An architectural historian, Paul Turner, had his own reasons for pursuing the elusive Ramée. The church in Antwerp was my contribution to Turner's list, in 1984, and he showed me the way to several other products of the association of his architect and my client. (Turner has subsequently discovered more works, in Europe and America, by Ramée, and is publishing his research as he goes.)

Ramée was a carrier across the Atlantic not only of architectural ideas but of mercantile associations as well. The client, Parish, introduced him to several other patrons among the participants in the Great Silver Scheme, and it was possible to find one or two of them through their Ramée connections even after the trail through financial records had become faint. (It happened that Ramée had provided for Talleyrand twenty years before he provided for Parish—as we shall see, he designed the largest ceremonial space ever to be put to ecclesiastical use by the bishop of Autun.)

Parish had the resources, ambition, and vision to transform the landscape of the Saint Lawrence Valley, and Ramée the talent. In 1986, the ruin of one of their magnificent, arcaded stone mills was sold for one dollar; it was an insurance hazard, though its site, a waterfall spreading glistening ripples into a little lake, provides fine swimming on a hot August afternoon. Another little church, perhaps by Ramée as well, standing on the opposite shore in a hamlet

---

*The only examples of this genre in America that could, with charity, be called successful were for Roman Catholic congregations and by Frenchmen: Joseph Mangin's Old Saint Patrick's, Maximilian Godefroy's Saint Mary's in Baltimore and chapel in Bardstown, Kentucky (see p. 296), and Joseph Ramée's Saint Peter's in Antwerp. Latrobe's essay in Gothic in Alexandria, Virginia, is, to be kind, unpersuasive; William H. Pierson, Jr., gives a judicious historian's verdict upon Charles Bulfinch's Federal Street Church in Boston: a "hopeless failure." John Holden Green's Saint John's in Providence is much grander, but not nearly so convincing or coherent a work of art as Ramée's. (See Pierson, *Technology*, p. 119.)

Ruined mill at Parishville

called Rossie, reminds us that Parish was America's most important client for neoclassical architecture next to Thomas Jefferson, and that Parish and his "French architect" anticipated Jefferson by creating America's first college campus with a rotunda at its center. Ramée's work at Union College in Schenectady was commenced five years before Mr. Jefferson's University of Virginia.

Ramée went to work in the Saint Lawrence Valley soon after he arrived in America, in 1811 or 1812. In the early spring of 1812, he and his patron were exploring the bluffs overlooking a frigid little stream flowing into the great river of the north, searching for a site for Parish's villa. At last they found one, "the most romantic situation you can imagine." Parish told his father that Ramée declared "he had never seen anything so fine." Since it is likely that Ramée had built a villa for the senior Parish in a superb situation near Hamburg, that was quite a statement.

In New York the chief arena upon which Ramée's talent was deployed is bounded by the towns of Ogdensburg, Parishville, and Rossie. (Rossie was to Parish what The Grange was to Alexander Hamilton; the Parishes professed to be descended from the lairds of Rossie in the same way Hamilton said he was of the line of the lairds of The Grange.)

For the first year or so, it seemed possible that northern New York might offer something of the same opportunity for grand schemes of architecture and

Barn at Duanesburg, New York, designed by Ramée(?)

land planning that had opened before Ramée in the ports of northern Europe. Parish provided him with a strong partner in Joseph Rosseel, another native of the Ardennes region of Belgium. Rosseel, like Ramée, had gone into exile rather than serve in the French revolutionary armies in Flanders. He now found himself working like a military engineer under the direction of Ramée, laying out roads from Parishville to Rossie and Ogdensburg. Parish subscribed to the Saint Lawrence Tollpike Company, to link his private roads to a larger network, and lobbied furiously with the state legislature for a highway to penetrate the Adirondacks. He built two schooners to make a water connection down the Saint Lawrence.

Meanwhile, he produced other clients for Ramée: Catherine Duane had him lay out her estate at Duanesburg—the barns on the property look very much like Ramée's work, though the house, built in 1813, does not—and the Ogdens developed a landscape on the scale of Stourhead or Fontainebleau.*

Northern New York was not to be left free of the contagion of warfare between Britain and the United States, as a co-belligerent of France, however. In a sideshow of a sideshow, the British attacked the barony of David Parish, exposed as it was, like an offshore island. Cut off by the Adirondacks from the rest of the United States, Parish nearly became a victim of that isolation. While he was directing Ramée's operations, a prowling British gunboat sent a round of explosives into Ogdensburg, barely missing the architect and the client.

---

*A magnificent centerfold in Ramée's monograph in the Union College Library depicts the plan. Once again, the barn, now destroyed, looked like a work of Ramée, though the house did not.

David Parish's villa in Ogdensburg, New York, as it appeared in 1857

The gunboat was driven off by American cannon fire; but in February 1813 a British force of five hundred men marched across the ice of the Saint Lawrence and routed the rag-tag garrison of Ramée's little unfinished fortification called Fort Oswagatchie.

After the British withdrew, work began again upon the interior of Parish's villa in Ogdensburg, and Ramée commenced the design of a new house upcountry. The villa, sometimes called the Red Villa to distinguish it from an older Parish residence called the Red House,* was an elegant, three-part, brick building, with a tall central section and two smaller wings. It has subsequently been remodeled and serves as a museum dedicated to the work of the painter Frederic Remington, who after Ramée was the most important artist to work in Ogdensburg.

Photographs of the country residence, and its immense barn, were rediscovered by Paul Turner in 1984. It was a frame building, in a Franco–Dutch scheme around a forecourt. The main structure had a gabled pavilion thrust forward over an arcade, like Ramée's Boursenhalle in Hamburg, and a little more like

---

*We will visit another Red House, designed for the pirate Jean Lafitte by Bartholomy Lafon, in Part Eight.

David Parish's country house, Parishville, New York

a design published by Ramée in Paris twenty years later in his *Country Cottages and Houses.* *

Montebello

One summer, probably that of the year 1900, a small boy in Baltimore was exploring a suburban area known as Garrett's Woods and came upon a "mysterious deserted house . . . Its stucco walls . . . streaked with huge weather stains." Its windows were like dead eyes, but it had "a dauntless gaity, proclaiming its . . . high breeding in language even a child could understand." Though the doors

---

*Since we are dealing with a man with a disinclination to explain himself equivalent to lockjaw, we are free to speculate: it appears to me likely that Ramée was showing us in the elegant and complex "Design #22" what he actually might have built for Parish had he not been frustrated by the intransigent locals, who had been building farmhouses for that terrain and climate, in their own ways, for a long time, and had no intention of adjusting to accommodate a fancy Frenchman.

There is a good deal of correspondence in the manuscript collections of Saint Lawrence University demonstrating that training by William Beckford and the comte d'Artois was not sufficient to overwhelm hard Yankee resistance to change.

were halfheartedly boarded up, the boy came to know "every inch of the echoing interior, by day and by night. In the shadows of what had been a stately dining room, he deeply relished the oval sweep of the walls." The great hall, thought by the boy to be a living room, was meant to impress: it was a cube twenty feet across, with a lantern to admit light from the top and two Venetian windows giving grace to two small anterooms.

Even in the mansion's ruined state, the boy, whose name was Gilman Paul, could enter the dining room by walking through the hall past the anterooms, into the lower floor of a narrow two-story section. On that summer day, he found his way up an oval staircase to the bedrooms, and

> stepping out through a shattered window to the roof of the living room, he shared with a thousand noisy bumble bees the flowers of the great white wisteria that was methodically wrecking the delicate wooden railing. Looking out through the tangle of the vine, he could see the distant city of Baltimore, already advancing in a relentless tide of two-story houses that was soon to overwhelm . . . the old house . . . [and] its majestic company of white oaks.

The oaks were all that was left of the garden design Samuel Smith watched grow into a gentle green landscape between 1800, when his villa was completed, and his bankruptcy in the bank crash of 1819. This was Montebello, named for the celebrated victory of Napoleon's Marshal Lannes over the Austrians, built by Smith just before his niece married Jerome Bonaparte.

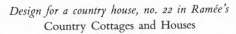

Design for a country house, no. 22 in Ramée's
Country Cottages and Houses

Montebello; hand-colored engraving, c. 1816 by William Russell Birch

We met Smith in his role as a Jeffersonian merchant-politician differing from the West Indian policies of his leader. In 1805, he was a congressman and the dominant political power in Baltimore. He was on the brink of his involvement in the Great Silver Scheme, so he was not quite so rich as he would be thereafter. He still walked warily, voting with the Federalists for a stronger navy, assuring his constituents that he did not wish to provoke the French unnecessarily, going along with the Republicans in appropriating funds for vigorous defense of merchant ships against the British.

Yet on December 20 he rose in opposition to his party leader, President Jefferson; he could not stomach Jefferson's policy of cutting off trade with the Black republic on Saint-Domingue. Toussaint was dead, the island prostrate; but its economy had life and profits in it yet. Smith and his constituents had no aversion to a black hand that held good currency, and it was with the approval of the merchants of Baltimore that he stood up in the House of Representatives to exclaim that the Blacks in Saint-Domingue had fought their own revolutionary war and that the United States should recognize their achievement. Having made a bow to the goddess of liberty, he went on to state the case for commerce:

many in Baltimore were dependent upon trade with Saint-Domingue. He estimated that half a million people in America had a stake in its continuance. When Jefferson put pressure on the Senate to comply with Napoleon's desire that the trade be suspended, other Republicans fell in line, but not Smith.

Jefferson was in retirement upon his own hillside when Smith reached the apogee of his fortunes, in 1818; for a moment; he was the greatest silver trader in the nation (David Parish had departed for Europe two years earlier). "An enormous speculator in stock of the United States Bank," he was also "an exporter of specie to India the half-million at a time," according to John Quincy Adams. Ten years earlier, Smith had established his fortune in concert with David Parish by moving masses of silver through two blockades and the stated policy of the government of Thomas Jefferson.

Jefferson's Monticello is a national monument; Montebello was destroyed, a victim of suburban sprawl, about 1916, the year David Parish's villa succumbed to neglect in the wilderness. The three had much in common: all were products of cosmopolitans, who had traveled much, absorbed much, and knew how to adapt the expensive neoclassical tastes of the Old World to simpler surroundings.

Ramée's house for Parish suffered the worst indignities; it was remodeled and

Floor plan of Montebello

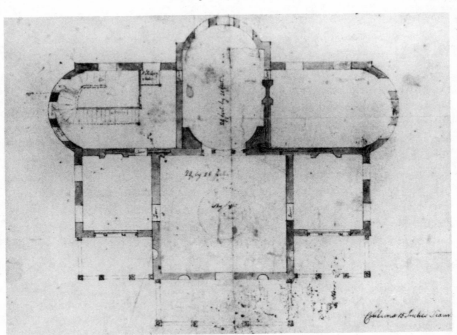

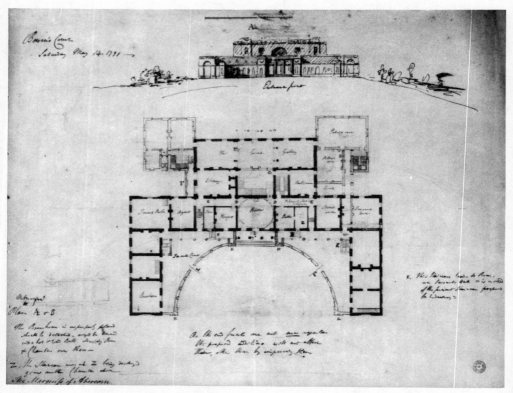

Sir John Soane's elevation and design for the ground floor of Baronscourt

extended to include its huge barn, half-timbered in the vernacular style of Denmark and Holstein, like those Ramée had earlier provided those of his clients around Hamburg who wanted something rustic. The house itself had become rustic by necessity; the Yankee millwrights and village carpenters who built it simplified the plans considerably.*

Not long before John Thurman made his architectural grand tour of Europe (see p. 54), Samuel Smith went there for the first time; after his father's shipment of flour was delivered to Le Havre, he explored Venice, Naples, Rome, Marseilles, and Barcelona, working his way along the Spanish coast to Lisbon. He spent the winter of 1774 in London and then traveled through the

---

*One of them, Daniel Whipple Church, left memoirs so full of acute observations, prejudice, humor, and energy that they deserve independent publication, perhaps coupled with the sketches of Mme de Fériet, which were made at the same time and in the same terrain. I hope to see such a project through, one day.

midlands to visit to the family home at Strabane, in the north of Ireland.

The most conspicuous mansion in the neighborhood of Strabane was Baronscourt, the Irish seat of the earl of Abercorn. It apparently stayed in Smith's mind—an example of the sort of thing he might build when he could. This recollection was reinforced when, shortly before he undertook the construction of Montebello, in 1798, he made use of Sir John Soane's sketches and floor plans of the remodeling of Baronscourt, executed for Abercorn after Soane visited there in 1791.

Montebello is a diminutive Baronscourt, bearing about the same relationship to its huge bulk as the first Monticello had to "American Henry" Hope's Welgelegen (see pp. 441–2). Both Abercorn's mansion and Smith's villa had high masses recessed behind porticos; Montebello's little curves at the side of its portico reverse the direction of Soane's massive sweep toward Baronscourt's dependencies, and Smith adopted Soane's peculiar version of a Venetian window, permitting himself a domed living room in the center of the house, where Abercorn had a larger but similar billiard room amid a profusion of ellipses and apsidal ends. Smith could afford only one or two.

And Gideon Granger's Villa

Northern European neoclassicism found its way to Canandaigua, New York, in 1818, where another villa in the latest fashion was built by Postmaster General Gideon Granger. Granger shared the political antipathies and architectural affinities of David Parish and Samuel Smith, and we will return for a fuller political explanation of the architecture of his villa on p. 285. Here we note only that Granger served Thomas Jefferson well, first as a party organizer in Connecticut and then as postmaster general and chief of Jefferson's secret service. Like Smith, he had no respect for Jefferson's successor, James Madison, in whose administration he also held the postmaster generalship. As we shall see, had it not been for Smith and Granger's differences with Madison, and the presence of Joseph-Jacques Ramée in an anteroom, Granger's house might have taken a much less interesting form.

22

PRELIMINARIES TO BUSINESS:
POLITICS AND ECONOMICS

The foregoing discourse has been, of course, "preliminary" to business only in a literary sense—architecture in the world outside books is a *consequence* of business. We must now go backward in time to find out how David Parish was able to afford the role of backwoods Maecenas, how Samuel Smith became the first great patron of neoclassicism in Baltimore, and Gideon Granger the first in Canandaigua.

We could start with Talleyrand, or we could start with the "prince of peace." Don Manuel Godoy, chief minister of Spain in the 1790s, earned that title by keeping his country out of the worst of Napoleon's wars from 1795 until 1808, when Napoleon determined to invade Spain. During the 1790s, the interests of Talleyrand and Godoy coincided in denying to the United States access to the silver mines of Mexico. After the destruction of the economy of Saint-Domingue, those mines once again resumed their primacy as the power center of the northern half of the Western Hemisphere.

Throughout the eighteenth century Louisiana was seen by both France and Spain to be a buffer between the ambitions and avarice of the Anglo-Americans and the treasures accumulating to church and state from those mines. Spain would have been bankrupt many more times had it not possessed Mexico. France, the ally of Spain, would have had far more to worry about in its contest with Britain had that enemy or the Americans acquired a ready source of specie and, with specie, the means to war and subsidized commercial competition.

Louisiana was to Americans an enormous stretch of territory open to settlement. To France and Spain it was a mere anteroom to a treasure chamber. The debt of the American people to Toussaint Louverture and five hundred thousand Blacks on Saint-Domingue was that they destroyed the garrison Napoleon intended to occupy that anteroom, and left Louisiana defenseless.

In 1801 and 1802, Napoleon mounted not one expedition to restore the empire of France in the New World but two. The first, under the command of his brother-in-law Leclerc, was to "rid us of these gilded Africans" by "annihilating the black government at St. Domingue." The second, as Henry Adams tells us, was composed of "ten thousand French soldiers, trained in the school of . . . Moreau, and commanded by a future marshal of France." The "marshal" was "Victor" (Claude Perrin) the future Duc de Bellone, and he and his men were to occupy "New Orleans and St. Louis before Jefferson could have collected a brigade at Nashville."

As we have seen, Thomas Jefferson assured Napoleon's emissary M. Pichon, as he did Robert Livingston, that "we entertain toward him [Napoleon] personally the most friendly dispositions." Whatever Napoleon might do, however he might traduce the liberties of France—or, of course, those of Saint-Domingue—the President of the United States would not object: "Whatever government they establish, we wish to be well with it."

Armed with these assurances, Napoleon proceeded with his plans. Once Saint-Domingue was secure, Louisiana was to be manned with the combined forces of Leclerc and Victor. Thus would be completed a stable triangle between France, the sugar islands, and Louisiana. The mainland possessions would supply food and markets to the West Indian plantations: "The system of this, as of all our other colonies, should be to concentrate its commerce in the national commerce . . . establishing its relations with our Antilles, so as to take the place . . . of the American commerce."

Keeping the Yankees out of the Antilles would be accomplished by Leclerc. The Spaniards, who remained in control of Louisiana despite the treaty "retroceding" it to France in 1795, were already moving to keep them out of the mainland base, soon to be raised "to a degree of strength" sufficient to allow it to defend itself "on its own resources." Victor's expedition was scheduled to depart Dunkirk in September 1802. Jumping the gun only a little, Don Juan Ventura Morales, intendant at New Orleans, forbade American shippers to deposit their merchandise there. The French ambassador in Madrid expressed Napoleon's "warm satisfaction" over this rebuff to what Napoleon described to Victor as "the pretensions of the United States and their usurpations over the Spaniards."

The Spanish exclusion of Yankee entrepôts, so "satisfying" to Napoleon, was in direct contravention of the Pinckney Treaty of 1795. Treaties were sometimes inconvenient; but until Toussaint wrecked his plans, Napoleon had no reason to regret his solemn assurances to the Spanish king: Spain could return Louisiana to France without fearing for Mexico. "You can declare in the name of the First Consul [Napoleon] that France will never alienate it."

Toussaint and the Blacks of Saint-Domingue resisted long enough to set these plans awry. The news of the death of Leclerc and the destruction of his army reached Washington at the same time Jefferson learned of the Spanish denial of trading rights in New Orleans. Bad weather and the British fleet baffled Victor. The Spanish action now became merely a provocative gesture in the face of an expansionary American government whose force, though puny in comparison with that of France, was entirely adequate to the task of "usurping" Louisiana.

Steadfastly, Talleyrand and Godoy had sought to create a "wall of brass"

between the Anglo-Americans and Mexico. Napoleon's assurance to the king
of Spain meant that he was taking back Louisiana to sustain that wall. But the
defeat of his plans in the West Indies, and the humiliation of what was in effect
a family expedition to establish a New World dynasty of Bonapartes, led him
to seek other means to secure for France the silver of Mexico. These means
would have to include a device to breach the British blockade.

Certain odds and ends had to be dealt with, however. Louisiana had to be
"alienated" for a price adequate to pay for Napoleon's next round of European
conquests or an assault upon Britain itself. Though the American government
was financially frail, it could, perhaps, borrow the money.

Through Du Pont de Nemours, Jefferson implied to Napoleon that even
he might consider a British alliance to eliminate a strong rival at the mouth
of the Mississippi. But a softer argument was also advanced. It was a common-
place of the time to think that the United States, gingerly governed according
to Jeffersonian principles and practice, and subject to the centrifugal impulses
of Jeffersonian ideology, would be likely to fall apart if it were to extend itself very much farther. What Jefferson and James Madison had to say on this
point was not sufficient to reassure Godoy, but it was certainly of interest to
Aaron Burr.

As late as 1821, Jefferson was still writing of "the individual States . . . as
independent, in fact, as different nations." Madison went to some pains to
communicate directly to Napoleon the view that "emigrations" across the
Mississippi into Louisiana would "weaken" the United States, for "no colony
beyond the river could exist under the same government, but would infallibly
give birth to a separate State having in its bosom germs of collision with the
East."

With the President and the secretary of state talking like this, what might
a disaffected vice-president be impelled to consider? Burr, the protagonist of
Part Seven, was offered an empire by the Louisiana Purchase, a transaction made
possible by Napoleon's breach of the constitution of France and of his solemn
assurances to the King of Spain. Furthermore, Burr and other American adventurers were thereby offered access to the silver hoard of Mexico in a Napoleonic
gamble, despite the advice of Talleyrand and the passionate remonstrances of
two other Bonaparte brothers, Lucien and Joseph.

In 1803, when Joseph protested against Napoleon's sale of Louisiana to
Thomas Jefferson's representatives in Paris, Robert R. Livingston and James
Monroe (for Monroe and architecture, see p. 417), he could scarcely have
anticipated that he himself would soon become king of Spain. And not even
in a Corsican fever of imagination could he have seen himself as he was later:
at once a landlord in the Adirondacks and the successor to Burr as a seeker after
Mexican wealth from a base in Louisiana. That is the story told in Part Eight.

By 1805, however, the chief end of Napoleonic policy toward the New

World was no longer a closed, triangular relationship between France, Louisiana, and the West Indies. Sugar could be left out of the equation. Louisiana and Saint-Domingue were lost. Napoleon was skilled at cutting his losses. Now the game was to be played for silver, and the players were to be precisely those merchants whose "predations" and "usurpations" had seemed so noxious when they were merely seeking a depository for merchandise in New Orleans.

Which brings us back to silver and to David Parish.

23

THE STAGE
AND THE FIRST SET
OF CHARACTERS

Specie—hard, lustrous, dense, tangible, readily measured; the kind of money one can test by biting and carry in hiding—only specie had secured for Europe the soft profusion of the East, its voluptuous garments, sweet scents, and delicate colors. It could also buy powder and ball, cannon, muskets—and mercenaries.

In the sixteenth century, Francis Drake, John Hawkins, and the poetic Walter Raleigh captained British men-of-war sailing the Spanish Main, interposing themselves between the Spanish enjoyment of such luxuries and the metal to purchase them. These celebrated seafarers pillaged the pillagers. To chastise them in their home ports in England, King Philip created the first Armada.

For another century, the Spanish seas were open to British warships and Spanish trade to British attack. Piracy at sea preyed upon piracy on land. Piratical swag was brought home to Holland and England to finance a great round of country houses. By 1800, private predation, financed by the crown, had become the occupation of fleets managed in London by gentlemen who never smelled gunpowder nor drew a sword.

Napoleon needed more than the revenues of France to finance his ambitions, more than the tribute he could levy upon all of Western Europe. His need for silver was satisfied by a set of financial adventurers from 1805 until 1809, when he destroyed their arrangements by his invasion of Spain. These entrepreneurs became very wealthy in the interval; a remarkable number of them became important clients for architecture, first in Europe and then in America:

David Parish became the patron of Ramée, the most gifted of all French designers to practice in the United States.

Ramée's other important private client, Denis Smith of Baltimore, received in his bank some of the deposits of the Silver Scheme, in all probability because of the intercession of Senator Samuel Smith, one of Parish's partners.

The Smiths' political crony Postmaster General Gideon Granger may have obtained a Ramée design and may have played a part in the Silver Scheme as well.

There is no question of the benefits of that scheme to:

Nicholas Biddle, by way of his father-in-law, John Craig, who named the family seat Andalusia to commemorate the silvery Spanish connection;

Stephen Girard;

Joseph Bonaparte;

The French architect Maximilian Godefroy, by way of Parish's partners the brothers John and Robert Oliver;

Robert Gilmor, a client of America's first native-born, professionally trained architect, Robert Mills;

Vincent Nolte, a client of B. Henry Latrobe;

Archibald Gracie, builder of the mansion now used by the mayor of New York city;

Nathaniel Amory, one of the Boston Amorys, clients of Charles Bulfinch, and connected by marriage to both Edward Stevens and William Lee (see p. 363).

After it was all over, new channels of international exchange had been opened; American bankers came to serve the hallowed roles of British pirates in transferring Mexican wealth through several way stations to China and India. But they did so in ways so notorious that it was important for Nicholas Biddle to be able honestly to state, later, that he was pure of any direct contamination from the speculations in the bank's stock carried out by his father-in-law's old partners. They had learned of such things from the French. In the 1820s, Biddle was very proud of devising partial substitutes for specie in payment for Far Eastern luxuries (bills of exchange called "India bills"); but a recent historian of his bank has pointed out that the bank still made huge exports of silver and therefore still required commensurate imports of Mexican silver. Thus, in effect, "the Bank of the United States," like Sir Francis Drake and Sir John Hawkins, "was an important channel through which the gold and silver of Spanish America was distributed to the rest of the world."

Outflanking the Wall of Brass

After their inglorious role as allies of the British against revolutionary France from 1793 to 1795, the Spanish Bourbons attempted neutrality. So did the king of Denmark. The British, however, made clear their intention to treat as enemies all neutrals who were also commercial competitors; in 1803, Admiral Cochrane seized neutral Spain's South American silver fleet in an act of piracy on a grand scale; and in 1807 Admiral Nelson's "friendly bombardment" laid waste to neutral Copenhagen's cathedral and much of the center of the seaport. Thereafter, Spain and Denmark became reluctant allies of France.

Spain had little to offer her allies after Lord Nelson destroyed her fleet at Trafalgar—except silver. The Spanish Bourbons attempted to buy with promises of that precious substance a measure of relief from the bloodier side of Napoleon's adventures: they committed their mines to pay six million francs a month, two million in supplies and four million in silver. The promise was of doubtful value, however, since the British fleet was in full control of the sea lanes between the Mexican mines and the ports of either Spain or France.

This was nothing new, of course. The military and architectural campaigns of the Spanish kings had been financed for three centuries by Mexican silver, but only when British pirates and privateers, and on occasion the British fleet in a formal sense, would let the flotas and galleons through. Louisiana, while it was a Spanish possession from 1763 to 1802 (in effect; legal title was more complicated), was always threatened by the Americans. As for Mexico itself, few Americans were yet as ready as Aaron Burr to move toward outright conquest. Most, like David Parish and Samuel Smith, regarded Louisiana as a base from which to expedite commercial transactions, legal and illegal, by which the appetites of Europe could be satisfied by the natural wealth of Mexico to the profit of the Americans.

In order to give some sense of the magnitude of the transactions to be laid before us, we must establish rough relationships among the kinds of money employed at the time. That is arduous enough, among other reasons because exchange rates wobble. We must also attempt to relate the purchasing power of those currencies to those of the date of writing (again, we must anticipate slippage to the date of reading). Purchasing power for labor differs from purchasing power for construction materials and for food. So the whole process is, shall we say, approximate.

Nonetheless, I suggest that in considering money transactions during the period under discussion we use the following formula:

1 pound sterling (1805) = 4 pesos (1805) = $4 (1805) = 15 francs (1805) = $80 (1988) *except* in architecture—see below.

A pound sterling* was worth about four pesos or dollars, or about fifteen

*A pound sterling was not a coin but an abstraction used for bookkeeping, balancing accounts, and in foreign-exchange transactions. "Pounds" were based upon an old troy pound of silver until Britain adopted the gold standard in 1816, when gold pounds became "sovereigns" and diverged from pounds. Other units of currency once based upon a pound of silver were the French livre, then almost identical with the franc, and the Italian lira.

Napoleonic francs. That pound had the financial purchasing power of about
eighty dollars in 1988. An 1805 dollar was worth about twenty dollars in
1988 *except* in building construction (architecture), where the equivalent of
an 1805 dollar would be about one hundred and thirty 1986 dollars. This
assertion is based upon the scientific method of direct observation: English
cottages with two bedrooms costing sixty-five pounds in 1805 were roughly
equivalent to those costing two hundred sixty dollars in the United States.
Their construction at the time of writing, in Washington, D.C., would have
cost about thirty-five thousand dollars. My other computations have been
relegated to notes.

The kings of Spain had their own computations to make; they had to find
the means for "protection payments" and thus to escape further harassment by
their burly "ally." Spain had suffered bad harvests, like the rest of Europe, and
the aforementioned disruptions in the flow of colonial remittance. Its revenues,
net of corruption, could barely defray royal expenses in moving from one
pleasure palace to another. Energy that had flowed into statecraft in the seventeenth century was now squandered in ludicrous but expensive pastimes.

The French economy was also in a shambles. Its financial markets had been
demoralized by speculation and by corruption reaching into the central banking
system and tax collection. (An incidental consequence was enriching an American poet; see p. 392.) French armies were drawing pay in encampments from
the Straits of Messina to the Vistula, from the Tagus to the Baltic. Silver was
desperately needed to finance not only those armies but also those of the Poles,
aroused to renew their ancient wars against Russia, those of the Germans,
continuing their squabbles in new combinations, and those of the Italians, who
ranged themselves on any side not including Austrians.

The British were in an equally sorry state. Their fleets had been in mutiny,
their cities torn by food riots. Wheat from Poland had been cut off by
insurrection and the wars of partition. Irish wheat had been scarce since the
French-led rising of 1798, and the population was surlier than ever. Wool, a
staple crop for exchange for food, was scarce as well; tens of thousands of sheep
had died in ice storms and blizzards. The provincial banking system had
collapsed. The Bank of England was driven to issue paper money, unsupported
by specie; and a government of agricultural magnates and city oligarchs had
gone so far as to support itself, and its allies under arms, by laying a progressive
income tax. The British had come to rely upon Mexican silver to the extent
that the image of King George III was simply imprinted upon whatever pesos
could be acquired. These numismatic palimpsests kept the armies of Russia,
Prussia, and Austria under arms in Europe, purchased the loyalties of the armies
of the Indian princes, and sustained the commerce of the East India Company.

The United States suffered its own silver famine: Louisiana had been purchased with borrowed money. These obligations were piled upon unpaid

Revolutionary War debt, unpaid "quasi-war" debt, and unpaid debt to finance the commercial war against the "Barbary pirates." North Carolina was yielding only a few bits of silver to architect-prospectors like Dr. William Thornton (see p. 206), while California and the Klondike slept on, their soil undisturbed by Yankee picks or sluices, their rivers showing their metallic sparkle only to moose and otter.

Such intense pecuniary craving, and such enormous resources for its satisfaction, are seldom long denied consummation.

This was a situation inviting expedients. To supply them, a new set of international financiers was emerging from the rubble of the old empires. These were the survivors and, from an architectural point of view, the chief builders of the period. Upon the rubble, new palaces arose in Paris and in the environs of Hamburg and Amsterdam. The well-tended countryside of the Home Counties of Britain is today dotted with houses built by these interconnected speculators, profiteers, commissaries, and war financiers. And so, ultimately, were the suburbs of Philadelphia, Boston, New Orleans, and Leraysville and Ogdensburg, New York.

Generals and men of sudden and dubious wealth, like those now before us, were not the only beneficiaries of the French Revolution, but they were certainly the most conspicuous. Huge fortunes were derived from the supply of armies, the levying of taxes, smuggling, cornering supplies of scarce materials and special information.

This was the incubation period of the great "houses" of modern finance, among them the Barings, who came from Emden to Exeter and became wool merchants and, finally, bankers; the Rothschilds and the Warburgs, moneylenders of the Rhineland and of the Hanseatic cities of the North Sea and the Baltic; the Hopes, who could call themselves French, Scottish, Dutch, or American as occasion demanded.

The merchants of Hamburg, Antwerp, and the ports of Holland sustained an ancient Hanseatic tradition of free ports linked by family ties and trade. Philadelphia, Baltimore, and New Orleans were drawn into this post-Hanseatic system. And though we describe the Great Silver Scheme from an American perspective, we should not forget that beside the Yankee packets in the harbor of Vera Cruz there were vessels whose captains had been known for years to the Parishes of Hamburg and the Hopes of Amsterdam: captains from Lübeck, Emden, Danzig, Stockholm, Gothenburg, Hamburg, and Copenhagen.

Those of us who have done business with the Barings and the Hopes of the 1980s think of them as merchant-bankers with the emphasis upon the term after the hyphen. But two hundred years ago, they were more important as traders in red and blue commodities than in green paper. Their ties to America were in staples like cochineal, a red dye made from pulverizing the females of a cactus-feeding tropical insect; and indigo, a blue vegetable dye largely produced in the French West Indies, despite a name derived from the Greek word for India. The Hopes also dealt in linens, grain, and timber, and silver became intensely important from 1798 to 1808. They lent when they had to, but trading was their preferred activity. They liked commissions better than interest—commissions come quickly!

A second necessary corrective to twentieth-century habits of thought is the recognition that these merchant-bankers cannot easily be described as of one nationality or another. They were identified more with families than with cities, more with cities than with countries. Their limbs were flexible and of very extended reach.

A Gathering of Giants

On land, Napoleon was without serious rivals.* The British lay at sea, sending subsidies to their allies ashore and blocking Napoleon's access to the products of other continents, such as silver and sugar. They consoled themselves for losses sustained in Europe by picking off occasional cargo vessels seeking to penetrate their blockade, and also picking off, around the world, the choicest island colonies of France and of the neutrals.

Napoleon attempted to seal off the Continent from British trade by a "Continental system" much resented by American ship owners who were carrying some of that trade. American resentment was about equal toward the British "orders in council" imposing a blockade across most apertures into the continent.

Resentment was not passive; American traders did as much smuggling as possible through both the British orders and the French system. The importance of sea running was shown during the interlude known as the Peace of Amiens, from 1802 to 1804. When peace broke out, legitimate commerce was possible, and the amount of goods transported by the American bottoms dropped by half. Except in such distressingly tranquil times, when American smugglers and blockade runners were forced to compete with British and French merchants, Hamburg was the focus of American ingenuity, so long as Napoleon left the city unoccupied.† After the French finally scooped up Hamburg, the British developed a base for smuggling on Helgoland, just over its horizon.

The merchants of Hamburg and Helgoland were led by the American consul, a Scotsman named John Parish—father of David—who had lent money to the

---

*In 1804, to consolidate his continental domain after he crowned himself emperor, Napoleon manufactured an instant military aristocracy of 31 dukes, 451 counts, and 1,500 barons. This explains why so many of the characters in this story were titled.

†For the same reasons, the People's Republic of China found it expedient to allow the British to keep Hong Kong as neutral trading ground.

thirteen colonies before independence and who afterwards encouraged many New England and Philadelphia merchants to enter lucrative blockade running off the coasts of northern Europe. Upon the outbreak of hostilities between revolutionary France and most of the rest of Europe, in 1793, these merchants distributed 2,000 ducats (about 14,000 marcs banco, or about $22,000 in 1988 dollars) to the nubile daughters of M. Lehoc, the French ambassador to Lower Saxony, the German state professing to rule the city. One thousand each went to the Austrian and Prussian ambassadors, "to ensure . . . good will."

The price of neutral trading rose, however, with each French success; the Hamburgers next distributed a much larger sum, 300,000 marks, to leading members of the French Directory, and to an interesting list of ladies: Mme Napoleon Bonaparte; Mme Tallien, the wife (not, in this case, the mistress) of one of the Directors of France; Mme Condorcet; and the wife—not the daughters this time—of M. Lehoc. "Good relations with the French were re-established."* (John Parish also served as paymaster to the Continental armies opposing Napoleon and as a transfer agent of Russian interest payments to creditors in The Hague and London, especially to the House of Hope.)

Hamburg was so succulent a market that a swarm of Yankee seafarers were drawn there. In the 1930s, Samuel Eliot Morison perused the registers of the port and found that American entries "increased from 35 in 1791 to 192 in 1799." He assured us that this "North-European trade was not without its cultural contacts": the Reverend William Bentley of Salem rejoiced in exchanging coffee for German enlightenment. Bentley's diary tells us the date when a "good Professor," first furnished him "some of the best Books which his country has yielded."

Upon that moment Morison placed his thumb, pronouncing it to be that when "German erudition entered New England." (That's the way history should be written; more of us should venture such certainties.)

Morison gives us the lead to a footnote and a transition. Erudition went one way; coffee, tea, cotton, sugar, tobacco, exotic woods, and rum went the other. Blockade, counterblockade, and embargo were permeable membranes, but they did resist the pressures of commerce. When, in 1809, the American Embargo Act was repealed, the urge to sell had only the British and French to outwit, and American merchants assaulted the northern coasts of Europe like Vikings of trade, joining the Danes in open defiance of the great powers. The Danish port of Tonningen became a proxy for Hamburg and Altona.

Morison was not much interested in buildings; his affinities were afloat. But from the point of view of an architectural historian, the most significant erudition to enter the United States from Hamburg, Tonningen, or Copenha-

---

*This was the method suggested by Talleyrand to secure "good relations" with the United States at the same time in the XYZ Affair (see p. 117).

gen was French, not German or Danish. It was architectural style, the reciprocal to trade in consumer goods.

American Hopes

Even more important than John Parish to the banking and smuggling system of northern Europe was American-born Henry Hope. Hope, like Parish, came of a family of Scots discomfited by the antics of Bonnie Prince Charlie and by the severe British response to Jacobite and dissenter rebellions.

The story of the Hopes is complicated. They are often said to be Scottish, like the Parishes. The diligent Dutch scholar Marten Buist tells us that they once may have been French but that there was a trading Hope in Edinburgh as early as 1538. They had a stake in France (again?) in 1619, and an Archibald Hop, or Hoop, was christened at the Scottish Church in Rotterdam in 1664. Archibald became a malt trader, doing business with a set of Scottish cousins who had acquired a baronetcy early in the century and enough wealth to establish themselves at Hopetoun. There they built—in stages—Scotland's grandest mansion (1721–54).

The fortunes of the Dutch branch were rising. About 1750, their stake in the West Indies increased as Thomas Hope was appointed to represent William IV, chief of state of Holland, as governor general of the Dutch West Indies Company. Twenty years earlier, the family had spun off one of its less successful members, Henry Hope of Rotterdam, to Boston, where he acted as the receiving end of a large family business in transporting emigrants to America, though the West Indies trade remained at the center of its affairs, as it was for the Lerays.

The son and daughter of the Boston Hope, Henry and Henrietta Maria, returned to Holland. Henry became the dominant partner in the firm and was succeeded by Henrietta Maria's son-in-law, John Williams, who assumed the family name of Hope.

"American Henry"* Hope—the son—was a grand fellow: "None ever more perfectly realised the idea of a merchant prince, diligent in gathering, delighted to distribute . . . refined mind . . . quick tact . . . singularly even, mild, engaging . . . amiable"—and tough. After his ascent to affluence, he remained detached from the broils of faction in Amsterdam and above any petty considerations of French or British partisanship that might impinge upon business judgment.

---

*The term is my own, derived from the custom of calling his cousin Thomas (a generation removed), the Hellenophile and art patron, "Furniture Hope," to distinguish him from other Thomases.

"The Hope Family of Sydenham, Kent," by Benjamin West

He was an American, he was prone to say. When his countrymen were in Holland, he received and dazzled them. Benjamin Franklin, after a visit, reported that "the Hopes . . . are Rank'd amonge the greatest Merchants of Europe." Benjamin West, the émigré American painter in London, learned of him from Sir Joshua Reynolds; Mr. Hope's collection of paintings, said Reynolds, "is acknowledged to be the first in Amsterdam."

The Hopes soon intermarried with the Barings, who came from Bremen, but who had become more British than the British after two generations in Exeter and London. The Hopes were Francophiles in the 1780s, though they became renowned as patrons of British art and architecture after 1800. The baron de Frénilly saw them in their city palace in Amsterdam, staffed by servants "dressed in gold-galooned livery and drawn up in a row along a white marble corridor . . . The Millionaires . . . prided themselves on being frenchified, spoke only French, and lived entirely à la Francaise."

In the late 1780s they built their country house at Welgelegen. This "Pavilion," which will become better known to us through its Jeffersonian associations (see p. 441), is the most significant large artifact calling our attention to the Hopes.* It did not remain long in their hands, however, for French republican forces invaded Holland in 1794, in a counterthrust to a call by the prince of Orange for Prussian and British troops to protect him from his own people, who wished to establish a true Dutch republic. After these invaders were defeated by the French counterinvasion, the prince, accompanied by the Hopes, fled to England.

Though the Hope family departed, the entire Hope fortune did not. The firm was bifurcated. Between the new headquarters and the old, a fleet of fast little vessels carried on business between the combatants. Speed was important, for remittances were very large indeed. They became even larger when swollen by the interest still being paid by the Russians on loans arranged by "American Henry" Hope.

With commissions came capital, and with capital came leisure, for some members of the family. Thomas Hope the younger, "Furniture Hope," was the initiator of the neo-Grecian "Hope style," which found its way to the White House in Latrobe's designs for the furniture burnt by the British in 1814. Hope was a patron of architecture, painting, and sculpture rivaled among the peculiar, passionate, and persuasive Hellenophiles of Britain only by another scion of a wartime financial fortune, Henry Drummond of Grange Park. In its tranquil Hampshire valley, this wonderful house, completed in 1810, was a dream of Greece. It was also the setting for a later scene in this story, when Vincent Nolte learned some home truths there, after it passed from the hands of Henry Drummond into the firm clutches of Alexander Baring.

24

THE SILVER SCHEME

In New Orleans in 1816, he was "a man of courtly address, cultured mind, young and unmarried . . . received in the best society and lionized as the young leading capitalist and cotton buyer in the community."

A decade later, he was "ruined, crippled and broken hearted," and twenty years further along, "a vain, garrulous, scandalous old fellow."

Vincent Nolte wrote a great picaresque autobiography, out of which, in the 1930s, Hervey Allen quarried his novel *Anthony Adverse*. Nolte's book is in

*The Hope diamond is its more compact counterpart.

some ways a novel, too; it is generous with imaginative detail about events that took place far out of his sight. But he saw so much: Robert Fulton's steamboat trials and David Parish's silver machinations; Napoleon's Italian campaign and Andrew Jackson's at New Orleans; Talleyrand and Nicholas Biddle; courtesans of London, Paris, Milan, and Ogdensburg, New York; Chateaubriand and Aaron Burr; the eruption of Mount Etna and an earthquake at Louisville; Seminoles and Hapsburgs; Lafayette, Louis Philippe, and the village police of Bessarabia; the piratic Lafittes and the banking Lafittes; Barings, Hopes, and the Pope.*

Nolte was an architectural historian as well: he observed the association of Parish and Ramée, and his residence was designed by Latrobe. After that great man's death, he tended the widow, as he had tended the common-law wife and children of Latrobe's gifted son.

To Nolte we owe an account of the turbulence in international finance wherein he became the richest and most celebrated cotton speculator in the New World. Earlier, he had been an agent of the largest transfer of hard currency in the face of a blockade known to the annals of finance. At the end, he was a translator of scraps of jargon for monks in Trieste, a bill collector in Odessa, and, finally, a penny journalist in Hamburg.

Nolte was at home there, at the brink of the northern waters. His great-grandfather owned woolen mills in Sweden. From the 1750s on, his grandfather and his uncles were principals in a mercantile firm in Hamburg. His father, John Henry Nolte, was sent to school in Exeter, where he became a staunch friend of Francis Baring; two Hanseatic boys found each other among the heirs of Devonshire woolmen. This friendship continued into the next generation; Vincent, son of John, was often rescued from what he called his "scrapes" by Francis's son Alexander, who became the greatest banker of his age, ennobled as Lord Ashburton.

At the age of eleven, in 1790, Vincent Nolte had his first walk-on role in an opera and contracted a permanent obsession with the theatrical. All his life he saw himself and others as figures in a drama: Napoleon, for example, whom he observed as a very young officer in Italy, seemed to him, in recollection, "diminutive . . . his complexion . . . pallid and of almost yellowish hue, and long, sleek, jet-black hair, like that of the Talapouche Indians of Florida." Only a man who knew Napoleon and who had, meanwhile, been shipwrecked among the Talapouche, as Nolte was, would think of such a comparison.

When Nolte was a schoolboy in Hamburg, he amused himself by writing "sketches" for a satirical paper and indulging his "mania for the play" by doing amateur theatricals among the French royalist exiles who filled the city. Nolte tells us that his mania "spread to the family" of his friend Peter Godeffroy,

*No child should be deprived of Nolte's book.

whose father's Wednesday-night soirées were the cynosure of émigré society. "At length . . . Ramée . . . who had built our first Merchants' Exchange, was directed to put up a stage . . . in the large establishment of Mr. Godeffroy, and there, in the course of the winter, we all made our debut." Among the debutantes was one of Godeffroy's daughters, who married Nolte's friend Richard Parish—brother of David and Charles, whom we meet below. These were the sons of John, the American consul (for whom Ramée designed a country estate).

It was at this point that Gouverneur Morris and Leray de Chaumont passed through Hamburg on their way to America. Morris, observing the prosperity of John Parish, suggested that Parish's son David might become a baron— indeed, a feudal lord—if he were to purchase just a few hundred thousand acres of Morris's surplus property in New York. The sale was made, and, as a result, Ramée was drawn into an American career.

In 1804, Vincent Nolte left Ramée and amateur theatricals behind. It was time to abandon Hamburg. The city finally had been plucked from its lucrative neutrality by "the iron hand of Napoleon, that deadly foe of all commerce." Nolte felt confined in a port held hostage. He set out for Paris and for Nantes. Left behind in Hamburg was his father's friend P. C. Labouchère, the brother-in-law of Francis Baring. As a French national, Labouchère could safely ride out the French occupation, managing the residuum of the house of Hope in Amsterdam after the Hopes themselves embarked for England. (Labouchère's younger brother, who presided over the affairs of the firm in Nantes, became the dominant figure in that city after the departure of the Lerays.) The Barings and the Hopes, in London, were therefore free to offer their banking services, at a suitable fee, to the British combatants, while the Labouchères were available to the French. The Noltes and the Parishes could provide American services either to the French or to the British. (The Rothschilds, with even greater dexterity, served both sides in the war in the very same suite of rooms. They financed Wellington's peninsular campaign against Napoleon through their Paris office.)

Gabriel Julien Ouvrard

Of all the financiers of this extraordinary epoch, the most resourceful was Gabriel Julien Ouvrard. Ouvrard was the son of a paper manufacturer; his life was one long exercise in the manufacture of paper, of one sort or another.

His first great fortune arose from a singular presentiment about the literary potentialities of modern democracy. He correctly perceived that the guarantees of free speech and press enacted after the fall of the Bastille would offer unprecedented incentives to the printing of newspapers and handbills. A swiftly organized oligopoly of unprinted paper stock made him rich the first time. He saw as well that revolution would disrupt the ordinary course of trade, causing prices to rise and hard currency to become scarce, and giving rise to the printing of a great deal of paper money. Revolutionary inflation rewarded him as much as revolutionary freedom of information.

With the capital acquired from a surfeit of democracy, Ouvrard next anticipated a shortage in sugar and coffee. Revolutions are seldom welcomed by their neighbors, and the French Republic was sure to come to blows with the monarchies of Europe. Britain, Ouvrard speculated, would cut off the West Indies from France, and scarce Caribbean commodities would rise in price. He was right, and rich, again.

Ouvrard was not only rich; he was charming, ebullient, and handsome. He became the lover of Mme Tallien; thanks to her, he was awarded the lucrative contract to supply the French fleet under the Directory and, thereafter, the Spanish fleet the French impounded at Brest. Neither Mme Tallien nor these large endeavors distracted him from supplying as well luxuries to Josephine, Napoleon's wife. His attentions to the consort of "the tyrant" put Ouvrard at some risk. He multiplied his exposure by becoming the principal financier of the empire. His position was precarious, for Napoleon understood neither finance nor why the celebrated Mlle Georges, an actress of great beauty, succumbed to the charms of Ouvrard more readily than to his own.

Ouvrard became the Maecenas of the empire, a spectacularly generous sponsor of composers and artists and architects. His château at Raincy was to Paris what the Esterházy Palace was to Vienna. His hostess was the daughter of the head of the central bank of Spain—a great convenience in many ways. Yet always, as the music played and the guests chattered, his mind, deep, subtle, and constant, was turning upon schemes to make money. His experience in supplying the Spanish fleet showed him how slow payments in Spanish silver could be.

So Ouvrard devised another plan.

The Scheme Unfolds

Ouvrard's scheme required synchronized exceptions to Napoleon's Continental system, Britain's orders in council, and President Jefferson's policy of discouraging American vessels from engaging in trade with either Britain or France. In addition, merchants must be found bold enough to put precious ships and cargo between the teeth of the combatants, risking a bite with the slightest change of political mood. Recalling Napoleon's success at securing a promise from the Spanish government to pay to France seventy million pesos, Ouvrard blithely suggested that the Baring-Hope connection advance most of the seventy million to the French treasury in large dollops (one can imagine eyebrows rising in Amsterdam), taking notes issued by the Spanish crown in return. These notes would then be farmed out to other Dutch banking houses.

And why would the Dutch invest? The Spanish notes would, if all went well, be paid in Mexican silver, carried in neutral (American) ships, with the complicity of the British, the Spaniards, and the French.

Commerce being what it was, there were already conventional illegalities of trade, familiar routes through blockade and counterblockade and in contravention of "nonintervention." Merchants were already taking Mexican silver in exchange for cotton, rice, or tobacco to be sold in Europe. If the Hopes and Barings could arrange for more of such goods to reach Europe, eager European buyers would then remit the credit equivalents of silver to the Hopes and their associates. Fees would be taken all around.

Ouvrard was, of course, not the only one with a plan. As soon as it became known that the Spanish Bourbons had pledged their Mexican silver to Napoleon, in 1803, other entrepreneurs made bids to arrange matters. Talleyrand suggested to Chancellor Robert R. Livingston, the American minister to France, that they go into business together; a merchant named Daniel Parker would be their agent to transmit silver from Vera Cruz to France. But though Talleyrand and Livingston were quite capable of securing the complicity of the French and American governments, they could not obtain the crucial British guarantee of safe delivery; the British had plans of their own. What was denied Daniel Parker and Robert Livingston became available to the firm of Gordon and Murphy.

The Murphys were a family of Irish merchants (like the Craigs and the Olivers) with branches in places like Cádiz and Vera Cruz. The Tory government, hearing that the Spanish branch of the Murphys had secured for Gordon and Murphy the rights to trade in Mexico and to ship silver directly to the Spanish crown, determined to put to the test the depth of Spanish need.

Bluff and hearty, the British government proposed that its fleet thrust aside all this folderol and go into the business of transporting silver to its enemies.

In December 1806, the warship *Resistance* was sent to Vera Cruz, bearing vouchers from the European Murphys to the Vera Cruz branch of the family. England and Spain were at war, but H.M.S. *Resistance* went home with more than three million pesos delivered under a Spanish crown contract, and the partners shipped an additional ten million pesos thereafter. Some of it went on conventional blockade-running packets by way of Jamaica, but most went in the holds of five ships of His Britannic Majesty's Navy, the *Resistance,* the *Thames,* the *Veteran,* the *Adamant,* and the *Topaz.*

For these services, Gordon and Murphy and the Admiralty took very large fees. Those of the Admiralty were used to shore up the Bank of England; and since the silver shipments went directly to the Spanish Crown, not to Napoleon,

Sir Francis Baring, John Baring, and Charles Wall by Thomas Lawrence

one could pretend that they were used only for Spanish domestic purposes. The most painful patriotic issues were avoided.

Six months after the *Resistance* appeared in the harbor of Vera Cruz, H.M.S. *Diana* dropped anchor there. This time the Mexican authorities were asked not to ship to Spain but, on order of the king of Spain, to the house of Baring in London. Would the Mexicans honor a demand to release silver to be carried to an enemy port on an enemy warship? They did; 3.8 million pesos in silver was delivered to the *Diana* with proper Spanish punctilio under the guns of the garrison. She dropped off 150,000 of the pesos in American ports to tease other merchants into the scheme, but the rest arrived at London in October. The Admiralty took another fee, duly paid to the Bank of England. The Barings took theirs (similarly deposited, one assumes) and paid the balance over to the Hopes, to transmit to France.

Such a quick, terrifying experiment was subject to more than political risk. The governance of Nature is not always so complaisant as that of human affairs. Not often would prudent men entrust 3.8 million pesos of silver to a single commercial vessel, and even the one-time profit of 830,000 pesos—about $16 million today—was not quite enough to justify that kind of risk.

On sober consideration, there was no avoiding the necessity to spread the risks across a fleet of neutral craft. Some neutrals were already operating in Vera Cruz, though not picking up silver deliveries for the British crown account. John Craig of Philadelphia had received Vera Cruz trading rights from the Spanish crown, through his Spanish son-in-law, Francisco Sarmiento. Craig enlisted a set of brothers-in-law, the Olivers of Baltimore. Craig and the Olivers made six expeditions to Vera Cruz between the issuance of their "exclusive" trading rights in December 1804 and the arrival on their doorsteps of Ouvrard's legate, bearing a new set of "exclusive" trading rights, with the British crown as an equal partner.

The British, Ouvrard, and the king of Spain proposed to profiteer from Mexican scarcities created by the blockade of the British fleet against the possessions of the Spanish crown. Profits would arise from sales by the Americans to the Mexicans. Having disposed of their goods, the American traders would carry home additional cargo beyond their extravagant trading profits: silver pesos sent under Ouvrard's crown contract. Shipments began. Silver pesos went into ballast, covered by a layer of trade goods for show. These products were unloaded in New Orleans, where the silver purchased other American products—increasingly, cotton—for the European market.* That market was starved and highly priced because of previous market imperfections caused by the fleets of both France and England.

These imperfections were sometimes violent, causing growing aversion to the risks of blockade running on the part of Mr. Jefferson's government. (Altercations with the British fleet would ultimately lead to the War of 1812.) To the conspirators in the Silver Scheme from 1805 to 1809, it was essential to induce a relaxation in Mr. Jefferson's aversion. The American government must take a realistic view, or American ships would sail home from Vera Cruz empty of silver ballast. This was already clear to John Craig and the Olivers. Reasons for finding exceptions to Jeffersonian policy, reasons of silver, must be shared with the Jeffersonian merchants of Baltimore and Philadelphia, such as Stephen Girard and Samuel Smith.

Once again, the support of Albert Gallatin, secretary of the treasury, must be secured, as it had been for merino sheep. Though differences with these merchants over aid to Toussaint were still fresh in everyone's mind, reasons could be found.

Who could be entrusted with the delicate task of arranging matters with these merchants and, with those arranged, doing more arranging with the government of the United States?

The Hopes, the Barings, and Ouvrard already had American connections.

---

*This is how Vincent Nolte, by then the agent of the Barings in New Orleans, entered the cotton business.

Ouvrard had a brother in Philadelphia. He had gone to Vera Cruz to "case the joint" and was shown millions in silver awaiting shipment. A Baring cousin was living in South Carolina. But Ouvrard's brother was Ouvrard's man, not the Hopes' or the Barings', and, for some reason undisclosed by the surviving documents, the South Carolina cousin, Charles Baring, was only briefly involved in the larger operations of the firm.

The *Diana* and Susan

In the first few drafts of this book, Charles Baring remained in the baffled sentence terminating the previous section. But Marten Buist's foraging about in the Hope archives has yielded the information that it was Baring who was aboard the frigate *Diana* in her hair-raising voyage from Vera Cruz to Portsmouth. From this single exploit in 1807, he and his brother, the future Lord Ashburton, collected personal commissions worth perhaps $2 million today. So he earned his way into the following admittedly parenthetical paragraphs:

Charles Baring was married, in Philadelphia, about 1798, to Susan Tudor Cole Heyward, a lady said to have been Welsh. In any case, she had been married several times; when Baring met her, she was the wealthy widow of James Heyward, a planter of Beaufort, South Carolina. After his affairs were put in order, thanks to the *Diana,* he and his wife settled down into Carolina planting "on a large scale," while he kept a casual hand in business in Charleston. A colleague in these ventures was the French consul in Charleston, the comte de Choiseul, himself a descendant of another family previously mentioned in these pages, the allies of the René Leray de Chaumont in the renaissance of the French navy.

About 1827, Baring and Choiseul joined with the Barings' primary Charleston correspondent, Mitchell King, in buying tracts of land in the foothills along the North and South Carolina border, near Flat Rock; between 1827 and 1830, they dominated a stretch ten miles long and eleven thousand acres in extent, where Baring built a summer house called Mountain Lodge. In the twentieth century it was remodeled and given eight slim columns, in pairs, across its portico—like that of Montmorenci, the mansion of a Warren County, North Carolina planter-merchant named William ("Pretty Billy") Williams, built about 1820 (see *Architecture, Men, Women and Money*).

Susan Tudor Cole Heyward Baring was a remarkable woman, of whom more should be known. She and her husband (it is said) designed a family chapel at Flat Rock. It became the community's Anglican church and remains in use to this day. After her death, and with it the end of income flowing from the Heyward estates, Baring was forced to give up Mountain Lodge; but he lived on, in the mountains, to the age of ninety-two.

The Craig Connection

Two other Baring brothers married daughters of the richest man in Philadelphia, William Bingham. With the Bingham daughters came easy connections to John Craig; his son-in-law the charming Sarmiento of Andalusia; and the resourceful Olivers, who already understood the high politics of trade.

Though history can barely perceive him beyond the bulk of his other son-in-law, Nicholas Biddle, Craig was a man worth studying. He commissioned Latrobe to remodel in "Regency Gothic" the summer house he called Andalusia, a name familiar to architectural historians but not often associated, as it should be, with Spanish silver.*

The threat of competition from the Craig-Oliver-Sarmiento group became known to the Hopes and the Barings, probably through Talleyrand. He had his own network of agents in places like Havana and Vera Cruz. He may have suggested that the Hopes engage someone who could deal not only with American complexities but also with the French government—that is, with Talleyrand, on his terms. Ambitious, resourceful, but already flawed by an overweening sense of his own importance and invidious wisdom, David, the third son of John Parish of Hamburg, stepped forward.

25

DAVID PARISH

David Parish had come to know Talleyrand during the bishop's exile in Hamburg, before he went off to America. Parish made his own departure from Hamburg soon thereafter and established himself in Antwerp. There is a persistent story that he acquired the capital for his new venture through a winning streak at whist.

Like Talleyrand, he loved high-stakes games. When the two were in partnership, they were not above fixing the deck. As the two-year Peace of Amiens between Napoleon and the British drew toward its end in 1804, Talleyrand visited Parish in Antwerp. The secret that Napoleon would shortly bring down

*The work was continued by his widow, with Robert Mills in charge for Latrobe, in 1807. Nicholas Biddle, who enjoyed a bantering exchange of architectural views with his mother-in-law, added piquancy to the estate with a Greek gazebo. Finally, Biddle called forth the Greek shell from Thomas U. Walter that one sees at Andalusia today.

David Parish (artist unknown)

upon himself, again, a British blockade, carried with it assurance that prices for West Indian trade goods would again escalate. Talleyrand was not a man to lose an opportunity like that. He informed Parish; they formed a corner on West Indian trade goods. They both grew notoriously richer—so notoriously that the Hopes could be quite certain that Talleyrand would not resist the Silver Scheme out of any animus against its American agent, and might, in fact, take a little piece of the deal himself.

Parish was allotted, for himself and useful friends, one-fourth of all benefits to flow from the scheme. Early in 1805 he set out for Philadelphia. In July, Vincent Nolte went to arrange matters in New Orleans.

It was the view of all the partners that their best representative in Vera Cruz would be another old friend of Nolte's, Armand Pierre Lestapis. Unfortunately, though he looked Spanish and spoke the language impeccably, Lestapis was French; the Mexicans were not hospitable to the French at that moment. Just in time, the partners heard of the death of one José Gabriel Villanueva, a Spaniard who happened to be of the same age, weight, and height as Lestapis. Lestapis became Spanish by becoming Villaneuva. Equipped with the identity and passport of his departed friend, he set out for Vera Cruz.

Lestapis, unlike Parish, was a romantic fellow, and he put the whole venture at risk. In Vera Cruz he fell in love with a local lady named Manuelita de Garay and revealed to her his true identity. He also revealed the possibilities before them. She responded by swearing them both to silence until the profits were reaped. She was not put off by marrying a man under a false name, so long as it was agreed that they would repeat the ceremony when it became propitious to do so. They were married under his real name, in Philadelphia, two years later.*

The Silver Fleet

In Philadelphia, David Parish and John Craig reached an accommodation: the members of the Craig-Oliver syndicate would give up their independent operation in return for a contract to do most of the carrying for Parish. They had attempted to secure, on their own, some assurances against the piratical British admirals and privateers operating in the Caribbean; but the British minister to the United States, who was not privy to his government's silver arrangements, protested that it was quite impossible for His Majesty to enter into a conspiracy with the king of Spain and these Yankee freebooters.

Higher levels of government must be reached. And there, smiling knowing smiles, were the Hopes and the Barings. Profits were great enough to provide for everyone, so the American merchants "cut a deal." They grumbled and gathered, grumbled and gathered more.

To gather the more expeditiously, they set upon the seas some of the loveliest objects ever made in America, trim craft built for speed rather than bulk, fit to voyage quickly to and especially from Vera Cruz. Modest carrying capacity was no deterrent when trade was in silver. The Craig-Oliver clan were adept in the design, construction, and navigation of ship-rigged, slim, sleek, and expeditious vessels. These "Chesapeake schooners" evolved into the famous Baltimore clippers.†

At first, all went smoothly. The proto-clippers slid around the sides of the North American continent, glistening in the sun, their white sails catching every breeze and their holds full of the moonlight glow of Mexican silver.

---

*Nolte found his own wife in New Orleans, somewhat later, and revealed, in his description of her, how trapped he was in the culture of his time. She was, he said, "remarkable not only for rare beauty, but for good tact—that substitute for a powerful mind which good Nature grants to women— . . . faithful, loving, steadfast, well-tried, and courageous." She bore him five children. The two boys died in early manhood, one of the daughters as a child. So he was left with this "steadfast" companion and the remaining girls, from whom, it seems, he expected far less than he might.

Though David Parish is not recorded as denigrating women in Nolte's way, he did not seem to be drawn to them, preferring, instead, a succession of young and handsome men (he left a portrait of one, John Ross, among his family pictures). One of them was William Courtenay, who served as supercargo on several of the voyages to Vera Cruz. It appears that this is "Kitty," the William Courtenay who became earl of Devon and lord of Powderham Castle. In his youth, Kitty had been involved in a scandal with William Beckford and was sent into temporary exile in America.

†My colleagues tending the National Water Craft Collection assure me that it is risky to use the word "clipper," as Vincent Nolte did, to describe Chesapeake schooners of 1805. On the other hand, they no longer hold to the traditional view that the first clipper ship was the *Ann McKim,* launched in 1833. The *Ann McKim* was not much different from predecessors of the Silver Scheme era.

No self-respecting merchant would let a merchant vessel go empty to Mexico. The manifests of the vessels bound for Vera Cruz showed shipments of calicoes, black velvet, "fancy chintz," cambric and corded dimity, German and Irish linens. British textile manufacturers happily contemplated their ledger books, and American manufacturers smiled in equal satisfaction. Vera Cruz welcomed fresh supplies of iron and steel, umbrellas, hats and gloves, fine writing paper and firearms, beer, wine, and brandy, olives and sweetmeats.

Payments in return were prompt. Customs receipts in the United States went far to reduce Mr. Gallatin's debt. In the period 1806 to 1808, four times more silver was deposited in branches of the Bank of the United States than was required for minting. Money supply, leveraged upward by silver reserves, rose enough to counteract some of the depression caused by Mr. Jefferson's inhibitions on other kinds of intercourse with the European belligerents. Mr. Gallatin was serving his party well; the Republicans had a better hold upon the southern and central ports to which silver shipments flowed. Federalist New England could howl about unequal protection of the laws: the Federal government was solvent again, wasn't it?

The Great Silver Scheme extended its benefactions to the farthest reaches of international finance. It refreshed the tired old East India Company and thereby enriched the merchants of Canton. British silver kept Austrian, Prussian, and Russian armies in the field against Napoleon. At the field of Wagram, in 1809, two armies outfitted by Mexican silver faced each other, the French and the Austrian. Cannon and uniforms, largely of Mexican fiscal origin, were stockpiled by Napoleon to be squandered in his Russian campaign. They might have been enough to bring victory to the French had Mexican silver not kept some Russian troops under discipline from 1809 to 1812, long enough to contend with Napoleon.

During the five years when the Great Silver Scheme operated, a sum of twelve million pesos reached the United States through Parish's agents. Only sixty thousand went directly to Europe in silver; the rest stimulated sales to Europe of American tobacco, rice, fish, and cotton. Silver was exchanged by agents like Nolte for these staples. In return, European merchants were pleased to issue notes, for "presentation" and collection to Europe. Once there, silver was converted by fiscal alchemy into paper.* Some of the paper clung to the hands of the British and Dutch financiers; some went into the Ouvrards' account in the Hopes' bank. Much of it eventuated in the war chest of Napoleon.

Seven hundred and twenty-one thousand dollars was divided between David Parish and his primary partners, Craig and the Olivers. By my computations,

---

*Lay persons like myself find it easiest to grasp such a point visually: the transfer of credits based upon metal became clear to me only when my wife and daughter and I went on a tour of the vaults of the Rothschild establishment in London and observed little cards, bearing the names of Arab states, shifted from one stack of ingots to another, as "calls"—rights to claim assets—shifted, though the assets themselves remained unmoved.

they could have built with that much money, at the time, a little city of six thousand two-bedroom houses.

The End of the Game

Napoleon's military expenses, like his frontiers, outpaced his receipts. Ouvrard was pressed to find additional sums and spent more and more time in Spain, pressing, in his turn, for more and quicker payments. He left his French affairs to a partner who substituted peculation for levitation. On the eve of his victory at Austerlitz, Napoleon was informed that the Bank of France was collapsing. Ouvrard was summoned home. He was blamed for the failure of his system to accommodate Napoleon's ambitions. At the end of 1807, he was forced into bankruptcy and then into prison.

The fall of Ouvrard put the Hopes to the test. Sitting in Amsterdam, with the emperor's noose around his neck, Labouchère told Napoleon's new chief of finance that he would not disgorge to the French government Ouvrard's private share of the Great Silver Scheme. According to Nolte, Labouchère said: "Whether we have money in our hands for Mr. Ouvrard or not, Baron, is not a matter for which we are obliged to render any account to you." Thereafter, the Hopes declined to continue their advances to the French government against the receipt of Mexican silver.

Napoleon ordered his own representatives in Philadelphia to try to induce Stephen Girard and others to accept the notes of the Spanish government and to start a new series of shipments of silver leaving the Hopes and Barings aside. The Americans declined.

Far more important, the Mexicans were tiring of watching their chief natural resource drained off to supply funds for royal extravagance and Napoleonic adventure. While no one could prove that their own king was a partner in profiteering from their distress, the merchants of Vera Cruz knew the price of "British manufactured goods which they sell at the most exorbitant profits." They complained of "illicit goods . . . the Jamaicans and Americans now lawfully import . . . in as large quantities as they please . . . and . . . sell at the prices they please . . . Foreigners enjoy every privilege, and the King's Subjects are alone oppressed."

It is no wonder that when the Mexicans heard that Napoleon had invaded Spain and set his brother Joseph upon the throne, they declined to load either H.M.S. *Melpomene* for Gordon and Murphy or the *Columbia* for the Hopes and the Barings.

The game was over. But David Parish and his partners were very, very rich.

Parish in the Woods

Another game now began. Among its participants were Gouverneur Morris, the man of poodles on ribbons and bright red shoes; Benjamin West, the painter; and James Leray de Chaumont. The million acres or so of scrub, rock, and swamp in northern New York that these gentlemen had acquired were somewhat more than they could use or readily market to purchasers of small farms. They searched the horizon for a buyer, and the perfect pigeon flew into sight, his pinions glittering with silver, rich and overconfident: David Parish. How beautiful he must have seemed to these three overstocked speculators. Headstrong, and possessing the modern equivalent of $25 million or more, Parish was much impressed with the scintillating Morris, often a guest of his father's in Hamburg, and with Leray, who could be quite charming.

In 1807, Morris drew Parish into an investment of fifty thousand dollars (possibly worth a million dollars today) in land he was willing to relinquish along the Saint Lawrence. Leray let Parish have one hundred thousand acres more. And Morris's kinsman David Ogden came forward and sold Parish an entire imaginary metropolis called Ogdensburg.

Upon the Pyrenean soil of the Adirondacks, Parish proposed to graze three thousand merino sheep. His role in the Silver Scheme earned him the right to call upon Albert Gallatin for a return of favors; and the secretary of the treasury permitted Parish, like the Du Ponts and Pierre Bauduy, to get his sheep through the Embargo Act, the blockade, and the counterblockade.

Parish was so caught up in "merino mania" that, according to Nolte, he came to believe the Adirondacks were "an exact repetition of the Spanish district where the merino sheep yield the most perfect wool." Nolte recounts the story that one day in 1808, he and Parish were en route from Philadelphia to Baltimore. "Parish was so possessed by this idea, that . . . as we passed a stretch of stony ground and saw some merino sheep skipping about over it, he exclaimed to me, in great glee, 'Look! Look there, Nolte! how they jump about! they yield splendid wool!' " (Perhaps that "stretch of stony ground" was one of the upland portions of the property belonging to Pierre Bauduy along the Philadelphia-Baltimore road.)

By the end of 1809, Parish had close to $370,000—worth perhaps $8 million today—invested in sheep and his empire of two hundred thousand largely barren acres. This was well within his share of the still undistributed silver profits. Nolte was dispatched to Europe to try to induce the Hopes and the Barings to permit Parish to retain their shares and commit them as well to the land venture. First, Nolte called upon the senior Parish, who was taking the

Parishville, c. 1838, by Salathiel Ellis

waters at Cheltenham. Parish was "out for a constitutional," wearing "a little velvet cap . . . in Polish style, with long wide sleeves and gold-worked braid, and a long Turkish pipe in his right hand; and in his left a silken leash, in which he held two skittish poodle dogs." It appears that Parish had acquired his taste in dogs from Gouverneur Morris, as his son had acquired his in land.

Nolte moved on, to report to Alexander Baring. Baring was in Bishopsgate, more drably clad than John Parish, and wondering what madness had overtaken the son of that prosperous old gentleman. He and his brother were already sitting on a million acres in the barrens of Maine inherited from William Bingham; so their response to Parish's proposition was: "He is welcome to it!"

Nolte next sought out David Parish's brother, Charles, in Helgoland, "the rendezvous of all the smugglers of the mainland," where Charles exhibited "his special fitness for the part of a mercantile matado," and where Nolte had no better luck. Finally, after a visit to Hamburg, he went off to Paris, where Labouchère "could not conceal a great deal of irritation against Parish." The lines were beginning to form. Nolte, sensitive to the opinions of his seniors, began noting "the vanity of Parish . . . throwing money about in all directions."

Nolte says he declined a partnership representing Parish in Liverpool and a counter-offer from the Labouchères. Instead, he became a representative of the Barings and the Hopes in New Orleans.

A State of Tranquility and Security

In 1810, David Parish made his own swing about Europe. He was finally willing to admit to his former senior partners that the land in northern New York was becoming a burden too heavy to carry alone. After hearing his proposals, they again politely refused. They had taken his measure and were disinclined to play, though they did offer him a seat on the board of Hope and Company. This he was too proud to accept. He resigned from his firm in Antwerp as well and set his face resolutely toward the Saint Lawrence Valley.

Parish returned to the United States in 1811. He told his father he was going to "the only country where a person could look forward to enjoy for half a century at least, a state of tranquility and security."

Though his fortune was tied up in sheep and land, Parish still behaved as the "omnipotent Jupiter of the American money-market," lavishing promises and impressions in lieu of cash. In America, impressions were almost legal tender.

The Philadelphia residence of David Parish was a mansion at the corner of Walnut and Little Seventh streets, on the west side of Washington Square. It stood three and a half stories high, with a flight of steps up to a fan-lighted doorway; George Ticknor of Boston thought it "the grandest house in the city." Within, things were grander still: Ticknor saw "for the first time in my life . . . a full service of silver plate, for twenty persons," with liveried servants tending a dining room "sumptuously furnished and hung with pictures of merit."

A frequent diner upon Parish's silver plate was the secretary of the treasury, Albert Gallatin, but by 1813 the two could no longer do much to help each other: the Treasury was as short of cash as Parish was. In February, in the midst of an unpopular war against the British, Gallatin told President Madison: "We have hardly enough money to last to the end of the month." He proposed to discharge the militia and restrict operations in the West to purely defensive maneuvering.

Six weeks later, on March 18, Parish told Gallatin that no "new appeal to the public" for funds would avail unless coupled with an assurance that the government would speedily withdraw from the war. "That," he said, might enable "me and my friends in our principal seaports to dispose of" a loan. A $10 million war loan was floated weeks later, but two-thirds of the necessary amount went unsubscribed. "The Olivers, Craig and others, who had to thank Parish for the origin of their wealth, did not feel inclined to risk, once more, the money they had accumulated." They met him with "shyness." Robert Oliver admitted to Nicholas Biddle that instead of investing in the war effort, he was sending "the principal part of my funds to England."

As Oliver and other merchants of the middle colonies bet against the survival of the government of the United States, the Federalists of New England went even further. They strove to push their own government toward insolvency, demanding payment of government debt in specie. Mr. Gallatin had none to supply.

Then Stephen Girard emerged from the shadows with a proposal: he would see to it that the necessary credit was found, even if he had to land most of the money himself.

Investment Banking

Parish put in no cash, but he took the major credit for underwriting Mr. Gallatin's famous war loan of $12 million.

This was how investment banking had its origins in America. Girard, Parish, and John Jacob Astor guaranteed to buy a very large amount of government debt and then sold off their obligations, and the government's, to a multitude of buyers.*

The three "underwriters" bought at a very heavy discount, with the intention of selling close to par, on the strength of their own names. Parish was still basking in his renown as a silver king, and Astor was known to be the proprietor of a fortune built on furs. The credit of these men replaced the ruined reputation of the United States government.

Girard had used his special relationship with Gallatin and Jefferson a year earlier to force other Philadelphia bankers to admit his private bank into the circle of those interchanging credits: thanks to his political connections, his bills of exchange could be backed by deposits of the United States government. (Gallatin understood Girard—they probably spoke their native tongue, French, to each other in private.) He now made a second assault upon the Quaker inner sanctum, using Parish as his crowbar. He made it plain to Parish that he wanted that harried man to deploy his friendship with Gallatin to secure the government deposits arising from the war loan. Indirection was unnecessary. Gallatin could calibrate power very precisely. He knew that Girard was in charge, not Parish: he told Madison, "My reliance upon Parish is not great."

---

*Donald Adams, who made this account possible by his researches into the loan, tells us that the subscription lists included a boarding-school operator, a clerk, a widow, a sea captain, a clergyman, a bookbinder, a jeweler, a brewer, a grocer, a shoemaker, a distiller, a tailor, and a miller. (D. Adams, *Beginning,* p. 114)

Albert Gallatin by Gilbert Stuart

Parish then overstepped. He wanted a share of the profits arising from investment of those deposits, resulting from "the arrangement I made for you with Mr. Gallatin." Girard, who knew better, rebuked him, reminding him that he, Girard, had all the money at risk in the underwriting. He had lent Parish every cent of Parish's subscription and charged no interest until Parish's obligations were long overdue. "A Gentleman," said Girard, "who does not contribute . . . cannot expect to participate." He had been forced to curtail his own operations in order to accommodate Parish, while he was harassed by a specie raid on his reserves by the Bank of Pennsylvania (operating in the stately headquarters—"si beau . . . si simple!"—designed by Latrobe).

Parish did not press; Girard did not forget. They joined together again, gingerly, a year later. The government was once again in need. "The Department of State was so bare of money as to be unable to pay even its stationery bill." A national bank was needed.

Parish dutifully performed his lobbying chores for the second Bank of the United States. Girard took the dominant role. In 1816, he repeated his investment-banking feat, disposing of nearly a million dollars of stock in the bank. David Parish, land poor, alienated from Girard, on edgy terms with the Barings and the Hopes, still spoke vaingloriously to the secretary of the treasury about his power to attract investors to purchase stock in the bank. But he was now so reduced in circumstance that he himself could not afford a single share. He was forced to "decline the proposition you had the goodness to make in relation to the Subscription to the Bank."

He was still trying to sell off his real estate, reducing the price from five

dollars to one dollar per acre. The collapse of the "merino mania" consumed
nearly all the resources remaining to Parish after he had built stores, houses,
mills, churches, taverns, and roads upon his endless acres of scrub and shale. The
War of 1812 destroyed his commerce upon the Saint Lawrence, and his iron
furnaces failed to produce a sufficiently commercial return. Settlers preferred
the deeper soil and kinder climate of Ohio and western New York to offerings
in the far North. Defeated, finally, Parish returned to Europe in July 1816, a
tarnished golden boy. After a desultory tour of England, he joined Fries and
Company, a new banking house in Vienna, under the protection of Prince
Metternich.

Metternich was master of Austrian foreign policy but no financial genius;
Parish was a daring speculator but no judge of character. The other partners
of Fries were, it seems, dishonest. Their rickety structure, sapped by peculations,
fell before the panic of 1825–26, a storm that also destroyed Vincent Nolte and
Co. in New Orleans. Nolte picked himself up and survived. Parish was not so
resilient as his old partner. Knowing that he had involved his elderly father in
his folly and that the family fortune was gone, he drowned himself in the
Danube on April 27, 1826.

26

COTTON AND ARCHITECTURE

Vincent Nolte returned to New Orleans in 1811. The three years of the War
of 1812 provided him a brief military career under Andrew Jackson, whom he
hated, and great opportunities to bite his nails. Commerce was dull. New
Orleans was bottled up by the British fleet prowling the Gulf of Mexico.

Wellington's victory over the French in Spain in 1814 permitted the release
of some of his troops to punish the Americans, who had been co-belligerents
with France. The British burned Washington and then sent a detachment of
Peninsular veterans to attack New Orleans, the capital of the former French
possessions recently acquired by the United States. That force was met and
defeated early in 1815 by Jackson's multinational army, an assemblage of Creole
pirates, Scotch-Irish backwoods riflemen, French republicans, monarchists and
Bonapartists, and merchants, economists, and artists of all countries, including
Vincent Nolte and Henry Latrobe, Benjamin Henry Latrobe's son.

Jackson was a fierce warrior, but he became an erratic military governor of
Louisiana after the battle, quickly forfeiting the respect of most members of
the coalition that had won him his celebrated victory. Colonel Toussard, once
the hunting companion of Irénée Du Pont, was acting as French consul in New
Orleans. Jackson arrested him in a fit of temper. Nolte assisted in extricating

Colonel Toussard from Jackson's arrest and built a reputation as someone to be trusted by men of all nations.

After the peace of 1815, Nolte's career careened upward. He became the most proficient cotton speculator in New Orleans, sometimes operating on his own account, but sufficiently busy in the interest of the Barings that when Francis Baring came to New Orleans in 1820–21, he found the levee "strewn from the upper to the lower suburb, with cotton bales, on which were stamped the marks of my firm." If Nolte's memory and my calculations of present value (neither more certain than the other) are correct, he was doing the equivalent in 1988 dollars of $25 million in cotton shipments every few weeks. "The most important commissions from France were . . . concentrated in our hands [and] those from England, in addition to the business entrusted to us from the northern states of America."*

The Last Act

The last paroxysm of the great postwar cotton inflation exploded in 1819. Vincent Nolte greeted Benjamin Henry Latrobe, who arrived in New Orleans in that year, with friendship and a succession of architectural commissions we will examine in chapter 41. After Latrobe's death, Nolte made a triumphal tour among his French customers. Near Nantes, in the summer of 1822, he

> saw the great Chateaubriand, then in the zenith of his glory, companion-less, wandering lonely and forsaken on the shore, pursuing his dreams . . . He merited this . . . neglect as little as I my distinguished welcome; that I felt in my heart. His merits rested on a pedestal that, as time progressed, would lift him ever higher; mine rested on a well-calculated lucky operation in the cotton market.

Nolte's "calculations" worked fairly well while prices oscillated in a relatively predictable range. Within that range, he deployed his credit liberally. But as his purchases followed prices upward in their last frenzied cusp, his system faltered. In the subsequent collapse, during the winter of 1825–26, his enormous holdings hung leaden and unsold. His British correspondents failed, along with more than a hundred banks in London. He was wiped out.

He went to Europe to explain himself. Francis Baring was "too busy" to receive him at The Grange and declined further credit. Baring did find time for a letter of consolation: "Of the various scrapes I have seen you in, that last which brought you down was certainly the one in which you had the least of

---

*"Commissions" from French textile manufacturing were as crucial a source of revenue to Vincent Nolte as to those cousins of Edgar Degas whom the painter sketched in New Orleans later in the century.

blame . . . I believe I once before told you that in my opinion you stand adversity better than prosperity, and this is the case with most people. Keep up your courage, my dear Sir." If Nolte's recollections are correct, Baring had things a little confused; Nolte was the author, not the object, of earlier sententiousness about prosperity and adversity. The object lesson had been David Parish.

Nolte returned to America, wound up his affairs, deplored the defeat of John Quincy Adams by "the filthy intrigues of a most unprincipled man—I mean, of General Jackson," and began again in Europe in 1829. After a lifetime collecting anecdotes, he died, in Hamburg, on the verge of the American Civil War.

I cannot deny you two of Nolte's vignettes. The first is about Talleyrand in the 1840s. The second is about himself, in the 1850s, on his last trip to the United States.

One day, when Talleyrand was near the end of his life, he was seen getting out of his carriage at the Chamber of Deputies. It was February 1848. He caught the eye of an acquaintance, who asked him whether he was going to swear loyalty to yet another new constitution for France: "You have done the same thing to fourteen others!" "My friend," Nolte has Talleyrand reply, "let us hope it will be the last."*

A few years later, Nolte traveled from Cincinnati to Philadelphia by coach with "a black-eyed, well-formed Italian lady," who, he said, "is now living on a country-seat near Ogdensburg, as mistress of a Hamburgher much younger than herself."

What delicacy. We shall have to identify that "much younger" lover, and return to the Red Villa left behind by David Parish in Ogdensburg. And there, patiently waiting for us to finish his story, is Joseph Ramée.

Enter M. Ramée

We have glanced at him as part of the entourage brought to the United States by David Parish, and then as the creator of the theater in Hamburg where Vincent Nolte first expressed his dramatic talent. He had traveled in even more exalted circles than these.

Ramée was trained as a member of the architectural staff of the brother of the king of France, the comte d'Artois, and learned stage design by working up pageants for the court at Versailles. The stage always attracted him. William Beckford, his most munificent patron, presented to him the opportunity to

*Talleyrand once included the commonwealth of Pennsylvania among the governments to which he pledged eternal fidelity.

design an entire village as a stage set, for an opera of Beckford's own composition.

Ramée began somewhat more modestly. He was credited with the design of a small theater in Paris before he was twenty, and he may have assisted in the design of a house for the actress and courtesan Sophie Arnould. If it had been built, it would have been next door to Ledoux's famous pavilion for the dancer and courtesan Mlle Guimard, a temple to Terpsichore and to Eros that was later remodeled by Ramée into a sober mansion for the banker Jean-Fréderic Perrégaux.

Our best information about Ramée (and about one of his rivals in Baltimore, Maximilian Godefroy) comes from the files of the French secret police and the courts. In 1800 Ramée tried, unsuccessfully, to prove that he had been a republican all along, so that he could return to practice in France. A number of his friends submitted affidavits describing his skill and reminding the Napoleonic police of the memorable "Fête de la Confédération," where Talleyrand and his three thousand priests officiated. When Lafayette led the National Guard into that celebration, they paraded to a central podium designed by Ramée. Pledges of loyalty to the republic were made at his cylindrical Altar of the Fatherland, upon a circular platform in the midst of a huge elliptical earthwork like a prehistoric fort.

Ramée had been quietly critical of the revolutionary regime; and after a brief service in the army of Flanders, he defected and went over to the Austrians, in company with Dumouriez and Louis Philippe. He spent nearly all the next twenty-three years in an exile neither harsh nor unrewarding. In the early 1790s, he was engaged by Beckford, the inheritor of incalculable sugar wealth from Jamaica. Beckford was the author, in French, of the Gothic novel *Vathek*. He was also creator of Fonthill, a cathedral of pleasure in Wiltshire with a twenty-seven-story-high tower, and, next, of a classic towerlet in Bath now set in the midst of a graveyard.

Beckford heightened his sensibilities with all manner of stimulants, including revolution. He was trained in music by Wolfgang Amadeus Mozart and in drawing by John Robert Cozens. He was in Paris in 1789, and again in 1790, vying with Richard Cosway (see p. 445) for the purchase of distressed artistic merchandise. He acquired an entourage of painters, cooks, and musicians, some of them, like the paintings touched up for resale by Cosway, left as the impedimenta of rapid aristocratic departures. In July 1792 he took his orchestra, his painters, and his cooks to the shores of Lake Geneva and set himself up at Evian, having escaped from "the most frightful confusion" in Paris. On the lakeshore he erected a little village of pavilions and tents, "planned, executed, & adorned by the first artists of Paris, who are all here in my suite." Among them was Ramée.

Buck Whaley, another Englishman of exotic taste, seldom awed by anything, acknowledged himself to be overwhelmed by what Ramée and Beckford offered their guests. During a "sumptuous" dinner, Beckford's twenty-four-piece orchestra performed. Very likely they played his own music, probably his creditable Mozartian opera called *The Arcadian Pastorale*. Afterward "the whole company was conveyed" into a "most delightful wood, in the midst of which was a garden laid out in the English taste, adorned with statues . . . Here, while we sauntered, our ears were often unexpectedly struck with the softest music" from invisible performers, "and the sounds . . . reverberated, with ravishing melody, by the echoing mountains . . . so that the whole appeared the effect of enchantment." What a relief from "frightful confusion."

After life with Beckford, it must have been a wrench for Ramée to return to the pedestrian tasks of landscape design for a series of minor German princes. He found his pace again in Copenhagen and in Hamburg, where he came to know a group of multinational trading families with American connections. Chief among these merchant clans were the Parishes.

Ramée's most famous work in Copenhagen was done for Constantin Brun, a barley-growing commission merchant who was director of the Danish West India Company. His remodeling of Brun's country villa, Sophienholm, was surrounded by a romantic garden that still remains, complete with one of its pavilions, a log cabin. Mme Brun was a renowned poet and proprietor of a salon; Ramée designed for her city mansion a bathroom in the classical style in which it was said she sometimes entertained, as Mlle Guimard entertained in her famous Parisian temple of the dance (see p. 439).

Until 1801, the hostility between Britain and France had profited Danish and American smugglers, who went armed to the gunwales against both the great powers. In 1801, as we have noted, the British simplified choices for Denmark by destroying the Danish fleet anchored in the harbor of Copenhagen (which means "merchants' haven" in Old Danish); and in 1807 they revisited the Danish capital with the same incendiary effects as those of their sojourn on the Potomac and Chesapeake Bay in 1814.

For nearly twenty years, armed Danish and American merchants had common cause and found common profits. Indeed, after Jefferson's embargo was finally abandoned in 1809 (it had become a perforated sham), the Danish port of Tonningen received one hundred and fifty American vessels in a six-month period, laden with what was, to the British, contraband coffee, tea, sugar, cotton, tobacco, and spices. Erich Erichsen, son of the lord mayor of Odense, became a great figure in Danish trade during this "period of glorious commerce." His good fortune has become our good fortune, because his city palace, richly ornamented by Ramée, is preserved very much as they left it, in the hands of one of the banks of Copenhagen.

Denmark, like the United States, was an undeclared co-belligerent with France, and though a few Danish fortunes were made in privateering, the

Danish West India Company lost its islands to the British. Norway, a Danish possession for centuries, was wrested away to be given to Marshal Bernadotte, the Gascon adventurer who became king of Sweden and an ally of Britain against France. The pool of capital in Denmark available for villa building or shipbuilding was sharply diminished.

Toward the end of the Napoleonic wars, and the end of Ramée's practice in Denmark, the enraged Danes turned against American shipping as well, scrapping for bones where once they had feasted, taking as prizes any foreign vessels that might be construed to be carrying British goods. Sugar from the West Indies found high prices in Hamburg, but the game was over. Impoverished Denmark was no place for an architect who was no businessman and needed effulgent clients like William Beckford, Constantin Brun, and Erich Erichsen.

With them, Ramée had done very well, but he was indeed a poor businessman. Though he shuttled between Copenhagen and Hamburg, by 1814 he was on the brink of bankruptcy and was delighted to come under the patronage of David Parish.*

Decorum, Ceremony, and Politesse

Parish was a good patron, thought by some to be "the champion, the pearl of all the businessmen of Christendom on both sides of the Atlantic." He did not forget his artists. When it was clear he could not himself underwrite a new architectural career for Ramée, he did all he could to find new clients. One was Dr. Eliphalet Nott, a late-blooming flower of the Enlightenment, who in 1804 had commenced a sixty-two-year tenure as president of Union College in Schenectady, New York, one of the first liberal-arts schools west of the Hudson River. Ramée designed its campus.

The term "liberal" requires a little elucidation in this context, as it always does. Nott was no more liberal than Thomas Jefferson, whose disciplinary theories he shared. Union's daring curriculum was imparted by tight control over its students, who lived with their instructors in patriarchal families. Nott endeavored to impart "the decorum, ceremony, and politeness of refined do-

---

*The meager records of his career permit the clear inference that it was at this time, and probably in Hamburg, that he first met Dr. J. B. Baudry, the agent for James Leray de Chaumont and the custodian of the portfolio of Pierre Pharoux in 1794.

It seems the good doctor was a friend to more than one architect. While my own guess is that the portfolio of Pierre Pharoux contained the plan for the house in Leraysville that Baudry built for Leray around 1806, it is also possible that the Leray villa sprang from a suggestion made by Ramée in Hamburg in 1802. Baudry and Ramée were both in Hamburg at the time; Ramée was at the height of his fame; and the north façade of the house (its old primary entrance) looks like the kind of villa being built by Ramée and his contemporaries in Hamburg and Copenhagen.

mestic life" by separating the mass of students and interjecting faculty among them.

A decade later, Thomas Jefferson, with the assistance of Latrobe and Dr. Thornton, sought to achieve the same ideal at the University of Virginia in Charlottesville, where "every professor would be the police officer of the students adjacent to his own lodge," taking care that his charges would be disciplined in "manners, morals and order."*

French educational theory was central to Nott's experiment;† it seems likely that he wanted to instill something more than Yankee courtesy, something more akin to courtly *politesse*. In Ramée, he must have found a gift of the gods: here was a man trained at the court of Louis XVI.

Like Pierre Pharoux before him, Ramée was more than an architect; he was a man of parts. As Pharoux had been welcomed by the Hudson River merchant-squires, Ramée had brought to the little courts of the German princes the final fruits of the ancien régime.‡ And there he was, looking for work in Schenectady with his fee paid in advance, ready to create a symbolic statement of the rule of Reason.

Not only would the students be tamed by the faculty; nature would be tamed by the hand of the great landscapist, and the campus disciplined into an arcaded unity. Superstition and monarchical pretension, which had been enthroned in baroque palaces, would at Union be replaced by Reason and Freedom.

The climate of northern New York, so wrong for merino sheep, was right for French educational and architectural theory. Union, unlike Oxford or Cambridge or Yale, had no religious requirements. By 1820 it had established a scientific, almost polytechnical, course, in defiance of the classical curriculum then almost universal in America. It substituted French for Greek in entrance tests. Its engineering diplomas were written in French instead of Latin. One of its seals proclaimed: "Sous les lois de Minerve nous devenons tous frères."

---

*Nott and Jefferson were gripped by the same educational theories as Joseph Lakanal (see p. 378). Nott, at Union, was successful in the experiments that failed for Lakanal in New Orleans.

†Despite the Francophilia of some Hudson River squires, and the attractions of French literary culture to others of the American elite, I doubt that it went very deep. An impressive list of links between France and the United States has been developed by literary historians like Bernard Fay, Howard Mumford Jones, and Van Wyck Brooks. French was studied at Harvard in 1732, at the University of Pennsylvania in 1754 (as the result of urging by Benjamin Franklin), and at Princeton in 1768. Jefferson, a prodigy in so many ways, studied French when he was five years old and made certain there was a chair in French at the University of Virginia.

My impression is that the laments of Latrobe about "violent prejudices among the Federalists against everything French" (see Talbot Hamlin, *Latrobe,* p. 386) were not limited to the Federalists, and that people like Nott and Jefferson were engaged in an uphill struggle. That struggle continued until the hill was climbed between 1917 and 1919, the summit being celebrated by the cry "Lafayette, we are here!"

‡Paul Turner is now pursuing Harold Larrabee's earlier leads as to Ramée's German career. Larrabee's research told us that Ramée's first client after leaving France was the prince-bishop of Erfurt. After the bishop came the dukes of Saxe-Meiningen, Saxe-Gotha, and Saxe-Weimar.

Union College as conceived by Ramée, 1815

Ramée's exquisite designs for Nott's campus are now in the Union College Library. It is just as well that they were preserved by Nott, for Ramée was averse to writing, aside from depositions for legal purposes. David Parish was once told by one of his subordinates that Ramée had promised "whole volumes of instructions" but "I suppose they will be verbal . . . and too late." Ramée did vouchsafe to posterity a one-line preface to his collected designs, in which he hoped they would be "more useful than the long and voluminous books written on this form of art."

His designs spoke for him, though the buildings based on them were only imperfectly and partially executed. At Union, even the designs were constrained by the foundations of two buildings already in place; Ramée had to go through a series of variations in French space planning in an effort not to lose coherence. These proto-buildings had not been intended for his Court of Honor or for an "academical village" like Mr. Jefferson's. They would have stood, four-square, like the domino clusters Americans substituted for monastic quadrangles. Yale was set out like that before 1930, a practical place for Yankees to learn in. Ramée's skill appears in the ways he linked such buildings together with sheltered walkways, in an undulating sequence of arcades.*

---

*It would be pleasant to be able to assert that in the center of it all would be a Pantheon of

Ramée's design for the Union College campus

There would be walkways and gardens throughout the sixty-seven-acre campus. In Schenectady, as in Hamburg or Copenhagen, Ramée, master of integrated designs, placed his buildings in a context of nature, but nature tamed, organized, made orderly, like the energies of students.

Union College was Ramée's last public building in America. That was not because he lacked skill or because Parish lacked a desire to provide clients for him. It was because there were few remaining men of means who would take the advice of David Parish. Among those who did, however, were the Smiths of Baltimore.

27

THE SMITHS OF BALTIMORE

Before he closed his public career by retiring as mayor of Baltimore at the age of eighty-six, Samuel Smith had fought with spirit and dramatic effect through two wars, forty years in Congress, a series of financial panics, and one of the celebrated bankruptcies of the young republic.

He was a tall man with a broad face and a rectilinear jaw. As he grew older, he acquired a demeanor of nobility, wisdom, and controlled ferocity, conveying an expectation of command. His face had an expression molded by that habitual receipt of deference which comes to young heroes who go on to become rich old men. These appearances are not to be trusted: Smith did not die rich, though he did die acclaimed and full of proud memories. He lost his money as he gained it, in swashbuckling speculation. We visited his Montebello on p. 228, noting that its name commemorates the exploit of another swashbuckler, Marshal Lannes, who drove the Austrians out of an Italian way station of that name on the way to the decisive victory of Marengo in June 1800.*

Colonel Smith was himself a hero. The defection of his Polish-French commander placed him in charge of one of the rare successes of the discouraging early years of the Revolutionary War, an effort to embarrass the British south

---

Enlightenment: a library, not a chapel. My first look at Ramée's plans suggested that the chapel was to be hidden away in an inconspicuous place. But Paul Turner has spoiled all this by determining that Dr. Nott (a clergyman, after all) did in fact intend the rotunda for religious purposes. We are indebted to Turner for the facts, though we can regret the loss of an architectural epigram. (Turner first spoiled my fun about the rotunda on a walk in Muir Woods, and later in a letter dated August 14, 1984.)

*I have counted Marengos in Iowa, Indiana, Wisconsin, Washington, and Saskatchewan. There may be more, to go along with the multiple Messénas.

General Samuel Smith in 1817,
by Rembrandt Peale

of Philadelphia. His assignment was to hold out as long as possible in a group of little forts between the city and the sea, to pick away at the supply lines to the continent's largest, and therefore hungriest, metropolis. Despite a painful shoulder wound, Smith was remarkably successful. He received a congressional citation as the hero of the fort at Mud Island and was able to return to his commercial activity, now amplified by privateering. (This was the fort that was turned into a respectable fortress after the revolution by Major L'Enfant, with murals in the Commandant's House by Pierre Bauduy; see p. 187.)

Baltimore had scarcely mattered before the revolution; the tobacco trade turned to Annapolis when it needed financing or supplies, and Philadelphia was then the second-largest city in the British empire, with an apparent hammerlock upon the wheat trade being developed by the German and Scotch-Irish settlers of the Pennsylvania hinterland. Now, brash Baltimore thrust itself forward, soliciting the wheat farmers to use its long wharfs, which could serve coasting schooners directly; it doubled its population between 1790 and 1800.

The new seaport on the Patapsco was led by seafaring traders, like Smith, casual about national loyalties and very sophisticated about architecture and finance. Several of them shared his passion for French literature.* It was Samuel

---

*One of them, Robert F. Smith, was Robert Morris's correspondent in Havana in the early part of the 1780s, engaged in smuggling silver specie through the British blockade. These operations apparently came to an end in 1782. The Baltimore records are very confused about this Smith; some

Smith's misfortune to have built Montebello before he could find the services of a good French architect; Ramée would have done him proud. (But, as we shall see, Ramée was on hand when another Baltimore Smith was ready for him.)

Samuel Smith's Francophilia was like Christopher Gore's, no deeper than aesthetics; it did not extend to commercial preferences or to statecraft. When, in 1801, the Spaniards, with the complicity of the French, shut off New Orleans to the merchants who were Smith's partners and constituents, he was disgusted by what he thought to be the timidity of Secretary of State Madison. He betook himself to a public dinner for Madison's rival James Monroe and offered this toast: "Peace, if peace is honorable; war, if war is necessary!"*

"War" in this case meant war with Napoleon, though Smith was the uncle of Mrs. Jerome Bonaparte. Mrs. Bonaparte was the unfortunate Betsy Patterson, whose marriage to Jerome lasted only long enough to permit John Quincy Adams to sniff at the pretensions of Baltimore upstarts: he referred to "Smith's nephew, the first Consul's brother." But a love of French architecture and furniture predated any Bonaparte connubialities. Smith's first major venture was selling a consignment of goods smuggled through the British blockade aboard a French privateer. Though much of the wealth that made Montebello possible was built upon privateering in the French West Indies, Smith's major fortune came from the Great Silver Scheme and its aftermath, when he went on to become "an exporter of specie to India." He grew poor again in 1819, in an affair that involved Denis Smith.

In 1814, the defeat of Napoleon freed the British to send a set of expeditions against the coastal cities of the United States. They burned Washington, captured Alexandria, and turned their attention to Baltimore. Monroe, newly appointed as secretary of war, made Smith the commanding general of the forces defending that city. They had little else to give them confidence beyond

---

authorities say he died in Havana, though recently Peggy Liss has found evidence of him in Saint-Domingue at the end of that year, still in correspondence with Francisco de Miranda (see p. 313), with whom he appears to have been engaged in other smuggling operations, and, perhaps, the early stages of insurrection as well.

Robert F. Smith is an intriguing wisp. I have been unable to discern how he was related, if at all, to Samuel Smith's brother Robert, later secretary of the navy and secretary of state. He was roughly contemporary with Samuel, born in 1760, but might have been the father of Denis Smith (see below), born about 1780. This would explain some of Denis's sudden wealth at the time silver smuggling once again became rampant (see also footnote on p. 280). Robert might be thought of as father to one aspect of our Silver Scheme, which connected Vera Cruz to northern Europe. (See the multivolume correspondence of Robert Morris, and references in Liss's *Atlantic Empires,* pp. 115–16, with useful notes on p. 284, and pp. 23–27 in Roy F. Nichols's *Advance Agents of American Destiny.)*

*As we will note in Part Eight, there were close political and economic connections between the Baltimore Associates and the New Orleans Associates.

the soundness of the French principles that had gone into the design of Fort McHenry and, perhaps, recollections of Smith's ability nearly forty years earlier to lead a ragtag force of raw recruits. Once again, he and his troops had before them a fleet and an army led by men seasoned in war against the French; once again, there were no natural obstacles among the sandspits and marshes he had to defend against amphibious assault.

After many a difficult day and the celebrated "perilous night," the defenses of Baltimore held, and Smith returned to politics and commerce, feeling free to differ from the leadership of his party when it came to trading with the West Indies. He had first gained national attention in 1798 defending the commonality of interest between Toussaint Louverture and the United States; his last public achievement was to rally support for a reciprocal agreement with Britain in 1830, which gave the Americans renewed access to the British ports in the islands. He differed as well in refusing to accept Jefferson's policy of unilateral disarmament in the 1790s—he was for supporting the kind of navy that could escort trading vessels to the Caribbean or silver ships to the Far East. And when it came to Albert Gallatin, he differed with everything that clever Genevese proposed. A common antipathy to Gallatin and disdain for James Madison* animated a cabal of Senator Samuel Smith; his brother, Robert, secretary of the navy; and Gideon Granger, postmaster general under Jefferson and (for a time) under Madison.

The cabal was united as well by an interest in architecture and by a lack of interest in the opinions of John Quincy Adams. Like Gallatin, Adams loathed Smith, and he deplored the fact that "the moral, political and commercial character of . . . Baltimore has for twenty-five years been formed, controlled, and modified almost entirely by" the family firm of "Smith and Buchanan [see below], their connections and dependents." Gallatin had caught Smith in an embarrassing association of government business and personal business, one of a series that his constituents ignored, believing in each instance that the culprits were Smith's partners, not the leonine hero himself.

The Crash of 1819

Alexander Hamilton's first Bank of the United States had been anathema to the Jeffersonians, as its successor, the second, would be anathema to the Jacksonians. Just as the silver kings of Colorado in the 1890s would forge an alliance with the Populists led by William Jennings Bryan to fight the gold

*Vincent Nolte, who along with David Parish shared these opinions, presented to Parish a caricature of Madison which Parish gave to Denis Smith.

standard, the proprietors of the mushrooming state and private banks of the early nineteenth century fought the implied competition and control of a national bank. Agrarians formed an alliance with local bankers and speculators who preferred flimsy and even corrupt little banks close at hand to a distant, cold, and powerful central institution—especially one modeled upon the Bank of England.

Thomas Jefferson pronounced the bank to be unconstitutional, a menace, an ogre, as he allowed its charter to lapse shortly after he became President. Upon its ruins a rank growth of state-chartered banks flourished: between 1811 and 1816 their number quadrupled. Albert Gallatin struggled to sustain some order in the nation's monetary system; but more orthodox Jeffersonians, in pursuit of a simple society with a weak government and low taxes, were disposed to believe that a central bank was no more necessary than armed forces any larger than a militia, a few bandit-hunting scouts, and a flotilla of pirate-resistant gunboats. Their aversion to industrial manufacturing exposed the citizens of the United States to whatever prices might be set on manufactured goods by the European traders.

Tariffs and patent protection for domestic producers who might compete with foreign manufacturers was the course preferred by Hamilton, outlined in his "Report on Manufactures," and demonstrated in his support for Major L'Enfant's second massive essay in city planning, after the District of Columbia, the company town of Paterson, New Jersey. But Hamilton lost, Jefferson won, and James Madison had to fight a war without either a system of war finance or armed forces capable of resisting British attack.

After the burning of Washington and the agonies of the Madison administration, some lessons were learned. It was obvious that the nation's economy had survived only through the generosity of European bankers, made somewhat more confident by their knowledge that a shrewd Genevese, M. Gallatin, was guiding Madison's shaky hand as best he could, and that "stakes" in the solvency of the United States were being taken by an equally shrewd French merchant, Stephen Girard, and a gruff, practical German, John Jacob Astor. A certain romantic confidence radiated by David Parish, of Hamburg and Antwerp (and lately of Ogdensburg and Philadelphia), did no harm.

The failure of the first set of war loans (see p. 261) demonstrated once again that a government cannot be run upon voluntary contributions. American currency became dangerously inflated. As Girard knew, a currency can be kept sound only by extracting substantial assets from citizens in the form of taxation or by being convertible into precious metals, which can in turn be converted into predictable quantities of goods—unless, as in 1988, foreigners have nowhere safer to lend their money.

American currency was by law convertible into silver pesos; but after the War of 1812, American credit continued to swell while the American specie supply was shrinking. Exporters of specie such as Samuel Smith were shipping it off to buy exotic products.

Larceny lurks in the mind under circumstances like this; always in the back of the American mind were the mines of Mexico. During the postwar years, however, that mind became distracted by a cotton bubble and a land bubble and a currency bubble. The second Bank of the United States was founded in 1817, upon bubbles. "If we had mines as rich as Potosi," said one economist at the time, "we should not be able to retain in the country even that small amount of silver necessary to keep banknotes convertible."*

Empty of scruples and full of expedients, a group later called "the Baltimore adventurers"† by Nicholas Biddle gained control of the Baltimore branch of the Bank of the United States and, through stock jobbing, came to influence the affairs of the central institution in Philadelphia. The adventurers were Denis Smith, George Williams, and Samuel Smith's partner, James Buchanan, president of the branch. The loans of the branch bank reached $12.5 million while its specie reserves declined to $26,714. A goodly portion of those loans went to the officers and directors of the bank.

Its stock was supposed to be widely spread; no more than thirty of the 40,141 shares sold in Baltimore could, under the law, be voted by one person. But Williams, a director of both the Baltimore branch and the central bank in Philadelphia, showed how to defeat that naive notion by taking up 1,172 shares as attorney for 1,172 names. Fifteen people came to hold three quarters of the Baltimore stock.

With the branch in hand, the Baltimore adventurers used its resources to blow up a bubble in the stock of the bank itself. They began by buying allotments accumulated for them by Denis Smith, 19,940 in June 1817 and 12,000 more in December. Sometimes collateralized by the stock itself, sometimes unsecured, this Smith and his friends borrowed nearly $6.5 million from the bank or the branch. In aggregate, they owned 47,000 shares, more stock than had initially been allocated to all of Baltimore. Buchanan and Williams even swept along James W. McCulloch, the cashier of the Baltimore branch, who borrowed $500,000 though he had no assets (except, perhaps, his future fame in American constitutional history).

William Jones, president of the second bank, joined in the bank stock jobbing and took $18,000 from the adventurers. He had been appointed by Madison though he was known to be stupid, weak, and a recent bankrupt.

Jones was not only venal; he was confused. Other directors in Philadelphia and Baltimore noted the fluttering of notes from one adventurer to another,

---

*Ultimately, California provided a remedy, but "ultimately" was thirty years off. In the period between the War of 1812 and the discovery of gold in the West, cotton had to serve as, in effect, currency convertible into English specie—except, of course, in 1825–26 and 1837–39, when the British refusal to export specie produced withdrawal symptoms in America.

†Not to be confused with the privateering Baltimore adventurers of the Gulf (see p. 274n.).

the transparency of their security, and the collapsing economy around them. Cotton, which had sold at 32.5 cents a pound in 1818, fell to 14.3 cents in 1819. Banks, chartered in every hamlet that could boast "a church, a tavern, a blacksmith's shop," reneged upon their notes and posted "closed today" signs for months in a row. Land prices descended; in 1819, Baltimore rents were half what they had been a year earlier; sale prices of Alexandria river-front property fell by 90 percent; the "United States Bank found itself owner of a large part of Cincinnati."

Land, cotton, bank stock, currency, and credit plunged down together. Jones struggled to get clear, embarrassed by the retirement from the board of Stephen Girard, who could not stomach what he saw there. Girard used straw men to sell three thousand of his shares, reversing the anonymous process by which Williams had bought his, and sold more stock into the maw provided by Denis Smith, Buchanan, Williams, McCulloch, and Jones. The adventurers tried to cover the loans, then tried to cover their tracks, and slipped from small, repeated deceptions into perjury and fraud.

Jones was replaced as president by the chilly and upright Langdon Cheves of South Carolina (see *Architecture, Men, Women and Money*), who contracted credit, cleaned up the bank's affairs, and drove Denis and Samuel Smith, Williams, and Buchanan into bankruptcy. He cleared the way for Nicholas Biddle, who succeeded him as president in January 1823.*

On March 6, 1819, the same day that Cheves relieved Jones of command, Chief Justice John Marshall handed down his decision in *McCulloch* v. *Maryland*. From the point of view of the Baltimore adventurers, it was a little late.

The chief issue in the case was whether or not Maryland could tax the now disgraced branch bank, as represented by the luckless McCulloch. Marshall had a constitution to expound and a commercial system to protect from both predatory state legislatures and outraged public opinion. His opinion said that Maryland had exceeded its powers. The Bank of the United States, however ineptly managed, was constitutionally established. It had been a "necessary and proper" expression of powers given Congress, and Maryland's proposed taxation was, said Marshall, "the power to destroy." States could not be permitted to destroy necessary and proper federal institutions, especially when those institutions served to sustain Federalist economies. Alexander Hamilton may have smiled in heaven; John Marshall had drawn heavily upon the arguments prepared by Hamilton to encourage President Washington to approve the first Bank of the United States, in 1791, over the arguments of Thomas Jefferson.

---

*Several other characters in our tale were involved along the edges of the bank stock bubble. George Graham testified to Congress soon after he became president of the Washington branch that Colonel George Bomford (see p. 395) held two hundred shares and that one of Denis Smith's brokers held shares for Henry Joseph "Steer" of Antwerp. This must be "Baron" de (or van) Stier of Riversdale (see p. 294). (See American State Papers, vol. 3, p. 313ff.)

Denis Smith

Denis Smith was one of the most important patrons of architecture in the first half-century of American independence. Yet he is known, if at all, as a scape-grace giving self-exculpatory testimony before the congressional committee investigating the collapse of the Bank of the United States, and as the butt of testimony given by others doing their best to pin the onus upon him. Smith does not come off well in the committee records; the facts seem to be that he remained a speculator to the end, caught with huge holdings of stock, perhaps as many as thirty-nine thousand shares, bought at much higher prices than the market would bear.

And he had offended powerful people along the way—the customary safety nets that salvaged the careers of Victor Du Pont, Samuel Smith, and William Scarbrough of Savannah (see *Architecture, Men, Women and Money*) were not extended to succor Denis Smith in his extremity. No insurance-company presi-dencies opened up, no courtesy directorships or forbearances of debt were vouchsafed. This is strange, since in so many other ways his fortunes moved in concert with those of the "ever popular" Samuel Smith.*

Perhaps, like Parish, he became haughty; perhaps he was thought to have gone beyond improvidence into dishonesty; perhaps he was an outsider grown too obtrusive, and therefore a fit nominee for election as scapegoat. He seems to have made a fundamental mistake: he drew down upon himself the displea-sure of Stephen Girard, who caused him to be admonished as early as 1813 that he was lending the funds of the National Mechanics Bank of Baltimore for "too long"—twelve to fifteen months. By 1817, Girard was speaking of

> that class of amateures who generally breakfast at 9 or 10 o'clock in the forenoon and immediately after are on the alert to borrow money . . . to renew before 3 o'clock the notes which they have due in Bank, and the remainder of the day with what they call their friends in eating, drinking, smoaking, talking of business which does not concern them and whenever some of their commercial operations prove disavantageous

---

*Stranger still, Thomas Govan, Nicholas Biddle's biographer, asserted that Denis (b. 1781) was a son of Samuel (b. 1752). No one else seems to have thought so, though the two shared a common name, lived in the same city, were both bankers, and both benefited from an association with David Parish. (See Govan, p. 57.) As suggested earlier, a better conjecture is that Denis was the son of the silver trader Robert F. Smith (see p. 275n.). Baltimore city records give Denis's approximate birth date and those of his marriage to Elizabeth Pressbury (1802) and then to Rebecca Smith, whom he married at her father's house, Poplar Grove, in 1806. His brother-in-law, yet another Smith, was Job Smith, Jr., a lumber merchant and president of the Maryland Savings Institution.

Calverton by Ramée, from his Country Cottages and Houses

which is often the case they attribute it to a bad luck . . . and . . . make up . . . a new accomodation which is discounted in Bank and renewed.

So disposed, Girard had, it seems, no remorse about unloading his own shares on Smith, in very large quantities and at prices advantageous to him but highly disadvantageous—indeed, fatal—to the financial fortunes of the "Baltimore adventurer."

The Mechanics Bank had been organized in June 1806 to become a Silver Scheme depository. Denis Smith was its cashier; he and his family lived above the bank, on Calvert Street, from 1807 until his country seat was finished in 1817. These were not cramped quarters, for M. and Mme Joseph Ramée and the family were his guests for an extended period in 1815–16.

Ramée was there to work on a number of projects, including the remodeling of a stone house that Smith had purchased west of Baltimore at a place bearing the aristocratic name Calverton. In 1812, when Smith insured it, the house had a plain front only forty feet long. When Ramée's design was complete, it was much larger, extending to two octagonal wings, set in extended romantic gardens—his most complex residential commission in America. Parish was generous; though he had not been able to scrape together the ready cash for

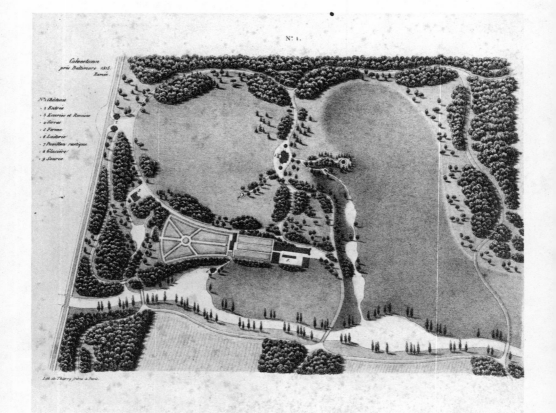

Ramée's estate plan for Calverton

something so ambitious for himself, he wrote Smith in January 1816 that "Ramée has shown me the plan of your Country House &c. with which we are all highly pleased here." In June, he paid Ramée's bill for $1,500 and debited Smith's account. (Did Ramée have a standard fee? Nott's was also $1,500.)

Ramée's Calverton replaced the old plain front with one of his characteristic scooped-out façades like that of the Hamburg Bourse, providing an outdoor living space that must have been like a columned garden pavilion. A visitor reached the pavilion by climbing a flight of stone steps and passing between columns about sixteen feet tall into a "room" perhaps thirty by thirty feet, recessed into the space left by the abutting of the two octagons.*

---

*Once again, the ghost of Pierre Pharoux rises up to remind us how long he has been forgotten. That friend to both Ramée and Pharoux Dr. Baudry could tell us much about them, and about their common penchant for octagons tied together with a rectangle at the back.

Calverton in 1874

Only from a distance could one observe that the visitor occupied the lower section of a much larger columned space, under a barrel vault, held aloft by two enormous square columns at the front and two square pilasters against the house. Then comes the symbolic dash: the whole huge volume was bisected horizontally by a floor, upon which sat a grand piece of sculpture. In old photographs it looks to us rather like Queen Victoria seated on her throne, but it was probably Justice or Reason (or perhaps the goddess of silver).*

Calverton was completed after the departure of Ramée for Europe, in 1816, by Robert C. Long, a local contractor-architect who was a director of Smith's bank. Though Latrobe did not get the commission for Calverton, he felt free to write to Smith recommending that the interior be finished by a friend of his and, though not given to such blandishments, spoke of Smith's role as a patron of the arts. The following fall, Latrobe was himself at work on a commission for Smith, a house in Washington (the plans have been lost). The two seem to have been on good terms, though Smith and Parish had sided with Ramée in competitions against Latrobe. When Ramée was not a contender, Smith went with Latrobe—he served on the building committees of the largest

---

*One may recall the muse of dance in a similar position, under the recessed vault of Ledoux's pavilion for Mlle Guimard (see p. 439). A figure of Virtue, or something akin to Virtue, was placed in the same posture in Maximilian Godefroy's Masonic Hall in Baltimore.

buildings constructed to Latrobe's conception, the Baltimore Cathedral and the Baltimore Exchange.

Smith, like so many of our characters, did not long enjoy the genius of his architects. Calverton was sold in 1819, as part of his bankruptcy proceedings—it became a poorhouse, then an orphan asylum, and burned down in 1874. Smith himself disappeared from the Baltimore city directories for a decade, then emerged in 1827, living obscurely on West Baltimore Street. The last entry for his name was in 1850, when his profession was given as "farmer."

28

OTHER CONNECTIONS

Ramée had high hopes for other work in Baltimore. In the competition for the Baltimore Exchange, in 1815, his chief competitors, Latrobe and Godefroy, knew they would win "if our friends can outvote Ramée's, that is Parish's, or Mills', that is Gilmor's." "Our friends" did outvote Smith and Parish, and Ramée did no better against Mills in another competition, for a monument to George Washington; his submission, an Arc de Triomphe, lives on, like most of his work, only as a beautiful drawing.

Parish tried again. He set Ramée up in business as an interior designer in Philadelphia, installing one of his secretaries as business manager (someone Ramée needed, judging from his experience in Hamburg). The venture was capitalized with as much as $40,000. That seems a large sum, about $850,000 in 1988 dollars; perhaps it was only a promise, which, like so many others at this time, Parish was unable to keep. He left the United States for Europe in June 1816, and Ramée went as well.

Ramée, at last discouraged, his patron discredited, had planned to go earlier. We know this as the result of the discovery of one of the very rare documents in Ramée's own hand, written to Parish's overseer and partner in Ogdensburg, Joseph Rosseel. It appears that Leray's agent and Ramée's friend, Dr. J. B. Bauduy, had been urging the architect to return to his European practice, specifically to Belgium. Ramée wrote Rosseel on February 11, 1815, that "I plan to return to Europe, and will probably reside near [Ghent,] the city where you were born." Ramée offered "to bring something to your relatives . . . [and] would visit them in any case as soon as I could." But the Waterloo campaign brought the final explosion of Napoleonic warfare into the Low Countries and caused a year's delay in Ramée's plans.

There is little more to tell. Ramée lived until 1842, working in Germany, Belgium, and France. Paul Turner is following his tracks and has turned up

Ramée's design for the Washington Monument

some of his surviving work. It is well worth finding, for of all Latrobe's contemporaries only Ramée offered real competition, with or without his friends, "that is, Parish's."

Gideon Granger

Aaron Burr was the Alcibiades of America's neoclassical age; some classicist should help us find an Athenian bureaucrat and political operator with whom to pair, in Plutarchian fashion, the ineffable Gideon Granger. Until that symmetry is provided, we will have to make do with a more contemporary pairing: Gideon Granger was the James Aloysius Farley of the Jefferson administration. What Farley was to Franklin D. Roosevelt, Granger was to Jefferson—a trusted political henchman without large ideological pretensions. He could, in general, be trusted, and was adept at the distribution of patronage.

Smith and Granger were, however, northern Jeffersonians. As noted earlier they might be personally loyal to Jefferson, but they did not share the desire of southern planters for expansion into the Caribbean if that were to occur at

Gideon Granger (artist unknown)

the expense of trade with the French West Indies or with the successors to the French there, such as Toussaint Louverture. That trade was exceedingly important to Granger's seafaring political allies and also to the inland, wheat-growing region of New York where he was accumulating land.

Granger's taste was Francophile, like that of many West Indies traders, of whom the most prominent were Stephen Girard and the Smiths.

Relationships were complicated among the Francophiles in the Jeffersonian party. The Silver Scheme had enriched the Smiths and, through them, sustained the precarious solvency of Ramée, while restoring public credit, much to M. Gallatin's own credit. Yet, though Secretary of the Treasury and Mme Gallatin were indebted to Granger's friends, they were on the cosiest of terms with the Madisons, while Mr. Granger was no friend to Dolley Madison, and the Madisons fervently returned the animosity.

Mrs. Madison wrote Mme Gallatin in 1814, recalling that ten years earlier Granger had made nasty references to her modest but possibly affectionate past, implying threats of exposure. At that time, Granger was using all the leverage at his disposal in a bid to succeed Aaron Burr as vice-president of the United States. In 1814, Granger was still a member of the Madison cabinet, having been inherited from Jefferson, along with his crony Robert Smith. Madison was finally ready to deal with him. The threat of Burr's intrigues had long abated. Mr. Jefferson was in retirement. Now!

The postmaster general walked into a trap. Without consulting the President, he nominated Senator Michael Leib of Pennsylvania for the lush postmaster's post in Philadelphia. Leib was a close ally of Granger and the Smiths, and vehemently opposed to the President.

Madison remonstrated, and the postmaster general showed his fangs: unless the President got out of his way, he would be forced to disclose a packet of letters from, to, or about Mrs. Madison. He had been holding it out of loyalty, he said, together with some gossip about Jefferson.

That second threat was what Madison needed: until Granger slipped on precisely that point, the President could not be entirely certain of the way the wind would blow from Monticello. Jefferson, for his own reasons, had kept his temper on the previous occasions.

In 1814 he kept it again, but barely. He wrote Granger two letters, rather fulsomely friendly in tone but concluding that "dragging such gossiping trash before the public" would do as much injury to Granger as to the Madisons or to Jefferson.

Granger backed off, but he did send Dolley a packet of copies—not originals—of the letters. Her heirs burned these copies. We do not know what Granger did with the primary evidence. Soon thereafter, he resigned from the Post Office and was replaced by Jonathan Meigs.*

What did Granger have to say about all this? In a letter to Jefferson, dated September 27, 1810, he alluded to

> one other subject from which my feelings have suffered more than from all others. One when I acted on the advice of General Dearborn. One when I sacrificed my own character & feelings to preserve the feelings and character of others, who were dear to you and me. My conduct was equally correct and honorable in 1808. I cannot be more particular. More than once have I determined to give my vindication to the World, but my prudence and regard for others restrained me . . . A cloud of suspicion has overshadowed me . . . and it has passed away . . . Sir, I have been accused of Burrism.

Burr, whose story, and architectural connections, we will pursue in Part Seven, was in Europe, and still dangerous. Granger reminded Jefferson that he had twice served Jefferson's interest in scuttling Burr's career: in 1800 (after carefully weighing his advantages), he had sent

> Mr. Erving to go to Virginia to warn your Electors of his intrigue— you know that in the Winter 1804 I acted in concert and in confidence with you and tho I was denounced to you in the Spring of that year, you knew that the denunciation was devoid of truth.

---

*Meigs's daughter was married to John Jackson, the widower of Dolley Madison's sister. Meigs was later the author of a letter about the disgraceful use of the spoils system by Andrew Jackson. Jackson, he explained, was forcing out people who had been appointed by the Virginians solely on the merits.

Someone close to Jefferson was the denouncer. Who? Granger knew:

> I have long known [though not from Jefferson, it seems] only by laying
> the facts together the Person who set that vile business on foot . . . He
> knew better, and happy will it be for him, if with all his importance he
> lingers two years without appearing as Burr did on the disclosure of his
> intrigue in 1800. I am not given to create suspicions[!!]. I know what I
> write and I know that intrigue did not go to Europe with Burr.

Now a clue to incriminating associations:

> You, Sir, know that I gave you authentic information of Burr's con-
> spiracy & how I got that information. You also know, sir, that it was by
> your advice & for what purpose I allowed the Federalist to assume free
> intercourse with me. It was to aid my Country & you.

Homesteads

Granger departed public office in March 1814, to become a country gentleman.*

Once he had thought of settling in Ohio, where the village of Cleveland
was thriving upon his land, but Mrs. Granger was unenthusiastic about living
so far to the west. He might have chosen Virginia, for even there he was the
owner of larger estates than Madison or Jefferson.† But among the friends of
Madison he would not have been welcome. He ultimately chose a homestead
in the midst of the land holdings most needing his attention, in Canandaigua,
in the lovely lake country of central New York.

I cannot find a record of the occasions when Gideon Granger came to call
upon his political ally Samuel Smith or upon Samuel's colleague Denis. Yet
I think it likely that Granger knew well the cashier of one of the main
depositories of the Silver Scheme and was acquainted with his residence above
the bank on Calvert Street. These are the interconnections: one cluster com-
prised Denis Smith, Ramée, Vincent Nolte, and Parish. A second included
Parish, his partner Samuel, and his depository Denis. A third was more overtly
political: Senator Samuel, his brother Robert, secretary of the navy, and Postmaster General Granger.

---

*He left behind him a comfortable, fanlighted, brick town house a block away from that of
William Lee, and not far from Joel Barlow's Kalorama. It remains to this day, as the Arts Club of
Washington, at 2017 I (pronounced "eye") Street.

†At his death, he still owned 114,000 acres in Randolph County in concert with others and 86,000
in his own name; 130,000 acres in Giles County, "patented to DeWitt Clinton 17th February
1796—also 38,322 in Franklin County patented to me." (Document dated September 24, 1821, quoted
in Arthur Hamlin, p. 65.)

Sophienholm as remodeled by Ramée, 1805–10

During the years that Granger was arranging matters for his retirement, Joseph Ramée was in Baltimore competing for commissions with Latrobe. As we have noted, he was "a guest of Denis Smith & . . . drawing his plan at his house," for Calverton. It is not unlikely that Samuel or Denis Smith, both enthusiasts for architecture and garden design, recommended to Granger that Ramée dash off for him sketches for the exterior elevations for the house he was thinking of building after his "retirement."

Calverton and the Granger Homestead were built at the same time. They do not look alike; but, for that matter, Calverton does not look very much like any earlier domestic design of Ramée's. The architect's own drawing of its unorthodox façade permits easy contrast to his signed drawings of villas near Copenhagen; these bear a more distinct family relationship to Granger's.

Among these were Sophienholm, which is closest in appearance to the Granger Homestead, and, more distantly, Oregaard, and Hellerupgaard. If Gideon Granger had built his house in Copenhagen, people might say that it was yet another demonstration of the "Ramée style."* (Though they might suggest that the careful little pilasters atop Sophienholm had degenerated into

*Another tripartite structure, not unlike these villas, and which I also think to have been designed in America by Ramée, is the barn to which we have referred, on the Duane estate at Duanesburg, for which he left a signed garden design.

The Gideon Granger house in Canandaigua, New York, 1815–18

three sets of Scamozzi columns on the Homestead, so it was unlikely that Ramée supervised its construction.)

In Canandaigua, we can strengthen this hypothesis by proceeding down the street to the Congregational church. It has a scooped-out front and an ornamented gable unique in America but similar to the upper stories of Ramée's Boursenhalle in Hamburg.* The church was under construction simultaneously with the house; Gideon Granger was a member of the committee that built it.

With this evidence before us, we are free to imagine an evening in Denis Smith's parlor above the Mechanics Bank, with Granger, Smith, and Ramée present. Perhaps Mrs. Smith and Mme Ramée were also there. (Mrs. Granger often remained in Connecticut during this period.) We do not require of this scene that it include Ramée's tossing off a complete set of construction drawings, as if he were Mozart wrapping up an overture over coffee and pastries. Neither Smith nor Granger was so thorough; Ramée did not even complete the design and supervision of Calverton, and the evidence suggests that Granger's Homestead was finished by the local builders who had built a house in Syracuse for Samuel Forman three or four years earlier.†

---

*The arcaded *lower* story of the Boursenhalle reappears in David Parish's villa at Parishville, built at about the same time as the church and the Homestead.

†The Forman house was recorded by the Architects Emergency Committee in 1937 among the

It is annoying not to find correspondence between Denis Smith of Calverton and Gideon Granger. We have no "How did those plans work out, Gideon?" Nor is there proof of a soirée above the bank. But in that apologia and compendium of subtle threats sent by Granger to Jefferson on September 27, 1810, pointed references were made to the Smiths and the Great Silver Scheme.

Granger reminded Jefferson of John Randolph's charge "that five hundred thousand pounds were made by the Embargo by the Smiths, which was divided between you, Mr. Madison and others (of which proof I believe will be public before long)." He knew full well that Jefferson and Madison took no personal rewards from the scheme; it is surpassingly unlikely that he was threatening Jefferson with a release of "proof" of such an outcome. The former President, who had retired in 1809, and his friend Mr. Madison, the incumbent, had, however, allowed huge profits to be made by their friends the Republican merchants in violation of the professed policies of the administration. It is interesting that Denis Smith, whose only previous known source of support was a salary of three thousand dollars a year as cashier of a bank, was thereafter able to commission the two leading architects of the nation to lay up for him very expensive plans indeed, and to offer an architectural inducement of forty thousand dollars more, as we shall see.

Neoclassical Townships

Properly situated in his grand house, Granger set himself up in a region permeated by French investment and French taste. He became a patriarch, a status that would have been problematical in Virginia, Ohio, or upon the "Yazoo" lands he and Wade Hampton had acquired by dubious means west of the Appalachians (see p. 325 and *Architecture, Men, Women and Money*).

Before his retirement, Granger had been the recipient of somewhat naive letters from David Parish. Parish wanted post offices to authenticate the civilized condition of his holdings and those of his neighbor Leray. But Granger joined the New York politicians led by De Witt and George Clinton in planning a canal to direct settlement westward, away from the Parish-Leray

---

"Great Georgian Houses of America." It has subsequently been destroyed, but its woodwork was carefully drawn and is identical to that of the Granger house. It also bears a similarity to that of Erasmus Hall in Brooklyn and to some of the baroque late-Georgian that one can see in houses of the time in the Connecticut River Valley.

We know nothing of Forman or his carpenters, but it is likely they were Stephen Wood and Edward Parker, to whom Granger paid bills, apparently for construction, in 1815. Wherever they got the fundamental shape, the carpenter-builders in Canandaigua could not resist little Ionic columns applied to the façade and pilasters at the corners.

The Boursenhalle in Hamburg, designed by Ramée, 1798
(drawing by J. Scheidel, c. 1840)

domain. He took his position with the winners and staked out for himself a very large area amid the classical landscape around Canandaigua.

Classical it was. Townships were called Lysander, Cato, Brutus, Cicero, Manlius, Sempronius, Fabius, Cincinnatus, and the like. Granger, the Yale-educated classicist, was at ease there: when he was writing political pamphlets in the 1790s one of his favorite noms de plume had been "Epaminondas." (The other was "Algernon Sydney.")

The state of Massachusetts owned a large section of New York, having acquired it while abandoning a political claim to the region. Granger's friends in his hometown, Suffield, Connecticut, had speculated there at three cents an acre in the palmy days of William Constable and Gouverneur Morris. Robert Morris had next taken a stake and sold it to a British syndicate headed by Sir William Pulteney. Then came the Franco-Dutch Holland Land Company, with its "XYZ" associations (see p. 117). Our old acquaintance Théofil Cazenove gave his name to Cazenovia: his Dutch clients, collectively, were immortalized in Batavia.

In 1814, Gideon Granger swept into this delightfully confused situation. Acting in part for the state of Connecticut, which had claims against the Suffield group, and in greater part (though in clear conflict of interest) for himself, he acquired "many large estates" and planned his neoclassical house at their core. Like the eighteenth-century British spoilsmen of the age of Walpole, whom he and Burr so much resembled, it was to be his "seat," his center of political power.

In the Senate of New York, which he entered for much the same private-spirited reasons that had taken Wade Hampton to Congress to press his and Granger's "Yazoo" claims, he "ably seconded De Witt Clinton in his efforts to organize . . . the internal improvements of the state," especially those that ran past his own door.

Alas, on the brink of success, on the last day of 1822, as the Erie Canal began construction, Gideon Granger died. His son benefited grandly from his exertions, however, and his daughter married first a Thayer and then a Winthrop of Boston.

First Congregational Church in Canandaigua, New York, 1816–18

29

FRIENDS AND RELATIONS

Not far from the headquarters of the early career of David Parish in Antwerp, Belgium, near the village from which came Joseph Rosseel and to which repaired Joseph Ramée after his return to Europe, there stands the Château du Mick. Unlike the enigmatic resemblances of a villa and a church in Canandaigua to the work of Ramée, those between the château and the Calvert Mansion, a villa near College Park, Maryland, are no longer a mystery. The house is a genuine multinational amalgam, built by an investor perhaps in the Silver Scheme and certainly in the subsequent speculations of the Baltimore adventurers, including the Bank of the United States.

The Maryland village is called Riverdale, a corruption of the true name of the house, Riversdale. The house has been a little corrupted, too; it also bears a superficial resemblance to Clifton, designed by Latrobe near Richmond, a fact noted as early as 1950 by a writer in the *Maryland Historical Magazine,* who went on to say: "Riversdale was a by-product of the French Revolution . . . Baron de Stier [the builder] . . . along with many of the nobility of his country, was faced with extinction . . . [after] the French Revolutionists . . . crossed the border into Belgium in 1794."

Susan Pearl has recently (1985) found correspondence and a set of floor plans in Belgian archives that show that Latrobe did indeed modify his Clifton design to accommodate Stier's desires, and, more important, provided new interior detail.

Charles Stier was not by Belgian practice a baron, it happens. He was a younger son, but his lineage was far more impressive than that of many barons. He was a direct descendant of Peter Paul Rubens and brought to America the most important collection of paintings to reach these shores until 1900, including many by Rubens himself. Unfortunately, they all went back again with him when circumstances in Belgium improved, and were dispersed in a famous sale in the 1830s.

For our purposes, however, Riversdale is chiefly remarkable for being the only large American house of the eighteenth or nineteenth century yet discovered that actually did reproduce, to any significant extent, portions of an "ancestral mansion" in Europe. This claim, part of a litany of filiopiety heard in many "historic homes," is one of the means by which American architects are deprived of their due. But fortunately, in this case, we have letters written by Stier to William Birch, who was laying out Stier's landscape garden during the same period he was at work on Samuel Smith's grounds at Montebello. Stier

Riversdale, 1818

explicitly states that the drawing room of Riversdale, with its blind arcades along the interior walls and a glassed arcade in the center of the exterior (where there was none in the Clifton design), was "based" on the Château du Mick, the Stier estate near Antwerp.*

This house is a real find. Along with David Parish, Joseph Ramée, and Joseph Rosseel, Charles de Stier provides a link between Francophone Belgium and the United States. (We should not forget the Walloon settlers of New Netherland.) It is also a lovely house, even as remodeled and execrably painted, even within its abbreviated grounds. What a marvel it must have been, with Birch's landscape and the Stier collection in place on its walls! As Charles de Stier wrote his daughter, the "painting room . . . would be unequalled luxury in America . . . You should realise that no individual in America has been able to acquire such a valuable collection as those you have there in boxes."

A Note on Maximilian Godefroy

Like Susan Pearl, Robert Alexander did the hard labor needed to patch together two difficult pieces of our story. It was Alexander who first cast doubt upon

---

*The exterior arcade remains upon both houses, though both have suffered remodeling on the interior.

the veracity of Marc Isambard Brunel, and it was also Alexander who has written as good a book as anyone is likely to compose about another architectural beneficiary of the Silver Scheme, Maximilian Godefroy. Scholars can find all they want in his book, but general readers may want to have a few of the facts of Godefroy's life stated here, in brief.

Godefroy was born in 1765, studied architecture, and commenced a practice on the eve of the revolution. Like Ramée, he served in the army in 1794–95. Though also a royalist, he stayed in France during the revolution, obscurely engineering and teaching. He was finally arrested by Napoleon's secret police in 1803, imprisoned for eighteen months, and in 1805 went into exile in the United States.

He found work in the booming city of Baltimore as a teacher of drawing, architecture, and fortification (the conventional grouping) at Saint Mary's College, the Sulpician institution under the strong-minded leadership of Father (later Bishop) William Dubourg (see p. 378). Baltimore had a strong French tone, imparted by émigrés. It was Godefroy's base, where he was secure under Dubourg's patronage.

Saint Mary's Chapel, by Godefroy, is a strange, classicized Gothic structure, somewhat like the equally uncomfortable Old Saint Patrick's in New York, by the Mangins. The commission for a Masonic hall was obtained by this royalist, Roman Catholic architect through the intervention of his friends among the freethinking émigrés; he also executed a chapel for another Sulpician college, in Bardstown, Kentucky. (Both chapels stand today.) He laid out the grounds for Jefferson's state capitol in Richmond, Virginia, in an inflexible French imperial style unlike Ramée's more romantic landscaping. He also constantly solicited military work, often with the help of Latrobe.

Godefroy was subsidized in Baltimore by "loans" from David Parish's partners the Oliver brothers. His family lived in a house on Hanover Street, provided by an Oliver associate, John O'Donnell, who was Mrs. Godefroy's uncle. It was probably through Parish and the Olivers that he broke out of his Roman Catholic circle; aside from the Masonic Temple, his largest commission on his own was for the Unitarian Church of Baltimore, close to Latrobe's masterpiece the cathedral.

The pure geometry Godefroy intended for the Unitarians, a sphere within a cube, produced such woeful acoustics that even these admirers of cool logic remodeled their auditorium into a more conventional interior, leaving Godefroy's original vault as a brooding omnipresence behind the dropped ceiling. One can imagine the remodelings away and wander between the cathedral and the church, recalling the brief friendship between Latrobe and Godefroy, two oddly coupled partners.

Their great joint project was the Baltimore Exchange, which survived until 1901; it was the largest commission either attempted, aside from Latrobe's work

The Baltimore Exchange, 1815–17

on the national Capitol. In 1815, the merchants of Baltimore agreed to subscribe for their own "Bourse," like Hamburg's but much larger. It was to be a complex of buildings under one classical shell: warehouses, insurance offices, brokers' offices, coffee house, reading room, meeting rooms, and exhibition hall, all situated around a central rotunda for the Exchange hall—another Pantheon, this time for commerce.

At the outset, things went well; Latrobe refused to carry out the plan without the partnership of Godefroy, writing to express admiration for Godefroy's "delicate feelings . . . genius and honor," though he admitted that differences might arise from his own experience in "mean contrivance" (survival in the hurly-burly of private practice) and Godefroy's "grand speculations in design" (in other words, his propensity for "visionary architecture").

Latrobe hoped these differences could be overcome with good will. Ramée was formidable competition, whom Latrobe knew to be "drawing his plan," supported by Denis Smith, a member of the building committee, we recall, of both the cathedral and the Exchange. Latrobe imagined a contest between two Frenchmen, Godefroy and Ramée, for the Francophile part of the community, while he contended with his former student Robert Mills for the support of the Anglo-Americans.

Latrobe wrote Godefroy that all this nationalism was foolish. Mills's chief backer, Robert Gilmor, was prone to argue that "native Americans should [bear] the palm away from foreigners," though he was an eager student of the architecture of Sir John Soane, often borrowing Soane's work from the Baltimore Library Company. Latrobe was usually classed with the French; he admitted to Godefroy that he had as much, or little, "of the Gallican spirit about me, [as] . . . you have . . . I am fool enough to lie awake & groan for hours over the state of France." But he had more immediate things to groan about. He heard that Denis Smith was offering "$40,000 more to procure Ramée the preference."

In the end, Latrobe and Godefroy bested Ramée and Mills; but they themselves soon fell out. Godefroy became an intense, unfulfilled, and unforgiving competitor against Latrobe. He was, at the outset, a dangerous one as well. He resigned his teaching post in 1817, to work on the Unitarian Church, a Battle Monument for the War of 1812, and the Branch Bank of the United States in Baltimore, which was to form a wing of the Exchange.

It was the management of that Branch Bank that was caught up in the speculative fervor of 1816–18. After it collapsed, they were forced out of the bank, and Godefroy's commission went with them. After Samuel and Denis Smith's bankruptcies, Godefroy set sail for England in 1819. He died in the summer of 1840, working on small municipal commissions in the French provinces.

Note on Ameriga Vespucci

You may have forgotten the dark lady in the carriage, Vincent Nolte's companion. She had been christened Elena Vespucci. When she arrived in America in 1839, she asserted that her first name was Ameriga and that she was the sole descendant of the publicist-explorer who had named the continent in communications to his patron, Lorenzo de' Medici. (Actually, she had a sister so named; but her sisters and brothers, back home, were willing to have her represent them and felt that she could do so best, apparently, by pretending they did not exist.) She was entitled, she seemed to think, to be rewarded for his achievements by the government of the United States, or by the states, taken one by one.

This she attempted to arrange by taking the states' leading male figures of America one by one. She became "much loved by the men, much hated by the women"; and, as some of the wives of the men she solicited discovered upon diligent inquiry, she had been so in Europe, too. She asserted that she had been the wife of a brave Italian (or perhaps Polish) revolutionary hero, acquiring

Ameriga Vespucci (artist unknown)

the charming little scar on her face while fighting beside him on the barricades. After his death, she had a number of male friends, including Prince Ferdinand, son of Louis Philippe.

She came to America to add to her list and to her fortune. Nicholas Biddle fell in love with her, to the dismay of his wife and his friends, and actually tried to get funds appropriated for her from Congress; she moved on to "Prince John" Van Buren, the swashbuckling son of the President. (Since she was a person without permanent address, our most telling glimpses of her in this period are in association with hostelries. She was seen at "her zenith" by the pianist and composer Louis Moreau Gottschalk: "a splendid young girl, of pale complexion, superb form, and a wealth of undulating ebony hair . . . one evening, on the balcony of the St. Louis Hotel in New Orleans, saluting, with the gesture of a queen, the crowd assembled to see her.")

But her star declined rapidly. In 1841 or 1842, while traveling with Van Buren, she stopped for the night at Hoover's Tavern in Evans Mills, New York, near the barony of George Parish, the nephew of David Parish, who, when he departed America for Europe, had left George in charge of his American affairs. A decade later, George had purchased his uncle's property and was living in and about Ogdensburg, in bachelor splendor. He too was spending the night at Hoover's Tavern; and according to a story widely circulated then (and recirculated in Walter Kellogg's novel *Parish's Fancy*), Van Buren lost Ameriga to Parish at cards.

She was then a woman of thirty-seven, still enormously attractive (we have

"A Winter Scene" by Salathiel Ellis
(the passenger in the sleigh is probably George Parish)

her portrait at this age). However they may have come together, she and George Parish stayed together for eighteen years, until he came into another inheritance—the lands, fortune, and title of another uncle, John, the brother of David. John had weathered the failure and suicide of David and had become a prosperous banker in Vienna, rewarded with the title Baron von Senftenburg. In 1858, George Parish succeeded him, left America and Ameriga. In 1860, he assumed his place at the imperial court, settling a comfortable allowance upon his former mistress, which enabled her to travel gracefully in the company of other aging charmers, such as Vincent Nolte.

In 1862, Gottschalk saw her again, in the Parish villa in Ogdensburg,

a house concealed in the midst of a shady park, surrounded by high walls, thus denying the curiosity of the indiscreet . . . [Inside, the] residence was sumptuous. French albums, Parisian engravings, and a crowd of those elegant little trifles and superfluities which are found only in French salons and which the morose and traditional taste of the Anglosaxons excludes from their parlors, at once told me that the mistress of the house was or had been pretty, that she had taste, and yearned for Paris.

When she entered the room, Gottschalk thought she was forty or forty-five; she was fifty-seven. " 'Paris,' she said to me, sighing, 'Paris!—without my fortune and twenty years less!' " And she led him to visit the "aviary, the library, the marble baths. I was dazzled." But she was like one of the inhabitants of her own aviary:

> The honest people of Ogdensburg had raised little by little around her one of those insurmountable walls made up of hatred, jealousy, and of secret malice cemented by the sour virtue of small towns. She never went out, saw nobody, and wept alone under the beautiful trees of her park, while the [wild] birds warbled on the branches.

Finally, she could tolerate Ogdensburg no longer; and though she could not recapture the years, she could make a dignified old age with what remained of her fortune. She returned to Paris, where she died on October 22, 1866. To the end, she corresponded with Ramée's friend Joseph Rosseel, who was still in charge of the Parish estate in Ogdensburg.

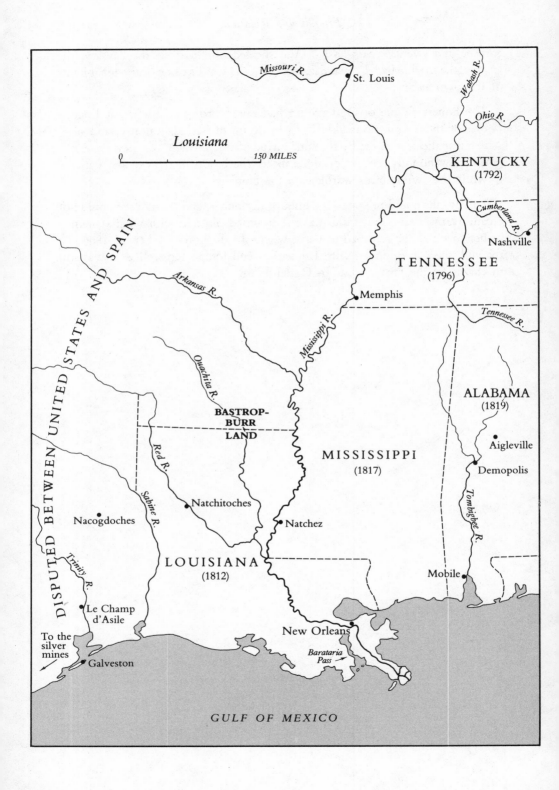

Louisiana

0 |————————————| 150 MILES

DISPUTED BETWEEN UNITED STATES AND SPAIN

Missouri R.

● St. Louis

Wabash R.

Ohio R.

KENTUCKY
(1792)

Cumberland R.

● Nashville

TENNESSEE
(1796)

Arkansas R.

● Memphis

Tennessee R.

Ouachita R.

Mississippi R.

**BASTROP-
BURR
LAND**

ALABAMA
(1819)

Red R.

MISSISSIPPI
(1817)

● Aigleville

● Demopolis

Sabine R.

● Natchitoches

Tombigbee R.

● Nacogdoches

● Natchez

Trinity R.

LOUISIANA
(1812)

● Mobile

● Le Champ
d'Asile

To the
silver
mines

● New Orleans

● Galveston

*Barataria
Pass*

GULF OF MEXICO

VII

THE "CONSPIRACY" OF
AARON BURR

The mines of Mexico beckoned as soon as galleons began bearing hoards of silver from those mines to Spain.

Sir Francis Drake and Sir John Hawkins, captains chartered by Good Queen Bess, demonstrated the cost-effectiveness of piracy, leaving the mining and refining to others. They seized the silver at sea. Spanish naval forces were later able to give some protection close to the source, but the direction of winds and currents required the passage of the silver fleet through a relatively narrow passage between what are now the coasts of South Carolina, Georgia, and Florida, and the islands of the Bahamas. French and British settlements were placed on those shores more out of a desire for pillage than for agriculture. Spanish occupation was largely intended to pre-empt the others.

The French settlers of South Carolina were exterminated by the Spaniards in the sixteenth century, but the British remained troublesome, and so did their successors, the Americans. At various stages in this narrative we will encounter several Frenchmen on other islands—and a Scot, Gregor MacGregor, who took the place of Drake and Hawkins; and, as we have seen, Napoleon I sought bases in Saint-Domingue and Louisiana to extend his American empire, with an eye to Mexico. Extending his policy of piracy on an imperial scale, the French continued to assault the Spanish possessions on the shores of the Caribbean well beyond the middle of the nineteenth century.

We would be getting too far ahead of our story if we were to deal at any length here with those efforts, but a few anticipatory notes may indicate the direction in which we are heading. We will come in Part Eight to an undertaking on the part of Napoleon's own officers to reach the mines by way of Alabama and Texas. They were not successful, though they had the advantage of an earlier reconnaissance on the part of Aaron Burr.

The Monroe Doctrine was a response to several perils, most directly one from the French (see p. 420). The war of 1846–48 trained a large corps of American officers for later, larger roles and deprived Mexico of half her territory. Though northern sentiment prevailed over southern in making a peace that stopped short of seizing the mines, Napoleon III took advantage of the civil war between those sections, a little more than a decade later, to install in the remainder of Mexico his own puppet ruler, the Austrian archduke Maximilian. The threat that Ulysses S. Grant would reappear upon the shore of Mexico, which he had left as a promising junior officer, as a hardened commander at the head of a veteran army, in 1865, induced the withdrawal of French support, and the pathetic end of Maximilian's rule (see p. 422).

We turn now to an interlude in this filibustering sequence, "Burr's Conspiracy," which flamed up in 1805–06. It was precipitated by the acquisition by the United States of the first Napoleon's holdings upon the mainland; it was a precursor to the resumption of French ambitions in America just after Waterloo; and it was contemporaneous with the Great Silver Scheme.

Biographers of Aaron Burr have not coupled his ambitions to the scheme. But the Spanish authorities did so, and carefully removed their hoard of silver from the coast, where it was exposed to his predation. Burr piously disclaimed any intention of raiding the banks of New Orleans, which were the temporary custodians of some silver already shipped. We have no precise information as to how much Vincent Nolte had on hand in the city at the time, though one of Burr's agents made a veiled threat to extort that which he had.

Burr had an affinity for French culture; much of his correspondence is in French. We have already noted his efforts to sustain French officers in charge of the primary coastal defenses of the United States (see p. 185). In his own "conspiratorial" entourage there were several more, including his chief of staff, Colonel Julien de Pestre. And it is entirely possible that the fundamental precept at the core of his "conspiracy" was hatched by a group of officers serving in the French army in the Low Countries early in the 1790s.

We will arrive there in a moment, after we have attempted to disentangle the web of ambitions on the part of the great powers along which, like insects of great boldness, men like Aaron Burr made their way.

30

WHOSE PLOT?

In the peace treaties of 1783, the British grudgingly assented to lines on the map drawn around what was asserted to be a "new nation" by their rebellious colonials. Many wise persons in London, and even in Philadelphia, expected that the undisciplined and overextended victors—especially after revolution in France deprived them of their most important international support—would fall to squabbling, and that only a little war would be necessary to erase those lines and bring the colonies back under the crown.

In 1788, the governor general of Canada, Lord Dorchester, sent an agent, Dr. John Connolly, to Louisville, on the Ohio River, to encourage westerners to detach themselves from the United States, attack the Spanish in New Orleans, and set themselves up as an independent buffer state. Connolly was betrayed by the ubiquitous blackguard James Wilkinson, and his plot came to nothing. Two years later, Dorchester tried another tack: he told the Indian tribes living north of the Ohio River that they should regard the Americans as intruders and that they could expect British aid in expelling them: "I shall not be surprised if we are at war with them in the course of the present year," he said.

This was a difficult time for the United States: the British policy of separating the transmontane West was a deadly danger to the American frontier; the British maritime policy of keeping Yankees out of the lucrative West Indies was even more dangerous, since this objective was shared by France. At the end of the 1790s, some of these perils, creeping through the forests and hovering on the seaboard horizon, were alleviated by Federalist policy. In 1795, John Jay negotiated a treaty of a kind of wary amity with Britain, and Alexander Hamilton conspired to the brink of treason to assure a concert of British and American interests.

Dorchester, twice baffled but now with some prospect of Federalist support, tried a third incursion upon the possessions of Spain in the Mississippi Valley, requesting that the Americans open the way for an expedition from Canada through the Ohio basin. The British and the Americans seemed ready to act together against Spain, however they may have bickered about the ownership of the territory along Dorchester's proposed line of march; their interests were already concerted in the nightmares of Hamilton's onetime friend Talleyrand.

As soon as he reached power after his unhappy American years, Talleyrand commenced soliciting a Spanish alliance devoted to erecting "a wall of brass forever impenetrable to the combined efforts of England and America." He hoped to place that barrier along the Mississippi, or, with luck, even farther forward, along the Appalachians.

But the Spanish empire, even with French support, was too exhausted to resist. Thomas Jefferson saw the Hispanic possessions falling from "feeble" hands "piece by piece." The question was: Would those pieces fall into the hands of the United States or into the clutches of the perfidious British? Or of Napoleon? Or of someone else with Napoleonic aspirations and Napoleon's indifference to nationality? The carcass of the Spanish empire lay exposed. The scent of carrion, of undefended frontiers, of easy offerings for pillage, brought forth from the United States a succession of adventurers, chief among whom was Aaron Burr.

The dissolution of the Hispanic empire proceeded so rapidly that the southern slaveholders of the United States, though they saw an opportunity opening before them, did not mobilize their resources rapidly enough to take advantage of it. James Monroe was urged by Thomas Jefferson to make his fortune in the western borderlands—and to get out of James Madison's path to the presidency. But Monroe coolly declined the opportunity; it went to Burr instead.

He was ready: Burr was a man of the mettle to succeed to the empire of Cortez by the methods of Cortez. His goal was to seize the silver mines of Mexico and to set himself up as a power in the West. He was never clear to others, and probably to himself, as to how independent he planned to become in a formal sense. National loyalties were not very intense among his contemporaries in any region, but in the West they could hardly be detected. In any case, his plan failed because of the defection of Wilkinson, a Spanish double-agent in his own camp, a man absolutely indifferent to patriotic considerations.

The Marcher Lords

Burr's "conspiracy" was not isolated or idiosyncratic. It was merely one of many to bubble forth from dislocations of the tectonic structure of power across all the fertile continents of the globe* between 1790 and 1820.

Napoleon was not alone; other French generals battled their way to thrones from Sweden to Sicily. Emboldened by these examples and rejoicing in like opportunities of their own, American marcher lords set themselves up in little frontier states in the mountains leading to the Mississippi Valley. These domains nominally belonged to Spain or to the United States, but they were in fact quite independent, for a little while at least.

---

*"Except Australia," one might demur—but that continent escaped only as a result of the miscarriage of a plan by Napoleon to assault it. His campaign against Egypt and Palestine, the first of three aborted efforts to conquer India, was followed by his foray against Saint-Domingue and schemes for the conquest of Mexico. He was drawn to weakness on an imperial scale by the instinct that led him to thrust, tactically, between the armies of his opponents at Austerlitz.

Such conditions were easily sufficient to induce a disappointed politician like Aaron Burr to find his own satrapy beyond the range of seaboard humiliations. He was encouraged to do so by the contradictory policies of the Jefferson administration, arising from contradictions in Mr. Jefferson's own character. The Sage of Monticello believed in a weak central government, and the frail economic base of that government during his administration made it certain that his prejudice would have a practical outcome. He could not afford what he did not desire. Yet, armed with such a small "stick," he nonetheless reversed Theodore Roosevelt's dictum and loudly exhorted his countrymen to expand forcibly to the south and the west.

Filibustering, like Burr's, flourishes when governments are frail and peoples bellicose, when the old empires are crumbling and the new have not yet emerged. Ambition abhors a vacuum—or perhaps one should say it rejoices in the occasion to fill one.

In the revolutionary period, even the admirals and generals of the powers resisting revolution took up filibustering and reverted to piracy, with and without the encouragement of their governments. The British fleet had advanced considerably in its technology since the days when Sir John Hawkins and Sir Francis Drake ravaged the Spanish Main for their silent partner, Good Queen Bess. But their lessons were well learned; and in 1804, Admiral Sir Alexander Cochrane, in a sheer act of piracy, looted the neutral Spanish treasure fleet of five million pesos. (It was Cochrane who later led the British assault upon Washington and Fort McHenry, Maryland.)

A year later, David Parish, the Hopes, and the Barings relieved the fleet of the need to return so blatantly to the devices of the sixteenth century. But the impotence of Spain was amply demonstrated when another British fleet seized Buenos Aires. It was symptomatic of the times that the people of Argentina drove them out again without any help from the viceroy, who had left the Argentines to their own devices.

Under such circumstances, Talleyrand's "wall of brass" failed even to provide an effective metaphor; and in 1803, Napoleon brushed aside such remonstrances and betrayed his explicit promise to the king of Spain to retain Louisiana.* He sold it to Thomas Jefferson, and reduced by five hundred miles the buffer between the ambitions of Aaron Burr and the silver mines of Mexico.

---

*France had colonized Louisiana after defeating Spain in competition to control the Mississippi Valley, and had then been forced by the British victories in the 1760s to relinquish to Spain the west bank of the great river and the vaguely known lands to the west. The British assaulted the Spanish garrison at Saint Louis during our Revolutionary War, when Spain was an ally to the American revolutionaries, but failed, and conceded Spanish rule. Spain turned the area back to France again ("retroceding" it) in a series of treaties between 1798 and 1801, on the explicit understanding that it would not be given up to the Anglo-Americans. This was the period of the "wall of brass."

The Adventurer

There is no "consensus profile" of Aaron Burr, no synthetic portrait like those generated by computer for police manhunt purposes. Each of us must think him through. As a politician, he might have been an English Whig of the time of Walpole; he was unfortunate in being born in the wrong time, in the wrong country, with an insufficient fortune. If he had turned his ambitions wholly, instead of partially, to getting rich through commerce, he would have made a good partner for the Hopes or the Barings.

And if we are to judge Burr, we must also arrive at our own conclusions about his shadow figure, James Wilkinson, to whom he wrote as "mon beau et cher Diable."

Let us begin with Burr, so celebrated when he was ascendant, so much the object of avid gossip when he was in decline, so systematically disparaged by nineteenth-century historians. His contemporaries knew every detail of his career. To the Jeffersonians, it was a compendium of horrors.

Burr, like Thomas Jefferson and Alexander Hamilton, was a lover of architecture and, we now know, wished to be a munificent patron. It is a pity that Marc Isambard Brunel's remodeling of Marble Hill was never completed (see p. 79). Now the house itself is gone. Monticello remains; even Hamilton's poor, bereft Grange remains. Nothing of Burr's remains, but there is evidence that he wished to be the sponsor of a city designed by Benjamin Henry Latrobe, and that is cause enough to follow his career.

Burr was born in Newark, New Jersey, the son of a divine who was president of the College of New Jersey, now Princeton University. His grandfather was the famous theologian Jonathan Edwards; his brother-in-law, the famous teacher of the law Tappan Reeve, with whom he studied. He served courageously in the revolutionary army and, in 1782, married the daughter of a British officer who had died in one of William Pitt's disastrous campaigns in the West Indies.

After the war, Burr rose rapidly in the Democratic-Republican, or Jeffersonian, party, and as a lawyer in the city of New York. He became attorney general of the state in 1789, and United States senator in 1791. Returning to New York to build his base, he was Thomas Jefferson's running mate in the election of 1800. As the result of a quirk that permitted the presidential and vice-presidential candidates to be treated as peers for the purpose of computation, the two received an equal number of votes in the electoral college, and for a few months the fabric of the new democracy was tested by Federalist intrigues. Though, in the event, Burr chose not to press the matter, and Jefferson was installed as President and Burr as vice-president, Jefferson already disliked

Aaron Burr (artist unknown)

Burr, and his feelings were not alleviated by the real possibility during the contentious interval that the Jeffersonians would have to use force to achieve the outcome clearly intended by the electorate. A man who simultaneously stood between Thomas Jefferson and the presidency and might require the order-seeking sage to employ violent means to get there was fit for the deepest Jeffersonian abyss. He might indeed be entrapped with a clear conscience.

Burr was serving as vice-president when he and Hamilton fought their duel on Weehawken Heights on the eleventh of July, 1804. Burr's career still had considerable energy in it; he had failed of election as President and as governor of New York, but he was still formidable. His tragedy was that he was also desperate; and, in desperation, he exposed himself to a partnership with James Wilkinson.

Wilkinson

Wilkinson, in his prime, was remembered for his open countenance, "mild, capacious, and beaming with intelligence . . . manly, and facile; manners bland, accommodating and popular; an address easy, polite and gracious . . . By these fair terms he conciliated; by these he captivated."

Even a more skeptical man than Burr might have been so captivated, and

James Wilkinson (artist unknown)

Burr was an easy mark. He gave the appearance of cynicism and imperturbable sophistication, but crafty Andrew Jackson once reflected upon Burr's character and said that though "as far from a fool as I ever saw . . . yet [he] is as easily fooled as any man I ever knew."

Wilkinson, a Maryland planter's son, was raised to be a physician but was never much interested in healing. He joined George Washington's army, was promoted rapidly, and was breveted a brigadier general by Congress. He was the lucky bearer of the tidings of victory at Saratoga in 1777. (Not all messengers are shot; some get outrageous preferment—it depends upon the news they bring.) Subsequently, however, he joined a group of conspirators who sought to replace Washington with Horatio Gates as commander of the American forces, and drunkenly betrayed them. He survived the ensuing duel with Gates but not an investigation of the honesty of his accounts, and was discharged. He then sneaked back into the army as clothier general, but was cashiered again for dishonesty. Sometime during these years, he opened a secret correspondence, in code and often in French, with Burr.

During the war, Wilkinson married Nicholas Biddle's cousin Ann. In 1784, with her money, he established himself in Kentucky. Three years later, he sold himself to the Spanish governor at New Orleans, becoming Agent 13 of the Spanish intelligence service. In 1788, he discovered the British plot to seize Louisiana conceived by the redoubtable Lord Dorchester. He insinuated himself among the plotters and betrayed them. In 1789, he betrayed to the Creek Indians the plans of the American government, of which he was a military officer, to build a road through Creek territory. The road crew was attacked, the road stopped, and the Creeks and their Spanish allies had another reprieve. (I have not sought synonyms for "betray" or "betrayal"; their very repetitions tell us something about Wilkinson.)

Wilkinson advised his Spanish clients not merely to retain defensive garrisons in territory contested with the Americans but to employ their missions for political as well as religious purposes. From these outposts, they should seek to detach the western provinces of the United States. The West was only tenuously tied to the eastern seaboard by paths across the Appalachians, an obstruction so serrated as to threaten, like a knife, the connecting fibers.

A series of "Spanish conspiracies" at one time or another involved every major leader of Kentucky and Tennessee. Wilkinson was the intermediary between those leaders and his Spanish employers. His recurrent and consistent role was inflammatory. Out of disorder would come his opportunities.

Other Plotters

In 1793, Thomas Jefferson encouraged "Citizen" Genêt, the French minister to the United States, to send a young botanist, André Michaux, upon a hapless filibustering expedition against Spanish Louisiana, in association with Jeffersonian politicians in Kentucky and Tennessee. Four years later, this scheme was renewed by Senator William Blount; another set of Jeffersonians assembled to assault Talleyrand's "wall of brass." Spain was fair game, even with the aid of the hated British. Though the plot failed, and Blount was expelled from the Senate, it brought James Wilkinson and Thomas Jefferson together. Two historians, I. J. Cox and, more recently, Milton Lomask, have suggested that "for years to come" Jefferson remained "subject to Wilkinson's influence." In any case it was this man, his reputation more stained than a butcher's apron, to whom, in the winter of 1804–05, Jefferson entrusted the territory of Louisiana, making him commander-in-chief of the American army in the West as governor.

Wilkinson had a capacity—one might say a satanic gift—of influencing men of otherwise sound judgment. His spell upon Burr may have begun to exert itself as early as 1796, according to Matthew L. Davis, Burr's only authorized biographer. Davis tells us it was at that time that Burr had various conversations with Governor John Jay of New York and expressed to Jay his intention to lead an expeditionary force in a war to take possession of Mexico. Jay, according to Burr, did not discourage him but, one suspects, may have even considered how he, and his political ally Alexander Hamilton, might bring the British into a concerted assault upon the "wall of brass." (Hamiltonians had even fewer compunctions than Jeffersonians about British alliances when Spanish possessions were the prize.)

If Edward Everett Hale can be believed, Hamilton was as close to the British as a member of the American government might honorably be, and was also "influenced" by Wilkinson. Hale claimed to have seen, in 1876, a trunkful of correspondence between Hamilton and Wilkinson. In these papers, dating from 1798, the year after Blount's plot was revealed, the two proposed to gather an army at Cincinnati to take New Orleans from the Spanish and, from there, to launch a concerted campaign against the rest of Spain's New World empire. The trunk, according to Hale, was offered for sale to the War Department. The department refused to pay the price required. The seller, in a fit of pique all historians may rue, burned the contents.

By 1798, Wilkinson was already corresponding, in code, with Burr; Jefferson was also in correspondence with Wilkinson, and Hamilton was vying with him for the privilege. During the quasi war with France, Hamilton had written to Secretary of War James McHenry of their President, John Adams: "the chief is too desultory . . . we ought certainly to look at the possession of the Floridas and Louisiana, and we ought to squint at South America."

31

THE PLOTS THICKEN

In 1802, the results of three years of secret diplomacy were made public, and the ownership of much of the territory coveted by Wilkinson shifted from Spain to France. Napoleon sold the region to the United States. When the Spanish governor was slow to effect the transfer—the French hardly took control—Jefferson mobilized the western militia to enforce "specific performance" of his contract with Napoleon.

The Spaniards, not for the last time in this story, acquiesced in the inevitable, but Jefferson soon called out the militia against them again, to threaten an invasion if they interfered with the expeditions he was sending into the lands along the vague borders of his newly purchased empire (see below). The militia, having effected the threat, went home but were to return yet again to arms, this time to be arrayed against Aaron Burr.

Wilkinson, the imp of chaos, was present in the Place d'Armes of New Orleans when, in 1803, the Tricolore went down and the Stars and Stripes arose over the city. In the spring of the next year, Jefferson's commander of the West urged Burr to make his play to gain control of New Orleans and, after that, the Mexican silver mines.

As we noted earlier, in a passing reference to the intrepid citizens of Buenos Aires, there were Latin Americans who had ideas about the future of their own countries. We will return to this point from time to time, even though our perspective is North American. It is impossible, however, to pierce the mysteries surrounding the intentions of Aaron Burr without introducing Francisco de Miranda to the story at this point.

Miranda was the partner with whom Wilkinson and Hamilton would have carried out their expedition to Venezuela, though it would have been more to his purposes than to theirs.

Miranda

A man of implacable energy, idealism, and ingenuity, Miranda was a true hero of South American independence. Some historians have depicted him as a gnat causing annoyance to Jefferson—Claude Bowers, for example, described him as a "queer little Latin-American soldier of fortune" in one volume, and in another as "the adventurer . . . as dependable as Burr . . . no more."

One can readily imagine a lofty Latino writing in such terms about George Washington if our revolution had failed and Miranda's had succeeded. But Aaron Burr's biographer Milton Lomask describes Miranda as "a man of overwhelming charm, with a vividly handsome face, articulate, learned, and dynamic . . . the only personage of his heroic age to participate in all three of its most memorable events: the struggle of the American colonies for independence, the French Revolution, and the liberation of Latin America." The Precursor, as he has been known since he received his own two-volume biography at the hands of William Spence Robertson in 1929, was no mere "soldier of fortune"; he was part statesman and part knight errant, and his career intersected with that of every great figure in the Atlantic community of his time, including Burr, Jefferson, and Hamilton. Like them, he even had time for architecture and garden design.

Born in Caracas about 1754, Miranda served in the Spanish army and joined in the expeditions against Pensacola and New Providence that supported American independence. He was quick to perceive lessons for his own countrymen, and in 1780 and 1781 he learned others of a more mercantile nature. In Havana, he joined with Robert Smith of Baltimore in several ventures, including the smuggling of silver by means anticipating one of the subthemes of the Great Silver Scheme. At this point, Miranda might have joined the ranks of the multinational merchants; but instead he went to the United States in 1784 to seek help in liberating his native region—not yet a country and much less a nation—from Spanish rule.

Alexander Hamilton and General Henry Knox (a client of Charles Bulfinch) encouraged Miranda. Knox drafted a proposal for five thousand unemployed veterans of the recent war with Britain to join in an attack on the Spanish rulers of Venezuela. Ships and money were needed, however. Stephen Girard, who might later have participated, was not yet grown to the fullness of his power. So Miranda went to London.

William Pitt and the merchants of "the City," though full of pleasant words, were not quite ready to throw Britain back into a Spanish war; so Miranda set out for Russia by way of Austria and Turkey. He was said to be among the lovers of Catherine the Great; certainly she gave him political encouragement. But Russian help was not enough. He returned to Britain when, in the late 1780s, there seemed a better promise of an Anglo-American alliance against Spain. Nothing came of that beyond letters of recommendation to the leaders of revolutionary France, where Miranda went next, in 1792.

Since the days when John Law inflated into vast speculations the hope of Louisiana's becoming as rich a province as Spanish Mexico, the French had been fascinated with such alluring possibilities. Citizen Genêt had hoped to "liberate" Louisiana for France, taking it back from the Spaniards, using American troops led by George Rogers Clark. In 1792, Dumouriez, as minister of foreign affairs, discussed the idea with the colleagues of another American hero, John Paul Jones, soon after Jones's death.

When Miranda found Dumouriez's successor in the foreign office unresponsive to his somewhat revised version of these schemes, he went off to speak to Dumouriez himself, at the headquarters of the French armies in Flanders. There he found more American revolutionaries, chief of whom was a New Yorker, John Skey Eustace, who had already reconnoitered Venezuela and was fluent in both Spanish and French. Eustace was a general in the French service, serving beside two other Americans, Eleazar Oswald, a colonel of artillery, and Lieutenant John Cox. (Also in the headquarters at the time were Louis Philippe and Joseph-Jacques Ramée.)

Miranda rose to the rank of brigadier general, commanding a wing of the French army. Dumouriez began to extol the virtues of "General Miranda's superb project" as one of the "diversionary tactics [to] . . . weaken the power of England and Spain," while American enthusiasts in Paris, like Thomas Paine and Joel Barlow, supported the propagation of "the principles of the French Revolution in Louisiana." As late as the end of 1793, Barlow submitted a plan to the French government entitled "How to Take Louisiana at No Cost to the Nation." Thus, in Paris and in Flanders there flourished the virus that later infected Alexander Hamilton, Aaron Burr, and Thomas Jefferson.

In 1791, the French government had held out the hope that after the frontiers of France were secure, Miranda might recruit six thousand Black troops in Saint-Domingue and, with French officers, return to Venezuela. But Robespierre executed Brissot, the leader of that government, and Dumouriez, Louis Philippe (and Ramée) went over to the Austrians. Miranda did not; he was consistent in his republicanism and would not truckle to monarchs. But though he had opposed the defection, only a spirited defense of him by Barlow before the Revolutionary Tribunal saved him from the guillotine.

Miranda was too radical for the Directorate installed in 1796; and Napoleon, at the outset of his regime, was determined to wring all the silver possible out

Francisco de Miranda; painting by Jean Lebarbier,
engraving by Charles E. Gaucher

of the Spanish Bourbons while professing a shared abhorrence of radicals like
Miranda. So in 1798 the "adventurer" went back to London.

From Paris, Miranda had corresponded with Alexander Hamilton, and once
in London he focused his formidable charm upon Hamilton's friend Rufus
King, who was representing the United States in Britain. King and Hamilton
did all they could to soften the resistance to Miranda's proposals on the part
of William Pitt and also of President John Adams; but they could not induce
an Anglo-American expedition to support Venezuelan independence. Miranda
then chose the unfortunate year of 1802 to make another try in Paris; Napoleon,
facing disaster in Saint-Domingue, wished to hear of no further Latin American
conceits.

In 1805, Miranda and Burr were both in New York, conspicuously recruiting
men and raising money for their respective "plots" against Spain. They conferred, but they did not conspire. Burr, who intended to go after the silver
mines of Mexico by way of New Orleans, and who needed all the assistance
he could muster among the floating population of professional soldiers and
mercenary sailors available, apparently saw Miranda as a competitor for recruits.
Miranda, simultaneously but not in concert, was laying plans to assault Venezuela by sea. Both were assured of the aid of the British fleet under Admiral

Cochrane, which had already demonstrated its profitable hostility to Spain; but Burr did not rely upon such assurances.

Miranda would have been wiser had he not, either.* He had important Federalist connections: though his old friend Hamilton was dead, John Adams's son-in-law William Smith had become his disciple. This did not please Jefferson, who was not ready to have the New York Federalists receive credit for liberating the Spanish possessions. Fully informed by Miranda of what he had in mind, the American government had ample opportunity to prevent him from accumulating ships, supplies, and men to lead against Spain. But it chose to let him proceed; in the same deliberate fashion it withheld rebuke of Aaron Burr for fifteen months after being informed of his designs. Once Miranda was at sea, in February 1806, Jefferson piously turned upon Smith and ordered him brought to justice.

Miranda was gone. Jefferson had Smith in his net. Burr and a colleague in New York politics, John Swartwout, rushed to his rescue. They turned the trial of Smith into a carnival of embarrassment for the administration. Smith became a hero of liberation of the Western Hemisphere from the hated Spanish and was acquitted. Jefferson alleged that the jury was packed by Swartwout; however that may be, the result was a humiliating rehearsal for the later trials of Swartwout himself, of his "accomplice," the French revolutionary hero Dr. Erich Bollmann, and of Burr.

Poignancies and Ironies

The trial of William Smith is an occasion of special poignancy for those who know something of the emotional life of Thomas Jefferson. Aaron Burr and Thomas Jefferson fought each other over the prostrate reputation of a hapless man whom Jefferson had known twenty years earlier, when they were both in love, for it was to Smith that he wrote the letters revealing the depth of his feelings for Maria Cosway (see p. 445). Smith entered the circle of Jefferson's friends by marrying Abigail, the daughter of John and Abigail Adams; Jefferson wrote to him as if it were Smith's romance, not his own feelings for Mrs. Cosway, that awoke in him the fires of youth and passion.

William Stevens Smith was not a character of great density or amplitude; but, almost alone among his generation of New Yorkers, he has left a legacy in architecture. In 1797 he was living in the Bronx, in a house still (in 1988)

---

*Miranda's expedition had some success until Cochrane suddenly—some might say, treacherously—pulled his fleet away. Miranda barely escaped, having done more damage to Cochrane's reputation than to the Spanish empire. He returned in 1810 for a final, tragic effort to liberate his country. He was defeated, captured, and died in a Spanish prison in 1816.

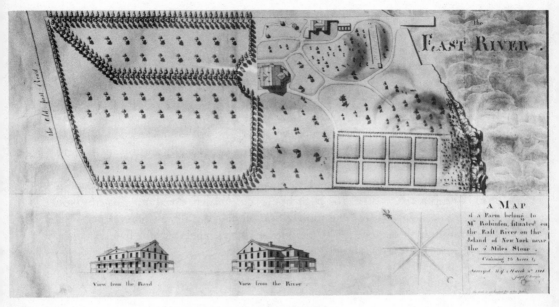

Joseph Mangin's 1806 drawing of Mount Vernon,
the William Stevens Smith estate in Manhattan
(known as the Smith-Robinson House)

extant at 3701 Provost Avenue, near 233rd Street. He made it available to Adams, his presidential father-in-law, during a yellow-fever epidemic in 1798. For two months it served as the executive mansion of the United States; one of the President's sons drowned in Eastchester Creek and is buried in the neighborhood.

Even a remnant of Mount Vernon, Smith's estate in central Manhattan, survives: the carriage house is still there. It is now a headquarters for the Colonial Dames, to be found amid high-rise apartments at 421 East Sixty-first Street. The main house burned in 1826. It was an ungainly thing, but so festooned with galleries in the French West Indian fashion that I was tempted to include it in Part One. It appears in a drawing by Joseph Mangin.

Smith is a sad figure. He was an embarrassment to John Adams and to Jefferson. Neither mentioned him when they resumed correspondence toward the end of their lives. In France in the 1780s, he had carried messages between them, and he accompanied them on their architectural tour of England. In this happier time, Jefferson wrote him many letters, including the famous one about "the tree of liberty [that] must be refreshed from time to time, with the blood of patriots and tyrants. It is its natural manure."

Poor Miranda. He held the same belief—and gave his blood to prove it.

An Architectural Note

Once, during his desperate efforts to recruit American aid, Miranda chanced to travel the coast of North Carolina. There he directed our attention to the first professionally trained French landscape architect to work in America, Claude-Joseph Sauthier (see p. 458). Miranda was impressed both by Governor William Tryon's house (now reconstructed for us to enjoy as well) and by its garden, designed by Sauthier in the late 1760s.

The Venezuelan visitor, though very much in a hurry, went to the trouble of obtaining a set of plans for both house and garden. At about this time, or earlier, he left with John Trumbull a fine sketch of a Greek-revival mansion which might have become the White House of Venezuela and the first residence erected in that style in the Western Hemisphere.

32

WESTERN ADVENTURES

What did Burr have in mind? To reach our own conclusions to that question (put, as it was, to a series of juries in 1806 and 1807), we must balance the well-known case of the prosecution against the less-known case those juries accepted as more credible. As often happens, the prosecution has written the history of the matter. The chief prosecutor was, in function if not in form, the President of the United States.

Many have come to believe that Burr was guilty as charged by Jefferson, guilty of treason and other high misdemeanors, guilty of wishing to purloin Louisiana, Jefferson's gift to the nation, to set himself up as emperor of the West.

In fact, however, Burr was acquitted of treason—not once but, in effect, four times,* though he went into a voluntary exile of four years. (He returned to New York, practiced law quite successfully, married a wealthy widow, and lived in reasonable comfort until his death in 1836.)

What was he about, then, in 1805? He was about what Dumouriez and

---

*Three grand juries failed to indict, and he was declared not guilty of treason in the final, famous trial of 1807. At the end of that trial he still had to face another for the misdemeanor of coveting the Spanish possessions, but no one bothered to pursue the matter. To convict him would have implied conviction of every major American political figure.

Miranda had plotted in Flanders, what Hamilton had been about in the 1790s, and what Jefferson himself was about: dismembering the Spanish empire. His plans, however, included an element lacking in Hamilton's: he was ready to remove himself to the West, accompanied by his successors (his daughter and grandson), and start a new career. By 1804, both Hamilton and Burr were passed-over politicians. They had lost the scramble for office in the settled states of the East. Hamilton repined but, at the time of his death, was not yet ready to adopt the traditional American remedy for wretchedness: picking up and leaving. Burr, on the other hand, like thousands of his contemporaries and millions of his countrymen afterward, attempted to make a new start, on a new "stake" in the West.

From that "stake" he would see what chance, guile, and James Wilkinson brought his way. He removed himself from the scene of his eastern afflictions, from juries in New Jersey acting as though his affair with Hamilton were not a matter of honor but of murder, from Jeffersonian politicians who had defeated him in his national ambitions and in his aspiration to the governorship of New York, from mobs, and creditors, and bitter memories.

The Bastrop Claim

Burr was not a man for small gestures. His "stake" was four hundred thousand acres set astride the present boundary of Louisiana and Arkansas, in the fertile valley of the Ouachita (sometimes called the "Washita") River. He had acquired his property from Abraham Morhouse, a Kentucky speculator and, at second hand, from Morhouse's partner Felipe Enrique Neri, also known as Baron de Bastrop.

Bastrop is a worthy member of our collection of international scalawags and filibusterers. We wish we knew more about him, so we could judge the truth of his assertion that he became a baron as the result of the affections of Frederick the Great of Prussia. He was apparently handsome, and his magnificent stature might actually have brought him to the attention of Frederick, who kept a stable of young six-footers for his personal guard.

The most credulous of Bastrop scholars, Aaron Sakolski, tells us that "Napoleon confiscated his property in 1795 and forced him to flee to America." But Napoleon came to power in France in 1799; in 1795 he was a young general, busy building a reputation in Italy. Some other propulsion must have ejected the "baron" from France, if that is indeed where this man with an Italian surname, a Spanish first name, and a title alleged to be Prussian actually was before descending upon Virginia. Perhaps the propulsion was political, or, perhaps, the discovery of a more than usually redolent fraud.

Sakolski tells us that after a period in Virginia, Bastrop took refuge in

Louisiana, "possibly for failure to pay his debts or because of passing out worthless bills of exchange." There he "became friendly with the Spanish governor," who, in 1795–96, granted him 1,200,000 acres on the Ouachita River.*

The pecuniary incentives for this "friendliness" caught the attention of higher officials, who put a stop to these relations and transactions in 1797. But that did not keep Bastrop from selling part of his claim to a group of Kentucky speculators, including Morhouse. Though even the friendly governor had required some limited settlement on the tract, and though Bastrop had never performed on this requirement, the speculators were unperturbed; and so, apparently, was a buyer of 400,000 of these acres, for five thousand dollars in cash and thirty thousand in assumed notes—Aaron Burr.†

Burr's ambitions were almost certainly based upon the Bastrop property (it has sprouted the little Arkansas city named El Dorado), though some newspapers of the day suggested that he intended to revive the much larger Yazoo claims. (These resulted from a somewhat earlier embarrassment, in which a suborned Georgia legislature had made huge concessions to speculators in Spanish lands east of the Mississippi. One of the Yazoo speculators was Gideon Granger; another, it was alleged, was Samuel Smith; and a third was Wilkinson. These are important figures in this tangled tale: one should bear in mind the close connections between Smith and Granger [see p. 285] and the fact that Burr entrusted Smith with his crucial proxy in the choice of the President in 1800.)

Burr told his friends he planned to settle upon the Bastrop claim and there watch for opportunities. Senator John Smith of Ohio later testified that Burr said to him: "If there should be a war between the United States and Spain, I shall head a corps of volunteers and be the first to march into the Mexican provinces. If peace should be profferred . . . I shall settle my Washita lands, and make society as pleasant as possible." His pleasure, it seems, included surrounding himself with neoclassical architecture of Latrobe's design.

Burr had found a lovely stretch of country. Dan Flores, its best chronicler, tells us that flocks of yellow and red parrots "flitted through the lofty bald cypresses and red cedars" of the Ouachita and Red River valleys. Whooping cranes gave their alarums to huge ivory-billed woodpeckers drumming on the

---

*Another grant, of 100,000 acres, went to a mysterious French émigré, the marquis de Maison Rouge. Perhaps the shadowy "marquis" was a client like David Parish, who named his house in Parishville the Red Villa, or like Jean Lafitte, whose residence at Galveston was called the Red House.

†For thirty more years, Bastrop left a trail of fraud and land speculation across the plains; he has been immortalized by the naming of a town in Louisiana after him, and one in Texas.

The ultimate purchaser of Burr's "Bastrop tract" was Stephen Girard, who invested $50,000 in improving it. He left it to charities, which lost their claims under a decision of the U.S. Supreme Court that Bastrop's title was defective.

virgin hardwoods. Passenger pigeons flocked so heavily together as to break the limbs of cottonwoods, and deer frisked in the shadows. The soil was rich, the deep sod unbroken; and on the river floodplains, shaggy bison feasted on the tall grass.

Burr never inspected the property, though he wrote Latrobe that "the excellence of the soil and climate are established to my satisfaction by the report of impartial persons."

Those impartial persons—the only explorers to give detailed descriptions of the Bastrop claim—had been provided by Thomas Jefferson. They were William Dunbar, of Natchez, and Dr. George Hunter, of Philadelphia, who explored the Ouachita Valley in the fall and winter of 1804–05. Jefferson arranged the expedition and persuaded Congress to pay for it. (Dunbar and Hunter exchanged scientific correspondence with the pirate-architect Bartholomy Lafon; see p. 399.)

The President, therefore, knew as much as or more than Burr about "the tract of country on the Washita." He said of it that it "was to serve as the pretext for all of [Burr's] preparations, an allurement for such followers as really wish to acquire settlements in that country, and a cover under which to retreat in the event of a . . . discomfiture . . . of his real design," the assault upon Mexico.

Jefferson also knew Burr's intentions. There was never a Burr "conspiracy" in the sense of a covert cabal. Burr operated with trumpets and drums. He reported to Secretary Albert Gallatin, the President's intimate adviser, when his land transaction was "about to be concluded." It is very likely that in his discussions with Jefferson himself, before he departed for the West, he gave his own description of the property and his plans for it—though he probably omitted his intention to wean away to it Jefferson's favorite architect.

Burr had a number of conversations with the President, one of them lasting more than two hours. No one knows what was said. I think it likely that the canny Jefferson held his tongue. Skillful silence might imply to Burr that his "corps of volunteers" would not be unwelcome along the paths traced out by Jefferson's system of "exploring" expeditions. In any case, Burr went ahead, corresponding and talking with every leading figure in the West, gathering boats and men and money.

Mr. Jefferson's Quasi-war: Preliminaries

Wilkinson, from his post as military commander in New Orleans, was meanwhile arranging matters for an "incident." According to the secretary of war, Henry Dearborn, many people believed some border fracas would permit "an attack on Mexico . . . under the direction of the Government of the United States . . . honor, glory and riches awaited every individual who would thus engage in the service of his country. Many honest and respectable men . . . kept the Executive [Jefferson] informed from time to time of the general movement."

Thanks to Wilkinson, the Spaniards were equally well informed. He was encouraging Jefferson's "explorations" and simultaneously urging his Spanish employers to "intercept Captain Lewis and his party"—the greatest of Jefferson's explorations, the Lewis and Clark expedition, had set out in 1804 to explore the northwest portion of the purchase—to fortify the posts along the Sabine. Wilkinson urged the Spaniards to "drive back every illegal usurpation" of her "most dangerous neighbor."

In February 1806, after one hundred and fifty Americans under Captain Edward Turner attacked the Spanish post at Los Adaes, the Spanish governor of Texas issued orders "to attack and destroy every Anglo-American party." In July, into this resistance he himself had provoked, Wilkinson dispatched Zebulon Pike, whose reconnaissance was to be up the Arkansas River toward the peak that now bears his name and then southward toward Santa Fe—and Mexico. He got all the way to "the Spanish peaks" north of Taos before the defending forces caught up with him.

Earlier, in the spring, Jefferson had sent another flying column into the Spanish lands. It proceeded up the Red River, pressing closer than had Dunbar and Hunter to the main "enemy" base at Nacogdoches. According to two of Pike's men, interviewed later in Santa Fe, their party was to rendezvous with Pike at the headwaters of that river. Jefferson selected Peter Custis, one of his stable of young Virginians, as chief scientist of this expedition, under the command of an experienced frontiersman, Thomas Freeman. Accompanied by a large military escort, it passed close by Burr's colony and headed up the Red River.

Freeman and Custis were instructed to test Spanish tolerance as boldly as they dared; Jefferson apparently wished to know the elasticity of the Hispanic imperial will. The incursion was under orders to relent only if it encountered "a superior force . . . arrayed against your further progress and inflexibly determined to arrest it." In March 1806 the expedition was outfitted, and word was sent by the President to Spanish officials in New Orleans that "any violence . . . offered the party by subjects of Spain . . . will have serious consequences."

Bastrop, a Spanish subject, did his best to warn his government of "the immediate movement of their [American] forces to invade the dominions of H[is] M[ajesty]." Jefferson might profess to be sending his expedition for purely scientific purposes, but Bastrop assured the Spaniards that the United States government was "merely awaiting the moment for running the boundary . . . before this work is undertaken."

The wonder of it all is that there were any guides and frontiersmen left for Burr. Indeed, many of the members of his little band of sixty or so came to him after being forced to choose one leader as against another in a race toward the same objective. Some switched sides. For example, John Smith of Ohio joined Burr's early planning but was enticed away by Jefferson and asked to suborn the loyalty of the Spanish governor of the Floridas. The President, he reported, told him that a war with Spain seemed to be inevitable. Though the cabinet postponed any military adventures against the Floridas in November 1805, Turner's attack on Los Adaes the following February suggested that the Americans had merely shifted their target.

The Spaniards replied with a great show of activity. They mobilized one force in Santa Fe, another on the Texas coast to head off Miranda (who was somewhere on the ocean at this moment, and no one could be certain of his destination), and a third concentrated around Nacogdoches. An army variously rumored to be a thousand men and twelve hundred (actually no more than seven hundred) was sent to the north (or east—the river turns south after running roughly eastward) bank of the Sabine River. The Sabine was far short of the frontier claimed by Spain after the "retrocession" of Louisiana. Spain asserted that it had relinquished only the land east and north of the upper Missouri.* It had not, however, organized resistance, despite Wilkinson's urging, until the Americans came perilously close to the old French base of Natchitoches, asserting they had purchased it with the rest of Louisiana. (Natchitoches is not to be confused with the old Spanish base at Nacogdoches. To help keep them apart, one can always remember that the *former* is pronounced "Nack-a-dush.")

Claims and Counterclaims

Mention of the French origin of the American claim to Natchitoches requires us to pause for a moment to touch upon the long history of such imperial contests for that region, and even more lightly (by necessity) upon its considerably longer mercantile history. The Spanish position was very ancient; in contesting it, the Americans were merely stepping into the almost equally ancient claims of the French.

There was considerable vagueness in the extent of those claims. At the farthest extent, the French and the Americans asserted a right to the Texas coast, resulting from the obscure explorations of René-Robert Cavelier, sieur de La Salle, more than a century earlier. La Salle himself is not obscure, of course; he even had an automobile named after him. But the exact locations of his brief

---

*In April 1804, in Madrid, the Council for the Fortification and Defense of the Indies, expressing stiffened Spanish resolve, had stipulated to its colonial governors the borders they were intended to defend. Mexico, said the council, began at the Missouri.

visits to Texas are still in dispute. It is probable that he stayed alive as long as he did only because the Spaniards knew no more about his whereabouts than do present-day scholars. Ultimately, in 1687, he was murdered by his own men, "by shooting him in the head with an arquebus." But the Spaniards had, all along, used about him the kind of language they later deployed upon his successor-in-interest Aaron Burr. La Salle's expedition was described to the viceroy as "these pirates . . . [who] would settle as far as New Mexico and make themselves Lords of many Kingdoms and Provinces."

By 1700, Spanish Franciscans, with escorts in armor and fully equipped for battle with more "pirates," had founded missions in the borderlands. They were met soon thereafter by the French, under Jean Baptiste Le Moyne, sieur de Bienville, who penetrated as far as modern Shreveport, Louisiana. The French attacked the Franciscans in the "Chicken War," but the Spaniards returned and built their capital of Tejas (Texas) at Los Adaes. The French under Benard de La Harpe ascended the Red River to the present site of Texarkana, Texas, and took their stand with a post there in 1719. They held it until about the time the Spanish moved their capital to San Antonio de Béxar in the 1770s.

The Native Americans were an important independent factor in these intra-invader contests. In the upper valley of the Red, the Taovaya-Wichitas and Comanches were greater powers than either the French or the Spanish. The former lived in large, settled villages of many hundreds of inhabitants, trading from the Mississippi to the Rockies. All the European contestants, Americans, French, and Spanish, went to great pains to woo them.

These two great groups of tribes were quite capable of defeating a large European army; they did so in 1758. Their loyalty to the French was an asset Jefferson tried very hard to inherit. Spain responded by offering appointments to former French officials, among them the great trader Pierre Vial, whose first assignment for Spain was shadowing the Lewis and Clark expedition and then arranging with the Pawnees to "dry gulch" it. Only an attack on Vial himself by another tribe saved those returning explorers. Otherwise, the southwest frontier would have seen a resumption, in a small compass, of the frontier battles of the middle of the eighteenth century we call the French and Indian War, and Andrew Jackson might have had the opportunity he desired to try to "conquer not only the Floridas, but all Spanish North America."

French traders and dispossessed frontier officials who had valuable Indian connections found employment with both sides in the quasi war with Spain. Some, like Vial, his partner Athanase de Mézières, and Bastrop, served the Spanish crown, while others led the Americans westward, like the Frenchmen who guided George Rogers Clark toward victory against the British in Indiana, during our revolution.

33

THE TURNING POINT

When Aaron Burr was an old man, he was asked if he had ever meant to divide the Union, and he replied: "No, I would as soon have thought of taking possession of the moon." What did he think he might achieve? "First, the Revolutionizing of Mexico, and Second, a settlement on what was known as the Bastrop lands."

Why did he believe, as he always insisted he did, that such a scheme might be agreeable to Thomas Jefferson, or if not agreeable, then at least achieved with Jefferson's forbearance? The President himself recalled later that he had once written Burr, "a little before my coming into office . . . a letter intimating that I had destined him for a high employ, had he not been placed by the people in a different one," the vice-presidency. In March 1806, Burr, in extremis and out of funds, reminded the President of that letter, saying that he needed employment, being "willing to engage in something . . . should [Jefferson] have anything to propose to him." Jefferson replied coldly that he had nothing to propose, adding the kind reminder that the public seemed to have lost confidence in Burr. According to Jefferson, whose account of the conversation is our only source, Burr blustered a little. Perhaps he said that he wasn't so weak as all that, and that he knew some things . . . about Jefferson's own plans? . . . about Gideon Granger's speculations in the western lands of the Yazoo claims?

Jefferson says he replied: "I feared no injury which any man could do me . . . I never had done a single act, nor been concerned in any transaction, which I feared to have fully laid open." Burr was on notice; all bets were off.

In those weeks, Jefferson was made aware that the Federalists of the West thought they too knew some things he would not wish to be "laid open." Joseph H. Daveiss, district attorney of Kentucky and brother-in-law of John Marshall, wrote the President a succession of letters about Burr's suspicious behavior. Daveiss became progressively angrier while he waited for a reply. Finally, he wrote James Madison, who counseled Jefferson to put nothing in writing, and to bury Daveiss's letters in his personal papers "to avoid the suspicions of which you seemed to be aware."

Those "suspicions" ultimately led Daveiss to write a pamphlet charging that there had been a secret understanding between Jefferson and Burr. If there was, it came to an end in that conference between the two in March. Thereafter, Burr set out, on his own, to find his way between the huge bulk of the United

States government on one side and the restive giant of Spain on the other. James Wilkinson beckoned him onward.

Jefferson vs. Burr

Not all Americans wished to go to war with Spain. Some, even in the South, were opposed to Jefferson's "secret expeditions, secret orders, and secret plans." Some, in fact, feared them more than the boisterous progress of Aaron Burr, for they were more comprehensive, more subtle, more Jeffersonian. The "philosophic mind" of the President found reasons for moral outrage, but he was not universally convincing. To many of his contemporaries and to some historians of our own day, he "sounded as though he had scotched Burr's plans for an invasion so that they would not interfere with his own."

And Jefferson's plans were bringing ever closer the prospect of war with Spain. His quasi war had already induced the prospect of hostilities between Pierre Vial and Lewis and Clark, and between the Spanish in the Red River Valley and Freeman and Custis. While Vial did not catch Lewis and Clark, in the last week in July 1806 the Spaniards on the Red found the second expedition and confronted it with a superior force. The Spanish commander told Freeman that "his orders were not to suffer any body of armed troops to march through the territory of the Spanish Government; to stop the exploring party by force." Mr. Jefferson's quasi war was at hand.

Freeman and Custis turned back. On learning the news, the American frontier flamed with indignation and humiliation. Then came the Spanish crossing of the Sabine in September. The leader of that little army explained to the commander of the American garrison at Natchitoches that he was responding to the provocation of Freeman, Custis, and their military escort.

Jefferson's messages to Congress about Spain were still so bellicose that Burr's expectations of a military opportunity for himself were hardly unreasonable. He was urged on by Wilkinson, still in command at New Orleans. Militia companies were mobilized, and the forts along the Mississippi were emptied of their regular soldiers, who were directed to assemble at Natchitoches. Burr wrote William Henry Harrison, a friend and appointee of Jefferson's: "All reflecting men consider a war with Spain to be inevitable."

Wilkinson told Secretary Dearborn that Pike's invasion, along the Arkansas, could "take possession of the Northern Provinces without opposition" at the very moment he was arranging for that opposition. The Spanish governor directed his forward commanders to treat "any expedition to the Colorado [Red] . . . [as] a hostile act." One of those commanders responded that, indeed, "irremediable damage . . . would result . . . if . . . the Expedition of the United States" were to unite with those Indians who had the habit of a French, not a Spanish, connection.

The actors were assembling for the final drama.

Wilkinson collected a large American force, ostensibly to contest the valley of the Sabine with the Spaniards but, he implied to Burr, also prepared to follow up victory there with a "March to the City of Mexico."* Burr was approaching, ready to lead such a march or, if it no longer seemed propitious, to set himself up, under Wilkinson's protection, in his four-hundred-thousand-acre bastion on the frontier. There he could await an equivalent opportunity, such as the arrival in New Orleans of a shipment of Mexican silver.

Suddenly, on September 27, 1806, the Spanish commander on the east bank of the Sabine turned around, recrossed the river, and left James Wilkinson and Aaron Burr without their incident. We know now, thanks to recent combing of Spanish government archives, that those Spanish troops were acting under orders from their superiors, who recognized how thinly spread were their defenses and did not actually desire a test of arms with the Americans.

Wilkinson next sought to pluck a rose from the thorns of disappointment—two roses, in fact, of different colors. First, on October 9, he began to "market" himself to Jefferson. His objectives were absolution and compensation. He asked protection against prosecution for his treasonous duplicities and eleven thousand dollars for his "expenses" in "crushing the conspiracy."

He recounted to his own deputy a self-serving version of Burr's "conspiracy." Then he set off to the Sabine, to make peace with the Spaniards, on whatever side of the river they might be. On the twentieth, he wrote his old correspondent Thomas Jefferson, painting a terrifying picture of the peril posed by Burr's handful of followers. He portrayed himself as capable of eliminating the Spanish threat and, that heroic action taken, as ready "to throw myself with my little Band into New Orleans, to be ready to defend that capital" from Burr. He actually commanded forces twenty times as great as Burr's.

Wilkinson may have known something about what was happening in Washington at the time. Between November 4 and 8, 1806, the Jefferson administration concluded an agreement with Spain and ordered Wilkinson to do what he had done already: arrange a truce with the Spanish forces on the Sabine.

Now for Wilkinson's other rose: While he was setting in motion his plan to collect on his old friendship with Jefferson, playing into the conditions leading the President to call a temporary halt to his predations of the Spanish frontier provinces, this commanding general and governor of lower Louisiana sent an aide, Walter Burling, to Mexico City, to try to reap from the Spanish a fat payment for the same actions.

Burling was to ask for $110,000 (roughly $2,100,000 in 1988 dollars) for "saving your country" by tranquilizing the Americans. Though the Spanish

---

*The phrase is not Wilkinson's but was employed by Wilkinson and Burr's agent in London, Charles Williamson, a British secret-service officer who met them while recruiting Americans for campaigns against the Spaniards in the Caribbean.

were not willing to go beyond the annual subsidies they had already sent Wilkinson and the "special" payment of $10,000 given him for a "special" report, he actually collected, later, $1,750 from the paymasters of the Jefferson administration for the costs of Burling's trip. He neglected to inform them, of course, of its purpose.

Silver, Napoleon, and Jefferson

What were the determinants of the outbreak of pacifism in Washington? What conditions in the larger world ordained respite from the imperial ambitions of the restive republic?

Thomas Jefferson, through his secretary of the treasury, Albert Gallatin, knew all he needed to know about the Great Silver Scheme. Gallatin must have discussed with him the exceptions that scheme required to the general inhibitions on trade with the European combatants, so that Mexican silver might help to eke out the Treasury's meager resources.

Jefferson also had the benefit of Wilkinson's regular dispatches about Burr.* His political intelligence system, organized among printers by Postmaster General Gideon Granger, served him well: a political ally in Philadelphia informed him that one of the principals in the Silver Scheme, John Craig of Philadelphia, had applied to some Philadelphia typesetters for pamphlet-printing equipment "destined for Mexico and calculated and cast for the Spanish language." The sellers "conclude that the types were intended for the conspirators." Jefferson, though probably not his Philadelphia correspondent, knew that there were two sets of conspirators, Parish's and Burr's, both doing business with Craig. The question was: What would happen if Burr's set entered into an accommodation with Parish's set and acquired more silver, in New Orleans or in Vera Cruz, than the national Treasury itself?

While this question was engaging some attention in Washington, another claimant to the hoard, in Paris, was preparing his own means to expedite its transfer away from any of the Americans. Napoleon was becoming impatient with the slow pace of the transmissions of Mexican silver by Parish, Craig, et al. To accelerate matters, and to "pacify" the Spanish people, he was plotting an invasion of Spain.

In 1806 Napoleon was at the peak of his pride. In December 1805 he had defeated the Austrian and Russian armies at Austerlitz and forced upon Austria a humiliating peace. He had abolished the Holy Roman Empire, after a

---

*So did the Spanish governor of Mexico, who, as noted earlier, prudently shifted the silver accumulating at Vera Cruz to an inland depository.

thousand years, and set up his brother Joseph as king of Naples, preparing him for the crown of Spain. In October, at Jena, he obliterated a Prussian army.

In Berlin, kings and grand dukes thronged to do him honor. At the cusp of his fortunes, pride overcame him, and he betrayed for the first time that failure to understand the power of commerce that led him, soon thereafter, to cashier Ouvrard, who would have been worth an army to a wiser monarch. "The sea will be conquered by the land," he intoned, perhaps the first ruler since Canute to believe such foolishness. And he issued his Berlin Decree, not only against British commerce but also, to his ultimate ruin, against all those who might trade with Britain. He alienated thereby the mercantile powers who might otherwise have rallied to support him against the predatory British.

"The British Isles are declared in a state of blockade. All trade and all dealings with them are hereby forbidden." Perhaps it might have made sense if he had had the power to enforce it. The British, with an immensely more powerful fleet, had been unable to close the ports of Europe against French commerce. Now one blockade was set against another.

Napoleon persisted. While his superb strategic sense drew him toward Russia, his faulty economic sense distracted him toward Portugal and toward that ultimate division of his forces which was his downfall. The interminable, deadly drain of French energies, men, and money in the Peninsular War was presaged by his warning to the Portuguese ambassador that if the king of Portugal did not close his ports to the British, "the House of Braganza will be off that throne within two months."

These signs of madness on the part of his great adversary would have gladdened the heart of William Pitt. No English statesman ever understood so well that trade is amphibious and capable, in Napoleon's terms, of conquering both land and sea. But Pitt had died in January, and the new foreign minister of Great Britain was Charles James Fox.

Perhaps that news had emboldened Napoleon. Now he had someone with whom he might strike a deal (to use a locution that would never have crossed his lips). The Americans also had reason to rejoice in the ascendancy of Fox. Spain might be detached from France; France and Britain might themselves arrange a truce in 1806, like that of 1802, a truce in the West to send Napoleon in the other direction, against Russia. (Does this evoke the ghost of Neville Chamberlain?)

On the other hand, of course, any British government, even one led by Fox, might fear a newly invigorated Franco-Spanish alliance. Burr's friends in London played upon this fear as well as upon the hope of turning the French toward Russia. Charles Williamson, in London, wrote Lord Granton that His Majesty's government might have to choose between "50,000 North Americans, with Col. Burr at their head, far on their March to the City of Mexico," and "a French force" getting "a footing in that Country."

34

THE "WALL OF BRASS" AGAIN

On both sides of the Atlantic, a British-American alliance was once again becoming a serious possibility. Again there was talk of Anglo-Saxons against Latins. An American alliance with the deceased Pitt would have been one thing, acceptable only to Federalists. But Fox was a hero to the Jeffersonians; his name was toasted, with Jefferson's, at their rallies. In the spring of 1806, Fox put James Monroe "more at ease" than he had "ever felt with any other person in office . . . in England." Fox was wont to say that he had been "accused of being too friendly to America."

Though Jefferson's emotional compass was usually steady in hostility to the British and in amity to the French, it wobbled when he faced southwestward. The ascension of Fox to power renewed a thought he had entertained, despite his Francophilia, when Napoleon took Louisiana from the Spaniards. Jefferson expressed the view that it was possible that "we must marry ourselves to the British fleet and nation" to prevent a French threat in the Gulf of Mexico. Under such circumstances, it might be a justifiable risk to mobilize all the forces available, including even Burr and Williamson, against the Spanish borderlands. They could travel the routes reconnoitered by Dunbar and Hunter, Lewis and Clark, Freeman, Custis, and Pike. Jefferson caused to be drawn a draft treaty to bring the United States into alliance with the British against Napoleon, in return for British support against Spain.

But as the year dragged along, Fox demonstrated to Monroe that though he was amiable, he was also weak. He could not carry his cabinet colleagues into an agreement to cease the impressment of American seamen, even though that impressment was going on at the mouth of New York Harbor, to the intense chagrin of all the maritime interests of the United States. Fox could have long, earnest conversations with Monroe, giving that rapt attention to American grievances which he had once given Latrobe's opinions about bricks. But he could not "deliver." Monroe reported him "sincere" but "checked in Cabinet."

Fox's weakness was worse than political. He was a very sick man. He died on September 13, 1806, and control of British policy swung firmly toward forces hostile to the American interest.

The Moment Passes

At this moment, Napoleon, with Talleyrand at his side, announced that he would not acquiesce in an Anglo-American filibuster. An assault upon Mexico would be taken as an assault upon France. The specter of a new "wall of brass" appeared along the Sabine. The American aggression would go no further without a fight, and this time might face a French expeditionary force.

Jefferson could not afford to make war upon France without British support. War against Britain, to end impressment, simultaneously with war against both France and Spain was unthinkable. He obtained a $2 million commitment from Congress to buy a peaceful settlement.* John Armstrong, one of the Livingston clan, whose French connections we observed in Part Two, was sent to Paris to ask the author of the concept of the "wall of brass" to melt it down: Talleyrand was to be bribed to arrange a truce with the Spanish government.

Isolated by these new arrangements, Aaron Burr was now an embarrassment. Once, perhaps, a useful instrument, he had always been an annoyance.† At the end of 1806, Jefferson's antipathy to him was being fed for their own reasons by Gideon Granger, Wilkinson, and the western Federalists. The time had come to stamp him out.

These were ugly days. Napoleon's backing of Spain deprived Jefferson's western policy of the fulfillment of the possibilities of extending the Louisiana Purchase by military force. Though Congress had been willing to appropriate the $2 million as an installment on another transaction (like the purchase) to buy Spanish territory from a French dictator (another "retrocession" might be arranged), it was becoming restive. The British were "policing the port of New York, firing shots across the bows of American vessels, and lining them up like suspects at a police station," to be searched for "deserters" from the British fleet.

Napoleon, recently so convenient to Jeffersonian policy as purveyor of Louisiana and extinguisher of the embarrassment of Toussaint, was now making threatening gestures. Under his yoke, France, beloved but formidable France, might actually replace feeble Spain in the Gulf and along the vague western frontiers of the United States.

Jefferson's sudden interest in a navy showed his desperation. His previous economies had so reduced the armed forces that there was no navy fit to respond

---

*It is only fair to report that Jefferson abandoned another set of principles at the same juncture: he recommended to Congress a large increase in expenditure for the navy. Millions for defense were to be spent along with millions for tribute.

†In 1804, Jefferson had written that Burr's "conduct . . . inspired me with distrust. I habitually cautioned Mr. Madison against trusting him too much. I saw afterwards . . . whenever a great military appointment or a diplomatic one was to be made . . . he was always at market." (Lomask, p. 107.)

to the British, no army fit to fight the Spaniards, much less the French.

The British stepped up their provocations, and so did the Spaniards. Jefferson grew impatient with Monroe, testing further a friendship already stretched by Jefferson's earlier effort to pack off to the western frontier this rival to his friend Madison. In the spring of 1807, Jefferson heard that Monroe had negotiated a treaty full of concessions to the British. A congressional delegation called upon him to find out when he would send to them Monroe's handiwork. His answer was: "Certainly not! Certainly not!" He would not transmit it, he cried, in a voice "ringing with an anger seldom heard from him."

A Western Policy

Policy for the western frontier grew erratic during the fall of 1806. On one October day, the cabinet was urged to mobilize all the scattered forces of the republic to pursue the miscreant Burr. On the next, Jefferson concluded that "the total silence of the officers of the government, of the members of the Congress, of the newspapers, proves [!!] he is committing no overt act against the law," and most of those orders were rescinded.

It was not until November 27, 1806, that Jefferson issued his famous proclamation charging "sundry persons" with "confederating together to . . . set on foot . . . a military . . . enterprise against the dominions of Spain . . . arming vessels . . . seducing honest . . . citizens . . . to engage in their criminal enterprises." To prevent further seductions, the President required "all officers, civil and military . . . to be vigilant in searching out, and bringing to condign punishment, all persons . . . engaged . . . in such enterprise." No mention was made of Burr, for none was needed.

"An enterprise against the dominions of Spain"—yet another. It was Gideon Granger who precipitated that presidential proclamation.

Granger did his best to divert attention from his own Yazoo speculations to those of Burr—that can be said without scrutiny of his character. Thomas Perkins Abernethy, one of the best historians of the Burr conspiracy, tells us that the "complacency of the Administration ended . . . when Jefferson received Postmaster General Gideon Granger's letter of 16 October." The postmaster general reported two things: first, that it was becoming widely believed that Burr was planning to invade Mexico and to separate the West from the Union; and second, that Wilkinson was a part of that plot.

Many people had reason to believe Granger to be no more savory a character than Wilkinson. Indeed, there were public charges that the postmaster general was another double agent, working for Burr as well as for Jefferson. But his letter did the trick. Jefferson knew his man, very, very well. And Granger knew his. Wilkinson played upon Jefferson's fear of Black insurrection, a fear made even more intense by the events on Saint-Domingue. So, it seems likely, did Granger, who was responsible for eliminating Black mail carriers from the postal service on the ground that they might form a network of conspirators, spreading sedition at government expense. Burr, it happens, had proposed abolition of slavery, at a fixed date, as far back as 1784, and had broken a tie in the Senate a decade later, voting against the Jefferson administration's embargo on trade with Toussaint. He could not be trusted.

Trials and Tribulations

In October 1806, Aaron Burr was in Kentucky, poised at the brink of his final western adventure. As he stood poised, Thomas Jefferson pounced.

Wilkinson, now an agent of Jefferson, had Aaron Burr, with fewer than a hundred motley followers, in his power. Though he proclaimed that Burr had seven thousand hardened desperadoes in his train, he knew that the full might of the United States—including the fleet under Captain Edward Preble and Commander Stephen Decatur, which was now mobilized—was no longer needed to deter any force Burr might assemble. John Graham, a Virginia gentleman often used by Jefferson on secret missions related to Spain,* was pursuing Burr downriver, having mobilized the militias of Ohio and Kentucky.

Jefferson wrote Wilkinson to assemble all the incriminating documents he could find, including coded exchanges with Burr, and ship them by trusted messengers to Washington "in order that the guilty may be convicted and the innocent [was Wilkinson paying close attention?] left untroubled." (The President sent a letter offering some of the same subtle reassurance to the equally equivocal Granger, who may have made his choice at the same time as Wilkinson.)

Burr was warned of Wilkinson's duplicity by reading the text of one of his coded communications in a newspaper. As we have seen, Burr's popularity in the western country was so great that, though he gave himself up to the civil authorities of Mississippi, they could not get a grand jury to indict him. But Wilkinson, encouraged by a suspension of habeas corpus voted by the Jeffersonian Senate,† was acting without constitutional constraints in New Orleans. Burr's friends were being arrested and imprisoned without trial and shipped off to Washington or Richmond under guard, at Jefferson's insistence. Burr did not dare to entrust himself to Wilkinson, whose character, and presidential backing, were now fully revealed.

---

*His brother, George Graham, served in similar ways. We will become more thoroughly acquainted with him in Part Eight.

†The Senate acted to authorize such action: habeas corpus was never actually suspended.

In disguise, Burr set out through the Mississippi wilderness for the unpatrolled border with Florida. He almost made it. But at the end of January 1807, he was caught by a little cavalry detachment. They too probably wanted to let him go; but, even on the frontier, discipline held. Burr was rushed by back roads, under armed guard, to Richmond, to stand trial for treason.

Though that trial resulted in no conviction, his political career was at an end. He went off to Europe, after a sojourn for recuperation with the hospitable and loyal Biddles of Philadelphia.

Burr in France

He arrived in Paris in February 1810, after wandering through Scandinavia. Talleyrand refused to receive him, either because he was powerless and unlikely to repeat, in reverse, the bishop's own transatlantic recovery or because Burr was the "murderer" of Hamilton. Undeterred, Burr made a characteristic mistake. He found common purpose with a scoundrel, Joseph Fouché, duke of Otranto and chief of Napoleon's secret police, who was guilty of treason one time too many just as Burr became his colleague. Fouché went into exile. There was no longer even a remote chance that Napoleon would distract himself with the scheme Fouché and Burr had been hatching for an alliance against the British and the Hispanic empire. The only outcome of this peculiar interlude was the filing in the Bonapartist archives of a mass of materials about Texas and Mexico that became useful later (see p. 344).

The long late career of Aaron Burr does not concern us; it was not so interesting as those of two others implicated in the "conspiracy" of 1805, Andrew Jackson and Henry Clay. Both cleaned their linen and went on to higher things. Wilkinson, perjuring himself at every turn but protected by the Jeffersonians, found his own appropriate glory in a ludicrous offer to duel with John Randolph of Roanoke. Thereafter, he faded out of the glare of history. After participating in two more filibustering expeditions against Mexico (the Magee-Gutiérrez campaign of 1813 and that of Dr. James Long in 1819), he died in a comfortable bed in Mexico City.

Assessing the character of Aaron Burr, John Quincy Adams described him as "brave, generous, hospitable and courteous" but "ambitious, rapacious, faithless and intriguing." When the danger was over, Jefferson, somewhat patronizingly, called Burr "a crooked gun . . . whose aim or shot you could never be sure of." He wrote Du Pont de Nemours that there never was much danger that "Burr's conspiracy" would "effect such objects by the aid of American citizens." Anyone who would think so "must be perfectly ripe for bedlam."

The danger passed in Washington, but it brought no respite from American threats against the Spanish possessions. One filibuster was removed from the scene, but many others rushed to take his place. In the midst of the Texas agitation of the 1830s, the elderly Burr remarked, perhaps recalling Talleyrand's comment about treason and timing: "You see? I was right! I was only thirty years too soon. What was treason in me thirty years ago is patriotism now!"

The Campaign Resumes

After Burr was in effect ostracized (like Alcibiades, but with more comfortable consequences), Jefferson turned directly southward, resuming his assault against the Spanish empire. He began what a recent historian has called a campaign of "persuasion, bribery and threat to seize Florida." He told Du Pont de Nemours in 1806 that, out of deference to France, he had withheld his presidential hand to "take or obtain our just limits." He was speaking of the shores of the Gulf of Mexico. But in 1807 he argued for a renewal of his quasi war with Spain. It would be easier now: "Our southern defensive force can take the Floridas, volunteers for a Mexican army will flock to our standard . . . our privateers [can] plunder their . . . commerce and coasts. Probably Cuba would add itself to our confederation."

Cooler temperaments prevailed, but Jefferson was unrelenting. In 1809, he tried to push the newly inaugurated Madison into attacks against the Spanish in Florida, and in 1811, he was back at it. Jefferson was not quite so bellicose as Theodore Roosevelt in his postpresidential furies, but the analogy is not as absurd as it may seem at first. Though war with Britain was imminent, and the country by no means united in the support of that contest, he urged Madison to take on Spain as well, arguing that the Georgia militia could capture Florida in a few weeks' time.

In this enthusiastic assessment he had an ally, who, for a century, has been united with him at annual fund-raising dinners of the Democratic party. What dinner partners: Thomas Jefferson and Andrew Jackson—the fastidious Virginian and the brawling Tennessean; the urbane plantation owner, with elegant French tastes, and the dueling, slave-dealing, bowie-knife-wielding frontier storekeeper-lawyer; the deist and the Old Testament prophet. But they did "dine together" in one respect: they had a common, and insatiable, appetite for the "derelict provinces" of Spain.

The Creoles Revolt

As we have twice before had occasion to observe, those provinces were not without energies of their own. In fact, it was because those energies were so strong that the expansion of the United States ultimately came to a halt at the

Rio Grande. It was not only the citizens of Buenos Aires or of Venezuela who became restive in the face of the weakening of Spanish imperium, nor did it open prospects only to idealists like Miranda.

The successful revolt of their neighbors in British North America offered lessons to the great plantation owners and merchants of the Spanish and Portuguese colonies. The *senhores de engenhos* (lords of the sugar mills), cotton growers and ranchers, were growing rich, restive, and independent. Like the serf-driving latifundiasts of Poland and Hungary, the slave owners of Latin America saw less and less reason to make remittances to an imperial system— Bourbon or Hapsburg—costing them much and defending them little.

In the Spanish as well as in the British colonies an intellectual class emerged at an immense remove from the home country, in part because the persecution of the Jesuits by the Spanish government in the 1760s deprived the colonials of a class of teachers who justified some deference to Europe. They had yet another reason to go it alone. A generation later, the traveling scientist Humboldt observed that Mexico City was the intellectual center of the New World. Not even the Philadelphia of Franklin, Rittenhouse, and Rush could compete: "No city of the new continent, without excepting those of the United States, can show scientific establishments as fine . . . as [those of] the capital of Mexico." And Vera Cruz was nearly one and a half times larger than New Orleans, and far more prosperous.

A proud, vigorous mercantile and mining oligarchy grown independent economically and intellectually will not long remain dependent politically. Local oligarchs were quite capable of setting themselves up as sovereigns of portions of ancient viceroyalties: Venezuela declared its independence in 1811; Brazil followed in 1815, Chile in 1816. Simón Bolívar became president of Colombia in 1821 and in the same year, Peru and Guatemala asserted their independence. Mexico became a republic in 1823.

35

ARCHITECTURAL ACCESSORIES

"One evening in June" of 1806, Benjamin Henry Latrobe later recalled, Aaron Burr visited his house in Washington. They conferred for hours. The architect later told Albert Gallatin, who had been sent to him to seek evidence against Burr, that their business was to discuss a canal around the falls of the Ohio.

Gallatin may already have had reason to doubt that this was the full story. James Wilkinson was busy spreading blame; he told officials of the administration that Latrobe was "zealously engaged" in Burr's "conspiracy."

When Gallatin pressed him, Latrobe admitted that he and Burr did not limit their discussions to the engineering of canals. They talked of

Miranda's expedition [against Venezuela in 1805], for instance, the rise & origin of which he was well acquainted with, & which he said he had from the beginning considered a most precipitate & ill considered scheme. And on this subject he told me many things which astonished me, both as to the names he introduced, and as to the light thrown upon many characters & much conduct, which the public appear to have viewed "through a glass darkly."

Latrobe himself had good reason, after the failure of Burr's scheme, to leave "the public" in some doubt about such "conduct" as ensued from their meeting that June evening. He was a family man, in precarious financial condition. Though he took on one job or another to eke out his salary, he was dependent for steady employment upon the surveyorship of the public buildings, a post that could be quickly withdrawn were he to fall out with Gallatin or Gallatin's superior, Thomas Jefferson.

Jefferson's feelings about Burr were already clear enough; he had forced him out of the vice-presidency and replaced him with another New Yorker, George Clinton. The President may have known that Latrobe had been Burr's candidate for the City Hall commission in 1802. He may have known as well that Latrobe had been sponsored by Burr to draw up a drainage plan for lower Manhattan in 1804. So when Burr approached the architect again in the spring of 1805, a month after he left the vice-presidency, Latrobe may have been apprehensive of further entanglements. But Burr seemed to be suggesting nothing that would be objectionable to Jefferson: would Latrobe journey to Louisville to survey the path of a canal around the falls? Warily, Latrobe put him off, though "nothing would be so agreeable . . . to my personal as well as my professional feelings."

Latrobe's excuse was that he was occupied in work upon the Chesapeake and Delaware Canal, but both men may have known that that venture was in financial trouble, heading for the suspension of its work that occurred within the year. In June 1806, Burr returned with an even better idea: would Latrobe sound out for a vaguely defined western venture the Irish canal workers who had become unemployed—hearty men all, and fit for many kinds of services? Might they not be willing to come to the West, perhaps to dig a canal, perhaps, as John Van Horne suggests in his notes to the *Latrobe Papers,* as a "substantial contingent of potential soldiers"?

Burr then requested advice from Latrobe on the proper craft (might one say troopship?) to navigate shallow western rivers, and received from Latrobe's office a set of careful designs. There is much controversy as to whether or not Burr's canal project was merely a "front" for his other western intentions in

1805; but he had dropped the plan by October 1806, when he wrote Latrobe again, with a clearer proposition.

This letter apparently was not available to Talbot Hamlin when he wrote his biography of Latrobe, and a strain of bafflement runs through that work as a consequence. Why was Latrobe subpoenaed as a government witness at Burr's trial, interrogated before the grand jury, held under bond, though never called to testify in court? Why was he subpoenaed again for the trial of Wilkinson but never called? Did Latrobe report to Gallatin his full relationship to the "conspiracy"?

Not quite, I think. Burr wrote that he had purchased four hundred thousand acres "of the tract called Bastrop's," and went on to say that it was his "intention to go there with several of my friends next winter. If you should incline to partake, and join us, I will give you 10,000 acres. I want your society; I want your advice in the establishment about to be made. In short, you have become necessary to my settlement."

What was the relationship of the "settlement" to the invasion of Mexico? Evidently, Burr meant to use it as his base. One can imagine it as a neoclassical base, a Latrobian capital-in-exile. That would have qualified Burr, unequivocally, for our list of politician-clients. It is pleasant to think of him playing viceroy to Latrobe's Lutyens or Nehru to Latrobe's Le Corbusier.*

Burr did inhabit, for a time, a huge public building designed by Latrobe, but it was not one designed to his specifications. During his trial in Richmond, he occupied a suite in the Virginia Penitentiary, one of the first of Latrobe's American commissions. It was seen by some observers as a castle, where Burr reigned with imperial confidence. His historical imagination and his sense of heroic irony were large enough to convert even incarceration into triumph.

Knowing Complicity?

How much of Burr's intentions were disclosed to Latrobe in 1806? A conspiratorial delight broke through discretion in some of Latrobe's correspondence in November 1806, a month after he received Burr's proposal. Even when he wrote about portrait painting, of all things, to a French military engineer, he could not resist adding:

> My Dear Sir, let's change the subject, and let me forget the drudgery of my trade. Can you tell me whether the Spaniards have retired across the Sabine, and whether Col. B still keeps his army and Gunboats in his pocket, or has begun to pull them out, and proceed toward Mexico.

*What wonders might have ensued if Burr had had both Marc Brunel and Latrobe at his disposal.

Six months later, he wrote again, this time to say, anxiously, that the earlier addition was intended merely to "ridicule . . . the expedition." But why did he feel a need to say such a thing in the first place? There is something more here than he cared to admit.

Latrobe was under intense pressure. He was still the architect of the Capitol. The President's friends were sorting each other out. On the night of November 14, 1806, Albert Gallatin demanded the explanation of Latrobe's relationship to Burr. On the following morning, Latrobe wrote to Gallatin the memorandum quoted earlier; of course, said Latrobe, he and the "conspirator" had other talks, for "I saw him nearly every day as he lodged near me." Latrobe showed Burr articles in the press trumpeting the charges of conspiracy. Burr, said Latrobe (perhaps intending the irony), attributed those charges not to Jefferson but to John Marshall, whose instructions to the jury would, in Burr's trial, assure Burr's acquittal of treason.

Latrobe told Gallatin that he had asked Burr about rumors that he intended to separate the western and eastern states, to which Burr responded that such a step would be imprudent. This was not what Gallatin wanted to hear—it would not help convince the court of Burr's treasonous intent.

Latrobe was not called as a witness in the Burr trial. Aside from the equivocal nature of his testimony, there may have been another reason for his escaping further interrogation. He made it clear to Gallatin that he was not without his own ties to Jefferson. His memorandum dropped the resonant fact that he had had dinner with the President on the night that Burr's chief of staff, Colonel Julien de Pestre, appeared on his doorstep.

Latrobe had just returned from the White House; de Pestre, now dispirited, was readying himself to abandon Burr in order to protect his brother-in-law, Louis de Mun, who was also one of Latrobe's favorite draftsmen. (It so happened that one of his assignments had been work to provide Burr with designs for his shallow-draft river boats.)

Though it was not used at the trial, Latrobe's affidavit to Gallatin is a document of considerable interest in tracing out the relationship of Burr to the French military émigrés to whom he was consistently drawn. De Pestre, according to Latrobe, had served "with first rate military talents" on Saint-Domingue; after "the wreck of an immense fortune" on the island, presumably after the ascension of Dessalines, he took refuge in New Jersey among the the relatives of Pierre Bauduy.

De Pestre's connection to Latrobe was through de Mun, who was born on Saint-Domingue, educated in France, served with de Pestre in the royalist army, and became his brother-in-law after they both took refuge in the United States. De Mun entered Latrobe's office as draftsman in 1802, served in various capacities until becoming embroiled in the Burr "conspiracy," and ultimately found himself engaged in land speculation west of the Mississippi.

It may be that Burr hoped that the presence in his entourage of distinguished men like these would be attracted to the French-speaking people of the Mississippi Valley, together with other refugees from France and Saint-Domingue. Among the relevant skills they might bring would be military engineering. Already, in New Orleans, Wilkinson had made good use of Bartholomy Lafon (see p. 399ff.), and there are shreds of evidence that Burr intended an alliance with the pirates of Barataria, the coastal region lying west of the Mississippi delta. Their leaders were the brothers Jean and Louis Lafitte, trained in the use of artillery in Saint-Dominguan waters. (One piece of such evidence is that Latrobe liked to refer to Burr's western colony as "Barataria.")

In the end, the French in the Mississippi Valley wanted little to do with more conspiracies and upheavals. Pirates among them were few; most were fur traders and small farmers and fishermen. They did not defer to officers and, like frontiersmen everywhere, were dubious about noblemen. De Pestre concluded that as "a frenchman he found himself looked upon with jealousy, even by those to whom Col. Burr most particularly had introduced him." Though the inhabitants of the French settlements "detested the american government," they had no appetite for insurrection; "tho' french they were ignorant, and he could never think of living among them."

So there was no French insurrection in the West. Aaron Burr went forward, with de Pestre by his side, and de Mun, wonderingly, following after. The Lafittes lay ahead, waiting.

Latrobe admitted to having "much conversation" as to Burr's affairs with de Pestre, but he did not press the point that de Pestre was chief of staff to Burr. Latrobe said only that de Pestre told him he had sold "part of his Jersey farm & intended to part with the remainder provided he could get more land of good quality for his money, even if it lay further back"—as far back as Arkansas?

Busily providing an alibi for de Pestre, Latrobe neglected to report to Gallatin that he himself, like de Pestre, had considered going to live on the Bastrop claim. Instead, he said he "advised" de Pestre to go to the "good land in Ohio," owned by his client Colonel Thomas Worthington of Adena (one of the few Latrobe houses remaining intact to this day, though mutilated in execution). Perhaps he did, but the key question is: at what stage of their discussions?

Burr had become a dangerous sort of friend; and his well-known affinity for French military engineers put several of them at great risk, including both de Pestre and de Mun. They were vulnerable, and even more sensitive than Latrobe to political pressure. De Pestre warned Latrobe of the powers being concerted against "B"* and urged him "not to accept . . . Col. B's offer." Latrobe thought

---

*"Bs" could be confusing, and thereby offered opportunities. After Burr was betrayed and was fleeing Jefferson's wrath, Wilkinson fiercely demanded that Vincent Nolte explain an anonymous note

it over and glumly reported to Gallatin: "I think that my presence is the only thing desired. The rest is sham."

Cleaning out his files, Latrobe then sent the designs of Burr's boats to the secretary of the navy. But he was not free of Burr's charm; he wrote a partner in New Orleans, in January 1807, after Wilkinson commenced his dragnet, that "Burr is not taken." (The tone is one of pleasure!) Perhaps he might yet find refuge in what Jefferson had told Latrobe was Burr's "impregnable Basin surrounded with mountains" (not a good description of the Bastrop claim, but a clear sample of Jefferson's fears).

Five years later, Latrobe insisted to his friend Erich Bollmann that "whatever Burr's plans were, God knows neither side have ever explained them to me." He also offered a shrewd appraisal of the "two most opposite characters" inhabiting the soul of Aaron Burr: "the most sanguine and the most suspicious; while he is careless of his interest, and even of public opinion, he is cautious to a degree of folly."*

Latrobe himself remained of two minds about Burr. He wrote Bollmann: "I love him still, tho' I would not trust him with the conduct of an intrigue to elect a common councilman." Still, in 1815, when Latrobe required a good lawyer to argue his lawsuit against Robert Fulton, he chose Aaron Burr.

---

he brandished that said that "B." had agreed to supply all the funds needed to finance Burr's attack on Mexico, pretending that he took "B" to mean Baring, Nolte's sponsor.

With quite uncharacteristic naiveté, Nolte took the ostensible cause of Wilkinson's bullying to be in earnest, though by that time Wilkinson had ample occasion to learn that there were deposits of silver in Nolte's custody in New Orleans and to carpenter together one of his extortion schemes. His inquiry actually implied to Nolte that he should make a little "advance" in return for the general's protection. But when Nolte did not seem to catch his meaning, and, a few weeks later, the final sparks of the Burr "conspiracy" flickered out, Wilkinson, with his usual niceness of calculation, assessed the costs and benefits of assaulting a friend of the Barings and dropped the case. Nolte was left to go after the silver remaining in Vera Cruz that Wilkinson and Burr might have used to finance their own plans.

*In the scatological style of the eighteenth century, Latrobe had other observations to make. Alexander Hamilton and Aaron Burr were both small in stature, but Hamilton was proud of his anatomical disparities, and Latrobe knew that both men were addicted to venery. He wrote a friend, John Lenthall, that he could imagine "Little Hamilton and Little Burr standing in the temple of Lingam (the Hindu Priapus) like the columns of Jakin and Boas in the temple of Solomon" (Hamlin, *Latrobe,* p. 275 n.; see also Burr to Mazzei on a comparison between the two, p. 591). Joshing about anatomical matters was not uncommon. The same attention to Hamiltonian detail appears in a letter, in French, written by Edward Stevens to Hamilton himself. It must have caused considerable bewilderment to Sir Henry Clinton, whose agents intercepted it during the Revolutionary War. It can be found in the Sir Henry Clinton Papers in the Walter L. Clements Library at the University of Michigan. (For Hamilton on the length of noses, etc., see Flexner, *Hamilton,* p. 260.)

VIII

THE
NEW THÉBAÏDE

While there were some gifted French officers available to design and command the coastal defenses of the United States after 1789 (men like Pierre Bauduy's friend Colonel Toussard, and those on the long list offered by Aaron Burr in defending them against Federalist attack during Jefferson's quasi-war; see p. 321), and while others (such as Pierre Pharoux, Charles Mangin, de Pestre, and de Mun) were on hand to provide engineering skills to speculators, architects, and filibusters, most Frenchmen with a talent for military activity were fully occupied in Europe.

In 1815, Napoleonic opportunities came to an end, and many more arrived in America—so many, in fact, that they could not be ignored as they gathered in Philadelphia, jostling peaceful merchants in the streets. There was General Jean-Joseph-Amable Humbert, who was famous for his brief successes, against great odds, as leader of the expedition to Ireland in 1798. There too was his second-in-command, who had risen, later, to become prince and marshal, Emmanuel de Grouchy. Beside them were the principal officers of the most fearsome corps of hardened soldiers in Europe, Napoleon's personal guard.

The term "old guard" has since been debased by application to tired politicians and refractory members of men's clubs. It was then terrible to those who hoped to preserve civility in Europe or America.

In the Quaker City, restless and fierce of mien, was Charles-François-Antoine Lallemand, veteran of campaigns from Egypt to Saint-Domingue. He had attempted a coup d'état against the Bourbons even before the emperor's return from Elba, seizing the arsenal of La Fère. His colleague in that rash venture, Charles Lefebvre-Desnouettes, general and count, was now also prowling Philadelphia. Charles Lallemand had commanded the *chasseurs* of the guard at Waterloo. His brother, Henri Dominique, had commanded the artillery of the guard; he too came to Pennsylvania, after seeking mercenary service in Russia, Turkey, and Egypt.

It was said that Lefebvre-Desnouettes had commanded the lancers at Waterloo "with a rage of desperation." Desperate still in America, these heroes rejoiced when, one day, they were joined by the irreconcilable General Antoine Rigaud, commander of a division at Waterloo that refused to accept defeat and had to be pursued by the allied armies all the way to Chalons.

These desperadoes were among the few Napoleonic officers who were actually condemned to death by the Bourbons. Others in Philadelphia were a little, only a little, milder. There was General Bertrand Clausel, count of the empire; General Dominique René Vandamme, commander of the Third Corps; and Count Pierre-François Réal, chief of Napoleon's police during the Hundred Days: seven generals in all, and, to support them, there appeared a veritable staff-college of thirteen colonels of the empire.

What did they have in mind? Not all of them agreed, but the ancient attraction of the silver mines of Mexico once again drew freebooters toward the southwest. Aaron Burr had failed, but he had left a set of plans in Paris with which others might prevail. Ouvrard, the Barings, the Hopes, and David Parish had been content with mere commissions; but there was no doubt at the court of Napoleon where lay the source of their wealth.

All that might be needed to rescue the emperor from Saint Helena was a fleet. And all that was needed to equip a fleet were silver pesos.

36

JOSEPH LAKANAL

Between the dusk of January 16 and the dawn of January 17, 1793, the National Convention of France debated the fate of the kindly, obese, vacillating, dull-witted man who had been King Louis XVI.

One by one, the delegates were polled; a majority spoke for the death penalty. Among those who did so eloquently was Jacques Garnier, a lawyer from Saintes.* When his time came, Garnier cast his vote "without appeal and without reprieve!" His reasoning? "The people, when betrayed, do not judge their kings; they hurl a bolt of lightning and exterminate them!" Garnier seemed always to declaim; he declaimed even when selling rum, whiskey, and cigars some years later in Indiana.

Joseph Lakanal, a professor of philosophy and rhetoric, having heard as much of this sort of thing as his professional standards could tolerate, cast his vote quietly. "A true republican," he said, "speaks little. The motives for my decision are there," as he placed his palm on his heart. "I vote for death."

Despite shows of heartfelt candor, Lakanal's motives were never fully disclosed. This was true even when the time came for him to find his own place of refuge in America, a little upstream from Garnier's grog shop. From there, in 1816, he wrote Thomas Jefferson, signing himself "Lakanal, of the Institute of France and of the Legion of Honor." "Here I am," he reported, "upon the banks of Ohio, upon an estate which I have just purchased: Gallatin County [Kentucky], in the vicinity of the French colony of Vevay. In this pleasant retreat I shall propose to divide my time between the cultivation of my lands and that of letters."

He did very little of either, preferring military adventure. As an intellectual, he had already done more than enough for any man; he was known for many achievements, including "Lakanal's Law," which laid the cornerstone of the modern French educational system centered upon the Ecole Polytechnique. In America, Lakanal became a link between two failed efforts to restore fallen leaders to power by the use of Mexican silver, conquered at its source. His strategy was that communicated to Napoleon six years earlier by the exiled Aaron Burr: the use of French officers experienced in European warfare to lead a volunteer corps of American frontiersmen to invade Mexico and seize its silver mines. They could then make their will known on the international stage, since they would have an asset under control as potent geopolitically as the oil of the Persian Gulf would be one hundred and seventy years later.

Though that concept had not commended itself to Napoleon in 1810, when he had no need for Burr or Mexico, in 1816, with some adjustments, it might bring Napoleon back from his own exile on Saint Helena. Even if the liberation of Napoleon was too much to achieve, Lakanal had the prospect of restoring Napoleon's brother Joseph Bonaparte to the throne of "the Indies," the Spanish possessions in Latin America.

Lakanal added an important new component to Burr's plan. This was an age of commercial as well as military adventurers, whose combined talents might redeem the failures of Napoleonic accounting and renew the glories of Napoleonic arms. Furthermore, a transition was apparent, even so early as 1816, from

*A town just a few miles north of the château of the Marquis de La Tour Du Pin.

Joseph Lakanal (artist unknown)

the age of the independent merchant-traders—men like William Constable, Robert Morris, and James Leray de Chaumont—to the reign of the manipulators of financial instruments, of whom the Hopes and the Barings were prototypes. (Stephen Girard and David Parish made this transition in their own careers, the former with greater success than the latter.)

Lakanal proposed to make use of the consummate practitioners of the old multinational—or nonnational—mercantile entrepreneurship, the pirates of Barataria, led by Jean Lafitte, in combination with the subtle master of abstractions, Stephen Girard, in what he called "the Napoleonic Confederation." For the "hands-on" military part of the operation he would rely upon a group of officers who had demonstrated their prowess at Waterloo; and for strategy, there was Lakanal and his old associates among the regicide intellectuals of 1789.

It was a grand proposition. Its difficulties, however, emerged in discussions between two of the military members of the partnership, Generals Clausel and Lefebvre-Desnouettes, and an unnamed "Philadelphia capitalist" (possibly Nicholas Biddle): men of finance and men of war have some difficulty in understanding one another. The capitalist had heard of Lakanal's plan and did not consider it a sound investment. The *National Intelligencer* of September 4, 1817, purported to record their discourse; the capitalist was said to have exclaimed: "I am astonished that such men as you who have money at command, should undertake such a Don Quixote expedition, when, by taking your stand upon the Exchange, you would get 20 percent on your money without trouble." Clausel was quoted as replying: "We have been accustomed to labor for the glory and happiness of our country, not to prey upon . . . other people's necessities." The reporter opined that this was "a reply which marks a noble mind."

The term "noble" has a vaguely feudal ring, and surely this conversation marks a stage in yet a larger transition, from the medieval world of direct military or mercantile entrepreneurship, given a final fling in the revolutionary era, to the cooler, larger strategies of capitalist abstraction.

Though this portion of our work is largely political and economic, architectural historians have three good reasons to be interested in Lakanal:

First, he was a real-estate speculator who sponsored the construction of an important example of French neoclassical architecture. In the garden room of that specimen of the style, Generals Moreau and Napoleon agreed to overturn the Directory.

Second, like Benjamin Henry Latrobe, Lakanal met, in the course of his career, many characters who left artifactual evidence of their passing, evidence on a grand scale. He is a handy guide to the lives of others who had significant effects upon the American constructed landscape.

Third, among the staff he assembled at the Ecole Polytechnique was the architectural theoretician Jean-Nicolas-Louis Durand, whose influence is still powerful today. Under Lakanal's aegis, Durand collected into a system applicable to architecture the theories of the late Enlightenment, available in America until that time only in bits provided by missionaries like Thomas Jefferson, Latrobe, and Joel Barlow, whose partial transmissions appeared in curricular changes (like the substitution of French for Greek and science for classics at Union College and at the University of Virginia) and in new campus designs: Union's, designed by Joseph Ramée, and the University of Virginia's, designed by Latrobe and Jefferson.

A generation later, the geometric neoclassicism of Ramée and Latrobe was reinforced by the intellectual grandchildren of Durand, arriving here among the "forty-eighters," who had learned Durandian concepts at the feet of his intellectual children, such as Friedrich Wilhelm August Froebel. And, after Froebel, as we all know, came Louis Sullivan and Frank Lloyd Wright.

Lakanal in Arcadia

Lakanal spoke of himself as a cultivator of letters, and he chose for his American "retreat" a place where he might have benefited from intellectual cross-pollination, had he remained there quietly. He was, for example, close to New Harmony, Indiana, where, in 1827, an experimental community was established by Charles Leseur, a naturalist from Le Havre, and by Robert and David Dale Owen, devotees, like Lakanal, of the philosopher Helvétius.*

At last, a quiet life, cultivating the soil and the mind: just the right note to strike with Jefferson, false though it was. Lakanal had learned to survive by dissembling; candor was a luxury few could afford in revolutionary France. When he had voted to send Louis XVI to be decapitated, he was careful to distance himself from "the rascal Lafayette and his intriguing accomplices . . . I have nothing in common with such people." He was, in fact, Lafayette's protégé; and twenty-two years later, his letter to Jefferson contained an intro-duction from that open-hearted man. Lafayette noted, without comment, Laka-nal's service "in the Representative Assemblies of France."

It went without saying that such service, when it included regicide, could not be pardoned by the Bourbons restored to power in 1815. Lafayette preferred to stress other achievements: Lakanal had been inspector general of weights and measures, aegis of the metric system, steward of the Lycée Bonaparte, author of the law establishing the primary and central public schools of France, and founder of the Ecole Polytechnique. He gave his country a copyright law to protect authors and artists a generation earlier than its counterpart was enacted in Britain; he was a defender of botanical research† and founder of that collection of specimens of human excellence—or at least eminence—the Insti-tute of France. In 1815, Lafayette told Jefferson, Lakanal was abandoning "these functions . . . and going to seek in the U.S., Liberty, Security and Happiness.‡

---

*It was Helvétius's widow who facilitated Thomas Jefferson's entree into the intellectual life of Paris. Helvétius's ideas, or at any rate his reputation, inspired Stephen Girard to name one of his best ships after him, one of his "philosophical flotilla."

†Norman Wilkinson's recent book about the botanical interests of Irénée du Pont (E. I. Du Pont, Botanist: The Beginning of a Tradition) is also informative on Lakanal, as the savior of the royal gardens of Paris as centers for botanical study. These jardins royaux were associated with the royal family, "and those revolutionists who wished to erase every last trace of the deposed Bourbon monarchy came very close to destroying them. Fortunately the influential M. Joseph Lakanal, president of the Committee for Public Instruction, opposed this senseless vandalism . . . and . . . prevailed upon the new government to save them" (pp. 13–14).

This explains why André Thouin, who had served as chief gardener of the Jardins Royaux, was willing to vouch for Lakanal to his old friend and correspondent Thomas Jefferson. Lakanal, said Thouin, was "a man to be recommended by his morality as well as by his learning, to whom our scientific institutions owe many debts" (quoted in Reeves, p. 30).

‡Another introduction from Lafayette was to his former aide Colonel Presley Neville. Presley Neville's father, General John, went to western Pennsylvania to represent Virginia's claims there, acquired large land holdings, and built a peculiarly West Indian house called Woodlands, in Collier Township, near Pittsburgh, in 1785. The general attempted to collect the whiskey tax from his neighbors and thereby provoked the Jacobin rising often called the Whiskey Rebellion, in 1794. The house was burned by a mob.

Violence in the United States directly partook of the spirit of the French Revolution. We are told by the Dictionary of American Biography that "Neville escaped and with other 'exiles' ['émigrés' might have done as well] returned with the army sent to put down the rebellion," led by Alexander Hamilton. Woodlands was restored; and in it, in 1797, the general received Louis Philippe and his

As Lafayette generously reminded Jefferson, Lakanal was the survivor of a group of theorists who nearly succeeded in creating a genuinely revolutionary school system for France; in the 1790s, Helvétius, Talleyrand, Cabanis, Destutt de Tracy, Condorcet, and Lakanal laid the ideological basis for the modern French educational system. When they were young, "the Revolution swept all minds and hearts along." The Terror changed all that; it was in the grip of another spirit. Destutt wrote his theories while under sentence of death; Condorcet committed suicide to avoid the guillotine. Cabanis was reduced to doing experiments to determine the exact moment of death when the weighted knife fell. Talleyrand went into exile; and even Lakanal, after a few months under the regime of Robespierre, thought it wise to seek a post in the distant southwest, presiding over the lands of departed aristocrats along the Dordogne (among them, it happens, the La Tour Du Pins). He returned to Paris after Robespierre had fallen, to execrate, safely now, "the new Pisistratus and his hired assassins," and to resume the creation of the revolutionary school system.

Lakanal as Patron of Architecture

Lakanal had time for architecture as well. His was a generation especially sensitive to symbolism; and, like many of his contemporaries, he knew that symbols are never singular in their implications. The buildings he commissioned manifested at once the ebullient speculative climate of his time in the application of geometric principles to the ordering of space and his recognition of a wonderful opportunity to make a killing in real estate—"speculation" in another sense.

His architect was Guislain Joseph Henry (1754–1820), manipulator of multiples of cubes and cylinders. For Lakanal and his brother, Jean-Baptiste, Henry devised one of his complex essays for a site along the rue du Mont-Blanc (now the rue de la Chaussée-d'Antin, nos. 18–22). There the Lakanals constructed a group of buildings around a courtyard and entry lane with a ground plan shaped like a keyhole.

One passed through a gateway and then proceeded down a narrow allée of poplars between nos. 18 and 22 to the court before no. 20. An old description assures us that "the inhabitants of the buildings at the side . . . were forbidden to throw anything into this avenue or under the trees." Order prevailed.

Having passed along the allée and thrust in the key, the visitor entered a half-circular court through a transition zone of quarter-cylinders under spherical vaults. Within the central structure, the exploring geometer passed through

brothers. The house has recently been restored, again. It would be nice to know if Lakanal actually visited this doughty old anti-Jacobin, but the records are mute.

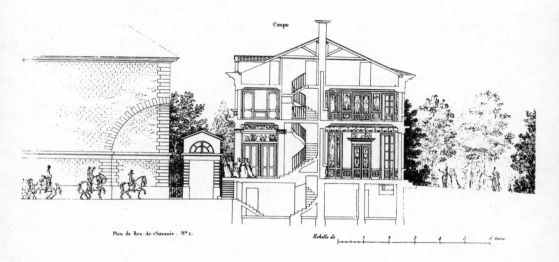

The Lakanal mansion in Paris

either a hexagon on the right or an octagon on the left to come into a circular room looking out upon the garden. (Today this very pretty set of ideas is buried within a new banking complex—but, if one presents the proper credentials, one is admitted to Lakanal's sitting room, quite intact, though tricked up with slide projectors, ashtrays, and podia.)

It is toward that circular sitting room, paneled in the "Grecian" taste, that one was meant to be led. Great things were meant to happen there, or if not there surely among the copses and bosky dells of the garden one once saw through the windows. Amid such calculated verdure, the Great Personage who inhabited all this geometrical perfection might relax from its intensity in a little thatched cottage with an aviary, where wild birds sang all day.*

Lakanal apparently met with financial reverses, for in 1799 the central house was no longer his property. Instead, it did in fact belong to a Great Personage, a man who might, so to speak, have been Napoleon: General Jean Moreau. It was in that house a plot was hatched that brought Lakanal's public life to an

---

*The Lakanal house is famous for kings—for twenty-eight kings. They were kings of Judea, who occupied niches on the façade of the Cathedral of Notre Dame until October 23, 1793, when the Commune of Paris decided they were images of kings of France. With an indiscriminate fervor that in France has often desecrated its sculptural heritage, the Commune ordained that the kings should be pulled down. They lay before the cathedral for almost three years, until Jean-Baptiste Lakanal thought it safe to spirit them away and bury them in the garden behind 20, rue du Mont-Blanc. They remained interred there until 1977, when the Banque Française du Commerce, then in residence, dug up what was left of them, and presented them to the Cluny Museum.

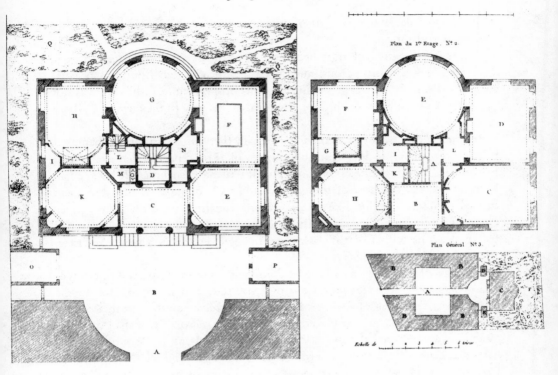

Floor plan of the Lakanal mansion

end, though this was not the plotter's intention. In the circular salon, on November 8, 1799, Moreau, whose victories in Germany matched Napoleon's in Italy, agreed to collaborate with Bonaparte in the coup d'état that put an end to the Directory. It might have brought Moreau to power instead of Napoleon, had he had the energy of his Creole wife (both Mme Bonaparte and Mme Moreau were from the West Indies), but after a brief partnership Moreau went to New Jersey, not to the throne.*

Socratic Evenings

At the crest of his career, in 1800, Lakanal was guilty of an indiscretion putting all in peril: he expressed to his superior the view that Napoleon was becoming a dictator. The superior was Cambacérès, who shortly became chancellor of the

---

*He returned to Europe in 1813, joining another defector, Bernadotte, once marshal of France but risen to be heir to the crown of Sweden, in directing the armies arrayed against the French at Dresden, where he was killed.

empire. This uncharacteristic fit of imprudence forced Lakanal into another period of rustication.

He emerged again in 1804, to become head of the Lycée Bonaparte. Ten years later he was again prosperous; and when a return of the Bourbons became increasingly likely, he "began converting his property into cash." He was not penniless when he boarded ship for America, on his way to the farm in Gallatin County.

It appears that he did not intend to remain there in isolation: one bemused boatman on the Ohio River, in the summer of 1816, reported that every time he turned a bend he came upon another boat bearing Frenchmen. If his eye had been trained for that sort of thing, he would have noted how many of them carried themselves stiffly, like soldiers. Some said they were on their way to confer with the man they called their "look-out," Lakanal; some were headed for rendezvous with Lakanal's associate, in regicide and in a new, American scheme, Garnier de Saintes.

Edouard de Montulé, one of the hard young men spotted by that Ohio River boatman, provided some indications of what they had in mind, and, in the process, a last sighting of Garnier. Desiring to purchase an interest in a colony in Alabama, where, he heard, were gathering the "heroes" who had survived Waterloo and escaped the firing squads of the Bourbons, de Montulé disembarked at Louisville to seek out a M. Garnier, land agent and whiskey merchant. Crossing a sand flat full of the debris of recent floods, he came upon "a log house, in fairly poor repair." In the "kitchen . . . bedroom, the living room—in short the only room," he was met by his host "with a spoon in one hand and a notebook in the other." Without ceasing to talk, Garnier "killed two chickens, dressed them, put them in to fricasee, doubled the amount of his beans, already cooking, [and] prepared a salad."

The notebook, entitled "Socratic Evenings," contained Garnier's reflections on the history of Europe from Henry IV to Bonaparte. We will never know what it might have told us about events in the recent experience of de Montulé, Lakanal, and Garnier. For soon after de Montulé departed, Garnier and his son attempted to follow the soldiers down the Ohio in a pirogue. They got caught in the rapids, and the boat capsized. The old orator of 1793, bearer of the Legion of Honor and a knighthood from Napoleon, went to his death clutching his "Socratic Evenings" to the last.

37

TO AMERICA

*". . . a free republic supporting with obedience the salutary
yoke of law . . ."*   LAKANAL to Jefferson, 1816

In the weeks after his final defeat, when neither he nor those who had won
at Waterloo could make up their minds what to do next, Napoleon and his
aide General Lavallette discussed seeking refuge in America. What a test of the
fragile polity of the United States that would have been! Bonaparte was still
only forty-six years old, considerably younger than the Caesar who crossed the
Rubicon. There was plenty of mischief in him yet.

As late as June 1815, the emperor's brother Lucien wrote their sister Pauline
that "he will depart for the United States . . . where all of us will join him."
Fortunately for James Monroe, John Quincy Adams, and Andrew Jackson
(especially for Andrew Jackson), Lavallette dissuaded Bonaparte from going to
America. He reminded the emperor that Moreau, his only true rival among
French soldiers of fortune, had "retired" to the United States.

The precedent of Moreau might be overlooked, but not a worse one:
Napoleon was unwilling to remind France of Louis XVI, who had tried to
desert his people in 1792. He responded to Lavallette, as a general and as a
monarch: he could not abandon "my brave officers who are so devoted to me."

Napoleon did not attempt to escape. He surrendered to his enemies the
British, who placed him as far away as possible, on Saint Helena, an islet in
the South Atlantic. But he did bestow upon America an opportunity for
hospitality to his family and, thereby, the honor of becoming a Bonapartist base
of operations: "My brother may leave," he said.

Kings and Princes

Of the three brothers who might have qualified for the role of advance man
in America, one, Jerome, had diminished his utility by his amatory escapade
in Baltimore (see p. 95). He would not have been welcome in a country where
his first wife had many friends. Another possibility, Lucien, was too unpredictable. He had a reputation as a Jacobin so radical that he would not accommodate
himself to the rule of his own brother. Just to be sure, the British had bottled
up Lucien in Malta.

Joseph Bonaparte (artist unknown)

The right man for America was the amiable Joseph, once king of Naples, then king of Spain and the Indies. Joseph had relinquished Spain but "forgot" to abdicate the crown of the Indies; nonetheless, he might be acceptable to the Americans. He was certainly acceptable to Stephen Girard, who arranged his passage and was rewarded with a bust of the emperor by Canova.

Joseph suggested that Girard also provide him with an annuity in exchange for the estate near Paris from which Bonaparte chose to take his inoffensive American title, the comte de Survilliers. Survilliers had, he said, "six thousand acres in one tract . . . the principal château with its green houses, orangeries, theater &c could not be built today for two million francs."

Girard gave a characteristic reply: "It does not suit me to figure as a great land owner in a country to which I shall never go, and under a government hostile to republicans." Here was a great moment in the dialogue between the consummate adventurers of statecraft, the Bonapartes, and the most foursquare of the adventurers of commerce, Girard. One recalls the seduction of old John Parish by Gouverneur Morris, who suggested that by relieving him of vast reaches of Adirondack real estate, John's son David might become a baron, not (like the Bonapartes) by conquest but (like a merchant—a Baring, for example) by purchase.

National boundaries did not inhibit trade, nor did oceans, loyalties, or laws. A former king of Spain might sell French real estate to Girard, a Philadelphia merchant, or buy New York real estate from Leray de Chaumont, a merchant of France, just as Morris might sell New York real estate in Paris to a Hamburg merchant. Commerce would have its way.

More Real Estate

Knowing Joseph's insatiable pecuniary appetite, Girard deployed David Parish to extricate from Switzerland some property left behind. Parish was in Europe at the time and arranged for the surreptitious movement to America of "a small package containing important objects." It arrived in May 1818 and was stored in Girard's vault.

Replenished by Parish, the comte de Survilliers settled in New Jersey, near the former home of General Moreau. With the assistance of Girard, he managed to accumulate there, in packets and portmanteaux, goodly portions of the wealth he had gathered in Naples and Spain, together with the residue of the silver earnings presented him by David Parish. He created a pleasant enclave of eighteen hundred acres, centering upon a house called Point Breeze.

If he had limited his real-estate ventures to New Jersey, as Parish urged, and resisted investing in upstate New York, he would have been wiser. Rumors would not then have arisen that he intended to transport Napoleon, after a rescue from Saint Helena, to the Adirondacks; these rumors were off the mark—as to destination, though not as to intent.

History does not record when it occurred to Joseph that he might establish a Bonapartist base in America. But in the busy days after Waterloo, he and his baggage train chanced to pass close to the Château de Chaumont, where the hospitable Leray received him and took off his hands a considerable sum in jewels, in hasty exchange for whatever extent of New York pine land Leray thought fair; after they both arrived in America, Leray sold him 150,000 acres more. Thus, the reluctant king and David Parish, the aspiring baron, became the successors to Leray and other, earlier speculators in the ownership of nearly 400,000 acres of the north country.

In the 1820s, Joseph Bonaparte built three houses upon this new domain; they were somewhat simpler than his château at Survilliers or his palace in Madrid. But he made use of them for hunting expeditions which were like the "pro-

"Point Breeze," by Charles B. Lawrence

gresses" of Hungarian magnates exploring the extremities of their Carpathian holdings.*

There grew up around Joseph's possessions in New York a colony of lesser Bonapartist expatriates, among them two "Murat princes," sons of Marshal Joachim Murat, Joseph Bonaparte's successor as king of Naples, and Caroline Bonaparte, Joseph's youngest sister. The more interesting of the two was Prince Charles-Louis-Napoleon-Achille Murat—the former crown prince of Naples—who came to America in 1823, explored the north country, and settled in Florida to grow sugarcane. He married a grandniece of George Washington, became an American citizen, speculated in Texas land, and practiced law in New Orleans. At his most effulgent, before the Panic of 1837, he owned plantations

---

*Also like a Hungarian magnate, Joseph bestowed progeny upon his remote possessions with less formality than that required for the establishment of the Baltimore Bonapartes by his brother. Annette Savage, Joseph's morganatic wife, gave birth to two daughters bearing the Bonaparte family names of Caroline and Pauline. Pauline died in infancy, but Caroline's birth was legitimized by Napoleon III in 1869. After Joseph returned to Europe in 1832, Annette married Henry Horr and moved to New York City. Caroline married Zebulon Hart, died in 1890, and is buried beside her husband in Oxbow, New York.

near Tallahassee and Baton Rouge and a town house in New Orleans. He died in 1847, leaving a plantation headquarters, Magnolia Mound, which still stands, on the campus of Louisiana State University.*

When we visit the Bonapartists in Alabama, we will hear tales of ladies in ball gowns and gentlemen in uniform, hewing wood and drawing water. To this day these same tales are told of those who settled in the town of Cape Vincent.

They may even be true, for one place or the other.

Next in rank after King Joseph and the Murat princes was Prince Grouchy. A mere marquis under the ancien régime, he became a Napoleonic prince though he was a cavalry officer with greater aptitude for the grand gesture than for following orders. This defect brought him too late to the field of Waterloo and made him a convenient scapegoat for that final defeat. Though the other Napoleonic exiles gave him scant credit for it, his achievement occurred after the battle, when he kept the remnants of the army together (thereby strengthening the hand of Talleyrand in negotiating a settlement with the enemies of France).

After his arrival in America, Grouchy brooded in isolation. Finally his theatrical instinct offered a device to rehabilitate himself: he would be purged upon the mountaintop at Monticello. It was a plot device anticipating Somerset Maugham (see *The Razor's Edge*). Thomas Jefferson seemed willing; any enemy of Britain might be a friend. The Treaty of Ghent, in 1814, had brought the War of 1812 to an end, but to him it was merely a truce, to be "terminated at the first act of impressment committed on an American citizen." An American "gauntlet must be forever hurled" at Britain. Britain alone could threaten American commerce upon the high seas. Experienced gauntlet hurlers could always come in handy.

Grouchy would have been welcome at Monticello, but he never completed his pilgrimage of purgation. The illness of one of his sons forced him to stop short of his goal, at Wilmington. There, for the last time, he experienced the sounds and smells familiar to his profession: he was present for one of the periodic explosions of the Du Pont powder works. His holdings in New York, purchased from Leray, led him to sojourn there, but later he tired of the sandy plains and retired to France.

---

*The most interesting architectural remnant of Bonapartist occupancy in northern New York was in Cape Vincent, a small, frame example of the geometric school of neoclassicism, so odd to the local eye as to be called the Cup and Saucer House. It was an octagon with a skirt of veranda around the first floor and (like an inverted cup) a two-room second story with a domed roof. It was built by the Napoleonic police-prefect of Paris.

A close equivalent to the Cup and Saucer House was Toscan's Bungalow, in Greenland, New Hampshire. Jean-Marie Toscan came to Portsmouth, in that state, as French consul in 1782 and built his Bungalow in 1800. It had an octagonal cupola, and a skirt of veranda only on the front—perhaps an apron rather than a skirt. I found an ancient picture of the house as this book was going to press and have been unable to discover whether or not it still exists.

Issuing to the Wars

We have followed Prince Murat, Prince Grouchy, and King Joseph beyond the chronological bounds of their debuts in America, straying into the 1820s and beyond, to put in place the tangible consequences of their residence in America. We now return to Philadelphia in 1816:

Though Napoleon was hors de combat, French patriots like Du Pont de Nemours set about to find other means to bring perfidious Albion to "a day of judgement." Their ardor was encouraged by Jefferson, who wrote to Lakanal that France would experience "resurrection." Joining the war chant, Garnier called for a "new Thébaïde," where there could be gathered the veterans "of the most beautiful of all causes, now at the mercy of the most cowardly of all their enemies."

The prospect of an American Thébaïde was not pleasing to Hyde de Neuville, the representative in the United States of the restored Bourbons; nor were the Bourbon governments of France and Spain beguiled by Joseph's apparently benign demeanor. The Spanish colonies were already in revolt. It was something to have Napoleon and his family of upstarts out of Europe, but Bonapartes were dangerous anywhere.

Though Napoleon was thousands of sea miles away, Neuville wrote the duc de Richelieu that American gossip was full of stories of plots to free the former

One of Joseph Bonaparte's houses near Lake Bonaparte in New York

Charles-Louis-Napoleon-Achille Murat
(artist unknown)

emperor and bring him to the new world: "I persist in thinking that only one man, Bonaparte, could operate there a great revolution. It appears that Joseph has been persuaded to dream of being King of the Indies." The Napoleonic exiles were "recruiting, scattering money and organizing secret expeditions." They had plenty of money to scatter; they came enriched by twenty years of pillaging Europe. They had plenty of energy, too; and Neuville was certain that after they paused to regroup they would find an excuse to renew the activity they enjoyed in Europe—gathering plenty of glory and plenty of swag.

The Quakers of Philadelphia must have felt some uneasiness as crowds of these unemployed military Frenchmen swaggered through their streets. Twenty years before, Wolfe Tone had recruited there for a French expedition against the British in Ireland; that expedition had left widows in Philadelphia and thirty thousand torn corpses buried in the Irish earth.

And what might be a "Thébaïde"? What did that term imply about their mission? In William Penn's city, proud of its classical learning, honest citizens were reminded of that Thebes described by Alexander Pope in his translation of the *Iliad*:

> The world's great empress on the Egyptian plain,
> That spreads her conquests o'er a thousand states,
> And pours her heroes through a thousand gates,
> Two hundred horsemen and two hundred cars
> From each wide portal issuing to the wars.

The worrisome news from Philadelphia reached the Federal City of Washington. Professor Lakanal and Colonel Nicolas-Simon Permentier, another quiet-spoken and apparently inoffensive man, urged Congress to adopt a policy like that of the French government, which a year earlier had hastened to get these restless spirits out of Paris. Keep them moving westward, suggested Lakanal and Permentier; these incendiaries should be placed beyond the fire wall of the Appalachians.

Former King Joseph the Mild entertained these heroes and introduced them, on best behavior, to his American friends. Vandamme, whose behavior could not be controlled—he was "renowned for his tenacity and fearlessness as a fighting general as well as for his frank rough manners and plundering and dissolute life"—was kept out of sight with considerable effort.

The complaisant Congress, taking pity upon the plight of these heroes and taking account of their bulging muscles, awarded them a land grant in central Alabama, at the junction of the Tombigbee and Black Warrior rivers.

Lakanal requested of Jefferson that he draw up their constitution, recalling that in 1789, the Sage of Monticello had been asked by the French revolutionary government for such a document. In 1817, he was more skeptical, declining the honor somewhat sardonically: "Is it proposed that this shall be a separate state? Or a country of a state? Or a mere voluntary association, as those of the Quakers, Dunkars [sic], Menonists [sic]?"

Though lacking a Jeffersonian charter, the heroes of Waterloo set out with apparent docility for their garrison in Alabama. The people of that territory (almost a state), flattered but wary, named a county Marengo after one Napoleonic victory and a town Arcola after another. Réal, perhaps unaware of the fate of Gallipolis (see page 92), called the Bonapartists' village Demopolis. Unfortunately, Demopolis was not within their congressional land grant, so these law-abiding citizens acquiesced in moving to a second village they called Aigleville.

Lakanal's Secret

While the more pacific of the Napoleonic exiles migrated to Alabama, Lakanal was providing cover for the militants. He wrote to Jefferson that his grief at the prospect of France under the heel of the British was assuaged by the spectacle of Americans "supporting with obedience the salutary yoke of law." He knew his man. Jefferson's image of a good society or a good university was a very orderly one. Lakanal sighed for a France ruled by Jefferson's "pacific genius." Sadly, said he, France got Bonaparte instead: "The ambition of a single man has brought the enraged nations upon us."

When Lakanal was writing of "the disasters of 1815" to friends in France, he took a different tone. He rejoiced that when he went scouting the West for a proper refuge for the officers of the old guard, he had chanced upon an Osage Indian settlement in Missouri, and "would you believe that on seeing us one of these savages cried out: 'Falanche babichile' (Frenchman friend), and immediately afterwards: 'Bonaparte! Bonaparte!' What a man! . . . The loss of the battle of Waterloo has not dampened in the United States the enthusiasm for this prodigy of our century."

Though Lakanal assured Jefferson he intended to cultivate agriculture and history, Simon Chaudron, one of the enthusiastic participants in the "Napoleonic Confederation," wrote him as "wise and illustrious master" to say that his "compatriots are accepting you as the look-out who serves them as the rallying point . . . [to lead them to] our national establishment . . . republican colonies in the interior of the country."

Whatever may have been Jefferson's impression of Lakanal, it fell to John Quincy Adams, secretary of state under President James Monroe, to cope with the notion of a new set of French colonies in the interior of America. Adams knew enough of Lakanal to expect that they would be located with geographical exactitude, for Lakanal was famous in his role in establishing reforms in weights, measures, latitude and longitude—modes of imposing order through metric measurements that had enraptured Adams when he began studying them, at the behest of Congress, in the spring of 1817.

Adams's deference to Lakanal, his *Report on Weights and Measures* (his proudest literary achievement)* was written just six months before Neuville demanded his attention to a packet of intercepted letters.† When the seals on those letters were broken, Adams learned that the admired proprietor of mathematical order in France, now in his advance post in Gallatin County, Kentucky, had become the author of a scheme for sedition and violence in Texas.

Lakanal was perhaps too much disposed to writing, too willing to trust messengers, too addicted to symbolism: on the cover of the packet of his letters, within the sealed envelope, he had affixed the seal of the regicide Convention, a liberty cap borne on a pike. Around the seal was this lettering: "Lakanal, Deputy to the National Convention."

---

*It is easy to understand why Adams was so compatible a secretary of state for James Monroe; his *Report on Weights and Measures* was fervent about a metric system spread in sweet dominion across the globe. Here is a sample (quoted in Dangerfield, *Good Feelings,* p. 161):

> If the Spirit of Evil is, before the final consummation of things, to be cast down from his dominion over men, and bound in the chains of a thousand years, the fortaste [*sic*] here of man's eternal felicity, then . . . the metre will surround the globe in use as well as in multiplied extension; and one language of weights and measures will be spoken from the equator to the poles.

†The *Report* was published in February 1821, on the same day that Adams concluded a transcontinental treaty with Spain. One of its purposes was surcease from the kind of filibustering proposed in those letters by Lakanal.

William Lee in 1812, by John Vanderlyn

The packet, addressed to Joseph Bonaparte, contained surveys of the topography, the Indian tribes, and the economic conditions of the Spanish possessions from Texas to Santa Fe, probably based on those deposited in Paris in 1810 by Aaron Burr, after the failure of his effort to interest Napoleon in an earlier version of the scheme Lakanal proposed. Lakanal's covering letter asserted that he had "already on several occasions entertained Your Majesty on these general dispositions." He professed "tender and profound veneration" for Bonaparte, whose skirts he promised to keep clean. "The common profession of our political faith is . . . : 'The King has nothing to do in this affair; it is our unbounded devotion to his Illustrious Dynasty which prompts us to act.' " Lakanal wound up by asking Bonaparte to defray some of his expenses and requesting that he be given a Spanish title* so that he might "affiliate himself in some sort with that nation." In that way he would better represent "Your August Majesty."

Neuville confirmed to Adams that the plot was to be "like that of Colonel Burr," thirteen years earlier: an "insurrection of the West," to seize control of the mines of San Luis Potosí. According to Neuville, Stephen Girard was this time a participant, an opinion soon confirmed when a New Orleans newspaper reported that he had given fifty thousand dollars to finance a filibustering

*One is reminded of the prudence of Lestapis (see p. 255).

expedition against Mexico, supplemented with very considerable sums from Joseph Bonaparte and "other distinguished Frenchmen."

Girard, unlike Nicholas Biddle, had no sympathy for Burr, though he had been willing to pick up, at a reduced price, the Bastrop claim and the ghost of Burr's imperial dream. But he had intimate knowledge of the affairs of David Parish, and of the possible benefits of control of the silver in San Luis Potosí and Vera Cruz. Those benefits had first been fully demonstrated by our old friend Gabriel-Julien Ouvrard.

(Henry Adams may have been right in the supposition, which apparently occurred to him sometime in the 1880s, that Ouvrard, along with Fouché, was listening when Burr, in 1810, attempted to solicit Napoleonic support for an assault on Mexico, to accomplish by force what Parish and Ouvrard had earlier achieved by indirection. This would couple Burr's "conspiracy" to the Great Silver Scheme, and add the dynastic dimension Lakanal recommended to Joseph Bonaparte—with a Bonaparte substituted for a Bourbon.)

William Lee

Stephen Girard had great weight. The financier of the War of 1812 and the second Bank of the United States was thought by many to be the richest man in the nation. Well acquainted with the Mexican trade through the Great Silver Scheme, he was perfectly capable of financing an opportunity to acquire Mexican silver by other means. Why else was this drab, dour, and powerful man consorting with the swaggering and bemedaled veterans of Napoleon?

President Monroe needed a bold and skillful man of his own to set against Girard. He could not find anyone so rich as the old man. But he could turn to William Lee and to Biddle, who were bound to him by friendships formed when they were all younger, and lonelier, in Paris. They had both demonstrated the energy, intelligence, and worldliness required to match the French desperadoes and the ingenious old West Indian trader.

Biddle had delighted Monroe in Paris and in London with his Byronic beauty of person and his classical learning. Though as yet no match for Girard in wealth, he was, in 1818, clearly a man on the rise in banking. Thanks in large part to Parish, Biddle's wife, née Craig, was rich (see p. 254). He had a prominent father with useful Federalist connections, and, more important, he had no financial stake in a Bonapartist conquest of Mexico.

In 1796, Monroe wrote that William Lee was "much my friend in Paris." Born in 1772, the son of a Tory merchant from Boston, he too came of a handsome lineage: the first Lee to reach Massachusetts was described as "very comely . . . gracefully beautiful . . . and has . . . good learning." William Lee, himself, was remarkably attractive to women; he married two fine examples of the strong American type and was a weekly dinner companion of Empress Josephine after her divorce from Napoleon. He once wrote to his wife about another female attachment: "What I feel for Madame Barlow* does not injure you . . . she deserves your esteem, as much for preserving her husband, as from her own merit. O! How I long to make you acquainted with her! When I want a friend, a consoling friend, I fly to your sex. Their bosoms only possess the healing balm . . ."

The wife to whom he wrote these lines was Susan Palfrey, daughter of William Palfrey, one of the aides-de-camp to General Washington. Palfrey became paymaster of the Revolutionary Army and would have represented Congress to France had he not died on his way to take up his post.

After returning to the United States, Lee made an unsuccessful effort to become Edward Stevens's successor as consul (really ambassador) to the government of Toussaint Louverture. (As we have seen, that presumably lucrative post went instead to Tobias Lear.) His friendship with Monroe did net him the consulship to Bordeaux, however; and, between 1801 and 1807, Lee was a merchant and "commercial agent of the United States." William and Susan Lee named their two sons Thomas Jefferson Lee and William Barlow Lee. The sons were a disappointment, but their two daughters were not (see p. 415).

Trade relations were chaotic in the time of Burr's "conspiracy" and the Great Silver Scheme, of blockade and counterblockade, of privateering and impressment. The British, the Americans, and the French raided each other's shipping; piracy was nationalized and richly rewarded. Diplomats such as Lee spent years negotiating for better French treatment of American shipping. Things went so slowly that he had ample spare time for dabbling in engineering; he almost talked Napoleon into building a bridge of Lee's design over the Garonne River. Though he did not quite succeed, he became in the process a favored figure at the court.

In 1810 Lee journeyed to Washington, stayed with the Joel Barlows at Kalorama, and rejoiced in the news that Barlow was returning to Paris as American representative. During this visit to Washington, he wrote to his wife of his amazement at how inexpensively one could sustain the grand manner in a nation not yet caught up in the worldwide inflation rising with Napoleon's ambitions. He and Barlow had befriended Robert Fulton in Paris, where the inventor was trying to dazzle the French revolutionary government into supporting his steamboat experiments. In 1810 Lee found Fulton at the peak of his fortunes, living in opulence in Washington. "My friend Fulton lives in a

---

*Lee met Mrs. Joel Barlow, "a very amiable woman," in March of 1796 in Paris, and the two families remained friends until death (Mann, p. 43). Lee's diary suggests why Monroe and the Barlows found him good company; it is full of sharp but benevolent observations on avarice, architecture, and the drama of life.

handsome three-story house, has four servants, two children," and a levee once a fortnight, all "for $4000 per annum."* And the Barlows were living like grandees at Kalorama, where they and the Latrobes welcomed the Lees into their cheerful Franco-American circle. Mrs. Barlow wrote Mrs. Lee that "my husband thinks nothing can go right if William Lee is not at his elbow." (In his will, Barlow left ten thousand dollars each to Lee's two daughters.)

Lee wrote his wife: "We are in a better situation than we ever have been since our marriage. My debts are all paid and I have something beforehand." He became an intimate of President Madison and his wife, who asked to have Lee's daughter Susan come and stay with them at the White House for the next two years (she went instead to Paris, with her mother). All these cozy arrangements came apart when Barlow and Lee returned to France, with the tragic consequences related elsewhere (see pp. 396–7). After the death of Joel Barlow, Lee went back to his mercantile interests in Bordeaux.

Lee remained so passionate a devotee of the Bonapartist cause, however, that after Waterloo he made an effort to spirit Napoleon away to America.† He was already non grata in Bordeaux, having written a bitter attack on the British during the War of 1812.

More Technology Transfer

By 1815 Lee had grown fat, not then a disability for a romantic male, and wealthy enough to finance the transfer of French technology to the United States. The United States was a "developing country." Lee, like Jefferson, Pierre Bauduy, David Parish, Leray de Chaumont, and the Du Ponts, wished to accelerate its development. He paid personally for the emigration of skilled dyers, one of whom "has discovered the means of printing woolens and cottons with various indelible colors, by one and the same operation." He wrote Monroe:

> Next week I shall embark a whole family, who carry with them ten or a dozen looms for manufacture of cotton and woolen hose, pantaloons, undervests, and petticoats . . . Their loom . . . is so simple that a child of twelve . . . may work it, whereas the German looms at present in use in the United States require a long apprenticeship.

Lee had work for Thornton, at the Patent Office:

---

*With the help of Barlow and Latrobe, Fulton was standing off the competition of Oliver Evans, who was Dr. Thornton's candidate for the first steamboat patent.
†In concert with General Bertrand Clausel (see p. 379).

It would prove highly useful were we to introduce into our patent law, as the French have done . . . a clause allowing the same privileges and advantages to the importers of useful machines and discoveries, as if they were the inventors thereof. By this means many useful arts would be carried to the United States . . . There are but few men of sufficient patriotism to pay several hundred dollars for a machine which, on its arrival in the United States, anyone may copy.

When Lee himself finally took ship to America, "he was accompanied by sixty manufacturers, fifteen of whom travelled at his expense." He had time for charity of a more direct sort, writing Jefferson to introduce a French expert on the teaching of the "Deaf and Dumb."

Though Jefferson asked Lee to establish a facility at the base of the mountain at Monticello, Lee decided to put the factory, employing French workers and French technology to produce oilcloth and stockings, near New York, and refused Madison's offer of a government post. But in November 1816, Lee had to admit defeat. The other shareholders reneged on their commitments; and, urged by his wife, who could stand no further risks and shocks, he went to work under George Graham in the War Department.

Madison soon found something better for his friend; Lee became second auditor of the Treasury Department on March 6, 1817, a post he held for the next twelve years. He moved into one of a row of houses near the Treasury offices, between the White House and Kalorama, numbered 1901 through 1911 Pennsylvania Avenue. It was this house that Latrobe remodeled for him, though the extant letters on the subject, in the Latrobe Papers, do not suggest anything very exciting.

Lee was a man of strong loyalties, leading to equally strong invidious antipathies. Barlow's house was his idea of a small palace fit for a republican capital. After the immensely rich Colonel John Tayloe refused a palatial design by Latrobe for his winter residence and chose instead the more modest "Octagon" by Thornton,* Lee derided Mrs. Tayloe as "a sordid creature, a penurious hag," and wrote ironically to his daughter of Tayloe as "our great spendthrift." Some years later he told her that "this old fellow and his hyena have fretted themselves to death because their negroes have fallen fifty percent in value, and wheat and corn are a drug."

He carried back to Washington the anticlericalism of revolutionary France, finding the town "full of parsons, 'a regiment of black coats,' as Red Jacket [the Seneca chief, a shrewd observer himself] calls them." He took note of John C. Calhoun's mother, who went one direction

with her carriage stuffed with reverends, and then returns with it stuffed with eatibles. There were fat priests and lean priests; scrub headed and bald

---

*The Octagon is now the headquarters of the American Institute of Architects.

headed, all running and bawling to and fro, with meagre Mrs. Lear, oily Mrs. Ramsey, fidgety Mrs. Calhoun and sweet Mrs. Hawley piping and swarming like blackbirds in a swamp.

Among these samples of William Lee's correspondence and in his Washington chronicles we find the first glimmerings of the French colony in Alabama (Lee called it "Proscripolis"). Even before coming to Washington, he had written Thomas Jefferson that "the Dukes, Counts and Generals, who were created by Napoleon, are very different from" the royalist émigrés who "brought from France and her colonies only their idleness, ignorance, debauchery and decorations." But the Napoleonic nobles "rose by their merit, not by hereditary right," and were ready, along with "those who . . . bring the arts and sciences [such as Lakanal] and manufactures . . . [to return] with ease to the source from which they came, and to the dignity of useful citizens."

Now, quite casually, one of his letters tells us that "M. Pénières, the celebrated ex-legislator, experimental agriculturalist and naturalist, has been dispatched . . . in search of a tract which will produce, among other things, the vine and olive." This was the expedition led by Lakanal which discovered Bonapartism among the Osage Indians (see p. 361).

Pénières was a lovable creature. Though he too had voted for the death penalty for Louis XVI, he was appalled by its consequences and campaigned against its use thereafter. As we have seen, however, that did not mean that, as he botanized his way across America with Lakanal, he was indifferent to politics. He was the sort of man Lee, in writing about his friends to Jefferson, described as "sober, amiable, and industrious." These friends had "civilization and good manners" and were not inclined to "meddling in our party disputes, or making a bustle at an election." Very reassuring.

Lee, in fact, served as vice-president of the Colonial Society of French Immigrants, formed in response to Garnier's call for a "new Thébaïde"—and the society sending Lakanal and Pénières on their western survey. While Lee was in Washington handling matters with the Federal land office, Pénières and Lakanal were disarming the natives in Alabama.

Dr. Thornton Meddles

William Lee may have slipped when he imparted his knowledge of French intentions to his friend Dr. William Thornton, in 1816 commissioner of the Patent Office, and occasional factotum for a sequence of Presidents. Thornton's chief occupation was geopolitical agitations. Among them was the effort to liberate South America using French soldiers of fortune. One Napoleonic exile wrote a friend in France that at Joseph Bonaparte's court-in-exile in New Jersey,

Thornton would often appear trying to turn the energies of the Bonapartist condottieri against the South American possessions of Spain.

As way stations, he had in mind Amelia Island, off the coast of Spanish Florida, and then Florida itself. Amelia was already in the hands of Thornton's friend Gregor MacGregor, a Scottish filibuster. MacGregor was trying to gather expeditionary forces to conquer the mainland. He solicited the assistance of the conspicuously underemployed officers of Joseph's court, who appeared remarkably immune to such stimuli. They had other things in mind.

MacGregor was a minor figure, a soldier of fortune who traveled without doctrines and whose filibustering was indistinguishable from piracy. He made the mistake of a small-time desperado in trying to compete with the established smuggling and privateering interests along the Georgia and Florida coasts. At their insistence, he was eliminated as a geopolitical force by Andrew Jackson.

Dr. Thornton did not give up, however. And neither did the Napoleonic exiles.

38

PLOT AND COUNTERPLOT

A curious set of emblems was selected for the allotment certificates of the Vine and Olive Colony—curious, that is, if the colony had been organized for the cultivation of vines and olives: a profile of Napoleon, in Roman style, identified as "Emperor of the French, King of Italy," and "guardian of the future"— the Latin inscription was "Mihi cura futuris." Since Napoleon's interest in agriculture had never been noteworthy, the future the colonists had in mind was, it appeared, somewhat more complex. Indeed it was: a four-step process. Only the first was to be an agricultural base, managed by the more pacific of the Napoleonic exiles, chief among them Lefebvre-Desnouettes. It was to support the second, an invasion of Texas, led by the more bellicose, such as the Lallemands and Humbert. The sale of agricultural land in Alabama was seen by many of its sponsors merely as one mode of financing an attack on Texas; after Texas they would (in the third step) assault Mexico. Once possessed of enough silver, they could purchase a fleet to set loose Napoleon from his prison on Saint Helena.

Monroe and Adams were severe with Lee and made clear to him where his responsibilities lay. Thereafter, the activities of the plotters were dutifully reported to the United States government, including meetings between Charles Lallemand and certain Mexican mine owners who were prepared to produce war chests of silver and to raise ten thousand troops "who only wait for French officers to discipline them."* The conspiracy included merchants in Charleston (who had armed two brigs), other entrepreneurs "at New York," and "two in Boston." While awaiting the silver to be provided by the mine proprietors, the Bonapartists would sell their shares in the Vine and Olive Colony to bankers in Philadelphia, thus acquiring working capital for their Texas expedition. To Adams, the transaction was "a perversity of delirium, the turpitude of which is almost lost in its absurdity." The United States expected French visitors to demonstrate complete respect for its laws.

Following Adams's instructions, Lee remonstrated with Charles Lallemand. The general cagily responded that "his brother and himself had determined not to engage in anything of this nature if disagreeable to" the American government. Lee saw the light and told Monroe: "This declaration I do not credit."

General Lallemand himself, buying time, also went to Adams to deny any plan to attack Texas. He added that he had no connection with Lakanal; nor did Joseph Bonaparte, who had refused to receive "letters from that schemer." Lallemand knew the cat was out of the bag; but a little embarrassment did not slow him down for long, for, according to Lee, he went on "purchasing arms and ammunition in New York."

Monroe then asked Biddle to join the fray. His assignments were to keep under surveillance the Lallemands, Girard, and Girard's private fleet, his "philosophical flotilla."

Biddle reported the sale of some of the Alabama lands and the departure from Philadelphia of a ship bearing one hundred fifty men "disciplined and prepared by the Lallemands." They were "not going to cultivate vines." Though he thought the Spanish government could have bought "the abandonment of the expedition by paying $12,000," the Spanish Minister to the United States, Don Luis de Onis, "would not however bid so high. Instead of buying off the party, he bought only the secret of their destination."

The secret of that destination was also important to Monroe. Like Jefferson and Andrew Jackson, he was a slave owner. The policy of these planters toward the southern frontiers of the United States is chiefly explained by that fact; though they feared domestic disruption by unemployed French soldiers, they feared other things more. Monroe in the White House and Jackson on the frontier were united in apprehension that the Spanish colonies could serve as a base for a Negro insurrection, a Negro-Indian alliance, or an effort to abolish slavery in the South.

Monroe need not have worried. Joseph Bonaparte had received instructions from Napoleon to aid an invasion of Texas directed against Spanish Bourbon interests, not to imperil the slave owners of the United States. This fact was

---

*Perhaps they had been waiting in disappointment that Aaron Burr had failed.

promptly conveyed by an informer in Joseph's Bordentown circle to Onis, who reported it to his superiors.

Onis went into direct negotiation with Lallemand, arguing that the project was "unworthy of their honor, and the glory they had won." A bribe from the Bourbon king of Spain would not be nearly so "unworthy," said he, offering cash and "an establishment in the Province of Texas . . . if they would live tranquilly as good vassals." Appearing to accommodate this expectation would get Lallemand and Humbert closer to the silver mines and to Mexican rebels against Spain; so he said he would wait past Christmas, 1817, for the Spanish subsidy. Then, he ominously told the minister, he "would respond to His Majesty from the Province of Texas."

Onis, still hopeful, provided a passport for Lallemand to go to the "Province of Texas" by sea, not by land—that way, he would not arrive with an army at his heels. The viceroy of Mexico, however, wanted no risks at all; he issued orders that Lallemand was to be seized if he came ashore.

Nicholas Biddle duly reported the departure of two more shiploads of Napoleonic officers from Philadelphia, one bearing the Lallemands and the other, General Rigaud. In New Orleans, Lallemand was awaited by an even more formidable figure, General Humbert.

Jean-Joseph Amable Humbert was very tall, very muscular, with a long, lean face, dark skin, and a bushy black beard. He was prone to "spells" and rages, but he was a great soldier. Born in destitution, he became a dealer in rabbit skins for the glove makers of Lyons before the revolution offered a new career. Humbert the rabbit skinner, elected an officer in the revolutionary army, found glory in Flanders and was promoted for his brutal efficiency in the civil war of La Vendée. Though his campaign in Ireland in 1798 was accounted an elegant failure, expensive only to the Irish, thereafter Napoleon feared and disliked Humbert as he did Moreau, and for the same reasons: they were possible competitors. Humbert had returned from Ireland a hero, Napoleon from Egypt under a cloud. Humbert was packed off to Saint-Domingue to be kept under the eye of Pauline Bonaparte's husband, Leclerc. After Leclerc's death, Humbert's attentions to the widow, and his reputation in other respects as well, became scandalous to the ears of the emperor, who had him exiled.

In 1813, he attempted to form a foreign legion in New Orleans to join the insurrection in Mexico led by General José Alvarez de Toledo; but his offer of aid was refused, and the general gave up soon thereafter. Humbert then served with distinction under Andrew Jackson at the Battle of New Orleans, and was authorized by Old Hickory to form a new legion, to be deployed to assist in another effort to free Mexico, this time a joint venture with the brothers Lafitte and their Baratarian pirates, under General Xavier Mina. Though it failed too, Humbert found much in common with the Lafittes and served as their "military governor" on the island of Galveston. On January 14, 1818, the

General Charles Lallemand;
engraving from a portrait by François-Henri Mulard

first contingents of the bearers of Napoleonic "honor and glory," led by the brothers Lallemand, landed on this island stronghold, set beyond the reach of any legal system save that of the Lafittes, in a misty land of marshes, bayous, and barrier islands stretching from the mouth of the Mississippi to that of the Rio Grande.

Lallemand's French-speaking land pirates were no match in guile for the French-speaking sea pirates of Galveston. The Lafittes had no desire for anyone to disrupt their profitable smuggling and privateering operations. They were enjoying an entrepreneurial delight: rich sea lanes effectively policed by neither Spanish nor American authority. Indeed, Pierre Lafitte had been receiving a regular stipend from the Spanish authorities. He earned it that January by informing them that Charles Lallemand and Humbert had left behind in New Orleans six hundred men and that their recruiters were seeking six thousand more. Lafitte warned his client-victims that these intruders planned to conquer Texas and, after Texas, Mexico; and he offered to betray his comrade-in-arms of 1815 while Humbert traveled to Galveston on one of his ships. Humbert reached his destination only because, in a fit of economy, the Spanish captain-general chose this moment to cut off subventions to the Lafittes. Having no motive for perfidy, they blandly completed their contract with the French, while Henri Lallemand, still in New Orleans, issued the usual pacific proclamations. One credulous Spanish official reported to his superiors that Lafitte's charges were unfair; the French proposed to move up the Trinity River from Galveston to make an "establishment which . . . is purely agricultural."

On March 10, 1818, the French moved from Galveston Island to the mainland on twenty-four boats provided by Lafitte. A sudden Caribbean storm struck them just offshore, scattering the flotilla and drowning a Colonel Vorster. They tried again by land and ran out of food; when they tried foraging, a hundred were poisoned by a plant they called "desert lettuce."

Then things improved: a passing Indian supplied another plant as an antidote, and they found their way to what appeared to be a fertile place, about eighteen miles upstream, bounded by woods and elevated above the flood plain of the Trinity, "a river as wide as the Seine, but full of alligators." By May, they had built a large fort supported by two smaller ones, mounting a total of eight cannon. These, they later testified, were "for protection against the Indians," though Lallemand told Lafitte something else: the guns were "a barrier against the ambitious designs of the United States."

Daily drills and strict discipline were ordained. There were evening recitals of Napoleonic glories. Lallemand issued a proclamation professing friendship and respect for the Indians but a willingness to fight anyone else who interfered with the colony he called Le Champ d'Asile. "We are armed, as the necessity of our position requires us to be, and as men in similar situations have always been," but, of course, "the colony will be purely agricultural and commercial in principle." Such a prospect required considerable faith; Le Champ d'Asile was situated upon a desert, no better fitted for the cultivation of the vine or the olive (well, perhaps olives might have grown, had anyone tried them) than the canebrakes along the Tombigbee.

Meanwhile, having marooned their rivals, the Lafittes proceeded to enter new negotiations with the wary Spaniards. The pirates' reputation was not good. As a local Spanish diplomat reminded his superior in Madrid, Jean Lafitte had subsidized Lallemand with plunder "from the robberies he has committed against ships of Spanish commerce . . . [he had] aided and sustained with supplies and other assistance the adventurers who, without his favor and aid, would surely have perished from hunger and misery in the deserts of Texas." Now Lafitte was asking to be paid to capture his own protégés.

The Spaniards, previously unwilling to buy off the French at low expense, now mobilized their creaking imperial apparatus. Four warships were ordered from Cuba. The viceroy of Mexico sent an army, though its commander protested that reaching Le Champ d'Asile would require traversing "two hundred leagues" of roadless Texas and "seven swollen rivers." An outpost with a hundred men was established twenty-five leagues from San Antonio, to delay any French attack against the city.

When the news of that force reached Lallemand, it was coupled with an earlier warning from Lafitte that the Spaniards were mustering their forces. Rumor swelled the Spanish array to "twelve hundred cavalry and several pieces of ordnance . . . rapidly nearing us." After their misadventure with desert lettuce, the French had "only one hundred men capable of bearing arms." Lallemand issued a Napoleonic proclamation that they intended "to repulse the foe, to fight them gallantly or die like Frenchmen."

The Spaniards sat trembling in their advance post. The French took this to mean that "the Spanish general, whether prevented by secret orders from taking the initiative or determined to draw a cordon round us . . . waited until disease and discouragement should undermine our not very formidable body."

Both sides waited. "No help came from Europe or the United States and we could not fight an enemy determined not to attack," the French chronicler tells us.

So, with great dignity, the heroes of Waterloo retired from the scene, "in the finest order, without confusion, without accident, save only the death of a single negro." At the end of July 1818, they abandoned their little forts and retreated, ignominiously, to Galveston.

A bedraggled Spanish army, actually smaller in numbers than the combined forces of Lafitte, Lallemand, and Humbert, arrived before Galveston in October. Emissaries were sent under a white flag to meet with the "officials" of the port. The Spanish negotiators needed only an hour or two to see that little additional push would be required to induce Lafitte to rid himself of his French visitors. However comfortable Galveston might have been for a small number of pirates living off the food they captured, it was too infertile to support the appetites of a battalion of healthy soldiers. The push was provided by a hurricane that flooded the island, and the survivors of Le Champ d'Asile retired to New Orleans, taking with them their remaining guns and ammunition.

Lallemand's abandoned forts were destroyed by the Spaniards in the last days of October; on November 12, the correspondent of the *Kentucky Reporter* wrote from New Orleans that "the establishment at Galveztown [as it then was called] has at length broken up, and General Humbert and his suite has arrived in this city; they were found on board of a vessel which has arrived in the river as a prize to the U. States ketch Surprise."

Arundinaria

The heroes of Waterloo did not have a dignified career in America. At each step they took, a foothold fell away under their weight. Then they had to pull their bulky forms out of the mire, brush off their uniforms, and start again. At each fall, they left coins upon the ground, enriching others, impoverishing themselves. They struggled on, reduced in dignity as well as in purse.

It did not help very much that the celebrated novelist M. Balzac turned them into bathetic characters in his trilogy of novels, *Les Célibataires,* presenting them as dupes, packed off to America through the machinations of the Liberal party in France: the resurgent mercantile bourgoisie wanted them out of the way when the next turn of political fortune came. It might be easier to dispose of sluggardly Bourbons than trim, tough Bonapartists. In fact, large sums were gathered in France to support them; paeans of praise for the wanderers appeared

General Count Charles Lefebvre-Desnouettes; copy of a portrait by Breslant

in the columns of a Bonapartist journal, *La Minèrve;* and a song about their adventures was very popular in the cafés of Paris.

But in Alabama those songs could not be heard. The settlers at Demopolis and Aigleville left behind after the collapse of the Texas expedition were now beyond the reach of Atlantic culture, transported into another, stranger world. The only road leading toward them, from settled places like Philadelphia, was the Natchez Trace, and it was two hundred miles distant, only a path that serpentined through boundless forests. The ornithologist Alexander Wilson said that between the Trace and White Bluff were the most horrid swamps he had ever seen, and depicted the French town sites as a prodigious growth of canes and high woods, which together shut out almost the whole light of day.

Arundinaria gigantia, the giant cousin of bamboo, as thick as an ankle, might have become good cattle feed; but the French had little experience with brush hooks and were not herdsmen. They did not know what was known to later settlers, whose hogs rooted out its understory and whose cattle consumed windrows laid down by expert cane cutters. Those among them who took seriously the establishment of an agricultural colony, and there were some, tried as best they could to grow plants familiar to them, olive trees and Bordeaux grapes. They did not know that thirty miles to the north a little rise in the land was festooned with a profusion of native grapes, which they might have grown to replace the Bordeaux strains that died of winter kill.

The leader of the peaceful group of Aigleville settlers was General Count Charles Lefebvre-Desnouettes, rich and very well connected. His brother was a brother-in-law of Napoleon's banker, Jacques Laffitte, and he was on friendly terms with Stephen Girard. "Vivacious and active, handsome in person and graceful in carriage and one of the best riders of his age," he was received as the beau ideal of the Napoleonic hero in Baltimore and Philadelphia. One of Napoleon's favorite aides, he had been at his side at Marengo (the battle after which the Alabama county was named). He had been awarded the Legion of Honor for gallantry at Austerlitz. He had ridden with Napoleon in his carriage on the retreat from Moscow, commanded a division against the British in Spain, and been made a count of the empire during the Hundred Days. When Napoleon took his leave from his weeping officers at Fontainebleau, after Waterloo, he embraced Lefebvre-Desnouettes for them all.

There are many stories of him after he settled in Alabama:

Item: Desnouettes dining "in a humble cottage in the wilds" with General Juan Rico, a fierce partisan leader of the Spanish republicans who had fought against the French led by Desnouettes at the bloody siege of Saragossa.

Item: Desnouettes drilling the local militia at the request of its leader, Manassey Finney, who called him "Captain DeSnouts."

Item: A report from his friend George S. Gaines that on their first meeting, Gaines happened to have, in his log headquarters, "some good, old French brandy and excellent claret." Later, he received return hospitality from the general, with food "cooked in the French style" (buttery, perhaps) and "very good" wine. It was on this visit to Desnouettes's five-hundred-acre estate that Gaines described his "mansion," a log house, and his "sanctuary," another cabin. There a ten-foot cedar slab was surmounted by a bronze statue of the emperor, and surrounded by flags and weapons taken in battle. A splendid figure, handsome and generous, Lefebvre-Desnouettes spent his personal fortune of twenty-five thousand dollars developing his lands on the Tombigbee. Finally dispirited, he responded to a request from Napoleon by booking passage for Europe upon a vessel bearing the fateful name *Albion*. It sank, with all aboard, off the coast of Ireland, not far from the bay where Humbert and Grouchy had attempted a landing back in '98.

The life of the Napoleonic exiles in Alabama has been sweetened and softened in sentimental stories of the Vine and Olive Colony, tales of "women dressed in ball gowns and satin slippers . . . dropping corn or wading in the mud to milk the cows," of officers who "ploughed, ditched and cleared land while dressed in their richest uniforms"; of ladies "in court dresses" and "gentlemen in gold braid tending their crops," who at the end of the day summoned their energy to "dance the night away" at balls, always "gay," always "brave." But their evenings were more full of mosquitoes than of the "gay grace and culture for which Paris is so famous."

As William Lee pointed out to Thomas Jefferson, these peasants or artisans had risen fast and far in Napoleon's revolution. It must have been hard to descend again so rapidly. Booty taken from Madrid to Moscow had for a decade

Aigleville: imaginative scenes painted in Paris, c. 1818, by an unknown artist;
from "The French at Aigleville or Foundation of the State," a five-panel mural

or so provided tables "loaded with luxuries." Now they were living like the
peasants of Russia or of Spain.

There were problems of title (land title, that is), one false start after another,
and then a slow, sad decline. The most energetic of the soldiers kept leaving
to do what they did best, to fight somewhere else. Among those who remained
in the colony for a while was the local ferryman, Colonel Nicolas Raoul. His
wife had been a marquise of the tinsel court of Joachim Murat and Caroline
Bonaparte at Naples. Finally, Raoul left Alabama and died fighting in Mexico.

Charles Lallemand only went as far as New Orleans with his brother. He
remained there to compose a celebrated treatise on artillery, then settled down
as a neighbor to Joseph Bonaparte in Bordentown and made the transition to
commerce by a marriage to a niece of the great Girard. The wedding must have
been full of nostalgia; it was attended by Joseph Bonaparte, Grouchy, Vandamme, and a battalion of other eminent exponents of the Lost Cause.

Henri Lallemand recovered from his indignities in Texas and went to war

*that hangs in the French Room of the State History Museum located in the
Archives Building in Montgomery, Alabama*

against the royal government of Spain in Spain itself. He was captured, was
released to live in poverty in Belgium, and returned to the United States to
run a school (probably subsidized by his merchant brother and, by extension,
Girard). Finally, he returned to Europe, recommended by Joseph Bonaparte to
Lafayette, and capped his career as military commander of Corsica. Grouchy
also returned to France, purged of his sins by the benediction of Neuville.

The Dean of the Academy

Not long after the collapse of the Champ d'Asile expedition, Joseph Lakanal
arrived in New Orleans from Kentucky. He had held himself aloof from pirates
and merchants and disasters all the while. He remained upon his own perch on
the Ohio, venturing neither to Demopolis nor to Aigleville nor to Le Champ
d'Asile, until after the fuss was over. In the fall of 1820, he was drawn to New

Orleans, the center of French culture in America, by an invitation to become president of the College of New Orleans and thus to resume his role as an educational reformer.

Out of the wilderness at last. In the great port city, some of his former associates among the insurrectionists were still picking fights in saloons; some enrolled in new schemes to "liberate" Mexico. Lakanal averted his gaze. He was no longer "look-out"; now he was *professeur*. Soon the College of New Orleans had a curriculum like the one Lakanal had sponsored for the Ecoles Centrales a generation earlier.

Supported by lotteries and revenues from "licensed gambling houses" (a term of some elasticity in New Orleans), Lakanal combined the liberal arts with technical education, assembling teachers skilled in the specific agricultural and navigational technologies useful in the waterlogged lowlands of the Mississippi delta.*

Grace King, a historian of New Orleans, tells us that though Lakanal was "known . . . for brilliant intellect and indomitable energy" he was also known as "a ci-devant priest [he had studied for the priesthood, like Talleyrand and Sieyès] and regicide." She goes on to tell us that "the good mothers of New Orleans" thought he represented, therefore, "the anti-Christ . . . the foul fiend would have been considered as good a director of youth."

Latrobe's *Journal* would have given Lakanal plenty of warning: he described in disgust the disarray of the diocese and the refusal of the local populace to accede to the authority of the bishop. That embattled Sulpician Louis-Guil-laume-Valentin Du Bourg (later known as William Dubourg) had arrived in Baltimore from Saint-Domingue in 1794 and had caught the eye of Latrobe's client for the Baltimore Cathedral, the first Roman Catholic bishop in America, John Carroll, who appointed him president of Georgetown College, then moved him on to Saint Mary's College (where Maximilian Godefroy was sheltered; see p. 296). In 1812, Carroll dispatched Dubourg to straighten things out in New Orleans, a task that was beyond even the capacity of this very able man; finally, he abandoned the fight and repaired upriver to Saint Louis, where he built another cathedral, and ultimately returned to France.

Though the college eventually closed as a result of the embarrassments Lakanal gave Dubourg, the regicide preferred to give a patriotic rather than a religious reason for the brevity of his tenure as president (he was forced out in 1823, the year his old ally Humbert died quietly down the street from the college). He said he had refused to relinquish his French citizenship; this affront was "demanded in order to preserve the Presidency of the University of Louisiana" (not quite the right institution; it was the College of New Orleans, but no matter).

---

*The experiments in education in the French style at Union College were under way at the same time.

From New Orleans, Lakanal went to the Vine and Olive Colony in Alabama, probably for the first time. Finding it too squalid, and perhaps too evocative of memories, he went to Mobile, where he remained until 1837.

In the 1820s, while France was being governed by the restored Bourbons, Lakanal had no hope of returning home. That "most inept . . . most cowardly . . . most odious government that ever weighed upon a civilized people" had good reason to rejoice in his indignities and those of his surviving co-conspirators. The minister of France in Washington received bulletins from Mobile from time to time reporting that General Clausel was there, neighbor to Lakanal, sowing and reaping "his homely crops of cabbage and potatoes as contentedly as the humblest peasant." The man with whom William Lee had conspired to break Napoleon out of the British trap, and who failed by only an hour, "brought his produce to town to dispose of it, forgetful of his former station," his brief glory under Bonaparte. (Ultimately, Clausel was recalled by Louis Philippe, now king of France, to become governor of Algeria. One colony for another: now the Algerians produced the cabbages.)

Lakanal hoped for something as good. In 1830 he tried to prevail upon the indulgent Lafayette—the "rascal" of 1792—to intercede for him with Louis Philippe. There is therefore some symmetry in our tale provided by a final salute, at Mobile, to Lafayette and Louis Philippe by "S. Chaudron, Esq." It was Chaudron who had proclaimed Lakanal the "look-out" of the "Napoleonic Confederation" in 1817. Now they were both in the produce business in Mobile. Chaudron delivered an ode "in French, written for the occasion," and Lakanal offered the toast to "the illustrious citizen of the two worlds, General Lafayette." Finally, Lakanal returned to France, where he was welcomed as the "Dean" of the Academy; he died there in 1845.

In his old age, did he visit the rue du Mont-Blanc? Did he experience, from time to time, the taut, disciplined geometry of the Maison Lakanal, with its sphere impaled upon a larger arc, its hexagons and octagons, its repeated coves and mini-spheres echoing each other? That precise, assured, urbane crystal of order was as well-proportioned and harmonious as was the cosmos in his theories. What a solace to the old man that architectural purity must have been, that balance and clarity, that confident rationality! If only he did not hear, in the back of his mind, the cries of an assembly lusting for blood and the *chunk* of the guillotine. Or was it his fate to hear instead the roosters who mocked him at dawn when, at last, he came to Aigleville? If he closed his eyes, amid the bustle of traffic, in the last days of the last of the Bourbon kings of France, Louis Philippe, could he imagine himself back in Alabama, hearing tales of Napoleonic heroism told by tattered veterans, watching the firelight pick up glints of mica among the pebbles on the dirt floor, while outside, the wind sang its ancient song in the giant cane?

39

THE PRESIDENT, THE BANKER,
AND THE GENERAL

The New Orleans correspondent of the *Kentucky Reporter*— the same newspaper that reported the return of Humbert and his men on the U.S. ketch *Surprise*— admitted ignorance of the "real cause" of Lallemand's abandonment of Galveston and Le Champ d'Asile. "Some say that an agent of the American government ordered them away . . ."

What was the nature of that government? What were its objectives? Who might that agent be, and what was his mission?

The so-called Era of Good Feeling, over which President James Monroe presided, was a time of exhaustion among political factions, of nervous irritability without the release of passion. No great causes stirred the blood, and there seemed to be no further necessities for heroic action. The founding fathers had done their majestic work, and little was left to be done by their sons. Such times often bring forth a stolid sort of statesmanship. This may explain why so boring a man as Monroe came to be President of the United States.

Tranquility, said John Quincy Adams of the President he so overshadowed intellectually, was "the pole star of his policy." A later observer, George Dangerfield, commented that Monroe, "more than has any other President before or after, seemed particularly able to personify tranquility."

Dangerfield took Monroe's measure with more precision than any other historian: Monroe was a man who "attained his eminence at some cost to his principles; but . . . who responded more to influences than to principles, and his principles had, in any case, been swallowed up in the grand notion of service." The difficulty of such a life was—and is—that "one may forget, in the ardours and delights of service, the ends to which that service is dedicated." This does not mean that Monroe was venal—not at all: "His motives were not lofty, but they were pure."

Like James Buchanan and Warren Harding, he looked presidential, the last of the Virginia dynasty, tall, and severe of mien. He carried himself stiffly, without the aristocratic assurance of Washington, Jefferson, or Madison. As if to give himself a gravity he felt he otherwise lacked, he wore, into the age of Jackson, the pantaloons and white-topped boots of the revolutionary years.

He was not universally admired. Aaron Burr called him "naturally dull . . . extremely illiterate; indecisive to a degree that would be incredible to one who did not know him; pusillanimous, and of course hypocritical." His soul, "turned inside out," might, as Jefferson asserted, disclose "no blemish," but it is difficult to discern what else might have been found upon its seamless surface. As Dangerfield put it, "he personified an interim." Carl Schurz, a man of unrelenting solemnity himself, thought Monroe "one of those respectable mediocrities in high public station, with whom people are apt to sympathize . . . especially when . . . attacked and humiliated by persons of greatly superior ability."

John Quincy Adams felt quite comfortable in harness with this stately, ambitious, impressive anachronism, since he, himself, drew forth from others less affection than admiration. While serving as secretary of state under Monroe, he could make the correct calculation that such a President would not be "too hard an act to follow" (to borrow a term from an art form beyond the range of Adams's interests), and another that the Virginia dynasty had sufficient energy left to carry its adopted son, Adams, into the White House. On his own, he would have been shriveled in the flame of Henry Clay's charm.

Adams was quite capable of that ironic penchant for obviously excessive praise that his grandson Henry raised to the level of literary art. In an effulgence of hyperbole, he compared Monroe to Augustus Caesar and drew our attention to his career as patron of architecture: "There behold him . . . strengthening his country . . . soothing her dissensions, and conciliating her acerbities . . . he was entitled to say, like Augustus Caesar of his imperial city, that he had found her built of brick and left her constructed of marble."

Monroe was important to architectural history, though not exactly in the same way as Augustus Caesar: he dismissed the greatest architectural genius ever to work for the federal government, Benjamin Henry Latrobe. On the other hand, he had the good sense to permit Adams and others to talk him into replacing Latrobe with Charles Bulfinch. And, as we will observe, Monroe received from a committee (contrary to all the laws of artistic probability) a design for his own house that ranks as one of the best of the neoclassical age in America.

As scholars have worked their way in recent years through archives in Spain, Mexico, and the United States, they have found cause to reconsider the apparently tranquil mien of James Monroe and to raise the possibility that Adams failed to understand the subtlety—one might even say "duplicity"—of his master. Alliances with pirates and soldiers of fortune might not commend themselves to Adamses but might appear unavoidable to a slave-owning planter, whose life was established upon violence, express or implied. So Monroe did not trouble to inform his secretary of state of everything he had in mind.

Virginian Diplomacy

From the results of a cabinet meeting in June 1818, we can infer something more than we have learned so far about what Monroe meant by "tranquility." That meeting deputized George Graham to take ship for Galveston.

Graham was an old Virginia friend of Monroe's, a nephew of George Mason of Gunston Hall, and husband of the widow of Mason's son and principal heir. He graduated from King's College, now Columbia University, in 1792, studied law, and made as grand a tour of Europe as was possible in the revolutionary years. He returned to Virginia in 1796, to practice law and land management. He and his brothers inherited more than four hundred thousand acres of land, much of it in Kentucky, requiring a youth spent in surveying, provision of slaves, and dexterous sale of property to eager settlers, including French émigrés. He served as a good Jeffersonian in the Virginia legislature, voted as a Jeffersonian elector for the Virginia dynasty after 1796, and was acting secretary of war in Madison's government for more than a year, after the disgrace of General Armstrong in 1814 and the burning of Washington.*

Graham administered the War Department until John C. Calhoun assumed it in 1817, six months into Monroe's term. Graham then was asked by Monroe to head the Washington branch of the Bank of the United States. He was accounted with possessing considerable skill in piecing together complex transactions—among them the provision of bank credit to James Madison, who (like Jefferson before him and Monroe after) entered retirement deeply in debt and died insolvent.

The Subhistorical Level

George Graham, like his brother, John, like Gideon Granger and William Lee, carried out the work of the Virginia dynasty at what might be called the "subhistorical level." They have not been celebrated, but without them the lives of the Presidents would have turned in quite different ways. So would the history of American architecture.

We can make George Graham a little more tangible by setting him among the buildings and builders he knew and we may know as well. It is a pity none of them were French, for he played a crucial part in Franco-American geopolitics.

---

*James Monroe was given the War Department in addition to that of State; Graham ran the former for him.

His youth was spent in the architecturally sophisticated household of the Masons, at Gunston Hall. Gunston is the work of William Buckland, who came as a servant indentured in architecture to the Masons and went on to become a prosperous architect and furniture maker. George Graham came down each morning at Gunston into Buckland's diminutive "Palladian Room" through the wonderful hall just reconstructed (1988). It is a tiny classical basilica, reduced from Lord Burlington's Assembly Room at York. In his maturity Graham lived at another Mason house nearby, Lexington, and he died at Highwood, the Maryland mansion of another kinsman, Robert Young Brent, son of Robert Brent of Brentwood, Latrobe's greatest residential commission in Washington city.

Interlude for George Graham, a Thimble, a Roan, Two Ladies, and Two Smugglers

There is a rumor that Dr. Thornton designed a house for Graham, but I have been unable, so far, to find its documentary proof. Graham had his choice of architects, for he lived on the edge of the Kalorama House circle, enjoying associations with Latrobe through the Brents, whose ancestral roots were intertwined with the Grahams', and with George Hadfield, through the Masons.*

As George Graham set out from Lexington for Galveston, on June 6, 1818, he passed Huntley and Arlington, whose occupants could have observed a "stout, a large-boned man, five feet eight, in his 49th year, and weighing about 170 pounds," riding a "gaunt-looking, raw-boned red-sorrel McKinney rone [*sic*]." His attendant, a twenty-year-old Black, had a better-looking mount, an "uncommonly fine looking cream colored horse with flowing white main [*sic*]

---

*Hadfield designed the Branch Bank of the United States in Washington, Graham was its president. Hadfield had many Mason connections. It is probable that one of his earliest "moonlighting" commissions, while superintendent at the Capitol, in 1796 or 1797, was to provide the design for the handsome house called Analostan, which only recently made way for a park on what is now Roosevelt Island. The owner was Graham's brother-in-law through marriage, and lifelong friend, General John Mason. Mason came to Washington in 1796 (like Hadfield, Latrobe, and Graham) from a mercantile career in Bordeaux and commenced building his house on the island in the Potomac between the Custis estate at Arlington, where Hadfield created his most famous house, and the future site of Kalorama.

Thomson F. Mason, Graham's nephew through marriage, built a villa called Huntley, on a ridge south of Alexandria. It still exists, though in a dilapidated state, causing arguments among architectural historians. Constructed between 1817 and 1826, it bears the stamp of a professional. That professional could have been Hadfield (who was at work on Arlington, for Mason's friend and wool-growing colleague George Washington Parke Custis) or Latrobe (who was then constructing Brentwood for the Brents).

and tail." This splendid animal carried, behind the Black, a large black-leather portmanteau.

Graham's portly frame and portmanteau were sorely tried by a journey across the Cumberland Road to the Ohio, where rest was possible at Graham's Station, in the midst of his holdings in Lewis County, near Lakanal's perch.* He probably went by boat down the Ohio and Mississippi to Natchez, and then, astride the McKinney roan, cross-country to the Texas shore, where he was conveyed by two smugglers across a bayou to Galveston.

George Graham left to his family a packet of "Galveston Papers." (They can be found at Gunston Hall.) They bring us closer to him, to his son, and to his contemporaries. Like William Lee, he loved anecdotes.

Item: With regard to his employer, John Quincy Adams. An infirmity of Adams's hand forced him to wear a silver shield attached to a tube to hold his pen. Jonathan Russell, one of his co-commissioners in arranging the Treaty of Ghent ending the War of 1812, saw fit to publish an attack on Adams. John Randolph of Roanoke exclaimed, when he read the article: "Ugh! What a fool! why Adams'll put on his thimble and sew him up in a minute."

Item: With regard to his horse. The roan had come to him from a friend, who said he "didn't know whether it would stand the journey or not, but . . . if this horse didn't . . . there wasn't another horse in the world that could."

It was one of the first horses on the East Coast carrying a brand, so it may actually have made the trip from Texas once before. Graham's son reported that having ridden the horse on the dry-land portions of the Galveston trip and back again, "Mr. Graham continued to ride him over the Blue Ridge and Allegheny Mountains each successive year to visit his farm . . . in . . . Kentucky, until the spring of 1823."

In 1823, Graham rented the farm and shipped his eighty slaves to Louisiana as part of his contribution to a partnership in Rapides Parish. He gave the roan to "an old lady-friend and neighbor there, Mrs. Bullock." In 1835, the roan and Mrs. Bullock were spotted again: a Graham cousin "met old Mrs. Bullock and her daughter, the two weighing 420 pounds, mounted on the old horse, going to meeting . . . and as I met them, I pledge you my word I couldn't see a particle of the horse except his face and ears, he was so completely covered up by the two old ladies and their clothes."

Item: With regard to the smugglers. These two "boatmen" who transported Graham to Galveston became respectable farmers near the plantation of a Graham descendant in Rapides Parish. When interviewed, they admitted that on that shore near Galveston they had not been easy of conscience when they first saw "a fine looking gentleman . . . in knee britches and fur-top boots, an a holster of pistols before him." One of them, Thomson by name, went on: "I was skeered! My heart went down into the bottom of my boots, for I

---

*I have not been able to find a deed for Graham to Lakanal. Pity.

thought he must shoorly be a custom house officer . . . but as soon as he spoke to us pilitely, an told us who he wus, an that he wanted us to take him roun' to Galveston to see the Frinch Gineral there . . . an I never wus so relieved in my life."

Galveston Revisited

Graham arrived in Galveston with formal instructions from the cabinet and, it is likely, informal orders from Monroe. There were rumors in Washington that the Bonapartists were getting out of hand; instead of adding to the annoyances of Spain, they might turn upon the Americans and raise a slave insurrection, which would be especially formidable when officered by White professional soldiers.*

This possibility was important to Monroe, a slave owner, like Jefferson and Andrew Jackson. They feared domestic disruption by unemployed French soldiers, but they feared other things more. The policy of these planters toward the southern frontiers of the United States is chiefly explained by their shared apprehension that the Spanish colonies could serve as a base for a Negro insurrection, a Negro-Indian alliance, or an effort to abolish slavery in the South. Though the abolitionist fervor of the early years of the French Revolution had abated, it might now be coupled to imperial ambitions and financed by Mexican silver.

Adams and Monroe were urged by Joshua Child, their Texas correspondent, to take steps to have the United States "take possession of their own soil [Texas, to begin with], and people it with a population that can defend it; thereby placing an inviolable barrier between slavery and the temptations of Mexico."

Adams warned Graham that things were complicated. Lallemand, the "wild and extravagant character contemplating the invasion of Mexico," had been "entertained by some individuals among the French refugees," Joseph Bonaparte and Girard. In addition, "more than one indication has reached us that the expedition was ultimately concerted [with the Spanish government] . . . This concert [is one] in which it can scarcely be doubted that the object of each party was to dupe the other."

---

*There was some basis for such fears. The French exiles had been ready before to put themselves at the head of armies of Blacks and mixed bloods. The British had defeated the Franco-American attack on Savannah, in 1778, with Negro assistance, and the tables were turned when the French led Negro troops from Saint-Domingue (including Henri Christophe) into battle against the British at Charleston. Victor Hugues, commanding an army of liberated slaves, led the French forces in the outer islands in 1793–95 and defeated the British as badly as did Toussaint, on Haiti, a little later. The British responded by raising their own West Indian regiments, led by White officers. The commissioners sent by Paris to Saint-Domingue in 1794 tried to place themselves at the head of forces led by Toussaint.

Adams told Graham to seek out Lallemand, Humbert, and their troops in Texas or New Orleans or wherever they were. He was to warn the "whole body" that they were on American territory and "express the surprise" of the United States that the French had "taken possession" of land within American "territorial limits." The claim of the United States to Texas was exceedingly dubious; the Spaniards were unlikely to acquiesce in it, so Graham was not to expose himself "to be captured by any Spanish military force." He was ordered to probe into the sources of "future aid and support" of Lallemand and Humbert, especially to determine how much was "supplied by Joseph Bonaparte, or by Mr. Onis, or by both."* And, finally, Graham could submit a bill "for your reasonable expenses, together with a compensation of five dollars a day."

Graham's first conversation with Lallemand in Galveston went rockily. Lallemand was confused. Then he professed delight that "the United States had determined to assert their claim to the province." Perhaps, he suggested, there might be an alliance between the Americans and his group of Frenchmen against Spain; indeed, he was about to declare war on his own hook, in retaliation for the attack upon him threatened from San Antonio. (One imagines the blood rising in his face as he set down a drink.) In fact, he said, he had planned all along to attack San Antonio.

Graham next had a chat with Lafitte. Recalling the glorious alliance between the pirates and Andrew Jackson in 1815, Lafitte declared his unwavering fidelity to the United States and his aversion to his recent Spanish paymasters.

There is some dispute as to what happened next. Harris Gaylord Warren, a historian reviewing the evidence in the 1930s, concluded that, instead of contenting himself with the remonstrance required by his official instructions, Graham proposed an alliance of the pirates, the heroes of Waterloo, and a group of volunteers he himself would raise in New Orleans. This dazzling array, based in Galveston, would seize "all the points on the coast to the Rio del Norte [the Rio Grande]." Graham's descendant George Mason Graham Stafford found such a thought disagreeable, and disagreed. He "read that article a number of times in an effort to discover some semblance of fact which would justify the author in his conclusions, but his search has been in vain." How could a "man of George Graham's character and reputation—a person trusted by men of Madison and Monroe's stamp . . . tell Lafitte one thing and report something entirely different to his chief [Adams]"?†

But there is considerable reason to wonder who, in this instance, was his chief. The Graham brothers were not accustomed to confidential service to

---

*One is struck by the similarity between this mission and that of John Graham in 1806 (see p. 333).

†Warren's thesis is stated at length in his book, cited above, and Stafford's in his on p. 74.

Adams; their duty was to the Virginians. John Graham had served Thomas Jefferson well in dealing with Aaron Burr, a Yankee of views unfriendly toward slavery (let us recall that in 1784 Burr proposed abolition) and a lamentable softness toward the insurrection of Toussaint Louverture. Graham had been sent on a confidential mission to Buenos Aires by Monroe to sniff out the intentions of the interlocked piracies and patriotisms of the Caribbean, for the Argentine revolutionaries were not so committed to slavery as the Brazilian. At the time, Simón Bolívar of Venezuela was being outfitted by the Blacks on Saint-Domingue.

George and John Graham had good cause to know that Monroe, without consulting Adams, had sustained Jefferson's bellicose policy toward the Spanish possessions. The planters were always seeking expansion room for their slave system.

Stanley Faye, who combed the archives in the 1930s, concluded that Monroe encouraged in secret both the Lafittes and Dr. Thornton's friend "Sir" Gregor MacGregor, "Brigadier of the Armies of the United Provinces of New Granada and Venezuela and General-in-chief of the Armies of the Two Floridas, commissioned by the Supreme Dictators of Mexico and South America." Adams, according to Faye, had to wait many months to learn "or at least to acknowledge to himself, how dearly President Monroe could cherish privateersmen who served his policy of provocation and oblique aggression against Spain."

There is no indication that Monroe was displeased by the traffic between MacGregor at Amelia Island and the Lafittes at Galveston. A regular exchange developed between the two offshore bases, each of which chartered "privateersmen" to capture Spanish vessels and supply the expeditions poking at the shorelines of Mexico and Columbia. Commodore Louis Aury, commanding one flotilla, was considerably annoyed when, in December 1817, Commodore Henley of the U.S.S. *John Adams* restored propriety by suggesting he cease and desist. Aury was even more baffled by the more vigorous action of Andrew Jackson, defender of legality, who found his way across the Spanish possessions, uninvited, to approach Amelia by land. He and MacGregor had underrated the lobbying power of their competitors among the dealers in contraband slaves in Savannah and Charleston.

Equally baffled was Dr. Thornton, as we have noted; Thornton thought he understood the intentions of the Virginia dynasty. Henry Clay had no difficulty in following the proceedings. Clay twitted the President from the floor of the Congress, asking why Monroe made such a grand gesture of liberating Amelia from privateersmen his own administration had put there, and why was he so shy of dealing likewise with the equally predatory Lafittes?

Though Monroe responded with formal messages to Congress deploring the dreadful Lafittes, the *John Adams* received no orders to execute its originally stated intention to proceed to Galveston. John Quincy Adams was left wondering. Faye suggests that George Graham, the "messenger to Galveston[,] had knowledge of what, although displeasing to the secretary of state, might not displease the secretary's chief."

Graham reported to Adams that he had asked the pirates to withdraw from Galveston, stop smuggling and privateering against American vessels, and that Lafitte, like a good boy, had agreed. Spanish Intelligence, with its own agents in Galveston, told quite a different story, however: "Graham promised Lallemand, No. 13 [Lafitte], and all the company the greatest advantages, both political and pecuniary . . . all sorts of assistance in order that they should extend their occupancy . . . as far as the Rio Grande, but on condition that after occupying these regions they should put them at the disposal of the United States . . . [and let them be] . . . made an integral part of the Union. General Lallemand has agreed to everything."

One little detail required some diplomacy: Graham suggested that Lafitte depart at his leisure and reposition himself on the other side of the sea lanes leading to Vera Cruz, on an island off the Yucatán. He would be furnished, as inducement, a charter by the revolutionary government at Buenos Aires, whose representitive in Baltimore, David Cortes De Forest, was known to feel that "the possession of a port on the Gulf of Mexico would be of great importance . . . as a means of annoyance to Spain." Adams had expressed the view that De Forest and his friends, the privateering Baltimore Associates (not Denis Smith's "adventurers"; see p. 274n.), were as shameless as Lafitte's friends, the New Orleans Associates, but Graham wrote him a pleasant letter introducing Lafitte's representative, George Garrot.

Graham's formal report admitted that with regard to "General Lallemand and Mr. Lafitte . . . it has been promised to these gentlemen that in the event of the occupation of this place by troops of the United States previous to their departure, they and the persons under their respective commands, shall be respected in their persons and property." And this pregnant note was sent by Graham to Adams: "I expect to see General Jackson on my way through Nashville to Kentucky. This letter will probably be handed to you by General Lallemand in person, whom I . . . recommend to your particular attentions and civilities . . ."

Adams, somewhat baffled, wrote in his memoirs that Graham "is for taking possession of Galveston, and so am I." He disapproved, he confided, of Graham's having suggested to Lafitte that the pirate sanitize himself by securing "a commission from Buenos Ayres," thereby acquiring the status of a leader of South American rebels against Spain. "I should not be surprised if we were to hear more of this hereafter, and not in a very pleasant manner. But it is all of Graham's own head . . ." Adams reported the whole matter to Monroe, who displayed unexpected pleasure, writing back that they had the Spanish government over a barrel. It was time, said Monroe, to tell Onis that "as he had rejected" their proposal for a peaceful settlement of the Texas border, "the United States must no longer be bound by it."

Graham and Lallemand left Galveston, presumably to drum up further support. Not long after they departed, nature intervened to terminate the possibility of a Napoleonic, piratic, and "volunteer" invasion of Mexico. A hurricane hit, drowning Galveston Island under four feet of gulf water, ruining the town, and destroying what little food was still left ashore. Lafitte's was one of only six houses left standing;* his fleet, "which had been riding at anchor in the bay, was scattered and lost." The cisterns were flooded with saltwater; thirst and hunger oppressed those marooned on the sandy islet, pirates and Napoleonic heroes alike.

A chance benefit of piracy relieved them. A Spanish schooner was captured in the nick of time, carrying water and a little food. Most of the French were happy to accept Lafitte's courtly invitation that they take this ship with them to New Orleans.

The great expedition was over.†

Humbert, the least romantic of men, might have spent in reminiscence some of the long, idle weeks and months to which history now consigned him. Perhaps he reflected upon the contrast between the humiliating denouement of the Champ d'Asile expedition in 1818 and his triumphs in Ireland in 1798, the "year of the French." At Castlebar, he had won an invader's victory over the British, one of the few since 1066; even after he surrendered to overwhelming numbers at Ballinamuck, courtesies were showered upon him by the British in Dublin; he had stood upon a hotel balcony in a blue coat with gold epaulets, gilt buttons, and a white cashmere waistcoat, acknowledging the admiration of the crowd.

In New Orleans, he was shabby, middle-aged, and ignored, except for an occasional arrest in piracy cases. He was dismissed as "indecorous and vagrant, forever in the taverns, surrounded by the rabble and attending them in their crimes." He may have felt, in New Orleans, that he was back almost at the beginning, before the revolution had offered a new career for a dealer in rabbit skins for the glove makers of Lyons . . . too much taken by drink, a man without profession and without pride, a prisoner . . . a bad joke.

---

*It had been well designed; see p. 399.

†I would be pleased to be able to assert with confidence what happened to Jean Lafitte. His brother Pierre wound up as a planter near Fort Jessup in Louisiana, on a plantation given him by Jean. Jean may or may not have taken up Graham's offer to help him "attach his destinies to the Government of British America . . . in any place or island which he may take from the Spaniards on the coast of the Spanish Main." He was rumored to have been killed by his own men after leaving Galveston. Other rumors said he set himself up again in business off Belize (British Honduras) and died of fever. Still others set him up as a businessman near Saint Louis.

40

JOEL BARLOW

In the 1790s, the French Revolution grew old and corrupt. Profiteers fed upon and decomposed the compost of both the old and the new regimes. They flowered in the moral putrefaction of the Directory. Speculators wagered fortunes upon each successive test of strength among the new politicians: the children of flux—swollen tradesmen, freebooting former clergymen, and subalterns grown overnight into generals.

The distended sanctions of the Church were ruptured, the shroud of aristocratic good behavior cast aside; the last, frayed continuities to the past seemed to have been severed by the guillotine.

Unsteady times grew more erratic; governments rose and fell, and so did government securities. A man who was quick to buy and shrewd to sell could make a fortune speculating in the instruments of government finance.

In France, privileged information was not one of the "privileges" abolished by the revolution. American statesmen, sent to Paris to reach accommodations with the corrupt and shifting sets of politicians, were not prepared for what they found. New World simplicities provided them with inadequate preparation for such a scene. Napoleon, in a rare moment of compassion—or, perhaps, patronizing as usual—said to one of them: "You have come to a very corrupt world."

Thomas Jefferson and John Adams, John Marshall and James Monroe, Nicholas Biddle and Christopher Gore were not naive men; but each, in sequence, was shocked by what he found in France. Several of them wondered how it was that their friend Joel Barlow was thriving there.*

Barlow was as witty as John Maynard Keynes, a later literary gentleman with a genius for currency speculation. Keynes, however, having access both to the telephone and to a remarkable intuition for markets, rejoiced in his successes, reporting them to the world, while Barlow had every reason to be shy of publicity in the presence of Robespierre, who decreed a death sentence for speculation.† We have therefore no record of Barlow's feats.

---

*Like Barlow, his friends Thomas Paine and Robert Fulton were well equipped for French adventures. They were like those birds that fly amid clouds of ash above a volcano, happiest amid explosions. Robert Fulton went to Paris precisely because it was unsettled; only when old orders are ruptured are sponsors likely to be found for radical new inventions.

†It is reasonable to think that Robespierre's downfall was as much a result of his restraint of profiteering as of his lack of restraint in the use of the guillotine.

Joel Barlow;
plaster bust by Jean Antoine Houdon

Success in speculation requires a peculiar talent cooled by disinterest: neither Keynes nor Barlow was addicted to it; both were entranced by something else. In Barlow's case that something was poetry; in Keynes's it was theoretical economics.

Barlow was a Connecticut lawyer, associate in education with Timothy Dwight (the poetic and opinionated president of Yale), and classmate of Noah Webster (the lexicographer). During one of his summer vacations from Yale, he fought the British on Long Island, but not long enough to delay his graduation in 1779. He wrote Webster (in words Mark Twain's Connecticut Yankee might have used) that they were both "without friends and without fortune to push us into public notice" (the key word is "push"). They were "men standing on their own merit," lucky to live in turbulent times, "a fine theater for the display of merit of every kind." Barlow became not only a lawyer but also the editor of the *American Mercury,* a journal he distributed from his book-and-stationery shop. He also wrote a new version of the Psalms. Toward the end of the War of Independence, he sallied forth as a chaplain, presumably on his strength as a psalmodist.

All the while—for eight years, in fact—he was at work upon his five-thousand-line *Columbiad,* an eight-volume epic that was, strange to say, immensely popular. So was he. Handsome, witty, and unfailingly cheerful, "in the midst of his busyness he . . . found time to be in love once or twice." Finally, he wooed and won, as the "rhyming lover," that splendid woman with whom William Lee fell a little in love. When he was away upon his embassies, he sent her messages by friends—a Mrs. Blackden, for example, who was instructed to "tell her I have not slept with anybody but God since I slept with her." Just before he died, he wrote her from Vilna: "I love my darling, first-begotten, long beloved wife better & more and harder & softer & longer & stronger than all the Poles between the north pole and the south pole."

Assignatic Interlude

Joel Barlow made a little money touting the Scioto Colony (see p. 91) and only a little more with *The Columbiad,* * but he had other occasions:

It is one of the wonders of Barlow's wonderful age that the revolutionary governments of France did not repudiate the enormous debts of the Bourbons. Everyone was aware that royalist corruption had piled illegitimate debt upon legitimate, that trade and colonial wars had been made even more costly by inefficiency and huge profits to courtiers and favorites. It was apparent that the management of public debt was inept.†

The governments in France in the 1790s, even that of the Jacobins, were governments of bourgeois revolution. To the bourgeoisie, the law of contract was mightier than the divine right of kings. Debts were honored, in a way. The French government wished to broaden the class of persons who would have "a stake in society," especially in the continuity of power. So they issued paper money called "assignats," originally much like mortgage notes, which could be redeemed, slowly, in land itself, but not in precious metals, like gold. As lands were sold, notes would be redeemed. Not all at once: land values must be held reasonably steady.‡

---

*If one were to capitalize the "opportunity lost cost" of the years expended in poetic composition, his rate of return was hardly worth the efforts of a man so fitted for currency speculation. (Aside from Alfred, Lord Tennyson, it is difficult to find a poet who waxed rich on poetry before the advent of Rod McKuen.)

†In 1792, some accounting was possible; and thirty-six of fifty-six "receivers general" of taxes were in default—and in very large amounts. Fifty treasurers and comptrollers had gone bankrupt, taking state funds down with them. Until 1800, there was no central bank in France to administer an orderly issuance of debt, though Holland, Sweden, England, Denmark, Prussia, and even Russia had such institutions.

‡It was the moderate colleagues of Brissot who commenced this practice, though one of them, Mirabeau, rightly required that, like a mortgage, the assignats be limited to face amounts of no more than half the underlying value in land. He told France the assignats were based upon "the most secure of all possessions, the soil on which we tread." In 1789, the king, though a prisoner, still added some creditworthiness. But Mirabeau's was the first of a succession of pledges to patriotic investors that depreciated faster than the flimsy paper upon which they were written. The decree that issued the first wave of these notes intoned a solemn promise of a debt limit—which was subsequently exceeded

Crown lands were sold, together with the properties of the Church and of émigré aristocrats. More and more assignats were printed. What was once, from the point of view of government finance, a sound idea (called by one historian "burying the past in the lands of the church") became a process of burying the patriotism of the credulous middle class in opportunities for the rich, especially those rich in special information.

Revolutionary budgets were even greater than royal ones, and so were revolutionary deficits in 1790–91. Annual expenditure exceeded tax receipts by more than a multiple of two. Assignats fell by two-thirds from face value by the end of the year, diminishing, of course, the real burden of debt, transferring it from government to those who had patriotically purchased the government's obligations. (This device has become a standard means of "taxation" in our own time.) It required, in revolutionary France, a remedy also familiar to us: issuance of still more paper, depreciating still more rapidly, driving commodity prices up. While assignats went to 10 percent of their face value, speculators noted that those issued by the royal government held their value better than those of the subsequent regimes; royal paper oscillated against republican paper, as prospects for a restoration came and went, with news of battles on the frontier.

After Robespierre went to the scaffold, his death penalty for speculation was abolished; so was all control of monetary policy. Governments hostile to France counterfeited assignats, using their printing presses to add to the confusion. By 1796, the assignats were valueless.

The Directory tried a new brand of paper—land warrants, which dropped a fifth of their face value on the date of issue, and at the end of six months were redeemed in coin at one-seventieth of face. Then, mirabile dictu, the credit of France began rapidly to improve; Napoleon's victories restored the faith of investors in the efficacy of a revolution—of sorts.

In this context, we come upon a remarkable juxtaposition in the *Dictionary of American Biography:* "Among the French [Barlow] was exceedingly popular. He . . . judiciously invested in French government consols . . . by 1794 he was a rich man." He had made a well-advised bet on a Corsican adventurer.

Joel Barlow was not sentimental about markets, but he was about politics. Like his friend and protégé Tom Paine, he offered himself for election as a deputy to the Convention, from the Savoy. The Savoyards chose one of their own, but Barlow digested the experience of the campaign and made of it a famous essay on the differing qualities of French and American life.*

---

by a multiple of 4,500. (Mirabeau is quoted in the entry for "assignats" in the *Encyclopaedia Britannica,* eleventh edition, by Professor Irwin of Trinity College, Dublin.)

*Paine took his politics at a higher pitch and antagonized Robespierre. He barely escaped the guillotine and languished in a Jacobin prison while Barlow saw through to publication Paine's essay *The Age of Reason.*

Kalorama, after remodeling by Benjamin Henry Latrobe

Consistent, good-humored tolerance of the vagaries of revolutionary French governments, and consistent capacity to profit from their rise and fall, made Barlow seem unreliable or worse to the Federalist party in the United States. During the quasi war between 1796 and 1801, John Adams thought Barlow "a more worthless fellow" than Paine, and George Washington was deeply suspicious of his motives. But Adams and Washington took seriously Barlow's mediation in bringing the quasi war to an end. Having sifted Barlow's letters "for suspicion of any ill design," Adams concluded that Barlow was right in declaring that the French Directory "is . . . sincerely desirous of restoring [good] relations . . . on terms honorable and advantageous to both parties," and began, at the end of 1798, to move toward an accommodation. That accommodation was completed over the prostrate form of Toussaint Louverture in 1801.

Barlow remained abroad until 1805, acting as the representative of the American government in such hot spots as Algiers. He helped Robert Fulton, the painter and inventor, to finance experiments with a steamboat. Not content with subsidizing Paine, he translated Brissot and Volney. Finally, he was ready, as his wife put it, "to go home and be respectable." In his account of Barlow's life, Van Wyck Brooks told of the means to proclaim respectability: he "went straight to Washington and established himself at 'Kalorama,'—a Greek variation of the too common 'Bellevue,'—on a slope overlooking Rock Creek with a house and an orchard, and Latrobe rebuilt the house . . ."

Latrobe went to work on a cubical mass so large that its construction had bankrupted Major Gustavus Scott and then proved too ambitious for William Augustine Washington, one of the general's nephews. Barlow had relieved Washington of the burden, at one of his characteristic discounts, in 1807. Latrobe fitted out the interior with marble fireplaces and added a long wing containing an orangerie, to remind Mrs. Barlow of Paris. And the old brick house was given a coating of smooth, neoclassical stucco, with one of those recessed coves above the portico that can be associated either with Mlle Guimard's bodice or with Pavilion IX at the University of Virginia (see p. 439).

The Latrobes lived just down the hill, and Lydia Latrobe declared her neighbor Mrs. Barlow to be "our particular friend." In the parlor at Kalorama occurred the meeting between Latrobe and "Toot" Fulton that brought them into a steamboat partnership with Edward Livingston. It did none of them much good. Fulton could leave nothing in repose; he dammed Rock Creek to form a testing place for one of his vessels, this time a submarine. But generally, life at Kalorama was tranquil. The gardens blossomed, the fruit in the orangeries prospered, and so did Barlow.

William Lee wrote his wife in 1810: "Barlow is elegantly situated here with an ample fortune . . . Barlow's house is a little palace . . . much in the style of Barrell's* at Charlestown. He keeps four horses, three carriages (one of which is devoted to me) and eight servants."

The warmth radiating from Kalorama can still be felt after nearly two centuries. The Lees, Madisons, Thomas Jefferson, and the Latrobes were among many who basked in the Barlows' friendship. Another important association for the future was established when George Bomford, of the Corps of Engineers, married Barlow's sister Clara. This was the Colonel Bomford who would resolve two dilemmas for James Monroe (see pp. 397, 419).

The Second Louisiana Purchase

Then it all came apart. In 1811, war with England appeared more and more likely. Barlow's friends the French were at the same time continuing their attacks upon ships under the United States flag, provoking some Americans to press for war upon both the superpowers. It was time for the old French hands to be pressed back into service. President Madison took Jefferson's recommendation that Barlow become the minister to Napoleonic France. The Latrobes saw him off at Annapolis, while Lee returned to his consulship in Bordeaux. Because of his extraordinary status at the court of Napoleon, he soon became Barlow's deputy in Paris as well.

*The published version of this letter says "Barrett's," but the original document in the Library of Congress refers to a real and important house by Bulfinch: the Barrell house.

Together, they hatched a plan as fantastic as that of David Parish and involving many of the same characters. Spain was in insurrection against the regime of King Joseph. Joseph's revenues were being siphoned off to feed Napoleon's other interests. Though Parish and Vincent Nolte had presented Joseph a bonanza in silver, very little remained in Spain. By 1810, Joseph felt poor again and wrote ruefully to his wife, "I am satisfied with having twice tried the experiment of being a king; I do not wish to continue it."

When Barlow arrived in Paris, Joseph's emissary there suggested that the reluctant king would be happy to dispose of Spanish Florida and her claim to a vast, undefined territory along the western boundaries of the Louisiana Purchase. The price to be paid Joseph personally would be a mere bagatelle: "six million acres out of the two hundred millions he gives you." Since it would take some time to sell off the six million acres so reserved, Joseph's "great distress for money for his domestic expenses" (as Barlow put it to President Madison) could be alleviated by a "loan" of one million dollars, secured by a mortgage on the acreage.

Barlow thought this as good a bargain as the original Louisiana Purchase, but Madison was uncomfortable; like Jefferson before him, he doubted the American public would approve a second transaction by which the Bonaparte family sold off Spanish territory for the purpose of funding their own comfort or campaigns.

The emperor was gathering the immense forces he was about to lead across Europe toward Russia; the ghost of Alexander the Great was calling him once

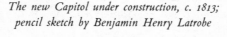

The new Capitol under construction, c. 1813;
pencil sketch by Benjamin Henry Latrobe

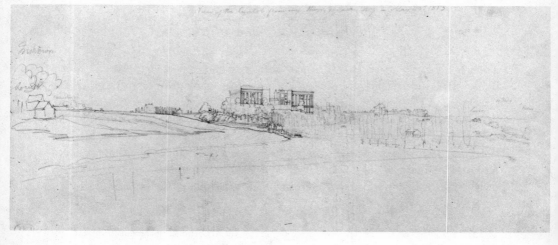

more toward Asia. As the Polish winds presaged the bitter winter of 1812, Barlow set out to meet the emperor at Vilna. When he reached Lithuania, Napoleon's Russian adventure was not going well. An American minister could wait; America was too far away to engage his attention. After Napoleon's defeat at Beresina, Barlow joined the retreat toward the west. The Polish cold, he said, reminded him of Connecticut.

On the way from Vilna to Cracow, traveling in a sleigh, he caught an inflammation of the lungs. In the little village of Zarnowiec, Joel Barlow died on Christmas Eve, 1812.

41

NEW ORLEANS

After Joel Barlow's death in 1812, the Kalorama circle drew more closely together, to protect the widow who had so often protected them. In 1816, she thought of marrying again. Latrobe told William Lee that Mrs. Barlow was considering "a col. Bull, an old grey headed batchelor; a jovial, sensible and good-hearted Soul, much beloved by his companions . . . [whose] only fault is, that like other bulls, he has very notoriously . . . lived on the common. But now he is going to be a good boy . . . They will probably spend Christmas in Joel's old mansion."

Lee was an intimate of both the outgoing President and the incoming; for Madison he had served as a special agent, and Monroe was a devoted friend from days in Paris. Latrobe used Lee as an emissary to both. He asked him to explain to Madison why the rebuilding of the Capitol, after its burning by the British, was going so slowly: "Our excellent[,] intelligent, and honest President . . . understands every thing better than Architecture."

A year later Monroe was in office, and, said Latrobe, "misled by I don't know who, expected the Capitol to be finished; of course he was disappointed, and in his first emotions would have ordered my dismissal, had he not been prevented by some disinterested friends."

Those friends included Lee, General John Mason of Analostan, George Graham's cousin, and Colonel George Bomford, Barlow's brother-in-law. Bomford was a friend of the Latrobe family, described by B. H. Latrobe's son John as "a small man of very soldierly carriage . . . devoted to his gun, and as a boy I used to be his companion in his shooting excursions into the 'slashes,' a tract of low and marshy ground" in what is now known as Foggy Bottom, below the Latrobe and Barlow houses.

Latrobe took a more adult view of Bomford, writing to Lee that the colonel "of the Engineers, a man of Science and worth," was "on the high road to preferment." With such personages taking his part, Latrobe survived awhile in the scuffles over control of the construction of the Capitol. But, as Latrobe wrote to John Trumbull, he still had "to do with a Commissioner and a very angry President."

The "Commissioner" was Colonel Samuel Lane, an infirm and irritable military hero, described by Latrobe's partisan and biographer, Talbot Hamlin, long afterward, as "a presumptuous little popinjay, who covered his ignorance with display of more than military arrogance."

It was probably Lee who proposed to Monroe the appointment of a commission, to include, alongside two trusted friends of Latrobe, Mason and Bomford, a confidant of the President's, Graham. The circle was small: it had been Graham and Mason who accompanied James and Dolley Madison in their retreat out of Washington during the British attack in 1814; Lee was an intimate of Madison's and an employee of George Graham, with whom he had served, as well, in the Champ d'Asile affair. Understanding Presidents, as they did, and each other, they ought to be able to work something out not too ruffling to Monroe's composure. All that was required, it seemed, was for a way to be found to keep Latrobe cool and Lane's pretensions under control.

On October 22, 1817, Lee wrote Charles Bulfinch that the commission had begun its work by recommending that Latrobe should be kept on the job.

Latrobe welcomed oversight by "these . . . honorable and good Men." But nothing could avert the ultimate tragedy. Latrobe was struck from an unexpected quarter: his beloved son, Henry, died of yellow fever in New Orleans.

His behavior became as distraught as William Tell Poussin had reported: he did indeed "spread poison with his actions."*

He was much provoked and insulted by Lane. Lane delighted in goading him, and he was already stretched to the breaking point by his financial disasters. At a meeting with Lane the architect lost his temper. He pulled the Commissioner up by the collar and, as Mrs. Latrobe reported years later, exclaimed: "Were you not a cripple I would shake you to atoms, you contemptible wretch! Am I to be dictated to by you?" Lane promptly went off to demand a new architect from James Monroe. Latrobe asserted that the Capitol's delay was not his fault but, on the advice of Bomford and Lee, acceded to the inevitable. He wrote Monroe on November 20, 1817, "I fear I have been the cause of much vexation while my only object has been to accomplish your wishes," and submitted his resignation.

---

*Poussin (1794–1876) succeeded Louis de Mun and a M. de Surville as a draftsman in Latrobe's atelier. His letter is among the Girard papers at Girard College.

A Fresh Start

In December 1817, Benjamin Henry Latrobe was forced into bankruptcy. After another year of fruitless struggle to right himself in Baltimore, he embarked for New Orleans, to complete a waterworks project left unfinished by his son.

The ship that bore him was named *Clio,* for the muse of history, a merciful muse who broods over New Orleans as a presence felt there more than in any other American city, and already memorialized in the Crescent City before Latrobe arrived. A street had been named for her by the most classically trained of the participants in George Graham's discussions at Galveston,* Bartholomy Lafon.

At the time, Lafon did not appear to George Graham to be a principal in those negotiations; little attention was accorded to his presence. Graham did not mention him, and he appears in other accounts only as "an unemployed architect from New Orleans," a mere onlooker. But the Lafittes did not operate a "sheltered workshop" for artists down on their luck. Lafon was not there casually, nor for the first time. He was a quiet but potent force on the island, called by the Lafittes its "civil governor" and judge of their picturesque "admiralty court."

Not long before, Jean Lafitte had written his brother in New Orleans that "our friend Lafon . . . is with me . . . reestablishing a new government in Galveston." (Their first "establishment" had been disrupted by a spasm of conscientiousness on the part of the customs authorities: a raid on Galveston that bagged Lafon, with geopolitical consequences to be addressed shortly.)

The capitol of this government was the Red House, Lafitte's residence, in which Graham conferred with Lallemand, Humbert, and the Lafittes. It served as Lafon's "courthouse" and governor's "palace"—more his than Lafitte's, since it had been built to his design and through his exertions.

The construction records of the Red House are among the most intriguing in architectural history, coming as they do from the reports of Spanish secret agents and the records of American authorities trying to intercept stolen goods. In September 1817, the agents told their superiors that "No. 13," Lafitte, was buying and loading aboard Lafon's schooner, the *Carmelita,* clothing and arms for forty soldiers, food, drink, and wood for building. The Americans reported shortly afterward that the *Carmelita* had "cleared . . . for Laguna, but really bound for Galveston, with provisions and materials for erecting buildings." A few months later, visitors were received by the Baratarians in what they reported to be Lafon's "pretty good house."

---

*These negotiations were going on as Latrobe was gathering himself for his journey to New Orleans.

Latrobe never had an opportunity to pass that judgment, for he did not reach Galveston before his career and that of Lafon ended—at the same time, and from the same cause, after those careers had been braided together in several curious ways.

Lafon the Architect

Lafon was born in 1769, in Villepinte, near Carcassonne, in southwest France, At some time, somewhere, he was trained in engineering, cartography, architecture, and enough metallurgy so that after a decade in New Orleans he could set himself up with Lafitte as an iron master and surveyor by 1790. He also built a large market for the beef trade, many residences, and provided the drainage projects for which Latrobe's waterworks were intended, a few years later, to provide the complement: Lafon's canals would have drawn out the swamp water, but the city's wells remained polluted and saline, and Latrobe's sophisticated steam-driven system was needed to provide fresh water.

To the extent that a few remaining drawings offer samples of Lafon's architectural style, it was similar to that of his contemporaries Pierre Pharoux, Stephen Hallet, and Joseph Mangin. In the subtropical climate of the Mississippi delta, however, he was forced to adapt stiff French classicism to more relaxed, damp, and torpid conditions. For example, the Bernini design for the Louvre, having shaped French thinking for a century after it was drawn in 1665 and having been carried over into Hallet's winning elevation for the United States Capitol, had another iteration in Lafon's plan for the New Orleans Public Baths. He inserted a platform under Bernini's Louvre to keep it from the delta damp, and enlarged its windows to receive any trifling breeze that might wander in from the gulf.

Like Pierre Pharoux, Bartholomy Lafon is known to us not so much from the scraps of documents and descriptions remaining in the literary record but from traces upon the landscape. Athens, New York, is still haunted by the ghost of Speranza, and the streets of Tivoli can still be traced in the dust; similarly, the upper and lower Garden Districts of New Orleans and the speculative village of Donaldsonville still carry the outlines of the grand designs of Bartholomy Lafon.

Unlike the prosaic Athenians on the Hudson, the citizens of New Orleans have retained the classical spirit of the age of Pharoux and Lafon, and many streets still retain the names Lafon bestowed upon them: Pritania Street is still there (a pritanium was a sanctuary to Hestia, goddess of the hearth, and Lafon apparently thought her to be the correct aegis for a great classical school, to be called a "Prytanium"). The Garden Districts were laid out by a pirate with a tenderness for female spirits; other streets of his invention still carry New Orleanians from home to work and back again—Terpsichore, Calliope, Eu-

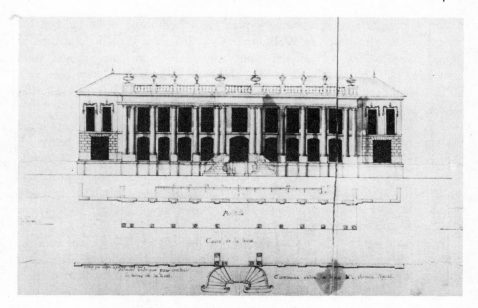

Elevation for the façade of the public baths in New Orleans,
by Bartholomy Lafon

terpe, Clio, and the other muses, together with all the Dryades. Along the canals
are byways named for the naiads (water nymphs). There are, as well, the gods,
Tritons and heroes we might expect of a man of Lafon's education.

Breaking away from the garrison-town plan of the Vieux Carré, Lafon
invented a system of canals, fountains, basins, and avenues to give grandeur to
a reclaimed but still pestilential swamp while it was drying out. New Orleans
has not followed all of Lafon's plans. The Prytanium and its neighboring
Coliseum were not built, nor was the amusement park that was to occupy a
circular island (another Tivoli) now deprived of its moat and called Lee Circle,
but William Donaldson of Donaldsonville, Louisiana, did so, and left us an
intact example of Lafon's planning skill.

Seen from the air, Donaldsonville, the lower Garden District, Esperanza-
Athens, and Tivoli—like the central portion of the District of Columbia—
might be French towns created, let us say, in Egypt or India, had Napoleon's
eastern schemes been successful.

Engineering of One Sort or Another

Lafon had demonstrated his competence as an engineer considerably earlier. In
1805, while Latrobe was still in charge of the construction of Federal buildings,

Lafon submitted a bold, openwork plan for a lighthouse to be built at the mouth of the Mississippi. In Washington City, Jefferson, Gallatin, and Latrobe found it too radical and offered suggestions for a more conventional, solid structure. This cooled things considerably: New Orleans has always been avid in its insistence upon local control of government contracts; and the local offer having been rejected, nothing happened.

Five years later, Latrobe himself entered into a contract to design and build his waterworks for New Orleans, to be powered by steam. He had begun his American engineering career with a similar venture in Philadelphia; and while New Orleans was notoriously the Macao of America, corrupt, plaguish, and violent, it was also a place where an old career might be revitalized or a new one begun. So Latrobe sent his son, Henry, at the age of eighteen, to represent the family and to oversee the work.

It might have been his great opportunity, for engineers were scarce in the booming West. The Latrobes were almost alone in understanding steam loco-motion; this was the age of the steamboat, and New Orleans was to become a steamboat city like Cincinnati and Saint Louis. The timing turned out to be good in another respect: Andrew Jackson was on the horizon, and the chief occasion for introduction to all the useful and potentially powerful of the West was to be service under Old Hickory in the Battle of New Orleans in January 1815.

The younger Latrobe did not have to await the occasion, for soon after he arrived in New Orleans, someone, perhaps Edward Livingston, introduced him to Lafon. By the spring of 1812, Lafon had arrived in Washington with letters of introduction of sufficient warmth to induce the Latrobes to take him in as a house guest.

Though small and "stocky" in stature, he was great in reputation. Latrobe wrote Henry that he had anticipated Lafon to be difficult, artistic, and proud, "riding a high hoof, full of himself," as L'Enfant had been. Instead, he was pleased to find him, "unassuming" and "agreeable," full of "politeness and fondness . . . not obtrusive." The perfect house guest—and, it turned out, the perfect mentor as well.

Lafon had just completed a term as alderman from the Third District of New Orleans, had published two city directories and a handsome city map. But certain problems had emerged in the titles to his own properties; he told Latrobe he was seeking to straighten them out with the authorities in Washington. Long conversations ensued between these two cosmopolitans of French extraction, in which Latrobe learned of the seamy side of doing business in New Orleans: "Anything . . . may be done by intrigue." What better intriguers might be found than Lafon and James Wilkinson, now briefly back in Washington, still tolerated, and indeed about to be promoted, by the Jeffersonians, again to reassume command in New Orleans. With a little pecuniary encouragement,

Lafon's Mississippi lighthouse

these two might "remove the opposition of the Mayor [to the cost of the waterworks] and render a majority [of the council] efficient."

This is not a phase in Latrobe's career when he was too fastidious about his partners. He was desperate, and had no illusions about either Lafon or Wilkinson, though he obviously approved of the former more than of the latter. Wilkinson, he said, was "an extraordinary man . . . [of] excessive indiscretion, and constant dependence on the best theft he can make for money to supply his profuse expenditures." Lafon did not seem to him a rogue but, instead, a delightfully wry guide to a corrupt society who had survived by knowing such things as that "the Secretary of the Mayor [w]as a very influential rascal whom the gift of a share will bribe to anything. Use this," he wrote to his son, "as you can and think proper."

Lafon took up residence with the Latrobes in April and was still there on June 10. His host reported that he had more esoteric work to do than mere land transactions. Maritime matters were much on his mind, and he was "engaged on a work on the hieroglyphical science of the ancients . . . he is a kind of enthusiast in that business, and will be laughed at, otherwise he is no fool."

A fool he was not; and only a fool would have been entirely candid about his reasons for being in Washington. His library may already have included the work on codes and code breaking its later inventory disclosed; the hieroglyphs he was after in Washington were probably not those of the ancients. It is more likely that he was there to get help with the Spanish maritime codes, possibly from the insurrectionary Dr. Thornton. He and the Lafittes had been capturing coded documents—the Spanish Intelligence service liked ciphers—and he had sound, businesslike reasons to wish to crack those ciphers. He was by this time a double agent of Spain and Barataria; it was important to him and his partners in piracy to check on the movements of the treasure ships of their employer-victims—while their employer-victims were checking on them. No one seems to have trusted anyone else.

Two months later, back in Louisiana, Lafon was observed by two fishermen as he directed the unloading of swag from Spanish ships into flat-bottomed bayou boats, probably taken from the Spanish brig *Nueva Dolores*. Shortly thereafter he was busy replenishing the provisions of a fleet of privateers at Barataria Pass, including the three vessels that had earlier surrounded the *Nueva Dolores* off the Louisiana shore and relieved her of twenty thousand pesos in silver.

This was during the summer of 1812; Latrobe was still writing Lafon in December as "my dear friend," and a full year later responded with pleasure to Lafon's request that he support Lafon's effort to secure a contract to sell oak timbers to the United States Navy—to supply pirate-hunting vessels for the gulf. Latrobe not only endorsed his character but also his note, "to any amount."

How much did Latrobe know about Lafon? About as much as he had known about Burr, that earlier Baratarian, perhaps (see p. 340). Probably not such details as that his "dear friend" and endorsee had acquired the *Carmelita* or other assets "forcibly and piratically," but almost certainly that he enjoyed a special relationship with the Lafittes.

Lafon and the Defense of New Orleans

Which brings us back to the confluence of the careers of the younger Latrobe, Lafon, Lafitte, Vincent Nolte, Humbert, and the gentry of New Orleans, led by the distinguished Edward Livingston, under the command of Andrew Jackson. We saw Livingston first as a potential client for Pierre Pharoux, and as mayor of New York. He was forced out of that post and into a new career in the West when an embarrassing defalcation occurred in the city accounts (though probably not to his benefit). In New Orleans, he became leader of the New Orleans Adventurers and counsel to pirates.

It required all of his wiles to extricate Lafon from jail after the customs raid on Galveston in 1814. It is said that his ultimate argument was that the British were about to attack the city and that Andrew Jackson, hastening down from the North to assume command,* would need all the experienced engineers he could find.

From 1812 onward, Lafon had been anticipating a seaborne enemy attack upon New Orleans and proposing the military architecture required to meet it. He had served as an officer in the militia since 1806 and as chief deputy surveyor for Orleans Parish. During the last days of Burr's "conspiracy," he had been asked by Wilkinson to proceed "briskly" to improve the city's fortifications both to the south, against the general's friends the Spaniards, and to the north, against his friend Aaron Burr.

For reasons lost to history, or at least to this historian, Wilkinson does not seem to have considered selling out to the British after 1806. Soon after he returned to his command in 1812,† he named Lafon "Chief Engineer of the department under my command," explaining to the secretary of war that he had found "the ablest one" to be had. This was one of Wilkinson's infrequent statements of fact, his last one of significance before he departed for the North.

Lafon made "a map of the vicinity of New Orleans" and commenced construction of parapets of mud, brick and heavy timbers far more useful than those "cotton-bale defenses" so beloved of mythologists of the Battle of New Orleans. He knew the terrain; the lines of the defenses of the city were laid out by him in advance of the battle. Jackson found especially useful, at a crucial

---

*Wilkinson had relinquished that command somewhat earlier, in order to accept a promotion to major general and an invitation from Livingston's kinsman Secretary of War John Armstrong to seek glory on the northern front.

†Wilkinson was probably bearing with him from Washington to New Orleans some stock certificates provided by Latrobe as douceurs to municipal officials, at the same time Lafon returned from his mysterious researches into "hieroglyphics" in Washington, which may have been of some interest for Wilkinson, as well.

moment, the moated embankments of Lafon's partially completed Fort Saint Philip.

The man known among the pirates of Barataria as "the engineer Lafon" not only drew up "plans for . . . [Jackson's] new batteries" but during the heat of the battle was "on hand to spur on . . . fortifications . . . [and] building a strong earthwork."

Two Engineers

Accounts of the battle refer repeatedly to both "Jackson's engineer Lafon" and "his engineer Latour." The two, who knew each other well, collaborated patriotically as they had piratically and had as much to do with Jackson's victory as the pirate artillerists, gamblers, planters, Black marksmen, Kentucky riflemen, economists, cotton speculators, and, of course, veterans of wars against the Indians who made up his army. Through the other Creole engineer at Jackson's side during the battle, Arsène Latour, Lafon and the younger Latrobe may actually have had a hand in bringing the Greek revival to New Orleans in 1816.*

By then, Lafon himself was no longer doing overt business in New Orleans.

---

*While we cannot pause too long to pursue a mere possibility, there is a Burrite connection here that may lead other researchers toward the discovery of relationships among Burr, Wilkinson, Lafon, and the Baratarian pirates. Back in 1809, Governor William C. C. Claiborne of Louisiana, barely out of his twenties but with a decade of dutiful service to Thomas Jefferson behind him, had seen fit to rehabilitate Jean Baptiste Thierry, the editor and publisher of the *Louisiana Courier*. Claiborne assured President James Madison that Thierry should be awarded a patronage contract to publish the Laws of Congress because, though some people attributed to him "some very improper and inflammatory publications" during the Burr "conspiracy," "three or four years hence . . . his politics have now assumed a very different aspect, and the paper which he conducts is the only one of eight in this city that gives support to the government." (Quoted by Samuel Wilson, Jr., in *Saturday's States*, a pamphlet printed in New Orleans, April 11, 1953.)

Claiborne, a Virginian by birth, succeeded Andrew Jackson as congressman from Tennessee when he was only twenty-one, though the Constitution of the United States stipulates that members of the House of Representatives shall be at least twenty-five years of age. Claiborne served so loyally in that body that Jefferson appointed him first to be governor of Mississippi, when he was twenty-six, and governor of Louisiana Territory, when he was twenty-eight. "He rendered distinguished service in moderating . . . factional troubles . . . and in controlling the negroes," we are told by Claude Bowers, always alert to such achievements (*Jefferson in Power*, p. 226).

Five years thereafter, Henry Latrobe and, it is generally supposed, Latour designed a house for Thierry that remains at 721 Governor Nichols Street in the French Quarter. Its Doric arcade (which re-emerged during a re-remodeling in the 1950s by Samuel Wilson, Jr., and Richard Koch) marks it as the oldest surviving Greek-revival building in the city (Samuel Wilson, Jr., in a letter to the author, December 15, 1986).

The forms of the arches, Mr. Wilson has suggested, indicate that the younger Latrobe had kept an appreciative eye upon the work of his father's pupil, Robert Mills, for the jail of Burlington, New Jersey. And this innocent little house reminds us that rehabilitation was always possible in New Orleans, a tolerant city, where people could pass from sedition of piracy to architecture and back again with grace.

"View from the window of my Chamber at Tremoulet's hotel, New Orleans,"
by Benjamin Henry Latrobe

His sojourn in jail was not much of a blemish; but his creditors had deprived
him of some of his residences and speculative holdings, and he may have found
it expedient to ply the architectural trade through Latour. The Red House
shows he had not abandoned the practice altogether, nor had his mapmaking
skill diminished: a beautiful map of Galveston Bay from his hand is to be found
in the Mexican archives; a copy of it probably served the Lallemand expedition.

Latrobe in New Orleans

Latrobe arrived at the mouth of the Mississippi in January 1819, not long after
Lallemand and Humbert reappeared from Le Champ d'Asile. He found quarters
in the boardinghouse of M. Tremoulet, who apologized for the "noise and
gabble" of a "vociferous" group of Frenchmen in the dining room, "some of
Lallemand's ruined party from the Trinity River." Though they were obstrep-
erous, Latrobe reported to his wife, "they are all decent men and two or three
of them seem to be . . . of excellent information, and polished manners." There
is a good chance that among them was Lafon, and that he advised Latrobe to

Latrobe's watercolor sketches of New Orleans "Market Folks"

move to another boardinghouse, with a larger apartment: the Rivière House, which he had designed.

Tremoulet's boarders sorted themselves out, the polished from the unpolished. In that cosmopolitan port, in 1819, it was as easy to put together a dinner party of good talk in many languages as it had been in New York in 1795. Lafon, for example, spoke German, French, and English and read both Latin and Hebrew.

There is no mention of Lafon in Latrobe's letters to his wife written from New Orleans. Bad luck in other friendships may have made him chary of telling her that he was consorting with pirates; he was more prone to acknowledge his acquaintance with respectable economists like Erich Bollmann and Vincent Nolte. But when he spoke of men "of polished manners," he could easily have referred to Lafon. The recently "civil" governor of Galveston was not alone in demonstrating that civility was valued among the pirates of Barataria. Jean Lafitte, the "Corsair," had been celebrated as such by Lord Byron and proudly gave to his friends copies of Byron's adulatory remarks. Lafon owned a library that included the works of Homer, Vignola, and Volney and the Koran. Alchemy, exorcism, and astronomy shared space on his shelves with politics, architecture, travel, philosophy, poetry, chemistry, meteorology and physics, together with codes and a set of law books.

By 1819, however, Mrs. Latrobe may have heard of too much of Lafon's second occupation. Lafon was no longer the architect-engineer but an unusually prosperous pirate.

Vincent Nolte to the Rescue

Henry Latrobe had died of yellow fever in 1817; two years later Vincent Nolte escorted his friend's father on a melancholy sketching expedition of the battle-field. Latrobe wrote his wife lengthy descriptions of that visit, omitting all reference to Lafon, though he would have been—and may have been—an even better guide. He also wrote her of another expedition, without mentioning their house guest of 1812; he went down the Mississippi to its mouth to offer suggestions for the completion of the lighthouse for which they had both produced designs. (This was also the project that embroiled Louis de Mun in the conspiracy of Erich Bollmann and Aaron Burr.)

Latrobe had little time for exploration, however. He set himself to build a municipal waterworks to be owned by private entrepreneurs, including himself. This was how he intended to recoup his fortunes. And he executed several other commissions, including improvements to the cathedral, a bank building (botched in execution after his death),* and a house—perhaps even two—for Nolte.

On March 20, 1819, Latrobe wrote his wife that he was "designing a house for Mr. Nolte . . . Mr. Nolte continues as kind or kinder than ever, and . . . sends for me if I miss his breakfast or dinner table." When Nolte had to return to Europe, Latrobe told Lydia that he would be lonely without his friend. "If I were to stay much after him, I should feel his loss greatly." They had the same quirky interests in words: Latrobe composed a little demonstration of French rhymed endings, drawn from the poems of Chamfort, which he dedicated to "Mon ami Nolte." And their antipathies were the same: both, for example, loathed Edward Livingston.

In his memoirs, Nolte says he moved into his "newly-built residence" in 1821. In his letters to his wife, Latrobe left a set of clues to where that house might be found, something tangible to record this friendship. Early in 1819, when he was living in Tremoulet's boardinghouse, he said that Nolte lived "about two squares" away. That affirms the notation in the New Orleans city directory of 1822 of a house at the northwest corner of Royal and Toulouse

---

*This is the building whose façade was like that built by Pierre Bauduy for the Bank of Delaware in 1816.

streets as the residence of "Vincent Nolte, merchant"; it is about the right distance.

Nolte acquired the property on May 6, 1818. We know he was in residence there well into the summer of 1821, a year after Latrobe's death. Remodelings have mitered the corner of the house to provide entrance to a store featuring Scandinavian crockery and glassware, and earlier mutilations destroyed the arcades of the ground floor; but the shape is there: a neoclassical design floating a stuccoed upper floor with little pilasters at the corners above the arcade. (The glassware is warehoused in the double parlor, which has Latrobian incised mantels of gray marble and shreds of ornament along the cornice.)*

There is a little courtyard at the side, known in 1988 as the Court of Two Lions, and containing a retail fountain store. On a summer evening, one can walk past the lion gateposts of Vincent Nolte's house to sit in his court, where there was no doubt a fountain playing. As the merchandise splashes away and pedestrians gossip outside the walls, one can imagine oneself there, gossiping with Nolte and Latrobe and possibly Lafon as well.†

While Latrobe was present to assist him, Nolte bought two warehouses, invested in cotton presses, wharves, and ships; Latrobe supplied designs for the hoisting machinery.‡ And there is one further project of Nolte's for which he may have received sketches, at least, from Latrobe: a "country seat situated about one league below the city of New-Orleans, & on the same side of the river . . . upon which have been but lately built an elegant, spacious and highly

---

*In the Historic New Orleans Collection there is a builder's estimate to turn the Nolte house into a bank building, dated June 3, 1829. It calls for two fireplaces, "interior ceilings of the bank plastered in plaster of Paris with handsome cornices," which might seem to date the shreds of present ornament and fireplaces to that remodeling, but it also calls for "a handsome staircase to ascend to the upper story," lit by "a large second story fan light." These do not appear to have been executed, so it is possible that none of this work was actually done and that the fixtures present date from Latrobe's work for Nolte.

†Land records record the purchase on May 6, 1818. There is a map (Marc Lafitte, n.p.) of April 28, 1819, showing the house for Mr. V. Nolte, and a notice of sale on March 9, 1821, but it was called "Mr. Nolte's" house by a newspaper, suggesting he was still in occupancy, when its cornice was damaged by lightning on July 16 of that year. (See Historic New Orleans Collection File for Block 62.) Though it is not the house where Nolte was living at the time of the notice of his bankruptcy auction, that may be because he had already sold it to lay his hands on cash during the panic of 1819, then leased it back from its new owner through 1821, and sometime thereafter moved into a smaller place on Saint Ann Street during his last desperate years. A notice in the *Louisiana Courier* for June 14, 1826, records a sheriff's sale of the real estate owned by Vincent Nolte, including "a small but Commodious dwelling house in St. Ann-street between Royal and Bourbon-streets, one story high," twenty-eight feet long, "and 57 feet deep, lying back on a passage 3 feet wide, leading to Bourbon-street."

‡One of Nolte's cotton-press ventures involved the demolition of a derelict Masonic Hall in the Faubourg Saint Mary. On May 8, 1819, Latrobe wrote that he had "been putting up some machinery for hoisting goods into his warehouse for Mr. Nolte." This letter was found by Samuel S. Wilson, Jr., among the Latrobe papers in the Maryland Historical Society, and provided to me by his kindness.

finished dwelling house, 56 feet front, by 32 feet deep, containing five rooms, two of which are papered, a commodious house for an overseer and family, kitchen, stables and out houses of various kinds." This was the sort of establishment where one might be proud to receive a visit from a Baring.

Yellow Fever

Nolte's country residence is described in the notice of his auction, but earnest searches have failed to produce any other record of it. Country residences were popular among the merchants of the city; they seemed to provide some relief from the scourge of yellow fever. This was the plague from which Edward Stevens rescued Alexander Hamilton in Philadelphia in 1794; it was only an occasional peril in New York, though it broke up the little assembly of Thomas Law, Hamilton, Talleyrand, and the La Tour Du Pins in the following summer. But in the swamps of the mouth of the Mississippi it came every spring with the fireflies, and death by fever remained a constant companion so long as the weather was warm.

Benjamin Henry Latrobe, his son Henry, and Bartholomy Lafon had many things in common aside from the profession of architecture. They were greatly gifted people of classical education, of broad interests. And they all died of yellow fever in New Orleans.

Henry Latrobe was the first to go, in 1817; Lafon was the last, in 1820. Each left a widow, who was Black, and children. Nolte supported the three Mulatto children of Henry until their architect-grandfather could assume that burden. Lafon, who died rich, apparently left enough to tend his family, whom he had legally acknowledged. (It was a New Orleans custom to solemnize a conjugal connection between a White man and a Black woman after there had been progeny.)

I say "apparently left enough" because he was no more interested in record keeping than he was in the formal spelling of his first name, which has been variously recorded as "Bartholomy," "Bartholomé," "Barthelomy," and "Bartholomew." This point is germane to a discussion of the disposition of his estate because he was probably known to his friends as "Thomy"—the name as well of the most prominent Mulatto philanthropist of New Orleans of the next generation.

Thomy Lafon was born in 1810, the son of Modeste Foucher, "a free woman of color" who was acknowledged by Bartholomy Lafon as the mother of his first two children by a testament executed the year before Thomy's birth. Thomy Lafon grew into a famous but very shy real-estate developer and founder of charitable institutions. By 1893, the year of his death, attitudes in the White community toward the acknowledgment and adoption of Mulatto children had changed. Thomy Lafon's obituary in the New Orleans *Daily Picayune* (embalmed in subsequent accounts) gave the name of his father as "Pierre Laralde Lafon" and gave Thomy's status as "colored," though it was apparently still acceptable to imply that he was Mulatto by description: he had "straight, steel-grey hair . . . olive complexion, and regular features." Though "many never . . . [had a] suspicion that he was not a Caucasion [*sic*], [and] although he never made any attempt to conceal that . . . [he was not, it] is said that this fact largely contributed to . . . his retired disposition."

There is a lifetime of innuendo in that set of phrases. Was it just the color of his father? What of the profession that provided the capital base for Thomy Lafon's real-estate investments? Thomy and his sister lived quietly together in a cottage, though owning "immense real estate interests," including several rented mansions. He had already "erected and endowed" a charity hospital, two asylums for orphans, an "old folks" home, and still had enough left over to bestow, in his will, another half-million dollars in further bequests to institutions serving Whites and Blacks, Protestants and Catholics; but he was most famous for private acts of charity for which he avoided "notoriety." He was a remarkable man, whose name still is carried by three charitable organizations and a public school in New Orleans.

Bartholomy Lafon, who seems to have been largely self-educated, went to some pains to assure a good French education to his son. Bartholomy was, as we have noted, a linguist; of Thomy it was said that his "style of conversation in the English, French and Spanish languages evidenced an excellent education. By some it is said he was educated in France . . . He was extremely courteous to everyone, and maintained a gentlemanly bearing and dignity in all his transactions." Like his father, he was "devoted to art, and was especially fond of music." He died from a fall after attending a concert given by the "colored violin virtuoso, Edmond Dede."

It is quite likely that when Thomy Lafon was eight or nine years old he met, at least once, his father's "dear friend" Benjamin Henry Latrobe, who was becoming acquainted with his own Mulatto grandchildren, as he learned to work among the handful of trained architects and engineers in New Orleans. After he arrived in the city, desperate to give his own and his son's family some financial stability, he struggled to complete his waterworks. He had been warned by the manner of Henry's death, but he ignored the swarms of mosquitoes rising from the river as he directed the work. He died of the fever they brought him, on September 3, 1820.

Vincent Nolte, who had tended Henry's widow and children, provided for Lydia Latrobe until she could patch up a life again in Baltimore. It is possible that Bartholomy Lafon would have offered assistance. But, twenty-eight days after the death of Latrobe, the fever killed him as well.

42

THE TRANQUILITY OF
JAMES MONROE

While William Lee had done all he could to help Latrobe keep his job as architect of the Capitol during the turmoil of 1817, he was also keeping his eye out for the interests of Charles Bulfinch.* He wrote his Boston friend that Latrobe was the victim of Monroe's impatience and also of an "unjust prejudice" on the part of Congress. "Latrobe has many enemies; his great fault is in being poor." Lee added that Latrobe was "an amiable, estimable man, full of genius and at the head of his profession," but that he and Monroe were unlikely to reach an accommodation.

Bulfinch was a consummate politician who had spent most of his adult years presiding over the Board of Selectmen of Boston; he could handle such matters. Lee went on: "While the President was here, you were mentioned in case Latrobe should be forced to retire, and I was happy to find Col. Bomford and others [Graham and Mason] thought such a solution would be judicious."

Bulfinch had met Monroe in Washington in January, and the President directed the construction superintendent to lead the visitor "over the ruins of the Capitol," burned out by the British in 1814. Monroe was so irritated by Latrobe that he refused to ask Congress for funds to finish the rebuilding.

That summer, Monroe hedged against his own commission (that of Graham, Mason, and Bomford). He went off to Boston for a tour of Bulfinch's public buildings. The official life of Bulfinch tells us that "the architect's modesty prevented him from elaborating on his role as host," but he himself made no claim to indifference. "My duty as Chairman led me to be almost constantly in company with the President during his visit of about a week."

In November, Bulfinch received Lee's letter about Latrobe's difficulties, but, as he wrote in his memoirs, "I declined making any application that might lead to Mr. Latrobe's removal." He did not have long to wait: "Before the end of the year . . . [Latrobe] determined to resign . . . On receiving information of this, in another letter from Mr. Lee, I made regular application through J.Q.A."—his old friend John Quincy Adams.

---

*George Hadfield's friends also became active on his account, and Latrobe tried to induce Robert Mills to apply for the job.

Charles Bulfinch in 1786, by Mather Brown

Bulfinch was too decent and secure a man to rise by climbing atop the reputation of a fallen genius. Soon after his appointment, he "received from Col. Lane a great number" of Latrobe's drawings, "beautifully executed . . . in the boldest stile." There were some things Bulfinch would do other-wise—broaden the stairs and passageways, diminish the "sombre" general ap-pearance of many rooms—but he knew he stood in the shoes of a master. "I shall not have credit for invention, but must be content to follow in a prescribed path: as my employers have experienced so much uneasiness of late, they are disposed to view me and my efforts with complacency."

After so much uneasiness, complacency: that was the theme of the Monroe administration.

In 1822, Monroe turned again to his friend George Graham. "Col. Lane died last night," wrote the President. "It has occurred to me that it might suit your views to accept the appointment."

When added to Graham's salary as president of the Branch Bank of the United States, "the compensation would be a respectable and comfortable support . . . I have not heretofore been able to make a suitable acknowledgment of my trust of your real merit." He would never be guilty of mere patronage—gracious, no! "I have been guided by general considerations, applicable to what I considered the strict line of my duty . . . applied to those most nearly connected with me."

Graham apparently declined, for soon afterward Monroe, always susceptible to the imperatives of duty, commissioned his friend to wind up the affairs of an abortive system of Indian trade and came close to adding another sinecure, opened by "the death of Mr. Meigs," his postmaster general. Meigs had not made nearly so effective use of the patronage possibilities of that position as Gideon Granger. Perhaps Graham could do better. But there were other and noisier claimants. Monroe did not give the postmaster's job to Graham, citing as his reason "the feverish state of the country"—disarray everywhere. Soon, however, Graham was securely installed as commissioner of the General Land Office.

These friendly arrangements persisted until Andrew Jackson replaced the courtiers of the Virginia dynasty with his own, and was charged with introducing a spoils system. John McLean, another former postmaster general, no stranger to the appointment process and a friend of Graham, wrote him in 1829: "The moral force of our institutions will soon be destroyed . . . General Jackson cannot be sensible of the vials of wrath which will soon be filled. How unfortunate that he has been called from his retreat to be used as a tool by contrasted, vindictive, and, I fear, unprincipled politicians."

The Rewards of the Principled

Graham went to live with his kinsmen the Brents, first at Latrobe's Brentwood, in the city, and then at the Highlands, in the country, where Graham, confidential agent to James Monroe, died after one year of the presidency of Andrew Jackson.

Charles Bulfinch retired gracefully to Boston, followed soon afterward by William Lee. Lee's wife had died. He was lonely. With the change of administrations, he was out of his job, an indignity duly reported by his daughter Mary: "Poor Papa! After serving his government faithfully for thirty years, that it should come to this." Mary Lee was married to a Russian diplomat with an estate in Courland, who offered to send her father a regular allowance to replace his government pay, an offer "from the Baron" that made him "weep with affection."

In 1830, his affectionate nature and a measure of prudence led him into a marriage with the very rich widow of the merchant John McLean (not the same as the postmaster), which brought him firmly into the circle of Bulfinch's friends. John Lowell, her brother-in-law, and her tribe of brothers were all his clients, as her first husband had been. For one of her brothers, Bulfinch laid up the greatest Boston mansion of the day, later remodeled into a townhouse for Christopher Gore. McLean, at his death, provided a huge bequest to convert Bulfinch's Barrell house into McLean Hospital, one of Bulfinch's last designs before assuming command of the Capitol. (The Barrell house was the building described by Lee to give his first wife a sense of the grandeur of Kalorama.)

The marriage of William Lee and the widow McLean, in her Beacon Hill

The east front of the McLean Hospital, showing Bulfinch's Barrell house;
c. 1820 (center); engraving by Abel Bowen

mansion, was attended by Daniel Webster and by John Quincy Adams, who described it:

> The parties are each about threescore years of age. I knew them both in the heyday of their youth . . . I then also knew their former partners, now in the grave . . . The couple thus united cannot have many years to live together. Their contemporaries, blooming in youth as I have seen them all, we are now some bending under the weight of years, and faces where I had seen roses in bloom were now furrowed, wrinkled and haggard . . . Cupid and Hymen! what worshippers of yours are these!

The former Ann Amory McLean was a true Boston lady, described by Lee as "enthusiastic, sincere, and immovable in her religious opinions, and believed in all the doctrines of that murderer Calvin. I have scolded her, coaxed her, persuaded her, but it was all in vain. You might as well attempt to throw a ray of light into a block of granite as into her mind." Ultimately, it seems, Lee, child of Voltaire, relented in his attempts to convert a child of Cotton Mather: he "came to a determination, as she had generously given herself and fortune to me, to yield to her . . . Next to Him she loved me most ardently, and seeing it I bent to all her wishes, to the astonishment of all her family and friends."

Her relatives shared Lee's disdain for the clergymen who fluttered about Ann Amory McLean Lee. After her death (Adams was right: they had only four years), her will was found to provide income only for her husband's lifetime, then a little for her relatives. All the rest went to the clergy. When the will was read, John Lowell rose and spoke for the assembled throng:

"Mr. Lee, since none of us are much benefited by this will, I hope you will live 100 years to enjoy the property left to you. . . ." Thereafter, the Amorys and the Lowells were, as Lee put it, "disposed to be very kind—excessively kind. Homo homini lupus (Man is a wolf to his fellow man)."

William Lee purchased a large brick house, of twenty-two rooms, at Roxbury. I have been unable to identify it, though he described it as standing "on an eminence which commands a view of Boston, its islands, harbor . . . and all the country round. It is a beautiful spot." The old Bordeaux trader added proudly, "I bought it of the widow and heirs, dog cheap." He put it in the name of his unmarried daughter, Susan, "so that when I am gone, she will be independent, as the rent will always support her."

He was gone three years later; he died on February 29, 1840.

Oak Hill

At the end of the presidency of James Monroe, Colonel Lane was still superintending construction of the Capitol, Bulfinch was still its architect, and George Bomford was still chief of the Corps of Engineers. (Bomford had given immortality to the magnum opus of his brother-in-law, Joel Barlow, by naming a cannon after Barlow's epic poem *The Columbiad*.) James Hoban, an earlier incumbent of both Lane's post and Latrobe's—and, at another time, architect of the White House—was now a prosperous contractor and real-estate speculator in Washington City. Thomas Jefferson was in retirement at Monticello, chiefly occupied with the planning of the University of Virginia. His friend James Madison was in retirement nearby.

Monroe owned property in Albemarle County, near Madison's and Jefferson's. As early as 1815, he was, like them, in deep financial difficulties. But he was a younger man; and adopting in his private affairs a strategy he had found effective in statecraft, Monroe assumed the offensive against his creditors. He went deeper into debt, acquiring two thousand acres in Loudon County, resolving to settle upon whichever parcel remained after his creditors forced the other into sale.

They took the Albemarle. He was left with the Loudon County property, where he lived in a hilltop cottage in a Cotswoldian landscape. The Blue Ridge could be seen receding southwesterly toward Mr. Madison and Mr. Jefferson,

Entrance and garden façades of Oak Hill

and a little tributary of the Potomac purled through grain fields toward the Capitol, in the other direction. From 1811 onward, while secretary of state and preparing for the presidency, Monroe rode out to his cottage on weekends, with his saddlebags stuffed full of papers. From the gallery of his cottage, he could look out upon lands long cultivated by Fairfaxes and Carters and gather his resources for a campaign to build his own manor house.

In June 1820, Thomas Jefferson sent him a letter, enclosing a drawing, now lost. Two years later, Monroe said the house then under way had been "sketched partly by Colonel Bomford, and partly by Captain Hoban, and partly by ourselves, or rather on suggestions by us all." He rejoiced that "for the plan I have paid not one cent."

Economy was the rule. Superintendent Lane supplied the brick maker; and the "plan of a house which Colonel Bomford has drawn for us, and which we very much approve . . . is a square building, with two wings, which both, being one story only, will take much fewer bricks than one entire building." Hoban was the general contractor; when he finished the portico, Monroe noted that it had cost only two hundred dollars and was "a new and distinct part."

Despite its design by committee, Oak Hill remains one of the most pleasant expressions of American neoclassical taste. Its entrance façade centers upon a very large fanlighted doorway, set into a broad recess of brick. It looks to me like something only Hoban, of that group, would have been likely to conceive. Perhaps Hoban also sketched the portico of five uncanonical columns, said to signify the fifth presidency, though it might have been an idea sent along by Jefferson, who considered, and rejected, something similar for Pavilion VII at the University of Virginia.

The building was for long painted very pale yellow, emphasizing that it was no longer Georgian and colonial; in this way it was similar to Tudor Place, the masterpiece of William Thornton, completed on a hilltop in Georgetown only a few years earlier. This might seem to suggest that Thornton was also consulted about the design of Oak Hill—and, indeed, at the time Thornton was everyone's adviser on architectural matters, as was Jefferson in matters political. But we can be quite sure Thornton had no hand in the design of Oak Hill: Thornton was a reminder not only of "Sir" Gregor MacGregor (see p. 368) but of something worse.

A President planning to cultivate retirement within a day's journey of Washington City would not like to be forced to recall too often the morning of August 28, 1814. William Thornton was the embodiment of the collapse of order, of safety, and of dignity on that day.

During the preceding weeks, while Secretary of War Monroe and President Madison and their little escort were dashing about the countryside trying to avoid British patrols, Thornton had remained in Washington, acting as mayor, though his only authority was as an honorary justice of the peace. Fears were quieted, looters resisted; the flames of buildings put to the torch by the British were extinguished. Shelter was found for those who had been unable to evacuate and whose homes had caught fire. Soon after the British pulled out, to gather their forces for an assault upon Samuel Smith's hastily assembled little army in front of Baltimore, President Madison, Secretary Monroe, and a muddy, dispirited entourage returned to the burned-out capital.

At 8:30 that night, an explosion was heard from the direction of Alexandria, down the Potomac. A new British squadron was demonstrating to the burghers of that port that they would do well to turn over the contents of their warehouses: the implied alternative was the fate of Washington, and, to add to the panic, rumor swept through the capital city that the British were coming back to finish the job! The French minister wrote Talleyrand, in Paris, that he was departing; he had no desire to receive the British at his dinner table for a second time.

Dr. Thornton had had enough as well. In the morning of the twenty-eighth, he sought out the President and Monroe and, making it clear that he had lost faith in their ability to protect the population, suggested that if they wished to pretend that they were still able to resist, that was all very well, but civilians might follow the example of the Alexandrians and surrender their town. Monroe looked him in the eye and told him that he would issue orders that if any delegations of citizens were spotted heading in the direction of the British, they were to be bayoneted.

So it is unlikely that, a few years later, William Thornton was James Monroe's architect for Oak Hill.

The Monroe Doctrine and a New "Wall of Brass"

By the fall of 1822, the world had turned. In the previous six years, Great Britain and the United States had hammered out a working alliance. Their opponents were the old partners of the "wall of brass," the Bourbon dynasties of France and Spain, now resurgent.

Anglo-American statesmen might have dismissed as poltroonery a French expedition to reinstall a monarchy in Mexico when Napoleon's unemployed soldiers attempted it in 1818. Five years later, it was no longer so easily brushed aside. This time the monarchy to be installed would be of the house of Bourbon, not of Bonaparte; and if this seemed a distinction without a geopolitical difference, for the first time since 1810—see p. 334—the French government was seriously contemplating a role in such a venture.

In April 1823, the French invaded Spain, for the same reason they had invaded in 1808, to install a regime more to their liking than any arising from the more liberal preferences of the Spanish people. The prime minister of

France, the comte de Villèle, spoke openly of a speedy conquest of the Hispanic peninsula followed by expeditions to install Bourbon princes in South and Central America. The idea was actually approved by the Council of State. French foreign policy in the Americas might now be synchronized with commerce for the first time since the days of Choiseul (see pp. 37–8).

The British responded for the same reasons as they had in the earlier case, though they did not send the duke of Wellington back into the peninsula with an army. Instead, they strove mightily to incite the United States to stand in the way of French commercial or political reinvasion of the Western Hemisphere. In this deployment of the United States to protect their own markets, British policy was successful. They provoked the Monroe Doctrine, and thereby justified the most memorable epigram of George Canning, foreign secretary in Lord Aberdeen's cabinet: "Contemplating Spain, such as our ancestors had known her, I resolved that if France had Spain, it would not be Spain 'with the Indies.' I called the New World into existence to redress the balance of the Old."

That was an unusually smug statement even for Canning; it had elements of truth, but there were other objectives to be served by the Monroe Doctrine. Among them was discouraging the aspiration of the czar of Russia to "guarantee the tranquillity of all the states of which the civilized world is composed" (including the future states of Washington, Oregon, and Alaska). The Virginians dominating the American government also desired to keep the British out of Cuba and Texas, so that those Spanish possessions might perform their manifest destiny to become slave states in the American union. But, to be fair to Canning, without his initiative the British might not have succeeded in preventing the French from becoming, once again, formidable competitors in the Western Hemisphere.

In his State of the Union message written in November 1823, in the study at Oak Hill, and delivered in December, James Monroe inserted scattered passages that together with subsequent amendments and elucidations have been consolidated into the Monroe Doctrine. He noted with pleasure the rising of the peoples of Spain and Portugal, "conducted with extraordinary moderation," and with displeasure how the French army had "interposed by force" foreign dominance "in the internal concerns of Spain. To what extent such interposition may be carried . . . is the question." What happened in Europe was one thing, but with "the movements in this Hemisphere we are of necessity more immediately concerned." Then his pen traced his great operative principle: "We should consider any attempt on their part to extend their system to any portions of this Hemisphere, as dangerous to our peace and safety."*

---

*Fifteen years later, French "interposition" again became "the question." This time it was a project of the Republic of Texas, and we may assume that it gave some wry satisfaction to the survivors

The Monroe Doctrine was received with contempt by the ambassadors and ministers of the Holy Alliance: words like "blustering" and "arrogant" were used in dispatches. But the combined British and American fleets were not so regarded; and, not for the first or the last time, cannons, including "Columbiads," converted dicta into doctrine.

For thirty years thereafter, the combined British and American fleets were strong enough to stand between any European power and the Americas. Then, during our Civil War, while the Americans were divided and distracted, Archduke Maximilian became emperor of Mexico in the last Bonapartist scheme for empire in the Americas. The people of Mexico rose against him; our Civil War came to an end; and the reunited American fleet was once again interposed to affirm the Monroe Doctrine. Maximilian lost the protection of a French military presence and died before a firing squad in 1867.

Blood and dust and gunfire at close range in a Mexican courtyard. History is full of ironic consequences, and strange juxtapositions: romantic Maximilian, the last emperor to reign in the Western Hemisphere, was sentenced to failure by the policy of the coolest of British statesmen, Canning, and by his imperturbable agent James Monroe—a man once compared, as a patron of architecture, to Augustus Caesar.

---

of the Champ d'Asile. Albert Sidney Johnston, Secretary of War for the Lone Star Republic—and later a general of the Confederacy—proposed creating twenty forts to guard its western frontier from depredations by the Mexicans or Indians. The Texas legislature was then asked by President Sam Houston to garrison them with eight thousand French soldiers, who would be given three million acres of land and all the mineral rights beneath—the mines again, always the mines. Despite Houston's backing, Texas pride and the recollection of earlier French expeditions brought forth a chorus of protest. *The Telegraph and Texas Register* of July 21, 1841, proclaimed that Texas would become "the tiny fraction of a French colony"; Houston was accosted by infuriated ladies on the streets of his capital, and, ultimately, the plan was dropped. (See Walter Prescott Webb, *The Great Plains.* New York: Grosset and Dunlap, 1931, p. 181.)

IX

SOLID
GEOMETRY

The first and greatest effect of the American Revolution in Europe was to make Europeans believe, or rather feel, often in a highly emotional way, that they lived in a rare era of momentous change.
    —R. R. PALMER, *The Age of Democratic Revolution*

The very nature of the Doric order . . . is intended to convey . . . duration . . . to bid defiance to the elements and to time itself.   —*The North American Review*, 1836

The principle assumed and acted upon was order.
                        —ROBERT MILLS

In the household of nature, something is always dying and something is always being born. From time to time, the pace of these processes increases, and there appears, rather suddenly, much more than usual that is new. The end of the eighteenth century was such a period—a "novus ordo seclorum," announced the Great Seal of the United States. The first French Republic was no less bold in its transforming ambitions, though its consequences bore little resemblance to the ambitions of those who first set in motion that series of shocks to France which (in the words of the British philosopher Sir Isaiah Berlin) "threw into relief the precariousness of human institutions . . . the poetry of action, destruction, heroism, war; the effectiveness of mobs and of great men; the power of chance; the feebleness of reason and the power over . . . fanatically believed doctrines; the unpredictability of events; the part played in history by unintended consequences . . ."

At the outset, it was possible to set out into this revolutionary era with confidence, fervor, and a propensity to believe that change was in its nature inclined toward "progress." Those benevolent revolutionaries who can be called "the Party of Hope" acted upon the belief that they could arrange the future to be better than the past. Charles James Fox and Mirabeau, for example, lived to the natural end of their days quite unembittered, perhaps because they died early and at the height of their political eminence. Others were not so fortunate. Robespierre, who went to the guillotine, was as much a member of the Party of Hope, in his humorless way, as Brissot, whom he sent before him to the scaffold.

The hopeful reinforced each other's enthusiasms. They shared a belief in salutary outcomes for both the French and the American revolutions. From 1778 to 1793, the Foxite Whigs of England smiled upon the Franco-American love affair from across the battle lines and across the oceans. There had been ample motives of ambition and of cold commercial policy for the French government to aid the revolt of the American colonies and for the Foxites to snap at the heels of the Tory government of Lord North, but, for a time, there was among people of liberal expectations a genuine infatuation with each other and with revolution. Statesmen, poets, and architects shared in the euphoria; even an aristocracy with few illusions about itself but yearning for purity—and novelty—daydreamed of American possibilities.

Enthusiasm for the untried swept from France across the English Channel. The essayist, philosopher, and painter William Hazlitt shared the sentiments of Jefferson and Brissot: "I set out in life with the French Revolution . . . Youth was then doubly such. It was the dawn of a new era, a new impulse had been given to men's minds, and the sun of Liberty rose upon the sun of Life in the same day." Fanny Burney, the bluestocking, joined a "Revolutionary Club." Many, following the lead of Fox, supported the cause of British reform and American revolt.

43

THE PARTY OF HOPE

Whether drawn by hope or driven by necessity, the Frenchmen whose stories we have been telling departed their own distressed country and embarked for America to reconstitute their lives. Royalists and republicans, anarchists and aristocrats made good their escape into the unknown as revolutions exploded about them. Change, to them, could only be for the better. Out of necessity rather than inclination, all these émigrés became members of the Party of Hope.

Because he wrote so powerfully, and out of such profound deliberation, we have often turned for guidance to this period to Henry Adams, at once its best and its most unnatural historian. Though he wrote in my own father's time, he seemed to write as one born well before his own great-grandfather John Adams, the last eighteenth-century President. Carrying, as he did, a renewed burden of Puritan skepticism about all human undertakings, this dour Yankee spent much of his life studying the Party of Hope, and it always seemed to him either naive or incomprehensible.

Jefferson was especially baffling, "in the somewhat affected precision of his French philosophy," proceeding with the most rigorous logic to the most outrageous conclusions. How could anyone believe that "fifty years hence the average man shall invariably argue from two ascertained premises where he now jumps to a conclusion from a single supposed revelation—that is Progress!"

It was Jefferson's hope that mattered, stated though it might be with "affected precision," Jefferson's fervor, contained by prudence, in a bloody and chaotic world. This is what Adams underrated. And it was also what he could not perceive in the architecture of the period under his scrutiny. Through nine compendious volumes, the man who could sympathetically unravel the mysteries of Mont-Saint-Michel and Chartres betrayed indifference to the constructed evidence of a period inimical to his own nature. This is strange, because there are subtle things in common between the early Middle Ages and the late Renaissance, things that make the architecture of the early Gothic appeal to the same spirits as that of neoclassicism. The commonalities, as Adams, of all historians, might have understood, had nothing to do with the tangible, and they defied the categories of "style." They had to do, instead, with such matters as courage and faith.

Despite its seamless surfaces and its ordered geometry, neoclassicism did not arise in any fabled springtime of the Western world, but in a bleak and confused winter. Civilization was blasted and shaken by imperial contests, religious massacre, and civil strife, yet it set itself once again to establish order. Part of this effort was made in a new continent, where there could not even be found the instructive ruins of a common past. Ruins there were, but they had been left by the ancestors of others, a fact of some psychological importance.

Goethe congratulated America on its absence of ruins:

> America, you're better off
> Than our own continent that's old.
> At tumble-down castles you scoff,
> You lack basalt, I'm told.
> Within, nothing daunts you
> In times rife with life,
> No memory haunts you
> Nor vain, idle strife.

But, of course, Goethe had never seen Poverty Point or the Great Pyramid of Cahokia.

The Reassurance of Antiquity

To the neoclassical generation, the ancient buildings of Europe and the Near East, pre-existing the Gothic by a thousand years and more, were admirable not only because of their pleasing proportions but because of their longevity. These structures were not unchanged, but they conveyed an impression of lastingness, and so provided symbols of pertinacity to new nations, new constitutions, new notions of science and religion. Neoclassical architecture was created to serve this need; it was compounded of hope and history.

Architecture very often comments upon its circumstances by stating a desirable opposite: for example, that aspect of their own epoch which the contemporaries of neoclassical architects felt most poignantly was its turbulence. The quality most evident in the work of those architects was tranquility.

Their world was being destabilized by immense demographic changes, as the birthrate surged in some parts of the globe, war and pestilence decimated other populations. Industrial societies were being created in the British midlands and the Brandywine Valley while those of India, dependent upon textile and steel manufacturing, were being destroyed.

The prosperous islands of Hispaniola and Ireland, which in the period from 1750 to 1800 had provided a final effulgence of wealth, descended into massacre, fire, and pestilence. Great populations were eradicated and deported, fertile fields laid waste. Geopolitics presented, on a grand scale, its lessons in the consequences of avarice and hate. Nations were formed and nations rent apart. A global transfer of wealth proceeded beneath and behind the flash and fire of global warfare, as antagonists struggled for advantage from Borneo to Labrador and from Patagonia to Saint Petersburg.

And architecture, to an unprecedented degree, proclaimed order and repose. With chaos all about, people turned, for respite and assurance, to clarity and to geometric purity, the qualities of classical buildings. The Gothic, as Henry Adams recognized, had been not only a religious expression but also, like the classical, the product of disciplined intelligence. Now, at the end rather than the beginning of an epoch, neoclassicism was the finest flowering of anxiety.

In the years between 1780 and 1830, great talent was made available to an American republic to provide a set of symbols implying pertinacity if not tranquility. A series of symbol makers came to the United States—most, it must be said, unwillingly. (Not so unwillingly as the Black slaves brought from Africa, or the White convicts sent from Ireland, Scotland, and France, or the conscripts impressed into German, British, and French armies and navies, but unwillingly nonetheless.)

Had he not suffered bankruptcy, it is doubtful that America would have had received the genius of Latrobe. Had there been no French Revolution, architects like Pierre Pharoux, Etienne-Sulpice Hallet, Maximilian Godefroy, Adrien Boucher, Bartholomy Lafon, Charles and Joseph Mangin, and Joseph Ramée would probably have gone about their business in Paris. Had there not been a race war on Hispaniola, Wilmington would not display to us the architecture of Pierre Bauduy. Once they were here, the bearers of neoclassical taste provided the energy, taste, and training to give the new American republic precisely the kind of face it required, testaments to courage as well as skill. They created, amid squalor and distress, serenity.

Their accomplishment is more than a phase in the history of form; it is the exposition of the role of solid geometry in the history of yearning. Responding to the turbulence about them, artists created very large symbols, frequently (but not always) habitable, as much to serve psychological as physical need. Sometimes, indeed, psychological imperatives overwhelmed physical comfort. Form often follows feeling.

As we approach the end of our story, three illustrations of this process come before us, the first a mere maquette, or model, of a huge building, the second nothing more than a scheme, but both powerful symbolic uses of the "Orders,"* and the third a prolific prototype of American uses.

The pyramid, the cylinder, and the dome were used in these instances to convey complex ideas symbolically, at points of interchange between France and the United States. In the case of the dome, the symbolic content included, at once, awe for French technological ingenuity and a deep inexplicit response to the female.

*I use this term very loosely, to include any architectural ideas derived from classical antiquity implying solidity of structure and balance, though this may offend those who insist that I produce at least the implication of a column and entablature.

Volney

Let us begin with the pyramid and the cylinder. Their appearance in America, among the friends of Thomas Jefferson and Benjamin Henry Latrobe, was due to a sudden and dramatic visitation on the part of that Frenchman who was known to have thought most about the buildings of antiquity and their symbolic application to revolutionary times. Constantin François Boisgirais was another of those mobile French intellectuals whose name changes marked their upward passage. He early exchanged his surname, derived from his father's farm, for "Volney." He spent a season amid the ruins of Baalbek, ruminating and writing, and, somewhat later, another, morose and surly, in Philadelphia. His descriptions of his travels in Syria and Egypt helped inspire Napoleon's campaign to conquer these regions for France, and his impressions of America imbedded certain clichés in the minds of French intellectuals, where they remain to this day.

The emperor made him a count, and the Bourbons elevated him to a peerage. This progression did not occur without stumbling and detours. One of the latter took Volney to America in 1795, to escape the fate of his friend Brissot. During his American sojourn, Volney renewed his friendship with Jefferson. The renowned traveler to Egypt presented the Sage with the model of a pyramid, proudly displayed at Monticello. In response, though after a considerable pause, Jefferson and Joel Barlow translated Volney's account of his American travels.

Needless to say, Volney's pyramid was not intended to evoke the stone monuments of the Mezzo-Americans nor even the more modest earthen ones of the Ohio Valley. For Europeans, these New World pyramids would merely have confused their repeated insistence that there were no ruins in America. Volney meant to compliment Jefferson by suggesting that they were both the linear descendants of the Egyptians, by way of the Greeks and the Romans. French architects of the time were suggesting pyramids as symbols of permanence for new republics (Ramée was among those who did so), and so, soon, would Americans like Robert Mills.

Jefferson and Barlow's translation was one answer, but it lacked the subtle symbolic return compliment inherent in the offering of Latrobe, who was befriended by Volney in Richmond in 1796, when both were at the nadir of their careers. Latrobe had just arrived from England and did not know the country as well as Volney, who encouraged him with multilingual gossip. Two years later, things had improved for Latrobe but not for Volney. He was becoming even more curmudgeonly than he had been in France. An elderly Quaker reported years later that he remembered Volney as displaying a "haughty and morose nature, jealous of the least appearance of slight and neglect . . . a timid, peevish, sour-tempered man."

Volney was not Brissot; he was not happy among Quakers, and certainly not among Quaker merchants, but when he gossiped with Latrobe, there was nothing morose about him, though the two had a good deal to be peevish about. To buoy up their spirits, Latrobe designed for him a cylindrical "hermitage" for some arcadian meadow beside the Schuylkill. There the acolytes of the great man, "the garçons philosophes . . . [would] live harmoniously together under one roof." Harmony—and, like the pyramid, stability. The cylinder, extended, becomes a column; and reduced to one dimension it becomes a circle, the sign of unity, wholeness, completion.

In France, an architectural folly joined a circle of ancient columns in a garden into a philosopher's roost. In America, Volney's pyramid or Latrobe's circular house would have to be created anew, and would therefore seem more artificial, and both would have the defect of being born of intelligence alone. The dome Jefferson gave himself was the gift of the heart as well.

44

MR. JEFFERSON'S TASTE

After a visit to Monticello in 1782, the marquis de Chastellux wrote that Thomas Jefferson was "the first American who has consulted the Fine Arts to know how he should shelter himself against the weather." Though, he went on, there were faults in the architecture; even allowing for snobbery and ignorance, that is an odd thing for an educated man to say.

The James River was lined with respectable brick houses built after consulting good English precedent. Annapolis, too, was a collection of such structures, thanks to the wide range of reading and sound English training of William Buckland. Philadelphia had several mansions suitable to a sidestreet off Pall Mall, and Charleston was not barren of taste.

What could Chastellux have meant? Jefferson was not even the first American to make intelligent use of French and British precedents of the eighteenth century. It must have been something else—perhaps that Jefferson self-consciously offered a field, or screen, upon which an aristocratic, artistic, and liberal French visitor could project his expectations of an American gentleman. The French have always admired those who admire the French.

Monticello was Jefferson's symbolic house, as the University of Virginia would later become his symbolic village. Their evocative qualities are felt by any sympathetic visitor, even today, though we are no longer able to enter into symbolic association as directly as did our forefathers. (This is a theme I tried to develop in *American Churches;* there is not space here to restate it at length, yet in dealing with Thomas Jefferson it is important to bear in mind that he had an almost medieval symbolic acuity. His themes were not theological; he was a man of another time, but he did employ architecture for moral instruction. For those ends, like others of his time and ours, he made use of the forms of eternity—that is to say, of geometry—in combination with the "Orders"—that is to say, the forms of antiquity.)

What Jefferson began with the capitol in Richmond he completed with an anthology of classical forms around the lawn of his University in Charlottesville. Though he left architectural historians an "academical village," he did not leave literary historians a book to make clear his point: it was "academical" both in the activity it was to house and in its own instructional function. He left to others to make that point obvious; he took on no more chores than his duty required. Besides, he knew that consciousness does not always require contentiousness; he got what he wanted in architecture without explaining himself too much.

Jefferson showed as little interest in composing books of his own on aesthetics as he did in visiting the remains of ancient buildings. There was a dry, practical—dare I say "Yankee"?—quality in him. He simply put architecture to symbolic use without discourse, experimenting with octagons, cubes, and spheres; but one can no more imagine a grammar of symbolism by Jefferson than one by Benjamin Franklin.

Still, Jefferson's abstractions were very powerful, especially when they combined the archetypal potencies of the dome of the sky and the feminine qualities of a contour composed of laminated curves. This is deep material. I do not enter it casually, but Jefferson is so central a figure in our history that each of us must try to come to terms with him as best we can, without being deterred either by his own reticence at key points or by the gorgons of specialized knowledge who stand in horrid custody of the precincts of "Jefferson studies."

So to complete this work, we offer some observations upon the development of Jefferson's taste, to the extent that it can be observed in his sketches, his buildings, and his very few comments. We even essay reconstruction of two moments in his aesthetic biography, believing that they shaped his life and, through him, the life of his country.

Jefferson is too important to be left to the specialists.*

---

*There is always something new to be learned. As I sat surrounded by the garden designs and estate plans of Pierre Pharoux, Claude-Joseph Sauthier, and Joseph Ramée, a friend read to me this passage from a book by two of the most generous and wide-ranging of Jefferson scholars, Ralph E. Griswold and Frederick Doveton Nichols (in *Thomas Jefferson, Landscape Architect,* Charlottesville: University of Virginia Press [reprint of 1981], p. 89):

> While Jefferson never pretended to be a landscape gardener, he was nonetheless the nearest equivalent to a landscape architect in the current fashion of early America. It was, however, not until the appearance of Alexander Jackson Downing, many years later, that the New World was to have a skillful designer in the landscape field, professionally identified as a landscape gardener.

The Young Jefferson

In his prodigious youth, Jefferson experimented with bold designs displaying a kind of home-grown geometrical architecture. Working alone, on his own estates, he found endorsement in reading the works of the circle of Masons who were sponsored by Lord Burlington from 1725 onwards. These "Burlingtonians" popularized the works of the ancients (by way of Palladio) and also contrived simple geometric structures, which Jefferson called "cubic architecture," uncluttered by the baroque excesses then prevailing in central Europe and in France.*

These Burlingtonian popularizers—the founding fathers of the sort of Carpenters' Guides that provided every hamlet in America with classical ideas a century later—made no secret of their desire to spread moral instruction through the use of architectural form; this was one of the lessons they learned from Palladio himself. Though Jefferson called Palladio's *Four Books of Architecture* his Bible, he knew his Palladio only by way of eighteenth-century English "apocrypha," free adaptations of Palladio's original. The architectural Bible Jefferson used was therefore like the religious Bible he recomposed with scissors and marginalia.

Jefferson owned a copy of *Select Architecture,* a book by the most famous of the Burlingtonians, Robert Morris, who abstracted from Palladianism a tight, clear, geometric set of patterns applicable to small houses and thereby inspired gentlemen-amateurs like Jefferson to build classically on a modest scale.

In the hands of American Freemasons, the act of building became a political statement as well as an aesthetic one. "Cubic" architecture, especially when smoothly stuccoed, repudiated the red-brick, foursquare, plantation architecture of the lower James River, which Jefferson thought tamely colonial and embarrassing. (Some of us think of it as provocatively Franco-Dutch [p. 459ff.]—but no matter.)

Archetypal Imperatives

Sooner or later, as one studies the work of artists, one has to make some guesses about the unconscious imperatives within their creative process, even without a complete set of dream notes or recorded conversations with their analysts. Jefferson was the least likely of artists to leave clues, even of an eighteenth-

---

*I must reserve for another book elaboration of a tangential point: Latrobe's English work is not Burlingtonian, Palladian, or neoclassical in the sense in which we have been using that term. His two country houses, Ashdown and Hammerwood Lodge, stand in another tradition, that baroque eclecticism running from Sir John Vanbrugh through Francis Smith.

century sort—Bernard Bailyn recently referred to his "hard glazed surface, so difficult to penetrate," and another of his biographers, Merrill Peterson, spoke of him as "an impenetrable man." Still, our responsibility to treat him as we would any other subject cannot stop at the point where both empathy *and* a century of analytical psychology can begin to help us. Therefore:

Jefferson's geometrizing permitted him to accommodate certain unconscious imperatives, quite constant in their effects throughout his life, while insisting that he was proceeding by strict rationality.

Apparent impenetrability is often a necessary protection against an acute sensitivity—as it was with Jefferson.

According to his friend Edmund Randolph, the young Jefferson wanted to adopt "a style of living much more refined than that . . . handed down . . . by his ancestors," but it is doubtful that what was meant by "refined" was that finicking prissiness implied by the word in late Victorian times. Instead, it is likely that Randolph meant "considered," or perhaps "rational," as Buford Pickens suggested not long ago, and that geometrizing was one of Jefferson's means of bringing "refinement" to his environment. His first, cubical design was for an outbuilding at Monticello (1769); then came an octagonal chapel project (1770); and in 1778 he used the abstraction of a telescope for an observatory of four cubes, each smaller than the last.

This quest for pure form led him next to experiments in neoclassicism, his scheme for a temple-form remodeling of the governor's mansion in Williamsburg at the end of the 1770s, and the Virginia capitol, devised after Jefferson had been long enough in Paris to become acquainted with the high priests (if the expression is not distasteful to Masons) of French Freemasonry. The revival of classical forms had acquired even more powerful moral and political meaning for him.

In an earlier draft of this text there followed here some pages about Clérisseau; his son-in-law, Jacques-Guillaume Legrand; Legrand's partner, Jacques Molinos; and an American client of Legrand, Christopher Gore. Though Legrand and Molinos were responsible for the design of the Paris Grain Market, which comes to have a major role in Jefferson's story, and though Clérisseau has been present with us since our opening pages, extended discourse about these gentlemen does not lie along the main corridor now to be followed; so they have been left on the cutting-room floor.

Fishing in Old French Books

Clérisseau, said Jefferson, had "given proofs of his skill and taste by a publication of some antiquities." The operative word was "publication." Jefferson's imagination had been furnished its examples of antiquity from books, not, as might have been the case had he grown up in Italy or southern France, from actual buildings. To the end of his days he remained a man of books. Latrobe complained in particular of his "prejudices in favor of the old French books, out of which he fishes everything." Below its irritable surface, this was an acute observation—Jefferson *was* bookish. That was the consequence of his early training, and it was also because he was intensely sensitive to real architectural space. French books were safe; French space was, for him, if not outright dangerous, then destabilizing.

So Latrobe was right, on the record. Jefferson's first old French book was Perrault's edition of Vitruvius—his first architectural purchase. Even before he set out upon his French mission, he had made a list of others he wished to procure, including Le Roy's *Images of Athens* and Desgodetz's *Ancient Buildings of Rome,* and these were among the first of his acquisitions when he reached Paris.

He drew forth Latrobe's annoyance by insisting on the authority of his library rather than deferring to Latrobe's long study of actual buildings. The young Jefferson, unlike the young Latrobe, did not have an inventory of antiquity all about him, or a Renaissance anthology of actuality readily at hand. When he did have a building of real merit to observe, like the Governor's Palace at Williamsburg, he did so with a finely honed sense of proportion—but books were his authorities. After Latrobe's death he continued to draw for suggestions for the University of Virginia upon books—those of a fellow amateur and book man, William Thornton, rather than turn to George Hadfield, who had spent years measuring and drawing Roman antiquities.*

The most frequently cited example given to contradict this argument is Jefferson's letter to his friend Mme de Tessé, reporting that he had gazed at the Maison Carrée in Nîmes "for hours, like a lover at his mistress." The chief mystery about this letter is why it has been taken by so many historians to be an unambiguous statement, since Jefferson made it clear in other correspondence that he was writing in code. Though he may have admired the building, he was not mooning about.

The revolutionary representative of the United States in Paris, a man with a lifelong passion for insurrection and a fascination with Latin America, was not inactive or "rapt" in Nîmes. In the shadows of an ancient temple, he was hard at work, hatching the first of his series of Latin-American plots. Though he did

---

*Jefferson's unwillingness to consult with Hadfield for the designs for the University of Virginia, as late as 1820, is still unexplained. He described Hadfield to Maria Cosway as "first after Latrobe in reputation." But Hadfield did not publish. No one would make *him* Dean of the School of Architecture.

I suspect that Hadfield's personal habits embarrassed Jefferson, or that Jefferson distrusted Hadfield's close connections with the arch-Federalist Custises, Peters, and Trumbulls. But how then can we explain his tolerance for the similar connections enjoyed by Thornton, whose most famous residential building was Tudor Place, designed in 1814 for the sister-in-law of George Washington Parke Custis? This puzzle must await another volume.

The Maison Carrée at Nîmes, as depicted by H. Robert

not ignore the Maison Carrée—and learned from it—he went to Nîmes to have a rendezvous with the Brazilian insurrectionist José da Maia.

He could not be expected to say so in a letter written through, and, in effect, to, the French censors. The Bourbons of France were allies of their cousins in Spain. Jefferson was writing to Mme de Tessé, who was sympathetic to his political objectives and was almost certainly privy to the same information Jefferson imparted to his superior in the diplomatic service, John Jay. There he explained that he "would go off my road as far as Nimes under the pretext of seeing the antiquities of that place."

Generally, however, he was led to confine himself to safe places, psychologically. Goethe, with whom Jefferson had much in common, set out to make his pilgrimage to Paestum (the most powerful remnant of Greek architecture known to men like him or Jefferson while Athens was still virtually inaccessible) in March 1787, at the same time Jefferson took the road to Nîmes. Goethe articulated his fears as Jefferson did not: "Once one takes it upon oneself to go" toward such a holy place, "and enters into a close interaction with it, one has to be very careful not to be swept away in a trance, or even go mad." Goethe had until then held himself back, with what German scholars call "a prohibitive fear of contact."

Goethe knew himself, measured his risks, and concluded that by that stage in his life he could resist the spirits hovering about Paestum.* In our own time, Carl Jung made his own calculations about the risks of visiting Rome and concluded, like Jefferson, that he would not expose himself to a test he could not pass. He did not venture upon a journey to Rome, nor did Jefferson journey to Palladio's Vicenza.

There was little risk of contagious madness in the country estates of the English aristocracy, a group for whom Jefferson felt little affinity, so he could allow himself a brief tour of English country houses and gardens with John Adams. He was thereby able to assess directly Lord Burlington's villa, and some refracted images of its exterior were coolly included in Monticello in its final form. Later, he traveled along the Rhine, where, as Marie Kimball notes, he "passed through all the great cathedral towns . . . without a word of what he saw."

Jefferson had no difficulty in maintaining his equanimity in Strasbourg, Nancy, Lyon, Bordeaux, Brittany, Normandy, and Burgundy. He lavished time upon the rice culture of the Po Valley, upon Turin, Milan, and Genoa. But he made no effort to reach Rome, nor did he go to see the houses of Palladio, a day's journey beyond the rice fields. So when Jefferson spoke to Latrobe of his "reverence for the Graecian & Roman style of architecture," he was speaking not of the sort of reverence that leads to pilgrimage but instead of the sort that is useful in argumentation, that which may be emulated.†

This is odd—the grand tour of the antiquities of Italy was considered essential to the architectural education of gentlemen of his time, his means, and his level of sophistication. And when he returned, he wrote to George Wythe: "In architecture, painting, sculpture, I found much amusement, but more than all in their agriculture, many objects of which might be adopted with us to great advantage."

---

*Egon Verheyen informs me that Goethe wrote about Paestum twice. The first time, he expressed disappointment, the second, he admitted satisfaction, as its unfamiliar proportions arranged themselves in his mind.

†According to Egon Verheyen, Jefferson reflected on this trip in his "Hints to Americans Travelling in Europe," insisting that Americans should observe carefully only the kind of architecture which might be emulated in American conditions. The "Notes on Virginia," of course, spoke of building to last, not merely to impress. In "Hints" Jefferson thought it "preposterous" to study what would be "too expensive . . . for us." (For "Hints" see *Papers of Thomas Jefferson,* Julian P. Boyd, ed., Princeton, N.J.: Princeton University Press, 1956, vol. 13, p. 264.)

What a dissembler he was, writing as if he were some shallow touring rustic, this man to whom architecture was a passion. He was, indeed, intent upon being "impenetrable." He could search literary precedents to justify predilections arising from depths in his nature. But, like anyone else who has learned of architecture from books, where it must be dried and shrunken into miniature plans and elevations, he was setting himself up to be overwhelmed by the real thing. As he was by the Halle aux Blés.

45

GRANDEUR IN THE EIGHTIES

The most exciting architecture in Paris of the 1780s—to architectural critics of the 1980s—has been called by many of those critics "revolutionary." The men who made it were, nearly all of them, firmly monarchist, reactionary, and opposed to the political ideas of Jefferson, Brissot, and Mirabeau, to say nothing of fiercer spirits like Robespierre and, at the leftward extreme, Babeuf. Let us take the cases of the most celebrated of these "revolutionaries," Claude-Nicolas Ledoux and Etienne-Louis Boullée.

When Ledoux referred, as he often did, to "the beauty of the masses," he was speaking only in architectural terms. In his days of glory he had rejoiced in standing "at the apogee" of royal favor. Ledoux became architect to Louis XV through the patronage of Mme Du Barry. His most famous commission was the building of a new wall around Paris, pierced by forty-seven gates and customhouses now much admired in engravings and in a few surviving examples. They were forty-seven variations on a theme: how art can serve internal revenue.

At the end of the 1780s, Jefferson was annoyed by the inconvenience posed by these "palaces by which we are to be let in and out." Though he was only inconvenienced, the hungry populace was angered. By exacerbating their resentment, architecture contributed to the revolutionary temper of the time. As the popular expression went, "Le mur murant Paris rend Paris murmurant." The farmers who brought produce to the inhabitants of Paris had to pay tribute at these gates to the "farmers general," the tax collectors asked by the improvident court to make up its expenses.

Some of this "revolutionary architecture" is known to us only in pictures of it burning; indeed, Ledoux himself might have been burnt had not the merciful death devised by Dr. Guillotin replaced the auto-da-fé as a means of public execution, and had he not narrowly escaped even the guillotine. He did no work during the revolution. His political preferences were made clear when he offered his services to Napoleon and dedicated a folio of his work to the czar of Russia.*

Most of the "revolutionary architects" were left during the revolution with little to do but indulge themselves in geometrical visions and an occasional commission for a festival or for temporary assembly halls. Their visions were large and stark. Perhaps because they were in life left so powerless, in art they endeavored to overwhelm.† Had much of their work been built, it would have made walking a street in Paris like traversing a fissure in the Greenland icecap: the winds would howl amid bleak and awesome expanses; seamless surfaces would deny the tiniest niche wherein to await a carriage.

Boullée was not popular during the revolution and became a member of the Institute of France only after the Jacobins were replaced by the Directory. Like Ledoux, he allowed himself to be "overpowered by an excessive love for the poetry of architecture." His Piranesian *Perspective View of the Metropolitan Cathedral* leaves no doubt that he intended us in such a building to be "overwhelmed by the extraordinary spectacle of inconceivable space."

Even in imperial France, after 1804, there was little scope for dreams like these; only Napoleon's Arc de Triomphe is of their scale. If Bonaparte had conquered the world, we might have seen the full expression of what is sometimes called "the architecture of the Enlightenment." Perhaps he might have spent the wealth of India to accommodate his own ambitions—and those of Ledoux or Boullée.

Revolutionary Architecture in America

The drawings and commentary of Ledoux had certain secondary and unintended effects in America. His ideas for communal dwellings ("condominia" would be a more appropriate title had it not been appropriated for other uses) were adopted, later in the nineteenth century, by the Saint-Simonians and the Fourierists, French utopian planners, who in turn contributed a set of notions to the communal villages of utopian Americans still later.

This is not a very impressive consequence of a style properly to be called "revolutionary." Neoclassicism, however, was broader than the work of a few interesting but largely unfulfilled architects in Paris; and even the excesses of the Parisian school could be redeemed by American poverty, which reduced

---

*The czar, who owned hundreds of thousands of "souls," was the proprietor of a number of Siberian model towns for which Ledoux would have been the ideal designer. There is a concentration-camp quality in the renowned village Ledoux designed around the royal saltworks in the forest of Chaux.

†It can be said for the baroque that it had sufficient movement and ornamentation to relieve its vastnesses. It could be grandiose and repetitive and therefore boring. But it was never so frigid as the buildings of the "visionaries."

its geometric clarity to a pleasant scale and left a legacy of beautiful small buildings.

Latrobe liked to tell the story that one day, as he passed by his newly completed Bank of Pennsylvania, he observed "two French officers standing opposite the building and looking at it without saying a word." He stepped into a doorway to hear their comments. "After some time one of them exclaimed several times, 'C'est si beau, et si simple!' . . . I do not recollect anything that has happened that has given me so much particular satisfaction."

The bank was tiny by Parisian standards. It could have fitted into the kitchen courtyard of a Parisian palace or acted as a construction hut for a project of a Ledoux, or as one of the speculative cottages of the duc d'Orléans. A son of the duke, Louis Philippe, was not pleased by American scale during his visit to Washington. Accustomed to palaces intended for processions, to staircases created for the entrances and exits of monarchs striving to appear larger than life, he thought "the front entrance" of the President's residence "ridiculously small." Taking the White House and the Capitol together, he gave his judgment that when finished, "the result will not be more beautiful than the pavilions at the new gates of Paris."

He was speaking of those tollbooths by Ledoux that Jefferson failed to admire, the tollbooths of the "farmers general" (one of these "farmers," it

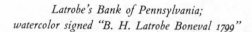

Latrobe's Bank of Pennsylvania;
watercolor signed "B. H. Latrobe Boneval 1799"

Ledoux's Pavilion of Mlle Guimard; drawing by Sir William Chambers

happens, was Boullée). Despite frequent allusions in architectural textbooks to the influence of a design by Ledoux upon the design for Pavilion IX at the University of Virginia, it is by no means sure that Ledoux had anything to do with it. It is true that, in a rare playful interlude in 1770, he had provided the dancer Mlle Guimard with a flirtatious little house with an inviting coved recess over its entrance.* It does have something in common with Pavilion IX, but they have a common original in a well-known Pirenesian print of a ruin in Rome.

Aside from its proximity to the Maison Lakanal—see p. 349—it is fair to note that the Guimard house was just down the Chaussée d'Antin from the residence of Jefferson's friend Mme de Corny and her husband, who had been commissary for the French army in America. (Among her other friends were Mrs. Cosway and Angelica Schuyler Church, whose husband had been enriched by the purchases of American produce by M. de Corny.) Mlle Guimard was notorious, and so was her house: one of its doors led directly to a bath chamber set behind a demure little classical screen like an inverted bodice. (Others see it as a screened apsidal arch.)

But never in his lifelong correspondence with either Mrs. Cosway or Mme

*This structure was replaced, around 1788, by a mansion designed by Ramée (see Turner, in *Art Bulletin*).

de Corny did Jefferson mention the Guimard house. Furthermore, a notation on the sketch for Pavilion IX indicates that it was Latrobe, not Jefferson, who suggested its façade. Latrobe did not need Ledoux. The form could be seen all over England, and had been deployed by many architects who had access to Pirenesi "prints." It was especially beloved by Robert Adam but used by James Wyatt and by Henry Holland—among other places, in a pleasant boudoir at Berrington Hall. It became very popular on both sides of the Atlantic. Variations appeared, some of them Masonic, in Baltimore and Philadelphia. Ramée offered one at Calverton, and Latrobe another at Kalorama, well before the university got under way. Others appeared in the work of Maximilian Godefroy, Robert Mills, and William Jay.

If Mlle Guimard's house were the prototype for a pavilion in the stern academic compound of Thomas Jefferson, this would be chiefly notable as a demonstration that Jefferson had a sense of humor; Pavilion IX was intended to serve as a station for a faculty member to police unruly students, more like a *barrière* than a courtesan's apartment.

Elevation and floor plans for Pavilion IX, University of Virginia,
by Thomas Jefferson (as suggested by B. H. Latrobe?)

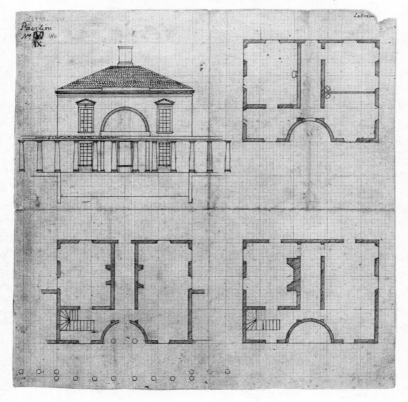

Hope and Respect

Jefferson was, however, very serious about architecture. He was not "impenetrable." His vulnerability to architecture was as poignant as his vulnerability to love. He knew himself well enough to keep himself protected from either those aesthetic or those romantic experiences that might distract him from his carefully measured, meticulously planned life. He was one of those people who are readily reached by the archetypal power of architectural space. (John Ruskin and Carl Jung were other such persons.)

Two experiences with actual buildings, both of them French in style, determined the course of his aesthetic development and that of his country. He memorialized the first of these in a sketch, the fervency of which tells us how deeply he was moved.

Monticello is seen by many people as the most French of American neoclassical buildings—not including, of course, those built by French architects. We might say something of the sort—with a word and a place substituted here and there—about Welgelegen, on the edge of the Haarlem Wood near The Hague. The English historian David Watkin describes it as the only full-scale example in Holland of the architecture of Louis XVI. Thomas Jefferson gave his version of that building in the most passionate drawing he ever made.

Welgelegen appeared earlier in these pages as the country mansion built by Henry Hope, banker of Amsterdam and Boston. (It now houses regional government offices.) Jefferson made his sketch in 1788, twenty years before the Great Silver Scheme; but with his usual eerie instinct for the significant phrase, he said at the time that the house "cost four tons of silver." After he became President he had good cause to associate the Hopes with silver, as subsequent Americans associate them with the great diamond now in the collection of the Smithsonian Institution.

Money, and financial embarrassment, would have been much on Jefferson's mind that spring day in 1788. He had been negotiating an extension of the debts of the United States by a Dutch banking syndicate. He and John Adams had gone to Amsterdam in fear of "our incurring something like a bankruptcy in Holland." They found things easier than they expected and "were able to set the loan agoing again." The fledgling nation could fly a little farther.

Monticello was on his mind as well: buoyed by his diplomatic success, Jefferson executed a second mission, purchasing, for his distant home amid the "savage" hills of the Blue Ridge, supplies not readily available in his base in Paris: a waffle iron, a pound of Hyson's tea, books, and a letter press.

Then he set forth to the countryside, for tulips and for architecture. He rode for hours through thousands of acres of tulips; their colors shone in the sunlight

Welgelegen

in a profusion extending across that Dutch flatness which eventuates but never seems to end as it enters imperceptibly the tides and mists of the sea.

Finally, this impressionable frontiersman turned a corner, around an edge of the Haarlem Wood . . . and he saw an apotheosis of his own vision of Monticello.

Jefferson had left his house unfinished, with its last design a "biloggial" one, with a temple-form portico above and a loggia below, three rooms wide and one deep. It was all he had been able to conjure out of his books, his experience with traditional Virginia cross plans, and his dreams.* Now, between the tulips and the woodland, he saw his little wooden house with a double portico grown into a huge Franco-Palladian palace. His wooden essay had been expanded into a vast actuality of marble.

Jefferson has left us a sketch, very shakily drawn, of the images fusing in his mind at that moment. It is usually said to depict Welgelegen, but it is no more a picture of Henry Hope's country mansion than it is the house in progress at Monticello.

*A form available to Palladians from the engravings of the master's Villa Cornaro at Piombino Dese and the garden front of the Villa Pisani at Montagnana. (Jefferson used it again at the University of Virginia.)

After he collected himself from his shock of recognition and made his drawing, Jefferson would easily have been able to detect differences other than scale between Monticello and Welgelegen. The palace before him centered upon a domed "tribune" flanked by two galleries for the display of Hope's paintings; the first Monticello had no dome. Welgelegen deployed the family and guest quarters in wings spreading opulently to the sides; the first Monticello had nothing like this.

How could the Virginian planter not have felt oppressed by a sense of the inadequacy of his country notions? Did he feel a pinch at his spine, something close to humiliation?

Already he had spoken of himself, to American friends, as being stretched to accommodate "new manners and new modes of living." In the presence of the splendor and the convoluted expectations of the Old World, he felt "savage enough to prefer the woods, the wilds" he once had thought to ornament by bookish Palladianism. On his mountaintop he had been building a pavilion in what he had thought was the latest mode. Even before he saw Henry Hope's *paviljoen,* he had begun to doubt himself and to tell others he was "a savage of the mountains."

We have only Jefferson's shaky sketch to record his state of mind, but it is difficult not to read it as the confession of a provincial abashed by an artifactual comment upon his tentative efforts at a cosmopolitan architecture.

After his return to America in 1789, Jefferson did not complete the Monticello he had designed in the 1770s. After he retired from George Washington's cabinet at the end of 1793, he commenced a new building campaign. First, he took down the upper portion of the house and commenced construction of the second Monticello. It had no double portico, no tripartite massing; it had a central domed mass, gallery spaces, and spreading wings.

These similarities to a mansion in the French style in Holland were much too subtle for anyone to compare Mr. Jefferson's house with a distant palace worth four tons of silver*—too subtle, perhaps, even for Jefferson himself to have associated Welgelegen and Monticello: sufficient to the day was his assertion that his experience in France had shown him that "all the new and good houses are of a single story."

After 1793, Jefferson composed a new and consoling form for Monticello, upon its "interior arrangement . . . of the French character,"† and upon a dome

---

*Only those who knew the contents of his sketchbook could observe the similarities between the new Monticello and the palace that Jefferson designed for the royal governor of Virginia at Williamsburg. It too would have had porticoes front and back, a "double pile" format, with a narrow little Palladian staircase toward the center. But, like Monticello I, it would have lacked the dome—the most compelling feature of Monticello II.

†At this point, Robert Mills's notes on architecture in Virginia sputter out with the words "He was . . ." What did he not quite say about Jefferson? This first committed Greek revivalist to be born

Final elevation of the first version of Monticello, 1771, by Thomas Jefferson

Jefferson's sketch of Welgelegen—and Monticello I(?)

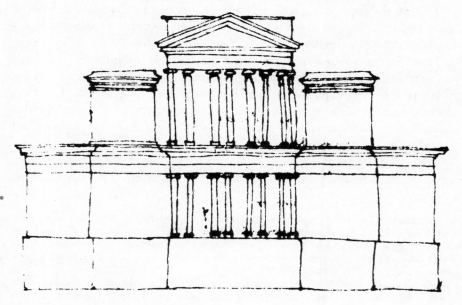

that owes its prominence more to a grain market, and a lady, than to any book, even to Welgelegen, or, for that matter, to any other mansion anywhere.

46

THE CURVE OF THE CORN MARKET

In the Paris grain market, the Halle aux Blés,* Thomas Jefferson met Mrs. Maria Cosway. It was a lovely day in August 1786. For him, she was the only person present, though she may have been accompanied by her brother, George Hadfield (the shy but charming man who became an architect of the Capitol in Washington), and by her ugly little husband, Richard Cosway, a painter of miniatures, who gained his wealth not so much as an artist but as a profiteer from art.

Maria and George Hadfield, children of tumult, were born in Florence. Their father, an English innkeeper, maintained establishments popular as way stations for gentlemen taking the architectural grand tour of Italy. The death of Hadfield senior drove the family to Rome and then to London, where Maria early learned how to survive in the demimonde of artists, courtesans, and courtiers dependent upon the prince regent. She could paint a little, speak a little in "five or six languages"; she was "active, ambitious, proud and restless." After rejecting the suits of at least one composer and another printer, at twenty-two she accepted Cosway, promiscuously bisexual, seventeen years her senior, but becoming rich. The painter James Northcote, who knew them well, later said "she always despised him."

Cosway gained those riches by means as characteristic of the time as the land-hawking of Joel Barlow or the globe-girdling smuggling operations of David Parish. Cosway accommodated the panic of those fearful French aristocrats who were buying land in America and selling their portable assets to establish bank accounts in London. John Walker, former director of the National Gallery in Washington, tells us that Cosway "was the Joseph Duveen of his time, and like that dealer he amassed a fortune. Pictures were cheap, and he even found a man in Belgium who sold them by the pound."

---

in America, tutored in this affinity by Latrobe, said of Jefferson in another set of reflections, at the outset of his autobiography, that "Mr. Jefferson was altogether Roman in his taste for architecture, and continued so to the day of his decease." (See appendices to Gallagher, pp. 158–59.)

*I have used Jefferson's plural form of the French word for grain or corn as he used it in writing to Latrobe about the Halle aux Blés. In his "Dialogue of the Head and Heart," written to Maria Cosway, he uses another plural, "Bleds," an eighteenth-century French spelling for "Blés." This is how Howard Rice, in his *Thomas Jefferson's Paris,* spells it. Others use the singular form "au Blé."

Cosway brought these "battered canvasses" home, "restored" them with his miniaturist's brush, provided new and suitable attributions, and sold them "for a handsome profit." Walker also suggests that bric-a-brac, furniture, and tapestries could be bought on the Continent "for a song," and that Cosway, "with his rich friends, placed his booty advantageously."

Maria, after a year of private training in the graces, was turned loose on the prince of Wales and other clients with potential for Cosway. It is said that there was once a secret passage from her bedroom, in Schomberg House on Pall Mall, to the prince's residence, Carlton House. This is geographically possible, and in character. Gouverneur Morris, the diplomat and gossip, reported that her house was always full of "princes and bohemians."

Her own habits were somewhat bohemian. In Paris, while she was Jefferson's companion, she was sufficiently accessible to others to be described as "like the fair Aspasia of old." In London, her lovers, aside from the prince, were reputed to include composers, painters, and one of the male members of the operatic family of Marchesi, with whom she traveled abroad. She had a daughter named Louisa Paolina, whose godfather—and probably biological father—was the Corsican general di Paoli, whom she met a little before she met Thomas Jefferson. She kept a vast collection of di Paoli's letters into her old age. We do not know what she kept of Jefferson's.*

This was the lady of "a form extremely delicate, and a pleasing manner," just twenty-six, who came to Paris in the summer of 1786 to join her husband on a scavenging trip. He came ostensibly to paint miniatures of the children of the duc d'Orléans—the children who, grown somewhat, later toured America as Louis Philippe and his brothers.

Autumnal Sweetness

The widower Jefferson had gone to the Paris grain market as he had gone to the delta of the Po, on one of his dutiful tours of facilities for the production and distribution of agricultural products. On this occasion he was accompanied by his friend John Trumbull, the painter, who happened also to have been a classmate, at the Royal Academy, of George Hadfield's, and could introduce the Virginian to Maria.

In the market, they all solemnly examined the new dome, one hundred and thirty feet across, erected with laminated wooden struts by Legrand and Molinos according to the method described by the Renaissance architect Philibert de l'Orme, or "Delorme."

Maria Cosway so intrigued Jefferson that by the end of the day he sent "lying

*Her records remain impounded in the Vatican, so we cannot be sure.

Richard Cosway, a self-portrait

messengers" to cancel his dinner with the duchesse de Rochefoucauld. Until early October, the tall American minister and the wife of the dwarfish Cosway had an idyll of sightseeing and picnicking and other "follies." Jefferson admitted to being so inspirited that he took to vaulting over fences. It is wonderful to imagine him so, though sad to relate that on attempting such a hurdle in the Cours-la-Reine, this middle-aged gentleman sprained his wrist. It was with his left hand, therefore, that he wrote his famous "Dialogue of the Head and Heart." Sadder still, the two of them had very little time; and his right hand never recovered sufficiently to permit him to resume playing the violin.

They became tourists of art, surveying the construction sites of Paris and the older monuments: the Galerie du Louvre, the Garde-Meubles, and the two fronts of the Hôtel de Salm suggested later by Jefferson to L'Enfant as models for the President's House in Washington City. Jefferson was a tireless enthusiast, thrilling, exhausting, and refreshingly naive.

The idyll could not last; Cosway insisted that she return with him to London. She was useful to him: her sweetness caught many bees. Jefferson returned to a suburban "hermitage" at a discreet distance from the center of things.

From August through December 1787, Maria Cosway managed to stand off her husband's scoldings and was able to find time to participate in more architectural and horticultural tours. Jefferson had come to know M. Thouin, chief of the king's gardens, and, during their first autumn, he and Maria made happy expeditions to the new fantasies erected in the garden of M. de Monville at the Désert de Retz, four miles from Saint-Germain.

Thomas Jefferson by John Trumbull

Gardens were important to both of them, and to others who have been important to us. (Jefferson was later able to exchange seeds with Thouin—and so was Irénée Du Pont—because Thouin and, as we have noted, his garden had been rescued from the Terror by Joseph Lakanal.) It is touching to find in the first of his responses to her, when their correspondence renewed in 1795, these lines: "I am eating the peaches, grapes and figs of my own garden & only wish I could eat them in your native country, gathered on the spot & in your good company . . . I am permitted from the innocence of the scenes around me to learn to practice innocence toward all . . ."

Rejected Visions

They also made a little "visionary" tour, visiting the pavilion at Louveciennes, designed by Ledoux for Mme Du Barry (and later haunted by her American tormentor, George Grieve; see p. 91). As for the renowned M. Boullée, he could be assessed as the architect of the country house of the comtesse de Tessé, Jefferson's correspondent about insurrection and architecture in Nîmes and aunt of Lafayette's wife. Jean-François Chalgrin's church of Saint-Philippe de Roule

Maria Cosway c. 1788, by her husband, Richard Cosway

remained in his mind sufficiently for him to simplify some of its elements for the only church he himself designed, Christ Church in Charlottesville.

In these last days of the old regime, the taste of Thomas Jefferson was becoming more conservative, not more revolutionary, perhaps because Maria Cosway was aesthetically antiquarian, as people at the edge of respectability often are (a point to which any seller of *boiserie* can testify), perhaps because of the resistance to "visionary" artistic ideas on the part of the circle of French Freemasons to which he was introduced by Benjamin Franklin. The taste of the duc de Chanteloup, the sculptor Houdon, and Lafayette had advanced no further than the English Masons of the circle of Burlington fifty years earlier.

Jefferson saw classical art largely through French eyes, but not the eyes of his own generation. The professors of architecture whom he met in the flesh were all, like Clérisseau, elderly Frenchmen. And when he turned to his "old

French books," many of them were old indeed. These were not the young geometrizers of neoclassicism.

After his return, Jefferson cautioned his countrymen against permitting any architect to stray far from precedent, "to draw an external according to his fancy." His early advocacy of archaeological (and paradoxically "advanced") neoclassicism for public buildings came to an end with his design for the Virginia capitol, as adjusted by Clérisseau. As we have noted earlier, Secretary of State Jefferson pressed L'Enfant to adapt to America that 1675 façade of the Louvre and one of the buildings beside what is now called the place de la Concorde. These buildings were old when he and Maria Cosway explored them. (Two hundred years had to pass before, unhappily, that concept was achieved along Constitution Avenue.)

Better the architecture of the Bourbons than too much novelty. "Experience shows that about once in a thousand times a pleasing form is hit upon." No, not for Virginia nor for the District of Columbia would there be "the brat of a whimsical conception never before brought to light." Instead, America should benefit from "some model already devised and approved . . . [or] copied from the most precious, most perfect model of ancient architecture," something that had gained "approbation—[for] nearly 2000 years."

Jefferson was no longer running "before the times" like the Jefferson of the 1770s. Only privately, and twenty years later, did he become free to experiment again, using French graph paper and recalling the experience, now safely internalized, of France before its revolution.

The Dome

Maria Cosway entered his life in a space that had been a sixteenth-century idea, materialized in his own time. The structural system had been proposed by Philibert de l'Orme in 1561, and was finally implemented in Paris in the 1780s. It produced what was, for Thomas Jefferson, "the most superb thing on earth!" For the rest of his life he tried to persuade architects to reproduce the "noble dome" of the Halle aux Blés. A little larger or a little smaller did not matter; it was that encompassing yet not suffocating, constant yet not boring, firm but luminous femaleness that counted.

Jefferson took home to America a copy of de l'Orme's Treatise of 1561 to help him explain to others how such things might be done. About 1801, he began constructing at Monticello a mysterious "skyroom" under such a dome. Its use is not readily apparent, except, perhaps, as a shrine to de l'Orme and to Maria Cosway and, it is possible, as an observatory. Jefferson did visit a similar space at the Greenwich Observatory, but Egon Verheyen kindly agrees with me that it may also be in that room that Jefferson wrote to Maria, as he did for nearly forty years.

Halle aux Blés; pen and wash drawing by J. B. Maréchal

His last letter went to her when he was eighty-one and she sixty-five. She had been made a baroness by the Austrian emperor for founding a convent school for girls at Lodi in Italy, like the one she had attended many, many years before. She was not herself interested in returning to convent life even then; she wrote her last letter to Jefferson from her palace in Florence, looking at the portrait of him she kept in her painted gallery. The palace was not distant from the building where her father had kept a boardinghouse.

A Romantic Obsession

Jefferson's feeling for their meeting place became a romantic obsession. He first suggested its form for a market at Richmond, and then in his own design for the White House. When the young Charles Bulfinch visited him in Paris, Jefferson encouraged him in what turned out to be a very brief flirtation with French ideas; in 1791 Bulfinch, back in conservative, Anglophile Boston, wrote his friend James Cutler, who was then in Paris, to send him old French books by the architectural historians Neufforge, Le Roy, and any new publications about de l'Orme domes. Jefferson was even so early as that arbiter of Franco-American architectural exchange.

After Jefferson became President, able to ordain large architectural ventures, he proposed a covered dry dock 175 by 800 feet in size, covered by a de l'Orme barrel vault. He sent for Latrobe, who produced a design reduced to approximately 165 by 780 feet internally, entered through Doric porticoes. Latrobe could rise to presidential suggestion, but such French visions were too vast for Congress. It refused to pay for the scheme.

Latrobe had offered Jefferson the proof he required, however. Clearly, the architect had the right instincts. In 1803, Jefferson appointed Latrobe Surveyor of the Public Buildings of the United States. Little could he know the persistence of Jefferson's determination to reproduce in America "the most superb thing on earth."

Soon the President was trying to force him to cover the House of Representatives with a de l'Orme dome, pierced with the kind of skylights used at the Halle aux Blés. Latrobe thought the scheme contrary to "conscience and common sense." While Jefferson was sojourning at Monticello, the architect went ahead, instead, to frame a wooden dome,* with a lantern, or cupola—perhaps as a temporary measure he hoped would become permanent.

Jefferson was not happy at what he saw when he returned to Washington. Latrobe was respectful, expressing the "deepest mortification that I have had the misfortune to displease you." But, though he was addressing the chief magistrate and no mean amateur of architecture, he did not concede: "I am convinced by the evidence of my senses in innumerable cases, by all my professional experience for near twenty years, and by all my reasonings."

Jefferson replied with an examination question for this "professional": what were the classical precedents for Latrobe's lantern? He got back a prickly answer: Latrobe knew his precedents, but he did not propose to do imitations of old buildings just because they were popular with Jefferson.

Archetypal Argument

Jefferson deployed every device of rationality and authority to be found either in his books or in his presidential position to induce Latrobe to accede to the architecture required by passion. He even argued that the dome of the Paris grain market was "like that of the Pantheon." Latrobe, who was one of the handful of people in America who had seen both the Pantheon and the grain market, knew better. Jefferson lost the point on the merits, but he was President and did not need to win that way. It is one measure of the man that he took the trouble to try.

Latrobe conceded, rhetorically, that if he knew an instance where "the Grecian style can be copied without impropriety," he would be content to be a "slavish copyist." But "the forms and distributions of the Roman & Greek

---

*The timbers were to be of the kind of New England white pine long used for the masts of His Majesty's warships.

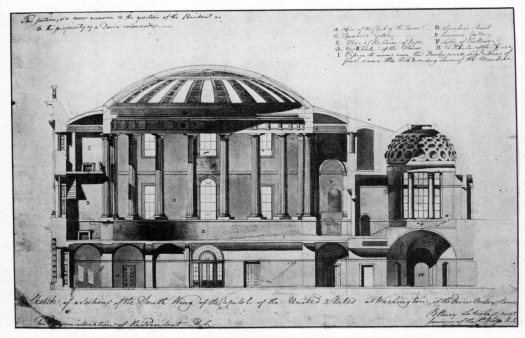

"*A Sketch of a Section of the South Wing of the Capitol of the United States
at Washington . . . for the consideration of the President U.S.*"
by "B. Henry Latrobe, arch."

buildings which remain are . . . inapplicable to the objects and uses of our public
buildings. Our religion requires a church wholly different from the temples,
our legislative assemblies and our courts of justice, buildings of entirely different principles from their basilicas . . ."

Jefferson was President. The striplights were built, producing conditions
perhaps acceptable for a grain market but not for a legislative assembly. In 1805,
with Jefferson's approval, the striplights were abandoned and replaced by panels,
each with a single light.

Latrobe, like most of Jefferson's contemporaries, mistook his man. He fell
into the error of thinking of a gifted and cosmopolitan amateur as merely
provincial; it was then that he complained to his brother of Jefferson's "prejudices in favor of the old French books, out of which he fishes everything."

Like so many people, Latrobe did not perceive the passionate man beneath
the don, the man who cloaked his preferences with precedents. Jefferson would
sometimes ride a runaway horse of emotion, but as he disappeared into the
underbrush, he could be heard reciting scraps of literary justification for his
predicament.

Jefferson's attempts "to force the state of things into the mould of his theories" were no more strenuous than his efforts to mold physical reality to accommodate the requirements of his emotions. As we all do, he found material means to reconstitute the forms that are most potent in the unconscious. As architects have known since antiquity, the experience of the spaces so created will thereafter invoke those forms and the archetypes behind them.

The Prepotency of an Idea

A number of strands in this story came together in 1811, when the theater occupying the site of Quesnay de Beaurepaire's old Academy Building in Richmond caught fire during a performance, burying in its embers the governor of Virginia, the mayor of the city, and more than seventy others who had been in the audience. A committee was formed to select an architect for a memorial and a church to be built to commemorate the tragedy. Latrobe and Robert Mills both contended for the job. Mills won, with a de l'Orme design, though Latrobe told a committee sensitive to the risk of fire: "As to covering the church with a wooden roof, you ought not to think of it."

But Jefferson was constantly thinking of it; after the "sky room" at Monticello had been completed, he had asked Mills to draw plans for a similar dome for a house for "a public officer," and in the following decades Mills went on to build five circular and domed churches, all invoking the ghost of the Paris grain market.* (As the years unfolded, four of these five churches with wooden domes were destroyed by fire—except, in mock of Latrobe's warning, the Monumental Church.)

The Monumental Church of Richmond and the sky room at Monticello were tributes, I believe, to Thomas Jefferson's recollection of a sunny day in August 1786, probably the happiest day, at the outset of the happiest two months, of his life.

Home at Last

After dinner at Monticello, in a haze of tobacco and wine, one might have felt oneself in a villa on a hilltop overlooking the Seine.

Mr. Jefferson's house was pervaded by nostalgia for France. He had brought back from Paris books, pictures, wine, furniture, and anecdotes. Jefferson shared

---

*It seems likely that Mills had the temerity to place one of Mr. Jefferson's de l'Orme vaults over the heads of six thousand Federalists for whom he designed Washington Hall in Philadelphia. We cannot be certain, for no structural analysis remains to us of this building, now long gone.

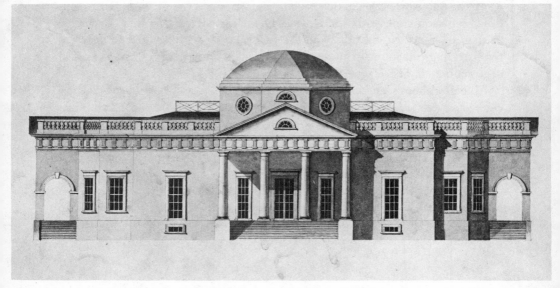

West elevation of Monticello, c. 1803; attributed to Robert Mills

a vanished past with Talleyrand; its recollection was "sweet" to them both. Had Talleyrand visited Monticello in the 1820s, he would have sensed this instantly, as he entered Jefferson's house as one did a French residence of the time of Louis XVI, through a foyer with a mezzanine.

Though Talleyrand did not return to America and could not call upon the Sage at Monticello, Jefferson's visitors did include Federalists, dissident Republicans, and Whigs who came to make peace with him—men like Edward Livingston and Daniel Webster. They found an old man whose table talk was all of Paris in the 1780s. Webster found touching the French customs at table, the French stories, and the French innuendoes, which, during the Whiskey Rebellion and the quasi war, when Jacobinism and nullification were in the air, would have seemed seditious to people of his persuasion.

Henry Adams was probably right: Jefferson "seemed during his entire life to breathe with perfect satisfaction nowhere except in the liberal, literary, and scientific air of Paris in 1789."

"Paris in 1789"—a phrase of some tenderness for an Adams. And if that Adams happened to be a historian, he would recall that one of the elements of Jefferson's "satisfaction" had been the beginning of a friendship with John Adams; both were serving as commissioners to the French government, though neither seems to have felt the other to be a competitor at this happy stage of their careers.

They rambled together about the city and on country walks. Abigail Adams called Jefferson "one of the choice ones of the earth"; her daughter concurred: "a man of great sensibilities," and the two men set forth on their celebrated tour of English country houses and gardens, followed by their successful negotiations in The Hague.

Abigail Adams's enthusiasm for Jefferson cooled as her husband and he entered a brief period of joint and very abrasive service in the second administration of George Washington. This was the autumn of their friendship.

There was a long winter. Adams was President from 1797 to 1801, constantly under criticism from Jefferson, who, in turn, occupied that office for the next eight years, barraged by salvos from Adams.

Then came a thaw during the troubled presidency of the amiable James Madison. Finally, in their old age, they had a second springtime and struck up a cozy correspondence, finding subjects to agree upon until they both died on July 4, 1826.

APPENDICES

I

Some Underrecorded Frenchmen

Some of the new fortresses of the American republic were built under the direction of French military engineers upon much older ruins bearing the marks of French military craftsmanship. As early as 1562, Jean Ribault built the first of the military installations on what is now the Marine training center on Parris Island, South Carolina. (John Reps, in the course of his inquiries into town planning in Virginia, suggested that Ribault's triangular fort was the model for the first English fort at Jamestown.)

Ribault's intruders were massacred by the Spaniards, on religious grounds rather than political—the French at hand were Protestant. French royal policy itself became more and more repressive of religious dissent after 1620, and Huguenot technocrats began to arrive in British America, ready to serve Protestant lords of any nationality.

Requiring a design for a fort at Yorke, on the York River, in Virginia, the settlers of Virginia compensated Nicholas Martieu (or Martiau), a skillful military engineer, with a new citizenship and a grant of sixteen hundred acres, including the terrain around Yorktown where, in 1781, French military engineers laid up the earthworks to besiege Lord Cornwallis. (Among the lineal descendants of Martieu was a surveyor whose military reputation reached its apogee at Yorktown—George Washington.)

Martieu's successor among French-educated practitioners of his profession in the English colonies of America was the uncle, tutor, and long-suffering guardian of Jean-Jacques Rousseau. Gabriel Bernard had served in campaigns against the Turks with James Oglethorpe, who became the proprietor of Georgia; he laid out eleven towns for Franco-Swiss emigrants in Oglethorpe's domain, and may have composed the plan for Savannah itself. After his death in 1737, he was succeeded by William Gerard De Brahm, who designed more towns and more forts and led German colonists to Georgia. In the 1750s, he was busy as far inland as Fort Loudoun, in Tennessee, and gave Savannah a new set of fortifications. It seems that he lived on another four decades, and died at the end of the century in Philadelphia.

Claude-Joseph Sauthier was a contemporary of De Brahm's and mapped North Carolina and New York as De Brahm had provided the first detailed maps of Georgia and South Carolina. He was an Alsatian who had published elaborate garden designs and cartographic studies by the end of the 1760s, when he came to North Carolina in the service of Governor William Tryon. Anyone who wishes to know the shape of the early seacoast towns of that state depends upon Sauthier's view of them. Tryon was a willful, vainglorious, and splendid gentleman whose expensive tastes in gardens (designed by Sauthier) and in mansions detonated the smoldering resentments of upcountry colonists in 1771 and brought Sauthier to the field of Alamance, the first skirmish of what would shortly become a civil war and then fuse into a larger war for independence. (We know of Sauthier largely because of a chance visit to North Carolina by a South American revolutionary supported by a West Indian architect working in the United States; see p. 318.)

Sauthier went with Tryon to his next post, the military governorship of New York, where he met Lord Percy among the British occupation forces. After the British withdrew from the city, he went off to become chief landscape designer for Percy in England, leaving behind him a hastily drawn map of New York that caused endless trouble to Pierre Pharoux.

The first coastal defenses of the American republic were largely built by French engineers; so was the academy already training their replacements, at West Point. "The First American System," of geometric fortresses carrying cannons on earthen parapets, was created by French engineers employed by state governments during the Confederation and the first presidency. After 1807, when war with Britain became likely, the "Second System" commenced, using more masonry and circular and semicircular forms (back to Edward I!).

Napoleonic experience with massed artillery, and new concepts in casement construction developed by Montalembert, permitted the stacking of "decks" full of artillery and supported by sophisticated masonry construction; American fortresses were developed under the guidance of former officers of Napoleon to compose our "Third System." Civil War photographs of the results of bombardments of these older fortresses, with blackened apertures in their immense walls, cleavages holding crippled cannons like cigars in the mouths of drunken soldiers, are images of Napoleonic engineering put to the test in the 1860s.

II

Franco-Georgian Examples

Shirley Plantation is situated in a county named for King Charles on a river named for King James between New Kent County on the north and Prince George County on the south. The house is approached ceremonially, like a Norman château; there it is at the end of a long avenue of poplars, lying beyond a tight, rectangular forecourt: a brick mansion under a mansard roof.

Shirley was built in stages, between the 1720s and the 1770s, by Charles Carter, son of John Carter of Corotoman, an important personage in the transmission of architectural style in America (see *Architecture, Men, Women and Money*). No one has been able to establish when, during this fifty-year span, either the buildings in the forecourt or the mansard roof went into place, so I am free to offer this hypothesis: they are the consequence of a visit by a Scots trader, one of many who swarmed along the James trading Glasgow textiles and chinaware for tobacco. Let us call him "Mr. MacX."

My hypothetical Scot brought something extra to exchange for a little of the famous Carter hospitality: training in architecture at the hands of workmen themselves trained by the masters of the Franco-Scottish style, William Bruce and William Adam, father of the more famous Robert. These seasoned practitioners formed their styles in France; their practice was nourished by the vitality of an "auld alliance" that was no longer political but was still so strong in Scottish aesthetics as to survive a sea passage.

Thomas Waterman associated Ashdown, a tall, isolated house in the Berkshire downs built by Lord Craven about 1665; Shirley; and an earlier Carter house, Corotoman. Gervaise Jackson-Stops has subsequently suggested that Ashdown comes from the line of Balleroy and of Dutch houses based upon Balleroy, or from Balleroy directly. We know that William Bruce derived his Franco-Caledonian houses from Balleroy and other French prototypes; there is an easy connection between Bruce's work and Mount Pleasant. So we have two streams proceeding from the same source and eventuating in America: one represented in the Virginia forms passed through Dutch intermediaries and the other terminating with Mount Pleasant, passing through Scotland.

William Bruce and Lord Craven's architects (probably the Dutchmen Balthazar Gerbier and William Winde) learned much from Mansart's Balleroy. The hypothesis offered here is that two Scotsmen, John Macpherson and my hypothetical Mr. MacX, learned much from Bruce. Though Waterman, a passionate Anglophile, found Shirley's floor plan inexplicable except in association with Corotoman, and Corotoman unique except for its connections to Ashdown, I think it is easier to see them all as based upon a common source, and that in Normandy.

While he completed the first stages of his own long building campaign, Charles Carter lived in Corotoman, his father's house. Corotoman burned in 1729 (with consequences ranging as far as Tennessee, detailed in *Architecture, Men, Women and Money*). But we know that like Shirley, Mount Pleasant, and Ashdown, it had a peculiar, close little forecourt. Moreover, its dependencies were jammed against the house, as if land were as expensive in Virginia as in Paris or Amsterdam—a striking arrangement on a site with a whole continent opening before it. This arrangement did not last long in Virginia. It was found to be much too cramped for a climate where windows must be open and buildings dispersed to permit the breeze (when it can move the heavy, humid summer air) to dispel noise and smells.

A similar arrangement is equally striking at Ashdown, a lonely place set amid the long sweep of the downs. Why were buildings clustered like this? There was no need for defense, as there was, for example, where similar groupings appeared in the West Indies. Why would people in the settled portions of the mainland English colonies, in the middle of the eighteenth century, be so chary of opening out in the fashionable English Palladian style, embracing and dominating its landscape? Why so tight a hold on dependencies?

This is not English, nor is it likely that Macpherson was aping the plantation-fortresses of Jamaica or Barbados. It is French, French by way of Scotland or by way of the burghers and aristocrats of Holland, who were practical men, and willing to take good things from the architectural styles of their deadly enemies the Bourbon kings of France.

One of those Dutch aristocrats became King William III of England, and king as well of England's colonies. As such, he became arbiter of their taste. Courtiers, both Dutch and British, followed his Francophile preferences, as accentuated by the acute observations made directly in France by his most gifted architect, Christopher Wren.

The Williamness of Williamsburg

Waterman and other teachers of architectural history used to encourage students to distinguish between "early" Georgian, "middle" Georgian, and (especially) "late" Georgian by pointing to the steep roofs of many early mansions in Virginia and the gentler ones that were laid up later. (There were other criteria useful at examination time, such as the use of giant orders and projecting porticoes.) Several of the early, steep variety are to be found around Williams-burg. Many more are to be found in France and in Holland. If we are willing to attend to what Dutch scholars tell us about this, we find that steep roofs are less interesting as mnemonic devices for early Georgian than as signs of the influence of French architectural taste upon Holland and thus upon those British colonies in North America ruled by a Dutch prince during the years when Americans first became able to build ambitious houses.

William III was offered the crown of England after the Scottish James fled to France in 1688, and his influence seeped through the British system long after his death in 1702: Macaulay's *History of England* is really an extended political biography of William, his hero. Macaulay, I am sure, would expect us to search for the effects of William upon his American colonies. Since those effects might well include an architecture grounded in the Franco-Dutch taste of his court, that search is part of our larger quest.

We find a good deal of it at colonial Williamsburg: a place distinguished for its Williamness, or more precisely, its Willemness—the degree to which it is not English. There is no other English colonial city in America built along an extended "mall" on axes, a "place d'armes." Williamsburg is as ceremonial in plan as Detroit or Montreal or Saint Louis; like these French villages in the New World, it aspires toward Versailles.

John Reps's wonderful studies of the history of the town did not bring him precisely to this point; but he tells us how Francis Nicholson, who commenced the creation of a grand design for the town in 1699, followed baroque prece-dents derived from Jean de La Quintinie (by way of the diarist John Evelyn). Nicholson, "in Honour of our most gratious & glorious King William," labored to introduce upon the Virginia thickets and marshes a plan carrying vast monograms of *W* and *M,* for William and Mary.* This undertaking, almost as ambitious in its way as the prehistoric Indians' tracing of lines across the desert landscape of Peru, was the extreme reach of Anglo-Dutch monarch-ical pretension in America.

It is due to the maps presented by Reps that we are able to see how similar were the outcomes of Nicholson's ideas for Williamsburg and Major L'Enfant's for Washington—the capitols and the chief executive's residence are in the same relationship in both. Some have suggested that both are derived from Versailles, where some of the same relationships obtain, but Versailles centers upon a single building, as Washington does not.

Nor are the public buildings of colonial Williamsburg very English. They too are Franco-Dutch, very, very sedate under their steep roofs. Dutch histori-ans of the period require us to focus on those roofs. Like those of the Dutch models upon which Americans built houses we misname for one King George

---

*Eighteenth-century architectural treatises often illustrated such monogramania.

or another,* these roofs "determine the shape of the buildings as much as the roofs of such French buildings as the chateau at Maisons and Vaux-le-Vicomte."

The palace at Williamsburg has a tight little Franco-Dutch forecourt, like Shirley; it was a fit headquarters for a governor bearing instructions from a Dutch prince.

The capitol at Williamsburg has become even easier to see as Dutch since it was given a moat of sand in its reconstruction. If it were placed in a real moat, with lily pads and diving ducklings, it would be precisely like a small, brick-turreted manor house in the Low Countries. Its contemporary the first New York City Hall looked like this too, before it was replaced by a sleek neoclassical building, largely of French design.

Wrenaissance

Historians of Williamsburg have long claimed an association with Sir Christopher Wren, who rose in royal favor in England during the end of the seventeenth century, before the full onset of either the baroque or the Anglo-Palladian styles. If "Willemite" will not do, then how about "Wrenaissance"?†

This most English of architects (as he is often described) sometimes worked in an idiom as French as the Franco-Dutch taste of his sovereigns. His only trip abroad was to France, where he saw the same châteaux visited by William Bruce. He is said to have consulted with the great Mansart himself; one of Wren's earliest works was a design for Trinity College, Oxford, with a mansard roof—like that at Shirley.‡

Long before Wren completed his French education, English patrons such as Lord Craven were drawing upon French sources by way of Holland; and more steep-roofed brick cubes came to England with Charles II when he returned from exile in Holland in 1660. His entourage included architects such as Hugh May, who had been trained in Holland—trained, as the Dutch themselves tell us, to be "nearer to the spirit of Levau and François Mansart than to Palladio."

---

*Sometimes they are called "Queen Anne," after William's successor and the immediate predecessor of the first four Georges. But if that lady had any strong ideas of architecture, she probably was sympathetic to her friend the duchess of Marlborough's baroque. The neat, red-brick-and-white-trim Willemite buildings of Williamsburg are not similar to the theatrical palaces of Queen Anne's reign, such as the Marlboroughs' Blenheim.

†The term was coined by Sir Edwin Lutyens, and the concept sketched here, centering upon it, was developed at some length in *Architecture, Men, Women and Money*.

‡No, I do not mean to suggest that Wren be substituted for my Francophile Scotsman as the Carters' architect.

BIBLIOGRAPHY

Adams, Donald R. "The Beginning of Investment Banking in the United States." *Pennsylvania History* 45, no. 2 (April 1978).

————. *Finance and Enterprise in Early America*. Philadelphia: University of Pennsylvania Press, 1978.

Adams, Henry. *History of the United States of America During the Administrations of James Madison*. 2 vols. Literary Classics of the United States. New York: Viking, 1986.

————. *History of the United States of America During the Administrations of Thomas Jefferson*. 2 vols. Literary Classics of the United States. New York: Viking, 1986.

————. *The Life of Albert Gallatin*. Philadelphia: J. B. Lippincott & Co., 1879.

Adams, John. *Diary and Autobiography of John Adams*. Edited by L. H. Butterfield. Cambridge: Belknap Press of Harvard University Press, 1961.

————. *John Adams: A Biography in His Own Words*. Edited by James B. Peabody. New York: Newsweek, distributed by Harper & Row, 1973.

Adams, John Quincy. *The Diary of John Quincy Adams, 1794–1845: American Political, Social, and Intellectual Life from Washington to Polk*. Edited by Allan Nevins. New York: Longmans, Green and Co., 1929.

————. *Memoirs of John Quincy Adams, comprising portions of his diary from 1795 to 1848*. 12 vols. Edited by Charles Francis Adams. 1874–77. Reprint. Freeport, N.Y.: Books for Libraries Press, 1969.

Adams, William Howard, ed. *The Eye of Thomas Jefferson*. Washington: National Gallery of Art, 1976.

Alexander, Robert L. *The Architecture of Maximilian Godefroy*. Baltimore: Johns Hopkins University Press, 1974.

————. "Nicholas Rogers: Gentleman-Architect of Baltimore." *Maryland Historical Magazine* 78, no. 2 (Summer 1983).

————. "The Union Bank, by Long after Soane." *Journal of the Society of Architectural Historians* 22, no. 3 (October 1963).

Almanach National. Paris: Berger-Levrault, 1782, 1789, 1790, 1791, 1792.

American State Papers, Documents, Legislative, and Executive, of the Congress of the United States, folio edition, Finance, vol. 3. Library of Congress, Washington, D.C.

Architects' Emergency Committee. *Great Georgian Houses of America.* Reprint. New York: Dover, 1970.

Arnett, Ethel Stephens. *Mrs. James Madison: The Incomparable Dolley.* Greensboro, N.C.: Piedmont Press, 1972.

Aubry, Octave. *Napoleon, Soldier and Emperor.* London and Philadelphia: Lippincott, 1938.

Bauduy, Mrs. Pierre. *Family Souvenirs.* Translated by Mimi H. Garesché. Unpublished pamphlet. Historical Society of Delaware, 1975.

Bauduy Papers. Hagley Museum and Library, Wilmington, Del.

Beamish, Richard. *Memoir of the Life of Sir Marc Isambard Brunel, Civil Engineer, Vice-President of the Royal Society, Corresponding Member of the Institute of France, etc. . . .* London: Longman, Green, Longman, and Roberts, 1862.

Becker, Carl. Review of *America and Culture, 1750–1848,* by Howard Mumford Jones. *American Historical Review* 33, no. 4 (1927–1928).

Beeman, Richard R., ed. *Beyond Confederation: Origins of the Constitution and American National Identity.* Published for the Institute of Early American History and Culture, Williamsburg, Virginia. Chapel Hill: University of North Carolina Press, 1987.

Beeson, J. W. "Characters and Incidents." *Demopolis Express,* February 7, 1895. State Department of Archives and History, Montgomery, Alabama.

Bemis, Samuel Flagg. *Pinckney's Treaty: A Study of America's Advantage from Europe's Distress, 1783–1800.* Baltimore: Johns Hopkins Press, 1926.

Bernstein, Harry. *Origins of Inter-American Interest, 1700–1812.* New York: Russell & Russell, 1945.

Biddle (Nicholas) Papers. Library of Congress, Washington, D.C.

Bizardel, Yvon. *The First Expatriates: Americans in Paris During the French Revolution.* Translated by June P. Wilson and Cornelia Higginson. New York: Holt, Rinehart and Winston, 1975.

Blackburn, Roderic H., and Ruth Piwonka. *A Visible Heritage, Columbia County, New York: A History in Art and Architecture.* Kinderhook, N.Y.: Columbia County Historical Society, 1977.

Bos, Harriet P. "Barthelemy Lafon." Master's thesis, Tulane University, 1977.

Bowers, Claude. *Jefferson and Hamilton: The Struggle for Democracy in America.* Boston: Houghton Mifflin, 1925.

————. *Jefferson in Power: The Death Struggle of the Federalists*. Boston: Houghton Mifflin Company, 1936.

————. *The Young Jefferson, 1743–1789*. Boston: Houghton Mifflin Company, 1945.

Boyd, Julian. *Number 7: Alexander Hamilton's Secret Attempts to Control American Foreign Policy with supporting documents*. Princeton: Princeton University Press, 1964.

Braham, Allan. *The Architecture of the French Enlightenment*. Berkeley: University of California Press, 1980.

Brillat-Savarin, Jean Anthelme. *The Physiology of Taste; or, Meditations on Transcendental Gastronomy*. Translated by M. F. K. Fisher. San Francisco: North Point Press, 1986.

Brodie, Fawn. *Thomas Jefferson: An Intimate History*. New York: Bantam, 1975.

Brooks, Charles B. *The Siege of New Orleans*. Seattle: University of Washington Press, 1961.

Brooks, Van Wyck. *The World of Washington Irving*. New York: Dutton, Everyman edition, 1950.

Brown, William Howard, ed. *The History of Warren County, New York*. Colens Falls, N.Y.: Board of Supervisors of Warren County, 1963.

Bruchey, Stuart Weems. *Robert Oliver, Merchant of Baltimore, 1783–1819*. Baltimore: Johns Hopkins University Press, 1956.

Brunel, Isambard. *The Life of Isambard Kingdom Brunel: Civil Engineer*. London: Longmans, Green, and Co., 1870.

Buist, Marten G. *At Spes Non Fracta: Hope and Company, 1770–1815: Merchant Bankers and Diplomats at Work*. The Hague: Nijhoff, 1974.

Burr, Aaron. *Political Correspondence and Public Papers of Aaron Burr*. 2 vols. Edited by Mary Jo Kline. Princeton: Princeton University Press, 1983.

Cassell, Frank A. *Merchant Congressman in the Young Republic: Samuel Smith of Maryland, 1752–1839*. Madison: University of Wisconsin Press, 1971.

Castorland Journal. Typescript dated December 1980 available from Oneida County Historical Society, Utica, N.Y.

Catterall, Ralph C. H. *The Second Bank of the United States*. Chicago: University of Chicago Press, 1903.

Childs, Frances S. *French Refugee Life in the United States, 1790–1800: An American Chapter of the French Revolution*. Baltimore: Johns Hopkins Press, 1940.

Clarke, Wood T. *Emigrés in the Wilderness*. New York: The Macmillan Company, 1941.

Clements, Paul. *Marc Isambard Brunel*. Harlow, England: Longmans, 1970.

Dallett, Francis James. *An Architectural Review of Washington Square, Philadelphia*. Frome, England: Butler & Tanner, 1968.

Dangerfield, George. *Chancellor Robert R. Livingston of New York, 1746–1813*. New York: Harcourt, Brace, 1960.

————. *The Era of Good Feelings.* New York: Harcourt, Brace, 1952.

Dawson, John Charles. *Lakanal the Regicide: A Biographical and Historical Study of the Career of Joseph Lakanal.* Tuscaloosa: University of Alabama Press, 1948.

Day, Stacey B., ed. *Edward Stevens: Gastric Physiologist, Physician, and American Statesman.* Cincinnati: Cultural and Educational Productions, 1969.

DeConde, Alexander. *The Quasi-War: The Politics and Diplomacy of the Undeclared War with France 1797–1801.* New York: Scribner, 1966.

Delafield, John Ross. "Montgomery Place." *The Dutchess County Historical Society Yearbook, 1929.* Poughkeepsie, N.Y.: Dutchess County Historical Society, 1929.

Delafield, Julia Livingston. *Biographies of Francis Lewis and Morgan Lewis,* vol. 1. New York: A. D. F. Randolph and Co., 1877.

Dictionary of American Biography. 20 vols. Edited by Allen Johnson and Dumas Malone. New York: Charles Scribner's Sons, 1931.

Dictionary of National Biography, The. 22 vols. Edited by Sir Leslie Stephen and Sir Sidney Lee. Oxford: Oxford University Press, 1973.

Du Pont, Bessie Gardner. *The Life of E. I. Du Pont.* 11 vols. Newark, Del.: University of Delaware Press, 1923–26.

————. *Lives of Victor and Josephine Du Pont.* Newark, Del.: Press of Kells, Inc., 1930.

Du Pont, Josephine. "Our Travels in America." Winterthur Manuscripts, group 3. Hagley Museum and Library, Wilmington, Del.

Du Pont Family Papers. Hagley Museum and Library, Wilmington, Del.

Dutton, William S. *Du Pont: One Hundred and Forty Years.* New York: Scribner, 1951.

Eberlein, Harold Donaldson, and Cortlandt Van Dyke Hubbard. *Historic Houses of the Hudson Valley.* New York: Bonanza Books, 1942.

Eckman, Jeannette, ed. *New Castle on the Delaware.* New Castle, Del.: New Castle Historical Society, 1950.

Ehrenberg, Richard. *Das Haus Parish in Hamburg.* 2 vols. Jena: Fischer, 1925.

Emden, Paul H. *Money Powers of Europe in the Nineteenth and Twentieth Centuries.* New York: D. Appleton-Century Co., 1938.

Fay, Bernard. *Revolutionary Spirit in France and America: A Study of Moral and Intellectual Relations Between France and the United States at the End of the Eighteenth Century.* Translated by Ramon Guthrie. New York: Harcourt, Brace, 1927.

Faye, Stanley. "The Great Stroke of Pierre Lafitte." *Louisiana Historical Quarterly* 23, no. 3 (July 1940).

————. "Privateersmen of the Gulf and Their Prizes." *Louisiana Historical Quarterly* 22, no. 4 (October 1939).

Fenwick, Hubert. *Architect Royal: The Life and Works of Sir William Bruce.* Kineton: Roundwood Press, 1975.

Flexner, James Thomas. *Young Hamilton: A Biography.* Boston: Little, Brown, 1978.

Flores, Dan L., ed. *Jefferson and Southwestern Exploration: The Freeman and Custis Accounts of the Red River Expedition of 1806.* Norman: University of Oklahoma Press, 1984.

Forbes-Robertson, Diana. "Asylum in Azilon." *American Heritage* 27, no. 3 (April 1976).

Fortescue, Sir John William. *A History of the British Army.* 13 vols. London: Macmillan, 1910–1935.

Fowler, Laurence Hall. "Montebello." *Maryland Architectural Review* 16, no. 11 (November 1909).

Fox, Dixon Ryan. *The Decline of Aristocracy in the Politics of New York, 1801–1840.* New York: Harper & Row, 1965.

Gaines, George S. "Gaines' Reminiscences." *Alabama Historical Quarterly* 26, no. 4 (Fall/Winter, 1964).

Gallagher, H. M. Pierce. *Robert Mills, The Architect of the Washington Monument, 1781–1855.* New York: Columbia University Press, 1935.

Gardien, Kent. "The Splendid Fools: Philadelphia Origins of Alabama's Vine and Olive Colony." *Pennsylvania Magazine of History and Biography* 104, no. 4 (October 1980).

Garesché, Louis Joseph. *Biography of Lieutenant Colonel Julius P. Garesché, Assistant Adjutant-General, U.S. Army.* Philadelphia: Press of J. B. Lippincott, 1887.

Garnett, Emmaline. *The Master Engineers.* London: Hodder and Stoughton, 1954.

Gay, Peter. *The Enlightenment: An Interpretation,* vol. 2. New York: Norton, 1977.

Gazette des Beaux Arts, 23 (1945).

Geggus, David Patrick. *Slavery, War and Revolution: The British Occupation of Saint Dominique, 1793–1798.* New York: Oxford University Press, 1982.

Gibson, George H. "Fullers, Carders, and Manufacturers of Woolen Goods in Delaware." *Delaware History* 12, no. 1 (April 1966).

Goedicke, Christian; Klaus Slusallek; and Martin Kubelik. "Thermoluminescence Dating in Architectural History: The Chronology of Palladio's Villa Rotunda." *Journal of the Society of Architectural Historians* 45, no. 4 (December 1986).

Golovin, Anne Castrodale. "Daniel Trotter: Eighteenth-Century Philadelphia Cabinetmaker." *Winterthur Portfolio* 6, 1970.

Gosse, Edmund, ed. *Conversations of James Northcote, R. A.* London: R. Bentley and Son, 1894.

Gottschalk, Louis Moreau. *Notes of a Pianist.* Edited by Jeanne Behrend. New York: Knopf, 1964.

Govan, Thomas P. *Nicholas Biddle: Nationalist and Public Banker, 1786–1844.* Chicago: University of Chicago Press, 1959.

Gowans, Alan. "Freemasonry and the Neoclassic Style in America." *Antiques,* 77 (February 1960).

————. *Images of American Living: Four Centuries of Architecture and Furniture as Cultural Expression.* New York: Harper & Row, 1976.

Griswold, Ralph E., and Frederick Doveton Nichols. *Thomas Jefferson: Landscape Architect.* Charlottesville: University Press of Virginia, 1978.

Hale, Edward Everett. *Memories of a Hundred Years,* vol. 1. New York: The Macmillan Company, 1902.

Hamilton, Alexander. *The Papers of Alexander Hamilton,* vol. 25. Edited by Harold C. Syrett. New York: Columbia University Press, 1977.

Hamilton, Allan McLane. *The Intimate Life of Alexander Hamilton.* New York: C. Scribner's Sons, 1910.

Hamlin, Arthur S. *Gideon Granger.* Canandaigua, N.Y.: Granger Homestead Society, 1982.

Hamlin, Talbot. *Benjamin Henry Latrobe.* New York: Oxford University Press, 1955.

————. *Greek Revival Architecture in America: Being an Account of Important Trends in American Architecture and American Life Prior to the War Between the States.* New York: Dover, 1944.

Hammond, Bray. *Banks and Politics in America, from the Revolution to the Civil War.* Princeton: Princeton University Press, 1957.

Harnsberger, Douglas. "In Delorme's Manner." *APT* [The Association for Preservation Technology] *Bulletin: The Journal of Preservation Technology* 13, no. 4 (1981).

Hay, Peter. *Brunel—His Achievements in the Transport Revolution.* Reading, England: Osprey Publishing, 1973.

Hibbert, Christopher. *The Days of the French Revolution.* New York: Morrow, Quill Paperbacks, 1981.

Hill, William H., comp. *The History of Washington County, N.Y., The Gibson Papers.* Fort Edward, N.Y.: Honeywood Press, 1956.

Hillairet, Jacques. *Dictionnaire historique des rues de Paris.* 2 vols. Paris: Editions de Minuit, 1963.

History of Greene County, with Biographical Sketches of Its Prominent Men. Cornwallville, N.Y.: Hope Farm Press, 1884; reprint, 1969.

Holland, Dorothy Garesché. *The Garesché, De Bauduy, and Des Chapelles Families, History, and Genealogy.* St. Louis: privately printed by the Schneider Print Co., 1963; separate mimeographed appendices available from Mrs. Holland.

Honour, Hugh. *Neo-Classicism.* New York: Penguin Books, 1977.

Hough, Franklin B. *A History of Jefferson County in the State of New York from the Earliest Period to the Present Time.* Waterton, N.Y.: Sterling & Riddell, 1854.

Hulbert, Archer Butler. *The Great American Canals.* 2 vols. New York: AMS Press, 1971.

Humphrey, R. A. "The Development on the American Communities Outside British Rule." In *The American and French Revolution, 1763–93. The New Cambridge Modern History,* vol. 8. Cambridge: Cambridge University Press, 1979 (paperback edition).

Hunt, Charles Havens. *Life of Edward Livingston.* New York: D. Appleton and Company, 1864.

Jackson, John, Jr. "The Mexican Silver Scheme: Finance and Profiteering in the Napoleonic Era, 1796–1811." Ph.D. dissertation, University of North Carolina, 1978.

James, C. L. R. *The Black Jacobins: Toussaint L'Ouverture and the San Domingo Revolution.* New York: Vintage Books, 1963.

Jefferson, Thomas. *Notes on the State of Virginia.* Chapel Hill: University of North Carolina Press, 1954.

————. "Writings." In *Literary Classics of the United States.* New York: Viking Press, 1984.

————. *Writings of Thomas Jefferson.* Edited by Saul K. Padover. Norwalk, Conn.: Easton Press, 1967.

Jones, Howard Mumford. *America and French Culture, 1750–1848.* 1927. Reprint. Westport, Conn.: Greenwood, 1973.

Judd, Henry A., and Lee H. Nelson, eds. "An Architectural Study of the Old Town Hall." Unpublished paper. Historical Society of Delaware, 1965.

Kaufmann, Emil. "Three Revolutionary Architects: Boullée, Ledoux, and Lequeu," *Transactions of the American Philosophical Society* (Philadelphia) 17, no. 3 (1952).

Kellogg, Walter Guest. Unpublished paper prepared for the Jefferson County Historical Society, apparently in 1945 or 1946, among the Kellogg Papers, Jefferson County Historical Society, Watertown, New York.

Kenin, Richard, and Justin Wintle, eds. *The Dictionary of Biographical Quotations of British and American Subjects.* New York: Knopf, 1978.

Kennedy, Roger G. *Architecture, Men, Women and Money in America, 1600–1860.* New York: Random House, 1985.

Kimball, Fiske. *Thomas Jefferson, Architect.* 1916. Reprint. New York: Da Capo Press, 1968.

Kimball, Marie. *Jefferson: The Scene of Europe, 1784 to 1789.* New York: Coward-McCann, 1950.

Kindleberger, Charles P. *A Financial History of Western Europe.* Boston: Allen & Unwin, 1984.

Kirker, Harold. *The Architecture of Charles Bulfinch.* Cambridge: Harvard University Press, 1969.

Kouwenhoven, John Atlee. *The Columbia Historical Portrait of New York: An Essay in Graphic History.* New York: Harper & Row, 1972.

Krafft, Johann K., and N. Ransonnette. *Plans, coupes, élévations des plus belles maisons et des hôtels construits à Paris et dans les environs.* Paris: Librairie d'Art décoratif et industriel, G. Hue, 1909.

Lahey, William C. "The Influence of David Parish on the Development of Trade and Settlement in Northern New York, 1808–1822." Ph.D. dissertation, Syracuse University, 1959.

Lamb, Martha J., ed. *The Homes of America.* New York: D. Appleton and Company, 1879.

Lancaster, Clay. "New York City Hall Stair Rotunda Reconsidered." *Journal of the Society of Architectural Historians* 29, no. 1 (March 1970).

Larrabee, Harold Atkins. "Joseph Jacques Ramée and America's First Unified College Plan." Franco-American Pamphlet Series No. 1. New York: The American Society of the French Legion of Honor, 1934.

Latrobe, Benjamin Henry. *The Journals of Benjamin Henry Latrobe, 1799–1820: From Philadelphia to New Orleans.* Edited by Edward C. Carter II, John C. Van Horne, and Lee W. Formwalt. New Haven: Yale University Press, for the Maryland Historical Society, 1981.

———. *The Papers of Benjamin Henry Latrobe: Correspondence and Miscellaneous Papers.* Edited by John C. Van Horne et al. 3 vols. New Haven: Yale University Press, for the Maryland Historical Society, 1984–1988.

———. *The Virginia Journals of Benjamin Henry Latrobe, 1795–1798.* 2 vols. Edited by Edward Carter II, John C. Van Horne, and Lee W. Formwalt. New Haven: Yale University Press, for the Maryland Historical Society, 1977.

Latrobe Papers (unpublished). Maryland Historical Society, Baltimore, Maryland.

Leech, D. D. T. *The Post Office Department of the United States of America: Its History, Organization and Working from the Inauguration of the Federal Government, 1789, to the Close of the Administration of President Andrew Johnson.* Washington, D.C.: Judd & Detweiler, 1879.

Lemagny, J. C. *Visionary Architects: Boullée, Ledoux and Lequeu.* Houston: Gulf Printing Co., 1968.

Leray Papers. Jefferson County Historical Society, Watertown, New York.

Lewis, Douglas. *The Drawings of Andrea Palladio.* Washington, D.C.: The Foundation, 1981.

Lincklaen, John. "John Lincklaen Journals," no. 6. (October 1983). The sixth of a series of selections from the journals of John Lincklaen, privately published by the Friends of Lorenzo, Cazenovia, N.Y.

Liss, Peggy K. *Atlantic Empires: The Network of Trade and Revolution, 1713–1826.* Baltimore: Johns Hopkins University Press, 1983.

Livingston Papers. New-York Historical Society, New York, N.Y.

Lloyd, Christopher. "Armed Forces and the Art of War." In *The American and French Revolutions, 1763–93. The New Cambridge Modern History,* vol. 8. Cambridge: Cambridge University Press, 1979 (paperback edition).

Lockwood, Alice G. B., editor and compiler. *Gardens of Colony and State; Gardens and Gardeners of the American Colonies and of the Republic before 1840.* 2 vols. New York: Published for the Garden Club of America by C. Scribner's Sons, 1931–34.

Lodge, Henry Cabot. *Alexander Hamilton.* Boston: Houghton, Mifflin, and Company, 1882.

Lokke, Carl Ludwig. "Jefferson and the Leclerc Expedition." *American Historical Review* 33, no. 1 (October 1927).

Lomask, Milton. *Aaron Burr.* 2 vols. New York: Farrar, Straus and Giroux, 1979–1982.

Louis Philippe, King of the French. *Diary of My Travels in America.* Translated by Stephen Becker. New York: Delacorte, 1977.

Lowry, Bates. *Building a National Image: Architectural Drawings for the American Democracy, 1789–1912.* New York: Walker, 1985.

Lyon, Anne Bozeman. "The Bonapartists in Alabama." *Gulf States Historical Magazine* 1 (March 1903).

Mann, Mary Lee, ed. *A Yankee Jeffersonian: Selections from the Diary and Letters of William Lee of Massachusetts, Written from 1796–1840.* Cambridge: Harvard University Press, 1958.

Martin, Peter. "Long and Assiduous Endeavors: Gardening in Early Eighteenth-Century Virginia." In *British and American Gardens in the Eighteenth Century.* Edited by Robert P. Maccubbin and Peter Martin. Williamsburg: Colonial Williamsburg Foundation, 1984.

McMaster, J. B. *The Life and Times of Stephen Girard, Mariner and Merchant.* 2 vols. Philadelphia: J. B. Lippincott Company, 1918.

Meynell, Laurence W. *Builder and Dreamer: A Life of Isambard Kingdom Brunel.* London: The Bodley Head, 1952.

Milbert, Jacques Gérard. *Picturesque Itinerary of the Hudson River and the Peripheral Parts of North America.* Translated by Constance D. Sherman. Ridgewood, N.J.: Gregg Press, 1968.

Miller, John Chester. *The Wolf by the Ears: Thomas Jefferson and Slavery.* New York: Free Press, 1977.

Minutes of the Common Council of the City of New York, 1784–1831, vol. 2. New York: M. B. Brown, 1917.

Montgomery, Elizabeth. "Reminiscences of Wilmington." In *Familiar Village Tales, Ancient and New.* Philadelphia: T. K. Collins, Jr., 1851.

Moreau de Saint-Méry, M. L. E. *Moreau de St. Mery's American Journey, 1793–1798*. Translated and edited by Kenneth Roberts and Anna M. Roberts. Garden City, N.Y.: Doubleday & Company, 1947.

Morison, Samuel Eliot. *The Maritime History of Massachusetts, 1783–1860*. New York: Houghton Mifflin Co., 1921.

Nichols, Frederick D. *The Early Architecture of Georgia*. Chapel Hill: University of North Carolina Press, 1957.

Noble, Celia Brunel. *The Brunels, Father and Son*. London: Cobden-Sanderson, 1938.

Nolte, Vincent. *Fifty Years in Both Hemispheres, or Reminiscences of the Life of a Former Merchant*. Freeport, N.Y.: Books for Libraries Press, 1972.

Norton, Paul F. "The Architect of Calverton," *Maryland Historical Magazine* 76, no. 2 (June 1981).

Norwich, John Julius. *The Kingdom in the Sun, 1130–1194*. New York: Harper & Row, 1970.

————. *The Normans in the South, 1016–1130*. London: Longmans, 1967.

Ott, Thomas O. *The Haitian Revolution, 1789–1804*. Knoxville: University of Tennessee Press, 1973.

Padover, Saul K., ed. *Thomas Jefferson and the National Capital: Containing Notes and Correspondence exchanged between Jefferson, Washington, L'Enfant, Ellicott, Hallet, Thornton, Latrobe, the Commissioners, and others, relating to the founding, surveying, planning, designing, constructing, and administering of the city of Washington, 1783–1818*. Washington, D.C.: USGPO, 1946.

Palmer, R. R. *The Age of Democratic Revolution: A Political History of Europe and America, 1760–1800*. 2 vols. Princeton: Princeton University Press, 1974.

Pancake, John S. *Samuel Smith and the Politics of Business, 1752–1839*. Birmingham: University of Alabama Press, 1972.

Parham, Althea de Peuch, ed. and trans. *My Odyssey: Experiences of a Young Refugee from Two Revolutions, by a Creole of Saint Domingue*. Baton Rouge: Louisiana State University Press, 1959.

Parish Papers, vol. 2. New-York Historical Society, New York, N.Y.

Parish Papers. St. Lawrence University Library, Canton, N.Y.

Paul, J. Gilman D. "Montebello: Home of General Samuel Smith," *Maryland Historical Magazine* 42, no. 4 (December 1947).

Perkins, Edwin J. *The Economy of Colonial America*. New York: Columbia University Press, 1980.

Philadelphia Society for Promoting Agriculture. *Memoirs of the Philadelphia Society for Promoting Agriculture*, vol. 3. 1814.

Pickens, Buford. "Mr. Jefferson as Revolutionary Architect." *Journal for the Society of Architectural Historians* 34, no. 4 (December 1975).

Pickering (Timothy) Papers, vol. 16. Massachusetts Historical Society, Boston, Massachusetts.

Pickett, Albert J. *The History of Alabama, and incidentally of Georgia and Missis-sippi.* Birmingham: Birmingham Book & Magazine Co., 1962.

Pierson, William H., Jr. *American Buildings and Their Architects: The Colonial and Neo-Classical Styles.* Garden City, N.Y.: Anchor Press, 1976.

————. *American Buildings and Their Architects: Technology and the Picturesque, the Corporate and the Early Gothic Style.* Garden City, N.Y.: Anchor Press, 1980.

Pilcher, Edith. *Castorland: French Refugees in the Western Adirondacks 1793–1814.* Harrison, N.Y.: Harbor Hill Books, 1985.

Pratt, Fletcher. *Road to Empire: The Life and Times of Bonaparte, the General.* New York: Doubleday, Doran & Company, 1939.

Pudney, John. *Brunel and His World.* London: Thames and Hudson, 1974.

Purcell, Carroll W., Jr. "E. I. Du Pont and the Merino Mania in Delaware, 1805–1815." *Agricultural History* 36, no. 2 (April 1962).

Pyle, Howard. "Old Times in a Quaker Town." *Harpers Monthly Magazine* 62, no. 367 (December 1880).

Quimby, Maureen O'Brien. *Eleutherian Mills.* Greenville (Wilmington), Del.: Hagley Museum, 1977.

Records of the United States Senate. Claim of Edward Stevens, February 6, 1826; Committee on Foreign Relations; Petitions and Memorials Referred to Commit-tees (SEN 19A-G6); 19th Congress, Record Group 46; National Archives, Washington, D.C.

Reeves, Jesse S. *The Napoleonic Exiles in America: A Study in American Dip-lomatic History, 1815–1819.* Baltimore: Johns Hopkins University Press, 1905.

Reps, John W. *Tidewater Towns: City Planning in Colonial Virginia and Mary-land.* Williamsburg: Colonial Williamsburg Foundation, distributed by the University of Virginia Press, Charlottesville, 1972.

Rice, Howard Crosby. *Thomas Jefferson's Paris.* Princeton: Princeton Univer-sity Press, 1976.

Richardson, D. "Profits in the Liverpool Slave Trade." In *Liverpool, the African Slave Trade, and Abolition.* Edited by Roger Anstey and P. E. H. Hair. Liverpool: Historic Society of Lancashire and Cheshire, 1976.

Robinson, Donald L. *Slavery in the Structure of American Politics, 1765–1820.* New York: Harcourt Brace Jovanovich, 1971.

Rolt, L. T. C. *Isambard Kingdom Brunel, A Biography.* London, New York: Longmans, Green, 1957.

Root, Edward W. *Philip Hooker: A Contribution to the Study of the Renaissance in America.* New York: C. Scribner's Sons, 1929.

Rosenbaum, Eduard, and A. Joshua Sherman. *M. M. Warburg & Co., 1798–1938, Merchant Bankers of Hamburg.* New York: Holmes & Meier, 1979.

Rosenberg, Jakob, et al. *Dutch Art and Architecture, 1600–1800.* Harmondsworth, England: Penguin Books, Pelican Series, 1966.

Rosengarten, J. G. *French Colonists and Exiles in the United States.* Philadelphia: J. B. Lippincott Company, 1907.

Ruppenthal, Roland. "Denmark and the Continental System," *The Journal of Modern History* 15 (March 1943).

Rush, Benjamin. *The Letters of Benjamin Rush.* 2 vols. Edited by Lyman H. Butterfield. Princeton: Published for the American Philosophical Society by Princeton University Press, 1951.

Sakolski, Aaron Morton. *The Great American Land Bubble: The Amazing Story of Land-Grabbing, Speculations, and Booms from Colonial Days to Present Time.* New York: Harper and Brothers, 1932.

Schachner, Nathan. *Alexander Hamilton.* New York: D. Appleton-Century Co., 1946.

Seeber, Edward D. "A Napoleonic Exile in New Albany." *Indiana Magazine of History* 44, no. 2 (June 1948).

Semmes, John E. *John H. B. Latrobe and His Times, 1803–1891.* Baltimore: Norman, Remington Co., 1917.

Serra, J. R., ed. *Paestum and the Doric Revival, 1750–1830: Essential Outlines of an Approach.* New York: National Academy of Design, 1986.

Smith, James H. *History of Dutchess County, New York, with Illustrations and Biographical Sketches of Some of Its Most Prominent Men and Pioneers.* Syracuse, N.Y.: D. Mason & Co., 1882.

———. *History of Warren County, with Illustrations and Biographical Sketches of Some of Its Prominent Men and Pioneers.* Interlacken, N.Y.: Heart of the Lakes Publishers, 1981.

Smith, Walter B. *Economic Aspects of the Second Bank of the United States.* Cambridge: Harvard University Press, 1953.

Sommer, F. "Emblem and Device: The Origin of the Great Seal of the United States." *Art Quarterly* 24, no. 1 (Spring 1961).

Stafford, George Mason Graham. *General George Mason Graham of Tyrone and His People.* New Orleans: Pelican Publishing Co., 1947.

Stein, Robert Louis. *Leger Félicité Sonthonax: The Lost Sentinel of the Republic.* Rutherford, N.J.: Fairleigh Dickinson University Press, 1985.

Stendhal. *Travels in the South of France.* Translated by Elisabeth Abbott. London: Calder and Boyars, 1971.

Stillman, Damie. "New York City Hall: Competition and Execution." *Journal of the Society of Architectural Historians* 23, no. 3 (October 1964).

Stinchcombe, William C. *The American Revolution and the French Alliance.* Syracuse, N.Y.: Syracuse University Press, 1969.

———. *The XYZ Affair.* Westport, Conn.: Greenwood Press, 1980.

Stokes, Isaac N. P. *The Iconography of Manhattan Island, 1498–1909.* 6 vols. New York: R. H. Dodd, 1915–1928.

Stuart, Reginald C. *The Half-Way Pacifist: Thomas Jefferson's View of War.* Toronto: University of Toronto Press, 1978.

Summerson, John. *Architecture in Britain, 1530 to 1830.* Harmondsworth, England: Penguin Books, 1970.

Talleyrand-Périgord, Charles Maurice de. *Memoirs of the Prince de Talleyrand.* Translated by Ralphäel Ledos de Beaufort. London: Farran, 1891.

Tansill, Charles C. *The United States and Santo Domingo, 1798–1873: A Chapter in Caribbean Diplomacy.* Baltimore: Johns Hopkins Press, 1938.

Tarrade, Jean. *Le Commerce colonial de la France à la fin de l'ancien régime: L'évolution du régime de l'exclusif de 1763 à 1789,* vol. 2. Paris: Presses Universitaires de France, 1972.

Thornton (William) Papers. Library of Congress, Washington, D.C.

Thurman, John. Letterbook 1771–1821. Unpublished. New York State Library, Albany, New York.

Torrey, Raymond H. "Hamilton Grange: Its History, Acquisition and Restoration by the Society, and Its Development as a Museum of Alexander Hamilton and His Time." *Scenic and Historic America* 3, no. 3 (April 1934).

Toussaint L'Ouverture Collection. Library of Congress, Washington, D.C.

Tunnard, Christopher. "Minerva's Union," *Architectural Review* 101 (February 1947).

Turner, Paul V. *Campus, An American Planning Tradition.* Cambridge: MIT Press, 1984.

———. "Joseph-Jacques Ramée's First Career." *Art Bulletin* 67 (June 1985).

Twentieth Century Biographical Dictionary of Notable Americans, The. 10 vols. Edited by Rossiter Johnson. Boston: Biographical Society, 1904.

Tyson, George F., Jr., ed. *Toussaint L'ouverture.* Englewood Cliffs, N.J.: Prentice-Hall, 1973.

Vaissière, Pierre de. *Saint-Domingue: La Société et la vie créoles sous l'ancien régime (1629–1789).* Paris: Perrin et cis, 1909.

Van Every, Dale. *Men of the Western Waters; a Second Look at the First Americans.* Boston: Houghton Mifflin, 1956.

Walters, Philip G., and Raymond Walters, Jr. "The American Career of David Parish." *The Journal of Economic History* 4 (November 1944).

Warren, Harris Gaylord. *The Sword Was Their Passport: A History of American Filibustering in the Mexican Revolution.* Port Washington, N.Y.: Kennikat Press, 1972.

Waterman, Thomas Tileston. *The Mansions of Virginia, 1706–1776.* Chapel Hill: University of North Carolina Press, 1945.

Watkin, David. *Thomas Hope, 1769–1831, and the Neo-Classical Idea.* London: Murray, 1968.

Whitfield, Gaius, Jr. "The French Grant in Alabama: A History of the Founding of Demopolis." *Transactions,* vol 5. Montgomery: Alabama Historical Society, 1904.

Wick, Wendy. "Stephen Girard: A Patron of the Philadelphia Furniture Trade." Master's thesis, University of Delaware, 1977.

Wiebenson, Dora. "From Palladianism to Greek Revival Architecture in America." In *Paestum and the Doric Revival, 1750–1830: Essential Outlines of an Approach.* New York: National Academy of Design, 1986.

Wildes, Harry Emerson. *Lonely Midas: The Story of Stephen Girard.* New York: Farrar and Rinehart, Inc., 1943.

Wilkinson, Norman B. *E. I. Dupont, Botaniste: The Beginning of a Tradition.* Charlottesville: Published for the Eleutherian Mills–Hagley Foundation by University Press of Virginia, 1972.

Williams, Eric. *From Columbus to Castro: The History of the Caribbean, 1492–1969.* New York: Vintage Books, 1984.

———. *Capitalism and Slavery.* New York: Capricorn Books, 1966.

Wilson, W. Emerson. "Artist-Soldier-Businessman Bauduy Planned Town Hall." *Wilmington Morning News,* July 9, 1964.

Wood, Peter H. "La Salle: Discovery of a Lost Explorer." *The American Historical Review* 89, no. 2 (April 1984).

Wright, Louis B. *The Atlantic Frontier.* Ithaca, N.Y.: Cornell University Press, 1964.

NOTES

I. A Way of Looking at Things

3 "a trifling Wager": Latrobe, note of September 8, 1799, in Latrobe, *Papers,* vol. 2, p. 147.

Among the unpublished Latrobe Papers is a document called "Remarks on the best form of a room for hearing and speaking," apparently dated around 1803, which contains references "from memory" of the acoustic qualities of "a few of the buildings which I have seen." They include the Pantheon in Rome, "churches in Italy, France, and Germany," the Anatomical Theater in Paris, and the "Hal au bled [Halle aux Blés] or Corn Market," in the same city. I am indebted to John Van Horne for bringing this to my attention.

1. *French Neoclassicism and Other Matters*

7 "rude, mis-shapen piles": Jefferson, *Notes,* p. 278.

"a pile of bricks": *Castorland Journal,* p. 125.

11 "Contacts of Americans": Becker, p. 884.

"Specifically French architectural details": Talbot Hamlin, *Greek Revival,* pp. 7–9.

2. *Architecture and Money*

15 Palladio designed villas as headquarters: Palladio's most easily recognized design, the Villa Rotunda, might seem to contradict these paragraphs. Unlike his other villas, it does not give the appearance of being the headquarters for a working farm. It was, instead, a pavilion for a retired prelate. A new view (in 1986) of its uses suggests that it was in fact more like the others than it appears; see Goedicke et al. In England, it was used as a precedent not so much by gentlemen farmers as by absentee landlords (like Lord Burlington) and by the builders of mausoleums, libraries, and "eye-catchers."

17 Mount Pleasant and William Bruce: The best book on William Bruce, illustrating his debts to France, is *Architect Royal* by Hubert Fenwick. I am indebted to Beatrice Garvan, who knows Mount Pleasant better than anyone else, for encouraging me in these speculations.

Thomas Waterman, who pioneered Virginia architectural history, associated Corotoman and

Shirley, two houses of the Carter family in Virginia, with Lord Craven's "shooting box," Ashdown, in the Berkshire Downs, west of London (*The Mansions of Virginia,* p. 111). The historian of Ashdown, Gervaise Jackson-Stops, in his essay in the guide to the house published by the British National Trust, tells us that Lord Craven, its builder, may well have based its design upon the same building in Normandy that attracted Bruce—Balleroy, designed by François Mansart and built around 1625.

In his book, Waterman was a little pre-emptory in saying that "the arrangement of the wings was unusual and rather unsatisfactory, and, except for Ashdown House, Berkshire, did not seem to occur elsewhere," because something like that arrangement was present at Mount Pleasant. Waterman recognized this in a later article in the *Gazette des Beaux Arts* 23 (1945), p. 112 (I am grateful to Pamela Scott for calling it to my attention); he wrote of "the apparent use of a design by Daniel Marot in the plan, facade, and dependencies of Mount Pleasant." I do not see the Marot plan and façade as having much to do with those of Captain Macpherson's house. It makes better sense to me to see Marot's work, together with that of Mansart and the other French architects who inspired William Adam and William Bruce, as being strained through the sensibility of Americans with roots in Scotland. Maybe that is because Waterman put more emphasis on architects than upon clients, and I would have it the other way around.

II.   The Multinationals

3.   *The Empire of Commerce*

page 29 "The scrapings of nationalities": Gowans, *Images,* p. 56.
Albany's garbage and pigs: Root, p. 15.
31 sugar warehouses of the Livingstons: Stokes, pp. 605–46.
34 "the very spot": Wright, p. 333.
"pinched an estate": "Lord Bellomont" in *Dictionary of American Biography,* vol. 11, p. 319.
35 a "hansom" plan: Janet Livingston Montgomery to Robert R. Livingston, May 29, 1802. Ruth Piwonka located this letter among the Livingston Papers.

4.   *The Men of the West*

36 Liverpool and Bristol as great slaving ports: Richardson, pp. 76–90.
United States dependence on West Indies: Bernstein.
"What commerce": ibid., p. 154.
"From the port of Nantes": Clarke, pp. 9–10.
37 "the most beautiful": ibid.
38 Jacques Leray as adviser to Louis XVI: ibid., p. 13.
"turned . . . especially": Lloyd, pp. 183–84.
"Whatever efforts are made": ibid., p. 174.
39 private war of the Leray family: Clarke tells us that the munitions were "bought by Chaumont with his own money or supplied from the national arsenals of which he had charge" (p. 17). Thomas J. Schaeper of Saint Bonaventure University, the expert on James Leray, tells me that Leray was not in charge of the arsenals (personal letter, February 24, 1986). Before I heard this, my note here ended: "Mr. Clarke can probably be trusted in this regard."
I am also indebted to Professor Schaeper for the information that the Lerays' losses were not in the form of debts owed by the American revolutionary government but in the far less tangible form of a claim for appreciation of depreciated currency.
40 "best known châteaux": Milbert, p. 154.
41 Vincent Le Ray and charades: letter dated October 5, 1813, Biddle Papers.

41 "intersecting footpaths": Clarke, p. 117.
42 description of the Hermitage: ibid., pp. 159–60.
   "rode for miles": ibid.
44 the young wife's unhappiness: ibid., p. 172.
   Leray to his creditors and to David Parish: Kellogg, pp. 12–13.
   Kellogg suggests (p. 13) that though David Parish and Leray "had carried on for several years a gracious and gossipy correspondence," in the 1820s "the tone of their intercourse changed. Mr. Parish became cold and calculating, demanding his money." It was not the same Mr. Parish: the Parish of the 1820s was George, not David. (See George Parish to Joseph Rosseel, February 3, 1822, Parish-Rosseel Papers.) George Parish, acting for both the Vienna and Antwerp branches of his family, was trying to salvage the solvency of old John Parish, head of the clan, which had been imperiled by David's ill-considered ventures. It is doubtful that George Parish was ever gracious or gossipy—that was David's way, not his.

5. Great Inventions

46 Simon Desjardins as an architect *expert-juré: Almanach National* 1782. For Pierre Pharoux, see *Almanach National* 1789, 1790, 1791, 1792.
47 "a tradition": John Ross Delafield, p. 23.
   Martha Lamb on Masséna: Lamb, p. 171 ff.
   "French domestic architecture": Eberlein and Hubbard, p. 105. The Chancellor called his residence Clermont, from an earlier Clermont (sometimes spelled "Claremont") on the same property, which was rebuilt in 1778 by Chancellor Livingston's mother on the site of a yet earlier Clermont, of about 1730.
48 "acute sensibility . . . and a love of approbation": Beamish, pp. 309–10.
49 "unable to obtain any notes": Noble, pp. 12–17. See also Beamish, p. 27.
   Castorland Journal: The original *Journal*, in French manuscript, was discovered in Paris in 1862 by an American tourist; it was given to the Massachusetts Historical Society. Three years later the society permitted a copy of the longhand translation into English to be made for the New York State Library at Albany. This version was in turn rescued from oblivion by Edith Pilcher and by the typists in Remsen. (My page numbers are references to this typescript version.) Pilcher's excellent summary was published in 1985 as *Castorland: French Refugees in the Western Adirondacks, 1793–1814.* Soon thereafter, Ruth Piwonka began assembling data for a comprehensive exhibit of the portraits of the Livingston family. Indefatigably conscientious, she also became the proprietor of a store of information about every conceivable source on the conjugal and commercial activities of the Livingstons during the period from 1793 to 1799, when they provided a series of commissions to Pharoux and possibly even to Brunel.
   Brunel's false passport: Beamish, p. 20.
50 "a good sailor": *Castorland Journal,* p. 44. For this account I have drawn, gingerly, on county histories and on Clarke.
51 "map of the city": *Castorland Journal,* p. 217.
   "a shelter of bark": ibid., pp. 156–57.
   "a little pond": ibid., p. 154. Fortunately, his plan for von Steuben is one of the few signed "Pharoux plans" to survive. It reposes close to the *Castorland* typescript in the Remsen-Steuben Historical Society.
52 "visited the two great rocks": ibid., p. 195.
53 Brunel and canals: Beamish, p. 32.
   "in later years": ibid., p. 30; see also Noble. It is fair to note that while Noble and Beamish were wildly off target, Brunel's grandson Isambard Brunel gave an account singular among Brunel biographies in the modesty and general accuracy of its claims for his grandfather's achievements, in his biography of his father, *Isambard Kingdom Brunel, Civil Engineer.*
   Pharoux on Schuyler and the canals: *Castorland Journal,* pp. 114–15. The canals' general trajectories had been discussed by Philip Schuyler and Gouverneur Morris as early as the Saratoga

campaign in 1777, and were debated continuously thereafter, until the portions under way in the 1790s were specified by the New York legislature, and money appropriated to Schuyler to supervise its construction, in 1792. For a good discussion of the history of the canals, see Fox or Hulbert. See also reports and correspondence about Schuyler's canal building, in the manuscript room of the New York Public Library.

page 54 "quit Trade and taken to settle": letter found by Eileen J. O'Brien in Thurman, p. 370.
descriptions of John Thurman: Beamish, p. 32; see also *Castorland Journal*, p. 120. Thurman was born on February 27, 1732.

55 Pharoux on Schuyler's "hydraulic endeavors": *Castorland Journal*, pp. 120, 132.
"inspect the labors": ibid.
"M. Pharoux embarked": ibid., p. 135.
Brunel's turning point: Beamish, p. 31.
"service for our friend . . . on his way": *Castorland Journal*, pp. 132, 152.

56 "engaged them": Beamish, p. 32.
contractors, Pharoux at Wood Creek: *Castorland Journal*, pp. 64, 212.
Brunel's "ingenuity": Beamish, p. 31.
"M. Pharoux concluded": *Castorland Journal*, pp. 119–20.
For Thurman, see James H. Smith, *Warren County*, pp. 550–51, and a great find, William H. Hill's "The History of Washington Academy," pp. 54–58. See also Brown, p. 249.

57 "for many years": Hill, pp. 54–58.
"the connection formed": Beamish, p. 32. Brunel sought to gain "a name." A name he did not gain was that bestowed upon him in most of his biographies, including one written as recently as 1974: he was never "chief engineer" of the state of New York or even of the city of New York. He may have done some engineering work for the brothers Mangin, or even for Major L'Enfant, after he left Pharoux; but never did he displace them as "chief." Never, therefore, could he, as "chief," have "organized an establishment for casting and boring ordnance which in itself was sufficient to place its originator in the foremost rank of mechanical engineers." (Beamish, p. 35.) Books hailing Brunel as the chief: Hay, pp. 4–5; Garnett, p. 14; Pudney, p. 8; Meynell, p. 19. Isambard Brunel, however, says severely only that his grandfather "obtained employment as a civil engineer. A few years afterward he was appointed engineer to the State of New York." (as quoted in Meynell, p. 2.)
"shortly became a busy architect": Noble, p. 16. See also Rolt, p. 10; Clements, p. 15.
the Capitol competition: Beamish, pp. 32–33. See also Clements, p. 15; Noble, pp. 16–17; Rolt, p. 10.

6.   The Further Career of Pierre Pharoux

59 "when New York demanded a play-house": Noble, pp. 16–17. Beamish's account appears on his p. 33.

60 "to make his talents known": *Castorland Journal*, p. 129.
newspaper accounts: The *Daily Advertiser* for June 5, 1793, reported that Nicolas Denise announced that "at great expense and under M. Boucher's directions a very convenient Bathing house . . . either fresh, salt, or warm water . . . [was to be built] at his house called Bellevue, on the East River." The issue for May 22, 1799, tells us that "the spacious New Bath in the rear of Trinity Church, is now open for the season." It does not say that it was not open the previous season, but there were no similar announcements from 1795 to 1798. The famous Arcade Bath, at 39 Chambers Street, appears to be a creation of about 1810.

As to the City Tavern, an engraving appears in the city directory for 1794. Though there is no confirming evidence that the building is by Pharoux, it is very much like the "Saint-Mémin" design for the tavern at Speranza. There is no dispute as to the City Tavern competition in 1794–95, but it can be confused with the Tontine Coffee House of 1792. As to the Mangins winning the contest for the Park Theater, see these newspapers, identified by Alexander in his unpublished manuscript on Brunel: the New York *Daily Advertiser,* January 31, 1798, and *Journal and Patriotic Register,* February 3, 1798.

What do we make of all this? Brunel and Pharoux may have painted flats for the actors in the old, wooden John Street Theater, their performing space until the Park opened in 1798. This may be at the core of Beamish's statement that Pharoux had occasion to "execute some of the decorative portion," perhaps the flats, of this obscure venture. Did Brunel take hand in creating its stage machinery? Beamish and other biographers pass along a complicated story of Brunel's devising a scene about a windmill for the Park. Maybe this sequence may explain the peculiar view of Clements (pp. 16–17) and Rolt (p. 10) that Brunel's Capitol scheme was so "well thought of" by New Yorkers that "a much modified version of it was used for their new Park Theater." Clements puts the Park Theater in the Bowery, though it was on Park Place and Broadway, many blocks from the Bowery; but the *Encyclopaedia Britannica* (eleventh edition [1910], vol. 4, p. 682), apparently in an effort to follow Beamish, refers to "the Bowery Theater," not built until 1826. Rolt struggles manfully with all this and calls the theater the "Palace, which was destroyed by fire in 1821." This will not work either, for reasons too complex to bother with here.

60 "also prepared plans": *Castorland Journal,* p. 129.
Edward Livingston did tell the Common Council: Minutes of the Common Council, pp. 94–95.
"residence at No. 1 Broadway": Hunt, pp. 56–57.
"My castle": November 16, 1793; Livingston Papers, roll number 5.

61 Harison's 227 Broadway is not quite at the corner of Broadway and Chatham (now Park) Place, where we might look for a Pharoux design on the basis of the clue given us in the *Castorland Journal;* but it was only a block off, on the corner of Broadway and Barclay. Harison's occupancy of 227 Broadway appears in the city directory for 1795. Pictures of the Hosack-Livingston house appear in Kouwenhoven, p. 102, and Stokes, plate 68A. John Livingston's dates are confirmed therein (though Stokes is not the last word) at p. 450.
houses not attributed to an architect: Attributions have been sought, and not found, in the files of the New York City Landmarks Commission.

63 Lamb's odd assertion: Lamb, p. 172. One view of the Hôtel de Beaumarchais, designed by Paul-Guillaume Lemoine in 1790, is found in Braham, p. 237.
"covered a great deal of ground": Julia Delafield, p. 200.
"Livingston sacrificed the dome": Lamb, p. 172. We cannot be sure when the octagon was sliced. Sometime before her death in 1810, Mrs. Livingston wrote her husband from the house asking him to bring up from the city "a Floor Cloth for the Octagon . . . and some pretty paper for it." She may have been "decorating" either the new upstairs room or the lower space before it became a library, paneled in mid-Victorian black walnut. The letter is undated, but it is found together with a group to her son dating from 1805–08, among the unpublished John R. Livingston papers owned by Victor E. Livingston.

It is impossible to tell from photographs if the arcaded orangerie that extended beyond the octagon in the 1850s was original. Perhaps it was another of the creations of Dr. Hosack or of Pharoux, or of both. It may have been among the accretions of the Aspinwalls, who perhaps remodeled the cornice of the dome.

63–4 Attribution of Arryl House to Brunel: Lamb, p. 171; also Eberlein and Hubbard, who put the date at 1783 (p. 105), when Brunel was fourteen years old. But even if we correct the date to accommodate its actual completion (on September 17, 1792, Chancellor Livingston wrote Samuel Mitchell that he was busy building his country house, and his account book for December 1793 shows him rounding out the last expenditures on the project), Brunel, Bunel, and Beaumarchais all remain distractions, or, at best, suggestions to look elsewhere, such as toward the Livingston family papers.

64 "The conservatory ran": Lockwood, vol. 2, p. 276.
"he embellished": *Dictionary of American Biography,* vol. 11, p. 324. I think Arryl House is more French–Northern European than English-Palladian—though it also has Franco-Polish analogs—but distinctions between the two are those of impression and general effect. Sketches made by

artists made it seem especially northern, rather like Joseph-Jacques Ramée's Copenhagen villas or the pavilion at Haga (1787–89) of Gustav III of Sweden. Those who prefer the English precedents can find them in drawings for Tottenham Park and Whitton Place, available at the Royal Institute of British Architects in London.

page 64 a plan from France: Janet Livingston Montgomery to Robert R. Livingston, May 29, 1802, Livingston Papers.

"power of attorney": *Castorland Journal*, p. 301.

67 Walter Livingston's "octagens": Blackburn and Piwonka, p. 52. Teviotdale had not, it seems, possessed dependencies; especially if they had formed a tight forecourt, it would have been the closest American equivalent to Lord Craven's Ashdown. By grace of the substitution for that Norman forecourt of neoclassical octagons, it would have entered much earlier into this text, and Appendix II to boot. The Franco-Caledonian phase of American architecture was passing; the neoclassical age was opening.

68 "planned by an . . . architect": John Ross Delafield, p. 23. The Hill was extensively remodeled in the 1820s, when adding porticoes was all the rage. General Delafield tells us, "It is probable that [Henry Walter Livingston's] widow Mary made many improvements in the house—the marble mantels and some of the cornices, the entrance hall and wide stairs are of a date later than its building" (p. 23 ff.). These were Greek-revival details of the 1820s or early 1830s. Mary Allen Livingston lived on into the 1850s. The map of The Hill can be found, thanks to Ruth Piwonka, in the Columbia County Clerk's Office in Hudson, New York (Columbia County Map, vol. 4, no. 319).

Pharoux bearing dispatches: *Castorland Journal*, p. 23.

The Hill, of 1796–99: The date of completion of The Hill is suggested by the fact that Henry Walter Livingston's correspondence no longer carries the address "The Hermitage" after June 1799.

Leray's house was also remodeled: The tale of that remodeling, between 1823 and 1828, is told at length in Kellogg. Our account of the house in its original form comes from the same Jacques Gérard Milbert whose *Picturesque Itinerary of the Hudson River and the Peripheral Parts of North America* gives us information about the lives and houses of the Livingstons. Milbert reported that the house had been rearranged between the time of his departure from America in 1823 and his writing in 1828. He does not speak of a portico addition. Nor does Kellogg; but all the other information given by the latter, suggesting that the house was repaired after some fire damage to it and other buildings in its compound, in order to make it "à la mode" for readier sale, and the timing of the work, corroborate my own observation of the structure of its attic and of the extra column capital reposing there.

69 "not finding his portfolio": *Castorland Journal*, p. 29.

Vincent Le Ray's letter: Hough, p. 444. Among Hough's notes is the original letter, dated September 29, 1853.

70 "a sketch of a plan": *Castorland Journal*, pp. 218–22. The given names are found in the Coxsackie tax list.

"the city of Speranza": ibid.

"worked on the plan": Infuriatingly, there seem to be no pictures or descriptions of the house John Livingston built in Speranza, "about 1796 . . . still standing" in 1884, according to the *History of Greene County*, p. 158.

71 "large map, made by one P. Pharmix": *History of Greene County*, p. 165.

When the Saint-Mémin engravings of four public edifices came into the Corcoran collection, late in the nineteenth century, the attribution to Saint-Mémin himself and the assignment to Asylum were made. This error was repeated in several subsequent publications, including Forbes-Robertson. It would have been as easy to get these locations wrong as to attribute the pictures wrongly. Neither point was very important to the founder of the Corcoran collection. He had bought nearly seven hundred Saint-Mémin sketches, intending to establish a national portrait gallery. The buildings came along with the lot.

75 "made me some proposals": *Castorland Journal*, p. 132. Pharoux's correspondence and meetings with Lynch: ibid., p. 222. The connection between Pharoux and Lynch invites further research,

as does Lynch himself, one of that group of Irish squires (William Duane, John Armstrong, William Constable, George Clinton, and Sir William Johnson were others) who imparted much Celtic color to the culture of New York in the eighteenth century. Lynch, the son of the mayor of Galway, made a fortune in Holland and was the most important single client of John McComb, Jr. (who provided him with an elegant country seat at Clauson Point in Westchester County, which became a military academy and lasted until 1926).

77 Château de Tivoli: Helen Wilkinson Reynolds, "Peter de Labigarre," in *Dutchess County Historical Society Yearbook, 1929* (Poughkeepsie, New York: Dutchess County Historical Society, 1929), p. 45 ff. A print of the Tivoli plan in this yearbook was taken from a print of Saint-Mémin's signed copperplate of 1795, in the possession of Mr. and Mrs. Johnston L. Redmond of Tivoli. See also James H. Smith, *History of Dutchess County,* p. 212 ff.

78 "saw M. de St. Mémin": *Castorland Journal,* p. 302.
report of Pharoux's death: Pilcher, pp. 15–16.
Pharoux's obituary: ibid., p. 68 ff.
tablet "To the Memory of Peter Pharoux": Hough, p. 51.
Brunel's account of his departure: Beamish, p. 33 ff.

79 "particular friend": Clements, pp. 16–17. It is not improbable that Brunel did enter into some form of comity with Hamilton, probably through the good offices of Pierre Pharoux, who knew both Hamilton and his canal-building father-in-law, Philip Schuyler.

Brunel told his biographers that the other person present at his dinner with Hamilton was "a Monsieur Delabigarre, who had recently arrived from England." This sounds like a garbled version of a story from Brunel about Pierre de La Bigarre, though he came not from London but from Saint-Domingue (see Clements, pp. 16–17).
The journal of Aaron Burr is in manuscript in the New-York Historical Society; the Library of Congress possesses an early-twentieth-century typescript, kept in its delicate-book department and therefore not reproduceable, but with an excellent index (see vol. 2, pp. 265, 277–79, 287, 296–97, 302–03, 306, 309, 311, 335, 364, 370). The Hurst Collection has made Brunel's sketch for Burr available to us through the good offices of Professor Richard Morris.
"many of the best families": *Castorland Journal,* pp. 124–25.

81 "hatred for foreigners": ibid.
von Steuben's anger: Bemis, p. 134 n.

82 Livingston told Constable: Robert R. Livingston to William Constable, August 6, 1799, Livingston Papers (discovered by Alexander). There is subsequent correspondence confirming the agency in Chancellor Livingston's microfilmed correspondence.
Brunel and the American cousins: Noble, p. 17 ff.
Richard Thurman's letter to Marc Brunel: Thurman, p. 414.

III.   Among the Great Ones

84 Nisbet's letter: dated May 18, 1797, and quoted in Childs, p. 32.
a man whose "form was perfect": from a report of Samuel Breck, quoted in Rosengarten, p. 208.

7.   Transatlantic Crossings

85 "Franklin is dead": My account is based on Bizardel, pp. 58–59.
86 I beg for liberty's sake: Lafayette quoted in Rice, p. 120.
86–7 Jefferson's protests to Jay: ibid., p. 121.
88 Brissot's Quaker-like appearance: Hibbert, p. 137.
"the growing luxury": from a report of Samuel Breck, quoted in Rosengarten, p. 205.

page 88 "You wish, sir": ibid.
   "free the people": Palmer, vol. 1, pp. 260–61.
89–90 Chateaubriand: Van Wyck Brooks does wonderfully well by Chateaubriand and less well by Crèvecoeur in his *The World of Washington Irving.*
   90 "there is something": This statement is included in the exemplary entry for Crèvecoeur in the *Dictionary of American Biography.*
   "Trade knows": Quoted in "Crèvecoeur on the Susquehanna," edited by H. L. Bourdin and S. T. Williams, in the *Yale Review,* April 1925; the same authors found the evidence of Crèvecoeur's Loyalist sympathies and published it in *The Nation* 121, no. 3142 (September 23, 1925).

8. *Innocents Abroad*

   91 George Grieve and Mme Du Barry: Bizardel, p. 198.
   "violent discussions": My quotations here are from Bernard Fay. What I have called "the strangest" was translated by Ramon Guthrie as "not one of the least strange," a locution a little too literally arch for my taste. The line, and the other comments, appear in Fay, p. 261.
   Lezay-Marnésia's views of America: ibid., p. 387.
   93 Rochefoucauld's description of Azylum, drawn from his travels: Childs, p. 71; his investment is described on p. 98.
   de Moré and Azylum: ibid.
   96 "proportioned to the greatness": Fiske Kimball's essay on L'Enfant in the *Dictionary of American Biography.*
96–8 Jefferson and L'Enfant: Padover, pp. 58–59, 159, 163, 178.
   98 "far exceeds anything": Lowry, p. 25 ff.

9. *A Feasting of Tigers*

   101 "Treason": Quoted in Hibbert, p. 317.
   102 "with a coffee-colored mistress"; "found himself dwarfed": Fay, p. 398.
102–3 Talleyrand's opinion of Americans: ibid., p. 400.
   103 "elephants": Henriette de La Tour Du Pin, quoted in Childs, p. 27.
   "they prefer isolation": Louis Philippe, p. 23. The 1971 edition has a puzzling introduction by Henry Steele Commager, who tells us "the prince dined with Talleyrand and Alexander in New York" (p. 7). Since Talleyrand left America in November 1796, and Louis Philippe arrived the following March, this seems unlikely.
   104 "most eccentric of Englishmen": quoted in Childs, p. 27.
   105 "exquisite type of Frenchwoman": F. Baldensberger, quoted in Childs, p. 28.
   " 'a school of American ways' ": Childs, p. 26.
   106 "She lived the life of a farmer-philosopher": Fay, pp. 384–85.
   La Tour Du Pin on Talleyrand: quoted in Childs, p. 203.
   La Tour Du Pin on Rochefoucauld-Liancourt: ibid., pp. 220–21.
   La Tour Du Pin on Lafayette: ibid., pp. 114, 132, 227.
   "She loved her farm": Fay, pp. 384–85.
   108 "a whole square": Rice, p. 15.
   "no pleasure at returning to France": quoted in Childs, p. 28.

10. *Alexander Hamilton*

   108 "I have just come from viewing": quoted in Schachner, p. 345.
   "divined Europe": ibid.
   "the greatest of modern statesmen": ibid.

110 "dark and insidious": quoted in Kenin and Wintle, pp. 353–54.
111 "A colossus": ibid.
"touch of the heroic": ibid.
112 "Monsr. Mainshin" and surveying: Stillman, p. 129.
113 Latrobe on his preference for Jefferson: Talbot Hamlin, *Latrobe,* p. 222.
Burr's assurance to Latrobe: ibid., p. 222. For this account I have drawn heavily on the extensive literature on the City Hall competition, especially Stillman and Lancaster, p. 33. Talbot Hamlin, in *Greek Revival Architecture in America,* says that Burr consulted Mangin on the defenses of New York and knew him well (p. 125). Curious—perhaps Burr knew Brunel through Mangin.
114 "a New York bricklayer": quoted in Talbot Hamlin, *Latrobe,* p. 188.
115 "would be copied from the new jail:" quoted in Bucher, Douglas, "Phillip Hooker, 1766–1836: Albany Architect" (Albany, N.Y.: privately published, 1978), p. 2.
117 Speculators involved in XYZ Affair: Stinchcombe, *The XYZ Affair,* p. 60 ff.
118 mansions for John Lincklaen: The best history of the work of John Hooker is in Lincklaen.

11. *The Grange*

119 "In neither size nor architecture": Alexander Hamilton, p. 41.
"never an architectural triumph": Allan Hamilton, p. 338 ff.
120 "always . . . a sweet asylum": ibid.
122 "Bastard brat": quoted in Schachner, p. 1. (His sources are often unreliable.) See also John Adams in *Diary and Autobiography,* vol. 3, p. 435.
123 "piazzas along the sides": Torrey.
Hamilton the Creole: Alexander Hamilton, pp. 481–82.

IV.   Saint-Domingue

126 French Assembly's abolition of slavery: In point of fact, it was the Convention dominated by the Montagne, the adversaries of Brissot's Girondists, that actually passed the abolition resolution in February 1794. But that was not because of any passionate interest in the matter on the part of Robespierre and his followers; it was merely the consequence of delays arising from domestic politics. The fulfillment of Brissot's policies came after his fall from power. (I am grateful for this point, and for many other sound suggestions, to Anne Perotin-Dumon.)
"The prejudice of race": Henry Adams, *History . . . Jefferson,* p. 316.

12. *The Benefits of Toil*

129 the West Indies sent home twice the value of goods: Eric Williams, *Capitalism,* p. 53 ff. The figures on these pages all come from Williams's remarkable book. Williams was a pioneer; his work has been confirmed or modified by a succession of scholars including Richard Sheridan, Seymour Drescher, and Roger Anstey, but these statistics remain useful.
"Sumptuous mansions": ibid., p. 61.
130 "the magnificent quay": Stendhal, p. 5.
"you are constantly": ibid., pp. 6–8.
"completely epicurean way": ibid., p. 13.
Eric Williams's figures: *From Columbus,* pp. 144–45.
slave revolts: ibid., pp. 193–94.
131 "If in no earthly spot": James, p. 46. James wrote fifty years ago, and other scholars have learned

things since; but many of his insights remain valid. For reconsideration of James's and Williams's direct connections between slave trading and the textile industry, see Tarrade.

page 131 There were about a hundred men: James, p. 10.

In the center of the garden: Parham, pp. 152–53.

132 There was no ingenuity: James, p. 12.

133 "de Vaudreils, a Chateauneuf": Vaissière, p. 217.

"at the same time": James, p. 114.

13. *Disaster*

133 "the social equilibrium": Childs, p. 12.

133–4 "dissensions" were "naturally kindled": Fortescue, pp. 74–75. For modifications of Fortescue, see Geggus.

134 John Locke and slavery: Williams, *From Columbus,* p. 202. Adam Smith on Negroes: ibid., p. 210. Condorcet on slaves: ibid., p. 212.

135 "to treat them as friends": James, p. 63.

136 "drunk with liberty": Ott, p. 30.

"extreme Jacobin opinion": Childs, p. 14.

"of the worst possible type": ibid.

"at once allied themselves": Fortescue, pp. 75–76. For a comprehensive view of Sonthonax's temperament, see Stein.

137 "indulged in a . . . policy": Childs, p. 14. See also Fortescue, p. 76.

"not brought . . . slaves": James, p. 122.

138 "aristocrats of the skin": ibid., p. 123.

Captain Bickford wrote: quoted in Ott, p. 49. Childs tells us that the commissioners "opened the doors of the city to the Negro brigands of the plain who poured in by the thousands—fire, pillage, and horror in their wake!" She presents the spectacle of "destitute white refugees piled into both warships and merchant craft." Reflecting the views of the dispossessed possessors of the Blacks who had risen against them, Childs informs us that when the British and their Patriot allies captured certain Saint-Dominguan towns in 1793, "the terms the English offered were good; slavery was to be on the same basis as in the English colonies." Describing the efforts of Napoleon to reimpose slavery upon Saint-Domingue, she calls it a "brave and futile attempt to regain control of the island" (p. 15, fn. 16.).

"Citizens, today the English": James, p. 142.

138–9 "ought to have shared": Fortescue, p. 370.

139 "one of the great personalities": James, p. 343.

"these pestilent islands": Fortescue, p. 385.

West Indian losses: ibid., p. 565.

140 "to re-establish slavery": James, pp. 196–97.

"General, I blame you": ibid., p. 235.

142 Hamilton on Blacks: quoted in Flexner, p. 258. It is only warily that I demur from this admirable writer on this point (see p. 142), but I think Hamilton's failure to join actively in the opposition to the three-fifths rule (for counting Blacks for representation) resulted from his sulking at the convention and was an indication of his willingness to concede almost anything to the slaveholders to bring them behind a strong central government, rather than a demonstration of his indifference to slavery. Further, his substitution, in another instance, of the word "injured" for "degraded" as the appropriate adjective to describe the condition of Black people resulting from slavery I take to show his refusal to consign them to a condition beyond redemption, rather than any palliation of the iniquity of their treatment.

Jefferson on Blacks: quoted in Miller, pp. 52, 57.

the dirty compromise: See Beeman.

143 "no morals to speak of": Bowers, pp. 428–29.

"[aligning] himself ardently": ibid.

14. *American Connections*

143 "very clamorous against our admission": Tansill, p. 4.
144 "crush the . . . insurrection": Tyson, p. 93; "the cannibals": ibid.
"87 cruizers . . . at sea": Tansill, p. 12.
Quotations from Timothy Pickering and John Quincy Adams: ibid., p. 13.
Jefferson's assurances: ibid., p. 8.
"avoid the explicit recognition": Ott, p. 95.
"We shall never receive": Tyson, p. 105.
145 "if left to themselves": ibid. See also Stinchcombe, *The American Revolution.*
146 "every student of the period": Lodge, p. 286;
"the remark had been made": ibid., p. 287.
The early friendship: Allan Hamilton, p. 274.
"a very able man": Henry Adams, *History . . . Jefferson,* p. 260.
"under God, [was due] to . . . Doctor Stevens": Day, p. 83
147 Stevens and Hamilton at King's College: Stevens was at King's College from 1770 to 1774. The dates of Hamilton's arrival on the mainland are much disputed (see Flexner, Appendix A), but he joined Stevens no later than the fall of 1773.

Stevens's career is described by Thornton in his pleadings for Stevens's expenses in Saint-Domingue, to be found among the petitions and memorials presented to the Committee on Foreign Policy of the United States Senate (Records of the United States Senate); we are indebted to Charles M. Harris, who is editing the Thornton Papers, for their discovery.

There is a file of Stevens documents in the National Archives appearing as Special List No. 7, pp. 172–75. Other sources for Stevens are Rush and Toussaint. The editor of the Rush letters, Lyman H. Butterfield, gives a good short biographical note on Stevens in vol. 2, p. 657.

Another group of papers related to Stevens were found for me by June A. V. Lindquist, librarian of the Von Scholten Collection of the Enid M. Baa Library on the island of Saint Thomas (some, in Danish, were translated by Fredrik C. Gjessing). Among them is a biographical note in Kay Larsen, *Personalia og Data* (Copenhagen: Royal Library, n.d.; microfilm reel 9), stating that Stevens was born on Antigua and came to Saint Croix.

Recent research by Betsy Bradley informs us that the Stevenses had been inhabitants of Antigua at least as early as 1727, when a Thomas Stevens sold thirteen slaves to a planter on Nevis. This Thomas Stevens was presumably the father of the Thomas Stevens born on Antigua in 1724, who was married to Anna Andsley in 1745 and was living on Saint Croix by 1758. He died in 1778, leaving three sons, Thomas, Edward, and Richard, and two daughters, Mary and Ann.

The first few drafts of this section had been completed when, to my delight, I found in the library of the American Philosophical Society in Philadelphia, a copy of Day.
"fought gallantly": Thornton to Henry Clay, September 1, 1825; in Records of the United States Senate.
Stevens's research on Puerto Rico: Thornton to Stevens, September 2, 1792; in Thornton.
"the unhealthiness of the Country": ibid.
148 "to conciliate the good will": Pickering to Thornton, January 4, 1826, in Pickering.
"it seemed apparent": Lodge, note A, p. 283. For Pickering's account I am generally following Lodge, p. 283 ff.
"General Hamilton's mother died": ibid., p. 283.
"In cases of this sort": ibid.
"meagre statement of Hamilton": ibid.
149 "the brother-in-law of Mr. Hamilton": Day, fn. 102. For appointments by Adams to the Hamilton family, see Alexander Hamilton, vol. 25, p. 196.
"Toussaint's clause," and "may be considered": DeConde, p. 136.

page 149 Pickering and Stevens on Toussaint: Tyson, p. 287. See also Day, pp. 98–101.
149–50 "Toussaint has on his Side" and Stevens on Mulattoes: Stevens to Pickering, June 24, 1799; in Day, pp. 98–101.
150 "invade the Island of Jamaica": Stevens to Pickering, September 30, 1799; in Day, pp. 98–101. Stevens and the *Experiment:* Stevens to Pickering, January 16, 1800; in Day, pp. 98–101.
"the French have been making war": DeConde, p. 127.
"caused a War": ibid., p. 129.
151 "to rid those seas": ibid., p. 128.

15. *The Slave Owners Attack*

152 "too great bias": Tansill, p. 78.
"convinced that all the West India islands": ibid., p. 10.
"We may expect": ibid., p. 18.
153 Gallatin's speech to the House: quoted in Tyson, pp. 95–96.
153–4 James Jackson and John Wayles Eppes on the issue of Saint-Domingue: Tansill, p. 105.
154 Mitchell and Logan: ibid.
"taking things just as they were": Lokke, p. 323.
"however advantageous": Ott, p. 123.
"The United Staes would withdraw": ibid., p. 120.
154–5 The governor of South Carolina et al. on Saint-Domingue: Ott, pp. 53–54.
155 M. Pichon's report on meeting with Thomas Jefferson: quoted in Lokke, pp. 324–25.
Addington and Talleyrand on common interests of the French and the British: ibid., pp. 326–27.
155–6 Napoleon on Toussaint's government: quoted in Ott, p. 144.
156 "We shall perish": James, p. 288.
Leclerc's instructions: ibid., pp. 292–93.
"We have no other recourse": ibid., p. 299.
157 "The population, corrupt": ibid.
"This is no longer a war": ibid., p. 359.
159 "in the extremest Distress": Stevens to Pickering, May 3, 1799; in Day, pp. 115–17. See also Stevens to Pickering, June 23, 1799, p. 122; June 24, 1799, p. 127.
Stevens on Mayer: Day, pp. 115–17.
Mayer to Philadelphians on Stevens: Day, p. 58 n.
"put a stop": ibid., pp. 115–17.
160 Washington to Clement Biddle: quoted in Day, p. 104. Handwritten original in possession of Mrs. A. J. A. Alexander of Spring Station, Kentucky.
Washington to the secretary of state: quoted in Day, p. 154.
Washington to Secretary of War Henry Knox (August 11, 1799): ibid., pp. 155–56.
Stevens to Secretary of State Marshall: ibid., pp. 156–57.
161 Stevens's claims were presented by Thornton, January 25, 1826; February 6, 1826; and March 4, 1826. See Records of the United States Senate.
letters of introduction: Stevens to Hosack, October 6, 1823, and July 1, 1829; Mrs. Thornton to Stevens, December 28, 1828; Stevens to Mrs. Thornton, January 2, 1824: ibid.
162 "frail and worthless fabric": Flexner, p. 451.
M. Pichon's report can be found in the Library of Congress, in the Ministère des Affaires Etrangers, correspondance politique, Etats-Unis, Part 6, pp. 330–32.

V. The Transfer of Art and Technology

16. *Stephen Girard*

167 French fashion and Philadelphia: Wick and Golovin have both suggested the importance of this transfer of French fashion to Philadelphia.

167 "may, I presume": Talbot Hamlin, *Latrobe,* p. 499.
169 "very important . . . venture": McMaster, p. 323.
 "moreover he is naturally disposed," ibid., pp. 324–25.
 "scandalous disregard": ibid.
170 "Oh, Revolution": ibid., p. 161.
 "nothing is impossible": ibid., p. 162.
 "for my part": ibid., p. 163.
 "The creatures now governing": ibid., pp. 169, 171.
 "You ought to remember": ibid., p. 181.
 "my fifty negroes": ibid., p. 183.
 "I am one of those": ibid., p. 198.
171 "the Work House": Moreau de Saint-Méry, pp. 87–88.

17. *Pierre Bauduy*

175 The tradition of Bauduy's design for Swanwyck runs back far into family memory, according to members of that family I have interviewed. The earliest written statement of it is in Eberlein and Hubbard (p. 215). In the *Wilmington Morning News* of July 9, 1964, another local historian, W. Emerson Wilson, stated that "Bauduy was the architect for Swanwyck, the home of his son-in-law, John P. Garesché, and helped design and build St. Peter's Catholic Church . . . At the request of city officials he drew up the plans for the new City Hall and designed other buildings in the city."
 The statement that "the house is believed to have been designed by a French refugee, Jean Garesché, between 1820 and 1830" appears in Eckman, p. 105. The credibility of this work is not high; its attributions and datings are frequently in error.
176 Quotations and information about the Saint-Domingue history of the Bauduy family are from Holland, p. 14 ff. I have also drawn upon family records and earlier privately printed family papers and sources cited therein, and from Mrs. Holland's two mimeographed supplements.
 Pierre "was . . . furious": ibid.
 "the most . . . violent": ibid.
177 "instead of flying": ibid.
178 "To avoid danger": ibid.
 "I leave . . . Ferdinand": ibid.; Madame's name is omitted in this source.
 "his Most Christian Majesty": ibid.
 "at the head of a troop": ibid.
179 "peacefully": ibid.
 "descended from a noble": Garesché, p. 24.
180 "the horrors of the Revolution": ibid.
 Birth and death dates for the family of Pierre Bauduy are to be found in Mrs. Pierre Bauduy, "Family Souvenirs," written around 1826.
 "mansion near the Delaware River": Holland, p. 28.
 "for shops and inns": ibid.
 "Ah, those French": Garesché, p. 24.
181 "Pierre Bauduy, gentleman coachmaker": Holland, p. 29.
 "an enterprising man": Montgomery, p. 112.
182 "Fruit trees": ibid., p. 251.
 Father Kenney's diary: The diary is in the possession of the American Catholic Historical Society of Philadelphia; a copy is in the Eleutherian Mills Historical Library near Wilmington.
183 "was dedicated under": Garesché, p. 25.
 "built . . . through Bauduy's efforts": Bauduy, p. 18. See also Eberlein and Hubbard, pp. 201, 211, 312; and Wilson.
 the Wilmington town hall attributed to Bauduy: See Eberlein and Hubbard, pp. 201, 211, 312; they do not give sources for their statements. See also Wilson. According to the records of the City Council, the first effort to produce a design led that body to two merchants, John Way

and Peter Brynberg, "to prepare a plan" (minutes of the Borough Council, February 24, 1792). But it was six years before municipal wrangling came to an end and the building was under construction, and it seems likely that by that time they had turned to Bauduy for help.

"An Architectural Study of the Old Town Hall," prepared for the Historical Society of Delaware in July 1965, by Lee H. Nelson and Henry A. Judd, refers to its history as "clouded by latter day, but undocumented, attribution to Pierre Bauduy." The report concedes that "it is possible that . . . [the builders] consulted Bauduy about the plan." I think Nelson and Judd go awry in their hypothesis that it was "the original plan," not Bauduy's suggestions, that "embodied certain embellishments or more architectural elaboration." In January 1798, the Borough Council did meet "to consider whether and what alterations were proper to be made in a Plan" then existing and concluded that "the doorway . . . be rusticated . . . that they be authorized to build a bow in the back front and windows in the ends of the House, etc." These are precisely the sort of additions Bauduy might have suggested. Possible sources of Way and Bryberg's "existing . . . Plan" were the Burlington County Court House in Mount Holly, New Jersey, and several similar buildings in Philadelphia, such as the Carpenters' Hall and the Congress Hall, as well as the city hall.

18.   *The Basis of Economics*

page 185 "A knowledge of order" (epigraph): quoted in Gay, p. 350.
186 "house damp": Pyle.
190 "If . . . Leclerc will arrange": Holland, p. 41. See also Bessie G. Du Pont, *E. I. Du Pont,* vol. 6, pp. 83–85.
the frustrated hunting expedition: John Rumm has suggested to me that this anecdote may be apocryphal and that Pierre Du Pont needed no hunting accidents to help him assess opportunity in the U.S. gunpowder industry.
"the country": Holland, p. 36.
191 "very eager . . . arrange naturalization": ibid., pp. 104–06.
"the ease of making": ibid.
192 "an American capitalist": Bessie G. Du Pont, *E. I. Du Pont,* vol. 7, p. 45 ff.; see also vol. 6, pp. 93–94.
"interfere with your idea": ibid.
"sell my property": ibid., p. 339.
"I salute you": Bessie G. Du Pont, *E. I. Du Pont,* vol. 5, pp. 318–20.
"If you settle" "esteem and . . . friendship": Holland, pp. 36–37.
"Above all": Bessie G. Du Pont, *E. I. Du Pont,* vol. 6, pp. 93–94.
193 "in purchasing materials": ibid.
"and his assistance": ibid., pp. 96–97.
"though his great energy": ibid., pp. 93–94.
"for three weeks": ibid., pp. 100–02.
194 "wishing to do you well": ibid., pp. 308–12.
"Bauduy is nervous": ibid.
"blame too severely": ibid., vol. 7, p. 15.
"I am responsible": ibid., p. 68.
"You are wrong": ibid., p. 90 ff.
"it is always a good thing": Holland, p. 59, quoting Peter Bauduy in a letter to Fortunée de Sassenay.
195 "the new consciousness": letter dated July 1800, in Holland, appendices.
"It is in his power": Bessie G. Du Pont, *E. I. Du Pont,* vol. 7, pp. 154–55.
"I saw at our meeting": ibid., p. 170.
"warmth and friendship": ibid., pp. 179–80.
"Do not be angry": ibid., p. 181.

19. *Architectural Matters*

196 found no mention: letter to the author, December 30, 1986. I am most grateful to Dr. Benson and Dr. Cooper for their efforts and for the use of illustrations of the bank from records of the Historical Society of Delaware.

198 "the highest point": Bessie G. Du Pont, *E. I. Du Pont,* vol. 5, p. 207.

199 "two drawings of the piazza": Quimby, p. 14

200 Irénée's correspondence with Victor Du Pont: letters dated August 22, 1802; August 26, 1802; and October [1802], Du Pont Family Papers.
   "the 'original drafting' ": Quimby, p. 11.
   "really astonishing": Bessie G. Du Pont, *E. I. Du Pont,* vol. 6, pp. 164–65.

201 "proportions, ceiling heights": Du Pont Family Papers, document 1265.
   Lower Louviers: W. W. Laird, the present owner of Lower Louviers, wrote me on June 7, 1984, that there was a family tradition that after Ferdinand Bauduy married Victorine Du Pont "he moved into the former Bauduy home on Chicken Alley," a row of houses on the Louviers side of the river.

202 "less a narrative": Bessie G. Du Pont, *Lives,* p. 205.
   "Soon a charming house": ibid.

203 "that E. I. designed, or had designed": letter to author, June 7, 1984.
   Marengo: the house appears in the Historical American Buildings Survey as "Latimeria."

20. *Gorky Park and Eden Park*

204 "injustice, bad faith": Holland, p. 71
   "a sportsman": Holland, appendices.

205 Don Pedro and "Seven Sheeps": Purcell, p. 92.

206 "and to bring back the Ram": ibid., pp. 92–93.
   "Pray remember": Bessie G. Du Pont, *E. I. Du Pont,* vol. 10, p. 87.
   "my thirty or forty thousand acres": letter dated September 2, 1809; Thornton.
   "I am not of the opinion": letter dated October 27, 1804; Thornton.
   "our worthy friend": Holland, p. 107.
   "very sheepish": letter dated September 2, 1809; Thornton.

207 "just from France": ibid.
   "examined his bags": ibid.
   "six ewes": Holland, p. 84.
   "Your government should realise": ibid., p. 85.
   "The greatest harm": Purcell, p. 94.

208 Pierre Du Pont's proposal to Jefferson: Bessie G. Du Pont, *E. I. Du Pont,* vol. 8, pp. 112–13.
   "I will show you": letter dated September 2, 1809; Thornton.
   "though I cannot obtain": ibid.
   "The embargo": Bessie G. Du Pont, *E. I. Du Pont,* vol. 8, pp. 159–60.
   "are spreading all over the country": ibid., p. 231.

209 "the heretofore barren hills": Purcell, p. 97.
   "in the neighborhood": ibid., p. 91.
   "immense strength, great mildness": quoted in Philadelphia Society, p. 372.
   "the wonderful woods": Holland, p. 97.
   "Mr. Jefferson lives": letter of September 2, 1809; Thornton.

210 "is a creation of wealth": Dutton, p. 49.

211 "amount to nothing": Holland, p. 62 ff.
   "among the scenes": Purcell, p. 95.
   I'll risque my fame: ibid., p. 96.

page 211 "many cloth manufacturers": Holland, p. 102.

212 "The government really hopes": Bessie G. Du Pont, *E. I. Du Pont,* vol. 10, p. 87.

"my partner": ibid., vol. 8, pp. 202–03.

"We have just signed": Holland, pp. 109–10.

212–3 decline of woolen manufacture in Delaware: see Gibson, p. 33.

Evidence on the tangled connections between the Bauduys and the Du Ponts in textile manufacturing is based upon documents in Hagley, from Bauduy family records contained in Holland, and, most usefully, from Gibson, especially pp. 37–39, and the additional authorities cited by him.

213 "Our new establishment": Holland, pp. 103–04.

"She is mismatched": ibid., p. 107.

214 "a very odd family": ibid., p. 109.

"this strange family": Bessie G. Du Pont, *E. I. Du Pont,* vol. 8, p. 267.

"been in love": Holland, p. 112.

"I left your house": Bessie G. Du Pont, *E. I. Du Pont,* vol. 8, p. 168.

"lent his credit": Dutton, p. 47.

"In addition to . . . the woolen business": ibid., p. 60.

215 "Bauduy was a shrewd business man": Bessie G. Du Pont, *Lives,* p. 182.

bickering between Bauduy and Irénée Du Pont: Bessie G. Du Pont, *E. I. Du Pont,* vol. 10, pp. 54–62.

"doing all he could": Bessie G. Du Pont, *Lives,* pp. 182–83.

"temperate, respectful letter": ibid., p. 183.

"came on to Delaware": ibid.

"took his place": ibid.

216 "my daughter Pusy": ibid., p. 192.

"Her letters": ibid., p. 193.

"copied Irénée's machinery": Dutton, p. 55.

217 Irénée's comments on Bauduy in Washington: ibid., pp. 200–02.

"without friends": ibid.

218 pensions paid by E. I. Du Pont: I am indebted to Eugene S. Ferguson for information on the pensions paid by E. I. Du Pont to the widows killed in the 1818 explosion.

"He attempted various projects": Holland, pp. 141–42.

219 Bauduy's obituary: ibid., p. 142.

"When cholera made its appearance": ibid.

VI.   Brass and Silver

21.   *Preliminaries to Business: Architecture*

222 David Parish's entourage: Nolte, pp. 105–06.

225 "the most romantic": letter dated December 1, 1812, Parish Papers, New-York Historical Society.

"he had never seen": ibid.

Paul Turner pointed out to me a letter in the Parish Papers in the New-York Historical Society from David to his brother Richard, dated June 1812, saying: "We are in daily expectation of the Fair Trader . . . from what you say about Ramée he and his family are on board." So we do not know if Vincent Nolte's fallible memory has Ramée's arrival wrongly synchronous with the others in 1811 or if Ramée came over that fall and then returned to Europe to bring over his family six months later.

Parish's account of building appears in letters quoted by Tunnard; only the enthusiastic Tunnard is the source of the attribution of the residence of Parish, Sr., to Ramée (p. 9); therefore one cannot be sure.

227 David Parish's Red Villa: My account comes from private communications with Paul Turner and from inspection of four photographs supplied by John Baule of the Saint Lawrence County Historical Association.

228 "mysterious deserted house": Paul, p. 253 ff.

229 Samuel Smith: The two biographies of Samuel Smith, by Pancake and Cassell, are both very competent, but without much interest in his architectural or aesthetic affinities. Neither Ramée nor Parish appears in either.

231 John Quincy Adams on Samuel Smith: John Quincy Adams, *Memoirs,* vol. 4, p. 325.

233 The visit to Strabane can be deduced from Fowler, who says that Smith designed Montebello to emulate "a villa near Strabane which appears in an 18th century architectural book." This led me to ask Desmond Fitz-Gerald, the obliging and erudite knight of Glin, to see what might be found in the neighborhood, and he came upon Baronscourt and John Soane's drawing for it in Soane's *Sketches in Architecture, London* (1793). This volume was to be found in the Library Company of Philadelphia in 1794, and the Baltimore Library Company possessed Soane's earlier (1778) work by 1798. These works were consulted by Smith and Robert Oliver, though we cannot assert with confidence when they arrived in Baltimore.

22. *Preliminaries to Business: Politics and Economics*

234 "rid us of these gilded Africans": Henry Adams, *History . . . Jefferson,* p. 267.
"annihilating the black government": ibid., p. 264.
"ten thousand French soldiers": ibid., p. 274.

235 "we entertain toward him": ibid., p. 278.
"The system of this": ibid., p. 307.
"to a degree of strength": ibid., p. 308.
"warm satisfaction": ibid., p. 314.
"the pretensions": ibid., p. 310.
"You can declare": ibid., p. 269.
"wall of brass": DeConde, p. 115. I have tried, without success, to find Talleyrand's first use of this phrase, which recurs often in secondary sources. It is an inspired expression, permitting tarnishing metaphors and the like, and I would be grateful for instruction as to the moment it sprang first from his lips or pen.

236 "the individual States": Henry Adams, *History . . . Jefferson,* p. 146.
Madison and emigrations: ibid., p. 295.

23. *The Stage and the First Set of Characters*

238 "was an important channel": Walter B. Smith, p. 91.
Outflanking the Wall of Brass: Jackson's unpublished Ph.D. thesis is the best source for information on the Great Silver Scheme. Scholars who wish to pursue the intricacies of the matters summarized in these preliminary pages may wish to consult some of Jackson's sources.

239 value of dollars in sterling: Drawing upon earlier research, Edwin J. Perkins, in 1980, estimated the then-present value in dollars of a pound sterling in 1780 to be $65 (p. 145 ff.). Wage rates rose somewhat between 1780 and, say, 1803–05, and there was a rush of inflation between 1980 and 1986. This suggests an adjustment to make that relationship one pound sterling in 1805 to $75 in 1986 dollars.

Kindleberger also has a go at the matter (pp. 474–75). John J. McClusker of the University of Maryland cautions (in personal communication) that it would be wiser to put the relationship at one pound sterling in 1790 to $50 in 1984. But, try as I have, I cannot content myself with the object-to-object contents of "baskets" of equivalent values. Buildings are not like wheat—so I have supplied my own guesses about buildings.

In 1790, 4.4 American dollars were stipulated by law to be equivalent to a pound sterling.

In 1805, a pound sterling may have declined to about $4 or 4 pesos or about 15 francs. The dollar/peso equivalency lasted until 1839, when, with Mexican-American relations at a low point, the peso ceased to be our legal tender. The United States, upon declaring independence two generations earlier, had replaced the pound sterling as our official money of account with the friendly Spanish peso, as represented by the coin known as a "piece of eight." Dollars of account, of course, varied widely with relationship to silver coins, but it seems to be true that the doblón, or doubloon, was generally, during our period, worth about a pound, or about four times as much as a piece of eight. For working purposes we may say that the piece of eight of 1790 had the purchasing power of $11.25 in May 1988 terms, and a doubloon about $41.50.

page 241 merchants of Hamburg: For the names of these firms, see Jackson, pp. 101, 306–07.

242 For John Parish, see Emden, p. 20; Kindleberger, p. 121; and German sources cited by Kindleberger, especially Ehrenberg.

243 My account of the merchants' largesse is indebted to that of Rosenbaum and Sherman, and to the German sources cited therein. "To ensure . . . good will" appears on p. 4; "Good relations" on p. 5.
"increased from 35": Morison, pp. 178–79.
trade in Tonningen: My information comes from Ruppenthal, pp. 11–12.

244 "None ever more": Buist, p. 16.

245 "the Hopes . . . are Rank'd": Watkin, p. 2.
"dressed in gold-galooned livery": ibid., p. 1.

24. *The Silver Scheme*

246 "a man of courtly address": *Biographical and Historical Memoirs of Louisiana* (2 vols., Chicago: Goodspeed Publishing Company, 1892; available at the Historic New Orleans Collection), vol. 2, p. 492.
"ruined, crippled": ibid.
"a vain . . . fellow": Nolte, p. xxii.

247 Nolte's description of Napoleon: ibid., p. 30.
"mania for the play": ibid., p. 39.

248 Ramée and stage: ibid.
"the iron hand": ibid.

250 Spanish Bourbons had pledged their Mexican silver: This portion of my account is especially dependent upon Jackson, p. 216.

250–1 details of silver shipments: ibid., pp. 212–19.

252 The Olivers' role in the operation: The best source for this is Bruchey, pp. 265–71.

253 Charles Baring and the *Diana:* Jackson, p. 213.

254 Craig and Latrobe: See Latrobe's letters to Craig, February 15, 1807, and April 16, 1807; and to Mills, July 6, 1807. Latrobe Papers.

25. *David Parish*

256 American products sold to Vera Cruz: See Bruchey, pp. 297–98.

257 Who got what from the scheme: Jackson has worked out the computations in detail; see pp. 270–95. See also Bruchey, pp. 328–332.

258 "Whether we have money": Nolte, p. 105.
"British manufactured goods": Jackson, pp. 225–26.

259 story about Parish and sheep: Nolte, p. 138.

260 description of John Parish: ibid., p. 155.
"He is welcome to it": ibid., p. 161.
"the rendezvous of all the smugglers": ibid., p. 162.
"could not conceal": ibid., p. 163.

261 "the only country": letter dated March 4, 1807, in Parish Papers, New-York Historical Society, p. 354.

261 "omnipotent Jupiter": Tunnard, p. 14.

Parish residence in Philadelphia: My information comes from Dallett, pp. 11, 33. The house had probably been built in 1807 for a West Indies merchant, Captain John Meany, at about the same time Latrobe finished a large house close by for the China-trader William Waln. The Waln house is described in Talbot Hamlin, *Latrobe,* pp. 197–99; Latrobe's letter to Waln of March 26, 1805, about the virtues of French house-planning as against the British, shows how thoroughly familiar he was with French practice (Latrobe Papers).

"We have hardly enough money": Donald R. Adams, "Beginning," p. 103

"new appeal to the public": ibid., p. 104

262 "The Olivers, Craig and others": Nolte, p. 187.

"the principal part": Govan, p. 45. Govan, a conscientious researcher, cannot be trusted for some details unimportant to him but important to us. For example, he associates the fall of Vincent Nolte with the crisis of 1839 (p. 361) when it occurred in 1820. He persistently spells the name of Thomas U. Walter with an "s" after the last name, and gives Ameriga Vespucci a male ending, as "Amerigo."

"my reliance upon Parish": Donald R. Adams, *Finance,* p. 30.

263 "the arrangement I made": ibid., p. 37.

"A Gentleman": ibid.

"The Department of State": ibid., p. 50.

"decline the proposition": ibid. Parish's ignominious failure to subscribe appears on p. 164 of the best, though factually flawed, account of Parish's financial career, Walters and Walters. The Walterses give citations, including works in German and references to Girard's letterbooks, not found elsewhere. Another useful source is Lahey.

26. *Cotton and Architecture*

265 "strewn . . . with cotton bales": Nolte, p. 273.

"The most important commissions": ibid., p. 269.

saw the great Chateaubriand: ibid., p. 283.

"Of the various scrapes": ibid., p. 328.

266 "the filthy intrigues . . . of General Jackson": ibid., p. 338.

"You have done the same": ibid., p. 346.

"a black-eyed . . . Italian lady": ibid., p. 426.

267 small theater designed by Ramée: Paul Turner has told me that this "petite salle de spectacle" may be the Salle de Concert added to the Hôtel Laval-Montmore in 1786, "similar in many ways to an auditorium that Ramée later designed for Union College" in Schenectady.

"planned, executed, & adorned": Beckford is quoted in Paul Turner's remarkable piece of research on the early career of Ramée, which I read in manuscript and which may have been published by the time this reaches print. I am very much indebted to Professor Turner for sharing it with me.

268 "the whole company": ibid.

Danish-American relations: See Ruppenthal.

269 "the champion": This is quoted, unattributed, by Tunnard, on p. 15; I have a dim recollection of seeing it elsewhere attributed to Ramée, but I cannot pin it down.

Union College: My Union lore comes from Larrabee.

269–70 quotations from Nott and Jefferson: Turner, pp. 68–69.

271 "whole volumes of instructions": Tunnard, p. 15.

27. *The Smiths of Baltimore*

275 Smith's toast: Henry Adams, *History . . . Jefferson,* p. 296.

John Quincy Adams on Samuel Smith: John Quincy Adams, *Memoirs,* vol. 4, pp. 325, 382; and *Diary,* vol. 1, pp. 284–85.

page 276 "the moral . . . character of . . . Baltimore": ibid.

278 "If we had mines": Dangerfield, *Good Feelings,* p. 184.

"the Baltimore adventurers": Hammond, p. 281.

Baltimore bank stock jobbing: Details can be found in Catterall, p. 39 ff.; see also Hammond, p. 260 ff. I did not find either of these accounts wholly satisfactory, because considerations of space dictated that they leave out many connections of the participants; so I turned to the American State Papers, p. 313 ff., wherein are found the reports of the congressional committee investigating the collapse of the second Bank of the United States.

With the branch in hand, etc.: My account is from Dangerfield, *Good Feelings,* p. 60 ff.

279 "a church, a tavern": ibid., p. 184, and many other of the sources cited above; the references to Baltimore, Alexandria, and the quotation about Cincinnati: ibid, p. 187.

Girard and his sales: Wildes, p. 223.

280 Girard and lending "too long": Donald R. Adams, "Beginning," p. 103.

that class of amateures: ibid., p. 111.

281 Ramée visiting Smith: Latrobe to Harper, quoted in Talbot Hamlin, *Latrobe,* p. 489. Nolte confirms the friendly relationship between Smith and Parish, and suggests further business relations, in his story of a sketch he drew for Parish, poking fun at James Madison as a warrior, which wound up in the hands of Smith. This is also a suggestion that Parish shared with Smith and Nolte the political opinions of Samuel Smith and Gideon Granger. See Nolte, pp. 181–82. "Ramée has shown me the plan": Norton, p. 117.

Robert Alexander found the insurance record of Smith's stone house and thereby demonstrated that Ramée's was a remodeling. See his "Nicholas Rogers," p. 101 and fn. 28. Ramée's sketch and plan, as reproduced in his volume of 1834, are to be found in the Union College Library.

281–3 Ramée and Calverton: The identification of this house as a work of Ramée was made certain by Norton in the face of considerable contention. Norton completed his description by telling us that there were two octagonal pavilions attached to the main house, bearing cupolas. Ramée's own sketch seems to me to show circular pavilions, but no matter.

283 Latrobe and Smith: Talbot Hamlin, *Latrobe,* p. 464. Hamlin describes Smith as a citizen of Washington and misnames Calverton as "Carrolton" in a note on p. 488.

28. *Other Connections*

284 "if our friends": Talbot Hamlin, *Latrobe,* p. 488.

"I plan to return": letter dated February 11, 1815, in Leray Papers.

286 Dolley Madison's reaction to Granger's blackmail, and reference to Granger's sordid past: letter to Mrs. Albert Gallatin, January 21, 1814, New-York Historical Society.

287 "dragging . . . trash": letters dated March 9 and 10, 1814, quoted in Arthur Hamlin, p. 49. one other subject: quoted in Arthur Hamlin, p. 40 ff.

289 "a guest of Denis Smith": Talbot Hamlin, *Latrobe,* pp. 488–89.

290 Gideon Granger's house: In Canandaigua, one is sometimes told that Granger's house was based upon houses in Suffield, Connecticut, his hometown. I have carefully checked both the extant and the departed buildings of that village, in company with William N. Hosley, Jr., the local architectural expert, and find no similarities whatever.

293 "many large estates": *The Twentieth Century Biographical Dictionary of Notable Americans,* 1904, entry for Gideon Granger.

"ably seconded": ibid.

29. *Friends and Relations*

294 Riversdale: Eugenia Calvert-Holland, "Riversdale: the Calvert-Stier Home," *Maryland Historical Magazine* 45, no. 4 (December 1950), p. 271 ff.

295 "based" on the Château du Mick: ibid., p. 281.
"painting room": ibid., p. 283.
296 Maximilian Godefroy: See Alexander, *Godefroy*.
296–7 Latrobe, Godefroy, and the Baltimore Exchange: This account and the quotations are from Talbot Hamlin, *Latrobe*, p. 488 ff.
298 "native Americans": Gallagher, p. 107.
Gilmor's borrowing of Soane: Alexander, "Union Bank," p. 137.
"of the gallican spirit about me": Latrobe to Godefroy, in Talbot Hamlin, *Latrobe*, p. 489 n.
"much loved by the men": Gottschalk, pp. 202–04.
299 "a splendid young girl": ibid.
300 a house concealed: ibid.

VII. Aaron Burr

30. *Whose Plot?*

305 "I shall not be surprised": quoted in Van Every, p. 195.
Hamilton's conspiracies: See Boyd.
"a wall of brass": DeConde, p. 115.
306 Jefferson on "feeble" Spain: quoted in Lomask, p. 8.
308 "mon beau et cher Diable": ibid., p. 27.
309 "mild, capacious": quoted ibid., p. 16.
310 "as far from a fool": ibid., p. 13.
311 Wilkinson's influence over Jefferson: ibid., p. 20.
312 Hamilton "influenced" by Wilkinson: See Hale, pp. 65–67.
"the chief is too desultory": Hamilton to McHenry, quoted in Schachner, p. 382.

31. *The Plots Thicken*

313 "queer, little Latin-American": Bowers, in *Jefferson and Hamilton*, pp. 427–28; "the adventurer," *Jefferson in Power*, p. 320 ff.
"a man of overwhelming charm": Lomask, p. 96.
   Miranda's career is well known to Hispanic historians, but the last biography in English is William Spence Robertson's *The Life of Miranda*, published in 1929 (2 volumes; Chapel Hill: The University of North Carolina Press). There are good, scattered references to him, a just appraisal, and much bibliography in Liss.
314 "General Miranda's superb project": Bizardel, p. 159.
the French government's hopes for Miranda: ibid.
317 "tree of liberty": Marie Kimball, p. 269.
318 Miranda on Tryon's house and garden: quoted in Martin. The Miranda sketch is among the Trumbull papers in the Metropolitan Museum of Art, New York.

32. *Western Adventures*

319 "Napoleon confiscated his property": Sakolski, p. 200. Sakolski is unreliable—for example, he calls Ramée "Renée." But, of course, economic historians are not often much interested in the spelling of architects' names.
320 "If there should be a war": Lomask, p. 112.
"flitted through the . . . cedars": Flores, p. xviii.

page 321 "the excellence of the soil": letter dated October 26, 1806, Latrobe, *Papers,* vol. 2.
"the tract of country": Flores, p. 199.
Jefferson on the Bastrop tract: ibid.
Burr reported to Gallatin: Lomask, p. 112.
"an attack on Mexico": Flores, p. 291.
322 "intercept Captain Lewis": ibid., pp. 81–82.
"to attack and destroy": ibid., p. 86.
Jefferson's instructions and warning to Spain: ibid., p. 56.
Bastrop's warning: ibid., p. 84.
323 war with Spain inevitable: Lomask, p. 66.
324 "by shooting him": Wood, pp. 322–23.
"these pirates": ibid.
French, Spanish, and Indians in Louisiana Territory: In my account, I am following the splendid
work of Dan Flores.
"conquer not only the Floridas": Lomask, p. 134.

33. *The Turning Point*

325 "No, I would as soon have thought": Lomask, p. 5.
Jefferson's account of his conversation with Burr: ibid., p. 108.
Daveiss's letters and Madison's advice: Bowers, *Jefferson in Power,* p. 384.
326 "philosophic mind": Flores, p. 54.
"sounded as though": Stuart, p. 41.
"his orders were not to suffer": Flores, p. 204.
"All reflecting men": ibid., p. 80 fn.
"take possession of the Northern Provinces": ibid., p. 30 fn.
"any expedition": ibid., p. 30.
"irremediable damage": ibid., p. 124.
327 "March to the City of Mexico": Lomask, p. 35.
Spanish acting under orders: Flores, p. 285.
"expenses" in "crushing the conspiracy": ibid., p. 287 fn.
"to throw myself": ibid., p. 286.
"saving your country" and Burling's expenses: ibid., p. 287.
328 Craig's type: Lomask, p. 114.
329 "The sea will be conquered": Napoleon as Canute, quoted (approvingly) in Aubry, p. 176.
"The British Isles": ibid.
"the House of Braganza": ibid., p. 233.
"50,000 North Americans": ibid., p. 39.

34. *The "Wall of Brass" Again*

330 "more at ease": Bowers, *Jefferson in Power,* p. 350.
"we must marry ourselves": Lomask, p. 21.
Jefferson's treaty: See Flores, p. 89.
"sincere" but "checked in Cabinet": Bowers, *Jefferson in Power,* p. 351.
331 "policing the port": ibid., p. 330.
332 "Certainly not": ibid., p. 359.
"the total silence": Lomask, p. 178.
Jefferson's proclamation: ibid., p. 180.
"complacency of the Administration": Abernethy, Thomas Perkins. *The Burr Conspiracy* (New
York: Oxford University Press, 1954), p. 185.

333 Granger and the elimination of Black postal servants: See Leech, p. 14.
"in order that the guilty": Bowers, *Jefferson in Power*, p. 390.
334 Adams's and Jefferson's opinions of Burr: Kenin and Wintle, pp. 122–23.
335 "You see?": Lomask, p. 4.
"persuasion, bribery and threat": Stuart, pp. 629–30.
"take or obtain": ibid.
"Our southern defensive force": ibid.
336 "No city . . . can show": Humphrey, p. 404.

35. *Architectural Accessories*

336 "One evening in June": Latrobe's account in Talbot Hamlin, *Latrobe*, p. 222.
"zealously engaged": Burr, vol. 2, p. 975.
337 "nothing would be so agreeable": letter dated April 17, 1805, Latrobe, *Papers*, vol. 2, p. 49.
"substantial contingent": ibid., p. 133.
338 "of the tract called Bastrop's": letter dated October 26, 1806, quoted in Latrobe, *Papers*, vol. 2, p. 276.
My dear Sir: Latrobe, *Journals, 1799–1820*, p. 123.
339 "ridicule . . . the expedition": ibid.
Latrobe's memorandum to Gallatin: Talbot Hamlin, *Latrobe*, p. 222 ff.
Latrobe on de Pestre: Latrobe, *Papers*, vol. 2, p. 295.
340 Latrobe on Barataria: ibid., p. 352.
as "a frenchman": de Pestre quoted ibid., p. 293.
"part of his Jersey farm": ibid.
de Pestre vulnerable: See Lomask, pp. 253–54.
"not to accept": ibid.
341 "I think that my presence": ibid.
"Burr is not taken": letter dated January 22, 1807; Latrobe Papers.
"impregnable Basin": letter dated January 5, 1807; Latrobe, *Papers*, vol. 2, p. 349 ff.
"whatever Burr's plans were": letter dated August 14, 1812; Latrobe Papers.
"I love him still": ibid.

VIII.   The New Thébaïde

344 "with a rage of desperation": Reeves, p. 28.

36. *Joseph Lakanal*

345 "without appeal and without reprieve": quoted in Gardien, p. 494.
"A true republican": Dawson, p. 10.
"Here I am": ibid., p. 102.
348 "the rascal Lafayette": ibid.
"Liberty, Security, and Happiness": ibid., pp. 96–97; see also Reeves, pp. 29–30.
349 "the Revolution swept . . . along": Gabriel Compayre, quoted in Dawson, p. 15.
"the new Pisistratus": ibid., p. 60.
"the inhabitants of the buildings": Hillairet, vol. 2, p. 33. I am indebted to Paul Turner for this reference.
349–50 description of Lakanal house: Kauffman, p. 184. The house is illustrated as plate 11 in Krafft and Ransonnette.

page 352 "began converting his property": Dawson, p. 92.
"a log house": Edouard de Montulé's report is quoted in full in Seeber, pp. 176–77.

37. To America

353 "he will depart": Reeves, p. 15.
Lavallette reminded the emperor: ibid., pp. 11–12.
"my brave officers": ibid., p. 16.
"My brother may leave": ibid.
Lucien Bonaparte on Malta: ibid., p. 45.
354 Joseph's description of his estate and Girard's reply are quoted in McMaster, pp. 327–28.
355 "a small package": ibid., p. 333.
357 Jefferson's intransigent views: Stuart, p. 57.
358 Jefferson to Lakanal: quoted in Reeves, p. 32.
"new Thébaïde": Gardien, p. 495.
359 "I persist in thinking": Reeves, p. 26.
"recruiting, scattering money": ibid., p. 25.
360 "renowned for his tenacity": The description of Vandamme is from the *Encyclopaedia Britannica*, eleventh edition (1911), vol. 27, p. 885—just before the entry for Cornelius Vanderbilt. They should have been partners, except that the latter was not remarkably dissolute.
"Is it proposed?": Reeves, p. 38.
"supporting with obedience": Dawson, p. 102.
361 "would you believe": ibid., pp. 104–05.
"wise and illustrious master": ibid., pp. 105–06.
361–2 Packet sent by Lakanal to Joseph Bonaparte: ibid., pp. 114–15.
362 "like that of Colonel Burr": Reeves, pp. 60–61, 582–83.
362–3 New Orleans newspaper report: See Warren, p. 195.
363 Burr, Ouvrard, and Fouché: Henry Adams, *History . . . Madison,* p. 169.
"much my friend in Paris": Mann, p. 2. Mann's is a glorious book, full of letters deserving to be very widely read.
"very comely": ibid., p. 1.
364 "What I feel": ibid., p. 43.
"My friend Fulton": ibid., p. 127.
365 "my husband thinks": ibid., p. 117.
"We are in a better situation": ibid., pp. 129–30.
"has discovered": ibid., p. 176.
Next week I shall embark: ibid.
366 It would prove highly useful: ibid.
"he was accompanied": Gardien, p. 492.
Lee on the Tayloes: Mann, pp. 191, 202, 220.
"full of parsons": ibid., p. 192.
367 "the Dukes, Counts and Generals": ibid., p. 181.
"M. Pénières, the celebrated ex-legislator": Gardien, p. 493.
Lee's warranties: ibid., p. 491.

38. Plot and Counterplot

368 "who only wait": Lee to Monroe, quoted in Reeves, p. 65. In my account of the conspiracy, I largely follow Reeves, p. 63 ff., and Faye in "Great Stroke," with aid from Warren.
369 "a perversity of delirium": Adams quoted in Warren, p. 198.

369 "his brother and himself": Lee's report on his interview with Lallemand, Warren, p. 198.
"This declaration": Reeves, p. 65.
"letters from that schemer": Warren, p. 198
"purchasing arms": ibid., p. 199.
"disciplined and prepared": Reeves, p. 78.
369–70 Napoleon's support for Lallemand, as reported to Onis, is accepted as fact by Warren (p. 194) and seems entirely likely.
370 Onis's offer: Warren, p. 200.
371 "establishment which . . . is purely agricultural": ibid., p. 212.
372 "a river as wide": Reeves, p. 84.
"for protection against the Indians": Warren, p. 213.
"a barrier against . . . the United States": Reeves, p. 86.
Lallemand's proclamation: ibid.
"from the robberies": Warren, p. 229.
The account of the end of Le Champs d'Asile: Reeves, pp. 91–92.
"seven swollen rivers": Warren, p. 222.
"twelve hundred cavalry": Reeves, pp. 91–92.
373 "the Spanish general": ibid.
"No help came from Europe": ibid.
"the establishment at Galveztown": *Kentucky Reporter,* quoted in Warren, p. 225.
374–5 description of Desnouettes: Whitfield, p. 352.
375 Desnouettes dining: Pickett, p. 631.
Desnouettes drilling: Beeson.
"some good, old French brandy": Gaines, pp. 184–86.
"women dressed in ball gowns": See Whitfield, p. 352, and Lyon, p. 333.
378 Lakanal as "anti-Christ": Dawson, p. 157.
Dubourg's career: See Alfred N. Hunt, *Haiti's Influence on Antebellum America* (Baton Rouge: Louisiana State University Press, 1988), pp. 57–58, and sources there listed. Hunt's fine book appeared after this manuscript was completed; I acknowledge its welcome presence in this last-minute note.
379 "most inept . . . government": Dawson, p. 157.
"his homely crops": Lyon, p. 333.
Chaudron's ode and Lakanal's toast: Dawson, p. 157 ff.

39. The President, the Banker, and the General

380 "real cause" of Lallemand's abandonment: *Kentucky Reporter,* quoted in Warren, p. 225.
Adams's and Dangerfield's comments on Monroe: Dangerfield, *Good Feelings,* p. 250.
"attained his eminence": ibid., pp. 96–97.
380–1 opinions of Monroe: Kenin and Wintle, p. 544.
381 "There behold him": ibid., pp. 543–44.
383 "stout, large-boned man": This description comes from the best source of information on Graham, *General George Mason Graham of Tyrone Plantation, and His People,* by the general's grandson, George Mason Graham Stafford (New Orleans: Pelican Publishing Company, 1947), p. 64.
384 "Ugh! What a fool": ibid., p. 80.
Account of the roan horse: ibid.
"a fine looking gentleman": ibid.
385 "take possession of their own soil": Warren, p. 216.
Adams's warning to Graham: Reeves, pp. 103–05.
386 Adams's instructions to Graham: Warren, p. 217, and Reeves, pp. 104–05.
Graham's first conversation with Lallemand: Warren, p. 217 ff.
Graham's chat with Lafitte: ibid.

page 387 "or at least to acknowledge": Faye, "Great Stroke," p. 67.
    Clay twitted the President: ibid., p. 52.
  388 "messenger to Galveston": ibid., p. 68.
    report of Spanish Intelligence of October 30, 1818: quoted ibid.
    "the possession of a port": ibid.
    Graham's formal report: *Louisiana Historical Quarterly* 20 (1937), pp. 642–50. For Graham to Adams, see Warren, pp. 220–21.
388–9 Adams's journal quoted in Reeves, pp. 105–06.
  389 "which had been riding": ibid., p. 107.
    "indecorous and vagrant": Faye, "Great Stroke," p. 94.

40. *Joel Barlow*

  390 "You have come": DeConde, p. 325.
390–1 Barlow's speculations: Milton Kantor, of the University of Massachusetts, has cautioned me about the absence of evidence for Barlow's speculation in currency, so I have tried to phrase my speculations about his speculations with care. I am grateful to Kantor, an expert in Barlowiana, for this and many other helpful suggestions and corrections of my text.
  391 "without friends and without fortune," etc.: These quotations, and the information for these brief biographical paragraphs, are drawn from the entry under "Barlow" in the *Dictionary of American Biography*.
    "in the midst of his busyness": Bizardel, p. 68.
  392 "tell her . . . ": ibid.
    "I love my darling": *Dictionary of American Biography,* "Barlow" entry (surely its most engaging line).
  393 "burying the past": The historian quoted is J. F. Bosher of Cornell, writing in *The New Cambridge Modern History* (Cambridge: Cambridge University Press, 1979, paperback edition), vol. 8, p. 584 ff. I am indebted to his account of French finance for these paragraphs. He makes the arresting point that the cost of the court, including pensions and gifts to courtiers, was only a seventh of the cost to the French of the war for American independence (p.598).
    "Among the French": *Dictionary of American Biography,* "Barlow" entry.
  394 "a more worthless fellow," etc.: For these quotations, and for illumination of this chapter in Barlow's life, I am indebted to DeConde, p. 175.
    "to go home": Mrs. Barlow quoted in the *Dictionary of American Biography,* "Barlow" entry.
    "went straight to Washington": This did not occur precisely the way Van Wyck Brooks describes it (p. 140). Brooks says Latrobe worked "in the Ionic style, suggesting the capitol at Richmond." We possess a number of drawings of Kalorama after Latrobe's remodeling; none of them depicts a building having the faintest resemblance to the temple form of the capitol at Richmond. It does not even seem that the little colonettes at the door, indistinct as they are, were Ionic.
  395 "our particular friend": Talbot Hamlin, *Latrobe,* p. 436.
    "Barlow is elegantly situated": quoted in Mann, pp. 129–30.
  396 "I am satisfied": Reeves, p. 115.
    "six million acres": ibid., pp. 130–31.

41. *New Orleans*

  397 "a col. Bull": Latrobe, *Papers,* vol. 3, p. 801.
    "Our excellent[,] intelligent, and honest President": ibid., p. 799.
    "misled by I don't know who": ibid., p. 953.
    John Latrobe on Bomford: quoted in Semmes, pp. 62–63.
  398 "of the Engineers": letter dated August 13, 1816, Latrobe, *Papers,* vol. 3, p. 799.

398 "to do with a Commissioner": letter dated October 10, 1817, ibid., p. 953.

"a presumptuous little popinjay": Talbot Hamlin, *Latrobe,* p. 476.

Latrobe on the commission: letter dated October 10, 1817, Latrobe, *Papers,* vol. 3, p. 953.

Latrobe's actions after his son's death: I am indebted to Charles Brownell for rescuing me from Talbot Hamlin's dramatic but hopelessly garbled account of these events, and supplying a better one. The story is told in Talbot Hamlin's *Latrobe,* p. 477.

399 "an unemployed architect": Faye, "Great Stroke," p. 38.

Lafitte on Lafon: ibid., p. 39.

building the Red House: ibid., pp. 45–46, 50.

400–1 Lafon as architect: See the remarkable Bos. Bos was assisted, as I have been, by Samuel S. Wilson, Jr., and relied, as I have, upon Stanley Faye, writing in the *Louisiana Historical Quarterly* a generation earlier. Faye wrote with dash, elegance, and delight in his subject, while making the most meticulous use of a wide range of archival sources; I cite Faye when his is the first discovery.

Bos offers a list of surviving buildings in New Orleans that are probably by Lafon:

Pedesclaux-Lemonnier House (c. 1795), 638 Royal Street

Bosque House (c. 1796), 617 Chartres

Isnard House (1801–06), 404 Bourbon.

402 Lafon's lighthouse: Latrobe, *Papers,* vol. 2, p. 31 n., pp. 69–71; vol. 3, p. 304.

"stocky": Faye, "Privateersmen," p. 69.

Latrobe on Lafon: Bos, pp. 51–52. For Latrobe's letters to his son on Lafon, especially, April 5 and June 10, 1812, see Latrobe, *Papers,* vol. 3, pp. 276–77, 305, 312, 325, 400.

Latrobe's long conversations with Lafon: Latrobe, *Papers,* vol. 3, pp. 276–77.

403–4 Latrobe on Wilkinson and Lafon: ibid., pp. 286–87.

404 "engaged on a work": Bos, pp. 51–52.

Book on codes in Lafon's library: reported by Bos, p. 5.

Lafon observed by fishermen: Faye, "Privateersmen," p. 60.

Latrobe endorsing Lafon, July 23, 1813: quoted in Bos, p. 52, n. 29.

Lafon's acquisition of the *Carmelita:* Faye, "Great Stroke," p. 38 ff.

405 Wilkinson and Lafon: See Bos, pp. 105–06.

"a map of the vicinity": Brooks, p. 86 ff., esp. pp. 99, 175, 259. Lafon's title at Barataria was reported by a Spanish secret agent; see documents in the Ayer Collection of the Newberry Library, translated by Harris G. Warren and published in the *Louisiana Magazine of History* 20, pp. 619–50, and 21, pp. 213–19.

407 Latrobe on the noisy Frenchmen and Lallemand's party: Latrobe, *Papers,* vol. 3, p. 175.

the Rivière house: Bos, p. 51.

408–9 contents of Lafon's library: See inventory of his estate, October 5 to October 30, 1820, in the records of the city of New Orleans, Philippe Pedesclaux Acts No. 13, Fol. 20–79; cited in Bos.

409 Latrobe's visit to the battlefield: Latrobe, *Journals 1799–1820,* pp. 197–99.

Visit to the lighthouse: ibid., pp. 284–88.

"designing a house": Latrobe, *Papers,* vol. 3, p. 1028

Latrobe's rhymed endings: Latrobe, *Journals 1799–1820,* p. 280.

"newly-built residence": Nolte, p. 281.

"two squares": Latrobe, *Papers,* vol. 3, p. 1026. Land records show that Nolte bought property in 1825 at 329 Royal Street, not at 39, and sold it in 1826—a little confusing, I admit, compounded somewhat by the fact that in 1823 and 1824 Nolte was listed in the city directories at 79 Canal Street. This may have been another business address. For 39 and/or 329 Royal, see entries under "329 Royal" in the Historic New Orleans Collection files for Square 64; city directory entries are available from that collection as well.

In the Historic New Orleans Collection there is an estimate to turn the Nolte house into a bank building, dated June 3, 1829. It calls for two fireplaces, "interior ceilings of the bank plastered in plaster of Paris with handsome cornices," which might seem to date the shreds of present ornament and fireplaces to that remodeling, but it also calls for "a handsome staircase to ascend to the upper story," lit by "a large second story fan light." These do not appear to have been executed, so it is possible that none of this work was actually done and that the fixtures present date from Latrobe's work for Nolte.

Land records record the purchase on May 6, 1818. There is a map (Marc Lafitte, unpublished) of April 28, 1819, showing the house for Mr. V. Nolte, and a notice of sale on March 9, 1821, but it was called "Mr. Nolte's" house by a newspaper, suggesting that he was still in occupancy when its cornice was damaged by lightning on July 16 of that year (see Historic New Orleans Collection file for Block 62). Though it is not the house where Nolte was living at the time of the notice of his bankruptcy auction, that may be because he had already sold it to lay his hands on cash during the panic of 1819, then leased it back from its new owner through 1821, and some time thereafter moved into a smaller place on Saint Ann Street during his last desperate years. A notice in the *Louisiana Courier* for June 14, 1826, records a sheriff's sale of the real estate owned by Vincent Nolte, including "a small but Commodious dwelling house in St. Ann-street between Royal and Bourbon-streets, one story high," twenty-eight feet long, "and 57 feet deep, lying back on a passage 3 feet wide, leading to Bourbon-street."

page 410 Nolte's investments: Nolte, p. 281. One of Nolte's cotton-press ventures involved the demolition of a derelict Masonic Hall in the Faubourg Saint Mary. On May 8, 1819, Latrobe wrote that he had "been putting up some machinery for hoisting goods into his warehouse for Mr. Nolte." This letter was found by Samuel Wilson, Jr., among the Latrobe papers in the Maryland Historical Society, and was provided to me by his kindness.

"country seat": Nolte's auction notice, in *Louisiana Courier,* June 14, 1826 (see p. 410 n.).

412 obituary of Thomy Lafon: New Orleans *Daily Picayune,* December 23, 1893, p. 3.

Thomy Lafon's benefactions and wealth: ibid.

"style of conversation": ibid.

42. *The Tranquility of James Monroe*

413 "unjust prejudice": Talbot Hamlin, *Latrobe,* pp. 451–52.

"While the President": ibid.

"over the ruins": Kirker, p. 321.

"the architect's modesty": ibid., p. 15.

"I declined making": ibid., p. 322.

414 "I shall not have credit": ibid., p. 323.

Monroe to Graham: Stafford, pp. 89–90.

415 Meigs's letter: ibid., p. 90.

McLean's letter: ibid., p. 93.

"Poor Papa" and the baron's offer: Mann, p. 230.

416 Adams on the wedding: ibid., pp. 233–34.

"enthusiastic, sincere, and immovable": ibid., p. 241.

417 Lowell on Lee's will: ibid., p. 240.

"disposed to be": ibid.

Lee on his house: ibid., pp. 244–45.

419 Monroe on the sketch for his house, etc.: Monroe to W. Benton, January 8, 1821, Monroe Papers, Library of Congress, ser. 1, reel 7.

Bomford's plan: Monroe to W. Benton, January 13, 1821, ibid.

"new and distinct": Monroe to Benton, August 12, 1822, Monroe papers, University of Virginia.

421 "Contemplating Spain": Dangerfield, *Good Feelings,* p. 306.

the czar is quoted: ibid., p. 297.

quotations from the Monroe Doctrine: ibid., pp. 302–03.

IX. Solid Geometry

423 "The first and greatest effect" (epigraph): Palmer, p. 239.

"The principle assumed" (epigraph): Talbot Hamlin, *Greek Revival,* p. 51.

423 the Great Seal: See Sommer, pp. 57–76.
424 "threw into relief": Honour, p. 184.
"I set out": Talbot Hamlin, *Latrobe,* p. 51.

43.   *The Party of Hope*

425 "in the somewhat affected precision": Henry Adams, *History . . . Jefferson,* p. 122.
428 "haughty and morose nature": Rosengarten, pp. 205, 208.
429 "the garçons philosophes": Talbot Hamlin, *Latrobe,* p. 128.

44.   *Mr. Jefferson's Taste*

429 "the first American": Rice, p. 61.
431 Masonic diffusion of symbolic geometrism: See Gowans, "Freemasonry"; Clay Lancaster, "Jefferson's Architectural Indebtedness to Robert Morris," *Journal for the Society of Architectural Historians* 10 (March 1951), pp. 3–10; and Weibenson.

In a letter dated May 29, 1987, Gene Waddell told me of his doubts that Jefferson was a Mason and suggested that good Masonic symbolism would suggest Ionic, rather than Corinthian, for the chamber of the House of Representatives and the library of the University of Virginia. He may be right; but so may Alan Gowans, in "Freemasonry," and the Masonic historian F. M. Hunter: Gowans suggests that Jefferson, aware of the novelty of a gleaming white, columned temple, sought ways to make his symbolic antiquarianism acceptable to his fellow citizens and reached out to Clérisseau, just the man to give authority to "an example of architecture in the classic style of antiquity" (pp. 245–46). Jefferson told the building committee this was the work of "an artist who had been employed many years in Greece, by the Count de Choiseul, Ambassador of France . . . in making models of the most celebrated remains of ancient architecture . . . " (See Marie Kimball, p. 76 ff.: quotations are drawn from his letters at the time or from his reflections in *Notes on the State of Virginia.* Waddell says the model itself was actually the work of Bloquet, not of Clérisseau.)
Jefferson's architectural library: For data on this I have relied upon Fiske Kimball. Jefferson also acquired the work of William Halfpenny, who had something in common with Morris, in 1778.
432 "hard glazed surface" and "an impenetrable man": I do hope Messrs. Bailyn and Peterson will not be offended if I have taken their quotations not directly but by way of Brodie, p. 5. One does not mention Fawn Brodie in some circles. She offended another Jefferson biographer, Dumas Malone, so much that while he includes a rebuttal to her work as Appendix III in the sixth volume of his life of Jefferson (which appeared in the same year as her ninth printing), he could not bring himself to print her name either there or in the index.
"a style of living," and my list of Jefferson's radical designs, are drawn from Pickens. Pickens's thesis is hotly contested, but it has value if not taken too straight, and if one admits the ingenuity of his drawings rather than assuming their accuracy as reproductions of Jeffersonian reality.
"given proofs of his skill": Marie Kimball, p. 73.
433 "prejudices in favor of": letter dated May 3, 1805, quoted in Talbot Hamlin, *Latrobe,* p. 294.
Jefferson's library: See William B. O'Neal, *Jefferson's Fine Art Library* (Charlottesville: University Press of Virginia, 1976).
434 Jefferson's "pretext" is discussed in Marie Kimball, p. 190.
434–5 Goethe and prohibitive fear of contact: Adolf Max Vogt in Serra, p. 172.
435 "passed through . . . cathedral towns": Marie Kimball, p. 223.
"In architecture": ibid., p. 218.

45.   *Grandeur in the Eighties*

436 Ledoux's announcement: Lemagny, p. 68. Kaufmann gives no evidence to support his assertion that though Boullée and Ledoux "did not play any active role in the political scene . . . they were men imbued with the great new ideals set forth by leading thinkers of the century, and

strove unconsciously . . . to express these ideals in their own medium" (pp. 433–34).

page 436 "palaces by which": Rice, p. 3.

437 Boullée on himself: Lemagny, pp. 16–17.

438 "two French officers": Talbot Hamlin, *Latrobe,* p. 157.

Louis Philippe's comments: Louis Philippe, p. 22.

441 Watkin's description of Welgelegen, pp. 3–4.

"cost four tons of silver," etc.: Marie Kimball, pp. 214–15.

Welgelegen: Architectural historians agree that Welgelegen was very important, though they do not agree on quite a few details about it. Watkin spells it "Weglegen," William Howard Adams "Welgelegen." Watkin says that it was sold to Louis Bonaparte in 1806; Adams et al. say 1808. Buist agrees with the latter in each instance. Nor do these sources agree as to who designed it. Buist (p. 42) says that it was "designed by the consul of the Sardinian Court in the Hague, Triquetti, who modelled it on the Borghese and Albani villas of Rome," and goes on to say that it is "the only example of a villa suburbana in the French classic style which exists in the Netherlands," which is not quite the same thing as Watkin's saying (pp. 3–4) that it is "the sole instance of the introduction of the Louis XVI style into eighteenth-century Holland." Triquetti is not the same, either, as Adams et al. . . . attributions—the Dutch architect Leendert Viervant and the Flemish master builder Jean-Baptiste Dubois.

Marie Kimball says Welgelegen has "a double frontpiece of columns, very much on the order of Monticello as Jefferson intended it to be," whereas Jefferson himself, in a portion of his report not quoted by her but in William Howard Adams, says that "there is no portico, the columns being backed against the wall of the front." This is an odd error for her to make, since her reports of Jefferson's travels in Europe are remarkable for their fresh sense of firsthand re-experience of what he saw. This passage reads as if she had contented herself with his elevation drawings, in this instance easy to misread. The two-dimensional effects are similar, but the glory of the first Monticello would have been its templelike openness. See Watkin; see also Marie Kimball, pp. 214–15; William Howard Adams, pp. 212–213.

"our incurring . . . a bankruptcy": Marie Kimball, pp. 214–15.

443 Jefferson's references to being savage: from sources quoted in Brodie, pp. 250–51.

"all the new . . . houses": from Gene Waddell's extensive treatment of the construction of the house in "The First Monticello," the *Journal of the Society of Architectural Historians* 46, no. 1 (March 1987), pp. 5–29.

46.   *The Curve of the Corn Market*

445 "five or six languages": James Northcote on Maria Hadfield quoted in Gosse, p. 99. I am indebted to John Walker, former director of the National Gallery of Art, for drawing my attention to this account, which also appeared in Brodie, (p. 254 ff.), and for providing me with a typescript of his work on Maria, as yet unpublished. Very much the same language is quoted by Bowers in *The Young Jefferson,* p. 448, citing George C. Williamson's *Richard Cosway* (London: G. Bell and Sons, 1905), p. 18. Bowers put too much sugar and too little discrimination in his account, wholly ignoring her affair with di Paoli and its consequence, Louisa Paolina. The birthplace, Mr. Walker has established, was Florence, not Leghorn, as has been reported elsewhere.

"she always despised him": ibid.

"was the Joseph Duveen": Quoted in Walker's manuscript (see above).

446 "battered canvasses": ibid.

"princess and bohemians": Bowers, *The Young Jefferson,* p. 451.

"like the fair Aspasia": Brodie, p. 285.

"a form extremely delicate": Northcote in Gosse, p. 94 ff.

447 Jefferson's suggestion to L'Enfant: quoted in Norton, "Thomas Jefferson and the Planning of the National Capitol," in William Howard Adams, ed., *Jefferson and the Arts: An Extended View.* (Washington, D.C.: National Gallery of Art, 1976), p. 194. There is an extensive literature about Jefferson, his tours of Paris, and the likely influence of French taste upon him. Perhaps the best

works are Rice and the essays by Norton and Frederick D. Nicols in *Jefferson and the Arts.*
447 Jefferson's "hermitage": Brodie, p. 288.
448 "I am eating the peaches": ibid., p. 366.
450 "to draw an external": Marie Kimball, p. 75.
"Experience shows": ibid., pp. 74–75.
"the brat": ibid., p. 74.
"the most superb thing": ibid., p. 162.
452 "conscience and common sense": Talbot Hamlin, *Latrobe,* pp. 273–74.
"I am convinced": ibid.
"like that of the Pantheon": ibid.
"the Grecian style": ibid.
453 striplights: I have found argument among authorities as to whether or not the striplights were
in fact briefly installed. The dispute is not significant enough to sustain here; I have relied upon
Gene Waddell's conclusion, stated in his letter of May 29, 1987, cited earlier.
Latrobe on Jefferson: Talbot Hamlin, *Latrobe,* p. 333.
454 "As to covering the church": For this discussion of the Monumental Church, I am indebted to
an unpublished manuscript by Douglas Harnsberger, the script for a discussion at Winterthur
on October 9, 1983, from which is taken Latrobe's comment, and to his monograph "In
Delorme's Manner."
house for "a public officer": The drawing for the house was marked "Shadwell," which has given
rise to the thought that it was a design for Jefferson's plantation of that name; since Gene Waddell
informs me (letter of May 29, 1987) that the drawing, now at Tulane, bears the inscription
"drawing is for a public officer," it seems likely that the "Shadwell" notation refers to the place
at which the drawing was executed.
455 "seemed during his entire life": Rice, p. 125.
456 "one of the choice": ibid., p. 94.

Appendix I

457 John Reps's inquiries: pp. 35–36. The English could have learned of the plan either directly
through John Hawkins, the piratical captain who visited Ribault's fort, or through the engravings of Jacques Le Moyne.
458 William Gerard De Brahm: There is some confusion about De Brahm's nationality. Governor
John Reynolds called him "a German Gentleman," and some records suggest that he was born
in Germany, in 1718. He may have been the child of Huguenot refugees or may have been
Franco-Dutch: see Mills Lane, *The Architecture of the Old South: Georgia* (Savannah: The Beehive
Press, 1986), pp. 22–23 and notes on p. 244, revising Nichols, pp. 11–12.
459 Shirley was built in stages: Dating Shirley is difficult. Waterman gives us his opinion that it
was completed in 1769 (pp. 173–74, 346–58, 422). There is a letter quoted in Emmie Ferguson
Ferrar, *Old Virginia Houses along the James* (New York: Bonanza Books, 1957), p. 90, which
says that it was being repaired in 1771; the forecourt could have been laid out as early as the
1720s, as suggested by the anonymous but scrupulous essayist in *Homes and Gardens in Old
Virginia,* edited by Frances Archer Christian and Suzanne Williams Massie (Richmond: Garden
Clubs of Virginia, 1953), p. 209 ff.
a Scots trader: There is wonderful reading available about the traders, ranging from John Barth's
novel *The Sot-Weed Factor* to powerful passages in Rhys Isaac's more recent *The Transformation
of Virginia* (Chapel Hill: University of North Carolina Press, 1982).
Waterman associated Shirley, Ashdown, and Corotoman: Waterman, *Mansions,* p. 111. More
recent archeological work by Theodore R. Reinhart demonstrates that the Shirley complex was
even more dense than Waterman knew. Two large brick dependencies—three stories high—
stood to the right and left of the main house. See Reinhart, "Shirley Plantation: Documentation,

Informants, and the Archeology," in the *Quarterly Bulletin of the Archeological Society of Virginia* 37, no. 3 (September 1982).

page 461 John Reps's wonderful studies: Reps, pp. 127, 146, 151, 169.

462 "determine the shape of the buildings": As to the Frenchness of eighteenth-century Dutch design, see E. H. ter Kuile's essay in Rosenberg, especially p. 396.

Wren's trip: It is Summerson who tells us of Wren's visit, and possible conversations, in France (p. 200).

"nearer to the spirit": See E. H. ter Kuile's essay in Rosenberg, p. 396.

INDEX

Page numbers in *italics* refer to illustrations.

Pages xiv, 3: Maryland Historical Society, Baltimore. Page 5: Courtesy Massachusetts Historical Society. Page 6: Museum of the City of New York. Page 15: Reproduced from *Great Georgian Houses of America* by the Architects' Emergency Committee, Vol. 1 (New York: Dover, 1970; reprint of 1936 edition). Page 18: Courtesy of the *Forbes* Magazine Collection. Page 22: French Government Tourist Office. Page 23: Photo by Charles W. Dunham. Page 25: Sketches made for the author. Page 31: The Brooklyn Historical Society. Pages 39, 41: Photos courtesy of The Watertown *Daily Times*, Watertown, N.Y. Page 43: From the collections of the Jefferson County Historical Society, Watertown, New York. Page 48: National Portrait Gallery, London. Page 50: The National Portrait Gallery, Smithsonian Institution; Gift of Mr. and Mrs. Paul Mellon. Page 52: Courtesy Oneida County Historical Society, Utica, N.Y. Page 54: The National Portrait Gallery, Smithsonian Institution; Gift of Mr. and Mrs. Paul Mellon. Page 58: Courtesy of Mr. and Mrs. Stephen Hurst. Page 60: Courtesy of The New-York Historical Society, New York City. Page 61: Bequest of Edward W. C. Arnold, 1954, The Edward W. C. Arnold Collection of New York Prints, Maps and Pictures, Metropolitan Museum of Art (Photograph courtesy of Museum of the City of New York). Page 62: Courtesy of The New-York Historical Society, New York City. Page 63: Courtesy of Rokeby Collection and John Winthrop Aldrich. Page 64: Courtesy of The New-York Historical Society, New York City. Page 65: New York State Office of Parks, Recreation and Historic Preservation/Clermont State Historic Site. Page 66: Columbia County Maps Vol. IV; Courtesy Columbia County Clerk's Office, Hudson, N.Y. Pages 67, 71: Sketches made for the author. Page 72: New York State Historical Association, Cooperstown. Page 73: *Courthouse Square:* New York State Historical Association, Cooperstown; *Court House engraved by Saint-Mémin:* In the collection of The Corcoran Gallery of Art, Gift of William Wilson Corcoran. Page 74: *Market Square:* New York State Historical Association, Cooperstown; *Market engraved by Saint-Mémin:* In the collection of The Corcoran Gallery of Art, Gift of William Wilson Corcoran. Page 75: In the collection of the Corcoran Gallery of Art, Gift of William Wilson Corcoran. Page 76: *Church Square:* New York State Historical Association, Cooperstown; *Church engraved by Saint-Mémin:* In the collection of the Corcoran Gallery of Art, Gift of William Wilson Corcoran. Page 77: Reproduced from the Dutchess County Historical Society *Yearbook*, 1929. Page 80: *Brunel's design:* Courtesy of Mr. and Mrs. Stephen Hurst; *Marble Hill in 1790:* Museum of the City of New York. Page 87: Clichées des musées Nationaux, Paris. Page 95: City of Bristol Museum & Art Gallery. Page 97: Museum of the City of New York. Page 98: Courtesy of The New-York Historical Society, New York City. Page 102: The Ford Collection/Miriam & Ira D. Wallach Division of Arts, Prints & Photograph/The New York Public Library/Astor, Lenox and Tilden Foundations. Page 104: Courtesy of Mrs. Van S. Merle-Smith. Page 105: Reproduced from *French Refugee Life in the United States, 1790–1800* by John Sergeant Childs (Baltimore, Maryland: The Johns Hopkins University Press, 1940). Page 107: Archives Municipales, Bordeaux. Page 110: National Portrait Gallery, Smithsonian Institution, Washington, D.C.; Gift of Henry Cabot Lodge. Page 113: I. N. Phelps Stokes Collection/Miriam & Ira D. Wallach Division of Art, Prints & Photographs/The New York Public Library/Astor, Lenox and Tilden Foundations. Page 114: The Edward W. C. Arnold Collection of New York Prints, Maps and Pictures, Metropolitan Museum of Art (Photograph courtesy of Museum of the City of New York). Pages 116, 117: Photos by author. Page 119: Courtesy of The New-York Historical Society, New York City. Page 121: I. N. Phelps Stokes Collection/Miriam & Ira D. Wallach Division of Arts, Prints & Photographs/The New York Public Library/Astor, Lenox and Tilden Foundations. Pages 137, 141: Schomburg Center for Research in Black Culture/The New York Public Library. Pages 167, 168: Stephen Girard Collection, Girard College, Philadelphia, Pa. Page 169: The Historical Society of Pennsylvania. Page 172: Courtesy of Maquita and Lee Driscoll. Page 174: Reproduced from *Great Georgian Houses of America*, Vol. 2 (New York: Dover, 1970; reprint of 1936 edition). Page 177: Photograph by Frances Benjamin Johnston; Courtesy of the Library of Congress. Page 179: Courtesy of Dorothy Gareschè Holland. Page 180: Courtesy of Maquita and Lee Driscoll. Page 181:

Courtesy of Dorothy Gareschè Holland. Page 183: Photo by author. Page 186: Courtesy of Maquita and Lee Driscoll. Pages 188, 190, 193: Courtesy of Hagley Museum and Library. Page 197: Courtesy of the Historical Society of Delaware. Pages 199, 200, 202, 205: Courtesy of Hagley Museum and Library. Page 207: National Gallery of Art, Washington, D.C.; Andrew W. Mellon Collection. Page 210: Courtesy of Dorothy Gareschè Holland. Page 217: Courtesy of Hagley Museum and Library. Page 223: Courtesy of Vici Zaremba, North-South Photography, Antwerp, N.Y. Pages 225, 226: Photos by author. Page 227: Photo courtesy Frederic Remington Art Museum, Ogdensburg, New York. Page 228: Photograph courtesy of the St. Lawrence County Historical Association, Canton, New York. Page 229: Schaffer Library, Union College, Schenectady, N.Y. Pages 230, 231: The Baltimore Museum of Art; Gift of the Friends of the American Wing. Page 232: By courtesy of the Trustees of Sir John Soane's Museum, London. Page 245: Abbott Lawrence Fund/Courtesy, Museum of Fine Arts, Boston. Page 251: Courtesy of Baring Brothers & Co., Limited. Page 255: Photo courtesy Frederic Remington Art Museum, Ogdensburg, New York. Page 260: Courtesy of The New-York Historical Society, New York City. Page 263: The Metropolitan Museum of Art, Gift of Frederic W. Stevens, 1908. Pages 271, 272: Schaffer Library, Union College, Schenectady, N.Y. Page 274: The Peale Museum, Baltimore, Maryland. Pages 281, 282: Schaffer Library, Union College, Schenectady, N.Y. Pages 283, 285: The Peale Museum, Baltimore, Maryland. Page 286: Courtesy U. S. Postal Service Library. Pages 289, 290: Photos by author. Page 292: Reproduced from *Interiordekorationer I Erichsens Paale* by Hans H. Madsen (Copenhagen: privately printed, 1968). Pages 293, 295: Photos by author. Page 297: Maryland Historical Society, Baltimore. Page 299: Photo courtesy Frederic Remington Art Museum, Ogdensburg, N.Y. Page 300: Courtesy of The New-York Historical Society, New York City. Page 309: The Detroit Institute of Arts, Gift of Mr. and Mrs. Arthur Fleischman. Page 310: National Portrait Gallery, Smithsonian Institution, Washington, D.C. Page 315: Photograph Bibliothèque Nationale, Paris. Page 317: Courtesy of The New-York Historical Society, New York City. Page 346: Reproduced from *Lakanal the Regicide* by John Charles Dawson (Tuscaloosa, Alabama: University of Alabama Press, 1948). Pages 350, 351: Reproduced from *Plans, coupes, élévations des plus belles maisons et des hôtels construits à Paris et dans les environs* by Johann K. Krafft and N. Ransonnette (Paris: Librarie d'art décoratif et industriel, 1909). Page 354: Stephen Girard Collection, Girard College, Philadelphia, Pa. Page 356: Courtesy of the Art Institute of Chicago. Page 358: Photo courtesy of The Watertown *Daily Times*, Watertown, N.Y. Page 359: From the collection of W. E. Groves. Page 362: Reproduced from *A Yankee Jeffersonian* by Mary Lee Mann (Cambridge, Mass.: Harvard University Press, 1958). Page 371: Courtesy Institute of Texan Cultures, San Antonio. Pages 374, 376, 377: Courtesy of the Marengo County Historical Society. Page 391: Courtesy of the Pennsylvania Academy of the Fine Arts. Page 394: The Columbia Historical Society, Washington, D.C. Page 396: Maryland Historical Society, Baltimore. Page 401: Louisiana State Museum. Page 403: The National Archives, Cartographic Branch, Records of the U.S. Coast Guard, Record Group No. 26. Pages 407, 408: Maryland Historical Society, Baltimore. Page 414: Courtesy of The Harvard University Portrait Collection, Gift of Francis V. Bulfinch. Page 416: Reproduced from *The Architecture of Charles Bulfinch* by Harold Kirker (Cambridge, Mass.: Harvard University Press, 1969). Page 418: Photos by author. Page 434: Musée du Louvre, Paris. Page 438: Maryland Historical Society, Baltimore. Page 439: Royal Institute of British Architects, London. Page 440: Thomas Jefferson Papers, Manuscripts Division, Special Collections Department, University of Virginia Library. Page 442: Government Information Service, The Hague. Page 444: *Final elevation of Monticello:* Courtesy of Massachusetts Historical Society; *Jefferson's sketch:* Reproduced from *The Eye of Jefferson: Jefferson and the Arts,* edited by William Howard Adams et al. (Washington: National Gallery of Art, 1976). Page 447: National Portrait Gallery, London. Page 448: The White House. Page 449: Cincinnati Art Museum, Museum Purchase. Page 451: Photograph Bibliothèque Nationale, Paris. Page 453: Courtesy of the Library of Congress. Page 455: Courtesy Massachusetts Historical Society.

A NOTE ON THE TYPE

The text of this book was set in Bembo, a facsimile of a type face cut by Francesco Griffo for Aldus Manutius, the celebrated Venetian printer, in 1495. The face was named for Pietro Bembo, the author of the small treatise entitled *De Aetna* in which it first appeared. Through the research of Stanley Morison, it is now generally acknowledged that all old-face type designs up to the time of William Caslon can be traced to the Bembo cut.

The present-day version of Bembo was introduced by The Monotype Corporation of London in 1929. Sturdy, well balanced, and finely proportioned, Bembo is a face of rare beauty and great legibility in all of its sizes.

Composed by The Haddon Craftsmen, Inc., Scranton, Pennsylvania. Printed and bound by The Murray Printing Company, Westford, Massachusetts. Designed by Peter A. Andersen.